Tax Law Design and Drafting

VOLUME 2

Tax Law Design and Drafting

Editor
Victor Thuronyi

INTERNATIONAL
MONETARY
FUND

1998

This book was designed and produced by Choon Lee, Philip Torsani,
and IMF Graphics Section and edited by Elisa Diehl

Library of Congress Cataloging-in-Publication Data

Tax law design and drafting / editor, Victor Thuronyi
    p.   cm.
    Includes bibliographical references (p.) and index.
    ISBN 1-55775-633-3 (vol. 2)
    1. Taxation—Law and legislation.   2. Tax administration and procedure.
3. Bill drafting.   4. Taxation—Government policy.   I. Thuronyi, Victor.
K4460.4.T37   1996   96-34672
328.3'73—dc20   CIP

Price: $25.00

Address orders to:
External Relations Department, Publication Services
International Monetary Fund, Washington D.C. 20431
Telephone: (202) 623-7430;   Telefax: (202) 623-7201
E-mail: publications@imf.org
Internet: http://www.imf.org

Summary of Contents

Volume 1

Volume 2

Contents

Volume 2

Chapter 15. The Pay-as-You-Earn Tax on Wages
Koenraad van der Heeden **564**

Chapter 16. Taxation of Income from Business and Investment
Lee Burns and Richard Krever **597**

Chapter 22. Taxation of Investment Funds
Eric M. Zolt   969

Chapter 23. Income Tax Incentives for Investment
David Holland and Richard J. Vann   986

Introduction

This is the second of two volumes dealing with tax law on a comparative basis. The present volume focuses on the income tax.[1] It also contains a bibliography of comparative tax literature and the most comprehensive listing available of the world's tax laws. The first volume concentrates on taxes other than the income tax, although many of the issues it considers also have a bearing on the income tax. It also deals with two specialized income tax topics—inflation adjustment and presumptive taxation. The reader is referred to the introduction to the first volume for a discussion of the genesis and general orientation of this work. The various caveats stated there apply equally to this volume. While complementary, the two volumes are designed so that they can be used independently; for example, volume 2 can be used in courses on income taxation. The index in this volume covers both volumes. Acknowledgments are stated in the first volume.[2]

As an orientation to the chapters in this volume, I begin by briefly examining the role of the income tax in developing and transition countries. I then consider comparative income tax law in broad outlines to set the stage for the more detailed discussion in the individual chapters.

I. Role of Income Tax

In the industrial countries, the individual income tax typically brings in a substantial share—in some cases, a majority—of tax revenues.[3] By contrast, in many developing countries, the bulk of tax revenue is raised from indirect taxes, principally taxes on imports or exports, and, increasingly over the last twenty years or so, from some form of value-added tax (VAT).[4] Moreover, in

---

[1]The term "income tax" is used here to refer to both the income tax on individuals and the income tax on corporations, which in many countries has a different name, for example, profit tax. In some countries, these taxes are governed by separate laws, and in others by the same law. *See infra* ch. 14, sec. II(B).

[2]In this volume we also include in footnotes a few comments by Prof. Leif Mutén, identified as L.M., who kindly reviewed much of the manuscript.

[3]*See* Tax Policy Handbook 294 (Parthasarathi Shome ed., 1995).

[4]*See id.* at 300–18.

developing countries, the corporate income tax represents a larger share of total income tax revenues than in the OECD countries; in many cases, more revenue is raised from corporate than from individual income tax, while the reverse is by and large the case in OECD countries.[5] This is not surprising in countries where many individuals fall below the poverty line.

At first glance, one might conclude that, in order to make developing country tax systems more progressive, the share of the individual income tax in overall tax revenues must be increased. This is not necessarily the case, however. In a system that relies heavily on indirect taxes for revenue, the income tax can supply progressivity at the top end of the income distribution scale. While critical in making the tax system more progressive, the income tax need not necessarily represent a large share of tax revenues in order to do so.

The above-described scheme, whereby the income tax supplements the VAT and other indirect taxes, may be appropriate for many developing countries because of its administrative implications. Only a small portion of the population would be required to file income tax returns. Instead of comprising most of the adult populace, as in a country such as the United States, the taxpaying population could be confined to relatively wealthy individuals and to businesses. By contrast, in many transition countries, the number of individuals who pay income tax tends to be higher than in developing countries, but most taxpayers would still not have to file returns because tax on wages and interest and dividends can be collected through withholding.

It is often said that, within the constraint of raising the desired amount of revenue, a well-designed tax system will satisfy the criteria of equity, efficiency, and simplicity. Equity means the establishment of a fair relationship between the resources available to a taxpayer and the amount of tax paid by that taxpayer. Efficiency refers to the effects that taxes have on economic behavior. Simplicity refers to the costs that a complex system imposes on both taxpayers (in complying with the laws) and the government (in collecting taxes). These criteria are merely one way of classifying the policy considerations that go into making decisions about tax law and should not be seen as excluding other factors. It should be clear that making decisions about taxation involves trade-offs among the relevant criteria and, hence, political or value judgments. For these, unique technically correct solutions cannot be dictated.

The primary role of the income tax is to provide horizontal and vertical equity to the tax system. The income tax is the only broad-based tax that can contribute significant progressivity (vertical equity) to the tax system. Of course, there are limits to the desirable degree of progression. Excessively high marginal rates are problematic because of their incentive effects and because of the difficulties they create for administration. For this reason, it is best to achieve progressivity by making sure that the tax base includes all income,

---

[5]See id.

rather than by imposing high rates on a tax base that is full of holes. The income tax can also make a unique contribution to horizontal equity (equal treatment of taxpayers in equal positions). Because the income tax is calculated on an individual basis, the definition of taxable income can be tailored to match a society's concept of equity among taxpayers. The challenge of income tax design is to give operational meaning to the concept of horizontal equity and to balance equity against other tax policy criteria (e.g., an income tax with too high rates will contribute to vertical equity but will lead to economic inefficiency; one that draws too fine distinctions between taxpayers may satisfy horizontal equity but will undermine simplicity).

How to design the income tax law in the face of these trade-offs is the topic of the chapters that follow.

II. Comparative Income Tax Law

Comparative income tax law can be pursued from different angles. Most studies have examined particular aspects of income tax law, comparing their development in different countries.[6] For example, Brian Arnold has traced the development of the taxation of the income of controlled foreign corporations and investment funds.[7] This kind of study can be helpful in the formulation of specific aspects of tax legislation.

In this introduction, I take a different approach—namely, to categorize families of income tax laws and to highlight some of the common characteristics within each family, and among families, as well as some of the differences. In advising a country on income tax design and drafting, it is important to be aware of the basic legal structure of the existing law so that any reform can build on it. As can be seen from the discussion below, the income tax law of most countries fits more or less clearly within one of several families. Legal concepts are inevitably shared within each family. Advice by a foreigner that is not based on an understanding of the family within which the law falls is not likely to be successful or appropriate to the country's situation. Of course, one must not fall into the opposite error either. Just because a law may be classified within a particular family does not mean that a country may not have developed rules of its own that differ radically from its brothers and sisters. Careful study is needed. More likely than not, however, particular rules, even if they cause the law to differ from the rest of the family, will be rooted in the common

---

[6]A recent exception is Hugh Ault et al., Comparative Income Taxation (1997), which considers a broad range of structural issues for the income tax of nine industrial countries, representing four of the eight families of countries identified in Table 1.

[7]Brian Arnold, The Taxation of Controlled Foreign Corporations: An International Comparison (1986); Brian Arnold, *The Taxation of Investments in Passive Foreign Investment Funds in Australia, Canada, New Zealand and the United States*, in Essays on International Taxation (Herbert Alpert and Kees van Raad eds., 1993).

Table 1. Families of Income Tax Laws

1. British	Antigua and Barbuda, Australia, Bahrain, Bangladesh, Barbados, Belize, Botswana, Brunei Darussalam, Canada, Cyprus, Dominica, Fiji, The Gambia, Ghana, Grenada, Guyana, India, Iraq, Ireland, Israel, Jamaica, Jordan, Kenya, Kiribati, Kuwait, Lesotho, Malawi, Malaysia, Malta, Mauritius, Myanmar, Namibia, Nepal, New Zealand, Nigeria, Oman, Pakistan, Papua New Guinea, St. Kitts and Nevis, St. Lucia, St. Vincent and the Grenadines, Samoa, Saudi Arabia, Seychelles, Sierra Leone, Singapore, Solomon Islands, South Africa, Sri Lanka, Sudan, Swaziland, Tanzania, Tonga, Trinidad and Tobago, Uganda, United Kingdom, Zambia, Zimbabwe
2. American	Liberia, Marshall Islands, Micronesia, Palau, Philippines, United States
3. French	Algeria, Benin, Burkina Faso, Burundi, Cameroon, Central African Republic, Chad, Comoros, Republic of Congo, Democratic Republic of the Congo, Côte d'Ivoire, Djibouti, France, Gabon, Guinea, Haiti, Lebanon, Libya, Madagascar, Mali, Mauritania, Morocco, Niger, Rwanda, Senegal, Togo, Tunisia
4. Latin American	Argentina, Bolivia, Brazil, Chile, Colombia, Costa Rica, Dominican Republic, Ecuador, El Salvador, Guatemala, Honduras, Mexico, Nicaragua, Panama, Paraguay, Peru, Uruguay, Venezuela
5. Transition countries	
a. The Baltics, Russia, and other former Soviet Union countries	Armenia, Azerbaijan, Belarus, Estonia, Georgia, Kazakhstan, Kyrgyz Republic, Latvia, Lithuania, Moldova, Russia, Tajikistan, Turkmenistan, Ukraine, Uzbekistan
b. Other	Albania, Bosnia and Herzegovina, Bulgaria, Cambodia, China, Croatia, Czech Republic, Hungary, Lao People's Democratic Republic, former Yugoslav Republic of Macedonia, Mongolia, Poland, Romania, Slovak Republic, Slovenia, Vietnam
6. Northern European	
a. German	Austria, Germany, Luxembourg, Switzerland
b. Dutch	Netherlands, Suriname
c. Nordic	Denmark, Finland, Iceland, Norway, Sweden
d. Belgian	Belgium
7. Southern European	
a. Portuguese	Angola, Cape Verde, Guinea-Bissau, Mozambique, Portugal, São Tomé and Príncipe
b. Italian	Eritrea, Ethiopia, Italy, San Marino, Somalia
c. Spanish	Equatorial Guinea, Spain
d. Greek	Greece
8. Miscellaneous	Islamic State of Afghanistan, Bhutan, Egypt, Indonesia, Islamic Republic of Iran, Japan, Korea, Syrian Arab Republic, Thailand, Turkey, Yemen

legal heritage and may be framed as an antithesis or modulation of rules that are part of that heritage. To understand those rules, it is helpful to know about the common family heritage.

Division into families is also of assistance to those seeking to understand the income taxes of different countries, whether for the purpose of comparative study or as part of tax practice. Identifying common characteristics of each family gives a head start to someone trying to sort out the law of an unfamiliar country. In the case of comparative income tax law research, the classification suggests that such research should include at least one country from each of the groups if it is to embody a truly global perspective.[8]

The classification scheme is not a novel one and largely tracks the classification of legal families by comparative law scholars. At the same time, the focus on the income tax means that some countries that might be grouped into different families for private law purposes may fall into the same family for the income tax because their income tax laws are similar.[9]

Virtually all the member countries of the IMF have some form of income tax law.[10] The families into which these appear to fall are set forth in Table 1.[11] The grouping is based on primary historic commonality or influence; much influence from one country to another is not captured in this grouping.

While there are considerable variations in the details of the income tax rules from country to country, it is important not to lose sight of the considerable commonality in the income tax laws of all countries, and the even greater commonality among the various groups of countries. Also, considering the systems of eight groups of countries is considerably less daunting than considering all the countries of the world individually. Therefore, obtaining a general overview of the income tax laws of the countries of the world is not as difficult as it may seem at first.

Historically, the income tax is a relatively new phenomenon and, in its modern form (late nineteenth and early twentieth centuries), the influence of three countries—Germany, the United Kingdom, and the United States—has

---

[8]Of course, by focusing on solutions adopted within the same paradigm, research confined to a single group can also be helpful.

[9]*Cf.* K. Zweigert and H. Kötz, An Introduction to Comparative Law 66 (2d. ed., Tony Weir trans. 1992).

[10]As far as I have been able to ascertain, only two IMF member countries (The Bahamas and Vanuatu) do not have an income tax. Several have an income tax of only limited application. Thus, Maldives has a tax on bank profits only. St. Kitts and Nevis has an income tax on corporations, but not on individuals. The United Arab Emirates, Oman, and Qatar have corporate taxes, but these apply mostly to oil companies and financial institutions. *See* 29 Tax Laws of the World 96, 110 (1987). Palau has a schedular and somewhat hybrid system, which includes a tax on wages, a modified turnover tax on businesses, and a tax on the net income of financial institutions.

[11]By way of disclaimer, I have not studied all these countries in detail, and it is certainly possible that the classification can be improved on the basis of further study and can be enriched by analysis of cross-family influences. Perhaps there is a doctoral dissertation here for someone?

been predominant. Other systems can for the most part trace their origins back to these three, in some cases in combination. For example, the original income tax law of France was influenced by that of Germany and the United Kingdom.[12]

At a general level, the degree of commonality in income tax is striking, given that the theoretical possibilities for different forms of income taxation are virtually limitless. For example, while there has been extensive academic discussion of a personal expenditure tax, even to the extent of working out the details of such a tax, no country has one. Most countries have a generally similar approach to taxing the chief forms of income (wages and business income), and perhaps a greater divergence of approach in taxing various kinds of income from capital, although the degree of variation is limited. This relatively broad similarity does not mean that there are not differences in technical detail. At the same time, there are substantial differences in policy on particular issues, more so than in the case of a tax like the VAT, which is much more uniformly applied from country to country than the income tax.

In the balance of this section, I highlight some basic structural differences in the income tax laws of the families of countries identified in the table.

The first group consists of countries whose income tax law has been influenced by that of the United Kingdom. For the most part, these countries fall under the common law legal system (in some of the countries, the legal system as a whole may not be common law but the income tax law has a common law influence). The income tax laws of a number of countries in the group go back to a British colonial model law of 1922.[13] Each country has modified its law independently since then; the extent of independent development varies. Countries that achieved independence from Britain before this time (Australia, Canada, New Zealand) developed their income tax laws independently and have not been influenced by the 1922 model.[14] For these countries, the common statutory language or structure is minimal, but there are similarities in the concept of income and allowable deductions that justify placing these countries into the same tax family as the United Kingdom. The income tax law of the United Kingdom itself of course has also undergone considerable independent development since the 1920s, which has not been closely followed by the other countries, except Ireland. Only the income tax law of Ireland therefore bears a close resemblance to that of the current U.K. law. Some of the countries in the group (Brunei Darussalam, Kuwait, Oman, Saudi Arabia)

---

[12]See Guy Gest, France, in Ault et al., supra note 6, at 39.

[13]Report of the Inter-Departmental Committee on Income Tax in the Colonies not Possessing Responsible Government, Cmnd. 1788 (Dec. 1922).

[14]The concept of income in these countries is, however, influenced to varying degrees by the same theories that lie behind English judicial decisions on the meaning of income. See Ault et al., supra note 6, at 8–10, 27–29.

have an income tax statute of limited application that has a common law in-fluence dating from a later period (after World War II).

Although the United Kingdom itself has separate laws for income tax and corporation tax, the 1922 model was a unitary law covering both individuals and corporations, and this approach of having only one income tax law is gen-erally followed by countries in the group.

The modern income tax originated in Great Britain in 1798.[15] Initially, the tax was imposed on a global basis. A schedular structure was introduced in 1803, but the tax again had a global form by 1842, although still based on a schedular definition of income.[16] The 1922 model ordinance represented a considerably simpler statute than the law then in effect in the United King-dom, namely the Income Tax Act, 1918. The 1918 act defined different types of income in schedules to the act and specified different rules for allowable de-ductions in each schedule. By contrast, the model ordinance provided unified definitions of income and deductions. There was a schedular element to the definition of income in the model, in that there were six paragraphs listing sep-arate types of income, so that any receipts not listed in one of these paragraphs were not subject to tax.

Many of the common law countries have departed from a schedular defi-nition of income. Income is often defined globally, and there is no segregation of rules for determining allowable deductions according to particular sched-ules. Instead, the rules for deductions are stated in terms that apply generally to all types of income. Even where the statute has adopted such a global form, however, judicial concepts of income may hearken back to the old schedules. Concepts of what is employment income, what is a capital gain, what is a busi-ness, what is a revenue item, and what expenses are deductible, among other matters, tend to be similarly treated in the judicial decisions, although in some countries these judicial rules have been overridden by statute. An underlying theme for the judicial concept of income (again, except as overridden by stat-ute) is the source concept, under which a receipt is considered to be income only if it is periodic in nature and derived from capital or from an income earn-ing activity.[17] The source concept is shared with continental systems and is in sharp distinction to the United States, which, despite earlier judicial flirtation with the source concept, has enjoyed a judicial concept of income that is broad in scope, reflecting any realized accessions to wealth. The source concept used to be most important for the taxation of capital gains, which are not consid-ered income under a source concept; however, by now many countries with a

---

[15]*See* Tiley, *United Kingdom, in* Ault et al., *supra* note 6, at 109. The tax was imposed by the Income Tax Act, 1799 (39 Geo. 3, c. 13). For a history of the law, *see also* 12 Halsbury's Statutes of England (2d ed. 1949).

[16]*See* Sylvain Plasschaert, Schedular, Global and Dualistic Patterns of Income Taxation 30 (1988). *See infra* ch. 14 for a discussion of the distinction between a schedular system and a global system with a schedular definition.

[17]*See infra* ch. 14, note 8.

source concept of income have overridden it by statute with respect to capital gains (or at least some capital gains).

The United States, together with the few countries whose income tax law is closely modeled on that of the United States, is listed as the second group. It shares with most of the countries in the first group the common law legal system. Therefore, some aspects of drafting, administrative law, and the role of judicial decisions are similar to those in the first group. In contrast with civil law countries, where concepts defined in codes tend to be applied uniformly in tax law,[18] the tax law in the United States and other common law countries tends to be autonomous from other branches of law.[19] However, the United States is categorized in a separate family because its income tax has developed along different lines. There was never an influence of the old U.K. schedules, because the U.S. definition of income was always a global one. Decisions in the U.K. courts on the concept of income and allowable deductions have had little influence in the United States. Although the influence of the U.S. tax rules on other countries in specific areas has been extensive in the past few decades, and although a number of countries—including, for example, many Latin American countries, Canada, Indonesia, and Japan—have taken some inspiration from U.S. tax law, only those few countries whose tax laws were modeled fully on that of the United States are included in the same group.

The United States is characterized by a global definition of income, a comprehensive system for taxing capital gains (although capital gains have been subject to tax at preferential rates, and although the realization rules are not as broad in the United States as they are in Canada, for example), a classical corporate tax system, a single law for corporate and individual income tax, and a worldwide jurisdictional approach based on both citizenship and residence, with the use of a foreign tax credit system for granting relief from international double taxation. The United States has some of the most highly developed rules in virtually all areas of income taxation, which have as a whole become impossibly complex to deal with. A good deal of the law—both basic concepts and detailed interpretations of the statute—is judge-made, probably more so than in any other country. The United States also boasts a high percentage of returns filed compared with the total population.

The third group consists of France and countries that have modeled their tax laws on those of France, largely deriving from a colonial period. There is a substantial degree of commonality among the income tax laws of countries in

---

[18]*See* vol. 1, at 91.

[19]In the United States, an additional factor has contributed to this tendency—namely, that under the federal structure while tax concepts are federally defined, corresponding civil law concepts are differently defined in different states, which are not even uniformly common law jurisdictions.—L.M. Similar considerations apply in Australia (also a federal state), Canada (a federal state, with both common and civil law systems), and to some extent even in the United Kingdom (which has two legal systems for private law—one applicable in Scotland and the other in the rest of the country). *See also infra* ch. 20, note 49.

this group. The resemblance generally is to the tax law of France at an earlier time rather than to the tax law of France today. In France and in many other countries in the group, the tax laws are all gathered into a single tax code (some countries have separate codes for direct and indirect taxes). However, the individual and corporate income taxes are set forth in separate chapters of this code and are considered to be separate taxes. The French definition of income is structured according to eight categories: income from immovable property; business income; remuneration of certain company managers; agricultural income; wages, salaries, and pensions; professional and miscellaneous income; investment income; and capital gains.[20] The rules for determining income and allowable deductions differ from one category to another. Before 1960, income in each schedule was separately taxed, and a global tax was superimposed on the schedular taxes (this is known as a composite system).[21] This composite approach has been replaced in France with a global approach. The scheme of division into schedules is similar to that of Germany (see below), except that Germany has an additional category of miscellaneous income that includes pensions. Capital gains in Germany are taxed under either business income or miscellaneous income. Apart from these and a few other details, however, the German and French schedules follow the same basic approach. The French system does, however, have a number of distinctive features, including a special "family quotient" method for granting relief for dependents,[22] the relatively extensive use of presumptive assessment methods,[23] the preferential treatment of business capital gains,[24] and its approach to taxing income earned abroad (exemption for business income of corporations; no foreign tax credit except under treaties).[25]

The Latin American countries share a similar legal system and the same or similar language. They do not belong in the same family as Spain and Portugal, however, despite the language similarity and colonial background, although they would be placed together if the topic were private law rather than income tax law. The reason is that colonial independence was achieved well before the development of the income tax. Therefore, the development of the income tax in Latin America, Portugal, and Spain occurred with substantial independence and along different lines.[26] Brazil's income tax resembles Argentina's much more than it does Portugal's.

---

[20]*See* FRA CGI § 1. The professional income category includes miscellaneous income: "sources of profits not included in another category of benefits or incomes." *Id.* § 92.

[21]*See* Guy Gest, *France, in* Ault et al., *supra* note 6, at 39. For a discussion of schedular and composite taxation, *see infra* ch. 14, sec. II.

[22]*See infra* ch. 14, sec. IX(B).

[23]*See* vol. 1, ch. 12.

[24]*See* Ault et al., *supra* note 6, at 198.

[25]*See id.* at 385.

[26]For a synopsis, *see* Plasschaert, *supra* note 16, at 32.

All of the countries in the group follow the approach of a single income tax law, covering both individuals and corporations. There are, however, substantial differences within the Latin American group, even in terms of the basic architecture of the income tax law. Some countries have a global definition of income; for example, in Colombia the global definition of income goes back to the origins of the income tax in that country in 1925.[27] By contrast, Chile still follows a composite[28] system of income taxation, under which schedular taxes on different categories of income are creditable against a global complementary tax.[29] The Chilean law divides income into only two categories: capital and business income (first category) and earned income (second category). In the middle fall countries like Argentina. The Argentine law follows continental Europe in defining income differently depending on whether individuals or companies are involved.[30] In the case of companies, any increment to wealth constitutes income (this brings about an equivalent result to the balance sheet approach of France and Germany).[31] In the case of individuals, the source theory is followed, under which an item is income only if it is periodic and comes from a permanent source.[32] Many of the Latin American countries have experienced substantial inflation and have enacted comprehensive inflation-adjustment rules (as contrasted with the ad hoc rules adopted in some European countries) that have by and large been retained even as inflation has declined in recent years.[33] These rules are quite similar in all the Latin American countries that have them. The Latin American countries have generally followed a territorial approach to international taxation, although several have now adopted a global approach. Many of the countries in the group have over the past decade enacted a tax on assets as a minimum business income tax.[34]

The fifth group consists of countries making the transition from a socialist to a largely market-oriented economy. Generally, these countries have separate taxes on the income of individuals and of legal persons. The group is divided into two subgroups, the first of which consists of the 15 countries that formerly made up the Soviet Union. The income tax laws of these countries have been subject to rapid development over the past six years. The pace of

---

[27]See id. at 30–31.

[28]See id. at 17.

[29]See CHL IR §§ 52, 56(3), 63.

[30]This discussion of Argentina draws on Enrique Reig, Impuesto a las Ganancias 24–25, 37–40 (1991).

[31]See infra ch. 16, Appendix A.

[32]See ARG IT § 2.

[33]See vol. 1, ch. 13.

[34]See Peter Byrne, The Business Assets Tax in Latin America—The End of the Beginning or the Beginning of the End? 15 Tax Notes Int'l 941 (Sept. 22, 1997); vol. 1, ch. 12, sec. III(C). Colombia has had a presumptive assets-based tax for some time. See McLure et al., The Taxation of Income from Business and Capital in Colombia 46–49, 140–44 (1990). The concept may have been borrowed from Italy. See infra note 47.

change is particularly noteworthy because all these countries started with virtually identical tax laws as of the time of the breakup of the Soviet Union in early 1992. This common origin justifies their inclusion in one group, at least as of the time of writing, even though there are now substantial differences among them. Since 1992, several members of this group have made radical changes to their income tax legislation (and other tax legislation). The Baltic countries, Georgia, Kazakhstan, the Kyrgyz Republic, and to some extent Uzbekistan and Moldova have adopted systems heavily influenced by international models. Russia and Ukraine have been slower to make fundamental changes, but have nevertheless enacted a substantial volume of tax reform legislation in the income tax area, as with other taxes.

The legislation in place in 1992 was appropriate to the tax system existing under the Soviet Union. Separate laws governed the taxation of physical persons and legal persons. The income tax for individuals had a limited role given the restrictions on individual property ownership and entrepreneurial activity. Under the 1992 legislation,[35] the definition of income for individuals is global in concept. Residents are taxed on their worldwide income, nonresidents only on their domestic-source income. However, a wide variety of exemptions apply covering many types of payments and benefits, including both items received from the state and also many benefits offered by employers (social benefits, pensions, compensation for injuries, severance pay, unemployment benefits, scholarships, interest on state bonds, lottery winnings, and interest on bank deposits, to mention only a few of the long list of exemptions). Under the Russian legislation, capital gains were in principle subject to tax, with exclusions. Enforcement of a capital gains tax is, however, difficult in the region, and some countries eliminated the tax.[36] Special exemptions apply for veterans, other individuals who provided heroic service of specified kinds, and the disabled. Deductions are provided for charitable contributions, dependency allowances, and home construction expenses. Despite the global nature of the definition of income, special rules (primarily having to do with withholding, but also in some cases specifying allowable deductions) were provided for wages received at the primary source of employment, wages received at other sources of employment, business income, income of foreign resident persons (i.e., noncitizens), and nonresidents. A number of the rules are holdovers from the former economy (e.g., special rules for noncitizens). The general orientation of the law was focused on collecting tax from withholding in all possible cases, even for business income.[37] This obviously made sense only in the context of the former economy, where little independent business activity existed.

---

[35]Russian Federation Act № 1998-1, Act on Income Tax on Natural Persons, Dec. 7, 1991.

[36]For example, both Kazakhstan and Georgia did not tax capital gains of individuals before adopting tax codes in 1995 and 1997, respectively.

[37]*See* Act on Income Tax, *supra* note 35, § 13(1)(a).

As the economy developed, it is therefore not surprising that substantial changes in the income tax would be made.

The tax on enterprises was designed with state-owned enterprises in mind. Its accounting rules and concept of income were the same as those under the accounting rules used for general purposes by state enterprises. Indeed, there was no conception that there *could* be a difference between financial accounting and tax accounting. The concepts involved developed out of a planned economy and had little to do with the concept of profit under a market economy. Under these accounting rules, many expenses that are normally deductible under European standards were not deductible. Advertising costs are one example; excessive wages are another,[38] the latter having to do primarily with concerns for regulating state-owned enterprises. Thus, what was required at the time of dissolution of the Soviet Union and transition of these countries toward market-based systems was a fundamental overhaul of these laws in short order. Even six years later, the process is only in its incipient stages in many of the countries in this group, although a few (particularly Estonia and Latvia) have advanced much further in the direction of European standards than the rest.[39] Even where progress has been made in reforming the law, administrative practice may take longer to change. The result is that the old Soviet accounting principles may still exercise an important influence in a number of countries. Those countries that have adopted substantially reformed laws may have freed themselves from these principles in theory, but now face the task of elaborating and applying the somewhat skeletal provisions found in the new legislation.

The other transition countries face similar issues, although they are distinguished from the former Soviet Union group in that they did not inherit the Soviet tax laws as of 1991. These countries similarly started with an accounting system designed for central planning. They have generally by now undertaken at least one round of fundamental revision of their tax laws, but further rounds lie ahead. In many cases, the definition of income under the individual income tax is global in form. To varying degrees, individual countries have looked to particular European countries as models. For example, the income tax law adopted by the Czech and Slovak Republics bears resemblances to the laws of Germany, and the income tax and profit tax laws adopted by (or being considered by) Romania resemble those of France.

---

[38]The concept of denying a deduction for excessive wages seems to have to do with a concern that managers of state-owned enterprises would pay excessive wages as an alternative to making profit distributions to the state.

[39]Kazakhstan adopted a comprehensive tax code in 1995, the Kyrgyz Republic in 1996, and Uzbekistan and Georgia in 1997. I worked on the codes for Kazakhstan and Georgia (the other two were modeled on the Kazakh code) and in my (biased) opinion, the Georgian code is the best of the lot at the time of writing. Even these relatively more modern codes respond to the stage of development of the tax systems of the countries concerned and will need to be upgraded in the future.

The sixth group (northern European) consists of countries whose law has been influenced to varying degrees by Germany and is further broken down into subgroups to reflect the degree of resemblance within each of these. Generally, these countries have separate taxes on individuals and on legal persons. Germany's definition of income is schedular in form and is based on seven categories of income; the same approach is followed in other countries in the same subgroup. The German categories are incomes from agriculture and forestry, business income, income from independent work, income from employment, investment income, rental income, and miscellaneous incomes.[40] The other countries in the group also use a basically schedular definition, but with fewer categories (three or four).[41] In these countries, there is generally no separate concept of capital gains in a business context; gains on the disposition of business assets are taxable as part of business income.[42] Germany has a very important concept (largely shared by other countries in the group and by France) that distinguishes between business assets and private assets. The withdrawal of business assets from business use is a realization event (this is also true in France). By contrast, gains on the sale of private assets are generally not taxable. Exceptions are made for the disposition of shares that represent a significant holding in a company and for short-term gains.[43] Accounting for business income generally follows financial accounting.

As with the northern European group, the seventh group (southern European) has separate taxes on individuals and on legal persons. In contrast to the global approach of Germany, the southern European countries have a history of schedular taxation.[44] Thus, the Italian system has historically been schedular (i.e., separate taxes with independent rate structures) and territorial, and has had a strong element of presumptive taxation.[45] The approach to taxation of capital gains has been similar to that of Germany: private gains are taxed only if attributable to speculative activity; gains of companies are taxed as part of business income. Italy has had a corporate income tax only since 1954.[46] This also had an important presumptive element in that it consisted of two components, the first being the assets of the company and the second being income that exceeds 6 percent of the taxable assets.[47] The income of

---

[40]DEU EStG § 2.

[41]For example, Dutch law divides income into business income, employment income, investment income, periodical payments, and profit from the disposal of a substantial interest. *See* Gerrit te Spenke and A. Peter Lier, Taxation in the Netherlands 22 (1992).

[42]Belgium is an exception. *See infra* ch. 20, sec. III(A).

[43]*See* Ault et al., *supra* note 6, at 199.

[44]*See* Plasschaert at 28–29. Greece also had a schedular system until 1955. The line between north and south is not a clean one, in the sense that Belgium and France had composite systems, going global in 1962 and 1960, respectively.

[45]*See* Harvard Law School, Taxation in Italy (1964).

[46]*See id.* at 196–97.

[47]*See id.* at 199–200. The assets tax has now been dropped. *See* ITA ISR § 89.

corporations was determined in the same manner as for individuals, that is, on a schedule basis. While the income and corporate taxes have now taken a more global form, the historical roots described above have influenced the form of these taxes. Spain also started with a schedular system, including presumptive elements, to which was eventually added a complementary global tax. Finally, the law of September 8, 1978, established the tax on a global basis, but still on a schedular definition of income.[48] Accordingly, the tax is imposed on the following types of income: income from labor, income from nonbusiness capital, income from business and professional activity, capital gains, and income taxed on a flow-through basis.[49] The corporate income tax in Spain goes back to the beginning of the century. By 1957, it was calculated on a global basis.[50] The tax law provides its own accounting rules (i.e., the tax law is autonomous from commercial accounting); however, in practice the differences between tax and commercial accounting are minimized because the regulations call for the commercial accounting rules to be followed for tax purposes unless the tax law stipulates otherwise.[51]

The final miscellaneous category represents countries whose income tax laws do not closely resemble those of any other group. Many of these belong to the Islamic legal family.[52] This is not to say that there has not been a substantial cross-country influence for this group. For example, Turkey has been influenced by Germany and perhaps France. Indonesia has been influenced in recent years by the United States, particularly in the 1983 reform of its income tax law. We also include in the miscellaneous category Japan and the Republic of Korea. There is a close resemblance between the tax laws of these two countries, which have been influenced by Germany and the United States, but have unique features of their own. In Japan, tax accounting for business income is determined by financial accounting, with such adjustments as are specified by the tax law.[53] There is a schedular definition of income, but the schedules differ from those used in Europe, consisting of Type I (corporate income), Type II (interest), and Type III (individual income).[54] The system of

---

[48]See César Albiñana, Sistema Tributario Español y Comparado 260–63 (2d ed. 1992).

[49]See ESP IRPF § 5.

[50]See Albiñana, supra note 48, at 203.

[51]See Reglamento del Impuesto Sobre Sociedades, § 37, reprinted in Código Tributario (Ollero et al. eds.; Aranzadi, 1995); Albiñana, supra note 48, at 208.

[52]An argument could be made for putting Islamic countries into a separate family, but it is not clear that there is sufficient commonality with respect to the income tax to warrant doing so. A feature that is unique to Islamic countries (since it is based on the Koran) is the zakat (whose form varies from country to country, but could be characterized as a hybrid income and wealth tax). In some Islamic countries, particularly Saudi Arabia, the zakat plays an important role in the income tax system, but the relationship between the zakat and the income tax differs substantially from one country to another.

[53]See Nakazato and Ramseyer, Japan, in Ault et al., supra note 6, at 79.

[54]See id. at 71.

taxing corporations is largely a classical one. The general approach to relief of international double taxation is a foreign tax credit system.

One could go on to identify numerous instances of legislative imitation (which in many cases involves borrowing from, or being influenced by, countries outside the group) beyond the influence of predominant countries in these groups, some of which may not be apparent from the legislative language itself. The grouping in the table therefore does not begin to tell the full story as to the influences of various systems on each other.

A Note on Terminology

With some exceptions, the terminology for legal categories of persons and things used in this book corresponds to that used in civil law countries:[55]

"Physical person" corresponds to "individual" in common law countries. "Legal person" is any person who is not a physical person. "Movable property" corresponds generally to "personal property" in common law jurisdictions. "Immovable property" corresponds generally to "real property" in common law jurisdictions. "Cost base" corresponds generally to "basis" or "tax cost."[56]

Acronyms and Citation Style

The citation style in the footnotes generally follows *The Bluebook: A Uniform System of Citation* (15th ed. 1991). This uses some Latin terms that may be unfamiliar to those not accustomed to this style: *supra* (above, in this book), *infra* (below, in this book), and *id.* (short for *idem*, in the same work). To avoid clutter, tax laws are cited using a standard abbreviated format: country abbreviation, abbreviation of law, and § (which refers to section or article, according to the context). Local style in many countries uses "art.," "s," or "sec." instead of §, but it seemed easier and understandable here to use the same format for all countries, since our abbreviated format in any event normally would not be the same as local citation style. Complete references to the laws are given in the bibliography.

The following acronyms are used in this volume:

CIS	Commonwealth of Independent States
EEIG	European Economic Interest Grouping
EPZ	export processing zone
EU	European Union
FDI	foreign direct investment
FIFO	first in, first out

---

[55]For a detailed discussion of these terms, *see* vol. 1, at 91–93.

[56]*See infra* ch. 16(V)(B).

FIFO   first in, first out
GATT   General Agreement on Tariffs and Trade (superseded by WTO)
IBFD   International Bureau of Fiscal Documentation
LIFO   last in, first out
OECD   Organization for Economic Cooperation and Development
PAYE   pay-as-you-earn
TIN   taxpayer identification number
UCITS   undertakings for collective investment in transferable securities
VAT   value-added tax
WTO   World Trade Organization

In numerical examples, "$" is used to refer generically to a country's local currency. If a reference to U.S. dollars is intended, US$ is used.

14

Individual Income Tax

Lee Burns and Richard Krever

> I suspect that if a million monkeys were put in front of a million
> typewriters, by Wednesday one of them would have come up with an
> improved version of the Income Tax Act.
>
> —*Paul Gerber, Senior Member,*
> *Administrative Appeals Tribunal*
> *(Australia)*

I. Introduction

This chapter addresses the design and drafting of the income tax law for
individuals.[1] The discussion covers the structure of the income tax, the definition of the tax base, the tax unit (i.e., identification of the taxpayer), the tax
rate structure, and the administrative and collection aspects of personal income taxation. The discussion of the tax base in this chapter focuses particularly on employment income, including fringe benefits. The taxation of
business and investment income is dealt with in chapter 16.

II. General Design

A. Schedular Versus Global Income Taxes

Two theoretical models exist for the structure of the personal income
tax—schedular and global. A schedular income tax is one in which separate
taxes are imposed on different categories of income. A global income tax is one
in which a single tax is imposed on all income, whatever its nature.

Note: Frans Vanistendael provided extensive input into an earlier draft of this chapter.

[1]This chapter uses the term "individual," commonly referred to in civil law countries as "physical
person" or "natural person," and refers to the tax as individual income tax or personal income tax.

In the benchmark schedular system, gross income and deductible expenses are determined separately for each type of income; in some cases, limited deductions or no deductions may be allowed. The rates of tax applicable to each category of income are then applied to the taxable amount of the income. The rates of tax may vary from category to category. Different procedures may apply to each category of income for the reporting, assessment, and collection of tax. Some types of income may be taxable only through withholding; others may involve the filing of returns. Schedular systems used to be more widespread; a few countries still have such a system, or one with substantial schedular elements.[2]

In the benchmark global system, there is no matching of particular types of income to the expenses incurred to derive the income. All income and expenses are considered together to arrive at a single net gain that is subject to tax. Thus, under a pure global system, the category of income is irrelevant.

Between pure schedular and pure global taxation, there are many possibilities. One of these has been called "composite," under which a global-type system is superimposed on a set of schedular taxes.[3] This approach involves combining some or most types of income for the purpose of imposing a progressive rate surcharge on top of the flat rates commonly imposed on the schedularized categories of income, as well as for the purpose of providing personal tax relief for family costs.

Many tax policy theoreticians consider the global income tax to be superior to the schedular system. It is commonly suggested that schedular taxation suffers from the following disadvantages:

---

[2]According to the latest legislation we could find (see Bibliography of Tax Laws), Burkina Faso, Burundi, the People's Republic of China, Eritrea, Ethiopia, Lebanon, Palau, Romania, Rwanda, Somalia, Sudan, the Republic of Yemen, and the Democratic Republic of the Congo (formerly Zaïre) have a substantially schedular individual income tax, in which different rate schedules apply to different major categories of income. Although Hungary has a global definition of income and a progressive rate schedule for the consolidated tax base (see HUN PIT §§ 4, 30), there are so many special rules and separate rates for different kinds of income that the tax should be considered substantially schedular. While the Philippines started out with a global system, a schedular system was adopted in 1981, with wages being taxed separately from other income. See Angel Yoingco, The Dynamics of Income Tax Reform (1985); and National Internal Revenue Code §§ 21, 28, and 29 (J. Nolledo, ed. 1985). Since then, there has been some movement back toward a global system, although substantial schedular elements remain. Schedular taxes are imposed on foreign-source income derived by nonresident citizens, and on interest, dividends, and capital gains, while other income is aggregated and subject to tax under a progressive rate schedule. See PHL NIRC § 21. A number of other countries treat certain income from capital on a schedular basis, for example, CZE ITA § 36 (special rates of tax applicable to interest and dividends); KAZ TC § 13 (interest, dividends, and liquidation gains subject to final taxes); LSO ITA § 158(2) (final withholding tax on interest). See also infra note 12.

[3]See Sylvain Plasschaert, Schedular, Global and Dualistic Patterns of Income Taxation 17 (1988). Examples of composite systems are those in Chile and Mozambique. The superimposed global tax is typically called a global complementary tax.

(1) The separation of an individual's income into more than one tax regime may make it difficult or impossible to impose progressive taxation and to provide for personal tax relief (in the form of exemptions, deductions, or rebates). Progressive taxation is commonly seen as the most effective way of levying taxes on an ability-to-pay basis, and, to the extent that ability to pay is indicated by an increase in total economic capacity, the tax should be levied on a taxpayer's total income. Under a schedular system, a progressive marginal rate structure may be applied to some categories of income only, leading to inequities between taxpayers who earn different types of income. Similarly, under a schedular system, personal tax relief must be either applied wholly against one category of income, such as employment income—in which case the relief may not be fully effective—or divided among various categories of income, which increases complexity.

(2) The schedular system is potentially more difficult to administer. Scarce administrative resources may be wasted on classification issues arising at the borders between the various schedules. For example, if income from employment and income from business are taxed under different schedules, then it becomes necessary to characterize a particular income-earning activity as being one of employment or business (self-employment). The border between an employer-employee and a customer-consultant relationship is difficult to draw.

(3) Any differences in the final tax burdens imposed under a schedular system on income in different categories will be exploited by taxpayers engaging in tax planning and restructuring to ensure that their income fits within the most advantageous category. Tax-planning activities of this sort not only impose economic dead-weight losses as resources are diverted into unproductive planning activities, but also may cause serious economic inefficiency as taxpayers opt for income-earning activities that may be less efficient, but more lightly taxed.

While a global income tax may be preferable from a conceptual perspective, the purest form remains a theoretical ideal only. In practice, all global income taxes contain some schedular elements and most existing income tax systems lie on the spectrum between schedular and global. While some countries with a global income tax define income without breaking it down into categories,[4] others have a schedular structure to the identification of taxable amounts, whereby such amounts are defined according to categories of income.[5] Such a definitional structure has two general implications. First, if an item is not included in any of the categories, then it is not included in income. Some countries may have a residual category, but even that is often not open-ended.[6] Second, it will often make a difference into which category an item of income

---

[4]*See* COL TC § 26; HUN PIT § 4 (*but see supra* note 2); RUS IT § 2; USA IRC § 61.

[5]*See* AUT EStG § 2; BEL CIR § 6; CAN ITA § 3; DEU EStG § 2; FRA CGI § 13; ESP IR § 23; GBR ICTA §§ 15–20; JPN IT § 22; LSO ITA §17.

[6]*See* DEU EStG § 22; LSO ITA § 17(1)(d); SGP ITA § 10(1)(g). *See also infra* secs. III(A) and VI.

falls, because each category has its own rules.[7] Even in jurisdictions that do not define income by reference to categories, judicial doctrines may classify income into different types.[8] Moreover, whatever the basic definition of income, distinctions are often made in the legislation for a range of policy and technical reasons. For example, if capital gains are included in the tax base, they may be treated differently from other types of income.[9] Similarly, different rules may apply to expenses incurred to derive different types of income,[10] or discrete sets of rules may be considered appropriate for particular types of income.[11]

Finally, the global systems of many countries have become partially schedularized by the use of final withholding taxes on certain types of income, particularly dividends and interest, and lower tax rates on capital income.[12] It has been suggested that in these jurisdictions partial schedularization may ac-

---

[7]*See, e.g.*, FRA CGI § 13(3).

[8]This approach is common in jurisdictions that have derived their income tax principles from the United Kingdom. For example, AUS ITAA (1997) § 6-1(1) provides that assessable income consists of "ordinary income and statutory income." Statutory income is any amount that is expressly included in assessable income under a provision of the tax law (ITAA (1997) § 6-10(2)). Ordinary income is income classified according to ordinary concepts (ITAA (1997) § 6-5(1)). The definition of income classified according to ordinary concepts has been elaborated by the courts. An amount derived is ordinary income if it has its source in an earning activity. The earning activities identified by the courts are the employment of one's labor, the investment of capital, or the application of labor and capital combined (i.e., the carrying on of a business). This has led to what is, in effect, a judicial categorization of income into employment, business, or property income. The courts have recognized that an amount derived that exhibits some of the essential characteristics of employment, business, or property income (such as periodicity and anticipation of receipt) may be ordinary income, although it does not have its source in an earning activity. Examples of such amounts are pensions and annuities.

[9]Capital gains may be distinguished because they are subject to preferential rates of tax, are partially exempt from tax, or are adjusted for inflation, or because restrictions are imposed on the deduction of capital losses.

[10]For example, many jurisdictions distinguish interest outgoings from other expenses for the purpose of imposing quarantining rules. *See infra* ch. 16. These rules may require further categorization of income types because interest expense incurred to earn a particular type of income may be deductible only against that type. Another expense-quarantining rule found in some jurisdictions is a restriction on the deductibility of employment expenses, which requires drawing a distinction between employment and business activity.

[11]An example is farming income, which is taxed on the basis of estimates in a number of countries. *See* FRA CGI § 64; DEU EStG § 13(1); AUT EStG § 21. In such countries, it will be important whether a particular activity is considered farming or nonfarming business. Obviously, this is also the case in countries where income from agriculture is exempt. *E.g.*, GEO TC § 43.

[12]Belgium effectively abolished progressive income tax on dividends and interest in 1985 and replaced it with a final withholding tax system; *see* BEL CIR §§ 171, 261, 269. Germany, which had a progressive tax on interest, collected very little on it and introduced a withholding tax in 1994 in order to be able to collect at least some revenue on interest income; *see* DEU EStG §§ 43, 43a. Scandinavian countries, led by Sweden, have recently moved toward schedularization and final withholding taxes on income from capital. *See* Leif Mutén et al., Towards a Dual Income Tax? (1996). *See infra* sec. XII, for discussion of final withholding tax on employment income. *See infra* ch.16 for discussion of final withholding taxes on investment income.

tually increase the progressivity of the income tax by eliminating opportunities for taxpayers to exploit timing differences and other preferential treatment that may apply to different types of income and expenses.[13]

B. Single or Separate Tax Laws

A basic structural question for income tax law is whether to have all income taxes in a single law or to have two separate laws, one for individuals and one for legal persons (companies and other taxable entities).[14]

A range of models exists.[15] In some countries, company income tax is levied under a separate tax law from individual income tax, and there is no cross-reference between these laws for the determination of the tax base.[16] A second model has company income tax levied in a law separate from that imposing tax on the income of individuals, but the rules for calculating the tax base are based on the rules in the individual income tax law,[17] or vice versa.[18] A third model has separate regimes for individuals and companies contained within a single act, with the company tax rules cross-referenced to the individual tax base rules so that the company tax rules in effect "piggyback" on those applicable to individuals.[19] A variation of this approach uses the same legislation and the same basic rules for determining the company and individual tax bases, but includes supplementary provisions with special rules applicable to companies or individuals.[20]

---

[13]See Mutén et al., *supra* note 12. The specific manifestation of this exploitation often is the deduction of interest expense and other losses against positive capital income. As a result of such deductions, the tax base for capital income may be very small without schedularization.

[14]Schedular systems may even have separate laws for different categories of income. This was more common in the past, but currently applies in Romania, for example, although it is proposed to consolidate these laws.

[15]In addition to the basic structural alternatives described, a look at the Bibliography of Tax Laws, *infra*, shows that many countries have, besides the basic individual and corporate income tax laws, other tax laws that contain rules related to income tax. Some of the Scandinavian countries provide examples of this. The resultant structure contributes to the complexity of the system, although it must be said in fairness that other countries (such as the United States) have managed to achieve a comparable if not greater complexity even though they have only one tax law.

[16]This is, for example, the case in Latvia, Romania, and Russia. Japan also has separate laws for individuals and corporations, with independent rules for determining income. In Hungary, the individual income tax law contains its own rules for measuring business income and expenses; the corporate income tax law refers to the amount determined for financial accounting purposes in the case of taxpayers keeping double-entry books. *See* HUN CTDT § 6. The tax code of the Kyrgyz Republic contains separate rules for individuals and companies, repeating most of the income-determination rules.

[17]See AUT KStG § 7(2); DEU KStG § 8(1); NLD Vpb § 8. Technically, the German company tax is not an income tax, but a tax on profits, the concept of income being reserved for the taxation of individuals.—L.M.

[18]See ESP IRPF § 42.

[19]See FRA CGI § 209.

[20]E.g., AUS ITAA; CAN ITA; COL TC; GBR ICTA; SWE SIL; USA IRC.

From a technical perspective, it is equally acceptable to use separate company and individual income tax laws or a single law, and both alternatives are compatible with either classical or imputation company and shareholder tax systems (these are described in chapter 19). It seems preferable, however, to abstain from separately setting forth the rules for individuals and companies, which would lead to duplication, complexity, and the risk of establishing divergent rules. More important than the form of the legislation is its substance. It is important that the tax base (and rates) of the company tax and the individual tax on business income be similar to simplify administration and discourage taxpayers from using a possibly less efficient business form only to secure tax savings arising from differences between the company and individual tax systems.

C. Charging Provision and Basic Terminology

The personal income tax is, as its name implies, a tax on persons, not on transactions or things. The charging provision in the income tax law should therefore impose the tax on persons. The tax is not imposed on all persons; rather, it is imposed only on those persons who have taxable income[21] for the relevant tax period.[22] Some countries impose the income tax on the taxable income of persons, rather than on persons having taxable income.[23] A charging provision of this type needs to be supported by a provision that imposes a liability to pay the tax on the person having the taxable income. The administrative provisions of the legislation will specify the due date for payment of the tax and include mechanisms for the collection and recovery of the tax due.

The charging provision sets out four central concepts underpinning the income tax. First, it identifies the *person* liable for tax, namely, any person who has taxable income for the tax period. The issues relating to identifying the taxpayer are discussed in section IX, below. Second, the charging provision imposes the income tax by reference to the *tax period*. This means that the taxable income of any person must be calculated separately for each tax period. Generally, the tax period for the income tax is a specific period of 12 months, commonly the calendar year or financial year of the relevant country. The periodic nature of the income tax means that it is necessary to provide accounting rules for allocating income and expenses to particular tax periods for the purpose of calculating a person's taxable income for the period. These rules are discussed briefly in section VIII, below, and in more detail in chapter 16.

---

[21]The term "taxable income" is used in this chapter to refer to the amount against which the rates of tax are applied. An alternative term used in some countries is "chargeable income." *See* LSO ITA § 13; SGP ITA § 38.

[22]*E.g.*, LSO ITA § 4(1).

[23]*E.g.*, USA IRC §§ 1, 11. Until recently, the income tax law in Australia followed this pattern; however, as part of the progressive rewriting of that law, the income tax is now imposed on entities (which is defined to include individuals): *see* AUS ITAA (1997) § 4-1.

Third, the concept of *taxable income* defines the tax base. Taxable income is a net concept determined by reference to the tax period. All income tax systems, whether global or schedular, generally seek to impose taxation on a net amount because this amount properly reflects a person's increase in economic capacity for the tax period.[24] The taxable income of a person for a tax period is therefore commonly defined as the gross income[25] of the person for the period less the total deductions allowed to the person for the period. A schedular income tax nets gross income and related deductible expenses on a schedule-by-schedule basis, while a global income tax nets gross income against total deductible expenses. The specification of the tax base is discussed in sections III–VII, below. Fourth, the charging provision should provide for the calculation of the amount of *tax payable*. In the ordinary case, this involves applying the relevant tax rates to the taxable income of the taxpayer and then subtracting any tax offsets that may be available to the taxpayer. Tax offsets are reductions in the amount of tax otherwise payable.[26] They are allowed primarily to reflect tax already paid through a special collection regime or as a concession to achieve certain social or economic objectives. Design issues relevant to tax rates are discussed in section X, below, and tax offsets are discussed in section XI, below.

By clearly specifying the central concepts, the charging provision will ensure that there is consistency in the use of terminology, thereby providing a coherent structure for the substantive provisions of the legislation. It is preferable that the charging provision be included at the commencement of the legislation so that the substantive provisions can then be developed as an elaboration of the central concepts specified in the provision. The importance of consistency cannot be emphasized too strongly. At best, failure to provide a coherent structure will lead to a confused application of the tax law; at worst, it will make the law unworkable. For example, it must be clear that charging provisions apply to taxable income and not to gross income.[27] Similarly, it must be made clear whether supplementary definition provisions include amounts in gross income or in taxable income.

---

[24]There are exceptions to this general rule, the most important being withholding taxes that are imposed on gross receipts. However, there is often little or no expense involved in deriving some kinds of income commonly subject to withholding tax, such as interest income. Also, withholding tax rates are commonly lower than ordinary tax rates, the difference being in part attributable to the fact that expenses are not taken into account when withholding taxes are imposed on gross receipts. The application of a lower rate against income that commonly involves few deductions means that the withholding tax is effectively a proxy for tax on a net basis.

[25]Also sometimes called "assessable income." *See* AUS ITAA (1997) § 4-15.

[26]Tax offsets are known by a variety of technical labels, including tax credits, tax rebates, and deductions of tax. For a discussion of the terminology used in various countries to describe tax offsets, *see infra* note 205.

[27]Unless, of course, it is gross income on which the tax is levied as with withholding taxes. It must be clearly stated when tax is imposed on taxable income and when it is imposed on gross income.

III. Taxable Income

The concept of taxable income effectively defines the income tax base. It was stated above that the taxable income of a person for a tax period is commonly defined as the gross income of the person for the period less the total deductions allowed to the person for the period.[28] The gross income of a person for a tax period is the total of amounts derived[29] by the person during the period that are subject to tax. The gross income of a person, therefore, will not include amounts that are exempt from tax. The total deductions of a person for a tax period are the total of expenses incurred by the person during the period in deriving amounts subject to tax plus any capital allowances and other amounts allowed as a deduction on a concessional basis (e.g., charitable donations). Consequently, there are three key elements in the definition of the tax base: first, the inclusion of amounts in gross income; second, the identification of amounts that are exempt income; and third, the allowance of amounts as deductions.

The definition of key concepts related to the determination of taxable income, drawing on commonly accepted understandings and notions in the jurisdiction, will depend in part on the structure of the income tax system to be adopted and in part on existing structures and concepts. Even when general definitions are used, they are inevitably supplemented by specific definitions, inclusion rules, exclusion rules, rules allowing deductions, and rules denying certain deductions. Thus, any consideration of general definitions must be made in the context of plans for specific rules.

A. Gross Income

Supplementary definition and inclusion provisions applying to the determination of gross income have proved increasingly important for the implementation of global tax systems. There are three reasons for this. The first is the circular definition of income that characterizes many global systems. As stated above, taxable income is normally defined as gross income less allowable deductions. But the definition of gross income may provide little guidance to the income concept, often including the term that it purports to define.[30] Second, and related to the first point, supplementary definition and inclusion pro-

---

[28]E.g., AUS ITAA (1997) § 4-15(1), ("taxable income = assessable income – deductions"); CAN ITA § 2(2) (taxable income defined as income plus certain additions and minus certain deductions); USA IRC § 63(a) (taxable income defined as gross income minus deductions).

[29]The word "derived" is used in this chapter to refer to the allocation of an amount to a particular tax period according to the application of tax accounting rules. *See infra* sec. VIII.

[30]E.g., AUS ITAA (1997) § 6-1(1) ("assessable income consists of ordinary income and statutory income"); CAN ITA § 3 (income defined as "the total of all amounts each of which is the taxpayer's income"); EST ITL § 9 ("the income of a resident taxpayer is all income derived. . . ."); USA IRC § 61(a) (gross income defined as "all income from whatever source derived").

visions may be needed to overcome the otherwise restrictive concept of income that would be applied by courts, particularly in Commonwealth or former Commonwealth countries, where courts rely on U.K. judicial doctrines.[31] Third, supplementary definition and inclusion provisions may be required in response to the growing complexity and variation of legal forms and transactions.[32]

Consequently, even under a global income tax, the inclusion of amounts in gross income will often be specified by reference to particular categories of income. For this purpose, income is commonly divided into employment, business, and property income. There are often supplementary definitions of each category of income and, in the case of property income, definitions of amounts included in property income (e.g., dividends, interest, rent, and royalties).

However, not all amounts derived by a taxpayer will fit neatly into one of these categories.[33] An issue arises, therefore, as to the specification of other amounts to be included in gross income. This is commonly done by separately listing out those amounts. As stated above, such a definitional structure means that any amount that does not come within one of the listed inclusions will not be included in gross income. This may be overcome by including a residual category of income. The residual category may itself be a separate category.[34] Alternatively, the list of amounts included in gross income may be expressed to be inclusive only so that a general formula may apply for including other amounts in gross income.[35] Regardless of how the residual category is identified, it is important that there be some certainty in the scope of its operation. Sometimes the word "income" is used to define the residual category.[36] In the absence of a definition of income,[37] such an approach can lead to uncertainty where the word is used in a jurisdiction in which it has no established mean-

---

[31]*See supra* note 8.

[32]For example, special definitional provisions may be needed to define as interest income certain types of gain realized on financial transactions. *See infra* ch. 16.

[33]*See infra* sec. VI for examples of amounts that may fall outside a classification of income into employment, business, and property income.

[34]*E.g.*, LSO ITA § 17(1)(d); SGP ITA § 10(1)(g).

[35]*E.g.*, EST ITL § 9(1) ("income of a resident taxpayer is all income derived by him/her from all sources of income during the period of taxation, including" seven specified categories of income. The inclusive nature of the provision means that any other amount derived by a resident taxpayer that is "income" is taxed); IDN IT art. 4(1) ("the Tax Object is income, meaning any increase in economic prosperity received or accrued by a Taxpayer . . . that may be used for consumption or to increase the wealth of such Taxpayer, in whatever name and form, including" 11 specified categories of income. Again, the inclusive nature of the provision means that any other amount that is "income" is taxed). "Inclusive" is used here to refer to a definition that takes the form of including specified items in a general concept, as opposed to offering an exhaustive definition of that concept.

[36]*E.g.*, EST ITL § 9(1); IDN IT art. 4(1); SGP ITA § 10(1)(g).

[37]IDN IT art. 4(1) is an example of a defined concept of income being used as a residual category. In that provision, income is defined to mean "any increase in economic prosperity." *See supra* note 35.

ing.[38] On the other hand, where it does have an established meaning, care must be taken to ensure that the use of the word "income" does not unduly restrict the intended scope of the tax base. A preferable approach may be to define the residual category broadly so that it covers all gains of whatever nature and to rely on the definition of exempt income to limit its scope.[39]

The discussion of the tax base below and in chapter 16 follows an approach that divides income into four broad categories: employment, business, and investment income, and miscellaneous receipts.

B. Exempt Income

There will be amounts that are not to be included in gross income. These amounts are usually identified as "exempt income." In providing for the basic charging provisions, it must be made clear that amounts defined as "exempt income" are excluded from the definition of gross income and thus from the calculation of taxable income.

While many different amounts may be treated as exempt income, such amounts can be classified into several broad categories. First, an amount or an entity may be exempt for social compassion reasons. Examples of amounts that may be exempt on this basis are welfare payments, scholarships, and compensation payments.[40] Examples of entities that may be exempt on this basis are religious, charitable, or education institutions of a public character.[41]

Second, an amount may be exempt as a result of international convention, agreement, or practice. For example, a country that is a signatory of the Vienna Convention on Diplomatic Relations is obliged to exempt from tax the official employment income and foreign-source income of a foreign diplomatic officer, consular officer, administrative or technical employee of a diplomatic mission or consulate, consular employee, member of the service staff of a diplomatic mission or consulate, or a private servant of a diplomatic mission.[42] The exemption also extends to the foreign-source income of family members and consular staff. As a matter of practice (sometimes only on a reciprocal basis), a similar exemption may be extended to other foreign government representatives working in the country.

---

[38]In the Anglo context, as a result of judicial decisions, for an amount to be income, it must have its source in an earning activity or exhibit the essential characteristics of an amount that has its source in an earning activity (*see supra* note 8). This is also the case in some continental European countries. In the United States, a broader notion of income has been developed by the courts, including any realized accretion to wealth.

[39]*E.g.*, IDN IT art. 4(1) and (3); LSO ITA § 17(1)(d) and §§ 21–32.

[40]*See infra* sec. VI.

[41]*See infra* ch. 19. The exemption may not apply to all income of the entity. For example, business income derived by such an entity from carrying on activities that are not related to the entity's religious, charitable, or educational purpose may be taxable.

[42]Vienna Convention on Diplomatic Relations (1961) art. 34 (500 UNTS 95).

Third, an amount may be exempt for structural reasons. This is primarily to prevent double taxation under the income tax or other tax legislation. For example, some amounts (e.g., interest) may be subject to withholding of tax at source as a final tax on the income. It is necessary to exempt such amounts from inclusion in gross income so as to avoid double counting. Another example is gifts, which may be subject to gift duties or capital transfer taxes. While such amounts need to be excluded from gross income, whether they are treated as exempt income for all the purposes of the income tax legislation will depend on the circumstances in which the concept of exempt income is relevant under the legislation.[43]

Fourth, an amount may be exempt for political or administrative reasons. An example of such an amount is a windfall gain.[44] Finally, an amount may be exempt as an incentive to encourage a particular activity. For example, the income of a retirement fund may be exempt from tax to encourage retirement savings. As indicated above, the concept of exempt income may be relevant for other purposes of the income tax law. For example, it is important in applying rules that deny deductions for expenditures incurred to derive exempt income.

C. Deductions

The third element in the determination of the tax base is the allowance of amounts as a deduction. The usual structure for allowing amounts as a deduction is to provide a general rule followed by supplementary definition and allowance provisions. The general rule commonly allows a deduction for expenses to the extent to which they are incurred in deriving amounts included in gross income. Consequently, the specification of amounts included in gross income also defines the basic parameters for the claiming of deductions. Supplemental provisions allow deductions for capital allowances (such as depreciation and amortization provisions) and as a tax incentive (such as charitable donations and retirement fund contributions).

D. General Principles

In specifying the basic structural rules of the income tax, there are some general principles for which provision may need to be made.

---

[43]For example, it is a feature (albeit unusual) of the Australian income tax that the amount of a loss carried forward for a particular tax period is reduced by the net exempt income of the taxpayer for that period, with the balance applied first against the net exempt income of the following tax period (AUS ITAA (1997) § 36-15). With such a feature, it is important that amounts treated as exempt income to prevent double counting be excluded from the calculation of net exempt income. Australian tax law has not always been consistent in this regard.

[44]*See infra* sec. VI.

1. Apportionment

The categorization of income (including the treatment of some income as exempt) gives rise to the need for apportionment rules, particularly for deductions. It is possible that a particular expense (such as interest) may be incurred to derive more than one category of income. Where different rules apply to different categories of income (e.g., expenses incurred in deriving investment income may be deductible only against that income), it is necessary to apportion such expenses between the different categories of income. It is generally sufficient for the law to state a principle that deductions are to be apportioned reasonably among the categories of income to which they relate.[45] If necessary in a particular class of case, more detailed rules can be provided by way of regulation or administrative practice. As stated above, some deductions may be allowed as a tax concession to encourage a particular activity (such as the making of charitable donations or contributions to retirement funds) and, therefore, do not relate to the derivation of any income. It may be necessary to make special provision for the apportionment of such deductions. Such a rule could provide for the apportionment of such deductions ratably among each class of income derived by the taxpayer.[46]

It may also be necessary to have an apportionment rule for income, although the derivation of composite amounts is probably less likely to arise than the incurrence of expenses to earn more than one class of income. One type of composite amount that is likely to be derived is a compensation receipt. It is possible, for example, in the personal injury context, that an undissected lump sum amount may be paid as damages for several losses, such as loss of earnings, physical impairment, and pain and suffering. In this example, to the extent that the amount is for loss of earnings, it should be included in gross income. A general rule of apportionment will achieve this result. In the absence of such an express rule, the courts may be willing to apply such a rule as a matter of general principle.[47] Alternatively, the courts may apply a single characterization to the whole amount.[48]

2. Recouped Deductions

Another example of an amount that may require a general inclusion rule is a recouped deduction (i.e., an expenditure or loss for which a deduction has been allowed that is subsequently recouped in whole or in part). It is common to find such rules in specific contexts, such as the recovery of amounts written off as bad debts or capital allowances recovered on disposal of the relevant as-

---

[45]E.g., LSO ITA § 46(1).

[46]E.g., LSO ITA § 46(2).

[47]See, e.g., Tilley v. Wales [1943] A.C. 386 (U.K. courts).

[48]See, e.g., McLaurin v. FC of T (1961) 104 CLR 381 (Australian courts have characterized such an amount as wholly capital).

set; however, it is preferable that a general principle be stated to ensure that all possible situations are covered. Such a rule would provide that any expenditure or loss (including a bad debt) that has been allowed as a deduction in one tax period but is recovered by the taxpayer in whole or in part in a later tax period is included in the gross income in that later period to the extent of the amount recovered. It should also be stated that the recouped amount takes the character of the income to which it relates. For example, the recovery of a previously deducted bad debt incurred in carrying on a business should be treated as business income. In the absence of such an express rule, the courts in some countries may be willing to apply such a rule as a matter of general principle,[49] but this may not always be the case.[50]

3. Valuation

It will be necessary in some cases to take into account for tax purposes an amount in kind. This is most commonly the case where income is derived as a benefit in kind (e.g., an employee fringe benefit). However, there are other contexts under the income tax where this will also be the case. For example, a deductible outgoing may be paid in kind, or an asset may be acquired or disposed of for consideration given in kind. In each case, the in-kind item must be valued for the purposes of determining the amount to be taken into account for tax purposes.

It is common for detailed valuation rules to be provided in the income tax law for the valuation of employee fringe benefits. However, as indicated above, the derivation of an employee fringe benefit is not the only circumstance in which an in-kind item will have to be valued for tax purposes. It is suggested, therefore, that a general valuation rule be included in the income tax law.[51] It is important that such a rule be of general operation so that it can apply in all circumstances where it is necessary to value an in-kind item. In other words, the rule should not be confined to the valuation of benefits as income. It is also important that the general valuation rule be subordinate to any specific valuation rule or rules that may apply in a particular context (such as those that may apply for the valuation of employee fringe benefits).

It is suggested that the basis of valuation under the general rule should be fair market value.[52] Where consideration is given in kind, valuation will ordinarily be necessary for both sides of the transaction. For example, if a person

---

[49]This is the position in the United States under the judicially developed tax benefit principle. *See* Hillsboro Nat'l Bank v. C.I.R. 460 U.S. 370 (1983); *see generally* Bittker & Kanner, The Tax Benefit Rule, 26 U.C.L.A. L. Rev. 265 (1978).

[50]*See, e.g.,* FC of T v. Rowe (97 ATC 4317) (Australia).

[51]Countries with a tax code may specify such a rule as part of the general provisions applicable to other taxes as well (such as value-added tax (VAT)). *E.g.,* Germany has a separate tax law known as the Valuation Law (DEU BewG).

[52]*E.g.,* LSO ITA § 65(1).

pays a deductible expense in kind, then the in-kind item will need to be valued for the purposes of determining both the deductible amount to the payer and the income inclusion amount of the payee.[53] Similarly, if a person acquires an asset providing consideration in kind, the tax cost of the asset acquired should reflect the value of the consideration given.

Special rules may need to be applied to the derivation of nonconvertible benefits. In jurisdictions relying on U.K. doctrines, the derivation of a non-convertible benefit raises two issues. The first is the characterization of the benefit as income and the second is the valuation of the benefit to determine the amount of income derived. For other jurisdictions, only the valuation issue arises.

The characterization issue arises in those jurisdictions relying on old U.K. doctrines because the judicial concept of income under those doctrines excludes benefits in kind that cannot be converted to cash.[54] In these juris-dictions, specific statutory inclusion provisions are necessary to bring noncon-vertible benefits into the gross income of the recipient. While nonconvertible benefits are most commonly provided in the employment context, they may be provided in other contexts, and the nonconvertible benefit rule applies equally in those other contexts.[55] Consequently, any statutory income inclu-sion rule applicable to nonconvertible benefits must be of general application and must not be confined to employee fringe benefits.

Where a nonconvertible benefit is characterized as income under either general principles or a statutory income-inclusion rule, the value of the ben-efit (and hence the amount of income derived) must be determined. In par-ticular, the issue is whether there should be any discount for the nonconvertibility of the benefit. On the grounds of equity and neutrality, the fair market value rule should apply equally to nonconvertible benefits.

---

[53]The in-kind payment may also involve the disposal of an asset (such as inventory) of the payer. Consequently, the valuation rule will need to apply also for the purpose of calculating any gain or loss on disposal of the asset by the payer. Similarly, the receipt of the in-kind item may also amount to the acquisition of an asset by the payee and the valuation rule will need to apply for the purpose of determining the tax cost of the asset. For example, suppose that A owes B $100 for rent of business premises. Instead of paying cash, A transfers to B inventory with a market value of $100 and that cost A $80. Under a fair market value rule, A will be re-quired to recognize a gain of $20 on disposal of the inventory and will be allowed to claim a de-duction of $100 for rental expense. This means that A is in the same position as if he or she had disposed of the inventory for cash that was then used to pay the rent. Under the fair market value rule, B would be required to recognize $100 as rental income and as the cost of the inventory acquired.

[54]This is a consequence of the doctrine from the decision of the House of Lords in Tennant v. Smith [1892] A.C. 150, where the taxpayer received free use of premises that he could not assign or let.

[55]See FC of T v. Cooke & Sherden 80 ATC 4140 (nonconvertible benefit provided in the business context); and Dawson v. Comm'r of IR (NZ) 78 ATC 6012 (nonconvertible benefit pro-vided as the return for an investment).

That is, there should be no discount for any restriction on the transfer of the benefit to another person or for the fact that the benefit is not otherwise convertible to cash.

IV. Employment Income

The main category of income derived by an individual is employment income. A number of technical and administrative issues arise in the taxation of employment income. The technical issues are discussed below and the administration issues are discussed in section XII.

A. Definition of Employment and Employment Income

The notion of employment is important in both schedular and global income tax systems. Under a schedular system, it is common for separate taxes to be imposed on income from employment and income from business, trade, or professional activities.[56] The rate of tax and the method of collection will generally differ depending on which tax regime applies. Consequently, the notion of employment under a schedular system is fundamental to the determination of the tax regime that is to apply to particular income derived. Under a global system, as stated above, there is often a schedular notion of income under which employment income is specifically included in gross income.[57] Even when there is a completely global notion of income, it is usual for there to be special rules applicable to employment income, particularly in relation to the collection of tax on such income.

In the absence of a tax law definition of employment, general law notions will apply. In civil law countries, employment will take the definition in the civil code or in a labor code.[58] In common law countries, employment will be defined by reference to tort jurisprudence applicable to determining an employer's vicarious liability. Neither type of definition will necessarily be appropriate for income tax purposes, where the objects of the legislation are quite different from those underlying the code or common law doctrines. For example, for income tax purposes (particularly the collection of tax), it is preferable to treat as employment relationships all service relationships where the remuneration paid is essentially for the labor of the service provider. This is the case regardless of the legal characterization of the relationship as that of office-holder or customer-client. These are relationships where the service provider incurs few deductible expenses in providing his or her labor and, therefore, should be subject to the collection regime applicable to income from employ-

---

[56]E.g., ERI ITP arts. 7 and 20.

[57]LSO ITA § 17(1)(a); SGP ITA § 10(1)(b).

[58]DEU BGB (Civil Code) § 611 *et seq.*; ESP Código Civil § 1544; ITA Codice civile § 2096 *et seq.*

ment.[59] Generally, nontax definitions will not be broad enough to cover all relationships that should be covered by the notion of employment for tax purposes and, therefore, a special definition for tax purposes should be provided.[60]

As noted above, even under a global system, employment income may be expressly included in gross income. In this case, it is necessary also to have a definition of employment income. Again, in the absence of such a definition, nontax definitions may apply in determining what employment income is, and these definitions may not be appropriate for tax purposes.[61] For example, nontax definitions of "salary" or "wages" may not include many employment-related receipts that should be treated as employment income for income tax purposes.

The definition of employment income may serve a number of purposes in a global or schedular income tax system, and the appropriate definition may differ depending on the use to which it is put. The definition may be used, for example, to identify a category of income for which special deduction rules apply. It may also be used to establish the base for withholding of tax at source by employers.[62] An important purpose of the definition in jurisdictions with a less than comprehensive judicial concept of income is to broaden the tax base. This is particularly the case in those jurisdictions that rely upon U.K. jurisprudence. As noted earlier, the income concept developed by U.K. courts was a narrow one. In the context of income from employment, the tests required a strict nexus between the provision of services and the receipt of consideration for the services so it could be said that the receipt was a product or an ordinary incident of the provision of services.

Thus, many gains that would be considered employment income in other jurisdictions were excluded from the U.K. judicial concept of employment income and, consequently, from the global concepts of income used in jurisdictions adopting U.K. jurisprudence. Examples include receipts that are characterized as being in the nature of a gift or "personal tribute" rather than as a product of the employee's labor and receipts that are characterized as being

---

[59]*See infra* sec. XII.

[60]*E.g.*, FRA CGI §§ 80–80 *ter*; HUN PIT § 24 (nonindependent activities include those of employment, legislative service, participation in association, and office holding, and activities of contributing family members); USA IRC § 3121(d). There have been substantial difficulties in the United States in the classification of workers as employees or independent contractors. Rev. Rul. 87-41, 1987-1 C.B. 296, sets forth 20 factors in applying the common law test for an employment relationship. *See also* Revenue Act of 1978, § 530, Pub. L. No. 95-600, which imposed a moratorium on the issuance of regulations on this issue. *See* Staff of the Joint Committee on Taxation, General Explanation of the Revenue Act of 1978, at 300–05 (1979).

[61]*See, e.g.*, FRA Code du travail § 140-2 (definition of salary).

[62]The withholding system applied to employment income is commonly called a pay-as-you-earn or PAYE system. *See infra* sec. XII; ch. 15. However, where employer withholding is a final tax on employment income, there should be complete identity between the definition of employment income for the purposes of the charge to tax and for the purposes of collection of tax.

in return for some consideration other than actual performance of labor, such as the giving up of valuable rights under an employment contract. Alternatively, the receipts may be characterized as capital amounts, paid to secure "negative covenants" from a past, present, or future employee not to compete with the employer or to divulge the employer's confidential information. Particularly in jurisdictions that rely on U.K. jurisprudence, therefore, the definition of employment income will need to be broad to avoid these interpretations.

The basic definition of employment income should include any compensation directly or indirectly related to the employment relationship. Depending on the drafting style used, it may be appropriate to enumerate for further certainty specific amounts,[63] including the following:

- salary, wages, or other remuneration provided to the employee, including leave pay, overtime payments, bonuses, commissions, and work condition supplements, such as payments for unpleasant or dangerous working conditions;
- fringe benefits;[64]
- any allowance provided by the employer for the benefit of an employee or in respect of any member of the employee's family, including a cost of living, subsistence, rent, utilities, education, entertainment, or travel allowance;
- any discharge or reimbursement by an employer of expenditure incurred by an employee other than expenditure incurred in the performance of duties of employment;
- consideration provided by an employer in respect of the employee's agreement to any conditions of employment or to any changes in the conditions of employment;
- any payment provided by an employer in respect of redundancy, any payment for loss of employment or termination of employment, and similar payments;
- any compensation received for a total or partial loss of employment income;
- retirement pensions and pension supplements;
- any consideration paid to secure a negative covenant from a past, present, or future employee; and
- gifts provided by an employer to a past, present, or prospective employee in the course of or by virtue of employment.

The definition of employment income can exclude certain fringe benefits and social benefits provided to employees that do not represent net economic

---

[63]Many income tax laws contain a nonexhaustive enumeration of various elements of income derived from employment. *See* AUT EStG § 25; BEL CIR §§ 31–32; DEU EStG § 19; ESP IRPF §§ 24–26.

[64]*See infra* sec. IV(C).

gains or that are to be exempted from the tax base in order to achieve certain social policy objectives.[65]

B. Employee Expenses

Because taxable income consists of net amounts, recognition of expenses incurred to derive gross employment income is as important to the definition of taxable income as are the inclusions outlined above. The rules regarding the deductibility of expenses incurred to derive employment income are relevant not only to the determination of net gains, but also to the design of the pay-as-you-earn (PAYE) withholding system applied to employment income. Recognition of employee expenses inevitably complicates the withholding system, making it difficult or impossible to use PAYE withholding as a final tax. Indeed, this is an example where tax policy may be dictated by decisions as to administrative design. If it is decided to make PAYE withholding a final tax for a majority of individual taxpayers, then it will be necessary to have either a standard deduction or a denial of employee deductions (perhaps compensated by rate adjustments)—see the discussion of this issue in section XII, below, and in chapter 15.

There are significant differences from jurisdiction to jurisdiction in the treatment of employee expenses. The trend, however, is to restrict employment-related deductions, given that they cause a number of significant administrative complications. First, as noted above, they make it difficult to apply withholding tax as a final tax on employment income. Also, they raise a number of difficult borderline questions—common trouble areas include expenses for education, commuting, travel, clothing, child care, and entertainment. Finally, given the large number of employees in any jurisdiction, it is inevitable that there will be many disputes over employment-related deductions—disputes that can tie up a disproportionate amount of administrative resources.

One solution that has been tried in some jurisdictions is simply to deny deductions for employee expenses[66] or to allow a flat deduction.[67] The impact of such rules will depend in part on the relative bargaining strength of employees and employers and thus on whether the additional tax payable by an employee faced with a deduction denial or restriction is actually borne by the employee or can be shifted to employers who are required to gross up wages to

---

[65]See infra sec. IV(C)(3).

[66]For example, in Canada, ITA § 8(1)(a) formerly allowed a standard deduction for employee expenses of 20 percent of employment income, to a maximum of Can$500. This provision was repealed in 1988, so that now there is no deduction for expenses incurred to derive employment income, except for very special categories of employment such as artists, clergy, and truck drivers. A similar position applies in New Zealand where no deductions are allowed for any expenditure or loss incurred in gaining or producing employment income (ITA § 105).

[67]See ESP IRPF § 28(2) (standard deduction of 5 percent with a cap of Ptas. 250,000 (approximately US$2,250) and a special standard deduction for handicapped employees; there is no provision for an itemized deduction).

offset the additional tax burden or assume responsibility for paying for the expenses formerly borne by the employee. If the employee bears all or some of the tax burden, two potential problems may arise. First, denying or restricting deductions for employee expenses may lead to inequities for some taxpayers, particularly those incurring large employment expenses. Second, it may open a significant distinction between employees who are not able to fully recognize employment expenses and self-employed persons and contractors, who are. The latter phenomenon may result in a significant restructuring of employment contracts as employers seek to have their relationships with employees recharacterized as independent contractor arrangements.[68]

A compromise approach is to allow taxpayers to choose between a standard deduction for employment expenses and a deduction for actual documented expenses when the latter exceed a specified threshold.[69] This is the solution most OECD countries follow.[70] It does not solve the problem, however, of the temptation of many taxpayers to opt for itemized and substantiated expenses, particularly when the standard deductions are set at a low level,[71] resulting in an inordinate volume of work for the tax administration. Therefore, if a system allowing taxpayers to choose between a standard deduction and the optional deduction of itemized and substantiated expenses is adopted, there

---

[68]The incentive to convert an employment relationship into an independent contractor relationship will depend on the scope of the definition of employment that applies for this purpose. As stated above, a broad definition of employment will include independent contractor relationships where the remuneration paid is essentially for the labor of the service provider.

[69]Jurisdictions that allow employees to choose between a standard deduction and an option to claim a deduction for itemized and substantiated expenses include Austria: AUT EStG § 16(3), which provides a flat deduction of S 1,800 (approx. US$180); Belgium: CIR § 51, which establishes a declining standard deduction of employment expenses ranging from 20 percent of employment income below BF 150,000 (approx. US$5,000) to 3 percent of employment income exceeding BF 500,000 (approx. US$16,500), subject to a maximum deduction of BF 100,000 (approx. US$3,300); France: CGI § 83 /3°, which provides an ordinary deduction of 10 percent of employment income, to a maximum indexed deduction (F 72,250 in 1993) and an additional standard deduction for specific forms of employment (artists, journalists, miners, construction workers, and traveling salesmen), which varies from 10 percent to 30 percent of employment income, also subject to a maximum limit; Germany: EStG § 9a (flat amount of DM 2,000 (approx. US$1,400)); the Netherlands: NLD WIB § 37, which provides a standard deduction of 8 percent of employment income, subject to a fixed minimum and maximum deduction and a special standard deduction for sailors; and the United States: USA IRC § 63, which provides a combination of standard deductions. A special feature of the U.S. employment income deductions is the adoption of a floor on deductions for certain itemized expenses, set at 2 percent of "adjusted gross income." *See* USA IRC § 67. A U.S. employee opting for the standard deduction in lieu of itemized deductions also gives up the right to itemized deductions that are not connected with employment.

[70]Two exceptions to this general rule are Australia and Canada. Australia permits deductions only for substantiated expenses and, as noted earlier, Canada does not allow any deduction for employment expenses.

[71]Examples of jurisdictions with relatively low standard deduction thresholds include Austria and the Netherlands.

are advantages to be realized by setting the maximum limits for standard deductions at levels that are high enough to dissuade all but a few employees from claiming deductions for itemized expenses.

A conceptually distinct problem is that of the so-called borderline expenses that have elements of both employment expenses and personal consumption. A number of legislative techniques have been used to minimize the problem, although none has eliminated it. To begin with, it is common for the general deduction rules to require a direct nexus between a deductible expense and the derivation of income.[72] This construction implies a distinction between expenses incurred to put a person in a position to derive income (e.g., commuting,[73] child care, and education), which are not deductible, and expenses incurred directly in the income-earning process, which are deductible. General rules of this sort are often also drafted to prohibit explicitly or implicitly deductions for personal expenses.[74] The general rules may be supplemented by specific ones addressing particular types of expenses.

Many jurisdictions have taken the position that social support is appropriate for some quasi-personal expenses such as child care or commuting expenses. At the same time, it is generally recognized that deductions for quasi-personal expenses will lead to an "upside-down" subsidy.[75] For this reason, some jurisdictions that wish to provide support through the tax system for quasi-personal expenses prefer tax offsets to deductions.[76]

An alternative approach for some quasi-personal expenses is to prorate the outgoings and allow a deduction for only a portion of the expenditure. This approach is taken, for example, with business entertainment expenses in some jurisdictions.[77] The proration approach has been criticized because of the administrative difficulties involved in substantiating entertainment expenses as legitimate business outgoings and because of equity concerns. Equity concerns are based on the indisputably high personal consumption value of the expenditure to the person incurring the cost, the fact that other

---

[72]E.g., AUS ITAA (1997) § 8-1; AUT EStG § 16(1); BEL CIR § 49; DEU EStG § 9(1); ESP IRPF § 41.

[73]Commuting expenses may be regarded either as travel to and from work (deductible) or as travel to and from home (nondeductible living expenses).—L.M. For a theoretical discussion, see William Klein, Income Taxation and Commuting Expenses, 54 Cornell L. Rev. 871 (1969).

[74]E.g., AUS ITAA (1997) § 8-1(2)(b) prohibits deductions for expenses of a "private or domestic nature"; FRA CGI § 83/3° limits deductions to expenses "inherent to the office or employment"; GBR ICTA § 198 allows "the holder of an office or employment" a deduction for expenses incurred "exclusively and necessarily in the performance of those duties" [of the office or employment]; IDN IT art. 9(1)(h) denies a deduction for "costs incurred for the personal needs of the Taxpayer and his dependents"; USA IRC § 262 denies deductions for "personal, living, or family expenses."

[75]See infra sec. VII.

[76]See USA IRC § 21.

[77]See CAN ITA § 67.1; LSO ITA § 35; USA IRC § 274(n).

persons benefiting from the expenditure will not be assessed on the value of the consumption benefit they receive, and the fact that the expenditures are incurred disproportionately by higher-income taxpayers. These concerns explain the prohibition on deductions for entertainment expenses in several jurisdictions.[78]

Full or partial denial of a deduction for entertainment expenses requires this category of expense to be defined. The concept covers all expenses incurred for the purpose of socializing with business associates, such as for meals, drinks, theater tickets, hunting, and yachting. In some countries, the concept of "representation" or "protocol" expenses is more meaningful.[79] These may include, in addition to entertainment, transportation and lodging expenses for one's own employees or for the employees of another company (e.g., a potential customer). Expenses for lodging and transportation should be treated in the same manner as business trip expenses, rather than as entertainment expenses. Thus, if a company pays for representatives of a potential customer to visit its headquarters, the costs of transportation and lodging should be deductible, while expenses for meals and entertainment should not be deductible if a deduction for entertainment expenses is generally denied.

C. Employee Fringe Benefits

1. Introduction

A "fringe benefit" is any monetary or nonmonetary benefit derived from employment that does not constitute cash salary or wages. Common examples of fringe benefits are employer-provided housing, the use of an employer-provided car for personal purposes, and the provision of discounted goods to employees.

The theoretical case for full inclusion of fringe benefits in the tax base is noncontroversial. Full taxation is a prerequisite to horizontal equity between taxpayers who are wholly remunerated in cash and taxpayers remunerated partly through fringe benefits. It is also a prerequisite to vertical equity because the incidence of fringe benefits tends to rise with taxpayers' economic incomes and employment status. Full taxation of fringe benefits is also a precondition to achieving an economically efficient tax system. It ensures that the tax system will be neutral between those employers able to provide fringe benefits and those not able to do so and removes the distortion in favor of providing goods and services that are not taxed. Finally, taxation of fringe benefits is important to protect the revenue base.

---

[78]AUS ITAA (1997) § 32-5; GBR ICTA § 577(1)(a); for a review of deductibility of entertainment expenses in several jurisdictions, *see* Ault et al., Comparative Income Taxation: A Structural Analysis 216–19 (1997).

[79]*E.g.*, GEO TC § 49(2) (representation); ROM PT § 6(2) (protocol).

The overwhelming theoretical case in favor of fringe benefits taxation is countered by a number of conceptual and political problems. A fundamental problem is that many taxpayers, and for that matter some tax administrators, do not perceive benefits in kind to be income with the same economic capacity as cash wages or salaries.[80] Subsidiary problems arise from the definition of fringe benefits, the difficulty in allocating general benefits among employees, and the difficulty in distinguishing genuine benefits from benefits that are consumed in the course of employment or that are a necessary condition of employment. The conceptual difficulties that arise with the income taxation of fringe benefits have often resulted in low levels of taxpayer compliance with, and administrative enforcement of, the tax law applying to these benefits. This in turn has led to a "tax culture" in some countries that regards fringe benefits as tax-free remuneration so that attempts to expressly bring the value of fringe benefits within the tax base are subject to political resistance.

2. Choice of Tax Method

Three methods have been used to tax fringe benefits. The first, and by far the most common, is to include the value of fringe benefits in employees' assessable income.[81] In civil code jurisdictions, the definition of salaries in the labor codes will usually include fringe benefits and this definition will in principle be applied for income tax purposes.[82] Similarly, fringe benefits will automatically be incorporated into income from labor in common law jurisdictions where the judicial concept of "income" is broad enough to encompass all net gains. In common law jurisdictions that rely on U.K. precedents, the judicial concept of income excludes benefits in kind that cannot be converted to cash[83] and values benefits that can be converted by reference to their value as secondhand goods or services.[84] In these jurisdictions, specific statutory inclusion provisions and valuation rules are needed to include the full market value of nonconvertible fringe benefits into the gross income of employees.

A second method of taxing fringe benefits is to impose a surrogate tax on the benefits by denying employers a deduction for the cost of providing them. This method is used in a number of countries for selected benefits, es-

---

[80]This is particularly the case with nontransferable benefits of a kind or quantity that the taxpayer would not have been interested in buying with his or her own money. An individual estimate of when this is the case is, however, too much for a mass procedure such as income tax assessment.—L.M.

[81]E.g., AUT EStG § 25(1)1a; BEL CIR § 31(2); DEU EStG § 19(1)1; FRA CGI art. 82; ESP IRPF §§ 24(2), 26; USA IRC § 61(a)(1).

[82]See International Fiscal Association, The Taxation of Employee Fringe Benefits 18–19 (1995).

[83]See supra note 54.

[84]Wilkins v. Rogerson [1961] 1 ch. 133 (an employee was provided with a suit worth £30, but was taxed only on its secondhand value of £7).

pecially those benefits that are difficult to allocate to particular employees, but is not used as a general method for taxing fringe benefits in any jurisdiction.[85] The principal disadvantage of denying deductions to the employer as a method of taxing fringe benefits is that it effectively taxes the benefit at the employer's marginal rate, which, for public sector employers or employers in tax loss positions, is nil. A deduction denial is equivalent to taxing the employee only if the same tax rate is imposed on employers and employees. Even then, equivalence is achieved only if the cost of providing a benefit is equal to its market value. Often, this will not be the case; some benefits, such as transportation on public transit vehicles operated by the employer, have little or no cost to the employer. The design of the company and shareholder tax system may also cause problems by "washing out" the effect of the deduction denial.[86]

A third method of taxing fringe benefits is to impose a separate tax (usually referred to as a "fringe benefits tax") on the employer, based on the value of benefits provided to employees. This method may be used as a basis for taxing specific benefits or as a general method of taxing fringe benefits. New Zealand was the first country to use a fringe benefits tax as a general method of taxing fringe benefits. The fringe benefits tax was adopted in New Zealand for political reasons in the context of a reform agenda based on a tax mix change.[87] The political authorities had concluded that the fringe benefits tax would be more viable politically than reform measures that included all benefits in employees' incomes. Similar considerations led to the adoption of a fringe benefits tax in Australia and to the adoption of separate fringe benefits taxes in some developing and transition countries.[88]

The fringe benefits tax imposed on employers as a general policy instrument for dealing with fringe benefits has been criticized.[89] It is particularly vulnerable to criticism that it undermines the measurement of employee income.

---

[85]It is used, for example, in Canada (ITA § 18(1)(b)) and the United States (IRC § 274) to tax some entertainment and recreational benefits provided to employees. In Belgium, art. 53/14° CIR denies a deduction for certain fringe benefits that are exempt in the hands of the employees on the basis of art. 38/11°, because (1) the beneficiaries of such benefits cannot be easily identified; (2) they cannot be considered as effective remuneration; or (3) they are small gifts and benefits at the occasion of weddings, birthdays, and other personal occasions.

[86]This is the case in Australia, for example. The deduction denial will cause the company to incur higher taxes, which in turn generates tax offsets (commonly referred to as "imputation credits") under an imputation system that shareholders may use to shelter tax-exempt income derived by the company. For a general explanation of "washout," see Charles McLure, *Must Corporate Income Be Taxed Twice?* 94–95 (1979).

[87]The concept of a fringe benefits tax has its genesis in the Report of the Task Force on Tax Reform 154–56 (1992) prepared by the McCaw Committee in New Zealand.

[88]*See, e.g.,* EST ITL § 33; LSO ITA §§ 115–127; MWI ITA §§ 94A–94D.

[89]*See* Richard J. Vann, *Some Lessons from Hussey and Lubick,* 7 Tax Notes Int'l 268, 268–70 (1993); Richard K. Gordon, *Some Comments on the Basic World Tax Code and Commentary,* 7 Tax Notes Int'l 279, 280–81 (1993).

While the employer-based fringe benefits tax might ensure that the benefits are subject to income tax, noninclusion in the employee's gross (and therefore taxable) income may allow the benefits to escape other taxes and contributions based on taxable income, particularly social security taxes. Also, employees' taxable incomes will be understated for the purpose of measuring eligibility for various means-tested benefits such as health benefits and education benefits. The understatement may also affect obligations based on taxable income such as support payments.

A separate problem with employer-based fringe benefits taxation is its inability to impose tax at the appropriate marginal rate for each employee.[90] A single rate must be applied to all fringe benefits, and this is usually the highest personal marginal tax rate on the assumption that most benefits are derived by persons in the highest marginal rate bracket. This approach presumes that employers will "cash out" benefits provided to employees in lower tax brackets, an approach that discourages the provision of benefits that might be provided more efficiently through employers. An example is medical insurance, which is less expensive when acquired through an employer-sponsored plan because of the discounts available to large group enrollments.[91]

There are two options as to the basic design of a fringe benefits tax. The first option is to design the fringe benefits tax independently of the income tax system, with no attempt to coordinate it. The second option is to carefully coordinate the income tax system to achieve the exact same overall tax burden on any given fringe benefit as would be the case if the employer paid cash to the employee instead of providing a fringe benefit. It is suggested that the second approach is preferable as it will ensure that the fringe benefits tax operates fairly and in a neutral fashion between those employees paid in cash and those paid in fringe benefits. If the tax burden is not the same for cash and fringe benefits, remuneration packages will be altered to achieve the best tax result, thereby giving rise to economic distortions and revenue losses resulting from the tax-driven alteration.

Fringe benefits taxes are usually imposed at a flat rate. For those countries with a progressive marginal rate structure, the setting of the rate is designed (at least initially) to achieve parity in terms of the final tax burden between the fringe benefits tax and the tax that would have been paid had the benefit been taxed in the hands of an employee subject to the highest personal marginal rate. Parity may be achieved under a system in which the employer is allowed

---

[90]This is only a problem where, as is usually the case, a progressive marginal rate structure applies to individuals. Estonia is the only country that imposes a fringe benefits tax to also apply a flat rate of tax to individuals. In Estonia, the fringe benefits tax rate is aligned to the individual rate of tax, which is currently 26 percent (EST ITL § 7).

[91]For this reason, if a fringe benefits tax is used, it may be desirable to exempt benefits of this sort. See LSO ITA § 124(3). Safeguards could be provided to prevent abuse (e.g., the Lesotho exemption applies only when the benefit is available to "all non-casual employees on equal terms").

an income tax deduction for the cost of the fringe benefit, but not for the fringe benefits tax imposed on the benefit[92] or under a system in which the employer is allowed an income tax deduction for both the cost of the fringe benefit provided and the fringe benefits tax payable thereon.[93] In the latter case, adjustments must be made to offset the value to the employer of the income tax deduction for the amount of fringe benefits tax paid. This can be done in one of two ways. First, the value of the benefit can be grossed up before the fringe benefits tax rate is applied,[94] or, second, the actual value of the benefit can be used and a higher rate of fringe benefits tax (i.e., the maximum marginal rate grossed up by an appropriate formula to achieve the desired parity) imposed on that value.[95]

One potential drawback with the flat-rate employer-based fringe benefits tax is that parity between fringe benefits tax and the alternative of taxing employees on the value of fringe benefits received can only be achieved with respect to one tax rate. That is, whichever system described above is used (nondeductible fringe benefits tax or deductible tax but subject to a gross-up of the value or rate), the parity formula is calculated to achieve parity with one tax rate only, usually the highest personal marginal tax rate for reasons explained above. If the employees receiving the benefits are subject to lower tax rates, the tax burden may be too high.

Another problem with an employer-based fringe benefits tax is its potential incompatibility with prevailing unilateral and bilateral international tax rules. If an individual from one country goes to work as an employee in a second country, both the country where the work is performed and the country where the employee is resident may claim taxing rights over the salary and fringe benefits derived by the employee. International tax rules to prevent double taxation have been devised on the assumption that fringe benefits are taxed to the employee in the country where the work is performed. If the employee's country of residence also seeks to tax the employee's remuneration, it will normally provide an offset[96] against the tax otherwise payable on employment remuneration (including fringe benefits) for any taxes imposed on salary and fringe benefits by the country where the work was carried out. However, if the country where the work was carried out imposes a fringe benefits tax on the individual's employer and the employee's country of residence seeks to tax the employee on the value of the fringe benefits received, the employee may not be able to obtain any double tax relief for the tax already levied by the other country on the same fringe benefits. This is because the country of resi-

---

[92]This is the method that applies in Estonia and Malawi. It is also the method that originally applied in Australia and New Zealand.

[93]This is the method that applies in Australia, Lesotho, and New Zealand.

[94]This is the method that applies in Australia (FBTAA § 136AA) and Lesotho (LSO ITA § 117).

[95]This is the method used in New Zealand.

[96]Generally referred to as a "foreign tax credit"; see infra ch. 18.

dence may not recognize the fringe benefits tax imposed on an employer in another country as an income tax paid by the employee. Since offsets are normally available only for foreign income tax actually paid by the employee, double taxation will result.[97] Similar difficulties arise in other cases where different countries assess different taxpayers for the same type of benefit.[98] Special treaty measures or unilateral rules can be devised to ameliorate the problem, although to date these problems have been largely ignored in those countries that impose a fringe benefits tax.[99] The international aspects of employer-based fringe benefits taxation are discussed further in chapter 18.

Another international law problem with an employer-based fringe benefits tax is that of imposing the tax on such employers as diplomatic and consular missions and certain public international organizations that are exempt from tax under a convention or other international agreement. It may be necessary to include a parallel regime for taxing employees of such organizations or entities; otherwise, the benefits provided to these employees may go untaxed.[100] The existence of parallel regimes for taxing fringe benefits means that the effective rate of tax on the benefits may differ depending on which regime applies. For developing countries with a significant presence by public international organizations that employ local staff, the need for parallel regimes may substantially detract from the advantages of the fringe benefits tax.

Notwithstanding these problems, a fringe benefits tax imposed on the employer does have the significant advantage of being more achievable politically in jurisdictions in which fringe benefits are not commonly perceived to be income that should be taxed in the hands of employees in the same manner as cash salaries. It may also be easier to implement in jurisdictions where cash salaries are low and employees would face liquidity problems if the cash remuneration were reduced by tax on both the cash payment and the benefits received. This may also facilitate the making of PAYE withholding a final tax on employment income. The choice of a fringe benefits tax system is thus likely to turn on political considerations as much as on technical tax ones. If

---

[97]The same problem can arise where the employee's country of residence provides relief from international double taxation by exempting foreign income from tax. This is because it is usually a condition of such relief that the employee has paid foreign tax on the foreign income.

[98]A leading example is in the area of pensions paid from pension or retirement funds, as the pensions may be double taxed if derived by a beneficiary in a country that taxes pension recipients from a country that taxes pension or retirement funds.

[99]One exception to this is the renegotiated Australia-New Zealand double tax agreement (signed Jan. 27, 1995), which was adopted in part to better coordinate the application of those countries' employer-based fringe benefits tax systems.

[100]Such taxation should, of course, apply only to those employees (typically, local staff) who are taxed on their employment income as a general matter. Another example of an employer who is generally excluded from a fringe benefits tax is a private individual who employs domestic staff (e.g., housekeeper, gardener, or chauffeur). However, in most developing and transition countries, the remuneration paid to such staff will generally be below the threshold for income taxation.

an employee-based fringe benefits tax system appears to be difficult to attain in the short term for political reasons, an employer-based tax may be considered as an interim solution. It may, however, be difficult to subsequently change to an employee-based tax. The New Zealand fringe benefits tax was originally recommended as a transitional tax, establishing the political acceptability of fully taxing fringe benefits, that would be phased out when taxation was shifted directly to employees.[101] The government did not accept the transitional aspects of the proposal, however, and there is no sign of an imminent or long-term future shift in approach in that jurisdiction.

One technical issue that may influence the choice of fringe benefits tax system is the difficulty of collecting the tax if fringe benefits are included in employees' assessable income. In theory, the tax may be collected on an assessment basis, when the taxpayer's final liability for tax for the year is determined, or on a regular basis throughout the year by including fringe benefits in remuneration subject to PAYE collection. The effective administration of either method requires the employer to provide tax authorities with information on the value of fringe benefits provided. Thus, from a compliance perspective, an employer-based tax is often less costly than one in which the tax is imposed on employees, since in the former case the employer can consolidate the value of benefits provided and does not have to report the separate value for each employee's benefits.

The choice among the three methods of taxing fringe benefits need not be resolved the same way for all benefits. All three methods can be used at once for different kinds of fringe benefits. Thus, fringe benefits can generally be taxed to employees, subject to exceptions for those benefits that may be excluded from employees' income for administrative reasons (an example might be *de minimis* benefits) or because of the difficulty in valuing the benefit derived by a particular taxpayer (e.g., recreational facilities that are available to all employees). Such excluded benefits may be taxed by way of deduction denial to the employer or under a fringe benefits tax.

3. Identification, Valuation, and Exclusions

Assuming a policy decision is made to tax fringe benefits fully, one might be tempted to recommend simply a general provision that all benefits in kind are taxable to the employee and that their value for income tax purposes is the fair market value of the benefit at the time it is derived by the employee. Experience in many countries shows that this strategy is not likely to be successful. Even if a taxable benefit is identified, requiring taxpayers to determine fair market value without providing further guidance on calculating that value will be a serious problem in many cases. A more fruitful strategy has proved to be to deal with different types of fringe benefits one by one, with explicit rules dis-

---

[101]*See* Report of the Task Force on Tax Reform, *supra* note 87.

tinguishing taxable benefits from those that are excluded from tax, and to provide easily applicable rules for the valuation of those benefits that are taxed. Valuation rules need not necessarily be in the statute, but could be provided in regulations. If most benefits are dealt with in this manner, then a residual catchall provision can provide for the taxation of benefits other than those specifically mentioned and further provide for their valuation at fair market value.

The first question to be resolved in the context of fringe benefits taxation by means of either an employee-based tax or an employer-based tax is whether the person receiving a benefit is an employee. In many cases, there will be an incentive for employers and employees to recharacterize the relationship as one of business and independent contractor.[102] Where fringe benefits are taxed at the employee level, characterization of the beneficiary as an independent contractor can take the person out of the PAYE system with respect to the benefits and enable the beneficiary to defer, and possibly reduce or avoid, tax payable on the benefit. Where fringe benefits are taxed at the employer level, characterization of the beneficiary as an independent contractor can defer tax and possibly reduce the rate if the beneficiary's marginal rate is less than the marginal rate used for fringe benefits tax purposes.

If fringe benefits are subject to a separate fringe benefits tax, either within the income tax legislation or as a separate tax, it is important that the definition of employee be used consistently throughout the legislation to ensure that there is neither overlap nor gaps between the tax applicable to other remuneration and that imposed on fringe benefits. Once it is determined that a person is an employee, it is necessary to see whether the person also enjoys another relationship with the employer (such as that of a shareholder of the employer, a friend of the employer, or a creditor of the employer) and whether the benefit is received in consequence of that person's employment or the other capacity.

A second issue to be addressed is the characterization of benefits, particularly cash benefits, as salary or wages or fringe benefits. The benefit that most often gives rise to difficulty is the payment of cash "allowances" or "bonuses." If these payments are considered salary, they will be subject to PAYE withholding. However, if they are treated as fringe benefits, they may not be subject to PAYE withholding if benefits are taxed at the employee level[103] and certainly will be exempt from PAYE withholding if benefits are taxed at the employer level. Specific rules will be needed to coordinate the tax imposed on cash benefits of this sort with any offsetting deductions that might be available to an employee as a result of the application of the amount received.

---

[102]See generally sec. IV(A).

[103]Where PAYE withholding is not a final tax, the value of fringe benefits provided may be excluded from the PAYE tax base, with the result that tax is deferred until assessment.

The third issue to be resolved is that of the value to be assigned to taxable fringe benefits. In theory, the preferable value for the taxation of a fringe benefit is the value of the benefit to the employee, because this is the cash or economic equivalent for the taxpayer. It is, however, impossible to levy a tax on the basis of the subjective valuation by a taxpayer, and so a surrogate must be used. The most appropriate value in this case is the market value of the benefit. It is logical to assume that for most taxpayers the value of benefits derived equals the amount other persons would pay for those benefits in a market transaction. Valuation based on market value best achieves the equity and efficiency objectives of fringe benefits taxation.

Determining the market value for common benefits can be a costly and administratively complicated procedure for employees and employers. Accordingly, it is common for tax systems to provide rules of thumb for determining market value for most common benefits. Depending on the legislative structure of the tax regime, valuation rules may be set out in legislation, regulations, or rulings. They may be provided in the form of valuation formulas or specific values for particular benefits.[104] The major categories of fringe benefits that are usually subject to specific valuation formulas include cars, housing, low-interest loans, debt waivers, expense allowances, shares acquired under an employee share scheme, and subsidized goods and services. Residual valuation rules may apply to other benefits.

In some cases, the valuation rules set out presumptive values that are lower than market values where the market value could impose an unreasonable burden on a taxpayer. An example is the provision of accommodation in a remote work site. If the value of this benefit were calculated as a reasonable rental value based on the cost of providing accommodation, the value of accommodation in, say, a remote jungle, a desert camp, or an offshore oil drilling platform would be very high. But the value to the taxpayer is the amount the taxpayer is saving by not paying for accommodation in an ordinary setting where the taxpayer would be if not for the job. The same is true of board. The cost of meals in a remote location could be high, but the saving to the taxpayer is the cost of meals where the taxpayer would live if not for the employment. Thus, in this situation, the value of accommodation and board is likely to be set at a figure based on the market value of the benefit had it been provided at a nonremote location rather than on its actual market value.[105]

Finally, special valuation rules may be needed in jurisdictions where it is difficult to allocate among employees such benefits as a subsidized cafeteria or

---

[104]For example, the value of automobile benefits may be determined by a formula that takes into account the cost of the vehicle, its age, and the distance traveled in the year.

[105]Some jurisdictions offer a range of exemptions for particular benefits for political reasons or to subsidize certain activities, particularly in remote areas. These exemptions take the form of indirect spending programs and, accordingly, are not considered in the context of devising a fringe benefits tax system.

employer-provided recreational facilities. Where benefits are taxed by means of a fringe benefits tax imposed on the employer, a surrogate value based on total usage may be used,[106] but where benefits are taxed at the employee level, some formula must be adopted to allocate the benefit to individual users. The employer could be required to keep strict track of actual usage by individual beneficiaries, but this may be an administratively expensive procedure. An alternative is to consider the benefit provided to be the right to use the subsidized facility rather than its actual usage and to assess employees on the notional value of that right. This approach poses two difficulties—valuation of rights that might not be used and imposition of a tax on persons who may not have wanted to be offered the right. An exclusion for socially desirable benefits provided to all employees on a nondiscriminatory basis (see immediately below) may avoid the problem in the cases of some benefits, but the difficulty will remain with others. It is a problem inherent in the employee-based tax.

Fringe benefits tax regimes may contain a range of exemptions. A common exemption is one for *de minimis* benefits, the value of which, after taking into account the frequency with which the employer provides similar benefits, is so small as to make accounting for them unreasonable or administratively impracticable.[107] Exemptions are also provided for benefits taxed under an alternative regime (deduction denial to the employer or fringe benefits tax). Sometimes exemptions are provided for socially desirable benefits such as subsidized meals, medical benefits, or child care facilities that are provided on a nondiscriminatory basis to all employees. Finally, an exemption is usually provided for benefits that would have been deductible to the employee had the employee incurred the cost of acquiring the benefit directly.[108] An example is the provision of work equipment to employees. Similarly, that portion of an allowance for which the employee has provided receipts or other proof of payment of expenses that are in the nature of business expenses for the employer should also be excluded.[109]

V. Business and Investment Income

Most of the fundamental issues concerning the taxation of business and investment income (inclusion of gains, allowable deductions, calculation and remittance systems for tax collection, and tax accounting rules) are equally relevant to such income derived by individuals and to that derived through part-

---

[106]*E.g.*, AUS FBTAA §§ 37A–37CF.

[107]For examples of exemptions on this basis, *see* LSO ITA § 118 and USA IRC § 132.

[108]*See* USA IRC § 132(d). For purposes of applying such a rule, any special rules denying all or a portion of employee expenses (*see, e.g.*, USA IRC § 67) should be ignored.

[109]*See* USA IRC § 62(a)(2)(A).

nerships., companies, and other entities or relationships, such as common law trusts. Accordingly, the examination of these issues in chapter 16 applies equally to the calculation of business and investment income derived by individuals.

As the discussion in chapter 16 points out, some particular issues raised in the context of business income can be of particular importance to individuals. For example, in jurisdictions that have adopted U.K. judicial doctrines, the judicial concept of business income is very narrow, and legislative base broadening in this area is necessary. Courts in these jurisdictions are often more likely to apply narrower concepts of income to individuals than to legal persons, so the statutory extensions can have a slightly greater impact on individuals than on companies. Similarly, some restrictions on deductions, particularly restrictions on personal and quasi-personal expenses, are sometimes more relevant to individuals than to incorporated entities, although these issues tend to be equally relevant to partnerships and, in many cases, to trusts. And finally, it is not uncommon to apply different tax accounting rules to small businesses, including most businesses operated by individuals, than are applied to large businesses, particularly companies and larger partnerships. These exceptions aside, the basic rules setting out measurement of business income apply to all taxpayers deriving business income, and, accordingly, these issues are not discussed separately for individuals here. For more information on these issues, see chapter 16.

One important issue relevant only to individuals is the characterization of income from a trade or profession. Some countries make a distinction between income from commercial trading activities on the one hand and income from professions and vocations on the other.[110] These distinctions reflect older divisions in civil law countries between commercial traders and members of the liberal professions; these may linger on in some areas of law, such as ethical rules and rules of professional organization.[111]

The definitions of business income in common law jurisdictions generally include income from professional activities,[112] and the distinction between business and professional income has not been maintained in all civil law countries.[113] There are no persuasive tax policy reasons for the distinction, which developed out of historical, nontax rationale; from a tax administration

---

[110]*E.g.*, DEU EStG §§ 15 (*Gewerbebetrieb*), 18 (*Selbständige Arbeit*); FRA CGI §§ 34 (*Bénéfices industriels et commerciaux*), 92 (*Bénéfices des professions non commerciales*).

[111]*See* Klaus Tipke & Joachim Lang, Steuerrecht 334 (13th ed. 1991). The former were supposed to trade for a profit, while the latter performed their services without profit motive, for only an "honorary fee."

[112]AUS ITAA (1997) § 995-1: "Business includes any profession, trade, employment, vocation or calling, but does not include occupation as an employee"; CAN ITA § 248(1); GBR ICTA § 18, sched. D, cases I and II.

[113]*See, e.g.*, ESP IRPF § 40 (both including professional income together with business income); NLD WIB § 6/2.

perspective, it is much simpler to have a single set of rules dealing with all business and professional activities. If necessary, targeted rules such as tax accounting rules for work in progress can be applied to professions without the need for a completely separate regime for professional income.

VI. Miscellaneous Receipts

The discussion above has centered around a schedularization of income into three categories: employment, business, and investment income. As stated above, not all amounts derived by a taxpayer fit neatly into one of these categories, and, therefore, an issue arises as to the specification of other amounts to be included in gross income. The legislative method by which this may be achieved is discussed in section III(A), above. The discussion below considers the treatment of some amounts that do not come within the categories of income discussed above.

A. Windfalls

Windfalls constitute unexpected accretions to wealth. While windfalls may constitute income under a comprehensive judicial conception of income,[114] they are not included in gross income in many jurisdictions. In most jurisdictions with schedular definitions of income, windfalls simply fall between the categories of income included in gross income. They similarly fall outside the judicial concept of income in jurisdictions that rely upon U.K. judicial precedents (as they do not have the necessary connection to an earning activity) and have usually been excluded from the coverage of later base-broadening legislation in those jurisdictions.

Although there are no persuasive tax policy grounds for excluding windfalls from the income tax base, political considerations and practical difficulties in assessing these gains most often explain their continued noninclusion in gross income in many jurisdictions. At the same time, their noninclusion in the income tax base does raise some administrative issues. The most problematic exclusion is gambling and lottery winnings. It is common practice for taxpayers facing assessment on the basis of a surrogate income measurement test, such as an assets betterment test (a test that presumes a taxpayer has derived enough income to explain the taxpayer's assets),[115] to claim their assets were acquired with nonassessable windfalls such as betting winnings rather than with unreported assessable amounts. While the assessment and enforcement rules may place the onus on the taxpayer to prove that gains are not taxable, the nonassessability of windfall gains does complicate the task of the adminis-

---

[114]*See* Cesarini v. United States, 296 F. Supp. 3 (N.D. Ohio 1969) (cash found in used piano is taxable).

[115]*See* vol. 1, ch. 12.

trators.[116] Other problems arise with taxpayers whose primary source of income is derived from gambling or betting activities, because tax administrators must then prove that taxpayers have crossed the threshold from persons who derive windfall gains from these activities to persons who carry out these activities as a business, thus generating assessable income.

The administrative solution to these difficulties in the case of gambling winnings may be to assess the gains but to collect the tax on most such winnings by imposing a final withholding tax at an intermediate rate.

A separate type of windfall payment is a prize or an award. Generally, tax systems distinguish between prizes and awards that are won by a taxpayer in a purely personal capacity, which are usually not taxable, and prizes and awards given in recognition of a taxpayer's business or employment activities, which are usually taxable. Thus, for example, the prize won by an architect who submitted a design to an architecture contest or a "player of the match" award won by a sportsperson would be assessable. The former is connected with an activity that is an integral part of the taxpayer's business (architects often enter design contests to achieve recognition and hence new clients), and the latter is an example of an award that enjoys a direct nexus with the taxpayer's employment responsibilities.[117]

B. Gifts

Although some have argued that gifts or bequests should be taxed,[118] they are generally not taxed as income. They may, however, be subject to gift or estate duties or capital transfer taxes.[119] Depending on the structure of the definition of income, it may not be necessary to provide an explicit exclusion for gifts. If the definition is schedular, gifts will likely fall under none of the schedules. If, however, there is a broad residual schedule ("any other income"), then providing an explicit exclusion for gifts bolsters a broad reading of this residual category.

If an explicit exclusion is provided for gifts, it should be limited.[120] It should not apply to the income from property that is transferred as a gift, unless

---

[116]A taxpayer may, for example, produce evidence of substantial winnings while omitting evidence of amounts lost. The latter may be difficult or impossible for the tax authorities to reconstruct.

[117]In 1986, the United States, which had previously made distinctions such as those outlined above, adopted a rule under which prizes and awards would be generally taxable. *See* USA IRC § 74.

[118]*See, e.g.,* Joseph M. Dodge, *Beyond Estate and Gift Tax Reform: Including Gifts and Bequests in Income,* 91 Harv. L. Rev. 1177 (1978).

[119]*See* vol. 1, ch. 10.

[120]*See* LSO ITA § 31. Where the statute has excluded gifts without any statutory limitation, the courts have had difficulty determining whether certain transfers, particularly those occurring in a business context, qualified as excludable gifts. *See* Commissioner v. Duberstein, 363 U.S. 278 (1960).

the income is attributed to the transferor, as happens in some antishifting rules.[121] Also, an exclusion should not apply to a gift or bequest of an income stream, such as, for example, a gift of an annuity or of the right to a royalty, unless (once again) the income is attributed to the transferor for income tax purposes as a result of the application of antishifting rules. In addition, an amount transferred by or for an employer to, or for the benefit of, an employee should not qualify as a gift but should be considered employment income. A similar rule could be provided for gifts made in a business context other than to an employee. Under such a rule, a gift made to a business associate would be treated as business income to the recipient.

C. Scholarships

Scholarships are another type of income treated inconsistently in different jurisdictions. In some jurisdictions they are generally taxable[122] and in others they are exempt from assessment, perhaps subject to limitations.[123] Once again, there are no persuasive tax policy reasons for excluding these gains from assessable income. Where scholarships are assessable and a taxpayer derives only scholarship income, much of the scholarship may be lightly taxed or exempt under the ordinary progressive income tax rate scale. Where a taxpayer derives significant income in addition to a scholarship, the exclusion of the scholarship from assessable income can seriously undermine vertical equity. Excluding scholarships can also lead to administrative problems, as employers can seek to characterize employment income as scholarships. This has affected, for example, graduate students working for the university where they are studying and employees asked to complete higher degrees directly relevant to their work.

If scholarships are to be taxed, they may have to be specifically listed if the definition of income is a schedular one, because they would not fall into the usual general categories of income. They will in any event have to be specifically mentioned if it is desired to exclude certain scholarships.

D. Damages

The tax treatment of damages (compensation awarded in a legal action) and settlement payments (paid to settle a legal action) will depend on the nature of the damages. The character of the compensation depends on what is being compensated.[124] For example, compensation for loss of a capital asset

---

[121]This is the case, for example, in AUS ITAA (1936) § 102B and CAN ITA § 74(1), where attributed income is excluded from the recipient's attributable income.

[122]See CAN ITA § 56(1)(n).

[123]See AUS ITAA (1936) § 23(ya), (z), and ITAA (1997) § 51-10; USA IRC § 117.

[124]A specific rule to this effect can be included in the law. E.g., LSO ITA § 70 ("compensation received takes the character of the thing that is compensated").

should be treated in the same manner as the proceeds on a disposition of the asset, subject to any rules allowing deferral of recognition of such gain. On the one hand, damages (other than for personal injury) intended to compensate a taxpayer for loss of employment or business income are usually assessable as direct substitutes for assessable gains. Damages for personal injury, on the other hand, are usually exempt from taxation on the basis that they represent no real gain to the taxpayer—they are merely compensatory for mental or physical losses of, or suffering by, the taxpayer.

In some cases, damages for personal injury are exempt from taxation because they fall outside general or judicial concepts of income and are not caught by any base-broadening statutory provisions. Where base-broadening statutory provisions would include damages for personal injury, it may be necessary to explicitly exempt these receipts where this result is desired.

One type of damage or settlement payment that gives rise to difficulty in many jurisdictions is compensation for the loss of a taxpayer's ability to earn income in the future. If a payment is made for the loss of income-earning capacity because of physical injury occasioned by negligence, it may be characterized as nonassessable compensation, even when the amount of damages is determined in part to be compensation for loss of future earnings. However, when a payment is clearly made in contemplation of lost income (without a physical injury), such as a payment for premature termination of employment, the amount should be treated as an assessable receipt. Drawing the line in this area is difficult and no fully acceptable solution exists.

E. Social Welfare and Analogous Benefits and Expenses

The tax treatment of social welfare payments and expenses differs markedly from jurisdiction to jurisdiction. It is an issue that can be evaluated only in the context of the jurisdiction's social payment system, because the tax treatment of benefits and expenses is an integral element of the overall social welfare system.

The development of theoretical tax positions is complicated by the different models for social welfare payments adopted by different jurisdictions. Some benefits are targeted to lower-income persons through means testing of income and assets. Others are provided on a near-universal basis. Some are funded from general revenues. Others are paid for from earmarked taxes or levies or from a combination of earmarked levies and general revenues. And in some jurisdictions, key elements of the social benefit system such as health are largely privatized, and services are paid for either directly by the user or by private insurance.

Some broad generalizations for possible tax treatment can be made. To the extent that benefits are tightly means tested, it may be appropriate to exempt them from taxation, because the recipients are quite likely to fall below the minimum tax threshold. Thus, means-tested welfare payments, unemployment payments, old-age pensions, and similar payments will normally be exempt from tax. This result is also consistent with considerations of tax administration.

In the case of other benefits funded through earmarked taxes or levies, parallel treatment of costs and benefits will provide for a generally neutral tax regime. For example, if unemployment insurance levies are imposed on taxpayers and these are deductible for income tax purposes, benefits received under the program should be taxable.[125] If the levies are not deductible, it may be appropriate to exempt the benefit from tax. In many cases, where contributions are not deductible, the benefit will be means tested and, therefore, would be excluded from income under the first principle, above.

In some cases, deviation from this general rule may be appropriate. One such case is where taxpayers make nondeductible contributions to an income support plan, but the benefits include an investment income component. An example of this arrangement is where taxpayers are required to make nondeductible contributions to a national old-age pension scheme. The benefits paid to members in this case in theory include investment income derived from the investment of the contributions. The most appropriate treatment of these benefits is as private annuity or pension payments, with the payments being fully taxed, subject to a deduction or exclusion for a pro rata return of the taxpayer's original nondeductible contribution.

Similar issues arise in the context of universally provided social benefits, such as free or subsidized public education, health services, higher education, and so forth. When the provision of these benefits is means tested, the preferable policy is to exclude the benefits from the income tax base, because benefits will accrue to lower-income taxpayers who are likely to be exempt from taxation. Exempting means-tested benefits will reinforce the vertical equity of the income tax system.

The appropriate treatment of such benefits as health care, public education, or higher education that are provided on a universal (i.e., non-means-tested) basis will depend on whether these are viewed as a social good, comparable to the provision of defense or police, or as social benefits intended to further the redistributive objective of taxation and expenditure. If they are viewed as social benefits provided in the context of redistributive objectives, including the value of the benefit in the income tax base can reinforce the progressivity of the income tax. Imposing a tax on the value of benefits effectively claws back the subsidy for middle- and higher-income earners that is inherent in the benefits. For a number of reasons, however, it is not efficient to use the income tax system to achieve or reinforce vertical equity in respect of these benefits. Most of these relate to the administrative difficulties in assessing benefits. These include problems of valuation (should the value of benefits be measured net of income tax previously paid?) and problems of attribution (is

---

[125]See, e.g., CAN ITA § 56(1)(a) (unemployment insurance benefits are included in computing the income of the taxpayer).

the value of, say, higher education a benefit to the student or the parents, and, if the latter, how should it be apportioned between the parents?). If the provision of these benefits is regarded as an element of the state's redistributive program, a far more effective and efficient solution to the problem of vertical equity is to means test the provision of benefits in the first place rather than to seek to claw back subsidies after the fact through the income tax system.

In terms of drafting technique, schedular definitions of income often do not include social welfare benefits, and their characterization also varies in jurisdictions that use global definitions.[126] When income is defined globally or with a broad catchall, and when an exclusion for some or all social welfare benefits is desired, it would be preferable to provide for such an exclusion explicitly in order to preserve a broad reading of the catchall, as suggested above for gifts.

F. Loans and Cancellation of Indebtedness

While the receipt of loan funds does not give rise to a taxable event (there being no gain because of the corresponding liability to repay), cancellation of indebtedness may give rise to the derivation of income. Upon cancellation of a debt, the taxpayer is immediately better off to the extent that he or she is relieved of an obligation, even though the taxpayer may not have been in a financial position to satisfy the debt had it not been canceled.

While cancellation of a debt increases the taxpayer's net worth, whether this constitutes income depends on the nature of the transaction. If, for example, the transaction is a private one, where cancellation is analogous to a gift, cancellation will not give rise to income to the relieved debtor, assuming that gifts are generally nontaxable.[127] Cancellation of loans made in an employment context usually gives rise to a taxable fringe benefit to the employee. Cancellation of loans made in a business situation generally gives rise to a gain that is included in business income, subject to any applicable special rules that defer or exempt such income in certain cases.[128]

G. Imputed Income from Owner-Occupied Housing

Only a few countries tax imputed income from owner-occupied housing.[129] In principle, this could be an important revenue source and an impor-

---

[126]The basis for their nontaxation in some global systems is sometimes obscure. The United States is an example of a jurisdiction where the rationale for exclusion is not articulated. *See* I.T. 3447, 1941-1 C.B. 191 (USA) (holding that social security benefits are not taxed, but no reason given).

[127]For example, cancellation of private debts (incurred in a nonbusiness or nonemployment context) does not result in the derivation of income in Australia, Canada, France, Germany, Japan, the Netherlands, Sweden, the United Kingdom, and the United States. *See* Ault et al., *supra* note 78, at 182–85. It may, however, be subject to gift taxation.

[128]*See infra* ch. 16.

[129]*See* Ault et al., *supra* note 78, at 172–75.

tant element in supplying progressivity to the income tax. However, practicalities suggest that this is generally not a feasible element for taxation for developing and transition countries because of administrative and valuation difficulties. This does not mean housing should be ignored. The provision of housing to employees should be taxed as a fringe benefit. Moreover, deductions should not be allowed for mortgage interest or other housing expenses. Finally, if preferential treatment is to be provided in respect of gains realized on disposal of a private residence, the preference should be narrowly circumscribed and subject to strict caps.

H. Illegal Income

It is likely that, as a matter of general principle, income from illegal activities would fall within the general inclusion provision under a global system or, in the case of a schedular system, one of the schedules.[130] However, if this is not the case, then it should be stipulated that income derived from illegal activities is still subject to tax. Where illegal income is taxed, a deduction should be allowed for amounts subsequently returned. In part, the possibility of taxing illegal income provides a tool for prosecution of crimes having nothing to do with taxation. Because criminals typically fail to declare their illegal income on tax returns, they can often be successfully prosecuted for tax evasion even when there is no specific proof as to how they got the money.

VII. Tax Relief for Personal Expenses

Under a comprehensive income tax, the taxable income of a taxpayer is the measure of the increase in the taxpayer's economic capacity during the relevant tax period. The way in which the taxpayer exercises the economic power resulting from an increase in economic capacity is irrelevant for the purposes of calculating the taxpayer's taxable income. In other words, the income tax is indifferent to the manner in which a taxpayer chooses to spend money provided the outlay was not incurred to derive gross income,[131] and, therefore, a taxpayer's taxable income should be the same regardless of whether the taxpayer saves the income derived, consumes it, or gives it to someone else to save or consume.

In addition to tax policy arguments, tax administration considerations also argue against allowing any tax relief for personal expenses, particularly in developing and transition countries. As discussed in section XII below, allowing such relief is inconsistent with a PAYE system under which most employ-

---

[130]*See* Ault et al., *supra* note 78, at 186–87.

[131]If an outlay is incurred to derive gross income, then it may be a deductible expense (*see* sec. IV(B), above).

ees (and therefore most income tax payers) pay tax through final withholding and do not file returns.

However, a number of countries do use the income tax system to provide relief for certain personal expenses. The main examples of such expenses are charitable contributions, interest, life insurance premiums, retirement fund contributions, and medical expenses. Tax relief for interest expense is discussed in chapter 16. The special nature of tax relief for charitable contributions warrants further consideration below.

Many countries wish to encourage the development of charitable organizations to fulfill various functions that are considered socially important. Some countries have chosen to do this through the tax system. While, as indicated above, strong arguments can be made that the tax system is not the appropriate means for granting such a subsidy, this is ultimately a political question that each country's legislature must address.[132] If tax relief is provided, then it may be provided in the form of either a tax deduction or a tax offset based on the amount of the contribution. Because a tax deduction is a subtraction from income, under a progressive tax system, the higher the individual's income, the greater the value of the relief. In other words, a tax deduction provides what is known as "upside-down" relief as the value of the deduction increases with the donor's income. In other words, the deduction is of greater value to those on higher marginal rates.

This has important implications for the subsidy given by the government for the contribution because the benefit of the tax savings resulting from the deduction does not flow exclusively to the taxpayer; rather it flows to another party, namely, the charitable institution. Consider, for example, a taxpayer on the highest marginal rate (say, 50 percent) who donates $100 to a charity. The taxpayer is entitled to a deduction of $100, which at the 50 percent rate results in a tax saving of $50 for the taxpayer. This tax saving lowers the cost of the gift to the taxpayer by $50, yet the charity received $100 from the taxpayer. In effect, the government gave $50 and the taxpayer gave $50. The upside-down nature of the tax deduction means that the government's contribution increases with the taxpayer's income and, hence, marginal tax rate. It also means that the government is making a smaller contribution to those charities chosen by taxpayers facing lower marginal rates.[133]

To avoid these problems, some countries have moved recently from a tax deduction system to a tax offset system for charitable contributions. Under a tax offset system, the making of a charitable contribution would not affect the determination of a taxpayer's taxable income, but rather would directly reduce

---

[132]*See generally*, Richard Krever, *Tax Deductions for Charitable Donations: A Tax Expenditure Analysis*, in Richard Krever & Gretchen Kewley eds., Charities and Philanthropic Organisations: Reforming the Tax Subsidy and Regulatory Regimes (1991).

[133]The experience in Australia is that about one-third of deductible gifts are made to private schools with a consequent benefit to the donor (Krever, *supra* note 132, at 20–21).

the tax payable on that taxable income. The amount of the offset could be set at any level;[134] once established, however, it would be the same for taxpayers in all tax brackets (i.e., the ratio of the government's contribution to that of the taxpayer would remain constant whatever the taxpayer's level of income). It is suggested that, if it is decided to provide tax relief for charitable contributions, then the relief be provided through a tax offset rather than through a tax deduction.

Whatever form of tax relief is chosen, certain limitations and restrictions should be considered so as to limit the administration problems that are likely to arise with such relief. First, a threshold can be provided below which charitable contributions are not deductible. The threshold, if set high enough, can prevent many returns from being filed while still encouraging individuals who make substantial gifts. Second, a cap should be placed on the amount of the relief available in any one year.[135] Third, in the case of contributions of property, it is important that the donation of the property be treated as a taxable disposal for market value so that the donor realizes for tax purposes all the gain for which a deduction or tax offset is sought. Otherwise the relief would be a vehicle for avoiding the capital gains tax and, moreover, can become a source of abuse by providing an incentive for overvaluation of property. If donations of property are not treated as taxable disposals for market value, the basis for the relief should be limited to the donor's tax cost of the property. Fourth, any scheme that allows relief for charitable contributions must define qualifying charities,[136] probably with a registration and approval requirement and with limitations on what qualifying charities may do (e.g., they may not provide benefits to any person other than as part of the exercise of charitable programs). It is also important to limit permissible distributees upon liquidation (i.e., only other charities or government bodies).

VIII. Timing Issues

A. Tax Period

As stated above, the income tax is imposed on a periodic basis. It is necessary for the legislation to specify the tax period, generally a period of 12

---

[134]*E.g.*, CAN ITA § 118.1 (amount of the tax offset is 17 percent of the first $250 of the gift and 29 percent of the excess above $250, subject to a maximum deduction of 20 percent of the taxpayer's total income for the tax period); NZL ITA § 56A (amount of the tax offset is 33⅓ percent of the gift subject to a maximum deduction of $500).

[135]*See supra* note 134.

[136]It is important that an organization qualify as a charitable organization only if it applies all or substantially all income and donations derived for charitable purposes so as to prevent individuals from using the exemption to build up a tax-free fund. In the United States, such a requirement is applied to private foundations, but not to all charities.

months, often set to coincide with the government's budgetary year or with the calendar year.[137] Some taxpayers may be permitted to use a substituted accounting period in particular circumstances. This is mostly relevant to business taxpayers and is discussed in chapter 16.

B. Persons Entering and Exiting the Tax System

Taxpayers may enter or exit the tax system during a tax period. Examples include persons immigrating or emigrating during a tax year, taxpayers leaving education for full-time employment, and taxpayers retiring from employment. Aspects of the tax system, such as tax concessions for the support of dependents (see section IX(D), below) and tax-free bands or progressive rate structures (see section X(A), below), are usually calculated on the basis of a taxpayer's total income over the tax period. When a person is effectively within the tax system for only part of the tax period, application of tax features such as concessions and tax-free zones to the taxpayer's income as if it were a full year's income can produce anomalous or inappropriate results. Accordingly, all structural aspects of the personal income tax should be reviewed and, if appropriate, adjusted so that a prorated formula will apply to taxpayers entering or exiting from the tax system in a tax period.[138]

C. Method of Accounting

The periodic imposition of the income tax requires a separate calculation of the taxable income of a taxpayer for each tax period. For this purpose, it is necessary to provide rules (referred to as tax accounting rules) for allocating income and expenses to tax periods. These rules identify the tax period in which income and expenses are to be taken into account in calculating the taxable income of the taxpayer for the tax period.

It is unlikely that a single tax accounting rule will apply to all taxpayers in respect of all items of income or deductible expense. Different rules will apply depending on the circumstances.[139] In general terms, income or expenses may be accounted for on a cash or an accrual basis. Ordinarily, salary and wage earners account for income and deductions on a cash basis, and business taxpayers above a certain size account for income and deductions on an accrual

---

[137]Various tax systems refer to the tax year in terms such as the "fiscal year," "year of assessment," "taxable year," and so forth. In composite systems, there may be more than one taxable period. For example, in Chile the tax on wages is collected monthly, while the taxable period for the global complementary tax is the calendar year. *See* CHL IR §§ 43, 52.

[138]*E.g.*, AUS ITRA 1986 §§ 16–20 (proration of tax-free threshold); CAN ITA § 118.91 (proration of certain deductions); CZE ITA § 15(7) (proration of tax allowances); FRA CGI §§ 166, 167 (treatment of income before establishment of residency and after departure); JPN ITL § 102 (computation of tax where a nonresident becomes a resident in the course of the taxable year).

[139]The rules of tax accounting are discussed in greater detail in ch. 16, *infra*.

basis. Under the cash method, income is derived in the tax period in which it is actually received by, made available to, or, in the case of a benefit, provided to the taxpayer. Similarly, expenses are treated as incurred in the tax period in which the taxpayer actually pays them. Under the accrual method, income is derived in the tax period in which the right to receive the income arises, and expenses are accounted for in the tax period in which the obligation to pay arises. Further, special rules may apply in particular cases (e.g., for long-term contracts or prepayments).

As different tax accounting rules may apply to the same type of income or expense depending on the nature of the taxpayer or to different types of income or expense of the same taxpayer, it is important that the charging and deduction provisions use generic terms to refer to the relevant tax accounting rules so as to properly accommodate all possibilities. The terms commonly used for this purpose are "derived" and "incurred." An amount is included in the gross income of a taxpayer in the tax period in which it is derived by the taxpayer. Similarly, an expense is allowed as a deduction of a taxpayer in the tax period in which it is incurred by the taxpayer.[140] The terminology therefore implicitly refers to the tax accounting rules, and which rule applies in a particular case depends on the circumstances. There should be consistency in the use of generic terminology in the charging and deduction provisions. For example, a situation where some charging provisions use the word "derived" while other provisions use other terminology such as "received" or "accrued" should be avoided because it may raise uncertainty as to whether all terms used are intended to be generic or are stating different tax accounting rules for different items of income. This is not intended to prevent use of specific tax accounting rules in particular cases; rather, specific rules should be provided for in the tax accounting rules and not in the charging provisions.

When an item of income is to be accounted for on a cash basis, it is important that the concept of "receipt" include a constructive receipt. This ensures that an amount that indirectly benefits the taxpayer or that is dealt with on the taxpayer's behalf or as the taxpayer directs is taken into account in calculating the taxpayer's income, provided the amount would be income of the taxpayer if it had been actually received directly by the taxpayer. Examples of situations that should be covered by a constructive receipt rule are an employer directly paying the school fees of an employee's child, the payment of part of an employee's salary or wages to the spouse of the employee, and the payment of part of an employee's salary or wages to a third party in discharge of a debt owed by the taxpayer to the third party. In each case, the application of a constructive receipt rule avoids the argument that, because the taxpayer

---

[140]In the United States, the term used for deductions is "paid" or "accrued." E.g., USA IRC § 162(a).

does not actually receive the payment, there is no derivation of income by the taxpayer.[141]

IX. The Taxpayer

The charging provision in the income tax law identifies the person liable for tax. A separate issue to be addressed in the case of individuals (as opposed to legal persons) is what individuals should comprise the appropriate tax unit. This section deals primarily with this issue. Initially, though, there are questions of terminology that must be resolved.

A. Terminology

Taxation law imposes different obligations on different categories of persons. These include the obligation to provide information to tax authorities about a person's own or another person's affairs, the obligation to file a tax return, the obligation to pay tax, and the obligation to withhold tax from payments to other persons.

Clear terminology should be used consistently throughout the tax legislation to refer to persons with tax obligations. Tax laws often refer to "person" or "taxpayer," but there is sometimes uncertainty about what these terms refer to in certain situations.[142] For example, the term "taxpayer" need not connote a person obliged to pay tax in a particular year.[143] A taxpayer may be required to file a return and provide other information to tax authorities even though the person did not have any taxable income for the year (as would be the case, e.g., if the taxpayer's deductions exceeded his or her gross income) or is not required to pay tax upon his or her taxable income (as would be the case, e.g., if the taxpayer's taxable income fell below a tax-free threshold). A broad definition of taxpayer as a person deriving an amount included in gross income would be more appropriate in these circumstances. Even that will not cover the case, albeit rare, of a person who incurs only deductible expenses. To be all-inclusive, the definition of taxpayer could be drafted to include any person who has incurred a tax loss for the tax period.

Similarly, a person other than a taxpayer may be required to satisfy that taxpayer's tax liability. This is the case, for example, where a tax liability is met

---

[141]There may be a derivation of an amount by some person other than the taxpayer, but the circumstances may be such that the amount derived does not have the character of income in the hands of that other person. For example, if part of an employee's salary is paid to his or her spouse, the amount derived by the spouse will not be employment income of the spouse because the spouse provided no services to the payer. This amount would constitute a gift.

[142]See, e.g., 1 William McKee et al., Federal Taxation of Partnerships and Partners ¶ 9.01[10] (3rd ed. 1997) (discussing whether reference to person or taxpayer includes a partnership).

[143]See also vol. 1, at 101.

by withholding at source. If the payer of gross income who is obliged to collect withholding tax from the payment is not the taxpayer in respect of that income, then alternative appropriate terminology should be used to apply to that person (such as "withholding agent" or "representative taxpayer"). Another possibility is that the taxable income of a person may include the income and deductions of another person. However, both persons may be treated as taxpayers for the purposes of collecting the tax on the taxable income.[144]

Given that taxable income is an algebraic concept determined periodically, it is appropriate to use a term such as "has" to describe the required relationship between a person and taxable income. Terms such as "derived," "earned," "accrued," or "received" are not appropriate for this purpose because they describe the required relationship between a person and individual items of gross income.

B. Individual, Spousal, or Family Units

The tax unit is the basis on which a person's taxable income is calculated.[145] Although a wide range of tax units is used in different jurisdictions for imposing tax on individuals,[146] the main possibilities are to treat as the tax unit individuals, married couples, or families. If couples or families (however defined) are treated as the tax unit, then taxable income is calculated by reference to the income and deductions of all persons included in the tax unit. While many tax theorists contend that the individual is the most appropriate tax unit for a benchmark income tax system, there is no consensus on the issue. The range of units used is largely the result of historical and political considerations.

The question of tax unit is closely tied to that of the tax rate structure. When individual tax rates are relatively flat, the differences between income aggregation and income splitting are minimal. However, large tax-free zones at the bottom end of the rate scale or significant low-rate bands exacerbate the differences in tax burdens between aggregation, splitting, and separate unit systems, described below.

The earliest income tax laws, such as the U.K. Act of 1799,[147] treated unmarried individuals and married couples as equivalent tax units because at

---

[144]This can occur, for example, under a system where a wife's income and deductions are included in the calculation of the taxable income of her husband, but the tax owed by the husband on the wife's income can be collected from both the husband and the wife (see ZMB ITA §§ 19(1), 85).

[145]A different meaning of tax unit refers to the person or persons against whom tax is assessed, that is, the legal taxpayer. The two need not necessarily be the same. For example, in some systems the taxpayer is the individual, but the tax is calculated on the basis of the joint incomes. This was previously the system in Sweden. See Martin Norr et al., Taxation in Sweden 83 (Harvard Law School, International Tax Program 1959).

[146]See generally Brian Arnold et al., Materials on Canadian Income Tax 39–44 (1993); John Head & Richard Krever eds., Tax Units and the Tax Rate Scale (1996).

[147]39 Geo. 3, c. 13 (repealed).

the time married women were not recognized as separate individuals for most legal purposes.[148] The Australian, Canadian, New Zealand, Swedish, and U.S. income tax laws, adopted more than a century later, recognized the individual, whether married or not, as the tax unit. The U.S. courts later allowed married persons in community property states to divide their income for tax purposes, and the U.S. Congress eventually extended to all married persons the right to divide income for tax purposes.[149] Equal splitting in the United States was eventually modified by the adoption of a special "joint filing" tax scale imposed on the combined spousal income.[150] The effect of this rate scale is that a married couple pays less tax than they would pay if their income were not combined, provided that their incomes are sufficiently unequal. If their incomes are relatively close together, then the couple pays more tax than they would pay if they were unmarried with the same incomes.[151] Married persons in the United States also have the option of filing separately rather than jointly, but the rate scale for married persons filing separately makes this option unattractive in almost all cases.[152]

Over the past few decades several members of the OECD that formerly used spousal units have moved toward compulsory or optional separate unit taxation for married persons. This shift has been made largely in recognition of social and legal changes granting equal rights to husbands and wives. In some jurisdictions, optional individual unit filing is available only for "earned" income, while investment income continues to be aggregated and taxed in the hands of the higher-income spouse.[153] In others, such as Germany, spousal in-

---

[148]For a historical review of family unit taxation and a comprehensive survey of the literature, see Neil Brooks, *The Irrelevance of Conjugal Relationships in Assessing Tax Liability, in* Head & Krever, *supra* note 146, at 35. While the United Kingdom finally adopted the individual as the tax unit in 1990, some of its former colonies still provide for the aggregation of a wife's income with that of her husband. *See* KEN ITA § 45 and ZMB ITA § 19(1).

[149]Each state of the United States has its own system of private law, including property and family law. In community property states, the income of a married couple is treated for property law purposes as if it accrued to each spouse, whatever the actual derivation pattern.

[150]*See* USA IRC § 1(a).

[151]This is because the rate bands for an unmarried individual are broader than one-half as wide as the rate bands of a married couple filing jointly. *See* USA IRC § 1(c).

[152]This is because the brackets of the rate schedule for married persons filing separately (as opposed to unmarried individuals) are one-half as wide as the brackets for joint returns (*see* USA IRC § 1(d)), so that the tax would normally be higher in all cases except when the incomes are evenly split, in which case the tax would be the same. However, this rate scale can be advantageous in certain cases where limitations on certain deductions based on a percentage of income would otherwise apply (e.g., when one spouse has a low income but high medical expenses, the latter being subject to a floor of 7.5 percent of adjusted gross income).

[153]For example, in Belgium and the Netherlands. *See* Sommerhalder, *The Taxation of Families and Individuals in Europe, in* Head & Krever, *supra* note 146, at 163, 166–79. Both Belgium and the Netherlands have hybrid systems that tax married couples separately for earned income, but also provide tax relief for couples. *See also* COG CGI §§ 89–95; CMR CGI §§ 117–123.

comes can be based on the individual unit[154] or joint filing,[155] with the rate scale applicable to joint filers yielding a tax burden similar to that which would ensue if incomes were equally divided for the purpose of applying the individual rate scales. The United Kingdom has an individual filing unit with a limited deduction that provides relief to married couples.[156]

The most radical position in terms of family aggregation is expressed in the *quotient familial* of the French income tax. In this system, all family income is aggregated and subject to progressive rates.[157] Before these rates are applied, however, the total family income is divided by a denominator of 2 or more. The basic denominator of 2 applies to a couple without children, and this figure is increased by 0.5 for each child (up to 2 children) and by 1 for each additional child thereafter.[158] The progressive rate scale is then applied to the resulting fraction of total income, and this liability is multiplied by the denominator figure to determine the tax liability imposed on the total income. The amount of tax reduction under this scheme is, however, limited to a specified amount per dependent.[159] One obvious effect of the French system, often cited as its intended purpose, is to bestow tax benefits on larger families.

If the married couple is the tax unit, then it is necessary to define whether the taxpayer is married.[160] A broad range of domestic circumstances can be identified. A taxpayer's civil law status may not always be clear. For example, a couple may consider themselves as married without entering into legal formalities, and they may or may not be considered married under the civil law of the jurisdiction where they live. A couple may also undergo a marriage ceremony without legal validity (e.g., if one of them is already married), or with questionable legal validity (if a divorce from a prior marriage of one of the parties has been obtained, but the validity of that divorce is uncertain). Two people may also marry, separate (without formal proceedings), and consider themselves no longer married, even if they are still married as a matter of law. Generally, where the married couple is the tax unit, the tax law relies on civil law rules for determining marital status. This means that couples (including same-sex couples) in marriage-like relationships not recognized under civil law are not treated as married for the purposes of determining the appropriate tax unit to be allowed to the

---

[154]*See* DEU EStG § 26a.

[155]*See* DEU EStG § 26b.

[156]GBR ICTA § 257A. The relief is referred to as the married couple's allowance and is provided to the husband, although under § 257BA the wife can elect to claim one-half of the relief. *See* Sommerhalder, *supra* note 153, at 186–92.

[157]*See* FRA CGI § 156.

[158]*See* FRA CGI § 194.

[159]*See* FRA CGI § 197(2).

[160]*See generally* Toni Robinson & Mary Moers Wenig, *Marry in Haste, Repent at Tax Time*, 8 Va. Tax. Rev. 773 (1989).

couple.[161] The approach taken to married individuals who are separated but not divorced varies. For example, in the United States, such persons are treated as married individuals,[162] whereas in Germany the election for joint filing applies only to married individuals living together. In Kenya and Zambia, the aggregation of a wife's income with that of her husband does not apply when the spouses are separated and the separation is likely to be permanent.[163]

Marriage, separation, and divorce occurring during the taxable year must also be dealt with (e.g., the status of a person could be determined as of the end of the year[164] or prorated for changes in status during the year). The complexity and confusion that can result from situations such as these argue against designating the married couple as the tax unit. A further consideration may be constitutional restrictions on discrimination on the basis of marital status.[165]

Even where the individual is the tax unit, it may be necessary to know the marital status of the individual. Marital status may be relevant to personal reliefs (see below) or to the definition of "associate" (which may apply, e.g., to prevent income shifting).

As indicated above, many countries have adopted separate taxation of persons, regardless of marital status—an approach that developed largely in response to the recognition of equal legal status for married and unmarried individuals. A secondary consideration that has proved of key importance in many jurisdictions is the disincentive effect of aggregate or joint filing on nonworking spouses seeking to enter the workforce. If spouses' incomes are aggregated, the tax rate imposed on the income derived by a spouse entering the workforce is based on the highest marginal rate of the principal earner. It has been argued that this effect discourages women in particular from entering or reentering the workforce following a period of child-raising responsibilities, and this concern has been a prime factor behind the move from aggregated or joint filing to individual units in many jurisdictions. Finally, administrative considerations are an important factor in favor of an individual tax unit. It is much easier, for example, to design a system of final withholding for employment income if the spouse's income does not need to be taken into account.

---

[161]For some purposes, some income tax laws also treat persons living in a partnership without being married in the same way that they treat a married couple. See AUT EStG § 33(4)(1); NLD WIB § 56. Rules based on whether two people live together can, however, be criticized on grounds of invasion of privacy.

[162]There is an exception to this for a married individual who has primary responsibility for the maintenance of a child (USA IRC §§ 2(c) and 7703(b)). This exception applies only where the individual elects to file separately and ensures that the rates of tax for unmarried individuals apply rather than those for married individuals electing to file separately.

[163]KEN ITA § 45(2) and (3); ZMB ITA § 3(1)(b).

[164]See USA IRC § 7703 (applies only to certain sections of the Code).

[165]See vol. 1, at 28.

C. Divorced and Separated Persons

The family law of many jurisdictions may require a higher-income spouse who formerly supported a lower-income spouse to provide support to the lower-income person for a period following separation or marriage dissolution. In many jurisdictions that use the individual as the tax unit, the payments are ignored for tax purposes—that is, the payer is not allowed to deduct the payment and the recipient is not taxed on it.[166] In effect, the payments are treated in the same manner as payments made within a marriage. Among other things, this rule ensures that there is no tax advantage to be gained from separation or divorce. Moreover, it is a simple rule to administer.

The treatment of support differs in jurisdictions that use spousal units and those that rely on joint filing. Systems that allow some splitting of income during marriage may continue to allow splitting following separation by allowing the payer a deduction for payments and including the amounts in the recipient's taxable income. In some cases, income shifting in this manner is allowed after divorce even though it is not permitted during marriage.[167] This approach is most often seen as a way of subsidizing support obligations with the object of providing a higher income for dependent spouses, particularly those with children. In recent years, this rule has been subject to strong criticism and many judicial challenges in jurisdictions that allow shifting of tax liability on support payments.

D. Recognition of Support for Dependents

Many tax theorists argue that, in the context of an income tax levied on the basis of ability to pay, expenses incurred to support dependents should be disregarded for tax purposes. Rather, it is argued that relief for the cost of supporting dependents is best provided through direct government assistance to families and not through the tax system.[168] Despite these arguments, most in-

---

[166]Ordinarily, support payments are not a deductible expense of the payer because they are not incurred in deriving income subject to tax. Consequently, it is usually not necessary to expressly provide for the denial of a deduction for such payments. In some jurisdictions, though, the receipt of support payments may constitute the derivation of income because of the periodic nature of the payments. It may be necessary, therefore, to expressly exempt such amounts from tax. E.g., AUS ITAA (1997) § 51-50.

[167]E.g., USA IRC §§ 71, 215; ZMB ITA §§ 17(h), 40. Full or partial deductions for alimony are allowed in Belgium, Canada, France, Germany, the Netherlands, and Sweden, and a limited tax offset is provided in the United Kingdom on the same basis as that for married couples. See Ault et al., supra note 78, at 276–80; Sommerhalder, supra note 153.

[168]A contrary argument is that relief for dependents is a way of implementing a policy whereby income is split among family members: "each family member should be taxed on items he actually consumes or accumulates, regardless of source." Michael McIntyre & Oliver Oldman, Taxation of the Family in a Comprehensive and Simplified Income Tax, 90 Harv. L. Rev. 1573, 1576 (1977). Under this argument, deductions for dependents should not be considered subsidies, and therefore do not suffer from the upside-down relief problem described in this section.

come tax systems provide some relief for the cost of supporting dependents. While the various tax relief systems adopted have been criticized as inefficient, inequitable, and administratively complicated, few jurisdictions have moved to replace income-tax-based relief systems entirely with direct grants or expenditure programs.[169] However, in most industrial countries, it is now common for tax support programs to be combined with direct expenditure programs (sometimes means-tested, sometimes universal) to ameliorate some of the drawbacks of tax-based support systems.[170] Relief for dependents through the income tax should be structured to take into account the existence of such programs and the level of benefits they provide.

Tax relief may be provided through income splitting with dependents, deductions for the support of dependents, or refundable or nonrefundable tax offsets for the support of dependents.[171]

To some extent, income tax systems recognizing spousal units (other than systems that simply combine the income of the spouses and tax it as if it were derived by one individual)[172] in effect use income shifting as a means of providing tax support for dependents. Only France extends this system of relief to the support of children through its *quotient familial* system.[173] This system provides upside-down relief as the tax saving from shifting income through the *quotient familial* system increases with the principal earner's income. That is, the greater the ability of the principal earner to support dependents, the greater the tax relief provided. Also, in the case of high-income earners, the relief provided by this method applies to discretionary income used for personal consumption or savings, but not for the support of dependents.

A common method of tax relief has been to allow individual taxpayers to deduct a specific amount as compensation for the support of dependents. The amount of the deduction may vary with the number of dependents. Because a tax deduction is a subtraction from income, under a progressive tax system, the higher the individual's income, the greater the value of the relief. In other words, relief through tax deduction suffers the same upside-down effect as relief through income splitting, in that relief is provided inversely with the taxpayer's need. Moreover, a deduction system fails to provide any relief for individuals with incomes below the lowest tax threshold. For these reasons,

---

[169]Sweden now provides all support for families through direct expenditure programs. Austria has an extensive system of family subsidies and very little tax relief for dependent children. *See* Familienlastenausgleichsgesetz 1967; AUT EStG § 33(4), (8).

[170]Examples include Australia, Belgium, Canada, France, Germany, Ireland, Italy, the Netherlands, Spain, the United Kingdom, and the United States.

[171]Tax offsets can be provided directly or indirectly by providing an extension of the lowest or tax-free threshold to taxpayers supporting dependents.

[172]As was the case under the earlier U.K. income tax regimes. *See* Brooks, *supra* note 148. This system has been largely abandoned, at least for earned income (i.e., income from employment, business, or the provision of services).

[173]*See supra* note 157.

some countries have moved away from deduction-based relief systems for dependents or have phased out the deduction for higher-income taxpayers.[174]

Some jurisdictions have replaced tax deductions with tax offsets as the method of relief for the support of dependents.[175] As with deductions, the amount of the offset may vary with the number of dependents. A tax offset is a subtraction from the tax payable by the individual (i.e., it is an amount taken into account after the rates of tax have been applied to the taxable income of the individual). A tax offset that can be applied against tax otherwise due is of the same value to all taxpayers who can use it and, therefore, avoids the upside-down effect of deductions.[176] However, like the deduction, it provides no support for taxpayers whose incomes are so low that they incur no tax liability under the ordinary income tax rate scale. This problem could be solved by making the offset refundable, but this solution has not generally been adopted.[177] Instead, reliance is placed on direct expenditure programs to assist these persons.

Tax policy in this area is likely to be influenced by administrative considerations. Particularly where relief is given outside the tax system, tax administration considerations argue in favor of relying on such relief and providing no deductions or offsets through the tax system. If it is decided to provide tax relief for the support of dependents, then the design of the relief should be kept as simple as possible. In some developing countries, the amount of the relief may vary with the number of dependents. Indeed, there may be separate reliefs depending on the nature of the dependent children, or if the dependents are handicapped or elderly persons. Administrators in some jurisdictions are concerned that taxpayers will simply claim the greatest relief possible regardless of the actual circumstances. For example, if the amount of the relief increases with the number of children up to, say, a maximum of three children, taxpayers may simply claim relief for three children regardless of the actual number of children they have to support, provided they believe the administration

---

[174]E.g., USA IRC § 151(d)(3) (deduction phased out by 2 percentage points for each US$2,500 by which the taxpayer's adjusted gross income exceeds the threshold amount (US$150,000 for a married couple)).

[175]See CAN ITA § 118.

[176]It is possible to design tax offsets that increase in value with income. For example, taxpayers in the Democratic Republic of the Congo are given a 5 percent reduction in tax otherwise payable (which is effectively a credit equal to 5 percent of the tax otherwise due) for each eligible dependent. The reduction is subject to two limitations—it is available for up to only nine dependents and a total monetary cap is imposed on the reduction: ZAR CDC § 89. Because the reduction is a percentage of total tax, which rises with total income, the benefits provided by the system increase with income.

[177]Exceptions include Canada and the United States. The Canadian goods and services tax credit, designed to provide relief particularly to lower-income persons for indirect taxes, is refundable; see CAN ITA § 122.5. In the United States, the Earned Income Tax Credit, which is partially designed to provide relief for the support of dependents, is also refundable; see USA IRC § 32.

does not have the resources to check these claims. This issue is particularly important where it is decided to make PAYE withholding a final tax.[178]

Those who argue for direct expenditure programs to provide financial assistance for persons supporting dependents cite a number of difficulties that apply to all tax-based relief systems. The first, and most important, is that of targeting. Whether a deduction or an offset-based relief system is used, the benefit will accrue to some taxpayers who require no assistance with support of dependents and will fail to reach some taxpayers very much in need of such assistance. Moreover, the tax system cannot provide controls to ensure that the relief is used to subsidize support. The taxpayer enjoying the relief may not be the taxpayer responsible on a day-to-day basis for supporting the dependent. This may be the case, for example, where tax relief is provided to a high-income taxpayer who fails to pass on the benefit of the relief to a lower-income spouse who is responsible for acquiring the necessities used to support the dependent. Depending on how it is structured, direct financial assistance may overcome this problem.[179] Finally, it may be more difficult from an administrative perspective to define dependents in an income tax system than in a social welfare system, because the concept of collective needs is different from the concept of ability to pay, and social support authorities may have more expertise, and social support laws more flexibility, in identifying dependency. This is particularly the case in respect of unrelated persons living with a supporter or where support is provided through extended families and family support networks.

If a tax-based system to provide relief for persons supporting dependents is chosen, it should be designed to minimize the upside-down, targeting, and administrative difficulties noted above. Proposals to provide tax relief for taxpayers supporting dependents should also be considered in light of decisions concerning the design of the rate scale. Adjustment of the tax-free threshold or lower brackets can be used to provide across-the-board "basic living expenses" tax relief to all taxpayers that is sufficiently generous to those supporting dependents.

A number of difficult definitional issues must be dealt with in any scheme for dependency relief through the tax system. Particular care needs to be taken with these because they can involve difficult factual and legal issues, and they will affect the majority of taxpayers who must apply the tests, usually without professional advice. The following issues are involved:

(1) Relationship. A basic issue is whether the right to claim relief for a dependent should be limited to relatives. If so, the relation must be specified, that is, just children, or also parents, or also a broader group of relatives. The argument for restricting relief to support of relatives is that otherwise too much

---

[178]*See infra* sec. XII; ch. 15.

[179]For example, the Australian home child-care allowance is paid to the parent actually caring for the child. The Swedish child subsidy is paid to the mother, if she is in charge.

may rest on the other possible test for dependency, namely, the amount of support provided. The level of support, particularly support in kind, may be rather complicated to determine, while relation is usually easier to determine. Some countries extend tax relief to persons living in the household of the taxpayer, even when they are not related to the taxpayer.[180] In countries with extended families and extensive family support networks,[181] this could result in serious administrative problems.

(2) Allocation of relief. Particularly in a system based on an individual filing unit, two taxpayers may often satisfy the entitlement rules with respect to a particular dependent. Only one should be allowed to claim the relief. Rules need to be provided to assign the right to the relief to one or the other spouse or for apportioning the relief between the spouses.[182]

(3) Support requirement. A decision must be made as to whether to extend entitlement to dependency relief automatically to, say, taxpayers with children or to limit automatic entitlement to cases where the taxpayer supplies the requisite amount of support. Support is a notoriously difficult concept to define and it would be best from an administrative point of view not to include it among the qualifications for dependency relief. It could be presumed, for example, that a person residing in the same household is receiving support.

(4) Income test. Dependency is often determined by reference to a dependent's personal taxable income (i.e., no recognition for dependency is allowed if the dependent's income exceeds a specific threshold). This rule is important if dependency is not restricted to those with a close family relationship, but is less critical if the relationship test is fairly narrowly defined. It raises a practical problem of administration, because it requires determining the income of one taxpayer in order to tax another. Where the test is specified, it is necessary to provide the time period for which it will apply. It is easier to apply if the dependent's income is tested for a period prior to that for which the deduction is allowed, but this may not adequately deal with changed circumstances.

(5) Period for relief. Another issue for the tax-free threshold as well as for the dependency deduction is whether they are applied annually or monthly. Some systems restrict the deduction to taxpayers who earn income in a given month. This facilitates the use of final withholding taxes. The entitlement to the deduction can be determined on a month-to-month basis, so that no need arises to adjust withholding for events taking place in prior months.

---

[180]*E.g.*, DEU EStG § 32; NLD WIB art. 46. These provisions include relief for foster children.

[181]The support networks might also be based on a clan, village, or tribe, or on other groups. In some cases support responsibilities may be allocated by law or custom to persons other than the parents. Application of a relationship test might be inconsistent with such support networks.

[182]For example, in Belgium and the Netherlands the deductions for dependents are automatically allocated to the higher-income spouse. *See* Sommerhalder, *supra* note 153.

X. Income Tax Rate Scale

A. Progressive and Flat-Rate Scales

A key issue in the design of the income tax rate structure is the progressivity, if any, to be incorporated into the tax rate scale. A progressive rate structure is one under which the effective rate of tax—the fraction of income paid in tax—increases as the level of income increases. A progressive tax can take the form of a graduated rate scale or a flat-rate scale combined with a tax-free threshold.

While setting the rate structure is a matter of economic and budgetary policy, as well as tax policy, and will often be influenced by political considerations, there are also technical considerations. First, the flatter the rate structure applicable to individuals, the fewer the incentives for such persons to engage in income shifting.[183] Second, if the rate of tax applicable to legal persons is not aligned with the maximum marginal rate for individuals, taxpayers may enter into income-diversion arrangements. For example, if the rate for legal persons is less than the maximum marginal rate for individuals, high-income earners may enter into arrangements to divert their income to entities that they own. This is discussed further below. Third, there may be administrative advantages to establishing a broad standard marginal rate into which most taxpayers with income tax liability will fall. This suggests that, apart from the zero bracket, there may be a need for no more than three or four positive rates: a standard rate, a rate below the standard rate, and one or two rates above it.[184] Even two positive rates might be adequate.

As noted in section II(A), above, some jurisdictions are moving toward imposing flatter rates of final withholding taxes on particular types of income, especially income from capital. Contrary to prima facie appearances, this trend does not necessarily undermine overall progressivity. While final withholding tax rates are usually lower than the highest personal marginal income tax rate, the effective rate of these taxes may be equal to or greater than the highest marginal tax rate, and, depending on the income bracket of taxpayers deriving income subject to flat-rate withholding, progressivity may even be enhanced by such taxes.

The effective rate of withholding taxes may exceed the highest personal marginal income tax for a number of reasons. The most important is that withholding taxes are levied on a gross basis, while the ordinary progressive rate scale is applied to net income. In the case of dividend income, in the absence of an imputation system, the effective tax rate imposed on dividends may in-

---

[183]See infra sec. X(C).

[184]A rate schedule with a larger number of brackets may appear to be more progressive, but in fact a schedule with three or four rates can be designed to offer a similar progression in the effective rate of tax.

clude a substantial underlying company tax. In the case of interest income, not adjusting for inflation may mean that nominal interest far exceeds the real income a lender enjoys.

A further tax rate issue to be resolved is that of a basic tax-free threshold, below which income is not taxed. Almost all tax systems provide such a tax-free threshold, either through a zero-rate bracket or through tax offsets or universal deductions. The size of the tax-free zone will depend on revenue needs—including the impact of other taxes, particularly on low-income taxpayers—and on administrative considerations. Significant administrative savings can be realized if a large number of low-income persons can be excluded from the tax net by way of a generous tax-free threshold.

B. Income Averaging and Antibunching Rules

The interaction of a progressive rate structure and a system of annual assessment can lead to tax rate anomalies in four respects. The first, noted earlier in section VIII(B), arises when taxpayers enter or exit the tax system during a tax year and possibly derive an inappropriate advantage by treating partial-year income as if it were full-year income for the purposes of the progressive rate scale. The three other anomalies apply to taxpayers who have been in the tax system for several years.

The second problem is a general one that follows from taxpayers' income derivation patterns. Taxpayers' actual annual earnings over the period in which they are in the tax system may be far different from their *average* annual earnings over the same period. Typically, taxpayers' earnings vary as they change employment, as they achieve seniority, and so forth. Application of the progressive rate structure to each year separately will yield a very different, and probably higher, result than would the application of the progressive tax rate structure to the average earnings over the period.

The third problem is similar to the second, but focuses on particular classes of taxpayers who are more likely than other taxpayers to derive income unevenly from year to year over the same period. Common examples of such taxpayers are farmers, artists, authors, and inventors. A taxpayer who derives widely fluctuating amounts of income from year to year may be subject, over a number of years, to a tax burden substantially higher than that faced by a taxpayer who derives the same overall income evenly.

The fourth problem is faced by taxpayers deriving lump-sum gains, such as capital gains or lump-sum retirement payments. These taxpayers may face a higher tax burden when the whole gain is taxed in the year of realization rather than annually as the gain accrues, pushing the taxpayer into a higher tax bracket. This is referred to as a "bunching" of the gain.

The problem of unequal lifetime income patterns and unequal derivation patterns by particular classes of taxpayers may be addressed through measures to average income. However, as explained below, it is common to direct these measures only at the third type of problem. The problem of income bunching can be addressed through antibunching provisions. These are also explained below.

1. Income Averaging

General income averaging may be used to address the problem of changing income-earning patterns. In simplified terms, general income averaging typically involves ascertaining the taxpayer's average income over a specific number of years, including the current year, and applying to the current year the marginal rates applicable to the average income. This procedure results in lower rates of tax for a year in which the taxpayer's income is abnormally high. A system of general averaging may impose considerable administrative burdens on revenue authorities. It would make it very difficult to treat PAYE withholding as a final tax on employment income. It can also provide unintended benefits for taxpayers who do not deserve relief.[185] Quite clearly, the case for general averaging is strongest when the income tax rate scale is sharply progressive. As the rate scale is flattened, the case for averaging diminishes, particularly when the potential benefits are weighed against the resulting administrative burden. For these reasons, jurisdictions that have used general averaging systems have moved to abolish those systems as the progressivity of the rate scales has been reduced.[186]

An alternative to general averaging is to confine income averaging to particular classes of taxpayers, notably primary producers, artists, inventors, and authors.[187] Averaging rules for specific types of income can be far less complicated for the tax system as a whole than general averaging rules, although they are complex for the taxpayers involved. Depending on how the rules are designed,[188] they may provide unintended benefits and distort taxpayer behavior as taxpayers seek to recharacterize transactions or income types to take advantage of income averaging. Unless the rate schedule is very progressive, it is best from the point of view of simplicity to eliminate any averaging rules.

2. Antibunching Rules

Similar concerns with distorted tax liability in the context of a progressive rate structure apply to lump-sum payments, particularly those that are attributable to gains, such as capital gains or lump-sum retirement payments, that have accrued over several tax years but that are assessable only in the year in which they are realized. In these circumstances, any increase in taxation re-

---

[185]For example, a young professional whose average income is depressed because he or she earned little or no income while in school.

[186]*See* CAN ITA § 118 (repealed 1980); USA IRC §§ 1301–1305 (repealed 1986).

[187]See AUS ITAA (1936) §§ 149–158L (farmers, artists, and authors) and §§ 159GA–159GDA (special "income equalization deposit" rules to provide further averaging for farmers); CAN ITA § 119 (farmers and fishermen).

[188]The design issues are similar to those for antibunching rules discussed in sec. XI(B), below, except that they involve taking into account the income of prior years.

sulting from the imposition of higher marginal tax rates on the lump sum may be seen as an appropriate, if somewhat crude, claw-back of the deferral advantage enjoyed by the taxpayer prior to realization. Nevertheless, for political reasons, some jurisdictions do provide special averaging rules for particular types of income, such as capital gains[189] or lump-sum retirement payments.[190]

Again, it is best to avoid such rules, but if they are provided they should be designed so as to minimize windfalls to taxpayers. The best way to do this, known as "top-slice" averaging, is for relief to be triggered only if, in the absence of any averaging rule, the derivation of a lump sum would be subject to tax rates that would not otherwise apply to the taxpayer. Thus, if a taxpayer's taxable income, apart from extraordinary gains, was high enough to ensure that the last units were taxed at the highest marginal rate, the averaging system would not be invoked because it would make no difference to the tax rate whether the gain were derived in one year or over a number of years. Typically, a top-slice averaging system slices a lump-sum payment into fractions (by dividing the payment by a number of years, which might be based on a notional determination of the period over which the payment has accrued) and determines the tax payable on the fraction, which is then multiplied by the denominator of the fraction to determine the tax payable on the entire lump sum. The system is best illustrated with an example. If the averaging system presumed that a lump sum should be averaged over, say, five years, the rules would determine the taxpayer's tax liability on taxable income without considering the lump sum and then considering the other income plus one-fifth of the lump sum. The difference between the tax payable on the taxable income without the lump sum and taxable income including one-fifth of the lump sum is the tax actually imposed on the one-fifth of the lump sum. This figure is then multiplied by five to determine the tax to be imposed on the entire lump sum.

If the taxpayer's taxable income without the lump sum is low enough that the addition of one-fifth of the lump sum still leaves the last units of taxable income subject to lower tax rates, those lower rates will be applied to the entire lump sum. If, however, the last unit of the taxpayer's taxable income, excluding the lump sum, is subject to the highest marginal tax rates, it will make no difference whether one-fifth of the payment or the entire payment is added to the taxpayer's taxable income when derived because the same rate will apply before and after the averaging system is invoked. Even this method can result in unintended benefits, for example, when a taxpayer derives on a steady basis capital gains eligible for averaging.

C. Income Shifting

Under a progressive rate schedule, there is an incentive to shift income to related parties, unless the type of income in question is taxed at a flat rate

---

[189]E.g., AUS ITRA sched. 7.
[190]E.g., Belgium, Germany, and the Netherlands.

on a schedular basis. As a result of income shifting, income that would otherwise be derived by a single taxpayer can be derived by two or more taxpayers who are then able to use more than once the tax-free thresholds and low rates applicable to lower levels of income. The income will be subject to much lower total taxation than if it had been derived by a single person.

A company tax rate that is lower than an individual's marginal tax rate may stimulate a related type of income diversion, from the individual to a company controlled by the individual or persons related to the individual.[191]

A number of countries have adopted measures to restrict income shifting. Experience has shown that, because a variety of income-shifting techniques are available to taxpayers, multiple responses are needed. Attempts to invoke universal responses, such as reliance on general antiavoidance provisions or tax authorities' discretions, have had limited success because they can be applied only on an ad hoc basis, following an audit. Moreover, general responses are administratively costly to apply and can often be defeated by apparent "business purpose" explanations for income-shifting arrangements.

At the heart of some countries' antishifting rules, of which the United States provides the leading example, are judicial doctrines that decline to recognize income-shifting arrangements as effective for income tax purposes, notwithstanding their validity under property law.[192] Judicial doctrines alone have proved insufficient to address the problem of income shifting, and a range of legislative approaches have been used. Separate rules are used for shifting income from investment and income from services.

The most sophisticated and, unfortunately, complex antishifting regimes are those that use attribution rules for non-arm's-length transfers of property or underlying income-generating property. Generally, these attribute to the transferor for income tax purposes income subsequently derived by the beneficiary of the transfer, whether income or property is transferred directly or through a trust.[193] A broader approach to preventing shifting of investment income is to attribute all investment income derived by married persons to the

---

[191]Whether there is such an incentive to divert income depends on a number of features of the corporate and individual income tax systems. *See infra* ch. 19.

[192]*See* Lucas v. Earl, 281 U.S. 111 (1930); Helvering v. Clifford, 309 U.S. 331 (1940); and Commissioner v. Harmon, 323 U.S. 44 (1944).

[193]CAN ITA §§ 74.1, 74.2 contain comprehensive attribution rules applicable to transfers to spouses and children whereby the income from property so transferred is taxed to the transferor. AUS ITAA (1936) §§ 102, 102A–102CA contain less comprehensive attribution rules when income is alienated through a trust or for less than seven years. In some cases, income is attributed directly to the transferor; in other cases it is taxed in the hands of a trustee at the transferor's marginal rate. In addition, AUS ITAA (1936), pt. IIIA imposes a tax liability on the transferor in respect of income-producing property that has appreciated in value as well as in respect of most transfers of income streams. GBR ICTA § 660 contains a rule disregarding dispositions over short periods, § 663 provides that any income from settlements for the benefit of minor children will be taxed as income of the settlor, and § 683 provides for a tax liability of the settlor when income is payable to any person but the settlor.

higher-income spouse.[194] Several jurisdictions have global antishifting systems, which impose either the highest personal marginal tax rate or the marginal rate of the parents on investment income derived by minors and, in some cases, on earned income in excess of the fair market remuneration that would be paid to these persons for services they provide.[195] At the price of some complexity, some systems provide exceptions for investment income that was clearly not derived as the result of an income-shifting arrangement. Examples of exceptions include income from property left in a bequest and income derived from property provided as settlement of a personal injury damages claim. An alternative approach for dealing with children's income used in some jurisdictions is to aggregate children's investment income with the income of the parent who claims the child as a dependent or with both parents' income in the case of joint taxation.[196] Constitutional or other restrictions may prevent the application of this approach in some jurisdictions.[197]

More sophisticated antishifting measures may be needed to deal with the various techniques used to shift business income. Excessive payments to spouses or children for "services" provided to the taxpayer may be countered with restrictions on deductions for payments to such persons.[198] Attribution rules can be used to counter income shifting through the use of partnerships involving related parties when one partner provides the bulk of the services from which the partnership derives its income and the other party has not provided any equivalent value.[199] Jurisdictions have had less success combating income shifting through service trusts or companies. These are trusts or companies that provide tax-deductible services to a taxpayer in a business context for a price much higher than the taxpayer would pay if the services were acquired directly. The beneficiaries or shareholders of the trust or company are

---

[194]This approach was followed in the United Kingdom, where before 1990–91 spouses were taxed on aggregate income, but could elect to be taxed separately on earned income. See GBR ICTA §§ 279(1), 283 (repealed by Finance Act, 1988); see also John Tiley, Butterworths U.K. Tax Guide 1990–91 ¶ 3.01 (1991). It still is the case in Belgium and the Netherlands. See BEL CIR § 126; NLD WIB § 5(1).

[195]E.g., AUS ITAA (1936) §§ 102AA–102AJ (unearned income of minor child taxed to the child at the maximum marginal rate); BEL CIR § 126 (income of children taxed together with parents' income); Gerrit te Spenke & A. Peter Lier, Taxation in the Netherlands 21 (1992) (unearned income of child, other than certain capital gains, taxed to parent with highest earned income); USA IRC § 1(g)(certain unearned income of minor child taxed at parents' rate).

[196]See, e.g., ESP IRPF § 89(3)(when parents opt for joint taxation, all income (earned and unearned) is aggregated); FRA CGI § 6 (same).

[197]For example, in Germany, owing to the constitutional clause in defense of the family (GG art. 6(1)), unearned income of the children is taxed separately rather than aggregated with their parents' income. See Tipke & Lang, supra note 111, at 54.

[198]See, e.g., AUS ITAA (1997) § 26-35.

[199]See, e.g., AUS ITAA (1936) § 94. This provision has proved of limited efficacy because attribution follows only if it can be shown that the person to whom income would be attributed "controlled" the partnership. Tax authorities have had more success in arguing that there was no actual partnership in these cases.

persons related to the taxpayer. Income shifting through this device could be combated by denying taxpayers deductions to related service companies or trusts in excess of the amounts those entities pay the unrelated parties who actually provide the services acquired.

Separate measures are needed to deal with the shifting of employment income by means of interposed companies or trusts. When the highest marginal tax rate imposed on individuals is higher than the rate imposed on companies, individuals may establish a company to provide services that they would otherwise provide as an employee. Income is derived by the company and is subject to a lower rate of tax. Experience shows that these arrangements cannot be combated through the use of judicial doctrines or general antiavoidance provisions alone and that specific antishifting measures are needed instead.[200] One approach is to impose a higher company tax rate on "personal service corporations," that is, on companies whose incomes are primarily attributable to services provided by an employee or employees who own the company or who are related to persons who own the company.[201] An alternative approach is to attribute income derived by personal service companies to the individuals providing the services for which the company is paid.

A related problem is that of interposed private companies used to derive investment income that an individual would otherwise derive directly and that would be subject to higher individual marginal tax rates. Once again, a number of different measures may be needed to address this problem. One technique is to deny private companies concessions, such as exemptions or tax offsets for intercorporate dividends, that are available to other companies.[202] Alternatively, or additionally, taxes may be imposed on undistributed investment income retained by private companies to encourage distributions of this income to the company owners.[203] And, finally, measures may be introduced to prevent companies from distributing to shareholders in a nontaxable way

---

[200]The Australian and U.S. experiences illustrate this point. Australian authorities first tried to combat shifting of this sort by imposing an undistributed earnings tax on private companies. (The tax was also adopted to protect the "classical" company and shareholder tax system—see infra ch. 19.) The undistributed profits tax was abandoned on introduction of the imputation system in 1986. At that time, company and highest individual rates were aligned. When a significant rate differential was reintroduced in 1988, authorities tried to use a general antiavoidance provision to combat shifting by means of interposed companies. That approach proved of limited efficacy, and in 1995 the government announced that new, comprehensive antishifting rules would be enacted. However, following a change in government, reform legislation was deferred indefinitely. U.S. authorities found it virtually impossible to combat income shifting by means of interposed companies. The problem was solved in that country when the company tax rate was roughly aligned with the highest personal income tax rate.

[201]See CAN ITA §§ 123(1), 125.

[202]This approach is used in Australia for "unfranked" dividends (dividends paid out of profits that have not been fully taxed in the hands of the distributing company) derived by private companies. See AUS ITAA (1936) § 46F.

[203]See USA IRC § 541.

income that was taxed only at the lower company tax rate. For example, loans from a private company to a shareholder or related party may be deemed to be taxable distributions by the company.[204]

XI. Tax Offsets

It was explained earlier that two types of subtractions are relevant to the calculation of the actual tax payable by a taxpayer. First, an amount may be subtracted from gross income in the calculation of the taxable income of the taxpayer. Second, an amount may be subtracted from the tax payable. It is common for a subtraction from gross income to be referred to as an "allowable deduction," and a subtraction from the tax payable as a "tax credit." However, the term "tax credit" sometimes does not translate well into other languages, perhaps because credit can also mean loan.[205] As explained in section II(C), above, the term "tax offset" has been used in this chapter to avoid these difficulties. Whatever terminology is used, it is important that the legislation clearly and consistently distinguish between these two types of subtractions because of the different tax consequences.

Four broad categories of tax offset may be allowed: (1) in recognition of tax already paid by the taxpayer (e.g., under a current payment system) or by another person on behalf of the taxpayer (e.g., by an employer through a PAYE withholding, another person paying income subject to withholding, or a trustee deriving income on behalf of a beneficiary); (2) in recognition of tax paid by the taxpayer or by another person on behalf of the taxpayer (through withholding tax) to foreign tax authorities;[206] (3) in an imputation system in recognition of tax previously paid by a company on dividends (or deemed dividends) distributed to the taxpayer;[207] and (4) for concessional purposes to support certain activities or responsibilities of the taxpayer, such as medical expenses,[208] child care,[209] charitable or political

---

[204]*See* AUS ITAA (1936) § 108.

[205]*Cf.* vol. 1, at 218, note 146 (tax credit versus deduction for VAT input tax). In France, the term *avoir fiscal* is used synonymously with *crédit d'impôt*. See FRA CGI § 158 *bis*. The draft tax code of Russia (art. 135) uses the term *nalogovi credit* (literally tax credit) to describe a postponement of the time for payment of tax, that is, in the sense of extension of a loan rather than in the sense of tax credit as it is used here. In referring to the crediting of foreign taxes, the draft tax code uses the verb *zaschitivat'* (counting toward, crediting), and uses the term "creditable amount" rather than "tax credit" (art. 560). The term used in Germany (*anrechnen* or *Anrechnung, see* EStG § 36) similarly has the sense of counting toward or charging. When a translation problem exists, the solution may lie in using a verb rather than using "tax credit" as a noun. However, when the verb used is equivalent to "deduct," then the problem discussed in the text—namely, the need to distinguish between deductions from income and deductions from tax—must be addressed.

[206]Such a tax offset is commonly referred to as a "foreign tax credit." *See infra* ch. 18.

[207]Such a tax offset is commonly referred to as an "imputation credit." *See infra* ch. 19.

[208]*See* AUS ITAA (1936) § 159P.

[209]*See* USA IRC § 21.

contributions,[210] support for dependents,[211] and retirement savings,[212] or to provide general relief to taxpayers with low earned income.[213] As was explained earlier, tax offsets may be used for these purposes in preference to deductions from gross income to avoid the upside-down effect of deductions, which provide greater tax savings to higher-income persons.[214]

Different rules apply to the recognition of tax offsets for taxes actually paid (the first three categories of tax offsets noted above) and tax offsets provided for concessional purposes. The latter have no nexus with income taxes actually paid and can be set by reference to independent criteria on the basis of the taxpayer's need for concessional support. One technique sometimes used to improve the targeting of concessional support tax offsets is to use "disappearing" tax offsets that decrease in value as a taxpayer's income increases.[215] Tax offsets that are intended to act as substitutes for direct social assistance payments may also be made refundable when they exceed the tax payable by a person entitled to the offsets.[216]

The extent to which offsets for taxes actually paid are recognized will vary. Offsets for advance payments of tax by the taxpayer are usually recognized completely; any amount that exceeds the final tax levied on the taxpayer is refundable in full. In contrast, taxes paid to foreign governments are usually recognized only to the extent of local taxes imposed on the foreign income with no refund of any excess offset.[217] Tax offsets for company taxes allowed under an imputation system may or may not be refundable depending on the design of the imputation system.[218]

In some cases, taxpayers may be allowed to carry forward to future years nonrefundable offsets that have not been recognized previously. Restrictions may be placed on the recognition of offsets for foreign tax and company tax paid that are carried forward, so that they may be used only to offset taxes on particular types of income. When different rules concerning refundability and carryover apply to different kinds of offsets, rules are needed to specify in which order offsets are taken.[219] These may require taxpayers to first recognize

---

[210]*See, e.g.,* CAN ITA § 118.1(3) (charitable gifts); USA IRC § 24 (political contributions— repealed).

[211]*See* AUS ITAA (1936) § 159J. *See supra* sec. IX(D).

[212]*See* AUS ITAA (1936) § 159SM.

[213]*See* USA IRC § 32 (earned income credit).

[214]*See supra* sec. VII.

[215]*E.g.,* USA IRC § 21(1)(2) (child-care credit).

[216]*See* text at note 177 *supra.*

[217]Further restrictions with respect to foreign income may divide that income into different income "baskets" on the basis of income type, the jurisdiction in which it was derived, or both these criteria, and may limit recognition of offsets for taxes paid on foreign-source income in a particular basket to local tax payable on that particular basket, with no carryover to other baskets of foreign-source income. *See infra* ch. 18.

[218]*See infra* ch. 19.

[219]*See, e.g.,* USA IRC § 38(d).

nonrefundable offsets and offsets that cannot be carried forward or transferred, so as to preserve the value of refundable offsets and offsets that can be carried forward or transferred.

XII. Administrative Aspects of Taxing Employment Income

Almost all countries collect the income tax payable on employment income (PAYE) on a current basis by withholding at source by the employer.[220] Employers collect the PAYE withholding tax, although the employees bear the liability because, under the PAYE provisions, employees whose salaries have been subject to PAYE withholding are deemed to have received the gross (pretax) amounts of pay they are due. Administrative and collection provisions impose the obligations to withhold and to remit on employers, and parallel penalty and interest provisions will apply to nonwithholding or nonremittance.

If the employer has withheld tax but has failed to remit it to the tax authorities, it is appropriate to relieve the employee of any further tax liability (because the employee has already effectively borne the tax).[221] In contrast, the provisions related to nonwithholding are usually drafted as parallel alternatives, allowing revenue authorities to collect the tax from either the employer or the employee, provided that it is collected only once.

If tax has been withheld, but the employer enters into bankruptcy or insolvency proceedings before the tax is remitted to the tax authorities, it is customary to give the government a priority interest in this fund, regardless of the general position that may be taken as to the priority given to tax debts owed by bankrupt or insolvent taxpayers. In effect, the fund is treated as being the property of the government rather than that of the employer.[222]

To be effective, PAYE collection and remittance obligations should be imposed on as broad a range of employers as possible. The objective, particularly if PAYE is to be used as a final tax on employment income, is to apply the system to every situation where payment is made substantially for the labor of the recipient of the payment—that is, where the person receiving payment will not be entitled to substantial deductions in respect of materials, equipment, and so forth. The definition of persons subject to PAYE with-

---

[220]This section elaborates on a few issues in PAYE taxation; for a full discussion, see infra ch. 15.

[221]E.g., USA IRC § 31(a) (credit allowed for the "amount withheld").

[222]The New Zealand position is not atypical: revenue authorities are given priority for PAYE and withholding taxes not remitted by an employer, but stand with other creditors for the employer's basic income tax liability (see NZL ITA § 365). A contrasting position was taken recently in Australia, where the priority for PAYE and withholding taxes was abolished. On the same theory, the failure to pay over the tax withheld can be made a crime, as was done in Sweden, on the basis that it is analogous to embezzlement. See Leif Mutén, Sweden Enacts Tax Account System, 15 Tax Notes Int'l 905 (Sept. 22, 1997).

holding is generally coextensive with the general definition of employee for income tax purposes, which is often broader than the labor law notion of employment.[223]

While the costs to an employer of administering PAYE collections are generally a small part of administering employee payrolls generally, PAYE obligations do impose a cost on employers, which is higher for small employers. In recognition of this fact and of the desirability of spreading the PAYE net as widely as possible, different remittance schedules can be applied to large and small employers, with the frequency of remittance falling with the size of employers' payrolls. Because employees are paid more often than the taxes are remitted to tax authorities, employers will obtain the benefit of the tax funds during the period between collection and remittance. This benefit can offset to some extent the costs of administering PAYE taxes, and the longer delay in remittance for smaller employers offsets in part the relatively greater costs faced by these employers. It must be recognized, however, that differential remittance dates do impose an additional administrative burden on tax authorities. When there is little or no computerization of the administration, a system of uniform remittance dates for all businesses may be easier to manage.[224] In Russia and certain other countries of the former Soviet Union, it is typical for remittance to be required simultaneously with the payment of wages. This is a holdover from the previous system of clearance accounts. It may still be justified under current circumstances because businesses are in extremely tight cash situations and temptations not to remit should not be offered. However, this should be changed when these circumstances no longer prevail.

Notwithstanding the desirability of extending the PAYE coverage as broadly as possible, most PAYE systems contain exceptions for particular types of employment. A common exception is for employment in respect of personal services for an employer that are not part of the employer's business or occupation. This exemption would apply, for example, to a housekeeper or a home gardener.

It was suggested earlier in this chapter that there has been a trend toward designing the PAYE withholding system so as to make such withholding the taxpayer's final liability. This has the administrative advantage of excluding a large number of salary and wage earners from having to file a return, thereby freeing up scarce enforcement resources for other purposes. For PAYE withholding to be the final liability on employment income, the amount withheld must be accurate, which means the employer must be made aware of the em-

---

[223]*See supra* sec. IV(A).

[224]There is, however, a compensating factor, namely, that the total number of transactions to be processed is smaller if small employers are required to pay less frequently. In developing countries, it is not uncommon for 75–90 percent of employers to fall into the "small employer" category, and a system that requires less frequent remittances from these employers may on balance require a smaller staff.

ployee's *taxable* income. This is usually done through an employment declaration, in which the taxpayer enumerates deductions, reliefs, or tax offsets that should be taken into account when determining taxable income. In some cases, the employment declaration may also provide the employer with information about other income derived by the taxpayer.

The use of employment declarations and withholding taxes as final taxes on employment income raises a number of technical and policy issues, which are discussed below.

A. Deductible Expenses

One of the main difficulties in making PAYE a final tax is the treatment of deductions. The tax is withheld from gross employment income, while in theory income tax is imposed on net gains, after recognizing deductible expenses incurred by an employee to derive the gross employment income.

It is impossible to take into account actual employment expenses when calculating PAYE withholding, as these will generally not be known at the start of the year. One possibility is to require employees to advise the employer of the incurrence of employment expenses so that they may be taken into account in subsequent withholdings. This approach has several problems. First, it may encourage employees to make inflated claims. This could be avoided by requiring the employee to produce documentary evidence to substantiate the claim to the employer. However, this requirement may impose an unreasonable and expensive compliance burden on employers. Also, the system imposes some obligation on the employer to assess whether or not the claim for a deduction is valid. Again, this may be an unreasonable and expensive burden to impose on employers.

Accordingly, if employee withholding is to be a final tax liability on employment income, a surrogate for recognition of actual expenses must be used. The alternatives of allowing a standard deduction or eliminating the deduction for employee expenses are discussed in section IV(B), above. Another option is to take no employment-related deductions into account in determining PAYE withholding, but to give employees an option to file a return if they wish to claim such deductions (in excess of any applicable threshold). The choice between these alternatives will be based on a balancing of equity objectives and administrative resources in the jurisdiction.

B. Personal Reliefs

Where it is decided to make PAYE withholding a final tax, it is necessary to keep the design of personal reliefs as simple as possible.[225] If dependent spouse support is to be offered through the tax system, from an administrative point of view, the best option is to have a single relief that is intended to com-

---

[225]*See supra* sec. IX(D).

pensate notionally for the support of a spouse, children, and other dependents. It is then available to all resident individual taxpayers. While this relief may represent a windfall advantage to those taxpayers with no dependents, many such taxpayers are likely to claim relief in any case if the administration does not have the resources to check such claims. For taxpayers with dependents, it avoids arguments as to who is a dependent (particularly where there is an extended notion of the family) as well as the problems that arise with a change of tax status during the tax period (see below).

If tax relief is to be provided for dependents through deductions or tax offsets related to the actual number of dependents, relevant information on an employee's dependents must be provided on the employment declaration form. The declaration forms should be filed annually if a taxpayer is claiming such relief and should contain enough information (full name, birth date, and so forth) to enable auditors to detect fraud by comparing declarations for different years. Allowing a taxpayer to claim a deduction for a dependent only if the dependent has obtained a taxpayer identification number has proved effective in combating fraud because this makes it possible to confirm both the existence of the dependents and their dependent status.[226] Also, the form should provide the taxpayer's spouse's taxpayer identification number if the spouse is not a dependent to enable auditors to determine when two persons are claiming the same dependents (if individuals are used as the tax unit).

One technical and policy problem raised by recognition of relief for dependents is a change of status during a year—a taxpayer may marry or separate, have a child or lose a child (or the child may cross an age threshold during the year), or a dependent may enter (or reenter) or depart from the household. The simplest approach for handling additions to dependency relief is to place the onus on the employee to provide information on increased support obligations by submitting an amended employee declaration at the time the increase occurs. Additional relief can then be taken into account for future tax withholding. This incentive does not apply to employees who lose a support obligation or an entitlement to relief during the year. Nevertheless, an employee could be obliged to provide information on changes in personal relief entitlement, and the information could be checked against the following year's initial employment declaration form. This process may be administratively onerous. The simplest alternative is to allow taxpayers to enjoy dependency relief for the entire year, even if their entitlement changes during the year (concomitantly, a taxpayer would not become entitled to dependency relief until the new year).

C. Multiple Employment and Changes in Employee Status

An employee's status may change during a year in a variety of ways relevant to her or his tax liability. For example, an employee may become a resi-

---

[226]USA IRC § 151(c)(3)(D)(I).

dent or cease to be a resident during an income year. Similarly, an employee may enter full-time employment or retire from full-time employment during this period. The employee may also change employment or accept positions with more than one employer. The PAYE system must be designed to cope easily with these types of events.

Changes in residency or entering or leaving the workforce are relevant only if benefits are prorated for persons changing status in these ways. Proration is sometimes used to prevent exploitation of benefits or the tax-free thresholds that are intended for persons enjoying a particular status for the entire tax year.[227] Only some types of proration can be handled in the context of a PAYE withholding system. It is in theory possible to take into account changes when a person commences employment (e.g., when a person leaves full-time education or becomes a resident), but impossible to take account retrospectively of changes when a person ceases employment (e.g., upon retirement or emigration). Recognizing changes of status poses a number of practical problems, of which the most significant is calculating withholding amounts. One key attribute of a PAYE system is the use of withholding liability charts that enable the employer to determine easily the exact amount of tax to be withheld from each salary payment. The charts are based on different levels of taxable income and are designed so that employers can take into account with relative ease such entitlements as personal allowances for dependent support. However, they cannot deal easily with a range of individual circumstances, such as variable tax-free thresholds. As a result, jurisdictions using these systems do not treat PAYE withholding as the final tax liability for employment income.

Problems also arise when an employee has more than one source of employment income. In this case, the total amount withheld will be accurate only if at least one employer knows the details of the employment income paid by others. While in some cases this may be possible, an employee may not wish to disclose the existence of other employment to his or her primary employer. In light of these problems, the system for final PAYE withholding for employees with more than one job is not likely to be fully satisfacftory.[228] One option is to require persons with more than one job to file a return so that their final tax liability can be determined.

A related problem area is that of taxpayers changing employment during the year. If the taxpayer's salary level is relatively unchanged following a change of employment, unobtrusive administrative procedures can ensure a continuity of appropriate PAYE withholding. If the former employer is required to provide the employee with a statement of his or her PAYE position at the date of leaving, the information can be provided to the new employer, who can use it as the basis for withholding to ensure accuracy for the year. This

---

[227]For example, Australia prorates the tax-free threshold for persons becoming or ceasing to be a resident and for persons ceasing full-time education. See AUS ITRA §§ 16–20.

[228]See infra ch. 15, sec. III(C).

system will not work when the salary level changes following a change of employment. While the new employer will know the taxpayer's total expected employment income for the year, the PAYE withholding charts will not show how withholding should be adjusted to compensate for the relative under- or overwithholding at the first place of employment (in terms of the changed total expected employment income). As a result, PAYE withholding cannot accurately be used as a final tax liability in this situation, and it may be necessary to require employees who change employment to file returns unless their salary level has not changed or income rate bands are so broad (or so flat) that a taxpayer's proportionate liability would not change with the change in income.[229]

D. Fringe Benefits

The taxation of fringe benefits in the hands of employees poses particular problems if employee taxation is to be based on a PAYE withholding tax that is intended to represent the taxpayer's final employment tax liability. From an administrative perspective, there is relatively little difference to an employer between the alternative fringe benefits tax systems—whether fringe benefits are taxed in the hands of employers or employees, it is common to require the employer to monitor and value all fringe benefits, although valuation is clearly much simpler when the employer can report total benefits and does not have to allocate those benefits to individual employees.[230] The principal difference is the impact of the tax on employee liquidity. Because withholding cannot be extracted from a benefit in kind, the tax on fringe benefits must be withheld from an employee's wages or salary, in addition to the tax payable on the wages or salary. As mentioned earlier, in the context of fringe benefits taxation, this process may have a significant effect on the employee's cash flow when the value of taxable benefits is quite high relative to the value of cash remuneration. Thus, one effect of imposing a final PAYE withholding tax on employee fringe benefits in such a situation may be to cause employees to "cash out" the benefits and restructure their remuneration packages to receive wages or salaries in preference to benefits in kind, even those that are most efficiently provided through employers because of the availability of group discounts, such as medical and dental insurance.[231] This possibility must be balanced against the obvious administrative advantages of using PAYE withholding tax as a final tax on all employment income and benefits derived by taxpayers.

If the cash-flow problems resulting from the introduction of PAYE withholding on fringe benefits are seen as transitional and the value of fringe benefits is not high compared with cash salaries, employers may be able to meet

---

[229]This problem could be taken care of if withholding were computerized instead of being based on charts, or if withholding were in any event done on a cumulative basis (*see infra* ch. 15), but this will be beyond administrative capacity in most developing and transition countries.

[230]*See supra* sec. IV(C)(3).

[231]*See* text at note 91 *supra*.

the initial cost of the PAYE deductions, recovering the funds over time from salaries as selected benefits are cashed out. The effect of this process is to transfer the cash-flow problem from employees to employers temporarily and to impose a real cost on employers. Whether this would occur depends on the relative bargaining powers of employers and employees.

A different problem arises with respect to the application of PAYE withholding to benefits that the employer may pay for once a year but that have the effect of providing a benefit to the employee continuously throughout the year. For example, an employer may provide employees with a health plan for which the employer accounts only once a year for the costs of operating the plan. Similarly, the valuation formula for a car fringe benefit will yield a single value for the year or perhaps a few values at the end of each mileage recording period if the formula takes mileage into account. In cases like these, it will be necessary to allocate part of the cost or benefit to each pay period of the employee. Rules of thumb will have to be devised to do this from the beginning of the year when the exact cost for the year will not be known until later.

One advantage of the fringe benefits tax discussed earlier is that taxation at the employer level facilitates the use of PAYE as a final tax and avoids the cash-flow problem noted above.

E. Other Income Sources

Unless the income tax rate scale is completely flat, PAYE withholding tax can operate as a final tax liability only for taxpayers deriving income solely from employment. In many developing and transition countries, this may be the case for a majority of employees. To the extent that employees do derive business or investment income, it is likely in most cases to be a *de minimis* amount relative to their employment income. Failure to reconcile the PAYE tax liability and the tax liability employees should incur if their complete employment and other income is taken into account will accordingly not seriously undermine the progressive tax system in most cases. The most likely scenario for an individual is that she or he will have a single job with her or his only other income being interest on a bank account. In this situation, it is possible to make PAYE withholding a final tax by taking steps to ensure the accuracy of PAYE withholding (as discussed above) and imposing a final withholding tax on interest income. Alternatively, PAYE can be used as a final tax on incomes up to a nominated threshold, on the assumption that persons above the threshold are likely to have income other than bank interest.

In some cases, failure to combine employment income and other income when determining final tax liability can prima facie violate the objectives of the progressive income tax. The extent to which treatment of the PAYE withholding tax as a final tax liability on employment income defeats overall progressivity depends on both the structure of the income tax rate scale (and in particular the degree of graduation) and the treatment of other income. In theory, the imposition of separate tax liabilities on business and investment income reduces the overall progressivity of the tax system, although in practice this may not prove to be true. In many cases, global taxation has in fact reduced progressivity because taxpayers have exploited shortcomings in the provisions by which income from capital is taxed to defer recognition of gains and to use deductions for investment income expenses to reduce their taxable income from employment. Unless the provisions for measuring business and investment income are well drafted and contain special rules for quarantining expenses incurred to derive those types of incomes (for further detail, see ch. 16), overall progressivity may be threatened.

The choice between using the PAYE withholding tax as a final tax liability in all cases or only when taxpayers do not also derive business or investment income will thus depend on a variety of factors, in particular the type of taxes imposed on business and investment income and the sophistication of the rules protecting the integrity of the business and investment tax systems.

15

The Pay-As-You-Earn Tax on Wages

Koenraad van der Heeden

> Although undeniably useful in immediately strengthening collections, . . .
> withholding does not obviate the need to strengthen the tax administration itself.
>
> —*Richard M. Bird and Milka Casanegra de Jantscher*

I. Introduction

Although all withholding taxes aim to tax income when it is earned, only withholding on wages is commonly known as pay-as-you-earn (PAYE).[1] This tax plays an important role in nearly all national tax systems.[2]

The PAYE is an important and easy-to-collect revenue item. Its claim on the resources of the tax administration is limited, particularly if return filing by employees is restricted to those who earn substantial other income or are entitled to significant special deductions, or both. A simple PAYE does not complicate the employer's wage administration. Compliance control can focus on employers only, rather than on individual employees. Nonconsolidation with other income is more acceptable when other income is also subject to withholding taxation.

A. Revenue Importance of the PAYE

The PAYE is a high-yielding revenue collector in many countries. It generates a lion's share of the personal income tax and, in industrial countries, usually exceeds the revenue of the general sales tax or value-added tax (VAT)

Note: The author would like to thank colleagues from the Tax Administration Division of the IMF's Fiscal Affairs Department, and Milka Casanegra de Jantscher, Emil Sunley, and Alan Tait for their comments on an earlier draft. This chapter appeared originally in the IMF's Working Paper series as No. 94/105.

[1]The basic mechanics of PAYE withholding are outlined in ch. 14, sec. XII, *supra*.

[2]Notable exceptions are France, Singapore, and Switzerland (for resident employees).

Table 1. Wage Withholding Tax

Country	As a Percentage of Personal Income Tax	As a Percentage of VAT
Belgium	76	146
Germany (west)	72	119
Luxembourg	70	104
Netherlands	86	144
United Kingdom	76	117
United States	88[1]	. . .

Sources: Organization for Economic Cooperation and Development, *Revenue Statistics of OECD Member Countries, 1965–1992* (1993); U.S. Internal Revenue Service.

[1]For the United States only, the number includes other withheld income tax and income tax to be refunded. The net number should be in excess of 80. The United States does not have a VAT.

by an ample margin. This is illustrated in Table 1 by the list of countries with mature personal income and VAT systems in tax year 1991.

In developing countries, personal income tax collected from wages represents an even higher percentage of total personal income tax revenue. However, depending on the actual rate structure, the VAT often generates more revenue in these countries than the PAYE. This is particularly true in countries in transition. In Russia, for instance, the wage withholding is nearly 100 percent of total personal income tax, but VAT revenue amounts to about three times the PAYE revenue.

B. Limited Use of Administrative Resources

More so than in industrial countries, developing and transition countries need to use their skilled administrative resources selectively. A relatively simple PAYE would allow the tax administration to collect a large share of the personal income tax with only a minor use of its resources. As such, the administration should aim at a final tax collection through the PAYE. Return filing should take place only when substantial other income or significant deductions occur and, therefore, when major adjustments to the withheld tax would need to be made. Collection of every "dollar" of taxes due can never be realized, and efforts to do so will not be cost-effective.

Because of the PAYE, more administrative resources can be deployed in those areas where tax revenue is more at risk than in wage withholding. In the area of personal income taxation, compliance control can focus more on auditing and collecting from self-employed persons; corporate income and sales tax payers can be better monitored.

The tax administration should focus its limited resources for PAYE purposes on the compliance control of the withholding agents, the employers. Instead of checking a large number of individual employees, the administration can focus on a limited number of employers. The employers must file monthly and pay the withheld tax on a monthly or more frequent basis. The administration should monitor the filing and payment records of the employers closely and follow up immediately whenever it is observed that one has stopped filing or paying. In addition to this kind of processing control, selective audits must be undertaken to ensure that tax is withheld from all wages paid and that the tax is properly computed.

C. Reduction in Return Filing

A PAYE substantially reduces the necessity of requiring employees to file returns. Employees with only wage income and standard deductions can be taxed on a final basis through withholding. Exemptions for minor amounts of other income and minimum requirements for special deductions can reduce return filing even further. However, practices differ substantially among countries.

In countries such as Australia, Canada, Sweden, and the United States, all wage earners whose income exceeds the exempt amount are still required to file an income tax return.[3] Tax withheld is credited against the total income tax due, and the difference is paid or refunded. Countries like Chile, Germany, Hungary, the Netherlands, and the United Kingdom, however, use the PAYE as a final income tax for most wage earners.[4] Administrative and compliance costs are lower under final withholding because many taxpayers are not required to file returns. These countries regularly implement additional measures to expand the finality of the tax. The withholding schemes are often modified to make them more compatible with the general income tax, and sometimes a limited filing threshold is applied to those with other income.

A different situation exists when a person's tax liability is based not on total income, but rather on separate tax schedules for each category of income.[5] In this situation, no special adjustment is needed for PAYE to be a final tax.

D. Other Withholding Taxes

Although this chapter deals only with the PAYE, it should be mentioned that withholding taxes on other income would allow further reduction of return filing. The fact that such other income is not consolidated with wage income is not necessarily a serious problem if (1) the wage income is modest, (2) the amount of other income is not too large, and (3) a withholding tax has been collected from other income.

---

[3]See USA IRC § 6012; CAN ITA § 150; AUS ITAA § 161; Graeme Cooper et al., Income Taxation 23–24 (1993); Harvard Law School, International Program in Taxation, Taxation in Sweden 579 (1959); Peter Melz, *Taxation of Individuals in Sweden, in* Taxation of Individuals in Europe (IBFD 1997).

[4]See *infra* sec. III(B).

[5]See *supra* ch. 14, sec. II(A).

Withholding taxes on dividends and interest are fairly common in national tax systems. Several countries have introduced withholding taxes on an even broader basis.[6]

II. PAYE Calculation Methods

There are three basic systems for calculating the amount of PAYE tax to be withheld: simple PAYE, cumulative PAYE, and year-end-adjusted PAYE.

The simple PAYE system applies the monthly withholding table on wages for that month, with no adjustments for wage changes in the tax year. Any difference between the tax withheld and the total income tax liability is accepted as the price of a simple tax system or is resolved by the filing of a return. The following example illustrates the simple PAYE mechanism.

An employee with a monthly taxable wage of $1,000 has an annual income of $12,000 and is subject to the following income tax rate scale:

Annual Income (In U.S. dollars)	Tax on Bracket of Income (In percent)
0–2,400	0
2,400–6,000	20
6,000–15,000	30
15,000 and higher	40

The tax period is the calendar year. The employee's income tax liability for the year is $2,520 ($2,400 at 0 percent, $3,600 at 20 percent = $720, and $6,000 at 30 percent = $1,800). Dividing the income tax liability into 12 equal monthly portions results in a monthly withholding tax of $210.

The calculation can be done each month. The monthly taxable wage is multiplied by 12, the annual income tax liability is computed, and that liability is divided by 12 for the monthly withholding. If, in the above example, the monthly taxable wage increased to $1,500 on July 1, the estimated annual income would be $18,000, the income tax liability would be $4,620, and the monthly withholding for the second half of the year would be $385.

Basically, multiplication and division by 12 represent nothing more than the steps for deriving a monthly withholding table from the annual income tax rate brackets. Therefore, most tax administrations have published monthly (and weekly) withholding tables as a service to employers—the withholding agents. In the above example, the monthly withholding table (dividing annual income by 12) would be:

---

[6]*See id.* sec. VIII(D).

Monthly Wage (In U.S. dollars)	Tax on Wage Bracket (In percent)
0–200	0
200–500	20
500–1,250	30
1,250 and higher	40

The withholding table can be, and often is, more elaborate. Many administrations publish tables for tax at small wage intervals of, say, $10. Standard deductions are often incorporated. For example, with a standard deduction of 5 percent of wage income, the tax withheld from a gross wage of $200 is computed on a wage of $190.

The monthly withholding tables assume that annual income is 12 times the monthly income (weekly income multiplied by 52). Monthly wages, however, may vary. If, in the above example, a monthly wage of $1,000 increases to $1,500 on July 1, the monthly withholding in the second half of the calendar year is based on an annual income of $18,000 rather than on the actual income of $15,000 (6 times $1,000 plus 6 times $1,500). The PAYE on the $9,000 earned in the second half of the year, therefore, is computed on the assumption that $1,500 is taxable at the marginal rate of 40 percent rather than 30 percent. The result is that the total amount of PAYE tax withheld exceeds the taxpayer's yearly income tax liability by $150.

Some countries—for example, Russia and the United Kingdom—continuously recompute the PAYE to make the tax withheld as close as possible to the actual income tax. This system is called the *cumulative PAYE*.[7] After a wage change, the PAYE of the next pay period is increased by the month's share of the difference between the income tax on total income prospectively to be earned during the tax year, and the tax already withheld in the tax year. Consequently, in the above example, the July 1 wage increase from $1,000 to $1,500 a month will increase the monthly withholding tax from $210 to $385. The tax liability on an annual income of $15,000 is $3,420 (six months at $1,000 and six months at $1,500), of which $1,260 has already been collected (six months at $210 a month). Still to be collected is $2,160 ($3,420 – $1,260). The monthly withholding for the remaining six months should therefore be one-sixth of this amount, or $360.

Several countries, notably Germany and Japan, apply a PAYE that is a hybrid of the simple PAYE and the cumulative PAYE.[8] During the tax year, this PAYE is similar to the simple PAYE; monthly withholding is based on the

[7]*See* appendix for a discussion of Russia and the United Kingdom. In the United States, an employee can request, and the employer can agree to apply, the cumulative system. *See* USA IRC § 3402(h)(3).

[8]*See* DEU EStG §§ 38–42b; National Tax Administration, An Outline of Japanese Tax Administration 26–28 (1993).

tables without regard to tax withheld in previous pay periods. At year-end, however, the final withholding is computed on a cumulative basis. The total wages paid and total tax withheld during the year are compared with the tax liability based on the actual wages paid, and a year-end adjustment is made.[9] The year-end wage payment can therefore differ markedly from the payments made during the year. This system is called *year-end-adjusted PAYE*.

In a simple PAYE, payment of substantial nonperiodic wage income by the employer (e.g., thirteenth month and annual leave allowances) may cause a problem.[10] Tax withheld from nonperiodic payments will be higher when the income is added to and taxed as ordinary wage income of the pay period than when averaged out over the tax year. A standard solution is to tax the nonperiodic payments at a proportional rate rather than at the progressive rate in the pay period. That proportional rate is based on the annual ordinary wage income of the employee and the additional tax due because of the additional nonperiodic payments.

III. Finality of PAYE

A. Preliminary PAYE

As mentioned earlier, countries like Australia, Canada, Sweden,[11] and the United States continue to require that all taxpayers with taxable income file a return, including wage earners with only one job who are not claiming a significant amount of special deductions. Why have these countries kept this filing requirement?

An argument in favor of return filing may be that the prospect of claiming tax relief (deductions or tax credits), however small it might be, gives taxpayers a satisfaction that can outweigh the burden of filing. Another argument is the awareness of paying taxes that comes with the filing of a return. As a taxpayer and a member of society, the person filing the return will be more aware of his or her tax burden and, therefore, better prepared to exercise his or her constitutional rights. A third argument is the prospect of a refund—because of deductions or imprecision in the withholding—which is inviting to the taxpayer. A May 1992 report of the U.S. General Accounting Office states that

---

[9]For a monthly wage that increases from $1,000 to $1,500 in July, the total tax withheld is 6 times $210 plus 6 times $385, or $3,570. The income tax liability is $3,420. Therefore, the PAYE in December is reduced by $150, from $385 to $235.

[10]A similar problem may occur in the year-end-adjusted PAYE when such wage income is paid before year-end.

[11]In Sweden, return filing has been facilitated by the rule that tax returns are prepared by the tax office, based on information returns received. The taxpayer has to supplement the return as needed, but if the return is correct, he or she just signs it. In Denmark, the taxpayer need not even sign if there is no change to make.—L.M.

final withholding would reduce refunds and, consequently, is not likely to be accepted by taxpayers because "many taxpayers look forward to receiving refunds and look upon the refund as a form of forced savings."[12]

A fourth argument may be the existence of income tax credits for lower-income taxpayers.[13] Given these credits as vehicles for income support, return filing generates the information needed for means testing. Examples are child support credits and credits to compensate for an assumed disproportionate burden of sales taxes.

The four countries mentioned above are actively exploring ways to reduce the compliance burden on taxpayers while retaining return filing. Because their tax administrations are largely computerized and their compliance control is based on information obtained from third parties (employers, companies, and financial institutions), these countries are considering systems where the initiative for the return lies with the tax administration. The tax administration would initially complete the return, based on the information available, and would then mail that return to the taxpayer for confirmation.[14] Such a system would require a considerable administrative effort. The tax administration would have to be fully computerized, as would its suppliers of information. A major concern, however, is whether taxpayers will promptly correct errors if the tax administration has prepared a return that underreports income.

Other issues that affect countries' choice of a return filing system are, first, the degree to which the existing income tax is schedular or global. In a fully schedular income tax system, a final PAYE will cause few problems, probably limited to situations where the taxpayer has a second job. In a global system, usually the progressivity of the tax rate and the tax exemption for a minimum income (personal allowance) make some return filing necessary. This also happens when a taxpayer can claim special deductions that cannot easily be included in the wage withholding.[15]

Second are the income tax rates. If they are steeply progressive, the accumulation of income from different sources may substantially increase the total tax liability. To determine this liability, a return is needed. If a taxpayer receives income from only one source, final withholding is still possible. The situation is rather different with a flat income tax rate. Final withholding is an option even in the context of a fully comprehensive income tax, provided that

---

[12]U.S. General Accounting Office, Opportunities to Reduce Taxpayer Burden Through Return-Free Filing (1992). Until 1992, the U.S. withholding system was designed to withhold more than was indicated on the annual income tax tables and, therefore, led to a large volume of refunds.

[13]E.g., USA IRC § 32 (earned income tax credit).

[14]See supra note 11.

[15]Many countries, even those that require all taxpayers to file returns, allow special deductions to be claimed through the withholding system. Examples are deductions for (extraordinary) medical costs, mortgage interest, and certain life insurance contributions. See supra ch. 14, sec. XII(A).

personal allowances are deducted only under the withholding scheme for full-time employment.

Third is whether the taxable base of the income tax is individual income or the joint income of a married couple.[16] When employment income is taxed individually, it is often possible to tax that income through a final withholding tax at source. Final taxation at source of the combined employment income of a married couple, however, is almost impossible. Whenever such income needs to be aggregated for income tax purposes, a joint return must be filed. This is an important reason why return filing in the United States is mandatory for all taxpayers.

Fourth is the distribution of nonwage income. In a society where a large portion of the population regularly receives investment income, the filing requirement seems appropriate. Where most of the population receives only wage income, however, final withholding is often appropriate.

B. Semifinal PAYE

A semifinal PAYE, through which at least some employees are taxed only through withholding and do not have to file a return, is the most common approach to wage taxation. Countries using this method apply different PAYE systems. For example, the Netherlands uses the simple PAYE system, Germany the year-end-adjustment system, and the United Kingdom the cumulative system.[17] Basically, the choice of system depends on the trade-off between the burden for taxpayers of filing returns and for employers of withholding.

The introduction of so-called filing thresholds can reduce the number of returns that must be filed. Only if other income surpasses a minimum amount does a return declaring all taxable income need to be filed. Below that amount, other income is not consolidated with the primary income from regular employment, and the tax on total income is that collected at source. For secondary employment income, that tax is the PAYE withheld by the second employer. Insufficient withholding at source results in a tax advantage for the taxpayer, which is not recaptured because of the filing threshold. Beyond the threshold, all taxable income is consolidated on the return, and insufficient withholding is offset by an increased income tax liability on assessment.

A filing threshold can also be applied to income tax deductions not included in the withholding scheme. Employees should not be allowed to file a return to obtain an insignificant refund. In considering comparable filing thresholds for other income (resulting in additional tax payable) and for deductions (resulting in a refund), it seems prudent to allow a higher threshold for the former than for the latter.

Filing thresholds can be used to keep the number of returns in line with the capacity of the tax administration. By initially setting the thresholds fairly

---

[16]See generally supra ch. 14, sec. IX(B).

[17]See appendix infra for the Netherlands and the United Kingdom; sec. II supra for Germany.

high, a developing country can apply a de facto schedular system to most employees. Only employees with substantial other income, including a well-paying second job, or with significant other deductions would file a return. With increasing administrative resources, a country can bridge the gap between the schedular system and the comprehensive system by gradually reducing the thresholds.

Filing thresholds are being used, for example, in Chile and the Netherlands.[18] Chile further reduces return filing by disallowing filing for refund purposes.[19] Tax withheld from wages is final, even when an individual was employed for only part of the tax year.[20] The filing of a return, with consolidation of total income, is required, however, when other income is received in excess of the filing threshold.

Other employment income can be taxed at source like the wages from the main source of employment. The same withholding tables are applicable. The person earning wages from two jobs, however, benefits from a second set of personal allowances and reduced progressive rates that is not available to the person who earns the combined wage income from one job. It may be desirable not to allow the employee to claim more than one set of personal allowances. For instance, in the United Kingdom, where the tax administration has to validate the personal allowance claim, only one claim form is validated.

C. Final PAYE

Theoretically, a final PAYE has a monthly withholding table that is not as such derived from an annual income tax rate. In practice, however, the annual withholding table (i.e., the monthly table, of which the income brackets are multiplied by 12) is similar to the income tax rate applicable to, for example, self-employed persons. The main characteristic of the final PAYE, however, is that income is taxed at source rather than in total.

Because the withholding table is not formally linked to the annual income tax levied on other taxable income, the tax period for withholding can be defined for that purpose only. The ability to pay tax can be based on annual income, as in the case of entrepreneurial income, but it can also be based on monthly income.[21]

---

[18]See CHL IR § 65(3).

[19]CHL IR § 65(3) is applied to this effect.

[20]The Chilean PAYE system is categorized as a semifinal system because of its "one-way" finality. PAYE withheld cannot be reduced (refunded), but it can be increased by additional income tax because of other income.

[21]The tax period is basically an accounting convention. Although a calendar year is generally used, many countries allow averaging of annual income over an extended period and most countries provide for a carryover (and also often a carryback) of losses into other years. See Richard B. Goode, Long-Term Averaging of Income for Tax Purposes, in The Economics of Taxation (Henry J. Aaron & Michael J. Boskin eds., 1980).

If the relevant tax period of the final PAYE is a month, wage fluctuations do not pose a problem because each month's wage is taxed independently. It is taxed independently not only of other income, but also of wages received in previous months or that will be earned in following months. In many developing and transition countries, this simple version of the final PAYE is used.[22] In Russia, however, the law stipulates that the final (monthly) PAYE should be levied cumulatively within the calendar year. The tax period for the PAYE is the calendar year, and, in principle, the employers apply the cumulative version of the final PAYE.

Many of the comprehensive income tax problems caused by other income are not found in the final PAYE. However, a major problem arises from wage income from a second job. In the comprehensive income tax, the filing of a return is the instrument used to address that problem. In the final PAYE, that instrument is not available. Either the problem should be resolved by the primary employer integrating all withholding (as discussed below, a complex alternative, but one that is stipulated in most countries of the Commonwealth of Independent States (CIS)), or income from each job should be taxed separately. In the latter case, the employee receives the personal allowances twice and escapes the full impact of progressivity unless a special mode of taxation is designed for secondary types of employment.

IV. Administrative Burden

With respect to the taxation of wage income, three parties are involved—the employee, the employer, and the tax administration. Their involvement varies from country to country, but the emphasis is on the employer and the tax administration.

Being the withholding agent by law, the employer is involved in collecting income tax from wages. To both the employee and the tax administration, the employer is rendering a tax service. Regarding the employee, it can be argued that the costs of providing these services are part of the costs of hiring labor. A reimbursement for these services by the beneficiary, the employee, is therefore not to be expected.

A different view could be taken with regard to the administrative services provided to the tax administration. The general practice of countries is to consider the obligation to withhold as part of general tax compliance obligations, the cost of which is not reimbursed by government. However, withholding may be better viewed as fulfilling part of the tax administration's tax collection function. The tax collection function is one of public authority, not under-

---

[22]In Chile, the comprehensive income tax requires that a return be filed when substantial other income is involved; however, a return for a refund of PAYE—because of short-term employment, for instance—cannot be filed.

taken in the interest of those who deal with the administration. Therefore, the tax administration should not charge a fee for its collection function and, where that function is partially delegated to the private sector, the private sector should be reimbursed for costs incurred. Yet employers rarely receive such reimbursement.[23]

Although explicit reimbursement of collection costs occurs only in exceptional cases, employers benefit from the lag between the time taxes are withheld and when they are transferred to the government. Without the withholding requirement, the employees would receive their wages in full at the end of the pay period. Because of the withholding, the employers retain use of part of the wage bill until it is transferred to the government. Assuming monthly wages, and payment of the withheld tax at the end of the following month, the employer's benefit is equal to the interest on a perpetual loan in the amount of the tax bill for one month.[24] In particular under conditions of high inflation, the time lag between withholding and transfer by the employer should be kept relatively short to safeguard the real value of the PAYE revenue.[25]

Given the expectation that employers will keep a basic accounting of their revenue and expenditure and, therefore, also of wages paid, a simple PAYE should not be a great burden to the employer. The tax to be withheld can be read from the withholding tables and deducted from gross wages.[26] The year-end adjustment system and particularly the cumulative system require much more work from the employer. It goes beyond withholding as such and borders on an assessment function.

The final PAYE systems applied in the CIS countries typically require the primary employers to include wages and tax withheld from secondary jobs.[27] Employers in Russia must also administer a cumulative PAYE. This workload is excessive for the employers.

As mentioned above, in all withholding systems, special allowances and deductions can be incorporated on an individual basis. Withholding adjust-

---

[23]In Switzerland, which applies the PAYE to nonresident employees only, the cantons allow employers to retain a small percentage of the tax withheld from employees as compensation for their collection service. See Cedric Sandford, General Report: Administrative and Compliance Costs of Taxation, 54b Cahiers de droit fiscal international 36 (1989).

[24]For large employers, a shorter transfer period may be applicable.

[25]See Vito Tanzi, Inflation, Lags in Collection, and the Real Value of Tax Revenue, in Public Finance in Developing Countries (1991).

[26]The appropriate bookings in the accounts are (wage $1,000, tax $210):

Withholding		Payment to Treasury	
(In units of domestic currency)			
Debit account "Wages"	1,000	Debit account "Wage tax"	210
Credit account "Cash"	790	Credit account "Bank"	210
Credit account "Wage tax"	210		

[27]RUS IT arts. 8–11.

ments should be based on authorization from the tax administration. This can result in substantial work for the employer, particularly if there are many special deductions and they change during the tax year; however, the inclusion of a few widely used deductions at fixed amounts for the tax year should not be too great a burden to the employer.

The decision on what type of PAYE scheme to adopt in a particular country should ideally be informed by data on the costs to the government and the private sector of collecting the personal income tax under alternative systems. A withholding tax implies a transfer of collection costs from the administration to the withholding agents, and more so with elaborate withholding schemes. Comparing the costs of the withholding schemes would help evaluate their efficiency. Unfortunately, few comparative data are available.

V. Social Security Contributions

Employers are also the payers of and withholding agents for social security contributions.[28] In many countries and for many employees, these contributions may be larger than the PAYE.

Withholding and paying of the PAYE and social security contributions are not usually integrated. Often, the base for the two levies is different, the accounting is separate, and the payments are made to different agencies. Integration of the two withholding systems is an urgent matter, with good prospects for administrative savings.

A first step toward integrating the two withholding systems is to combine the payment and control systems of the PAYE and social security contributions.[29] If employers indicate the amounts of PAYE and social security contributions, they can then transfer the total amount withheld to one government account, which the authorities can distribute between budget and social security funds. In addition, government control of the withholding could be delegated to the audit functions of the tax administration only. The audit of the PAYE would be extended to social security contributions as well, so that the social security administration would not run its own audit program, which would largely overlap with PAYE audits.

Further integration of the two systems requires the harmonization of the base on which PAYE and social security contributions are levied. Currently, because social security contributions are often deducted from the PAYE base, employers must compute PAYE and social security withholding separately. With a harmonized base, total withholding can easily be calculated.

---

[28]See vol. 1, at 392–94.

[29]In Canada, Sweden, and the United States, for example, the tax administration is also responsible for collecting social security contributions from employers.

The scope of the integration of income taxation and social security contributions could be extended to self-employed persons. For the generally applicable contributions (i.e., payable by all individuals), the income tax rate could then be combined with these contributions into one income levy. The shares of income tax and social security contributions, with a distribution to the budget and the social security authorities, could be preserved by enacting annually the two relative percentages separately.

The Netherlands recently integrated the collection of income tax and generally applicable social security contributions. A simple rate structure is used, with one base for both income taxation and social security levies. The resulting income levy contains a social security component to finance social security funds and an income tax component.

The social security component is payable only up to a certain income level. Beyond that level, only income tax is collected. For both the income tax and social security purposes, the same threshold applies. The most difficult integration issue was the transfer of the employer's share of social security contributions to employees with a compensating increase in wages. That transfer was necessary to establish one base for the new combined levy and equal circumstances between employed and self-employed persons. A onetime transfer with compensation on a certain date was rejected because it might have increased the social security burden on employees in the future. A compromise was reached, involving transfer and compensation over a transition period, the amount of the transfer and compensation being based on the current contribution rate for the year in question.

VI. Administrative Constraints of Developing and Transition Countries

In industrial countries, the administrative capability of the tax administration, employers, and employees allows for flexibility in shifting the administrative burden from one participant in the collection process to another. Electronic data processing permits heavy involvement of both tax administration and employers. A comprehensive taxpayer education and taxpayer compliance program allows substantial employee participation. For these countries, administrative constraints are usually not a major issue in the design and operation of the collection system.

Although the workload of the tax administration, employers, and employees may vary among countries, the focus of every PAYE is on employers as the withholding agents. They initially compute, collect, and account for the income tax on wages and deposit the tax into the treasury accounts. It is their performance of these duties that determines the quality of the PAYE system. The tax administration monitors the filing and payment compliance of employers and ensures that they have complied with the law in computing and transferring the withheld tax by carrying out audits where necessary.

In developing and transition countries, a limited number of large employers may have the administrative capability, experience, and personnel to administer a relatively complex PAYE. It is prudent, however, to assume that on average most can manage only a fairly simple PAYE. Also from the point of view of control by the tax administration, the PAYE should be accessible to simple audit techniques and should not require highly skilled audit input.

Regarding the PAYE in the context of a comprehensive income tax, tax administrations of developing and transition countries do not have the means to process and assess large numbers of employee returns. Therefore, the emphasis in these countries should be on a PAYE that is as final as possible. With the PAYE collected, the income tax liability of the majority of the taxpaying employees should be met and no further collection required. Only a relatively small number of employees should be required to file an income tax return, either because these employees are in the highest income brackets or because they receive substantial amounts of other income. The thresholds above which returns must be filed should be based on the tax administration's ability to process returns. Whether or not all of the employees' other income is accounted for in the overall income tax is an issue on which compromise is necessary if the income tax collection system is to be manageable and reasonably equitable. It is better to enforce a reasonably equitable system properly than a perfectly equitable system poorly.

In the countries where the PAYE does not function in the context of a comprehensive income tax, but is the final income tax on wages, employees file returns only if they have other income. The need to limit the number of returns filed is as important for the schedular income tax as for a comprehensive income tax; therefore, equally high thresholds should be set for filing. Where income is derived from a second job, a return cannot be filed to combine the wages. However, the alternative of integrating the two withholding schemes by requiring the main employer to include the second job wages and the PAYE in the withholding would overly complicate the PAYE system. The only possible adjustment is to disallow the claim of personal allowances from the second job.

The fact that no returns are filed with the administration implies that tax administrations cannot verify against the return tax actually withheld and paid by employers.[30] Final taxation of employees through a PAYE system,

---

[30]In most countries, employers must file a PAYE return together with the payment. The return should contain information on the total wage bill and the tax withheld. Annually, the employer should supply wage and tax information for each employee. That information, however, is not sufficient for audit purposes.

therefore, requires regular auditing of the employers' withholding records. These audits should check withholding procedures and transfer of the with-held tax, but should also serve as a check on employees' claims on personal al-lowances and other deductions.

VII. Impact of Inflation on Withholding

Many countries in Latin America and the CIS countries suffer, or have suffered, from high inflation. In some Latin American countries, the PAYE rate brackets and the personal allowances are adjusted monthly to reflect price increases; in the CIS countries, such adjustments are generally made less fre-quently, but do occur within the tax year.[31]

In a final PAYE, as is applicable in many CIS countries, the tax period is essentially a month instead of a year. What happened in the preceding months and will happen in future months are not relevant for wage taxation in the current month. A recomputation of wages and tax of an earlier with-holding period into values of the monetary unit at year-end is therefore unnecessary.

In Latin American countries, the PAYE functions as a withholding in-strument of a comprehensive tax on a calendar year's income. With full infla-tion accounting, the tax liability should be computed in year-end values of tax rate and personal allowances, although current values have been used in the monthly withholding. For a simple illustration of this, it is assumed here that wages and personal allowances increase monthly by 10 percent because of in-flation. Given a wage of $100 at the end of January, and personal allowances (the monthly share of it) of $20, the numbers at the end of each quarter are as follows:

	Mar.	June	Sept.	Dec.
	(In units of domestic currency)			
Wages	121	161	215	285
Personal allowances	24	32	43	57

For income tax purposes, the personal allowances for the year are 12 times $57, or $684. Taxable wages at year-end values are 12 times $285, or $3,420. However, wages may also have changed in real terms, so total wages for the year in year-end values cannot simply be computed by multiplying the year-

---

[31]These adjustments prevent real increases in tax revenue solely because of inflation. Real de-creases in revenue resulting from collection lags may occur because of late transfer of the with-held tax by the employer. *See* Tanzi, *supra* note 25; *See also supra* vol. 1, ch. 13.

end wage by 12. It is necessary to recompute each monthly wage and withheld tax at the year-end value.

In the example above, the recomputation of each monthly wage in year-end values does not reduce or add to the tax already paid. Provided that the tax brackets are properly adjusted for inflation, the tax already withheld matches the year-end liability when revalued in year-end prices. In many cases, in fact, a recomputation is not necessary, as it would result in only minor changes that would not justify the complex cumulative system. In Chile, for instance, the system of inflation accounting has been greatly simplified.

Additional difficulties arise when other income, including other wage income, is involved and a return must be filed to declare the cumulative income. Wage income is generally evenly spread over the tax year, while this may not be true of other income. This raises the question of how to compute that income in year-end values. The administrative burdens involved for both the taxpayer and the tax administration necessarily lead to a limitation of return filing. Only in cases where substantial other income is received should returns be filed.

VIII. Withholding Systems: Country Examples

The PAYE systems of nine countries—three industrial, four developing, and two in transition—are described in the appendix. The industrial countries are the Netherlands, the United Kingdom, and the United States; the developing countries are Chile, Indonesia, Kenya, and the Philippines; the countries in transition are Hungary and Russia.

As the appendix shows, a fairly large number of different PAYE models have been implemented in national tax systems. A clear pattern of models used by industrial countries on the one hand and developing and transition countries on the other hand cannot be distinguished. Nor is there any evidence that developing and transition countries are using simpler models than industrial countries. Cumulative systems are used by all groups, as are year-end adjustment systems. A reduction of the number of returns filed is an objective in most countries.

Although the authorities may have designed (and legislated) a sophisticated tax system, lack of administrative expertise and resources may render it quite basic. In a number of countries where employees are required to file income tax returns, the tax administration does not do much with them. In Russia, employers are supposed to administer a cumulative assessment procedure of overall employment income; however, the practice of withholding by a Russian employer may be not much more than a flat-rate payroll tax on wages paid by that employer.

In Tables 2 and 3, the main characteristics of the PAYE systems of the nine countries are summarized.

Table 2. Characteristics of PAYE Systems in Nine Countries

Country	Type of PAYE System			Finality of PAYE			Involvement of Tax Administration	
	Simple	Cumulative	Year-end-adjusted	Preliminary	Semifinal	Final	Personal allowances	Other deductions
Chile	X				X[1,2]			
Hungary			X		X			
Indonesia			X		X			
Kenya	X				X			X
Netherlands	X				X[1,3]			X
Philippines			X	X				
Russia		X				X		
United Kingdom		X			X		X	
United States	X			X				X

Source: Appendix at the end of this chapter.
[1] Filing thresholds are applicable.
[2] PAYE is not refundable.
[3] If income exceeds a certain level, a return must be filed.

Table 3. Additional Characteristics of PAYE Systems in Nine Countries

Country	Included in the PAYE Are				Personal Allowances Disallowed for Second Job	Integrated with Social Security Contributions
	Personal allowances	Other deductions	Other wage income	Other nonwage income		
Chile	X					
Hungary	X	X				
Indonesia	X					
Kenya	X	X	[1]	[1]		
Netherlands	X	X	[1]	[1]		X
Philippines	X				X	
Russia	X	X	X			
United Kingdom	X	X	X[1]	X[2][1]	X	[3]
United States	X	X	[1]	[1]	X	[3]

Sources: Appendix and laws cited therein.
[1]Other income may limit other deductions.
[2]Included to some extent.
[3]Payment and audit programs are integrated.

IX. The PAYE Recommended for Developing and Transition Countries

Tax legislation should be compatible with the standards used by the tax administration, withholding agents, and taxpayers, in the sense that the compliance required is at par with available and enforceable compliance. Tax legislation requiring high voluntary compliance and administrative control, but executed by a weak tax administration and inexperienced withholding agents and collected from uncooperative taxpayers will not yield the budgeted revenue or realize the intended distribution of the tax burden or achieve the intended distribution of the tax benefits.

Such legislation will hamper economic development and further reduce the population's willingness to comply with government policies.

Given developing and transition countries' administrative constraints, a simple PAYE should be given preference over any other PAYE system, regardless of whether the PAYE functions in the context of a comprehensive or a schedular income tax system.

A. A Simple PAYE

It is very important that the PAYE be simple. The tax administration, not the employer, should perform the assessment function. A simple PAYE therefore implies that an employer is not required to

- administer other income of the employee, whether that other income is wages from a second job or nonwage income. The PAYE covers only wages earned from the employer administering the withholding. That coverage is complete, however, including earnings in cash and in kind. For wages in kind, the employer is provided with clear and explicit valuation guidelines by the tax administration.[32]
- assess or withhold tax from accumulated taxable wages earned in periods that extend beyond the regular pay periods of a week or a month. Personal allowance and wage changes from one pay period to another do not affect the withholding for a given pay period. The employer is not obliged to add pay periods together and adjust the tax withheld for those periods into a tax assessed for the whole year. Cumulative and year-end-adjusted PAYE systems are not simple.
- compute the tax to be withheld from wages paid. The employer is able to work with withholding tables that are designed, produced, and provided free of charge by the tax administration. The tables are easy to use so that the employer can read the PAYE straightforwardly from them. Following a column of taxable wages, columns of tax to be withheld for each personal allowance group (e.g., single, married, one or

---

[32]*See supra* ch. 14, sec. XII(D).

more dependent children) list the applicable tax amount. The wage column has small wage steps, and variations of wages between steps do not affect the amount of PAYE.

A simple PAYE system permits final income taxation of an employee who holds only one job, is entitled to personal allowances, and may claim only widely used other deductions for income tax purposes. Such an employee does not have to file a return. Therefore, the employer is required to

- collect from the employee information on the personal allowances to which he or she is entitled. Although the tax administration provides the forms to be completed by the employee and randomly checks the information during employer audits, the forms are filed with and kept by the employer.
- compute wages for withholding purposes, deducting a proportional share of personal allowances and widely used deductions. The employer includes widely used deductions to limit further return filing by employees. The simple PAYE, however, is not used for special deductions claimed by only a small number of employees; for these deductions, a return must be filed.
- maintain wage withholding records for each employee, containing entitlement to personal allowances, other deductions authorized by the tax administration, totals of taxable wages and PAYE withheld in the tax year to date, and payments to the treasury. Taxable wages include those in kind, valued on the basis of clear and explicit tax administration guidelines. If (as it generally should) the tax administration uses a taxpayer identification number (TIN), the records are identified by that number.
- deposit the tax withheld each month in the treasury, accompanied by a document listing the total number of employees, amount of taxable wages, and PAYE withheld.
- send at the end of the tax year a report to the tax administration, and an individual statement to the employee, on wages paid and PAYE withheld and paid for each employee. The annual reporting is more detailed for comprehensive than for schedular income taxes.

To increase the finality of wage withholding, the employee is required to file a return only if substantial other income is earned and is allowed to file a return only if significant additional deductions are claimed.

In addition, to maximize the finality of the wage withholding, an employee whose wage income varied during the tax year or who received income for only part of the tax year may not be allowed to file a return for the purpose of a refund.[33]

---

[33]This aspect of the final PAYE of the CIS countries is used in Chile. Such a rule can be criticized as unfair. In deciding whether to adopt it, policymakers need to estimate the degree of unfairness that is likely to be involved given the rate schedule and weigh the unfairness against the administrative costs of allowing return filing in the context of the system as a whole.

B. The PAYE and a Comprehensive Income Tax

In a comprehensive income tax, the PAYE is not a tax entirely by itself. Wages are consolidated with taxable income subject to tax, and the PAYE withheld is credited against the tax on total taxable income. Given the similarity between PAYE withholding rates and the income tax rate schedule, in the absence of other income and special deductions, in principle, a credit after consolidation results in a zero liability. In short, the whole income tax exercise with return filing and assessment is essentially redundant. Therefore, most countries applying the concept of a comprehensive income tax do not require return filing in that case. The PAYE is a final tax in these circumstances.

In most countries with a semifinal PAYE, individuals must file returns when they earn other income, including wages from a second job.[34] Some countries have introduced so-called filing thresholds, stipulating that below a certain amount of other income a return need not be filed. A second job, however, more or less automatically requires the wage earner to file a return regardless of total income earned. As mentioned above, sometimes a filing threshold is required for return filing for a refund. Returns for small refunds are not accepted.[35]

In developing and transition countries, taxpayer compliance is at an early stage, and the tax administration's processing and enforcement capacity is not yet up to handling a large number of returns. It is therefore urgent that return filing be restricted to those cases where the consolidation of employment income with taxable income from other sources yields substantial revenue and markedly improves the equity of the system. Generally speaking, returns should therefore be filed only by employees who (1) receive a sizable amount of other income or have significant other deductions, or (2) are in the highest income brackets. Although it can be argued that high-wage employees are properly taxed in the PAYE, it is prudent to include all relatively high income earners in the income tax assessment system.[36]

Sizable other income, significant other deductions, and highest income brackets can be defined according to the circumstances. In an emerging market economy, with a weak tax administration and a majority of the employees working at near-subsistence levels, the filing thresholds should be fairly high. In time, as the tax administration gains experience, income tax consolidation can be given a higher priority.

A second job is a frequent source of other income in developing and transition countries. The fact that such income is not consolidated with regular

---

[34]In the United Kingdom, however, other income is, at least to some extent, included in the year-end-adjusted and the cumulative PAYE.

[35]An individual whose wage income varied during the tax year may not file a return for a refund of PAYE in Chile.

[36]E.g., LSO ITA § 129(b)(i).

employment income results, inter alia, in the unintended benefit of a second set of personal allowances. To eliminate that benefit without resorting to income tax consolidation, the use of personal allowances must be restricted to the main employment. Some industrial countries—for example, the United Kingdom—have solved that problem by issuing allowance claim forms that are identified by the TIN and can be used to obtain only one set of personal allowances. If the nonfiling employees are registered with the tax administration, other countries can also use this system. Without such a registration system, however, the administration has limited means to control the multiple use of personal allowances in the withholding stage.

C. The PAYE and a Schedular Income Tax

In terms of the preceding section, a PAYE in the context of a schedular income tax is similar to the PAYE of a comprehensive income tax if, in the latter, sizable other income, significant other deductions, and highest income brackets are defined so that no employees meet the criteria for consolidation. This situation also indicates the difference between the two systems: in the comprehensive PAYE, consolidation of employment and other income is possible but not necessary for all taxpayers, whereas in the schedular PAYE, income from different sources is not consolidated.

Although the schedules presume that accumulated employment income will be taxed by the schedular PAYE, consolidation is not possible within the employment income schedule. The PAYE is a withholding instrument that individual employers use for wages paid. It is not suitable for withholding from the aggregate of employment income received by each employee. In the CIS countries, the main employer theoretically includes in the PAYE wages and withheld tax from a second job; however, this process is unenforceable and, moreover, is very much at variance with the concept of a simple PAYE.

Because the PAYE cannot be used for consolidation purposes, a fully schedular PAYE is an inadequate instrument for distributing the overall tax burden based on the individual ability to pay tax. Therefore, a long-term objective should be a global income tax structure in which a single rate schedule applies to an individual's total annual income. Within that objective, many employees could still be taxed in a schedular fashion, provided that persons with sizable other income are required to file a consolidating return or persons with significant other deductions are allowed to request a refund.

In conclusion, taxation of income, including employment income, should be comprehensive, and the return filing rules should be pragmatic. Initially, the filing of a return could be exceptional, limited to employees in the highest income brackets; later, it should be extended to taxpayers who regularly receive significant income from more than one source.

Appendix. Description of National PAYE Systems

The following description of national PAYE systems focuses on (1) the withholding rate versus the income tax rate, (2) the inclusion of special allowances and deductions in the withholding system, (3) the treatment of income from secondary employment and other income, (4) the withholding from wage increases and nonperiodic wage income, (5) the withholding for social security purposes, (6) the distinction the systems may make between lower and higher wage income, and (7) the information the employee and the employer must furnish to one another and to the tax administration.[37] It is based on the situation in 1995.

Industrial Countries

This section presents the PAYE systems of the Netherlands, the United Kingdom, and the United States, which have a comprehensive income tax. In the Netherlands, about 50 percent of employees file returns; in the United Kingdom, about 10 percent; in the United States, nearly 100 percent.

The filing of returns by nearly all employees (as in the United States) allows for a rather simple PAYE. The administrative burden is shared by employees, employers, and tax administration, without a principal role for any of them. Where employers have a larger share of the burden (as in the United Kingdom), one would expect relatively lower overall administrative costs of tax collection. Because more returns are filed, the administrative costs of tax collection should be higher in the United States. In fact, however, these costs are much lower in the United States than in the United Kingdom (about 0.5 percent of income tax receipts, versus 2 percent in the United Kingdom),[38] probably because of the high degree of computerization of the U.S. tax administration. Assessing returns is not a time-consuming issue for that administration, and a final withholding system is therefore not a priority for the administration.[39]

Netherlands

In the Netherlands, an employee must submit to the employer an annual statement regarding his or her personal allowances (the so-called employee's statement). An employee who wants the withholding reduced because he or she has deductible expenses (e.g., mortgage interest) requests the tax administration to authorize the employer to do so. The tax administration authorizes a reduction only where it is likely that other taxable income will not outweigh

---

[37]For a general discussion of some of these design features, see *supra* ch. 14, sec. XII.

[38]*See* John A. Kay & Mervyn A. King, The British Tax System (5th ed., 1990).

[39]The cost of complying with the obligations to complete and file a tax return is not included in the comparison.

the reduction. Only through a (reduced) authorization for other deductible expenses does other income have an impact on the withholding. The personal allowances claimed in the employee's statement are not affected by other income. If no statement is submitted to the employer, personal allowances are limited to the entitlement of a single person.

Withholding tables are based on the income tax rate, with the inclusion of a standard allowance. The tables are applied in a noncumulative fashion. The relevant pay period is basically the tax period for PAYE purposes. The tax consequences of a changing wage level, for example, are not resolved at the PAYE stage. Changes in the personal circumstances of the employee are reported to the employer by a new employee's statement. The withholding is adjusted for future pay periods only.

Each job stands on its own, regardless of wages earned in another job or income received from other sources. The withholding is taken from the wages as though these wages were the employee's only taxable income. Nonperiodic wage income is taxed at a flat rate, based on the total wage earned by that employee at that job.

Although the social security funds are outside the government budget, the generally applicable social security contributions are fully merged with the income tax rate and, therefore, also with the PAYE withholding. Part of the resulting income levy is transferred to the social security funds. The remainder, being the old-style PAYE, is recorded as income tax. The tax administration is solely responsible for collection and compliance control. The social security funds are charged a fee for the administrative services rendered by the tax administration.

The Netherlands income tax law contains strict rules regarding the filing of income tax returns. If there is an excess of PAYE withheld over income tax due (because of a varying wage level, wages earned during only part of the tax year, an increase in personal allowances during the tax year, or deductions not claimed or not permitted for PAYE purposes), a return can be filed for a refund provided the refund is not insignificant.[40] When a wage earner has other income (including wages from a second job), he or she must file a return to assess the additional income tax due if the additional income exceeds the filing threshold.[41] Wage earners whose income exceeds a certain level must also file a return.[42]

Each month, the employer must transfer to the treasury the tax withheld and file a return with the administration. Each year, the employer must inform the administration and the employees about tax and social security contributions withheld and the amount of taxable wages paid. Each employee is iden-

---

[40]*See* NLD WIB § 62.
[41]*See id.* § 64.
[42]*See id.*

tified by a TIN (used for tax and social security purposes). If employees need to file a return, they include that information in the return.

United Kingdom[43]

When starting to work for the first time, the employee must file an information form (a coding claim form) with the tax administration. On that form, the employee informs the administration about his or her income tax position in terms of personal allowances[44] and other income. Based on that information, the administration determines the employee's tax-free allowance.[45] In principle, this allowance is the sum of personal allowances reduced by the amount of other taxable income on which no withholding is applicable and that is rather certain to be received. Subsequently, the tax administration informs the employer and the employee about the tax-free allowance in a "notice of coding." De facto, the involvement of the administration takes the form of an advanced income assessment.

The employer deducts the PAYE from taxable wages in a cumulative way: for each pay period, the tax to be withheld is the income tax due for the tax year inclusive of the current pay period, with a pro rata allocation of the tax-free allowance reduced by the tax already withheld in the preceding pay periods of the year. If an employee changes jobs during the tax year, he or she receives from the previous employer a statement about the tax-free allowance (the coding), wages taxed, and tax withheld; based on this statement, the new employer continues the cumulative withholding for the remainder of the tax year.[46]

The coding claim forms are filed with and checked by the tax administration. If the form is not filed, a notice of coding cannot be issued, and the employer must withhold tax based on a so-called emergency code. That code allows only the basic personal allowance of a single person. In this case, only the tax-free allowance attributable to the remaining pay periods of the tax year can be used, whereas a notice of coding allows the use of the full annual allowance. An employee is required to file a new coding claim form every five years or immediately after a change in the employee's personal circumstances.

For a second job, a form is filed separately with the tax administration. Because the information on other income includes wages earned in principal employment, the notice of coding issued for the second job contains no tax-

---

[43]For a general discussion of the United Kingdom's cumulative PAYE, see John Tiley, Butterworths U.K. Tax Guide 1990–91 ¶ 6: 115 (1990).

[44]Other general deductions are limited in the United Kingdom and, if allowed, take the form of a reduction at source. For example, mortgage interest is reduced by the percentage that is the basic income tax rate when receivable by a qualified lender, who can, in turn, claim a refund from the administration. GBR ICTA § 369.

[45]See Income Tax (Employments) Regulations 1993, Regulation 7.

[46]See id. Regulation 18.

free allowances. The coding could indicate that the tax is to be withheld at a rate higher than the basic rate.

Other nonwage income of the employee is included in the withholding by the employer to the extent that (1) it is reported in the claims form, (2) withholding is not applicable on that income, and (3) other income is equal to or smaller than the personal allowances. Therefore, other income can reduce personal allowances to zero, but cannot increase the taxable income subject to the PAYE.[47]

Social security contributions are withheld separately from the PAYE on a noncumulative basis and are partly deductible for PAYE purposes. The generally applicable contributions are payable to the tax administration. Compliance control is shared by the tax administration and the social security administration. Both administrations may make field audits.

The PAYE is deposited with the treasury on a monthly basis.[48] The tax administration is informed annually by employers of the employees' taxable income and tax withheld.[49] Each employee is identified by a social security number. Sometimes, insufficiently withheld income tax is carried forward to the following tax year (through a lower coding); in other cases, the employee is sent an income tax return.

The United Kingdom has not issued strict rules regarding the filing of income tax returns by employees. Generally speaking, taxpayers are required to inform the tax administration about income that is not taxed or is insufficiently taxed at source. The tax administration then chooses between an adjusted coding for PAYE purposes and/or an "invitation" to file a return. Taxpayers who regularly receive substantial other income are required to file a return.

United States

The withholding process begins with the employee completing a form for his or her employer, stating the number of standard personal allowances he or she is entitled to and the special expenses that are deductible from income (such as mortgage interest, local taxes, and extraordinary medical expenses).[50] Special deductions in excess of the income tax standard deduction are expressed as a multiple of the standard personal allowance and are added to the number of such allowances.

Based on this form, the employer deducts from the employee's wages an amount equal to the number of claimed personal allowances multiplied by the standard allowance and applies the appropriate withholding table.[51] The with-

---

[47]Currently, the U.K. tax administration is contemplating using "negative tax-free allowances" when other income exceeds personal allowances.

[48]*See* Income Tax (Employments) Regulations 1993, Regulation 40.

[49]*Id.* Regulation 43.

[50]*See* USA IRC § 3402(f)(2)(A).

[51]*Id.* § 3402(a).

holding tables are derived from the income tax rate brackets, but include the standard deduction.

The above-mentioned form is copied to the tax administration only if an employee claims a relatively high number of personal allowances. If the employee does not submit a form to the employer, withholding is based on only one personal allowance and no special deductions. The employee must submit a new form when a change in personal circumstances results in a reduction of the number of personal allowances and may submit a new form if there is an increase in the number of personal allowances.[52]

An employee with two jobs must submit a form to both employers. Because the personal allowances can be claimed only once, the employee must choose where to claim them.[53]

The employer does not include the employee's other nonwage income in the withholding. However, the amount of estimated nonwage income, such as dividends and interest, reduces the number of additional allowances.

Tax from nonperiodic wage income is withheld at a flat rate rather than at the progressive rate on which the withholding table is based. At the request of the employee, however, the employer may agree to apply a cumulative withholding system.[54] The employee may also request that this system be applied if his or her wage increases.

Although social security contributions in the United States are not integrated with the PAYE, they are payable together with the PAYE. To some extent, the social security administration is involved in reconciling the payments of each employee and employer. Only the tax administration, however, audits employers.

After filing their returns, employees often receive a refund, as many taxpayers do not claim all the withholding allowances they are entitled to. To compensate for the relatively high withholding, the U.S. tax administration in 1992 began using withholding tables that are somewhat lower than those based solely on the income tax rate.[55]

Depending on the amount of the PAYE, the tax withheld is deposited with the treasury each quarter, month, week, or day using depository coupons preprinted with the employer's name, address, and identification number.[56] Payment summaries for each employee are filed with the tax administration each

---

[52]Id. § 3402(f)(2)(B).

[53]See id. § 3402(f)(7).

[54]See id. § 3402(h)(3).

[55]See 54 Tax Notes 486 (Feb. 3, 1992).

[56]If the employer's employment taxes for the preceding year are over $50,000, the employer must make semiweekly deposits of employment tax; if less than $50,000, the employer makes monthly deposits. Under the semiweekly rule, if the payroll date is Wednesday, Thursday, or Friday, the tax must be deposited by the following Wednesday, in other cases by the following Friday. If the employer accumulates $100,000 in employment tax, the tax must be deposited by the end of the next banking day. See Treas. Reg. § 31.6302-1.

quarter, with the employees identified on the basis of social security number. Annually, employers provide their employees with a withholding statement for return filing purposes. A copy of this statement is also forwarded to the tax administration.

Developing and Transition Countries

This section describes the PAYE systems of Chile, Hungary, Indonesia, Kenya, the Philippines, and Russia. These countries were selected because of regional representation.

Chile, Hungary, Indonesia, Kenya, and the Philippines[57] operate their PAYE in the context of a comprehensive income tax, as do the industrial countries. Russia has implemented a schedular income tax system, in which the schedule for employment income provides final taxation through the PAYE.[58]

Chile

Because of a simple system of only one standard personal allowance (the zero-rated bracket of the rate schedule) and no other deductions, the employee does not need to inform the employer about his or her personal circumstances. The employer simply applies the monthly withholding tables. Although the traditionally high inflation is now close to a single-digit number, the brackets of the withholding tables are defined in so-called monetary taxable units.[59] Their values in Chilean pesos are adjusted monthly.

The PAYE functions within a comprehensive income tax: the taxable period is the calendar year. The income tax rate is defined in monetary taxable units of which the value in pesos is expressed in end-of-year values. All income earned during the year is recalculated in end-of-year values.

The withholding system is a simple PAYE with final withholding on a monthly basis. In effect, the tax period for employees who are not required to file a return is the calendar month.[60] The employer does not have to adjust the

---

[57]Although the income tax of the Philippines has substantial schedular elements (*see supra* ch. 14, note 2), for this purpose it can be considered comprehensive in the sense that wage income is consolidated with other income, such as business income.

[58]This is a simplification of the actual situation, which has changed over time and which now has moved away from a final tax for employees. While art. 13 of the individual income tax law calls for globalization of income, the precise extent of globalization has varied over time. *See, e.g.*, Presidential Decree No. 2129 of Dec. 11, 1993, which provides that employees with income from several sources whose total income falls within the standard rate bracket do not need to file a return. Article 18 of the law used to be somewhat ambiguous about the filing requirements of employees. It used to state that employees did not have to file returns. However, a sentence was subsequently added stating that this provision did not apply to employees who also had business income.

[59]*See* CHL IR § 43.

[60]*See id.*

withholding of previous months of the tax year on a cumulative or an end-of-year basis. Differences between tax withheld and final income tax liability must be resolved through return filing.

Although all employees holding a second job are required to file a return, the obligation to file returns is substantially reduced by the following provisions: (1) employees with only one job and no other income never have to file a return,[61] (2) a filing threshold applies to other income up to a specified amount,[62] and (3) employees cannot file a return solely to obtain a refund of PAYE.

Social security contributions are withheld from wages and deposited with the social security authorities. The tax and social security administrations each have their own audit programs to ensure proper withholding.

Each month, the employer must transfer the withheld tax to the treasury. Each year, taxable wages and withheld tax for each employee, identified by TIN, must be reported to the tax administration. Each employee receives information about his or her annual wage income and PAYE withheld.

Hungary

Upon commencing employment, the employee must notify the employer of his or her personal circumstances. From this information, the employer determines the employee's entitlement to personal allowances. Other deductions are not included in the employer's monthly withholding scheme. The withholding tables are based upon the income tax rate.

An employee with other income, including other wage income, must file a return with the tax administration at year-end. In this case, a simple PAYE is applicable without cumulation or year-end adjustment. An employee with no other income, but claiming deductible expenses, must file a form with the employer at year-end. In that form, the employee must confirm that he or she received no other (wage) income during the tax year. Based on this form, the employer will "assess" the employee's income through the year-end-adjusted PAYE. The employer must make all forms available to the tax administration for audit purposes.

Through this year-end adjustment, changes in personal allowances, nonperiodic wages, and other deductions are taxed at the withholding level for employees with single wage income. Employees with other (wage) income are assessed by the tax administration after they file a return.

The employer also withholds social security contributions. The contributions are administered separately from the PAYE and are paid to the social security funds. The tax administration is not involved with auditing this withholding system.

---

[61]See CHL IR § 47.
[62]See CHL IR §§ 43, 44, 65.

Each month, the PAYE withheld must be paid to the treasury, and a return filed to the tax administration. At year-end, taxable wages and PAYE for each employee are reported to the tax administration. All employees, whether assessed by the employer or filing a return, receive information at year-end on their taxable wages and PAYE withheld.

Indonesia

A person who begins a job must inform the employer, in the so-called employee's statement, about the personal allowances he or she is entitled to.[63] That statement is valid until the employee's personal circumstances change and a new statement is submitted.[64]

The withholding tables, which are based on the income tax rate,[65] apply to the relevant pay period only, without cumulative adjustments for tax withheld in preceding pay periods. The noncumulative system, however, is supplemented at year-end through an adjustment of the withholding based on the tax already withheld and the income tax due on the total of taxable wages paid during the tax year.

An employee with any amount of other income, deductions, or a second job must file a return for income tax purposes at year-end.[66]

Employers also withhold from wages a small fraction of social security contributions, which are payable to the social security administration on a monthly basis. The tax administration is responsible for compliance control regarding the PAYE; the social security administration controls the collection of social security contributions.

Each month, the employer deposits the withheld PAYE in the treasury and files a return with the tax administration. Each year, the employer must inform the tax administration of wages paid and PAYE withheld for each employee, the employees being identified by their TIN. The employee receives a statement from the employer for return-filing purposes with his or her taxable wage and PAYE.

Kenya

Employees must complete a personal relief claim form to inform the employer about the personal allowances they are claiming.[67] On that form, they can also claim other relief, such as deductible life insurance premiums. These

---

[63]*See* IDN IT § 21(III).

[64]*See* IDN IT § 21(IV).

[65]The PAYE from employees paid daily and weekly, however, is fixed at the basic income tax rate of 15 percent.

[66]*See* IDN IT § 21(VIII).

[67]For an example of such a form, *see* Republic of Kenya Income Tax Department, Employer's Guide to Pay as You Earn in Kenya 14–15 (1991).

deductions, however, must first be approved by the tax administration. To that end, the claim form should be presented for approval to the administration.

During the tax year, the personal relief claims cannot be changed. The employee must wait until the following tax year and include the change in the new form he or she submits for that year.[68] A failure to complete the claim form will result in withholding without any form of personal relief being granted.[69] The personal relief takes the form of a tax credit rather than a deduction from the taxable wage and is deducted from the PAYE according to the withholding tables. These tables are based on the income tax rate.

Other income is not included in the PAYE withholding; however, in approving deductible expenses to be included in the PAYE, the tax administration may consider existing other income as it is known to the administration. A second job also does not affect the amount of tax to be withheld in the principal job. In principle, the claim form can be submitted only for the main job; therefore, no relief is granted in the PAYE regarding the second job.

The PAYE is noncumulative for the pay periods of the tax year, a year-end adjustment is not made by the employer, and personal allowances remain unchanged during the tax year. When, because of various circumstances, the PAYE is lower or higher than the income tax due, the employee must (or may) file an income tax return.

An employee's social security contributions are also withheld at source and are paid by the employer to the social security fund. The fund is responsible for compliance control regarding the contributions.

The employer registers the PAYE for each employee on tax deduction cards.[70] At year-end, the employer sends these cards to the tax administration.[71] The administration may use the cards for income tax assessment purposes. The employee receives a copy of his or her card for return-filing purposes. The PAYE withheld is paid monthly to the treasury, and a return is filed with the administration.

Philippines

In the Philippines, an employee must submit to the employer a withholding exemption certificate that states his or her personal circumstances and hence the entitlement to personal allowances.[72] If there is a change in circumstances, a new certificate must be submitted.[73] If no certificate is submitted, the withholding is based on zero allowances.[74]

---

[68]Id. at 10–11.

[69]Id. at 7.

[70]See, e.g., id. at 16–19.

[71]Id. at 9.

[72]PHL NIRC § 72(d)(2)(A).

[73]Id. § 72(d)(2)(B).

[74]Id. § 72(d)(2)(D).

Withholding tables are based on the income tax rate; special average rates are applied to nonperiodic wage income. Although the withholding system is noncumulative with a view to subsequent pay periods of the tax year, the employer is obliged to make a year-end adjustment.[75] Against the income tax due on the wage income for the entire year, the PAYE withheld until the last pay period will be credited and any remaining tax will be the PAYE of that last period. In theory, the net wage of the last period could be zero, and the employer is responsible for an excess of PAYE over gross wage.

Other (nonwage) income does not affect the PAYE. The employee receives the full amount of personal allowances regardless of any amount of other income he or she may be entitled to. If an employee has more than one job, the personal allowances can be claimed only with the principal employer.

Social security contributions are also withheld from wages, but are deposited with the social security administration. That administration is responsible for compliance control regarding collection and payment of the contributions.

The fact that the income tax liability of the employee is fully covered by the PAYE does not affect the employee's obligation to file an annual return with the administration. The wage content of that return is based on information received from the employer.[76] At year-end, the employer must report to the tax administration on each employee's wage income and PAYE withheld.[77] The employer transfers the withheld tax monthly to the treasury and files a return with the administration for compliance control. Employees and employers are identified by one unique numbering system.

Russia

In Russia, the PAYE is basically a matter between employee and employer. Employees are not registered with the tax administration. The PAYE is the final income tax for employees.[78]

The employer in effect takes care of the assessment function regarding employment income.[79] The employee must report all allowances and deductions to the employer, and the employer computes the appropriate withholding. The employer uses the income tax rate designed for employment income. The employment tax rate is almost identical to the tax rate for self-employed persons.

This essentially simple system, however, suffers from the flaw that the income base is compartmentalized in, on the one hand, employment income and, on the other hand, other taxable income. A person with income from several sources is likely to pay less income tax than one with the same income

---

[75]*See id.* § 72(h).
[76]*See id.* § 76(a).
[77]*Id.* § 76(b).
[78]As discussed in note 58, *supra,* this is no longer the case for employees with business income.
[79]RUS IT § 8.

from only one source. Administrative ease and a not-yet-established market economy, however, are strong arguments for keeping this simple system for a certain time.

The implementation of this PAYE system is far from simple, however. The system seeks too high a level of accuracy for employment income as a whole and for the tax year in total. First, the primary employer is expected to include in the withholding scheme the wages and tax withheld from secondary employment on the basis of information supplied by the employee. Second, the withholding is based on the cumulative system.[80] Withholding for the current pay period is computed on an annual basis, with a credit for tax already withheld during the tax year.[81] Because the tax administration is not involved, the employer carries the heavy administrative burden of a rather comprehensive system. Whether all employers have the administrative capacity to do so is questionable.

The employer also withholds social security contributions and transfers them each month to the social security administration. Audits of PAYE and social security withholding are carried out by the tax administration and the social security administration, respectively.

Each month, the employer deposits the withheld PAYE in the treasury. The employer is not required to provide information on individual employees or to submit an annual report to the tax administration.

---

[80]See id.
[81]See RUS IT § 8.

16

Taxation of Income from Business and Investment

Lee Burns and Richard Krever

> Lobbyists know that a 0 percent tax rate on capital income is not, in fact, the lowest possible rate.
>
> —Joel Achenbach

I. Introduction

This chapter addresses the design and drafting of the income tax law as it applies to business and investment income.

While employment is an activity exclusively engaged in by individuals, business and investment activities may be engaged in by individuals or legal persons. Consequently, the rules for taxing income from business and investment cut across the taxation of individuals and legal persons. Countries with separate tax laws for individuals and legal persons need to coordinate the rules for taxing business and investment income, even though these may not always be uniform.

Regardless of the overall design of the income tax,[1] it is common to provide special rules for taxing business or investment income. These rules primarily relate to the tax base, timing of the recognition of income and deductions, and collection of tax. By far the most important are the timing rules. Particularly in the business context, these rules must negotiate the difficult terrain that bridges financial accounting and taxation. While uniformity between tax and financial accounting may seem desirable, countries have adopted

---

Note: Contributions to this chapter were made by Frans Vanistendael. The appendix is by Victor Thuronyi, with contributions by David Williams. Thanks also to Emil Sunley.

[1]Global, schedular, or composite; and single or separate tax laws for individuals and legal persons. See supra ch.14, sec. II.

quite different approaches: some countries have achieved substantial uniformity; in others, tax and financial accounting are substantially independent.

II. Business Income

The characterization of an amount as business income is important in both schedular and global income tax systems.[2] Under a schedular system, it is common for separate taxes to be imposed on employment, business, and investment income. Consequently, the characterization of an item of income determines which tax regime applies to it. Under a global system, there is often a notional schedular breakdown of income types under which business income is specifically mentioned as a type of income that is included in gross income. Even if the notion of income is completely global, special rules, particularly tax accounting rules, may apply to business income. Other types of income derived by individuals may be calculated using different rules.

The starting point in determining whether an item of income is business income is to determine whether the activity giving rise to the income is properly characterized as a business. This issue is considered first below, followed by a discussion of inclusion rules related to business income. The third topic covered in this section is deductions for business expenses.

A. Definition of Business

In the absence of a definition in the income tax law, the term "business" will have its ordinary meaning.[3] In broad terms, a business is a commercial or industrial activity of an independent nature undertaken for profit.[4] The concept of a business may overlap with the notion of employment for tax purposes.[5] Whether this is the case will depend on the definition of employment that is included in the law. For administrative reasons, employment should be defined for income tax purposes to include all continuing service relationships where most or a significant part of the service provider's income is derived from one customer and that income essentially represents remuneration for

---

[2]*See also supra* ch. 14, sec. V.

[3]While the word business is commonly used in income tax laws, some countries use other expressions, such as "entrepreneurship," to identify independent economic activity. *See, e.g.,* EST IT § 9(1) (income derived from entrepreneurship).

[4]Some systems have distinguished a trade from a profession or a vocation. *See, e.g.,* GBR ICTA § 18 (sched. D, case I (trade) and case II (profession or vocation)). *See also supra* ch. 14, sec. V. As discussed in ch. 14, it is preferable not to draw such a distinction. Therefore, business should be defined to include both trade and professional activities. *E.g.,* AUS ITAA (1997) § 995-1; CAN ITA § 248; IND ITA § 2(13); KEN ITA § 2; ZMB ITA § 2.

[5]In the United States, employment is considered to be a business, but other systems generally do not follow this approach. This is in any case largely a semantic point in the United States, which distinguishes the business of employment from other businesses.

the service provider's labor.[6] This will include some independent contractor relationships (i.e., relationships that are within the ordinary meaning of business). Where employment is defined in these broad terms, the definition must be coordinated with the definition of business so that the same economic activity is not characterized as both a business and an employment for income tax purposes. This could be achieved by providing that a business does not include an employment.[7]

B. Definition of Business Income

The definition of business income may serve a number of purposes in a global or schedular income tax system, for example, to identify a category of income for which special deduction or timing rules apply. It may also be used to characterize a particular item of income as business income where the income may otherwise be characterized as investment income. An important purpose of the definition in jurisdictions with a less than comprehensive judicial concept of income (e.g., those that rely on U.K. jurisprudence) is to broaden the tax base.

The relationship between income characterization and timing rules is an important factor in the design of the income tax rules applicable to business income. In turn, the timing rules depend on the relationship between tax and financial accounting rules. Because of the importance of this latter relationship in determining business income for tax purposes, this relationship is discussed first below. There then follows a discussion of specific inclusion rules relating to business income.

1. Financial Accounting and Business Income Taxation

Two basic models are used to determine the taxable income arising from business activities (referred to as "taxable business income") of a taxpayer[8] for a tax period: the receipts-and-outgoings system and the balance-sheet system. Under the receipts-and-outgoings system, generally used in common law countries, the determination of taxable business income is based on the calculation of all recognized income amounts derived by a taxpayer in the tax period and all deductible expenses incurred by the taxpayer in the tax period. Under the balance-sheet method, common in many European civil law jurisdictions, taxable business income is calculated by comparing the value of the net assets in the balance sheet of the taxpayer at the end of the year plus dividends distributed by the tax-

---

[6]*See supra* ch. 14, sec. IV(A).

[7]*E.g.*, AUS ITAA (1997) § 995-1; CAN ITA § 248; KEN ITA § 2.

[8]In this discussion, the reference to "taxpayer" is intended to include a partnership, although, generally, a partnership is not a separate taxpaying entity. However, it is usual to calculate the taxable income (or the gross income and deductions) arising from the partnership's activities as if the partnership were a separate taxpayer in respect of that income for the purpose of determining the tax liability of the partners. *See generally infra* ch. 21.

payer during the year with the value of the net assets in the balance sheet of the taxpayer at the end of the previous year.[9] A positive difference constitutes táxable business income, while a negative difference is a business loss.

While the two models may sound quite different, in practice they are similar in many respects. In theory, the starting point for the balance-sheet method is the taxpayer's financial accounts, while the receipts-and-outgoings system starts with gains and expenses that are recognized for tax purposes. In practice, however, most taxpayers in receipts-and-outgoings regimes use accounting records of commercial profits and losses as a starting point to show gross income and expenses. The recorded income and outgoings are then adjusted as necessary to reflect the differences between tax and commercial accounting rules. Similarly, while the balance-sheet method explicitly commences with commercial accounting records, these must be adjusted to reflect differences between tax law and commercial accounting practice. In some circumstances, the two systems may yield the same determination of taxable business income.

Not all business taxpayers are required to compile comprehensive accounting records that include balance sheets. Accordingly, in jurisdictions that use the balance-sheet method to calculate taxable business income, smaller businesses operated by sole traders and self-employed persons (particularly those that account on a cash basis)[10] may be allowed to calculate income as the difference between taxable receipts and deductible expenses.[11]

The relationship between the determination of business income for tax purposes and financial accounting rules is analyzed in detail in the appendix to this chapter. Those materials note that the principal purpose of financial accounting is to provide an accurate analysis of the profitability of an entity to the managers and owners of an entity, as well as to creditors and potential outside investors. Income tax, in contrast, is concerned with the measurement of the net economic gain of a taxpayer in a fixed period for the purpose of collecting a portion of the gain as tax. These differences explain why classifications used in one system may not be relevant to the other. For example, because financial accounting is concerned with presenting owners, creditors, and investors with an accurate reflection of the ongoing profitability of an entity, it places some emphasis on classifying gains by reference to their regularity.[12] Distinctions of this

---

[9]*See infra* appendix.

[10]*See infra* sec. IV(B)(1) for a discussion of cash-basis accounting.

[11]*See, e.g.,* DEU EStG § 4(3) (taxpayers who are not required under commercial law to keep double-entry books and do not keep such books).

[12]For example, financial accounting may distinguish between ordinary gains and extraordinary gains (which often equate to "capital gains" in income tax concepts) to ensure that readers of the accounts are not misled into thinking that extraordinary gains will be regularly received by the business. Often, extraordinary gains realized upon disposal of an asset have accrued over many years. *See* Financial Accounting Standards Board (USA), General Standards I17.106 and I17.107 for an example of the criteria used in financial accounting to identify extraordinary gains. The key criteria in U.S. financial accounting standards are the "unusual nature" of the transaction yielding the gain (I17.108) and the "infrequency of occurrence" of the transaction (I17.109).

sort that are drawn for accounting purposes are generally not carried over for tax purposes in jurisdictions that use the balance-sheet method of calculating taxable income.[13] The accounting distinctions are, however, relevant in some jurisdictions that use the receipts-and-outgoings method of determining taxable income.[14]

A second area in which financial and tax accounting rules differ is the treatment of income to which a future liability may attach or income that is related to goods or services to be provided in future years. This difference is relevant to both methods of determining taxable business income. Financial accounting uses a variety of means to ensure that the calculation of income does not present a distorted view of true long-term profitability when a taxpayer's right to retain income is contingent on the provision of goods or services in the future or is otherwise associated with potential future liabilities.[15] Income tax rules, by way of contrast, are not as concerned with qualifying or deferring recognition of income for the purpose of noting the taxpayer's future obligations. Instead, they tend to recognize income when the taxpayer has command over the gain, while deferring recognition of the consequent obligation until it is actually satisfied.[16]

The relationship between tax and financial accounting is important in the design of income tax rules in developing and transition countries. These two types of jurisdictions differ from each other in key respects in terms of their financial accounting systems, and both types of jurisdictions differ again from industrial countries.

Most developing countries have relatively comprehensive financial accounting rules, usually based on the systems of one or more of the member countries of the Organization for Economic Cooperation and Development

---

[13]However, several countries draw a distinction between capital gains and other business income. See *infra* ch. 20, sec. III(A).

[14]For example, in common law countries, gains that are characterized as extraordinary gains for accounting purposes are commonly treated as capital gains for tax purposes, where the tax system provides different treatment for capital gains and ordinary income gains.

[15]In some cases, this is done by recognizing receipts as income but then appropriating part of the amount received to a "reserve" to indicate that it is not actually available for use or distribution, but is being held for eventual application to satisfy a contingent or potential liability. Alternatively, an amount received may be treated as unfettered profits but be subject to a notation to the accounts indicating that it is subject to a contingent or potential liability and may not, therefore, reflect actual gain. This might be done, for example, where goods are sold subject to the purchaser's right to rescind the contract within a fixed period. A receipt related to the provision of future goods or services is likely not to be treated as income at all for financial accounting purposes. Instead, it will probably be credited to a "prepaid revenue account," which is a liability of the company (offset by an increase in cash). As the goods or services are provided, the liability will be diminished and amounts will move from the prepaid revenue account to the income account. Income tax treatment of advance payments may accord with the accounting treatment or may require inclusion of the payment in income. See *infra* sec. IV(C)(1).

[16]See *infra* sec. IV.

(OECD). In many cases, however, local accounting rules have not evolved in line with changes in industrial countries that were adopted to reflect changes in commercial practice. A different situation exists in most transition countries, where financial accounting rules were designed for application in a centrally planned economy and are now undergoing or have undergone reform. The adoption or reform of accounting laws has ameliorated the problem, but the accounting laws alone are not sufficient for income tax purposes. In many cases, statutory regimes are not supported by developed commercial accounting practice or judicial precedents that can be used to fill in the gaps in accounting statutes. Accordingly, it may be necessary for income tax laws of developing and transition countries to include characterization and timing rules, instead of relying on financial accounting. Tax accounting issues that should be addressed in income tax laws are reviewed below in section IV(B).

2. Specific Inclusions

It was stated above that a key purpose of the definition of business income is to broaden the income tax base, particularly in jurisdictions that rely on U.K. law or precedents. Jurisdictions that use U.K. concepts[17] measure taxable business income using the profit-and-loss method, based on taxable receipts and allowable deductions. In these jurisdictions, only receipts recognized as business income under judicial precedents or specific rules in the statute are included in gross income from business.[18] The judicial concept of business income in U.K. law characterizes gains as income from business if the receipt is a product or an ordinary incident of the carrying on of a business. Judicial precedents for determining whether gains satisfy this test emphasize the characteristics of the receipt, such as periodicity, and the subjective intention of the taxpayer with respect to the derivation of the gain.

A gain may thus be income from business if it arose from a transaction that was entered into by the taxpayer with a business or profit-making intention.[19] Such a gain is said to arise from an adventure or concern in the nature of trade.[20] Under this approach, gains from "one-off" or isolated transactions such as immovable property sales and speculative financial transactions are

---

[17]The U.S. courts have taken a broadly similar approach to the issues discussed in this paragraph, although there are some differences in the approach of the case law—hardly surprising given the extensive amount of litigation on these issues.

[18]Also sometimes called "assessable income." See supra ch. 14, note 25.

[19]See Rutledge v. Commissioner, 14 T.C. 490 (1929); Martin v. Lowry [1927] A.C. 312.

[20]Some income tax systems derivative of U.K. principles include an "adventure or concern in the nature of trade" in the definition of business. E.g., KEN ITA § 2; CAN ITA § 248; IND ITA § 2(13); ZMB ITA § 2. This has its source in U.K. tax law in which trade is defined to include "every trade, manufacture, adventure or concern in the nature of trade" (GBR ICTA § 832).

particularly difficult to imbue with an income character, and the disputes concerning the characterization of gains from such transactions account for a high percentage of taxation cases in jurisdictions relying on U.K. judicial concepts. In these jurisdictions, gains from transactions that fall outside the business income concept are likely to be considered capital gains and hence outside the judicial concept of income. Rather than define business income expansively to overcome this problem, many common law jurisdictions have simply accepted the judicial characterization and grafted capital gains tax regimes onto the basic income tax system[21] or adopted a separate capital gains tax.[22]

In jurisdictions that use the balance-sheet method to calculate taxable income, the business income concept is typically formulated to encompass both gains from ongoing commercial activities and gains on the disposal of business assets, including immovable property and machinery.[23]

A broad definition of business income can also be helpful in transition jurisdictions that use evolving accounting standards and accounting codes as the basis for calculating taxable income. It can achieve certainty and simplicity in the income tax base and avoid the application of significant administrative and judicial resources to issues arising from the uncertain boundaries of business income. Choice of an appropriate drafting technique to accomplish this objective will depend upon the drafting norms followed in the jurisdiction.

A wide inclusion provision should treat as business income any gains arising on the disposal of business assets.[24] It should be made clear that the inclusion rule applies to all assets of a business and not just those used in the normal operations of the business. Thus, the concept of business asset should include not only assets physically used in, or held by, the business, but also investment assets related to a business activity. For example, a person carrying on a construction business may make short-term investments with advance payments received, and these investments should be considered business assets and not investment property. For companies and partnerships this effect can be achieve by a rule that treats all assets of such entities as business assets. For individuals conducting business activities, that may be achieved through a broad definition of business asset that includes all assets used, ready for use, or held

---

[21]For example, the inclusion of capital gains in AUS ITAA (1936) §§ 160AX–160ZZU and CAN ITA §§ 38–55.

[22]*E.g.*, GBR TCGA.

[23]The following definitions of business income for commercial and industrial enterprises are based on a net-increment-of-assets theory (*théorie du bilan*) and include all gains on assets used for business purposes: AUT EStG § 4; BEL CIR § 24; FRA CGI §§ 34, 36, and 38/1 and 2; DEU EStG §§ 4 and 5; CHE LIFD § 16; ESP IRPF § 41. NLD WIB § 7 taxes any advantage, whatever the name or the form, derived from an undertaking.

[24]*See infra* sec. V for a discussion of the timing and calculation rules relating to gains on the disposal of assets.

for the purposes of a business. As a practical matter, it may be difficult to draw the line between the business and investment activities of an individual. Nevertheless, making the distinction will be necessary if gains on the disposal of investment assets may be either untaxed or subject to some form of tax concession.[25]

The inclusion in business income of gains arising on the disposal of business assets needs to be coordinated with any special regimes applying to specific types of assets, particularly inventory and depreciable or amortizable assets, as such regimes may have their own inclusion rules. Even if these regimes do have their own inclusion rules, it still should be made clear that the amount included under those rules is characterized as business income. This should also be the case for amounts included in gross income as recapture of excess depreciation or amortization.[26]

The business income inclusion rule should also cover any gain arising in relation to a business debt.[27] Ordinarily, if a person receives money with an obligation to repay, the receipt of the money is not regarded as income because of the offsetting liability to repay the amount received. However, if a debtor is able to discharge a business liability for less than the face value of the liability,[28] there needs to be some adjustment to the debtor's tax position to reflect the increase in the debtor's net worth. The simplest way of making this adjustment is to include the difference between the face value of the liability and the discharged amount in the business income of the debtor in the tax year in which the debt is discharged.[29] If the discharge has come about because the debtor is in financial difficulties, it may be appropriate to defer recognition of the gain by applying it to reduce the debtor's loss carryovers or asset costs, rather than including it in income.[30] Applying the gain in this way will reduce the debtor's deductions or cost recognitions in later tax years, thereby increasing the debtor's taxable income in those years.

Other items that can be explicitly enumerated in a definition of business income include the following:

---

[25]See infra sec. VI(C).

[26]These amounts may also be referred to as balancing charges or as claw-back. See infra ch. 17, notes 170–71.

[27]See generally supra ch. 14 sec. VI(F).

[28]Where the debt is a fixed-interest security, this may come about because a general rise in interest rates has resulted in a reduction in the value of the debt, so that the debtor is able to repurchase the debt for less than its face value. It may also come about under a debt-defeasance arrangement whereby a borrower liable to repay a loan at some future date pays a third party an amount approximating the present value of the loan in consideration of the third party's agreeing to pay the amount owed by the borrower when it becomes due. Finally, it may come about because the value of the debt has decreased because the debtor is in financial difficulties.

[29]E.g., LSO ITA § 19(2); UGA ITA § 19(1)(a); USA IRC § 61(a)(12).

[30]E.g., UGA ITA §§ 19(3), 39(3) (insolvency); USA IRC § 108 (insolvency or in formal bankruptcy proceedings). Some countries apply this rule in all cases and not just to debtors in financial difficulties. See, e.g., AUS ITAA (1936) sched. 2C; CAN ITA § 80 et seq.

- amounts received as consideration for accepting a restriction on the capacity to carry on business;
- amounts received as an inducement payment to enter into a contract or business arrangement (e.g., a lease "inducement" payment received for entering into a lease of business premises);
- gifts received by a person in the context of a business relationship;
- recovery of amounts previously deducted as business expenses, including bad debt claims; and
- amounts received in respect of lost business profits under a policy of insurance or a contract for indemnity or as a result of a legal action.[31]

As stated above, a specific inclusion rule may also be used to give priority to the characterization of a particular item of income as business income where the income may also be characterized as investment income. For example, investment income will usually be defined to include interest income. However, where interest income is derived by a person in carrying on a business of banking or money lending, it is appropriate to treat the income as business income and not investment income. It is also appropriate to treat interest income as business income when its derivation is incidental to business operations. This would be the case, for example, with interest derived on a business's normal bank accounts or short-term investments. The same can apply to rental income where the business of the person deriving the income is the holding or letting of property.

The proper characterization in these circumstances may be relevant to the application of rules that quarantine deductions against particular classes of income.[32] Where income is derived from foreign sources, the characterization of the income may also be relevant to the calculation of the foreign tax credit limit.[33] It should be provided that the treatment of such income as business and not investment income for inclusion purposes does not preclude the income from retaining its characterization as interest or rental income for other purposes of the legislation. This ensures that any specific provision applying to such classes of income (such as nonresident withholding tax) is not avoided by an argument that the income is not interest income but business income.

C. Deduction of Business Expenses

In theory, all costs incurred to derive business income should be recognized for the purpose of determining net income, although the timing of rec-

---

[31]It may be preferable to deal with the last two of these specific inclusions with general inclusion rules applying to all types of income (and not just business income). If general rules are used, it will be necessary to provide rules concerning the category of income into which these items fall.

[32]For example, it may be provided that expenses incurred in deriving investment income may be deductible only against investment income. *See infra* sec. VI(A)(3).

[33]In some countries, the limit must be calculated separately for different types of income. *E.g.*, USA IRC § 904.

ognition may vary for different types of expenses.[34] Early income tax laws often used restrictive language such as "ordinary and necessary" when defining deductible expenses.[35] Phrases such as this invite a subjective ex post facto analysis as to the desirability or effectiveness of business expenses. Other early income tax laws referred to expenses that were "wholly and exclusively" incurred to derive income subject to tax.[36] Terminology of this sort opens the door to a complete denial of a deduction for dual-purpose expenses, such as those incurred to derive both exempt income and income subject to tax, or those incurred for both personal purposes and to derive income subject to tax.

Generally, courts in jurisdictions that employ restrictive language of the sort described have read the provisions creatively and refrained from applying them to deny taxpayers deductions for genuine business expenses. The courts have adopted flexible interpretations of terms such as "ordinary and necessary" to discourage tax officials from second-guessing business decisions and denying a deduction for what subsequently proved to be ineffective or inappropriate outgoings.[37] Similarly, courts have applied language such as "wholly and exclusively" in a pragmatic fashion. Under such an approach, an expense that can be apportioned may, in relation to a part of the expense, be seen as incurred wholly and exclusively for the purpose of deriving income subject to tax.[38]

An alternative model for the design of a deduction provision commences with broad, nonrestrictive language and then supplements the general rule to allow deductions (the "positive" limb or limbs of the deduction provisions) with specific restrictions on deductions (the "negative" limb or limbs).[39] To accommodate dual-purpose expenses, the positive limbs should contain apportioning language—for example, "expenses are deductible *to the extent* that they are incurred in the production of income subject to tax." To ensure that the broad objectives of the positive limbs are achieved, it may be useful to refer to alternative bases for deductions—for example, deductions may be allowed for expenses incurred in the production of income subject to tax *or* incurred in the operation of a business carried on for the purpose of producing income subject to tax. Many outgoings incurred by a business are necessary or appropriate to the operation of the business but not consumed directly in the income-earning

---

[34]*See infra* sec. IV(D). The issues raised here are similar to those that arise under the value-added tax (VAT) for input credit, and the reader might usefully compare the discussion in vol. 1, at 219–20.

[35]USA IRC § 162, for example, has retained the phrase "ordinary and necessary expenses."

[36]This was the rule in early Australian and Canadian income tax laws. GBR ICTA § 74(a) has retained this phrase. It is still also found in many income tax laws derivative of U.K. principles. *E.g.*, KEN ITA § 15; SGP ITA § 14; ZMB ITA § 29.

[37]This has been the experience in the United States. *See* Welch v. Helvering, 290 U.S. 111 (1933) and Commissioner v. Tellier, 383 U.S. 687 (1966).

[38]In the case of GBR ICTA § 74(a), *see* Ransom v. Higgs [1974] 1 WLR 1594.

[39]*E.g.*, LSO ITA § 33.

process of the business. A specific reference to expenses of a business will ensure that all legitimate business expenses are deductible.

Negative limbs, prohibiting deductions for particular types of expenses, fall into three broad categories: restrictions on deductions for personal expenses, restrictions on immediate deductions for capital outgoings (incurred to derive long-term or long-life benefits), and restrictions on deductions motivated by policy considerations. It is important in drafting to state clearly the relationship between provisions denying deductions and any specific rules allowing deductions (such as depreciation provisions).[40] Ordinarily, the prohibition rules override general rules for the allowance of a deduction, but are in turn subject to specific rules allowing deductions. For example, the prohibition on immediate deductions for capital outgoings overrides the positive limb allowing a deduction for business expenses, but, as explained below, the prohibition may in turn be overridden by measures that allow the outlay to be deducted under a depreciation or amortization regime.

There are two advantages to a general deduction provision designed with broad positive limbs followed by specific negative provisions that specify the types of nondeductible outgoings. First, this technique avoids the impossible task of enumerating the endless list of expenses that may be incurred by a business.[41] It is impossible for legislative drafters to anticipate every type of expense that will be incurred, and, as a result, a system that allowed deductions only for enumerated expenses would inevitably prejudice some businesses. Second, and more important, the drafting approach that commences with a broad general deduction measure followed by specific deduction-denial measures provides a logical and sound framework for taxpayers, tax administrators, and tax adjudicators and makes the task of characterizing unusual expenses simpler for all parties.

1. Personal Expenses

The first category of deduction-denial measures applies to personal expenses and is relevant only to unincorporated businesses, because companies are inherently incapable of incurring personal expenses.[42] In the context of individuals deriving business income, it may be redundant to restrict the deductibility of personal expenses, since by definition a personal expense will not satisfy the criteria for deduction as a business expense. Nevertheless, as indi-

---

[40]*See* Commissioner v. Idaho Power Co., 418 U.S. 1 (1974) discussed in ch. 17 *infra* at note 57.

[41]The exhaustive-list approach seems to be favored by jurisdictions with a history of central planning. *See, e.g.,* MNG BEIT § 5(1); CHN EIT § 6.

[42]There is, however, a line of U.K. judicial authority that suggests that some business expenses, such as damages or fines, may be incurred by traders (including legal persons) in a personal capacity. *See* Strong & Co. Ltd. v. Woodifield [1906] AC 448 (brewery company held to incur damages in its capacity as householder rather than innkeeper). This authority now has little impact, particularly outside the United Kingdom, as later courts have distinguished the decision and largely confined it to the particular facts of the early cases.

cated in chapter 14 in the context of employment expenses,[43] statutes often prohibit deductions for personal expenses. Courts in particular find negative provisions of this sort useful for reinforcing decisions to deny deductions for personal outgoings. Further specific restrictions are sometimes used—for example, restrictions on deductions for "luxuries" where the value of the outgoings will not be taxed to the beneficiaries of the expenditures.[44]

Another type of personal expense to which specific restrictions are often applied is a "hobby" expense. A hobby is a personal activity that in other circumstances might constitute a business. For example, a holiday or weekend property could be nominally operated as a farm. Similarly, a taxpayer might pursue a recreational hobby, such as photography, sculpture, racing, or gambling, that constitutes a business for other taxpayers. Restrictions are needed to prevent taxpayers from deducting the expenses associated with such properties or activities.

Restrictions on the deductibility of hobby expenses may be achieved in two ways. First, reliance may be placed on a suitable definition of "business," drafted to exclude investments or activities that are not primarily intended as income-earning ventures. This approach has proved to be of little utility because courts in jurisdictions using this approach have found it almost impossible to map a clear line between genuine businesses and hobbies that are conducted with businesslike features.[45] A second approach is to allow expenses of any activity to be deducted only against income generated by the activity unless the taxpayer can demonstrate, by reference to objective criteria set out in the legislation or in regulations, that the activity constitutes a business.[46] Further, under such an approach, a rule based on profitability can be applied to determine that an activity is a business. For example, it can be provided that where the activity is the taxpayer's principal source of livelihood, it will not be considered a hobby and expenses will be deductible in future years, subject to loss-carryover rules.[47] Alternatively, an activity can be presumed to be a business based on profitability over several years—for example, three years out of five.[48] Care must be taken that such rules do not prevent a genuine business activity from being treated as such during an extended period of recession or

---

[43]See supra ch.14, sec. IV(B).

[44]See BEL CIR § 53/10; DEU EStG § 4 V 7; Klaus Tipke & Joachim Lang, Steurrecht 261–63 (13th ed. 1991).

[45]This approach is used in Australia. The limited efficacy of this approach prompted the government to adopt specific hobby expense restrictions in 1985, but political and technical difficulties led to their withdrawal, and tax authorities continue to rely on the business definition as the sole means of restricting deductions for hobby expenses.

[46]E.g., USA IRC § 183. The regulations under § 183 list nine factors to consider in characterizing a taxpayer's activities. It is made clear in the regulations that the list is not exhaustive and that no one factor or even a majority of factors is decisive.

[47]See infra sec. IV(A)(2).

[48]See USA IRC § 183(d).

of adverse seasonal factors.[49] Given this caveat, this approach prevents abuse of the deduction measures while recognizing the start-up costs and profit fluctuations that legitimate businesses may encounter.

2. Capital Expenses

The second category of deduction-denial measures applies to capital expenditures, which are incurred to acquire assets or benefits[50] with a life extending beyond the tax period. In principle, measures preventing deductions for capital expenditures are not intended to impose absolute prohibitions on their recognition. Rather, they are supposed to prevent immediate deduction for outgoings relating to long-term benefits, and other provisions in the law should allow for their recognition on a more appropriate timing basis. However, in some countries, the effect of rules preventing immediate deductions for capital expenditures is to prevent any deduction for these expenses.

A properly designed system will provide for the recognition of all types of capital expenditures. Under such a system, the method of recognition depends on the nature of the asset or benefit acquired by the expenditure and, in particular, on whether the asset or benefit "wastes" over time. An asset or benefit wastes if it declines in value through usage or over time. Examples are buildings, plant, machinery, patents, and contractual rights of a limited life (such as an agency dealership for a fixed term). For such assets or benefits, the cost should be recognized by way of depreciation or amortization deductions allowed over the life of the assets or benefits. Depreciation and amortization rules are discussed in detail in chapter 17.

An asset does not waste if its value does not decline through usage or over time, although it may vary in response to market conditions. Examples are land and shares. For such assets, the cost of acquisition should be recognized upon disposal of the asset, through provisions that allow the cost base of the asset to be deducted in computing gain or loss on the disposal. Rules for cost inclusion and gain calculation are discussed in section V, below.

The design of a comprehensive regime for the recognition of capital expenditures must adequately provide for expenditures yielding benefits with uncertain lives. For example, a person may incur substantial expenditures in fighting the license application of a potential competitor or defending title to an asset already owned. Given that such expenditures may result in long-term

---

[49]For example, a farmer may be forced to take a job in town during a period of adverse seasonal conditions or a period of depressed commodity prices. During this period, the farming activity may not be the farmer's principal source of livelihood nor may the farming activity be profitable, but this should not prevent the farming activity from being treated as a business.

[50]A benefit is a business advantage that does not involve the acquisition of any asset, such as, for example, the reduction of competition. See Graeme Cooper et al., Cooper, Krever & Vann's Income Taxation 10-34 to 10-54 (1993).

benefits, they may be characterized as a capital expenditure; because the life of the benefit is uncertain, however, they may not fit within the ordinary amortization rules. To deal with such expenditures, it is suggested that a residual amortization rule be included to allow recognition over an arbitrary period of any capital expenditure for wasting or uncertain life benefits not covered by specific depreciation or amortization rules, or that it be included in the cost base of identifiable assets.[51]

An alternative approach that can be used in jurisdictions that have separate capital gains provisions for business taxpayers is to recognize the expenditure as a capital loss when the benefit acquired by the expense has expired.[52] However, this approach suffers from several major flaws. First, recognition of the expenditure is deferred until the asset or benefit expires, so that there is not a proper matching of expenses to revenue. Second, the expenditure is then recognized as a capital loss that, under the capital gains rules, may be applied only against capital gains. Third, even under a comprehensive regime for the taxation of capital gains, some capital expenditures will not be covered—namely, expenses that are not related to the acquisition of an identifiable tangible or intangible asset.[53]

The cost of inventory is not considered a capital expense in the ordinary sense because inventory is related to ongoing business operations. Nevertheless, inventory does not waste, and, therefore, the cost of acquiring inventory should not be recognized until it is sold.[54]

3. Policy-Motivated Restrictions

The third category of deduction-denial measures applies to expenses that satisfy the positive nexus test for deductibility but that the legislature chooses, for various reasons, to disallow as a deduction. One reason the legislature may choose to do this is to discourage or penalize a particular activity for public policy reasons. Examples include prohibitions on the deductibility of fines and similar penalties[55] and bribes and similar illegal payments.[56]

---

[51]For example, Canada uses a residual amortization rule that allows a taxpayer to recognize expenditures for wasting benefits not covered by other depreciation provisions on a 7 percent declining-balance basis. Not all the cost is recognized; see CAN ITA § 14.

[52]Australia, for example, has adopted this approach.

[53]Such expenditures never recognized for tax purposes are sometimes known colloquially as "nothings" (as in Canada prior to the adoption of the residual amortization rule in that jurisdiction), or "black holes," the term gaining currency in Australia.

[54]See infra sec. IV(D)(4).

[55]See, e.g., AUS ITAA (1997) § 26-5; EST IT § 16(4); LSO ITA § 33(3)(e); UGA ITA § 23(2)(h).

[56]See, e.g., GBR ICTA § 577A (expenditure incurred in making a payment where the making of the payment constitutes the commission of a criminal offense); USA IRC § 162(c); OECD, Implementation of the Recommendation on Bribery in International Business Transactions, 4 OECD Working Papers, No. 34 (1996).

A deduction-denial rule may also apply to income tax paid to other domestic or foreign jurisdictions, as well as to the domestic tax itself.[57] The treatment of foreign taxes will depend on the international tax regime.[58] The problem of other domestic income taxes arises most commonly in federal jurisdictions. The treatment by the federal or subordinate governments of taxes paid to the other level of government will depend on the fiscal support arrangements in place in the jurisdiction. In some jurisdictions, the two or more income taxes operate in parallel; in others, one level of government provides a deduction or credit for income taxes paid to the other.[59]

Other policy-motivated deduction restrictions may be designed to reinforce tax administration. A common example is the denial of a deduction for payments made by the taxpayer that are subject to withholding tax if the taxpayer has failed to withhold tax as required.[60] Another example is payments that are not properly substantiated by documentary evidence.[61]

The legislature may also choose deduction denial to deal with borderline expenses that have elements of both business expenses and personal consumption. Such expenses are discussed in chapter 14 in relation to employment,[62] but the issues are equally relevant where the expenses are incurred by a business for the benefit of a customer, client, or other business associate. The main examples are entertainment, meal, and refreshment expenditures. For these expenditures, a deduction may be disallowed to the extent that the amount is not included in the income of the beneficiary of the expenditure (subject to exceptions where, for example, the benefits are provided to paying customers or given to a broad cross section of the public as samples).[63] Alternatively, some countries limit the deductible portion of ex-

---

[57]*E.g.*, EST IT § 16(3); LSO ITA § 33(3)(b); SGP ITA § 15(1)(g); UGA ITA § 23(2)(d).

[58]*See infra* ch. 18.

[59]*See* vol. 1, at 68. It may be concluded that no explicit deduction prohibition is needed where deductions are not to be given for income taxes paid to another level of government as the payment may not satisfy the positive nexus tests in the deduction provisions (because the tax is not considered an expense of earning income). This means that if recognition is to be provided for another domestic income tax by way of deduction (*e.g.*, USA § IRC 164), a specific allowable deduction or tax offset provision will be needed.

[60]*E.g.*, AUS ITAA (1936) § 221YRA(1A) (no deduction for royalties paid to a person outside Australia until withholding tax paid to the Commissioner).

[61]*E.g.*, AUS ITAA (1997) § 900-70 (car expenses) and § 900-80 (business travel). These rules apply only to individuals and partnerships in which an individual is a partner.

[62]*See infra* sec. IV(B).

[63]*E.g.*, AUS ITAA (1997) § 32-5 (entertainment expenses deductible only if the value of the benefit is included in the recipient's income, is subject to fringe benefits taxation, or in other limited cases); UGA ITA § 24 (entertainment expenses deductible only if the value of the benefit is included in the recipient's income or the entertainment is supplied to the public as part of the taxpayer's business).

penses to a fixed amount specified in the statute.[64] Similar limitations apply in relation to costs incurred in providing leisure facilities maintained for the benefit of employees and business associates, and the payment of social club membership fees for the benefit of employees.[65] A limitation may also be included on the deductibility of the cost of a gift made directly or indirectly to an individual if the gift is not included in the individual's income.[66]

Other examples of policy-based deduction-denial rules are some interest expenses;[67] contributions to nonapproved pension, superannuation, or private social security schemes (to encourage contributions only to schemes with rules that achieve the government's retirement income policies);[68] and contributions to political lobbying organizations or to political parties.[69]

III. Investment Income

As with employment and business income, the characterization of an amount as investment income[70] (or as a particular type of investment income) is important in both schedular and global income tax systems.[71] Under a schedular system, characterization determines which tax regime applies to the income. Under a global system, there may be a specific inclusion rule for investment income or special timing or administrative rules.

There are two broad approaches to the inclusion of investment income in gross income. First, the inclusion rule could refer to investment income, which is then separately defined by reference to specific categories of income, such as annuities, dividends, interest, rent, and royalties.[72] Where capital gains on the disposal of investment assets are included in the income tax base, investment income may also be defined to include such gains.[73] Alternatively, the inclusion rule may refer to specific categories of investment income rather than to a collective notion of investment income.[74] Even under this design, it may still

---

[64]E.g., CAN ITA § 67.1 (deductible amount is 80 percent of the expenses incurred); IND ITA § 37(2) (first 10,000 rupees is deductible plus 50 percent of the excess); LSO ITA § 33 (deductible amount limited to 50 percent of the expenses incurred); NZL ITA § 106G (deductible amount is 50 percent of the expenses incurred); USA IRC § 274(n) (only 50 percent of expense is deductible).

[65]E.g., AUS ITAA (1997) §§ 26-45 (recreational club facilities) and 26-50 (leisure facility or boat); CAN ITA § 18(1)(l); NZL ITA § 106G.

[66]E.g., UGA ITA § 23(2)(f).

[67]See infra sec VI(A).

[68]E.g., LSO ITA §§ 95, 96.

[69]E.g., CAN ITA § 18(1)(n) (political contributions).

[70]In some jurisdictions, the term "property income" or "capital income" may be used.

[71]See also supra ch. 14, sec. IV.

[72]E.g., LSO ITA §§ 17(1)(c), 20; UGA ITA §§ 18(1)(c), 21.

[73]E.g., LSO ITA § 20.

[74]E.g., EST IT § 9; IDN LCIT § 4; SGP ITA § 10.

be necessary to define investment income for particular purposes under the income tax law.[75]

Under either method of inclusion, the specific categories of investment income may be the subject of supplementary definitions. While these supplementary definitions will be relevant to the income inclusion rules, they may in fact be more relevant to other aspects of the income tax, particularly withholding on payments such as interest and royalties paid to nonresidents. Given the flexibility of modern commercial law contracts, a nonresident may derive income that is functionally equivalent to interest, royalties, or rent, but is not within the ordinary meaning of those terms. In the absence of broad definitions of interest, royalties, and rent, this income may not be subject to tax.[76] In these cases, there may be no doubt that what is derived is income, but it may not be covered by the definition of interest or royalties for the purposes of the relevant nonresident withholding tax.

In light of this, the drafting of supplementary definitions of specific categories of investment income, such as royalties, may be influenced by international practice, particularly that reflected in the OECD Model Tax Convention on Income and Capital[77] (OECD Model Treaty).

Supplementary definitional rules for annuities, interest, rent, and royalties are discussed below. The definition of dividends is discussed in chapter 19, section VI.

A. Annuities

In common law jurisdictions, annuities were originally developed in the context of trust law, where they were used to impose a support obligation on an estate. The obligation required the estate to pay a fixed stipend to a beneficiary, using both income derived by the estate and capital, if income was insufficient to satisfy the payment obligation. Commercial or purchased annuities are a more recent development. A taxpayer purchasing a commercial annuity provides an "annuity provider" with a capital sum that is returned with compensation conceptually similar to interest in fixed payments over a specified term or, in the case of a life annuity, over the taxpayer's life.

A taxpayer must be allowed to recover the cost of purchasing an annuity, so that only the profit portion of the gain is taxed. The usual procedure is to recognize the cost of the annuity on a pro rata basis over the life of the annuity. The cost recognized as a portion of each annuity payment is determined by dividing the cost by the total number of payments for a fixed annuity and by the total number of estimated payments for a life annuity. This can be done by first

---

[75]*See supra* text at notes 24 and 25.

[76]If the nonresident withholding tax rules do not apply, then it is often fairly easy to structure the transaction so that the income derived by the nonresident has a foreign source.

[77]*See infra* ch. 18, note 9.

prorating the payments and recognizing only a part of each payment as income or by recognizing the entire annuity payment as income and allowing an off-setting deduction for the cost component attributed to the payment.[78]

This method of cost recovery results in a deferred taxation of annuity income. This deferral makes annuities an attractive investment vehicle for both individuals and businesses. In particular, it is possible to structure an ordinary commercial loan so that it takes the legal form of an annuity, and thereby take advantage of deferred taxation. From an economic perspective, fixed-term annuities are in many respects the functional equivalent of a "blended" loan in which the borrower repays the loan principal over the period of the loan. In a blended loan, each payment contains a return of principal and an interest component, but the interest component of the initial payments is high compared with the repayment of principal, while the interest component of the last payments is small, since most of the principal on which interest is calculated has been repaid by the time of those payments. Given the functional similarity between blended loans and annuities, commercial lenders may try to characterize an ordinary commercial blended loan as an annuity in order to defer recognition of interest income by recognizing interest income in equal installments over the life of the transaction rather than predominantly in the initial payments.

Under normal circumstances, a borrower would prefer to enter into an ordinary loan arrangement rather than an annuity arrangement, because the former entitles the borrower to larger deductions in the early period of the loan. However, if the borrower is a tax-exempt person (or is in a net operating loss position), a loan offers no advantages over an annuity because there will be no tax advantage from recognizing the higher interest component at the beginning of the loan. If the borrower is indifferent between a loan and an annuity, the lender may suggest the annuity option and offer a reduced rate of interest in return for the deferral opportunity.

Many common law jurisdictions vulnerable to this practice have enacted antiavoidance provisions to prevent exploitation of the annuity rules in this manner. The simplest solution is to restrict the annuity treatment described in section III(A), above, to limited categories of annuities such as retirement annuities and to define other annuities as ordinary compound interest blended payment loans for tax purposes, whatever the legal designation given to them by the parties. This will allow tax authorities to notionally dissect annuity payments into interest and principal components, as if the payments were made pursuant to an ordinary commercial loan contract.

B. Interest

Interest is the compensation earned by a creditor for the use of his or her money during the period of the loan. Fundamental to the ordinary

---

[78]E.g., AUS ITAA (1936) § 27H; ZAF ITA § 10A.

notion of interest is that there is a debt obligation. To make this clear, interest may be defined by reference to a debt obligation with a separate definition of debt obligation in the law that includes accounts payable and obligations arising under promissory notes, bills of exchange, debentures, and bonds.[79]

As indicated above, modern commercial law contracts make it possible to convert interest on debt or quasi-debt obligations into a variety of other forms, including discounts and premiums in respect of loan principal. Thus, interest is often defined for tax purposes to include commonly used interest substitutes such as discounts and premiums. However, even terms such as these have a recognized legal meaning, and, like the notion of interest itself, characterization as discount or premium may be avoided. Consequently, it is suggested that the definition of interest include a general formula to more effectively cope with the flexibility available to taxpayers in the way they structure their financial transactions. For example, interest could be defined to include "any other amount that is functionally equivalent to interest."[80]

C. Royalties

The definition of "royalties" for tax purposes is complicated by the fact that the term has diverse meanings across jurisdictions, and, even within a jurisdiction, may be applied to fundamentally different types of payments. One meaning is a payment for the use of a person's intellectual property. Thus, an author may be paid royalties for the right to print and sell books containing the author's copyrighted material, a musician may be paid royalties for the right to produce and sell tapes or compact discs containing the musician's work, or an inventor may be paid royalties for the right to produce and sell the inventor's patented system. Royalties may also be payable for the right to sell products bearing a trademark or copyrighted identification marks, or for the right to use know-how. In each of these cases, royalty payments are normally based on output (so much for each unit sold or produced).[81]

A related type of royalty is a payment for the sale of intellectual property. Rather than licensing a publisher to print a book with an author's work, the author may sell the copyright to a publisher, with the proceeds from the sale being paid as royalties based on sales. In essence, the copyright is sold for an unknown price, to be determined and paid as the books are sold. This sort of royalty is fundamentally different from the first one in that it is consideration for a sale, not payment for the use of the recipient's property. However, despite the legal difference, there may not be much of an economic difference in some cases. For example, the sale may cover only a limited geographic area or a lim-

---

[79]E.g., UGA ITA § 3 (definitions of interest and debt obligations).

[80]E.g., UGA ITA § 3 (definition of interest).

[81]See generally Murray v. ICI Imperial Chemical Industries Ltd. [1967] 2 All E.R. 980, at 982–83.

ited period of time and may therefore have essentially the same effect as a license covering this area and period of time.

A third type of royalty is paid for the exploitation of natural resources connected with land, most commonly mineral resources (including petroleum), gravel, or timber. Calculation of the amount of royalties payable is normally based on the quantity or value of the resources taken, for which these royalties are effectively a purchase price.

Because royalties encompass so many different types of payments, the characterization of amounts as royalties for tax purposes varies from jurisdiction to jurisdiction. In particular, not all countries classify royalties as a category of income in its own right. Some countries classify some kinds of royalties as rental income[82] or, for royalties received by individuals for intellectual property created by personal exertion, as income from independent labor.[83] Other countries classify royalties as investment income subject to the same basic rules as interest income.[84]

The definition of royalties for tax purposes may also be influenced by international practice. There is a definition of royalties in article 12 of the OECD Model Treaty, which applies to transactions between the Contracting States. This definition has been included in the domestic tax law of many countries either generally or in relation to the taxation of nonresidents.[85] The article 12 definition includes payments for the use of, or right to use, intellectual property rights or know-how. It also includes payments for the provision of technical assistance ancillary to the use of intellectual property rights or know-how.[86] The definition does not include natural resource royalties. This is because such royalties are treated as income from immovable property under the OECD Model Treaty and, therefore, are dealt with under article 6 rather than under article 12. This reflects a distinction between royalties related to property that has its origin outside the jurisdiction (such as technology rights), for which there may be limited source-country taxing rights, and royalties related to immovable property located in the jurisdiction (such as the taking of natural resources), for which there are full source-country taxing rights. If natural resource royalties are excluded from the domestic law definition of royalties, they may be included in the definition of rent (which is not usually

---

[82]AUT EStG § 28 (1)3; DEU EStG § 21(1).

[83]NLD WIB § 22/1 (b).

[84]BEL CIR § 17 par. 1/4.

[85]*See generally infra* ch. 18, sec. IV(E).

[86]Prior to 1992, the definition of royalty in the OECD Model Treaty also included amounts received for the use of, or right to use, any industrial, commercial, or scientific equipment (i.e., amounts received under a lease of movable property). The OECD Model Treaty was amended in 1992 to exclude such amounts from the definition of royalties with the intention of bringing them within the business profits article. Notwithstanding this, the definition of royalties in the domestic tax law of some countries still includes such amounts. *See, e.g.,* AUS ITAA (1936) § 6; KEN ITA § 2; LSO ITA § 3; UGA ITA § 3; ZMB ITA § 2.

subject to nonresident withholding tax) or treated as a separate category of income.

A definition of royalty based on the use of, or right to use, certain rights can be avoided by structuring the transaction as a disposal of the right. For this reason, some countries also define royalties to include the gain arising on the disposal of rights or property covered by the royalty definition.[87]

D. Rent

Under ordinary principles, rent is an amount received as consideration for the use or occupation of, or right to use or occupy, immovable property or tangible movable property. As indicated above, the scope of the definition of rent for the purposes of the income tax may depend on the definition of royalties. If rent from the lease of movable property is included as a royalty, then the definition of rent may be confined to consideration for the lease of immovable property. Similarly, for the reasons given above, natural resource royalties may be treated as rent rather than as royalties.

As with transactions involving the payment of interest, it may be possible to structure a leasing transaction so as to convert rent into other forms, such as premiums on leased premises. Thus, a definition of rent for income tax purposes should include commonly used rent substitutes, such as premiums.[88]

IV. Issues of Tax Accounting

A. The Tax Period

1. Annual Measurement of Taxable Income

Given that the income tax is imposed on an annual basis, it is necessary to specify the income tax year. The tax year will normally be specified as the calendar year, or as a fiscal year set to complement the government's fiscal year. In the discussion below, this is referred to as the "normal tax year."

In many jurisdictions, taxpayers may be permitted to substitute a different 12–month period as their tax year.[89]However, allowing taxpayers to choose a tax year that differs from that of other taxpayers may result in some revenue loss if taxpayers are able to exploit the inconsistency.[90] It is suggested, therefore, that a taxpayer should be allowed to use a substitute tax year only with

---

[87]JPN Corp TL § 138(7); KEN ITA § 2; UGA ITA § 3. *See further infra* ch. 18, sec. IV(E).

[88]*E.g.*, UGA ITA § 2 (definition of rent).

[89]*E.g.*, AUS ITAA (1936) § 18; EST IT § 6; IDN LCIT § 12; LSO ITA § 49; UGA ITA § 40.

[90]An example is the use by a partnership of a substitute tax year to defer tax. *See infra* ch. 21, sec. II(B)(4). Another example involves taxpayer A paying at the end of its tax year a deductible expense to taxpayer B. If B is on a different tax year, B may not be taxed on the payment until later.

the permission of the tax administration, and, for this purpose, a procedure for applying for permission should be provided in the law or regulations. Permission should be granted only when the taxpayer demonstrates a legitimate need to use a substitute tax year.[91] To ensure that there is no loss or unacceptable deferral of tax resulting from the move to or from a substitute tax year, the tax administration should be allowed to prescribe conditions for the use of the substitute tax year. The right to apply for permission to use a substitute tax year may be restricted to corporate taxpayers or may extend to other business taxpayers (although cases where a sole trader can demonstrate a need to use a substitute tax year are likely to be rare).

A taxpayer using a substitute tax year may wish to cease to do so or to change to another substitute period (perhaps as a result of takeover). A procedure for making such changes may be provided, and, ordinarily, the rules outlined above should also apply to such applications.

Special rules are needed for "transitional" years when a taxpayer changes its tax year. The transitional period should be specified as the period commencing at the end of the taxpayer's last complete tax year to the beginning of the changed tax year. This ensures that the different years mesh with the rest of the legislation and prevents transitional problems, such as an extended tax year (greater than 12 months) when a taxpayer changes from one tax period to another.

The tax law is typically enacted (and amended) for application to the normal tax year. For example, changes to the income tax law may be stated to apply to the calculation of tax liability for a particular year and all subsequent years. Where taxpayers may use a substitute or transitional tax year, it is necessary to specify the law that is to apply to that tax year. For example, it may be provided that the law applicable to a normal tax year applies also to a substitute or transitional tax year that commences during the normal tax period.

2. Loss Carryovers

The annual measurement of income from economic activity that extends over a number of years is likely to lead to fluctuating measurements over the years, and this, combined with fluctuations in economic performance, may result in tax years in which allowable deductions exceed gross income (i.e., a taxpayer suffers a net loss for the year).

The tax law may provide for a net loss to be carried forward and allowed as a deduction in a subsequent tax year or carried back and allowed as an additional deduction in a previous tax year. The carryback of a net loss requires reopening the taxpayer's assessment for the prior tax year. From a theoretical perspective, taxpayers may be allowed virtually unlimited carryback and carry-

---

[91]For example, a case for using a substitute tax year may be established by a corporate taxpayer where the taxpayer belongs to a group of taxpayers (including foreign entities) with a group balance date for business accounting purposes that differs from the normal tax year.

over of net losses for recognition in years other than the years in which they are suffered,[92] but this theoretical case is tempered by two practical considerations.

First, there are significant divergences between the actual tax system adopted in any jurisdiction and the theoretical ideal. So long as it is impossible to guarantee the integrity of a comprehensive income tax base, safeguards against "bottomless holes" must be adopted; limitations on loss carryback or carryover are important elements in the safeguard armory.[93]

Second, unlimited carryback or carryover of net losses is possible only with sophisticated administrative resources, resources much greater than those available to taxpayers and administrators in most jurisdictions. For this reason, it is suggested that only loss carryovers be allowed. There may be some advantage in setting the loss-carryover period to coincide with the period in which the tax administration can amend an assessment (this period will also usually coincide with the period for which a taxpayer is required to keep records), but a longer period may also be specified. In countries where loss carryover is limited, examples of periods allowed are 5,[94] 7,[95] 8,[96] and 20[97] years.

Under a schedular income tax, carryover of losses will be provided for by reference to classes of income separately dealt with in the schedules. Even under a global income tax, carryover of losses may be to some extent schedularized.[98] Further, the carryover of losses by companies (and other entities as appropriate) whose ownership changes may be restricted to prevent trafficking in "loss" entities.[99]

---

[92]*See generally* Dale Chua, *Loss Carryforward and Loss Carryback, in* Tax Policy Handbook 141 (P. Shome ed. 1995). Examples of unlimited loss-carryforward rules are AUS ITAA (1997) § 36-15; GBR ICTA § 393 (there is also a three-year loss-carryback rule in ICTA § 393A); NZL ITA § 188; ZAF ITA § 20; SGP ITA § 37; ZMB ITA § 30. Other countries with unlimited carryovers include Belgium, Germany, Ireland, Luxembourg, and Sweden. *See* Commission of the European Communities, Report of the Committee of Independent Experts on Company Taxation 242 (1992).

[93]For example, a large backlog of loss carryovers, which resulted from a combination of factors, such as inadequate definition of inflation adjustment and abuse of tax holiday provisions, threatened to undermine the corporate income tax in Argentina in the late 1980s and early 1990s. *See* vol. 1, at 464–65.

[94]*See, e.g.,* EST IT § 21; FRA CGI §§ 156(I) and 209(I); HUN CTDT § 17(1); IDN LCIT § 6 (the Minister of Finance may decree that an eight-year period applies to specific types of businesses). Five-year periods are also allowed in Denmark, Greece, Italy, Japan, Portugal, and Spain. *See* Commission of the European Communities, *supra* note 92, at 242.

[95]*See* CAN ITA § 111 (a three-year carryback rule also applies); CHE LIFD § 67(I); Commission of the European Communities, *supra* note 92, at 242.

[96]*See* IND ITA § 72.

[97]*See* USA IRC § 172.

[98]*See infra* sec. IV(B)(5) (foreign currency losses); VI(B) (capital losses); USA IRC § 469 (passive activity losses).

[99]*See infra* ch. 20.

B. General Timing Issues in the Recognition of Income and Deductions

1. Method of Accounting

The use of a tax year to measure, on a year-by-year basis, income from economic activity that extends over more than one tax year requires rules to allocate income and expenses to particular tax years. Under both the balance-sheet method and the receipts-and-outgoings method, the allocation of income and expenses is made by reference to cash- or accrual-basis accounting systems. Both systems measure income when it is derived and recognize expenses when they are incurred, but the time at which a taxpayer is considered to have derived an amount or incurred an expense can differ significantly under the two systems.

Under the cash-basis system, income is derived when it is actually received by, or made available to, or applied to the benefit of, the taxpayer, and expenses are incurred when they are paid. Under the accrual-basis system, income is derived when the right to receive the income arises, and expenses are incurred when the obligation to pay arises.

Practices for determining the appropriate method of tax accounting to be applied by a taxpayer vary. In some countries, the law leaves the matter to be determined according to financial accounting principles[100] or by the courts.[101] In other countries, the tax law may, within limits, give taxpayers a choice in the method of accounting to be applied.[102] Whatever practice is adopted, salary and wage earners would normally account for income and deductions on a cash basis, and legal persons conducting businesses account for income and deductions on an accrual basis. Individuals conducting business typically enjoy some flexibility. In particular, it may be appropriate and simpler for smaller businesses to use cash-basis accounting. However, if small businesses are allowed to use cash-basis accounting, the threshold between cash-basis and accrual-basis taxpayers must be set out.[103]

When taxpayers are allowed a choice of accounting method, they may change their basis of accounting, particularly if a threshold is set above which

---

[100]See *infra* appendix (France, Germany).

[101]In Australia, the courts have made it clear that a taxpayer's method of accounting is to be determined according to legal principles and not according to generally accepted accounting principles. Nonetheless, the courts have developed legal principles that, in most cases, bear a close relationship to accounting principles.

[102]E.g., EST IT § 37 (an individual may use either the cash or the accrual basis of accounting for business income, but other taxpayers must use the accrual method); LSO ITA § 50 (a taxpayer may account on a cash or an accrual basis except when gross income for a tax year exceeds a monetary threshold, in which case the taxpayer must account for business income on an accrual basis in all subsequent years); UGA ITA § 41 (a taxpayer may account on a cash or an accrual basis, provided that the tax method chosen conforms to generally accepted accounting principles and subject to the tax commissioner's power to prescribe otherwise in particular cases).

[103]E.g., LSO ITA § 50. See *supra* note 102.

accrual-basis accounting must be applied. Changes in accounting methods can also arise from changes in the law, which may require all taxpayers to change the way they treat particular types of transactions.[104] When a taxpayer changes its method of accounting, transitional measures are needed to prevent lacunae or overlaps. A lacuna can arise, for example, when a taxpayer changes from a cash to an accrual basis because amounts billed but not received in the tax year prior to the change may escape taxation. This is because no amount has been received in the tax year in which the cash method applied, and no entitlement to receive has accrued in the tax year to which the accrual method applies.

It is suggested that transitional rules relating to a change in accounting method be drafted in broad terms because it may not be possible to anticipate every area needing such rules. In particular, the rules should not be confined to income and deductions because issues may arise in relation to tax offsets or other aspects of the income tax. A broad rule should permit adjustments to be made to the income, deductions, offsets, or other items as necessary to ensure that no item is omitted or taken into account more than once. It is also necessary to specify the tax year in which the adjustment is to be made. Ordinarily, this would be the first tax year under the changed method.[105] To properly monitor a change in tax accounting method, it may be provided that the change can be made only with the permission of the tax commissioner.

To minimize problems of administration, it may be decided to stipulate that once a taxpayer has been required to use the accrual method, the taxpayer must continue to use that method even if his or her gross income is less than the applicable threshold in a subsequent year. Some jurisdictions allow taxpayers to change back and forth between systems provided their income rises above or falls below the threshold for a number of consecutive years.[106]

The timing of recognition of income and expenses is crucial to the calculation of taxable income under both the receipts-and-outgoings system and the balance-sheet system. Under both systems, the choice between cash-basis accounting and accrual-basis accounting will have a significant effect on the measurement of taxable income. So, too, will the rules that govern exactly when receipts and expenses are recognized under cash- and accrual-basis accounting.

---

[104]For example, suppose the law is changed to require capitalization of certain costs of producing inventory that could be deducted under prior law as current expenses. An effect of this rule would be to increase the value of opening inventory for the tax year in which the changed method is first applied. This would lead to a gap because the opening inventory would exceed the prior year's closing inventory (valued under the old method).

[105]*But see* USA IRC § 481 (three-year spread).

[106]For example, Hungary requires taxpayers who are above the threshold for two consecutive years to change from cash-basis accounting to accrual-basis accounting and allows, at the taxpayer's option, unincorporated taxpayers to switch from accrual-basis accounting to cash-basis accounting if their taxable incomes fall below the threshold for two years. *See* Act XVIII of 1991, Accounting Act § 13.

In Anglo-American jurisdictions, the financial accounting rules are typically established by generally accepted accounting principles devised by the accounting profession through self-governing autonomous professional bodies. In civil law jurisdictions, the rules may be established by an accounting act or by the commercial code, supplemented by generally accepted accounting practices or by regulations. In both cases, it may be necessary or appropriate for the income tax law to specifically address particular types of transactions whose accounting treatment may be vulnerable to manipulation intended to distort the measurement of taxable income (usually by accelerating recognition of deductions or deferring recognition of income). It may, therefore, be desirable both to reinforce fundamental tax accounting rules with clarifying statements of principle and to adopt more detailed tax accounting rules for particular types of transactions. The extent to which specific rules need to be articulated for tax purposes, therefore, will differ from case to case and will depend on the clarity and specificity of the financial accounting rules. This qualification applies to much of the discussion below. Thus, while it is suggested that a number of rules be specified for tax purposes, in many jurisdictions it may not be necessary to provide an explicit tax rule because the matter is already taken care of appropriately by the accounting rules.

Specific tax accounting issues that may be addressed in the income tax statute are reviewed below.

2. Currency Translation Rules

A taxpayer's income, deductions, and offsets[107] must be measured in the national currency. With the greater integration of the world's economies, it is increasingly likely that a taxpayer will derive income or incur expenses in a foreign currency. The income tax law should therefore include rules for translating amounts denominated in a foreign currency into the national currency.

The basic rule should provide for currency translation on a transaction-by-transaction basis. Under such a rule, each receipt of income denominated in a foreign currency should be translated into the national currency at the time the income is derived. Similarly, each deductible expenditure denominated in a foreign currency should be translated into the national currency at the time the expenditure is incurred. The basic rule should be broadly stated so that it can apply to other amounts taken into account for tax purposes. For example, the translation rule should apply to foreign tax when a foreign tax credit applies.

If multiple exchange rates apply at the time the foreign currency is to be translated into the national currency, it is necessary to specify which rate is to apply. For example, when a buying and selling rate is specified for the relevant day (as is usually the case), it could be provided that the exchange rate midway

---

[107]For an explanation of tax offsets see ch. 14, sec. XI.

between the two for that day is to apply.[108] In other cases, there may an official exchange rate and a market rate, in which case a discretion may be provided to the administration to require the taxpayer to use the exchange rate that most accurately reflects the taxpayer's income.

A requirement to translate amounts denominated in a foreign currency on a transaction basis may be too onerous for a taxpayer who enters into multiple transactions in a foreign currency. For example, a taxpayer may have a foreign branch that engages in many transactions daily in the foreign country in which the branch is located. The branch's financial accounts are most likely to be maintained in the currency of that jurisdiction, and the tax law may allow the taxpayer to keep its tax accounts in that currency as well. In this case, the taxpayer will be permitted to calculate the taxable income of the branch in the foreign currency (referred to as the "functional currency" of the branch). The taxable income of the branch will be translated into the national currency at a specific exchange rate. Ordinarily, the rate specified would be the average exchange rate for the tax year. It may be desirable to permit tax authorities to substitute alternative translation formulas in special circumstances, such as when dealings are in a particularly volatile currency.[109] Alternative formulas may include the use of weighted averages (taking into account when most transactions take place) or even requiring translation by reference to shorter averaging periods, such as a month, a week, or even a day. Because the functional currency is the currency of the country in which the branch is located, when the foreign branch derives amounts denominated in a currency other than that currency, the ordinary transaction-based rules should apply to translate that other currency into the functional currency.

The currency translation rules apply only for the purpose of reporting in national currency any foreign currency amounts derived, incurred, or otherwise taken into account for tax purposes. Foreign currency transactions themselves may generate gains or losses for a taxpayer. These are discussed in section IV(B)(5), below.

3. Claim of Right

Taxpayers often receive or pay amounts that are disputed or potentially subject to dispute because, for example, the amount is received by mistake, is erroneously computed, or is the subject of a controversy about, say, performance or quality. The question is when these amounts should be recognized as income or deductions.

In the broadest sense, all amounts received and payments made are contingent in that they may later be subject to dispute. The income tax would not be workable if there were no recognition of receipts and expenses until the

---

[108]E.g., UGA ITA § 58.
[109]See vol. 1 at 460–62.

payments were settled (in some cases, this could involve waiting until the expiration of lengthy statutory limitation periods). To solve the problem, it is usual to require taxpayers to recognize amounts for which they make an initial claim of right and expenses that they are initially obligated to satisfy. This rule eliminates arguments by taxpayers that the recognition of an amount for tax purposes is unclear because its legal status is uncertain.

A claim-of-right rule may arise under general principles[110]or through specific legislative provision.[111] Under a claim-of-right rule, the normal tax accounting rules as to when income is derived or expenditures are incurred[112] apply to an amount even if there is a dispute or potential dispute as to entitlement or obligation.

When a claim-of-right rule applies, an issue arises as to the treatment of repayments made or received should it ultimately be found that the taxpayer is not entitled to receive, or obliged to pay, the amount. Two broad approaches may be identified for dealing with such cases. First, the assessment for the tax year in which the income or expenditure is recognized can be reopened and adjusted, so that the original inclusion or deduction and the repayment are treated as a single transaction; or, second, the adjustment can be made in the tax year in which the claim of right or obligation to pay is withdrawn.

While the first approach may be theoretically correct and is used in some industrial countries, it may not be administratively feasible for developing and transition countries to adopt such a rule. Consequently, the second approach is considered preferable.[113] Again, the basis of the timing of the adjustment will depend on the tax accounting rules applicable to the taxpayer. In the case of a cash-basis taxpayer, an adjustment is made to eliminate income and expenses when payments are refunded to the appropriate party. In the case of an accrual-basis taxpayer, the adjustment is made when the claim of right is given up. It will be necessary to coordinate the claim-of-right rules applicable to deducted expenditure with the general rules on recoupment of deductions.[114]

4. Price Uncertainty

It is not uncommon in commercial transactions for the determination of the price to be subject to some contingency. In this case, the uncertainty relates not to the existence of a right to receive or obligation to pay, but to the

---

[110]This is the case in the United States. See North American Oil Consolidated v. Burnet, 286 U.S. 417 (1932).

[111]E.g., UGA ITA § 45(1).

[112]See supra sec. IV(B)(1).

[113]This approach was adopted by the courts in the United States. See U.S. v. Lewis, 340 U.S. 590 (1951). In certain circumstances, under IRC § 1341, an adjustment is made to the current year based on the tax reduction that would have resulted by excluding an amount from income in the prior year.

[114]See ch. 14, sec. III(D)(2).

amount that is ultimately receivable or payable.[115] Contingent prices may be based on either "positive" contingency conditions or "negative" ones.

Positive contingency conditions usually establish a fixed base price and a further payment obligation in line with criteria such as productivity and profitability. For example, mining rights may be sold for a lump sum or installment payments plus an amount for each ton in excess of a floor amount mined. Similarly, a business may be sold for a lump sum or installment payments plus a percentage of profits for a given period following the sale.

A negative contingent price establishes a fixed base price that is subject to downward variation if a condition is not met. For example, mining rights may be sold for a lump sum or a series of installment payments that presume a certain tonnage will be available. In the event that the property produces less than the amount expected, the price will be adjusted downward by a particular amount for each ton.

A simple way of dealing with positive contingent prices is to dissect the sale price into two components—a right to receive or an obligation to pay a fixed amount (either as a lump sum or in installments) and a right to receive or an obligation to pay additional amounts contingent upon the occurrence of a specific event—and to recognize the two elements separately. The fixed amounts are recognized according to normal tax accounting rules (including those relating to installments, if relevant). The later contingent amounts are treated as though they attach to contingent rights or obligations that crystallize when the condition precedent to further payments is satisfied.

Negative contingency obligations are treated similarly in respect of the initial fixed payment or payments, but offsetting deductions or adjustments are made available when it becomes clear that the original payment was not correct.

While the approach suggested above for ignoring contingencies until the time they are resolved may result in some use of contingent terms to defer accrual of income, it is suggested that, from an administrative point of view, this is the most appropriate way for most developing and transition countries to deal with contingent amounts.

5. Foreign Currency Exchange Gains and Losses

While the translation of foreign-currency-denominated amounts is dealt with above, this section deals with gains and losses on foreign currency exchange transactions (and similar transactions described below). The primary issue in relation to such gains and losses is timing; although, for those income tax systems derivative of U.K. principles, there may also be characterization is-

---

[115]See *supra* sec. IV(B)(3), and *infra* sec. IV(C)(1) and (D)(1) for the treatment of amounts due or payable that are subject to uncertainty as to legal rights or obligations.

sues (i.e., whether the gain or loss is recognized under general principles or whether specific statutory recognition rules are needed).

The simplest type of foreign currency gain or loss is that realized in respect of foreign currency holdings. A taxpayer may have foreign currency holdings as a consequence of engaging in international transactions. For example, a taxpayer may receive foreign currency as payment for services rendered or goods supplied or may acquire foreign currency to meet a business expenditure.[116] Alternatively, a taxpayer may keep foreign currency holdings as a hedge against inflation or as an investment. In each case, the foreign currency is an asset of the taxpayer so that a gain or a loss will accrue as the value of the foreign currency fluctuates relative to the local currency during the period in which the foreign currency is held.

From the perspective of a comprehensive income tax base, the ideal tax treatment of foreign currency holdings is an annual valuation and recognition of gains and losses on an accrual basis. Many industrial countries are moving toward recognizing gains and losses related to financial instruments through an annual valuation commonly known as "mark to market."[117] If accrual-basis taxation is adopted for financial instruments, it may be important to recognize foreign exchange gains and losses on both the asset and the debt side on an accrual basis as well, so as to avoid serious distortions in the treatment of financial instruments generally. This is particularly important in highly inflationary economies.[118] However, unless the remainder of the income tax system measures gains consistently on an annual accrual basis, accrual-basis taxation of foreign currency holding gains and losses may be out of step with the remainder of the income tax system and may impose a considerable administrative burden on revenue authorities with limited experience in relatively sophisticated accrual measurement systems.

For these reasons, foreign currency holding gains and losses are often taken into account on a realization basis. Provided that foreign currency is treated as an asset, all dealings in foreign currencies (acquisitions, disposals, and conversions into other foreign currencies) can be dealt with by the provisions for recognizing income and losses that apply to ordinary property transactions.

A second source of foreign currency gains and losses arises from foreign currency loans and debt claims. Under a realization-based system, no special rules are needed for interest payments or interest receipts. If these are made in foreign currency, they are translated into local currency under the general

---

[116]While the foreign currency translation rules discussed in section IV(B)(2), above, apply in determining the amount in national currency of the income derived or the expenditure incurred in these cases, the taxpayer may actually hold the foreign currency for longer than the exchange day.

[117]For example, Canada, New Zealand, and the United States have adopted accrual-basis taxation for some financial instruments, and Australia proposes to do so.

[118]See vol. 1, ch. 13.

translation rules. With respect to repayment of principal, provision should be made for lenders and borrowers to recognize as a gain or a loss (as appropriate) the difference between the value in local currency of a loan principal at the time the loan is made and its value in local currency at the time it is repaid. Once again, however, if accrual-basis taxation is used for financial instruments, it may be more appropriate to recognize foreign exchange gains and losses on an accrual basis as well, by incorporating these changes into the annual valuation rules for obligations and debt claims denominated in foreign currency.

Special rules may be needed for rollovers or refinancing of foreign debt, which arises when a foreign debt owed by a taxpayer is rolled over or refinanced by a new loan in the same foreign currency from the same lender. In theory, there is no reason to treat this arrangement any differently from one in which a borrower repays a foreign currency loan by borrowing from a completely different borrower. However, in some jurisdictions, this type of arrangement may be treated for tax purposes as an extension of the original loan and may thus not be recognized for the purpose of measuring foreign currency gains or losses.

A third type of foreign currency gain or loss arises as a by-product of the separation of income and expense recognition and actual receipt or payment in accrual-basis accounting. Accrual-basis taxpayers will initially record the amount of income derived in a foreign currency or expenses incurred in a foreign currency by translating those values into their national currency at the time the income is derived or the expense incurred.[119] If there has been movement in the national currency against the foreign currency between those times and the times at which income is actually received or expenses paid, the amounts recorded in the taxpayer's accounts and the amounts actually received or paid will differ, and an adjustment must be made to "correct" the original amount recorded.

There are, in theory, three ways this can be done. First, the taxpayer's accounts can be reopened and recalculated, with the actual income received or expenses paid (as translated to the national currency) substituted for the amount originally recorded by the accrual-basis taxpayer. However, in many cases this correction requires reopening a previous year's accounts. As has been explained earlier, it is very rare for tax systems to adopt procedures involving reopening accounts of previous years because of the administrative burden this imposes on both taxpayers and tax officials.

A second solution is to correct the taxpayer's accounts by attributing the difference between the income or expense originally recorded and the amount actually received or paid to the specific account to which the amount relates. Thus, if an income amount turns out to be more or less than originally recorded, it is corrected by adding an amount to income or subtracting (as an al-

---

[119]*See supra* sec. IV(B)(2).

lowable deduction) an amount, depending on which way the currency moved. Similarly, if an ordinary deduction turns out to be more or less than originally recorded, the correction takes the form of an addition to income or an additional deduction, as the case may be. If the amount refers to the acquisition of property—either inventory, depreciable property, or nondepreciable property—the correction is made to the relevant property account. That is, if the expenditure is on inventory, an adjustment is made to the closing value of inventory in the year in which the expense is paid and the currency difference crystallized. Similarly, if the expenditure is on depreciable property, the tax value of the asset is adjusted in that year, and if the expenditure is on nondepreciable property, the cost base is adjusted in that year.

The second solution is the preferable option from a theoretical perspective, because it achieves the correct timing recognition of currency rate differences attributable to the purchase of property. Because the difference is attributed to the actual property acquired, it will be recognized in line with the recognition of the expense generally—for example, if the expense is for depreciable property, the cost of the property is adjusted and correctly recognized over the life of the property. Similarly, if the expense is for nondepreciable property, the corrected cost is recognized when there is a disposal of the property.

Whatever its theoretical merits, the second solution is not commonly used, probably because of the administrative costs it involves. The third solution, adopted in most jurisdictions, is by far the simplest from an administrative perspective. Under the third approach, when a foreign currency difference crystallizes because previously recorded foreign currency income is received or a previously recorded foreign currency expense is paid, the difference is simply recognized as a foreign currency gain or loss without any attempt to change underlying accounts by attributing the amount to the underlying transaction.

A realization system of recognizing foreign currency gains and losses should be accompanied by a quarantining system. This can be accomplished by treating foreign currency gains and losses as capital gains and losses, so that foreign currency losses are subject to the same limitation as capital losses.[120] Such a quarantining system is necessary to prevent taxpayers from entering into "wash" transactions intended to generate paper foreign exchange losses without any real change in the taxpayer's economic position. Without a quarantining system, if the local currency falls in value against a foreign currency in which a taxpayer has borrowed, the taxpayer with the foreign debt can trigger a recognition of a paper loss simply by refinancing the loan. By borrowing an additional amount in the foreign currency sufficient to repay the loan principal, the taxpayer is able to extinguish the original debt and claim a deduction for the difference between the value of the principal in local currency when the loan is made and the value at the time the loan is "repaid."

---

[120]See infra sec. VI(C).

Quarantining rules will not be needed if foreign exchange gains and losses are taken into account on an accrual basis. In this event, depending on the rules for interest income and expense and any inflation-adjustment rules, it may be appropriate to provide that foreign exchange gains and losses are treated as interest income and expenses, respectively. The rationale for this is that the exchange difference plus the actual interest paid on a foreign currency debt will be roughly equivalent (on an ex ante basis) to interest paid in domestic currency on a domestic currency debt. If foreign currency losses are not treated as interest expenses, then transactions can easily be structured to circumvent limitations on the deductibility of interest expense.

6. Bad Debts

For tax purposes, debts fall into two broad categories. The first comprises amounts recognized by an accrual-basis taxpayer as income on an account yet to be satisfied.[121] The second consists of amounts due on a loan provided by the taxpayer. Both types of debts represent a liability to the debtor and an asset to the creditor. In the ordinary course of events, if the debt proves unrecoverable, the creditor should be able to recognize a deduction or loss when the debt or loan is written off as unrecoverable. However, it is usual for special rules to be adopted to deal with both types of debt.

In some jurisdictions, losses on assets such as debts owing to the taxpayer will not be addressed by the general rules for measuring business income. In other jurisdictions, the loss may otherwise be recognized, but a specific rule is adopted to control the timing of loss recognition or to impose conditions on the recognition. The primary purpose of the special rule applying to loans that subsequently become uncollectible is to control the timing of the loss recognition. In some jurisdictions, only taxpayers in the business of money lending are allowed to recognize bad debts related to loans.[122]

There are two approaches to the calculation of bad debt deductions: the charge-off method and the reserve method.[123] Under the charge-off method, taxpayers are able to recognize bad debts only on previously recognized income amounts or on nonrecoverable loans when the debt owing to the taxpayer is determined to be worthless. The reserve method, by way of contrast, allows a taxpayer to partially recognize debts when they become doubtful and before they are fully written off for financial purposes. In other words, under the re-

---

[121] A cash-basis taxpayer who has provided a customer with goods or services may find it impossible to collect payment. Usually, tax systems provide no special rules for debts in this situation, although the taxpayer may be able to recognize the loss under general provisions or, in some cases, under capital gain and loss rules.

[122] E.g., AUS ITAA (1997) § 25-35; CAN ITA § 20(1)(p) (moneylenders and insurers); IND ITA § 36(1)(a), (2) .

[123] See generally Julio Escolano, *Loan Loss Provisioning, in* Tax Policy Handbook 145 (P. Shome ed. 1995).

serve method, taxpayers will be allowed a bad debt deduction for an outstanding loan before the debt is formally treated as nonrecoverable.

It is suggested that the charge-off method should be used by all taxpayers other than financial institutions to recognize losses on loans. The difficulty in applying the reserve method is that it requires an accurate estimation of debts that are most likely to prove worthless. Because of the nature of their business and the standards imposed by external regulatory bodies requiring continuous monitoring and maintenance of accurate information on outstanding loans owed to them, financial institutions should be able to determine with a reasonable degree of accuracy the percentage of loan debts owed to them in the tax year that will ultimately prove bad. Further, the determination of the bad debt reserve can be based on the classification of the institution's loans made according to the rules of the central bank or other regulatory agency. It should be possible to ensure, therefore, that the bad debt reserve claimed by the financial institution accurately reflects potential bad debts. For other taxpayers, under the reserve method, the bad debt reserve is likely to be an arbitrary percentage of outstanding debts at the end of the tax year.[124] For many taxpayers, such a rule simply results in an unwarranted deferral of recognition of a portion of the taxpayer's income to the following tax year.

The key issue in applying the charge-off method for recognizing a deduction for a bad debt is when a debt has become worthless (as discussed below, this is also relevant for the reserve method). Determining whether a debt is bad usually involves considering all the circumstances, including continual nonperformance, adequacy of security, and the financial state of the debtor. To prevent abuse, the law could provide that a taxpayer must have reasonably pursued without success certain avenues for recovery before the debt is written off for income tax purposes.

Where a bad debt deduction has been allowed under the charge-off method and the taxpayer subsequently recovers all or part of the debt, the amount recovered should be reincluded in gross income. Reinclusion in gross income may be pursuant to a specific rule to that effect or a rule applicable to the recoupment of deductions generally.

The reserve method contrasts with the charge-off method in that it allows recognition of some losses on debts before they are written off as nonrecoverable. Under this method, a reserve is established as an allowance against the eventuality that some outstanding (nonperforming) loans may prove to be uncollectible. The bad debt deduction in the reserve method thus includes recognition of doubtful debts that have not turned "bad" in the sense of being

---

[124]In countries that use the reserve method, the law may stipulate that the bad debt reserve is such amount as the administration considers reasonable given the taxpayer's circumstances. With such a rule, though, the practice often develops that the administration allows all taxpayers to claim an arbitrary amount as the bad debt reserve. Taxpayers who want to claim a reserve in excess of that amount then have to make a case to the tax commissioner.

written off. The method uses a formula that takes into account debts that are sufficiently doubtful at the end of a year to be recognized for commercial financial accounting purposes under relevant financial institution rules, doubtful debts that are finally recognized as nonrecoverable and written off during the year, and recoveries of debts previously written off.

Under a normal reserve method, regardless of how the actual reserve is calculated, the tax deduction for bad debts is computed as follows:

	(i) closing reserve (amount of doubtful debts at end of year),
less	(ii) opening reserve (amount of doubtful debts at end of prior year),
plus	(iii) debts written off during the tax year,
less	(iv) recoveries of previously written off debts,
equals	(v) bad debt deduction for the tax year.

The closing reserve for one year becomes the opening reserve for the following year. Determining the tax deduction for loan losses based on a reserve method may appear, at first, to provide a double deduction for loan losses. Each loss, however, is deducted for tax purposes only once. There is no double deduction because, once loans are written off, there is no end-of-year reserve with respect to those loans. The end-of-year reserve relates only to loans outstanding on the books at the end of the year. When a previously written-off amount is subsequently recovered, the deduction otherwise allowed must be reduced by the recovered amount. Thus, the previous deduction is reversed.

For example, suppose a taxpayer has at the end of its first year of doing business $1,000 of doubtful debts. No debts have been written off during this year. The taxpayer's bad debt deduction for the year would be calculated as follows:

Closing reserve = $1,000
Opening reserve = 0
Bad debt deduction = $1,000

Further debts that become doubtful during year 2 will be taken into account in determining the amount of the reserve, as will debts that were recognized as doubtful in year 1 and actually written off as nonrecoverable in year 2 and formerly doubtful debts that subsequently proved recoverable. If the taxpayer had another $1,000 of debts that became doubtful in the second year and wrote off half of the previous year's doubtful debts ($500) while collecting one-fourth of the previous year's debts that had been classified as doubtful, the second-year reserve deduction would be calculated as follows:

	(i) closing reserve ($1,250),
less	(ii) reserve at the beginning of the tax year ($1,000),
plus	(iii) debts written off during the tax year ($500),
equals	(iv) bad debt deduction for the tax year ($750).

The closing reserve for year 2 is the amount of doubtful debts remaining at the end of the tax year. This would comprise $250 from the previous tax year ($500 of the previous year's doubtful debts is no longer doubtful, because it has been written off, and $250 is no longer doubtful because it was subsequently collected) plus $1,000 arising in year 2.

Some of the previous year's reserve amount representing doubtful debts ($500 worth) has actually been written off. The reserve is reduced by that amount, and the same amount is included directly in the bad debt deduction by adding it to the formula for deduction of bad debts.

Where a previously written-off amount is subsequently recovered, the deduction otherwise allowed must be reduced by the recovered amount. Thus, if we assume in year 3 that the taxpayer encounters another $1,000 of doubtful debts as of the end of the year, writes off no further debts, and recovers $200 of a previously written-off debt, the taxpayer's doubtful debt deduction for year 3 would be as follows:

	(i) closing reserve (amount of doubtful debts remaining, $2,250),
less	(ii) reserve at the beginning of the tax year ($1,500),
plus	(iii) debts written off during the tax year (0),
less	(iv) recoveries of previously written-off debts ($200),
equals	(v) bad debt deduction for the tax year ($550).

Note the closing reserve for year 3 (and thus the opening reserve for year 4) takes into account doubtful debts, but is not affected by recoveries, while it was affected by debts written off. Debts written off will no longer be included in the reserve, while recoveries have no effect on the amount of doubtful debts held by a taxpayer. All that has happened is that part of a previous deduction has been reversed.

C. Timing Issues in the Recognition of Income

1. Income Subject to Potential Claims or Charges

Financial accounting attempts to measure the income of a continuing business over an extended period. Tax accounting, by contrast, measures *annual* net gains to determine a net amount that should bear a tax liability. The different objectives of the two accounting systems explain why they often diverge significantly with respect to their treatment of income when there is some doubt about the taxpayer's right to retain the income or when the receipt of income is tied to possible future outgoings.

Cases for which there may be some doubt about the taxpayer's right to retain the income fall into two categories. The first is attributable to the attendant risk in business that once a service or product has been delivered, the customer may demand a refund because of dissatisfaction with the service or product. This category is addressed through the claim-of-right rule discussed in section IV(B)(3).

The second type of doubt arises in respect of income that relates to the future provision of services or goods. An example of doubt about a taxpayer's right to retain income is the receipt of an up-front payment for a service or product that will be delivered over a period of years—for example, under a contract to provide continuing lessons or a contract for a multiyear magazine subscription. Similarly, a taxpayer may accept a refundable deposit for delivery of a product or service in a future year. An example of a case where the receipt of income is tied to possible future outgoings is the sale of a product, such as a car, subject to a multiyear warranty. Financial accounting rules often treat both types of situation similarly, while it is not unusual for tax accounting rules to prescribe greatly different treatment of the two situations.

Financial accounting rules tend to spread recognition of income over the periods during which the retention right is uncertain or the possibility of related expenses remains. This is normally done through reserves. Where a business derives income in either of these situations, it will establish a notional reserve in its financial accounts to indicate that part of the income received is not available for use or distribution, but rather is being held to satisfy a possible repayment obligation or to cover anticipated future costs associated with the income. The net income reported for financial accounting purposes will not include amounts in reserves.

Tax accounting rules often distinguish between the two situations and sometimes allow taxpayers to defer recognition of income that is subject to possible repayment while denying deferral of income merely because its receipt may give rise to future expenses.

The rule allowing taxpayers to defer recognition of income that is subject to possible repayment may reside as a general tax accounting principle established by the courts or may be incorporated into the tax legislation if it is not normal for the courts in a jurisdiction to adopt tax accounting rules outside the statute. Where the rule is based on judicial doctrines, it is usually established by interpreting the term "derived" with respect to income as meaning a right to retain income without the risk of return. Thus, in the case of a prepayment for the provision of future services, a taxpayer will be treated as deriving the income not when it is received but rather on a year-by-year basis, as services are provided and customers lose their rights to refunds.[125] If the rule is established through legislation, it is important that the onus be placed on the taxpayer to demonstrate, on the basis of previous experience or statistical evidence, that there is a genuine risk that the taxpayer's customers will cancel the contract for future services or products and upon cancellation will be entitled to a refund of amounts previously paid.[126]

---

[125]For example, the rule is established by judicial doctrine in Australia.

[126]*E.g.*, CAN ITA § 20(1)(m), which requires that payment be for goods or services that it is "reasonably anticipated" will have to be delivered or rendered after the end of the year. *See also* USA IRC § 455 (deferral of prepaid subscription income).

This approach is not universal. In some countries, tax authorities have interpreted tax accounting principles to require immediate recognition of prepaid amounts. This approach may be modified in particular instances.[127] However, taxpayers are usually not required to recognize refundable deposits or security deposits (such as those paid to utility companies to guarantee payment of accounts or to landlords to cover possible damage to the premises). Rather, these are treated as akin to loans or receipts over which the taxpayer has no claim of right.[128]

The focus on annual measurement explains why tax accounting rules make no similar provision for potential future expenses, such as warranty expenses connected with current derivation of income. Once again, the lack of recognition for possible future obligations can be the result of judicial doctrines or specific statutory prohibitions.[129]This approach is consistent with the concept of economic performance discussed in section IV(D)(1), below.

2. Installment Sales

Where a taxpayer sells property on an "installment" basis, payment may be made over a number of tax periods. Some jurisdictions have allowed both cash-basis and accrual-basis taxpayers to recognize income from the sale over the period of payments, under the so-called installment method.[130]Where this system is used, taxpayers recognize gain on a pro rata basis over the payment period, assuming that each payment contains an equal return of cost and each payment therefore also contains an equal percentage of the total profit realized.[131]

The installment method involves a number of serious tax policy problems. Some problems are relevant to all disposals of property, while others are relevant only to disposals that give rise to capital gains, particularly if capital gains are treated preferentially relative to other gains.

If capital gains are treated more preferentially than interest income, vendors may seek to disguise all or part of the interest component of installment payments as a capital gain by raising the total price and reducing the interest charged. To combat this, special measures may be needed to "carve

---

[127]For example, in the United States, tax authorities have interpreted tax accounting rules to deny deferral of income related to goods and services to be provided in future years, but have adopted some exceptions, such as a ruling that allows taxpayers to recognize income for services over two years in some cases (Rev. Proc. 71-21, 1971-2 CB 349) and to defer recognition of payment for the sale of some types of inventory and other specified assets (Treas. Reg. § 1.451-5).

[128]See supra sec. IV(B)(3).

[129]See, e.g., CAN ITA § 20(7).

[130]E.g., USA IRC § 453.

[131]It has been observed that the U.S. rule results in a reduction of tax liability compared with a vendor who receives the whole price at the time of disposal. This is because no account is taken of the effect of time on the value of money in determining the amount of each taxable installment. See Marvin A. Chirelstein, Federal Income Taxation 284–85 (1994).

out" the implicit interest component of each payment so it can be taxed as interest.[132]

Even if capital gains receive no tax preference compared with interest income and appropriate interest is charged on installment payments, or if gains on the disposal of property are treated as business income, the installment basis of income recognition can lead to serious inequity and inefficiency. This is because it effectively subsidizes vendors providing vendor finance relative to vendors who sell for cash, leaving the purchasers to finance the acquisition from third-party lenders. The taxpayer selling on an installment basis (and thus providing vendor finance) can defer recognition of gain and payment of tax until payments are made, while the vendor selling for up-front consideration enjoys no tax deferral. If the tax savings from deferral are passed on in part to the purchaser (through a lower sale price or interest rate), installment sale vendors will also enjoy a market advantage compared with those unable to finance the sale of their own property.

The solution to this problem that some jurisdictions have adopted is to recognize the entire sale price at the time an installment sale contract commences.[133] This has the effect of treating the installment sale as a sale for full value to the purchaser, supplemented by a loan from the vendor to the purchaser.

3. Long-Term Contracts

It is not uncommon for businesses to enter into contracts that extend beyond the tax period and that require both performance and payment to be made over the life of the contract. These contracts are referred to as long-term contracts.

In a long-term contract, the total payment to be received by the taxpayer is often set out in the contract.[134] In a sense, the taxpayer is therefore "entitled" to receive the money upon entering into the contract, although the taxpayer is not entitled to actual payment at that time. However, unlike with an installment sale, the taxpayer has not performed all that is required under the contract. The various rationales set out earlier for up-front recognition of gain on an installment sale do not apply to long-term contract arrangements, because the arrangement is not a substitute for the up-front payment that would otherwise take place, as with an installment sale. In economic terms, it may be appropriate to recognize a certain amount of income upon signing the contract based on the present value of the profit that the taxpayer is expected to make. However, this amount will often be impossible to measure.

---

[132]*E.g.*, AUS ITAA (1936) § 256; CAN ITA § 16(1); USA IRC § 63(b).

[133]*E.g.*, AUS ITAA (1936) § 160ZD(1)(a); USA IRC § 453(b)(2), (e), (g), (k) (providing circumstances under which installment method does not apply).

[134]This will not always be the case. For example, a contract may be of the cost-plus type or may involve an incentive fee.

The adoption of specific rules for long-term contracts can avoid confusion, particularly for accrual-basis taxpayers, about the recognition time for income and deductions arising under a long-term contract. Two accounting methods commonly used for long-term contracts are the percentage-of-completion method and the completed-contract method. Under the percentage-of-completion method, profit is recognized in proportion to the progress made on the contract during the relevant accounting period. In other words, the profit is recognized as it "emerges" over the life of the contract. Under the completed-contract method, profit is not recognized until the contract is substantially performed. Accounting standards now clearly favor the percentage-of-completion method as a better measure of "periodic accomplishment" over the life of the contract. From a tax perspective, the completed-contract method gives rise to an unwarranted deferral of tax.

The principal issue under the percentage-of-completion method is, not surprisingly, how to measure the percentage of the contract completed during the taxable year. A relatively administrable, although somewhat arbitrary, rule is to assume that the percentage of completion equals the percentage of total contract costs incurred during the year.[135]

Example

A contractor enters into a construction contract to be completed over three years. Under the contract, the contractor expects to incur expenses of $500,000 and to derive gross income of $1,500,000, for a taxable net profit of $1,000,000. In the first year of the contract, the contractor incurs expenses of $200,000. The contractor's expected taxable net profit is allocated to each tax year in a pro rata fashion, using the ratio of actual expenditure to expected total expenditure as the key. Thus, in this example, the recognized taxable profit in the first year would be $1,000,000 × $200,000/$500,000 = $400,000. If expenses of $200,000 were also incurred in the second year, recognized taxable profit in that year would also be $400,000.

Long-term contracts that envisage performance and payment made over a number of tax years fall into the broad categories of fixed-price and cost-plus contracts. Under the former, the total consideration for the contract is agreed on before work begins; under the latter, the customer agrees to pay the taxpayer a consideration based on costs incurred plus a profit margin.[136] The formula used to determine annual recognition of profits under the percentage-of-completion method will initially use estimates of total profit in fixed-price contracts or total profit and total costs in cost-plus contracts. As the contract proceeds, the calculation must be revised to reflect the changed base figures

---

[135]E.g., UGA ITA § 46.

[136]A variant is the cost-plus-incentive-fee contract, where the contractor's profit margin may vary depending on the extent of cost overruns, timeliness of completion, or other factors. The various kinds of contracts are described here for information; they should not be defined as separate categories for tax purposes.

and an adjustment made for what turned out to be the incorrect amounts previously recognized. An adjustment may also need to be made where profits change because, for example, the contractor is paid an "incentive fee" for early completion.

The correction for changed expenses or profit can be done two ways. Some jurisdictions use a sophisticated "look back" method to reallocate contract profits over the years of the contract at the time it is completed.[137] While this method is useful for minimizing tax avoidance, it is probably too complicated to be advisable for most developing and transition countries. A simpler alternative is to revise the calculation and make adjustments when the change becomes known. The revision approach can lead to a loss in one year even though the total project yields a profit. The phenomenon can be illustrated using the example provided above and assuming that costs in the final year run to $300,000 instead of the expected $100,000.

Example

If there were no cost overrun in the final year, the contractor's taxable income for the third year would be $1,000,000 × $100,000/$500,000 = $200,000. However, if the costs were $300,000, the total profit on the project would be only $750,000 ($1,500,000 gross payment less $750,000 total expenses). The taxpayer has already recognized $800,000 in profits in previous years. Thus, in the third year of the contract, the taxpayer would recognize a loss of $50,000.

The loss recognized in the final year can be dealt with under the normal rules for loss carryovers. One problem that may emerge for developing and transition countries is that the contract may be the taxpayer's only income-producing activity in the country, so that there is no benefit in a loss-carryover rule. To overcome this problem, a special loss-carryback rule for long-term contracts can be formulated.[138]

The definition of a long-term contract subject to the long-term contract income-recognition rule should include any contract for the manufacture, installation, or construction of property (including a contract for the performance of services related to such manufacture, construction, or installation), provided the expected term of the contract extends over more than six months and the contract is not completed in the tax year. This would ensure the rule applies to, for example, the construction of buildings, bridges, dams, pipelines, tunnels, and other civil engineering projects; construction management contracts in relation to such projects; the construction of major items of plant; and contracts for the refurbishing of hotels and other business premises. The long-term contract rules would not apply to most service contracts, however.

---

[137]*E.g.*, USA IRC § 460.

[138]*E.g.*, UGA ITA § 46 (loss carryback allowed only with the permission of the tax commissioner).

D. Timing Issues in the Recognition of Expenses

1. Economic Performance and Recognition of Expenses

A fundamental principle that merits reinforcement is the nexus between legal and economic liability for accrual-basis taxpayers and between payment and economic liability for cash-basis taxpayers. It was noted earlier that an accrual-basis taxpayer is normally understood to have incurred an expense when the obligation to pay arises, and a cash-basis taxpayer is treated as having incurred an expense when it is paid. It is important that the "obligation to pay" for accrual-basis taxpayers and "amount paid" for cash-basis taxpayers be interpreted in an economic sense, not in a strict legal contractual sense.

This means that the act of legally entering into a contract that will obligate a taxpayer to make future payments should not in itself cause an accrual-basis taxpayer to be treated as if it had incurred the payments. In an economic sense, an obligation to make payment in the future is not actually "incurred" until there has been an economic performance that gives rise to the obligation to pay. While a taxpayer may commit to make a payment in the future for services to be provided in the future, the obligation is not actually incurred until the services are provided, as the obligation is only contingent prior to the provision of services. For example, a taxpayer can enter into a long-term contract to rent premises for a number of years. The rental obligation with respect to each of the future years is not actually incurred until those years. Similar principles apply to cash-basis taxpayers who actually make payments for services or goods that will be received over several years. Insofar as the payment relates to future years, it does not represent an expense incurred at the time of payment. Rather, it is akin to a security deposit to the recipient to guarantee the price for the goods or services to be delivered in the future. If, for some reason, the contract is terminated before delivery, the taxpayer should be entitled to a refund, either under the contract itself or under contract law principles in most jurisdictions.

The basic deduction provisions in many income tax systems may not be interpreted to operate in this strict way. In particular, immediate deductibility under the general deduction provision is normally not restricted to expenditures that are consumed in a tax period.[139] Consequently, in the absence of a specific rule to the contrary, an accrual-basis taxpayer that enters into a long-term commitment for the purchase of goods or services may be allowed to deduct the entire amount payable under the contract. Similarly, a cash-basis taxpayer who makes a prepayment for the future delivery of goods or services may be able to deduct the entire amount paid. To prevent this result, some coun-

---

[139]An exception is Indonesia, where it is provided that costs of earning income that have a useful life of more than one year may not be deducted at once, but rather are to be deducted under the amortization rules. The position under the Indonesian income tax conforms closely to the theoretical model outlined in the text. See IDN IT §§ 6(1)b, 9(2), and 11(10).

tries have added to their income tax laws a supplementary rule, sometimes known as an economic performance rule, to reinforce the principles that accrual-basis taxpayers should recognize expenses as incurred when the obligation to pay has crystallized and not when the agreement creating the obligation is entered into, and that cash-basis taxpayers should recognize expenses as paid when the contracted good or service is provided and not when initial consideration is given to the supplier. The economic performance rule provides that an expense will not be treated as incurred before economic performance with respect to the expense occurs.

If it is thought that a general economic performance rule applicable to all taxpayers is not needed because under general principles accrual-basis taxpayers are considered to have incurred expenses only in the years in which goods or services are provided, then a prepayment rule applicable to cash-basis taxpayers should be provided.[140]

2. Accruing Liabilities

A taxpayer's ongoing business will normally give rise to accruing liabilities that will not have to be satisfied until a future tax year. Common examples include the liability of borrowers to pay compounding interest when a debt matures, the liability of insurance companies to pay insurance claims related to the current year when the claim is settled in a future year, the growing liability of extractive industries to restore property when mining is completed, and the obligation of employers to pay future benefits to employees on the basis of current work.

No consistent approach is universally adopted to address these issues. It is generally the case that accruing liabilities that give rise to actual debts can be recognized as they accrue. This is true, for example, with a compounding interest obligation, where compounded interest is treated as a new deposit by the lender. While there are exceptions to the rule, discussed below, taxpayers generally are not permitted to recognize accruing liabilities where no actual debt is created by the accruing liability. In some cases, however, tax legislation may allow recognition for specific types of accruing liabilities, such as to fund environmental restoration or to provide pension or retirement benefits to employees where the funds are notionally allocated to a reserve by the taxpayer.

The simplest statutory approach to the problem is to enact a general rule that, subject to specific exceptions,[141] denies taxpayers deductions for an accruing liability until the liability has crystallized into an actual obligation to pay or created an actual debt of the taxpayer. Possible exceptions can then be

---

[140]*E.g.*, AUS ITAA (1936) §§ 82KZL–82KZO. This applies to all types of prepayments, but does not apply where the benefit is provided within 13 months of the date the expenditure was incurred, where the prepayment is required by legislation or court order, or where the prepayment is less than A$1,000.

[141]Such as for bad debts of financial institutions. *See* secs. IV(B)(6) and VI(D).

considered on a case-by-case basis where the interests of the taxpayers can be balanced against the revenue costs of the exceptions. Appropriate conditions can be attached to each exception allowed. For example, to qualify for recognition of an accruing liability, a taxpayer may be required to establish an actual reserve in its accounts and insulate those funds from encroachment to satisfy other liabilities of the taxpayer.

3. Repairs and Improvements

An area that gives rise to disputes in a number of jurisdictions is that of expenditures for repairs and improvements. It is common for income tax systems to distinguish between expenses for these two purposes and to allow deductions for the former, while the latter are capitalized into the cost base of the assets to which they relate and recognized over time through the depreciation system or as part of the cost base when calculating a gain or loss on final disposal.

From an income tax perspective, the distinction between repairs and improvements is quite artificial. The complicated and contradictory case law in many jurisdictions illustrates well how impossible it is in practice to establish mutually exclusive camps and to classify categorically work on assets as either repairs, improvements, or acquisitions of new subassets that are incorporated into larger assets.[142] Even if a satisfactory method of distinguishing repairs, improvements, or acquisition of replacement parts can be devised, the distinction is unlikely to yield appropriate tax treatment; as often as not, the classification has no relevance to the life of the benefit acquired, which is the principal criterion determining recognition and timing for business expenses.

The application of the expense recognition principle—recognition over the life of the benefit—is almost impossible to apply to many repairs, alterations, or improvements, because there is often no way in which the effective life of these benefits can be estimated. Accordingly, a surrogate formula is needed to determine the tax treatment of such outgoings.

The simplest rule is one that eliminates the need to distinguish between repairs, improvements, or the installation of replacement parts through the use of a simple mathematical formula (sometimes known as a repair allowance).[143] The formula system presumes that, on average, the amount of repairs needed will bear a relatively fixed relation to the total value of depreciable property. Any excess over this amount can be presumed to be an improvement. Thus, it is logical to presume that high expenditures relative to the value of the relevant property are likely to give rise to benefits that enjoy a life approximating that of the underlying property, while low expenditures relative to the value of that property are likely to enjoy briefer lives. For example, expenditures on repairs or improve-

---

[142]See infra ch. 17, sec. II(B).
[143]See infra ch. 17, note 50.

ments that exceed, say, 5 percent of the value of an asset can be considered to be the purchase price of a long-term benefit and added to the cost base of the asset, while expenses less than that threshold can be considered to be costs incurred to derive short-term benefits and deducted immediately.[144]

If the traditional approach of immediate write-offs for repairs and capitalization of improvements is adopted in preference to a repair allowance, a special rule for initial repair expenses should be considered. Where a taxpayer acquires a used asset and incurs initial repair expenses to prepare the property for use in the taxpayer's business, it is arguable that the initial expenses should be wholly capitalized and treated as part of the acquisition price for the asset. If the vendor incurs the repair expenses and sells the property in a ready-to-use form, the costs would be directly incorporated into the cost of the asset. A purchaser should not be able to accelerate deductions by purchasing property not ready for use and then repairing the property to bring it to usable form.

There are three ways in which a rule of this kind can be formulated. First, one could establish a bright-line rule under which all repairs within, say, six months of an asset's placement in service are treated as capital costs, regardless of the facts of the individual case. Alternatively, one could establish a presumption that repairs undertaken within a certain period are capital in nature, which the taxpayer can rebut by showing that the repair is genuinely a repair rather than a set-up cost. A third approach is to adopt a cost formula similar to the repair allowance described above. For example, the rule can apply only to repair costs incurred within one year of the acquisition of an asset and allow a deduction for repair costs of up to 5 percent of the original acquisition cost while requiring taxpayers to capitalize repair costs in excess of that amount incurred within that year.

4. Inventory

Income tax systems commonly measure gains and losses from the acquisition and disposal of inventory separately from gains and losses arising from the disposal of other property.[145] The essential purpose of tax accounting rules relating to inventory is to ensure that a deduction is not allowed for the cost of acquiring inventory until the inventory is sold.[146] This policy objective is consistent with the general rules regarding gains and losses from the disposal of nonwasting assets, but separate rules are adopted for inventory in recognition of the continual turnover of this type of property.

---

[144]Where a pooling depreciation system is used (see infra ch. 17, sec. III(G)), the 5 percent threshold can be applied by considering expenditures on all assets in a pool relative to the value of the pool.

[145]See generally Dale Chua, Inventory Valuation, in Tax Policy Handbook 139 (P. Shome ed. 1995).

[146]See supra sec. II(C)(2).

As with other tax accounting rules, the rules relating to inventory may be based on commercial accounting standards or may be specified in the tax law or in regulations. An initial issue that should be addressed in the inventory rules is what is encompassed in inventory and thus subject to those rules.[147] In some jurisdictions, inventory is not defined and, therefore, takes its normal commercial meaning.[148] In other jurisdictions, it is defined, but in terms largely declaratory of its normal commercial meaning.[149] Essentially, inventory is anything that is turned over in the ordinary course of business (i.e., it is the things in which a business trades). Inventory may be bred or grown (such as livestock and agricultural produce), manufactured, purchased, or otherwise acquired (such as through a barter transaction). Inventory is not confined to finished goods. It includes goods in the process of production (i.e., work in process), and raw materials and supplies that are to be consumed directly or indirectly in the production of goods.

Inventory is not limited to tangible movable property. In particular circumstances, immovable or intangible property can be inventory. Generally, there is nothing in the intrinsic nature of any particular item that gives it the character of inventory. The same item may be inventory in the hands of one person but not in the hands of another. For example, a motor vehicle may be inventory in the hands of a motor vehicle dealer but not in the hands of a person who purchases it from the dealer. In fact, a person may hold the same type of item in different capacities. For example, the private motor vehicle of a motor vehicle dealer will not be part of the inventory of the dealer, nor will a vehicle acquired to deliver parts or pick up customers.[150]

The system used to defer recognition of the cost of inventory will depend on whether the income tax system generally uses the receipts-and-outgoings method or the balance-sheet method to determine business income. There are two equivalent systems for measuring the cost of inventory in jurisdictions in which the receipts-and-outgoings method is used to calculate taxable business income. The simpler of the two systems is based on financial accounting principles.[151] In this case, a deduction is allowed for the cost of goods sold during the tax year calculated according to the following formula:

(Opening inventory + cost of purchases) – closing inventory.

An equivalent system used in some jurisdictions is to allow a deduction for the cost of inventory acquired during the tax year, followed by a reinclusion

---

[147] In jurisdictions that rely on British legal concepts, inventory is commonly referred to as "trading stock."

[148] Singapore is an example of such a jurisdiction.

[149] E.g., AUS ITAA (1997) § 70-10.

[150] It is possible that an asset may change status. For example, a motor vehicle dealer may take his or her private motor vehicle into inventory, or vice versa. The tax consequences of a change in status of an asset are discussed in sec. V(E)(1), below.

[151] E.g., UGA ITA § 47.

in gross income of the value of closing inventory.[152] The reincluded amount is the excess for the tax year of closing over opening inventory. Where opening inventory exceeds closing inventory, a deduction should be allowed for the excess to ensure that expenses incurred in prior years are recognized when stock is eventually sold.[153]

It should be provided that the value of closing inventory for a tax year becomes the value of opening inventory for the next tax year. Items included in inventory should follow the accounting rules for purchases and sales. Thus, if the taxpayer has recognized the cost of inventory that is not yet physically received, it should nevertheless be included in inventory, and, if the taxpayer has recognized income from the sale of inventory, it should not be included in inventory, even if physically on hand at the close of the year.

In many jurisdictions, taxpayers are able to value closing inventory at the lower of cost or market value. Thus, if the market value of inventory falls below its cost,[154] a taxpayer can recognize the loss in the tax year in which it occurs without actually disposing of the inventory. In some jurisdictions, taxpayers can also use the higher of market value and cost to value closing inventory, to bring forward recognition of gain prior to disposal.[155] There is no persuasive policy reason in favor of the latter concession, and it may be used for tax minimization or avoidance purposes by generating gains to offset losses that might not otherwise be recognized for tax purposes. Accordingly, while the choice between the lower of cost or market value may be incorporated into the inventory rules, a choice of higher of cost or market value is not recommended.

In the ordinary case, closing inventory will be valued at cost. Two particular issues arise when valuation is based on cost: first, the identification of amounts included in the cost of inventory that is manufactured or constructed by the taxpayer; and second, the valuation of closing inventory where the cost of inventory has varied and it is not possible to trace individual items of stock.

The first issue with cost concerns the extent to which ancillary costs such as labor costs or factory overhead costs should be included in the cost of manufactured or constructed inventory. If such costs are included in the cost of manufactured or constructed inventory, they will not be recognized until the inventory is sold. Two basic models are used to determine the cost of manufactured or constructed inventory. Terminology differs from jurisdiction to jurisdiction, but the fundamental features of the two models are similar across tax systems. Under the simplest method—commonly known as the prime-cost method—the cost of inventory is the sum of direct material costs, direct labor

---

[152]E.g., AUS ITAA (1997) § 70-35.

[153]A variation on this approach applies in New Zealand where taxpayers are allowed a deduction for the cost of inventory and a deduction for the value of opening inventory, while the value of closing inventory is included in gross income. See NZL ITA §§ 85, 104.

[154]This may arise, for example, because of damage, deterioration, or obsolescence.

[155]E.g., AUS ITAA (1997) § 70-45; NZL ITA § 85(4).

costs, and variable factory overhead costs. Direct material costs are the costs of materials that become an integral part of the inventory produced. Direct labor costs are the costs of labor directly involved in the production of inventory. Variable factory overhead costs are those factory overhead costs that vary directly with the volume of production. Under the more complex method—the absorption-cost method—a percentage of fixed factory overhead costs (such as rent) is included in the cost of inventory. Where absorption costing is used, rules must be adopted to distinguish costs that are attributable to the inventory and costs that should be considered general overhead expenses (and are thus deductible without reference to the inventory provisions).[156]

Different rules may be adopted for cash-basis and accrual-basis taxpayers with respect to the amounts included in the cost of inventory. A cash-basis taxpayer may be allowed to determine the cost base of inventory using either the prime-cost or the absorption-cost method, while accrual-basis taxpayers are usually required to use the absorption-cost method.[157]

The second issue that arises when valuation is based on cost relates to the identification of items of inventory that are on hand at the end of the tax year. This is necessary where the cost of acquiring, constructing, or manufacturing different units of inventory has varied. For unique products, businesses can trace the actual movement of stock and thus ascertain the exact cost of closing inventory. More commonly, businesses buy and sell generic stock, and there is no record of the movements of individual items. Thus, for inventory other than unique traceable stock, a presumptive tracing rule must be applied. While a number of variations are used in different jurisdictions, most fall into one of three inventory tracing methods, the first-in-first-out (FIFO), average-cost, or last-in-first-out (LIFO) system. Under the FIFO method, the cost of inventory on hand at the end of the tax year is determined on the assumption that items purchased or produced first are sold first, so that the items on hand at the end of the year are those last purchased or produced. Under the average-cost method, the cost of inventory on hand at the end of the tax year is determined by reference to the weighted-average cost of all items on hand at the beginning of the tax year and purchases during the year. Under the LIFO method, the cost of inventory on hand at the end of the tax year is determined on the assumption that items purchased last are sold first, so that items on hand at the end of the year are the earliest items purchased or produced. In a period of

---

[156]Ordinarily, general, administrative, and selling expenses are not included in the cost of inventory. *See, e.g.,* USA IRC 263A and the regulations thereunder (in 1986, the types of expenses required to be included in the cost of producing inventory were substantially broadened). As an economic matter, however, all costs incurred by a firm should ultimately be recovered as part of the cost of production, so that arguably all expenses of a firm should be allocated to costs of production. Such a rule would also be simpler to administer, because it would minimize the requirement to draw distinctions among different types of costs. *See* Victor Thuronyi, *Tax Reform for 1989 and Beyond,* 42 Tax Notes 981–96 (Feb. 20, 1989).

[157]*E.g.,* UGA ITA § 47(5).

moderate inflation, the use of the LIFO method for valuing trading stock will provide taxpayers with a simple compensation for the effects of inflation on measuring profits.[158] However, the LIFO method is complex and results in undervaluation of inventory.[159]

5. Research and Development

The longevity of benefits derived as a result of expenditure on research and development is incapable of measurement at the time the expense is incurred. It may be presumed, however, that some long-term benefit is realized as a consequence of any research and development expense. For example, even if a research and development outlay yields no direct, relevant results, the expenditure may provide long-term benefits by narrowing down options and suggesting possible paths for other research initiatives.

Because it is not possible to estimate accurately the useful life of benefits resulting from research and development expenses, a hypothetical life must be adopted. In many jurisdictions, doubts about the longevity of benefits from research and development expenses are resolved in the taxpayer's favor through the use of relatively short amortization periods, or immediate deductions, for these outgoings.[160] Such treatment is also seen as a tax expenditure (i.e., tax concession) that encourages research and development.[161] An additional argument in favor of allowing an immediate deduction for research and development costs is that it may be difficult to distinguish them from other general business expenses. There are, however, disadvantages to the use of an amortization period for research and development outgoings that is significantly shorter than the period applicable to other capital expenses. Most important, generous treatment of research and development expenses will lead to taxpayers recharacterizing expenses as research and development outlays to accelerate the deduction of these expenses. This may happen, for example, with equipment that is used both in manufacturing products and in developing new products. To limit the scope for recharacterization, it may be provided that research and development expenditure does not include the cost of acquiring a depreciable or intangible asset, the cost of acquiring land or buildings, or the expenditure incurred for the purpose of ascertaining the existence, location, extent, or quality of a natural deposit.

---

[158]Special rules for valuing closing inventory apply under comprehensive inflation-adjustment systems. *See* vol. 1, ch. 13.

[159]*See* McLure et al., The Taxation of Income from Business and Capital in Colombia 239–40 (1990).

[160]E.g., AUS ITAA (1936) § 73B (immediate deductions range from 100 percent to 125 percent of the relevant expenditure incurred); LSO ITA § 40 (immediate deduction); UGA ITA § 33 (immediate deduction); USA IRC § 174 (at the taxpayer's election, research and experimental expenditures may be immediately deductible or amortized over five years).

[161]*See generally* Stanley S. Surrey & Paul R. McDaniel, Tax Expenditures 211–12 (1985).

A possible hybrid approach is to prescribe a limited amortization period for research and development expenses and to allow an immediate deduction of that part of the expense that is attributable to any project or line of inquiry pursued by research if the project is abandoned without generating results.

V. Issues Relating to the Taxation of Assets

A number of issues arise in the design of the income tax as it applies to assets.[162] Some issues may be specific to particular classes of assets,[163] while others may be relevant to all assets. It is suggested that the asset rules be structured so that the rules common to all assets are included in a single regime of general application. These rules include those for determining the cost base of assets, realization and recognition rules, and rules for determining gain or loss on disposal. In systems based on the balance sheet, they will include rules for determining the balance-sheet value of assets. Specific rules for particular classes of assets can then build on these basic rules. This approach not only ensures that rules are provided for all assets, but also means that there is a fundamental consistency in the basic treatment of different classes of assets. An alternative approach in some countries is to provide detailed rules for a particular class of asset (such as investment assets), with much briefer rules provided for other assets. It is recommended that this approach be avoided.

A separate asset regime of general application is supplementary to the operation of the inclusion and deduction provisions in the law. It is not the purpose of the regime to bring amounts to tax or allow amounts as a deduction. Rather, its purpose is to elaborate the meaning of concepts used in the inclusion and deduction provisions. The main areas that can be dealt with in a separate asset regime are timing and calculation matters. The timing rules identify the tax year in which the inclusion and deduction provisions apply to an asset, and the calculation rules provide for the determination of the taxable or deductible amount. Depending on the asset, the taxable amount may be a gain calculated by subtracting the cost base of the asset from the consideration received for the asset, and the deductible amount may be a loss calculated by subtracting the consideration received for the asset from the cost base of the asset. In other cases, such as inventory, the taxable amount may be the consideration received, and the deductible amount may be the cost of the asset. In either

---

[162]The concept of an asset is used in this discussion in preference to the concept of property that is used in some tax laws (e.g., IDN IT § 4(1)d ("gains arising from the sale or transfer of property")). In its ordinary meaning, an asset is any thing that may be turned to account. Depending on general law meanings, the notion of property may not be interpreted this broadly. For example, legally enforceable rights that are purely personal in nature may not be regarded as property.

[163]For example, specific rules may apply to inventory, depreciated or amortized assets, and assets subject to capital gains taxation.

case, the asset regime should provide for the determination of the cost base of, and consideration received for, assets.

The main matters that may be dealt with in a separate asset regime are discussed below.

A. Timing Rules for Realization of Gain or Loss

Ordinarily, gains or losses arising in relation to assets are taxed not as they accrue, but rather in the tax year in which the taxpayer realizes the gain or loss. In most cases, a gain or loss is realized at the time the taxpayer ceases to own the asset. While a taxpayer will normally cease to own an asset as a result of the sale of the asset, there are other ways in which this can occur (e.g., as a result of an in-kind exchange, a gift, or a distribution of the asset). Thus, it is suggested that the concept of disposal, rather than a narrower concept like sale, be used to state the basic realization rule. In its ordinary meaning, disposal covers all situations in which the ownership of the asset changes. Even so, an extended definition of disposal will be necessary to cover all intended realization events in relation to assets, particularly those relating to intangible assets. The definition of disposal should include the redemption, expiry, cancellation, surrender, loss, or destruction of an asset. It should also be provided that the disposal of an asset includes a partial disposal. An example of a partial disposal is the sale of a lot that has been part of a single block of land that has been subdivided.

The disposal rules may also provide for gain or loss recognition where an asset that is outside the tax system is brought within the tax system, or vice versa. This can occur because a change in the taxpayer's circumstances changes the tax status of assets held by the taxpayer. For example, a nonresident taxpayer may become a resident taxpayer. If the new country of tax residence taxes worldwide income, then the change in residence may bring assets held by the taxpayer at the time of the change within the tax system of the new country of residence (these assets previously being foreign assets of a nonresident). Alternatively, a resident taxpayer may become a nonresident taxpayer. The effect of the change may be to take some assets held by the taxpayer at the time of the change outside the tax system of the taxpayer's former country of tax residence (these assets now being foreign assets of a nonresident). A similar situation can arise where an exempt person becomes a taxpayer, or vice versa. This can happen as a result of a change either in the taxpayer's circumstances or in the law.

In these situations, there is no change in the ownership of the asset, and so there is no disposal in the ordinary meaning of the word. If an entry or exit from the tax system is to be treated as a realization event, then it will be necessary to include deemed-disposal rules to cover this situation.[164] Comprehen-

---

[164]Rather than artificially "deem" that a disposal has occurred when one has not, an alternative approach is to define the situations in which gains and losses are brought to account as taxation "events"—*see, e.g.,* AUS ITAA (1997), proposed Div. 104.

sive deemed-disposal rules can be difficult to enforce and may not be necessary for developing or transition countries.[165] However, it will be necessary to include some such rules, particularly to prevent taxpayers from obtaining a tax deduction for what is essentially consumption expenditure (e.g., if a personal-use asset becomes a business asset, there should be a deemed disposal and reacquisition to ensure the decline in value due to personal use is not recognized for tax purposes). The effect of a deemed-disposal rule is to treat a particular event as giving rise to the disposal of an asset for a consideration equal to either the market value or the cost base of the asset at that time depending on the circumstances.[166] If relevant, the taxpayer will also be treated as having immediately reacquired the asset for the same consideration. This then becomes the new cost base of the asset for tax purposes.

B. Cost Base

The basic rule is that the cost base of an asset is the consideration given for the acquisition of the asset.[167] This should include any borrowed funds used to acquire the asset. Where the taxpayer has given consideration in kind for the asset, the market value of the in-kind consideration at the time of the acquisition should be included in the cost base of the asset. The cost base of an asset should include any ancillary costs incurred in the acquisition of the asset, such as legal and registration fees relating to transfer of the ownership of the

---

[165]It is suggested that this is the case for residence change situations. *See* ch. 18, sec. VI(E).

[166]Market value consideration will be recognized when an asset moves in or out of the tax system (*see supra* sec. V(A)), while consideration equal to cost will be recognized in most cases when an asset changes tax status (*see infra* sec. V(E)(1)).

[167]While much tax terminology is similar in different countries, this is not the case for "cost base" and its equivalents. It is in fact more than a difference in terminology and has to do with differences in the structure of income tax laws. The United States has an underlying concept of "basis" (and adjusted basis), which is used throughout the income tax law for such purposes as computing capital gains or depreciation deductions (e.g., the term adjusted basis is used more than 300 times in the Internal Revenue Code). The concept is defined in USA IRC §§ 1011–1016. Similarly, Australia has the concept of cost base of assets, which is defined in AUS ITAA (1936) § 160ZH, but this concept is not as pervasive in the tax law as is the American concept; it does not govern depreciation deductions, for example, which are determined according to the cost of plant. *See* ITAA (1997) §§ 42-60 to 42-90. The Canadian approach is similar. *See* CAN ITA § 54 (adjusted cost base). Most countries do not have a formal underlying concept of basis. They might refer to the cost or acquisition cost of assets in rules for determining capital gains. For example, the Spanish law refers to the acquisition value in its capital gains rules. *See* ESP IRPF § 46. France similarly refers to the acquisition price. *See* FRA CGI § 150 H. The United Kingdom uses the concept of cost both for capital gains purposes and for purposes of determining qualifying expenditure for depreciation purposes. In contrast, Germany, like the United States, has an underlying concept for the valuation of assets, namely, *Buchwert* (book value). The concept of *Buchwert* is used both for purposes of computing capital gains and for purposes of the balance-sheet method of determining taxable income (for which, see appendix *infra*). *See* DEU EStG §§ 6, 6b(2). In most cases, the *Buchwert* of an asset for purposes of German tax law will correspond to the concept of adjusted basis as used in U.S. tax law.

asset, transfer taxes, agent's fees, installation costs, and start-up expenses to make the asset operational. The cost base of an asset should also include any capital expenditures incurred to improve the asset and expenses incurred in respect of initial repairs.[168]

When there is a partial disposal of an asset, it is necessary to provide rules to apportion part of the cost of the original asset to the part of the asset sold. For this purpose, the cost of the original asset should be apportioned by reference to the market values of the respective parts of the asset at the time the asset was originally acquired.[169] It may be difficult to apply this rule when an asset was acquired without contemplation of part disposal. The information may thus not be available at the time of disposal to apportion cost on the basis of market values of the respective parts of the asset at the time of acquisition. In this case, the original cost can be assumed to be allocated on a pro rata basis by reference to relative market values of the part sold and the part retained at the time of disposal.[170]

A taxpayer may hold a number of assets of the same type. When the assets have been acquired for different costs, and the taxpayer disposes of only a part of his or her holdings of the asset, it will be necessary to know which asset or assets have been disposed of for the purposes of determining the cost of those assets. Ordinarily, outside of inventory, it should be possible to identify the particular asset or assets disposed of so that the actual cost of those assets is used. However, there may be some types of asset for which actual identification is not possible. Examples include shares of a company that is not obliged to use registration numbers and holdings of precious metals. For these assets, a presumptive tracing rule needs to be provided. While several possible tracing rules may apply when the asset is inventory,[171] an identification rule based on first-in-first-out is suggested for noninventory assets.

Cost-base rules should cover two special cases. The first case is where a taxpayer acquires an asset in circumstances in which the acquisition constitutes the derivation of an amount included in the taxpayer's gross income. For example, a taxpayer may be remunerated with an asset rather than with cash. In this case, the cost base of the asset should be the amount included in gross income plus any consideration given by the taxpayer for the asset. The purpose of this rule is to prevent double taxation.

---

[168]*See infra* sec. IV(D)(3).

[169]*E.g.*, UGA ITA § 53(5).

[170]*E.g.*, AUS ITAA (1936) § 160ZI. Another approach, not recommended, is to allocate cost on a pro rata basis using features of the property sold, such as the size of a part of immovable property sold compared with the size of the part retained. Given that it is only by chance that there would have been a consistent movement in the market value of the respective parts of the asset since the original asset was acquired, this approach is likely to lead to inappropriate allocations of original cost.

[171]*See supra* sec. IV(D)(4).

The second case is where a taxpayer acquires an asset in circumstances where the acquisition of the asset is the derivation of exempt income. In this case, the cost of the asset should be the exempt amount plus any consideration given by the taxpayer for the asset. The purpose of this rule is to ensure that the exemption is not clawed back on a subsequent disposal of the asset.

C. Consideration Received

The basic rule is that the consideration received for the disposal of an asset is the price received for the asset, including the market value of any in-kind consideration. Where borrowed funds are included in the cost base of the asset, any relief from the debt by the transferee must be treated as part of the consideration received on disposal of the asset.

Where a taxpayer disposes of two or more assets for a single undissected consideration, it is necessary to provide for the apportionment of the consideration among the assets. For this purpose, the consideration received should be apportioned by reference to the market values of the assets disposed of as of the time of the disposal.

In some situations, the consideration for a disposal of an asset may be nominal or zero. For example, a taxpayer may give an asset (such as inventory) to a customer or a client as a sample or as part of a promotion. Where the parties are genuinely unrelated and the purpose of the dealing is not to shift value to some related, but tax-preferred transaction between the parties, the actual consideration received (if any) should be treated as the consideration for the disposal of the asset. The treatment of non-arm's-length transactions is discussed in section V(D), below.

The consideration rules must correspond to the notion of disposal that applies for the purposes of the law. For example, it was stated above that the notion of a disposal should extend to situations where an asset has been lost or destroyed. For these disposals, there may be no consideration received for the disposed asset, or the taxpayer may have received insurance proceeds or damages (see below). There are a number of different rules in different jurisdictions that apply in these circumstances. Often, however, these are explicable by reference to particular historical factors and are of little precedential value. In the absence of special circumstances, the simplest and fairest rule is to measure losses arising from such involuntary disposals by reference to the actual consideration received, if any. If no consideration is received, then the taxpayer will have incurred a loss on the disposal equal to the cost of the asset.

Where a taxpayer is subject to a deemed disposal in respect of assets moving in or out of the tax system, a market value rule should apply to the disposal. This means that the taxpayer is treated as having disposed of the assets for their market value at the time of the deemed disposal and to have immediately reacquired them for the same amount. This ensures that only the gain or loss arising while the asset is within the tax system is recognized.

Special rules may be needed for compensation (such as insurance proceeds or damage awards) received in relation to assets. Where compensation is received in respect of the loss or destruction of an asset, the amount should be treated as the consideration received for the disposal constituted by the loss or destruction of the asset. For this purpose, it is necessary to ensure that the definition of consideration received is drafted broadly so as to cover such amounts.

Compensation may also be received for damage to an asset where the asset has not been lost or destroyed. If the amount of the compensation equals the cost of repairs (e.g., fixing the car after an accident), then no gain should be recognized in relation to the compensation amount. Where the compensation offsets damage that cannot be repaired, it should be recognized through a reduction in the cost base of the asset.

D. Non-Arm's-Length Transfers

In the absence of prophylactic measures to control the amount of cost and consideration for tax purposes, related parties may choose transfer prices in the hope of achieving a variety of tax objectives—minimizing recognition of gain to defer taxes, inflating gains to absorb losses that were carried forward, value shifting to transfer gains to a lower bracket or exempt taxpayer, and so forth. Objectives unrelated to taxation, too, may also influence transfer values. For example, taxpayers may wish to shift value to improve their balance sheet for the purpose of obtaining debt finance.

To prevent manipulation of transfer prices, rules for determining the deemed market value consideration are needed for non-arm's-length transactions. In broad terms, an arm's-length transaction is a transaction in which the parties act completely independently of each other and seek to put their own interest first. A transaction between related parties would be presumed to be a non-arm's-length transaction because one or both parties may be willing to subordinate their own interest to that of the other party or a related third person for the purpose of achieving an overall tax saving. However, this is only a presumption because related parties can enter into a transaction on arm's-length terms. The nature of the transaction is usually tested by reference to the price that would be expected if unrelated parties entered into the transaction.

Non-arm's-length transactions require complementary deeming rules. The person disposing of an asset in a non-arm's-length transaction should be treated as having received consideration for the disposal equal to the market value of the asset at the time of the disposal. The same amount should then be treated as the cost base of the asset for the person acquiring the asset.

While gifts are usually non-arm's-length transfers, they raise special conceptual issues. Genuine gifts occur most commonly within families; most "gifts" outside the family involve some sort of quid pro quo. The case for treating gifts in the same manner as other non-arm's-length transactions (i.e., as a disposal for a deemed market value consideration) is strong. Any other treatment introduces inefficiencies and inequities by distinguishing between persons who dispose of property or services for arm's-length consideration and make a gift of the proceeds and those who provide the property or services directly.

The argument commonly raised against deemed market value consideration in respect of gifts is the alleged liquidity problem faced by the donor. Often, the lack of liquidity is at the choice of the donor, given that the donor could have disposed of the property at market value. A secondary argument focuses on the alleged valuation difficulties encountered in a transfer for no consideration. The problem is no greater than that encountered in any non-arm's-length transfer, however, and tax administrators can apply to gift transactions the expertise developed to value all other non-arm's-length transactions.

Similar issues apply to testamentary gifts. While it seems intuitively inappropriate to treat the taxpayer who makes a gift of property differently from the taxpayer whose property transfers on death, a distinction between inter vivos and testamentary gifts is not unusual. Often, jurisdictions that provide a deferral in respect of testamentary transfers impose death duties or similar taxes, and it may be thought that liquidity problems could be exacerbated as a result of the two tax liabilities. Similar treatment of inter vivos and testamentary gifts is desirable, however, in light of the inequities that would follow from a complete exemption from recognition of accrued gains on death (by means of a cost-base step-up for recipients of property) and the economic lock-in inefficiencies that would follow from a deferral of recognition (by means of a cost-base rollover for the recipient). Liquidity problems, if any, can be addressed through, for example, installment payments of tax subject to ordinary finance charges.

E. Nonrecognition Rules

There may be situations in which a taxpayer has realized a gain or a loss on disposal of an asset, but recognition of the gain is deferred until a later event occurs. Similar deferral may apply when property changes its tax status. In some jurisdictions, these nonrecognition rules are referred to as providing rollover treatment. The tax position of a taxpayer or asset is rolled over into another taxpayer or asset, as the case may be. This is done by deeming the taxpayer to have disposed of relevant property for consideration equal to its cost and to have reacquired the property (if there has been no actual disposal of assets) or to have acquired replacement property for consideration equal to the original cost.

Tax laws commonly provide for rollover treatment in four types of situations, described below.

1. Changes in the Tax Status of Assets

An asset can change its tax status in a number of ways. For example, a trader may take some stock from inventory for personal use or consumption (or vice versa, although this is much less common). An item of inventory can also become a business asset of another type, such as depreciable or amortizable property, or vice versa. Similarly, property acquired as business assets or inventory may subsequently be held as an investment asset, or vice versa,[172] and in some cases may thus be subject to different tax rules.

Rollover treatment, which can be applied to most changes of tax status, is the equivalent of saying that the asset was originally acquired for its ultimate use, and so the interim period in which the asset was held for some other use is thus ignored. A deemed disposal for cost will normally lead to no gain or loss recognition. For example, if an item of inventory is removed for personal consumption by the taxpayer, the taxpayer will be treated as having disposed of the stock at the time it was taken out of inventory for cost,[173] which will offset the deduction obtained for the cost of inventory. Some systems (e.g., Germany), however, treat a withdrawal of assets from business use as a disposal for market value.[174]

A special rule is needed when a personal-use asset that would be depreciable property if it were a business asset is converted to a business asset. If rollover treatment were applied in this case, the taxpayer would be able to recognize some personal consumption costs for tax purposes. For example, if a taxpayer converted a machine from personal-use property to inventory, the decline in value due to personal use could be recognized as a loss if the property were rolled over at cost. Such conversions should be treated as disposals for market value.

2. Disposals Intended to Trigger a Loss

While the income tax system tends to recognize gains and losses only when there is a disposal of an asset or a prescribed tax event giving rise to a deemed disposal, the value of assets changes continuously. The realization event aspect of the income tax system can provide taxpayers with opportunities to reduce tax liability by accelerating recognition of losses on assets that have declined in value while deferring recognition of gains on assets that have appreciated over the same period. If the disposals are genuine market transactions to unrelated parties, the losses will normally be recognized for tax purposes. In some cases, loss recognition will be denied, however, and rollover treatment will be imposed.

The first loss situation in which rollover treatment is prescribed is for below-cost transfers to related persons, even if the price reflects market value. Losses are generated even though the asset continues to be owned by the same group of companies or the same family. To prevent such artificial generation

---

[172]This possibility can be confined to individuals carrying on a business, because all assets of a company or partnership should be deemed to be business assets. *See supra* sec. II(B)(2).

[173]*E.g.,* AUS ITAA (1997) § 70-110.

[174]This approach corresponds to the deemed disposal on conversion of assets to business assets—*see supra* sec. IV(A).

of a loss, the transferor should be treated as having disposed of the property at cost, and the transferee should be treated as having acquired the asset for the same amount. This preserves the accrued loss, which will be realized when the transferee eventually sells the asset outside the group or family.

The second loss situation in which rollover treatment is prescribed is for "wash sale" situations. A wash sale is when a taxpayer disposes of an asset that has declined in value and immediately thereafter acquires the same or a similar asset. The transaction costs may be minimal compared with the tax savings resulting from the realized loss. The abuse of such transactions can be avoided by prescribing rollover treatment to wash sales that involve the taxpayer's reacquisition of the asset within a designated period.

3. Involuntary Disposals

A nonrecognition rule may apply to an involuntary disposal of an asset when a replacement asset has been acquired. Examples of involuntary disposals to which this rule may apply are the loss or destruction of an asset (e.g., through fire or theft) and the compulsory acquisition of an asset by a government authority. There are usually two conditions to the application of the nonrecognition rule. The first condition is that the proceeds of the disposal (such as insurance proceeds) must be used to acquire a replacement asset of a kind similar to the disposed asset. The second condition is that the replacement asset is acquired within a specified time of the involuntary disposal, say, one year. The nonrecognition rule should apply only to the extent that the proceeds of the involuntary disposal are used to acquire the replacement asset. If the proceeds of the involuntary disposal exceed the cost of the replacement asset, then the excess of the proceeds over the cost of the replacement asset should be recognized as a taxable gain arising from the involuntary disposal. Where the nonrecognition rule applies, the cost of the replacement asset is the cost of the involuntarily disposed of asset plus the amount (if any) by which the consideration given for the replacement asset exceeds the consideration received on the involuntary disposal. The nonrecognition rule that applies to involuntary disposals is illustrated by the following example:

Example

A taxpayer owns an office building that cost $1,000,000. The building is destroyed by fire. The taxpayer receives $1,500,000 under an insurance policy, which is wholly used to acquire a replacement office building. Under the nonrecognition rule, no gain or loss is taken into account on disposal of the building to the extent that the insurance proceeds of the disposal are used to acquire the replacement building. The tax cost of the replacement building is $1,000,000— that is, the cost of the destroyed building at the date of its destruction. This means that recognition of a $500,000 gain made by the taxpayer on disposal of the destroyed building is deferred until the taxpayer disposes of the replacement building.

If the actual cost of the replacement building was $1,600,000, then the tax cost of the replacement building would be $1,100,000 (the cost of the destroyed building plus $100,000 paid by the taxpayer for the replacement building in addition to the insurance proceeds). Recognition of a $500,000 gain made by the taxpayer on disposal of the destroyed building is still deferred until the taxpayer disposes of the replacement building.

If the replacement building had actually cost $1,400,000, then the cost of the replacement building would still be $1,000,000, but the difference between the insurance proceeds and the cost of the replacement building ($100,000) would be included in the taxpayer's business income. This is because this part of the insurance proceeds has not been used to acquire the replacement building. Recognition of the other $400,000 of gain in relation to the involuntary disposal is deferred until the taxpayer disposes of the replacement building.

4. Spousal Transfers

A nonrecognition rollover may be provided to facilitate the transfer of assets between spouses (or former spouses) on the breakdown of a marriage. The transferee spouse takes over the original cost of the asset so that recognition of any gain or loss that has accrued prior to the transfer is deferred until a subsequent disposal of the asset by the transferee spouse.

F. Transitional Basis for Assets Previously Outside the Tax Base

The reform of income tax legislation often brings into the tax base gains on assets that were not previously subject to income taxation. To avoid the retrospective application of the tax law, transitional measures should prevent or at least minimize the taxation of gains that have accrued prior to the introduction of the new tax. From a theoretical perspective, the ideal rule is one that sets the cost of assets previously outside the tax base as their market value at the time the new tax reform comes into effect. To prevent market confusion and potential disruption between the unveiling of the new tax rules and their effective date, some jurisdictions that have expanded the tax base in this manner have used the market value as of the time the new measures were unveiled or shortly before.

A rule based on market value when the tax base is broadened is feasible only if market value information is readily available at that time and accessible when there is an eventual disposal of the property. Experience in industrial countries that have adopted this approach shows that few difficulties emerge when this rule is applied to "publicly listed assets," such as publicly traded shares or precious metals, or to assets included in databases that can be used to estimate closely the value of an asset at the time of tax reform. An example of the latter is real estate where property records will show the sale price of neighboring properties sold around the time of the tax reform. However, valuation is a prime source of dispute and litigation in the case of assets involving intangible elements such as goodwill (e.g., businesses or shares in private companies). In industrial countries, these values are normally determined by financial indicators, such as comparable rates of return in similar businesses. In developing and transition countries, it is more appropriate to use a surrogate measure of value when the tax base is broadened. The simplest rule for assets acquired prior to tax reform is to deem cost to be the original cost adjusted by a factor such as inflation adjustment. Even this surrogate measurement may be difficult to apply in some cases, for example, when assets have been acquired long before tax reform or through inheritance.

One country attempted to broaden its tax base by introducing measures on a prospective basis so that they applied only to assets acquired after a certain date.[175] This approach is not recommended because it creates arbitrary differences in the treatment of assets depending on when they are acquired. These differences encourage taxpayers to enter into transactions to shift value from taxed to untaxed assets. Further, this approach creates a lock-in effect in that persons holding assets acquired before the relevant date are encouraged to hold onto them.

VI. Special Regimes

A. Interest Income and Expenses

It is common for tax legislation to contain special rules for interest income and expenses. As discussed in section III(B), it is usual to define interest broadly to ensure that amounts functionally equivalent to interest (such as discounts and premiums) are treated as interest for tax purposes.

It is necessary to include special timing rules in relation to interest. These rules serve two purposes. First, they ensure that the different amounts within the broad definition of interest (such as discounts and premiums) are subject to the same recognition rules. In the absence of special accounting rules, it might be possible for a taxpayer to recognize a gain relating to a discount or premium when the gain is realized—that is, upon redemption or repayment of the loan. Thus, even if the discount or premium is taxed as interest, the recipient may still enjoy a significant deferral advantage over ordinary interest. Special accounting rules are needed to deem the recipient to derive the gain represented by a discount or premium as if it were compound interest derived over the life of the loan.[176]

Second, special rules are necessary to prevent taxpayers from taking advantage of timing mismatches that can arise in accounting for the various forms of interest. For example, a mismatch can arise when a financial institution issues a

---

[175]AUS ITAA (1936) § 160L.

[176]AUS ITAA (1936) §§ 159GP–159GZ; CAN ITA § 12(3), (4), and (9); ESP § 37 Uno 2(A) *(rendimientos implícitos)*; *but see*, to the contrary, FRA CGI § 125-0 A (capitalized interest taxed only at the time of the expiration *(dénouement)* of the contract, so that the taxpayer has a timing advantage in capitalizing the interest).

security to an individual under which the payment of interest is deferred for, say, five years. In the absence of special rules, the financial institution may be permitted to deduct the interest expense as it accrues, while the individual accounts for the interest income when it is paid (under cash-basis accounting). To avoid such mismatches, it may be provided that both the lender and the borrower must account for interest income on an accrual basis, regardless of the taxpayer's general method of accounting. An exception may be provided if the interest is subject to withholding tax. Both the lender and the borrower may be required in this case to account for the interest on a cash basis.[177]

Limitations on the deduction of interest expenses may be desirable for a number of reasons. In principle, like other expenses incurred to derive business income, interest expenses should be deductible in full. However, restrictions on interest expenses may be used

- to prevent taxpayers from exploiting the full deductibility of interest in periods of high inflation;
- to prevent taxpayers, particularly foreign taxpayers, from exploiting different tax rates on interest and dividends; and
- to prevent taxpayers from exploiting differences in the treatment of interest and capital gains.

Finally, in common law jurisdictions in particular, special rules may be needed to prevent taxpayers from exploiting the different treatment of "blended" payment loans and annuities.[178]

1. Inflation Benefits

In the absence of special rules on interest deductibility, taxpayers who borrow in a high-inflation environment may derive a significant tax advantage from debt financing. Most of what is nominally interest expense may in fact be repayment of a portion of the loan.[179] A system of global inflation adjustment can be used to address this problem.[180] However, because most countries will not adopt such a system, partial adjustment for interest could be considered, although the case for inflation adjustment of interest expense is not appreciably stronger than the case for inflation adjustment of the cost of inventory, depreciable assets, and other property. Nor is there a reason why inflation adjustment rules (or surrogate rules) imposed on borrowers paying interest ex-

---

[177]Some countries do attempt to apply accrual tax rules although the payment of interest is subject to withholding tax. When payment of interest is deferred by capitalizing it into discounts, premiums, or other forms of capital gains, the rules on withholding tax should provide that the tax becomes due by the payor on any portion of the gain, premium, or discount that has accrued during the taxable period. In such cases, withholding tax is to be paid on an annual basis before effective payment of the income. *See further* BEL CIR §§ 19(3), 267.

[178]*See supra* sec. III(A).

[179]*See* vol. 1, ch. 13, sec. IV(A).

[180]*See* vol. 1, ch. 13, sec. IV(D).

penses should not apply equally to lenders deriving interest income. Selective recognition of the effects of inflation on only one element of the business income equation will introduce new and potentially more significant distortions into the income tax system. This fact should be kept in mind when proposals for adjusting allowable deductions for interest expenses are evaluated.

2. Thin Capitalization

If the domestic company and shareholder income tax regime is based on a classical tax system, comprising separate taxation of company income and distributions to shareholders, there will be an incentive for taxpayers to invest by way of debt instead of equity. Distributions are thus deductible to the company and are taxed only once in the hands of investors. Extensive reliance on debt financing is known as thin capitalization.

Adoption of a partial imputation system reduces the incentive to recharacterize equity as debt and dividends as interest payments. Adoption of full imputation almost eliminates the distortion in respect of domestic shareholders, provided both dividends and interest are subject to similar tax treatment. If interest is subject to a different regime, such as low domestic withholding tax, shareholders in companies deriving income that will not carry imputation credits are likely to structure their investment as debt in order to convert their returns to interest.

Unless imputation is extended fully to all foreign shareholders, an incentive to engage in thin capitalization will remain for these taxpayers. Even then, a bias toward debt investment will exist if the final tax imposed on interest income is different from that imposed on dividends, as is often the case.[181] Alternative solutions to the problem of thin capitalization as applied to foreign shareholders are discussed in chapter 18.[182]

If rules designed to counter thin capitalization arrangements are to apply to all shareholders, they are best located in the statutory provisions applicable to companies. If the rules are to apply only to foreign shareholders, they can be included with other international tax measures. Thin capitalization rules can also be used in lieu of explicit inflation adjustment of interest expense, which may be considered too complicated to apply. In this case, the rules should apply to the deduction of all interest expenses.

3. Interest Quarantining

A problem confronted in many tax systems is the difficulty of matching interest expenses to corresponding income attributable to those interest expenses. Interest is generally deductible as incurred, while income is recognized as derived. Taxpayers may enjoy considerable tax benefits if they may deduct

---

[181]For example, lower rates of tax on interest, including zero rates, may be prescribed by treaty.
[182]See infra ch. 18, sec. V(G)(2).

interest outgoings in the period before the years in which the resultant gains are taxed. The benefits are increased if the income qualifies for a preference— such as partial exemption, special rates, or inflation adjustment—while nominal interest is deductible in full against nonpreference income subject to ordinary rates of tax.

In some cases, it is relatively easy to identify the period of deferral of income. For example, an investment asset may yield no current income, its entire return taking the form of capital gains that will be taxed when they are realized. Another case is when interest expense is incurred to finance the construction of property, such as heavy equipment, a public utility plant, or a building. In this case, because of the passage of time, the taxpayer expects the finished project to be worth at least as much as the incurred costs plus interest on those costs up to the time the property is placed in service or sold.

Other cases of deferral may be more difficult to identify. For example, a taxpayer may acquire immovable property for the dual purposes of using it as business premises and deriving business income during the period of occupancy and of realizing a further gain upon disposal. Alternatively, a taxpayer may acquire property for the dual purposes of deriving rental income during the lease period and deriving a further gain when the property is sold at the expiration of the lease term. In these cases, the property is generating income that is currently taxed, but there is also an element of appreciation in value that will not be taxed until the gain is realized.

Two measures can be used to minimize the mismatch of interest deductions and consequent income. First, interest incurred in respect of the acquisition or construction of property before the property generates income can be capitalized into the cost base of the property. Second, quarantine rules can be applied to interest incurred to derive dual-element income, such as rent or business income and capital gain. Because investment income is most likely to involve dual elements, it is common to restrict quarantining rules to this type of income. Normally, quarantining will limit interest deductions that are incurred to derive investment income to the amount of investment income derived during the taxable year, with an indefinite carryover of undeducted interest. When taxpayers carry on business in a personal (not incorporated) capacity, it will be necessary to separate business credit from personal credit.[183] Some countries, in principle, still permit unlimited deductions of interest even on personal loans,[184] which result in a considerable loss of revenue.

B. Finance Leases

A lease is an agreement under which the owner of an asset (the lessor) grants another person (the lessee) the right to use the asset for a stated pe-

---

[183]BEL CIR art. 14; CAN ITA § 20(1)(c); FRA CGI art. 31/1 (d); USA IRC § 25. The U.S. provision is considered by some commentators to be excessively complicated.

[184]See NLD WIB § 45/1 f, with some limitations in arts. 45/3 and 5; CHE LIFD § 33(1)(a).

riod. As consideration for the right, the lessee agrees to make rental payments to the lessor. At all times, the legal ownership of the asset remains with the lessor. The commercial accounting treatment of a lease and its tax treatment will depend on whether the lease is a "finance lease" or an "operating lease."

A finance lease[185] is an arrangement that is legally structured as a lease, but has the same economic effect as a sale on credit and purchase of the leased asset. Thus, under a finance lease, the lessor effectively transfers the benefits and risks of ownership of the leased asset to the lessee while retaining legal title in the asset. An operating lease is one in which the legal and economic ownership of the leased asset remains with the lessor so that the lease payments are genuinely for the use of the leased asset.

Under tax law, three broad approaches to the use of finance leases are adopted. One approach is to give effect to legal form, so that all leases are effectively treated as operating leases for tax purposes. This means that the lessor would be treated as the owner of the leased asset and thus the person entitled to claim depreciation and other deductions relating to ownership. The rental payments are treated as income of the lessor and a deductible expense of the lessee.[186]

The other two methods broadly accord with commercial accounting treatment of finance leases. In contrast to the strict legal approach, commercial accounting rules recognize the economic reality of a finance lease by treating it as a sale and purchase of the leased asset. Thus, the lessee (not the lessor) is treated as the owner of the asset, which is entered into the lessee's books as an asset of that taxpayer. The lessor is shown for accounting purposes as having made a loan to the lessee, the rental payments being treated as payments of principal and interest on the loan.

Treating a finance lease for tax purposes in the same way as other leases gave rise to arrangements under which such a lease could be used to transfer tax benefits from a person who could not use them to a taxpayer who could. Consider, for example, a person who wishes to acquire an item of substantial plant. The person does not have sufficient funds to self-finance the acquisition and will thus need to borrow. In the ordinary case, the person will be able to deduct the interest expense and claim depreciation deductions in relation to the cost of the asset. Suppose, however, that the person is not in a position to use these deductions, or at least not immediately. The person may not expect to earn enough income for several years to take advantage of the deductions, so that the benefit of the deductions is deferred. Alternatively, the person may be a tax-exempt entity, such as a government instrumental-

---

[185]The term "finance lease" is commonly used in tax literature. Commercial accounting rules use the term "capital lease."

[186]See Gustav Lindencrona & Stephan Tolstoy, International Fiscal Association General Report, *Taxation of Cross Border Leasing* 21, 30 (75a Cahiers de droit fiscal international) (1990).

ity, which cannot utilize the deductions at all. Another possibility, particularly in developing and transition countries, is that the person may be entitled to a tax holiday, and so, again, cannot use the deductions. In these cases, arrangements can be entered into whereby a financier acquires the asset and leases it to the person under a finance lease. Because the financier is the legal owner of the asset, it is entitled to claim deductions related to ownership. The effect of the finance lease is to transfer the tax benefits associated with ownership to the financier, although, through the terms of the lease, the economic benefits and obligations are with the lessee. The availability of the tax benefits means that the financier is able to provide the lessee with a lower cost of funds. The arrangement, however, is detrimental to the revenue because it results in the full utilization of what would otherwise be unused tax benefits.

Tax law treatment of finance leases in a manner similar to accounting treatment can be accomplished in two ways. In some jurisdictions, courts will use general interpretation principles to read the tax law as giving effect to the underlying economic form of a lease, not its apparent legal form. In others, the tax law has been drafted to achieve this result explicitly.[187] It is recommended that this approach be adopted in developing and transition countries.

Tax laws drafted to achieve a result similar to commercial accounting practice should make it clear that for tax purposes, the arrangement is treated as a sale on credit from the lessor to the lessee, and so the lessee is treated as the owner of the property and the lessor as a financier. The deemed purchase price is the present value of the rental payments to be made under the lease, and the price is treated as financed through a loan from the lessor to the lessee. Each payment the lessee makes under the lease is treated as a repayment of principal and interest under the loan. The interest component is calculated according to actuarial methods on the principal outstanding at the commencement of each payment period, with the balance of the payment treated as repayment of the principal.[188] The interest component of each payment is treated as an interest expense of the lessee and interest income of the lessor.

The central issue is the determination of whether a lease is a finance lease. It is suggested that several alternative tests based on commercial accounting rules be prescribed. The essence of these tests is to identify cases where economic ownership of an asset effectively passes to the lessee. Under these tests, a lease will be treated as a finance lease if any of the following circumstances is present:

---

[187]*E.g.*, CAN Income Tax Regulation 1100(1.1); LSO ITA § 68; UGA ITA § 60.
[188]*See supra* sec. III(A).

- The term of the lease (including any period under an option to renew) is equal to or greater than 75 percent of the estimated economic life of the leased asset.
- The lease contains an option to purchase the leased asset at the end of the lease for a fixed or determinable price.
- The estimated residual value of the property to the lessor at the end of the lease term is less than 20 percent of its fair market value at the commencement of the lease.
- The present value of minimum[189] lease payments equals or exceeds 90 percent of the fair market value of the asset at the commencement of the lease term.
- The leased property is custom-made for the lessee and, at the end of the lease term, will have little or no value to anyone other than the lessee.

C. Capital Gains

While the concepts of capital gains, their historical basis, and the terminology used vary from jurisdiction to jurisdiction, distinctions between capital gains and other gains are common. In many countries, capital gains (or certain categories of gains) are treated preferentially for tax purposes. Preferences may include lower rates, partial or even complete exemptions, averaging, and inflation adjustment that are not available for other gains.[190]

Even when capital gains are fully taxable in the same manner as other income, the distinction is often retained for the purpose of quarantining capital losses against capital gains. Quarantining is necessary because capital gains are taxed on a realization basis. In the absence of quarantining, taxpayers can defer the recognition of gains and accelerate the recognition of losses to reduce taxes payable on other income.

In some jurisdictions, the concept of a capital gain is legislatively defined, while in others (for the most part the United Kingdom and former U.K. colonies), it is largely a judicial concept defined by tests set out in case law. In former U.K. colonies, in particular, great care must be taken when drafting the definition of capital gains. One problem almost unique to these jurisdictions arises from the fact that the flexibility of property and contract law enables taxpayers to engineer many transactions to give rise to gains that would be characterized by the courts in some of the jurisdictions as capital gains under the governing judicial concepts and thereby excluded from the ordinary income tax base. Because these gains are not generated by disposals of property as those are normally understood, they can be brought into capital gains provisions only with terribly complex deeming provisions. A far simpler approach is to

---

[189]The term "minimum lease payments" is intended to include regular "rental" payments plus any supplemental mandatory payments (e.g., the amount of a lessee guarantee of residual value).

[190]See generally John King, Taxation of Capital Gains, in Tax Policy Handbook 155 (P. Shome ed. 1995).

modify the definition of income to ensure that these gains are included in the tax base.[191]

In many jurisdictions, all gains derived from the disposal of assets by legal persons and from the disposal of business assets are treated as ordinary business income.[192] Under this approach, capital gains derived in the context of a business are not subject to any preferences that may be available to individuals deriving capital gains on investment portfolios. Exceptions may be made for disposals involving the liquidation of the business, which may be taxed preferentially.

There is a large body of literature debating whether capital gains should be given preferred treatment or taxed at all, and it does not seem useful to repeat the arguments here. Any distinction between capital gains and other gains will of course involve definition problems. Long experience in OECD countries suggests that a completely satisfactory definition cannot be found. Inevitably, taxpayers alter their behavior to exploit tax concessions in ways not originally intended by the legislation. Transactions are altered to recharacterize income not subject to the concession as gains that do qualify for special treatment. This, in turn, leads to calls for complex antiavoidance provisions, to considerable litigation, and to significant dead-weight losses from energies diverted to tax planning.

At the same time, in the context of limited administrative capacity in developing countries, there are persuasive arguments for excluding from the tax base many types of capital gains and losses derived by individuals. Because capital gains and losses may accrue over many years and are generally recognized on a realization basis, taxpayers may not have maintained adequate records for calculating the amount of the gain or loss. For this reason, and coupled with notorious difficulties of enforcement, it may be appropriate to exclude from the tax base most capital gains realized and losses suffered by individuals, apart from gains and losses attributable to assets such as shares and other financial investments and immovable property. Other exclusions are desirable for tax policy reasons. Thus, for example, losses on personal-use assets such as cars and appliances whose value declines as a result of use should be excluded to ensure that taxpayers are not able to recognize capital losses on what is essentially personal consumption.[193]

---

[191]Australia provides an excellent example of the problems that can be encountered if capital gains provisions are used to catch gains that fall outside the judicial income tax base, such as payments for entering into negative covenant (noncompetition) agreements and payments for agreeing not to pursue contractual rights. In Australia, this was first attempted by resort to complex and highly artificial deeming provisions. The courts rejected them as virtually meaningless. A second, and more complex, redraft was needed. Rather than simply adding these gains to the ordinary income tax base, the government now proposes to replace the artificial deeming provisions with legislation defining capital gains "events."

[192]Examples include many European jurisdictions.

[193]Examples of jurisdictions with exemptions for these assets include Australia and Canada.

The drafting approach adopted to achieve exclusion of these gains or losses will depend on the general drafting structure; whether a jurisdiction is based on a schedular or a global model; whether the background or judicial concept of income would otherwise include these gains or losses; and, if the jurisdiction uses a global income tax system, whether global taxation is achieved by means of separate inclusions for employment, business, and investment income. If the exclusions are to be legislated through a specific exclusion measure, that provision can refer to all nonbusiness assets owned by physical persons apart from listed assets (which would then include intangible property and immovable property). An alternative approach is to exclude personal-use property other than immovable property, with personal-use property defined as property acquired primarily for the personal use and enjoyment of a physical person or his or her family.

D. Farming Income

It is not unusual for jurisdictions to provide special rules for determining farming income, because of, in addition to political considerations,

- the possibility that farmers will not retain business records in the same format as other businesses;
- the practical difficulties in auditing farmers;
- the difficulties of valuing farm produce and livestock inventory; and
- the fact that farmers are more likely than other businesspersons to take items out of inventory for family consumption.

An important consideration in the design of the farming tax regime will be the administrative capabilities of tax authorities. In developing countries in particular, surrogate measures of income using presumptive criteria may be the most efficient method of determining tax liability,[194] at the potential cost of some equity.

Special rules will also be needed to deal with consumption of a farmer's own produce. Several competing policies must be considered in this situation. It is arguable on equity and efficiency grounds that consumption of self-produced inventory should be treated as a disposal at market value. This policy would achieve equity between taxpayers who sell their produce to purchase other types of food in the market and those who consume their own produce. It would also eliminate a distortion in favor of consuming one's own goods as opposed to participating in the market. At the same time, however, it is true that persons other than farmers are able to produce foodstuffs for themselves without tax consequences. If the same treatment were accorded to farmers, it would be necessary to distinguish inventory from production intended for personal use. Also, it could be argued that farmers, by virtue of their knowledge

---

[194]See vol. 1, ch. 12.

of the industry, could purchase produce for a value much lower than the market price faced by other taxpayers.

These problems are most easily resolved by treating consumption of inventory as a disposal at cost instead of at market value or, equivalently, by disallowing a deduction for the cost of self-consumed produce.

E. Non–Life Insurance Companies

Under a short-term[195] insurance contract, the insured person will pay a premium to the insurer as consideration for the insurer, upon the happening of a specified event within a given time, paying to the insured or a nominated person either an agreed sum or the amount of the loss caused by the event. The period of cover under the insurance contract is usually one year, after which the insurance contract is simply renewed. Depending on the sophistication of the local non–life insurance market, insurable risks may be limited to loss of property or may extend to virtually any risk other than loss of life.

The taxable income arising from short-term insurance activities is generally calculated in the same way as the taxable income arising from other business activities, with premiums derived included in gross income and claims incurred allowed as a deduction. However, three features of short-term insurance activities may justify special tax treatment. These are discussed below.

1. Income-Recognition Rules

Income-recognition rules must take into account that some part of the premiums received during a tax period will cover risks for a period after the end of that year (referred to as "unexpired risks"). This is because, in many cases, the period of the insurance policy will not coincide with the insurance company's tax year. The accounting practice is for insurance companies to treat a portion of their short-term insurance premium income received during a year as relating to unexpired risks as of the end of the year. This amount is not regarded as having been earned until the following year and, therefore, is excluded from their income for that year and included in income in the following year. A similar approach may apply for tax purposes. This may be an aspect of the accrual tax accounting rules,[196] or a specific deductible allowance may be provided for premiums in respect of unexpired risks (with a reinclusion rule for the following year).[197]

---

[195]Short-term insurance as used here includes property and casualty insurance and term life insurance, provided the term of insurance is not beyond one year or so. Life insurance with longer terms raises other issues that are beyond the scope of this book.

[196]Premiums paid in respect of unexpired risks may be treated as unearned income.

[197]E.g., UGA ITA § 17 and fourth sched.; ZAF ITA § 28(2); ZMB ITA § 25 and third sched.

2. Deduction-Recognition Rules

On the expense side, deduction-recognition rules must take into account the three types of claims that may arise during a tax year for a company carrying on a short-term insurance business. The first type of claim is one that arises and is paid out during the tax year. This is allowed as a deductible expenditure of the company. The second type of claim is one that arises during the year, but that has not been paid out as of the end of the tax year. This type of claim is also allowed as a deduction under accrual tax accounting on the basis that the obligation to pay has arisen during the tax year. The amount of deduction is based on established insurance practice for assessing the likely amount payable on a claim. The third type of claim is one that is unreported as of the end of the tax year; it relates to an event that has occurred during the tax year but that has not been reported to the insurance company, either because a third party has not made a claim against the insured or because the insured has not reported the claim or the happening of the event. This type of claim may also be allowed as a deduction under accrual tax accounting on the basis that the happening of the event crystallizes the liability of the insurance company to pay, even though the claim has not yet been reported to the company.

3. Contingency Reserves

For financial accounting purposes, companies carrying on short-term insurance retain a contingency reserve to meet the exceptional level of claims that may arise from a catastrophe. It is not recommended that a deduction for tax purposes be allowed on the basis of the creation of a contingency reserve for financial accounts purposes. As noted in section II(B)(1), reserves are used in financial accounting to provide an accurate picture of the long-term profitability of a business. Tax accounting, on the other hand, is concerned with the accurate measurement of net gains on an annual basis. The establishment of a contingency reserve does not represent a sufficiently certain liability to be recognized for income tax purposes.

VII. Administrative Aspects of Taxing Business and Investment Income

Taxes imposed on income from business are normally self-assessed,[198] which imposes on the taxpayer, in the first instance, responsibility for calculating taxable income and the tax due on that income and for making installment payments at designated times. The taxpayer's calculations are reviewed by revenue officials when returns are filed and may be subject to further audit. The self-

---

[198]In other words, the taxpayer determines (assesses) the amount of tax due and files (lodges) the tax return.

assessment system may be supplemented by a withholding system applicable to certain business payments. The withholding system is discussed further below.

A. Advance Payments of Tax

The most crucial element of the system for collecting business tax is the formula for determining installment payments. The object of the system is to require businesses to pay tax on a regular basis throughout the year as income is derived, not when final liability is determined after the end of the tax year. This formula ensures revenue flow to tax authorities, prevents deferral of tax payment, and minimizes the risk of disbursement of income before the appropriate proportion is remitted as payment of a tax liability. Related issues are mechanisms for adjusting payments if the taxpayer's business income changes during the year and reconciliation of installment payments with the final tax liability.

The frequency with which installments of business income tax must be made varies significantly among countries. In many jurisdictions, different frequencies are used for different types of businesses (unincorporated or incorporated) or different sizes of businesses (based on taxable income or turnover). The use of variable installment payment frequencies has two objectives: (1) to minimize administrative costs for smaller businesses; and (2) to reduce financing charges for smaller businesses that face a number of biases in the capital market and, accordingly, tend to place greater reliance on cash flow to fund ongoing operations. In light of these objectives, a frequency distinction based on the size of a business is more logical than one based on legal form. However, rules based on size may be manipulated by taxpayers establishing multiple companies. This practice may be combated through consolidation rules, but this tends to add complexity to the system. An alternative approach is to base payment schedules on a combination of business size and form. The simplest approach is to use the same rule as that used to determine when businesses are required to use accrual accounting, or to use the same form of rule with a different threshold.

There are four basic models for the formula used to determine business tax installments. Two systems rely on the previous year's taxable income as the basis for estimating the taxable income of the current year, and two use data from the current year to estimate total taxable income for the year.

The simplest system is based on the previous year's taxable income, divided by the number of installments. (Alternatively, the formula can be based on the previous year's tax liability, adjusted, if necessary, by any change in tax rates.) A slightly more sophisticated system is one based on the previous year's taxable income (or tax liability), adjusted by an "uplift" factor that is based on the actual or projected inflation rate or on a measurement of expected growth in nominal incomes generally.[199]

---

[199]The uplift system is used, for example, in Australia for individuals deriving business and investment income.

The simplest system relying on current-year data is based on records of turnover for the installment period. The turnover for the period is multiplied by the ratio of the previous year's taxable income to turnover for that year to estimate the probable taxable income that will ensue from the known turnover for the current year. A more sophisticated system draws on an estimate of actual taxable income for the year based on income derived and expenses incurred in the year until the end of the installment period.

Systems for determining installments on the basis of the current year's income provide a more accurate calculation of a taxpayer's probable total liability for the year and the appropriate installment payments to be made. However, the potential administrative burden they impose on taxpayers is considerably greater than for systems based on the previous year's income. Also, these systems, particularly ones based on a running determination of taxable income for the year, are possible only if taxpayers have access to relatively sophisticated accounting and tax expertise. Accordingly, a system based on actual income for the year is more easily applied in industrial countries than in developing or transition economies. Nevertheless, a number of transition countries require payment of tax according to results for the current period.[200]

Systems based on income of the current year are self-adjusting in terms of changes in business fortunes. If the taxpayer uses prior-year information to calculate liability for current-year installments, some adjustment mechanism is needed if the taxpayer's taxable income for the year is likely to differ significantly from the estimated income on which installments are based. To protect taxpayers from undue hardship in the event of falling business income, the taxpayer should have the option of nominating an expected taxable income that is lower than that yielded by the presumptive formula or of altering the estimate downward if circumstances make this appropriate during the year. Rigorous interest and penalty measures will discourage taxpayers from deliberately nominating lower-than-expected incomes to reduce installment payments and thereby deferring payment of some tax until a final reconciliation payment at the end of the year. These measures should impose a charge significantly higher than the prevailing interest rate to ensure that taxpayers do not use underestimation as a means of securing finance (in effect "borrowing" tax due until the close of the year). Countries with serious tax collection problems may not want to provide any option for taxpayers to reduce required installments, if there is a concern that any reasonable penalty would be ineffective in deterring abuse of such an option.

While most installment systems that are based on taxable income of the previous year provide taxpayers with the option of substituting a lower estimate of expected income, it is not usual to require taxpayers to uplift their estimates if financial information during the year indicates that income will be

---

[200]*See, e.g.,* KAZ TC § 51.

greater than that yielded by the presumptive formula.[201] Not requiring taxpayers to uplift provides taxpayers with a deferral advantage in times of increasing income. To avoid the problem, taxpayers can be required to use an installment calculation system based on current-year information, such as turnover.

One particular problem with both systems is that of taxpayers commencing business. In the absence of any special provisions, these systems allow such taxpayers to defer tax on the income derived in the first year until the end of that year. Because it is common to allow taxpayers to substitute lower estimates when they believe income is falling, taxpayers leaving business suffer no corresponding overpayment of taxes when closing business operations. Although the deferral by taxpayers commencing business undermines the installment system, most jurisdictions that rely on a formula of installment payments that is based on statistics from previous years do not make any effort to address the problem. Because taxpayers commencing businesses are not likely to earn substantial profits in the first year, the approach of not providing a special rule for these taxpayers is justifiable. However, the absence of a special rule may provide significant windfall benefits to some categories of taxpayers, such as lawyers or accountants, who are invited to join the firm as full partners (and hence become business proprietors). It also opens a potential door to abuse if business owners move the business operations to a new company on a regular basis (or even annually) to defer payment of tax. However, this is not likely to emerge as a serious problem until an economy is fairly advanced.

B. Withholding

A domestic withholding system can be applied to payments made to some self-employed persons, although it is not administratively possible to apply such withholding taxes to all payments made to those persons. For example, given that the tax is withheld by the payer of the income, it is not feasible to apply the tax to all payments to a self-employed person with a large number of small-value customers, particularly nonbusiness (i.e., final-consumer) customers. Even if such customers complied with their obligations to withhold the tax and remit it to revenue authorities, matching the large number of small withholdings to particular taxpayers would be an extremely onerous task for the administration. Withholding tax on self-employed persons, therefore, is usually confined to those industries with a small number of business customers. Even then, there is generally a value threshold before withholding applies and, possibly, an exclusion for contracts with nonbusiness consumers. The most common industries to which withholding tax applies are construction and transportation.[202] An exception may be provided for taxpayers with a satisfac-

---

[201]Provisions for uplift estimates need not be explicit. The United States imposes an implicit requirement by levying additional tax on large corporate taxpayers whose estimated tax payments are less than actual tax. See USA IRC § 6655(d)(2).

[202]E.g., AUS ITAA (1936) §§ 221YHA–221YHZ.

tory compliance record. Consolidation measures may be needed to prevent taxpayers from splitting contracts into multiple contracts, each generating payments below the withholding threshold.[203]

Withholding on payments to self-employed persons is generally at a flat rate applied against the gross amount of the payment. Because the rate is applied against gross income, some amount of deductions is notionally taken into account in determining the rate. This is important because taxpayers in the industries to which such withholding applies are likely to claim substantial deductions for the cost of inputs. If the rate of withholding on gross receipts is set too high, then the withholding tax may ultimately exceed the taxpayer's chargeable income for the year of assessment, causing serious cash-flow problems for the taxpayer.

Withholding on income derived by self-employed persons who are resident taxpayers will generally not be a final tax. A taxpayer will be required to file a return showing taxable income for the tax year and tax payable thereon, and a tax offset will be given for the withholding tax.

C. Withholding on Income from Capital

Final withholding taxes on gross income are the usual method for assessing nonresidents on income from capital. A final withholding tax means the recipient is not required to file a return or face additional assessment in the source jurisdiction with respect to income subject to the tax. The recipient may be subject to additional tax in the recipient's country of residence. In most countries, final withholding taxes are imposed on interest and dividends paid to nonresidents. They are often extended to royalties and less commonly to rental income paid to nonresidents[204] and to distributions from trusts.[205]

The use of final withholding taxes on income from capital paid to resident taxpayers is a growing phenomenon, but the practice is far less common than for nonresidents. Reluctance to use final withholding taxes for resident taxpayers primarily stems from equity concerns. The use of any flat rate will prejudice taxpayers whose incomes would be subject to lower rates if the ordinary rate structure were applied and will provide a windfall to taxpayers whose incomes would otherwise be subject to higher rates.

The widespread use of final withholding taxes on different categories of income effectively creates a schedular system with what are, in effect, separate taxes on different categories of income. The system may, in fact, become a hybrid system with flat-rate taxes on some categories of income and progressive rates on others. In theory, the system may be designed so as to minimize the loss of progressivity by applying withholding taxes as a final tax only if the tax-

---

[203]*See, e.g.,* Regulations for the Implementation of the Individual Income Tax Law § 21 (State Council, People's Republic of China, Jan. 28, 1994) (consolidation of payments).
[204]*See, e.g.,* CAN ITA §§ 212(1)(d), 215(1).
[205]*See, e.g.,* CAN ITA § 212(1)(c).

payer's income is primarily of the category subject to progressive rates (and therefore not subject to final withholding taxes).[206] In practice, however, such a system would be difficult to implement.

There is no doubt that final withholding taxes on income from capital are preferable from the perspective of administrative simplicity. As was noted in chapter 14,[207] flat-rate withholding taxes on income from capital may not undermine progressivity as much as feared. The important point is that, if income from capital is segregated in this manner, taxpayers are unable to minimize tax by mismatching gains and losses and exploiting inconsistencies in timing or treatment of different types of expenses and gains. In fact, some studies from Scandinavia hold that the movement toward "dual income taxes" (i.e., flat-rate taxes on some types of income from capital and progressive rates on other income) may actually increase progressivity by precluding taxpayers from exploiting arrangements to minimize their tax in these ways.

The choice between separate withholding taxes or ordinary assessment for income from capital will depend on a range of political and administrative considerations. Essential to the effective functioning of either system is a high-integrity taxpayer identification number (TIN) system. This is important for an ordinary assessment system for auditing purposes. The TIN system serves several different functions if withholding taxes are used. One purpose is to facilitate auditing. While tax authorities may no longer be concerned with attributing income from capital to the correct taxpayer if final withholding taxes are used, they will be interested in comparing income from capital with other income sources to ascertain whether the taxpayer declared enough income to explain the investments now generating investment income.

A second purpose of TINs in a system that uses withholding taxes is to give taxpayers the option of filing in appropriate cases. While optional filing complicates the administration of the withholding tax, it can be used to protect the interests of lower-income taxpayers who are subject to ordinary assessment tax rates that are less than the withholding tax rates. It can also be used to protect taxpayers who incur significant expenses to derive their income from capital. This may be the case with, for example, taxpayers deriving rental income.

An alternative to optional filing sometimes mooted to protect lower-income taxpayers from the impact of withholding taxes that are higher than their marginal tax rate is a limited exemption from withholding. The exemption is usually suggested for interest on accounts in financial institutions up to a designated amount. However, because it is impossible for financial institutions to know of other accounts that depositors may hold, higher-income tax-

---

[206]*See, e.g.*, Charles McLure & Santiago Pardo, *Improving the Administration of the Colombian Income Tax, 1986–88, in* Improving Tax Administration in Developing Countries 124, 126–27 (Richard Bird & Milka Casanegra eds. 1992).

[207]*See* footnote 28 and accompanying text in that chapter.

payers are likely to exploit the exemptions by opening multiple accounts. A high-integrity system of taxpayer identification numbers will enable tax authorities to identify these cases, but a very sophisticated system for cross-referencing data is required. Also, additional tax can be collected only by means of an assessment levied on appropriate taxpayers. The use of mandatory withholding tax coupled with optional filing by lower-income persons is administratively simpler, because it transfers the onus for further action to the taxpayer. Such a system would not be desirable, however, if a large number of additional returns had to be filed. Either system can be used to identify taxpayers who may be involved in shifting arrangements. Appropriate targets for antishifting audits can be identified by comparing claims for lower or zero tax rates with returns of spouses and other family members.

Optional filing for income from capital raises a number of issues. First, it must be decided whether optional filers can elect to have a lower or zero withholding tax imposed or whether they are subject to the withholding tax, with the two being reconciled after the tax year when a return is filed. In that case, a refund of excess withholding tax may be made. Allowing taxpayers to seek a lower or zero withholding tax rate by submitting an appropriate form to income payers ensures that there is no overpayment of tax during the year. However, such taxpayers would have to be required to file returns at the end of the year to ensure that they are entitled to the lower rates or exemptions they claim. This further filing imposes some burden on taxpayers and an additional administrative burden on income payers, who must provide revenue authorities with details of all cases in which taxpayers seek lower withholding rates or exemptions. It also imposes further administrative burdens on tax authorities, who must cross-check with individual returns those cases of lower or zero withholding rates in order to ensure that taxpayers are entitled to the benefits they claim. Measures are needed to discourage taxpayers from deliberately or inadvertently claiming entitlement to lower or zero withholding tax rates. These include interest payable on the deferred payment of tax and penalties depending on the culpability of the taxpayer. Finally, if the choice is between an exemption from withholding and full withholding, taxpayers subject to tax rates even only slightly below the withholding rate would enjoy a significant deferral on their tax liability.

If taxpayers are not given the option of seeking lower or zero withholding rates subject to reconciliation when a return is filed, it must be decided whether refunds of withholding tax should be accompanied by compensation for the use of the taxpayer's funds prior to the refund. Compensation in the form of interest imposes additional administrative burdens on tax authorities, but promotes equity. Only a limited number of persons are likely to file returns to obtain refunds.

If the system of mandatory withholding tax subject to reconciliation when a return is filed is adopted, an exception should be made for exempt taxpayers, who should be able to claim an exemption in any case. Also, the final withholding tax should not be used for interest paid to financial institutions, because these taxpayers will incur significant expenses to derive interest income and their net margin on interest payments will be much smaller than the gross payment.

It is not necessary to choose between a final withholding tax and a withholding tax subject to reconciliation for all classes of income from capital. For example, a final withholding tax can be imposed on interest income and dividends, while taxpayers subject to a withholding tax on rent can be allowed to file a return and seek reconciliation if withholding tax rates are higher than the taxpayers' personal rates.

The taxation of income from royalties is complicated because royalties encompass several conceptually different types of payments, which are classified differently by different countries.[208] The categorization is important, not so much for the definition of income as for the deduction of losses and expenses. The extent to which taxpayers incur expenses to derive royalty income will vary significantly depending on the type of royalty. Depending on the structure of the tax system and the characterization of royalty income, taxpayers may be entitled to deductions for itemized expenses, a standard deduction, or no deduction at all. This treatment will in turn determine whether a withholding tax can be applied to some or all types of royalties.

If royalties are assessed under a schedular tax system or are subject to a final withholding tax, there is a good case for an effective tax burden in line with the maximum tax rate in the personal income tax and the normal rate of corporate income tax. Any substantial discrepancy between the tax rate for royalties and the rates for other income will cause taxpayers to recharacterize payments as royalties, or as something other than royalties, depending on which alternative leads to the lowest tax burden. Also, any preferential treatment or rates for royalties will encourage multinational businesses to withdraw profits in the form of royalties rather than as dividends or interest.

Appendix. Relation Between Tax and Financial Accounting Rules

A. Introduction

Commercial companies keep accounts for the information of their owners and creditors. These reflect the assets and liabilities of the company on a balance sheet as well as the profits for the preceding year. The relevance of a company's profits for commercial accounting purposes and for tax purposes is broadly similar. For purposes of the income tax, profits are considered to constitute taxable capacity. Profit is, of course, an imprecise concept. It is a tem-

---

[208]*See supra* sec. III(C).

poral concept, requiring measurement against a defined period of time. Although the basic purpose of measuring profit is shared by commercial accounting practices and by the tax rules, the purposes of tax and financial accounting are not exactly the same. Because of these differences in purpose, and in the light of different legal and commercial traditions, different countries have developed different systems for relating the tax rules and the commercial accounting rules.[209] How they do this is a critical issue for the drafting of the rules for determining business income. At one extreme, business income can be measured according to an entirely self-contained set of rules that are included in the income tax law and regulations. At the other extreme, the income tax law can state simply that income for tax purposes is the same as income as determined under the rules for commercial accounting. As we shall see, in practice most countries adopt a combination of rules.

B. Evolution of Commercial Accounting Rules

In the two centuries since joint-stock companies came to be widely used, pressures have been applied to define how business profits are identified. Membership of businesses has been drawn more widely, and members now require formal checks on the accounts of their businesses. External controls have been imposed, usually by legislation, and include independent audits. Further, many members of a business are portfolio investors, requiring—as do the markets— greater transparency of performance of a business. These accounting regulations have not been applied universally: smaller corporate businesses and noncorporate businesses are often exempted wholly or partly from these obligations.

The original lack of a required form of accounting has been replaced in all OECD countries by a combination of law and accounting practice designed to produce some consistency and objectivity in the presentation of company accounts. There are, however, distinct national differences both in the rules and principles adopted and in the legal or professional forms that those rules and principles have taken. The tendency in civil law countries has been to adopt rules within the commercial code or a law on accounting. By contrast, in common law countries, much of the content of accounting rules has been left for professional bodies or expert committees to produce.

Accounting laws and practices are being coordinated at regional and international levels, as well as being imposed more strictly at the national level. A comparative discussion of the effectiveness of accounting standards for tax purposes may start with an examination of the International Accounting Standards (IAS), produced since 1973 by the International Accounting Stan-

---

[209]*See generally* Commission of the European Communities, Report of the Committee of Independent Experts on Company Taxation 50–51, 195 (1992); Guido de Bont et al., Fiscal Versus Commercial Profit Accounting in the Netherlands, France, and Germany (1996).

dards Committee, an autonomous body, but associated with the International Federation of Accountants (IFAC), a nongovernment body of professional accountants. Some thirty standards have been issued—a mixture of general principles (e.g., prudence, substance over form, and materiality)[210] and specific rules (such as the information to be disclosed in financial statements).[211]

Within Europe, the countries of the European Union apply a series of company directives that require set principles and formats for company accounts.[212] Some officials of the European Commission attempted to adapt some of these rules into a format to provide a common definition of the tax base for income tax, but the attempt failed even to secure support within the Commission and was never officially published.

Progress has been made in recent years, but accounting norms are inconsistent, incomplete, and evolving. It is too early to expect a common definition of profit at the international level, although one is starting to emerge. But for public companies in states with developed capital markets, there are standard formats, principles, and rules for presenting accounts. The growing internationalization of business reinforces this trend.

C. Current Practice

1. Overview

Some states base their determination of the taxable capacity of companies on the commercial accounts of those companies. In these states, the precise form of company accounts is typically laid down in the commercial code. Subject to some specific exceptions in both tax legislation and jurisprudence, compliance with the commercial law also amounts to compliance with the tax laws, and tax is levied accordingly. The profit that the company declares to the market is closely related to the profit on which it is taxed (although, in practice, the extent of the profit declared to the market may be driven by tax considerations).

Other countries have a tax definition of profits that may be markedly different from the company's own view of its profitability for the purposes of payments of dividends and publication to the market. Historically, these countries have taken a more relaxed view to the detailed form of company accounts for general legal purposes, but have imposed rules requiring specific accounting treatment of both additions and diminutions to wealth for tax purposes only. With limited exceptions, what a company does for accounting purposes is totally irrelevant to its income tax position. As a consequence, the income tax

---

[210]IAS 1.

[211]IAS 5.

[212]*See* particularly the Fourth Company Directive—78/660/EEC, and the Seventh—83/319/EEC.

law and regulations must govern in detail the methods of accounting for all the elements that enter into the determination of taxable income.

To clarify the matter, we will review the rules applicable in Canada, France, Germany, the United States, and several transition countries. The topic is a complex one, and the reader should be warned that the discussion below does not capture all the subtleties of each system, which would require a much more in-depth examination.

2. Germany

In Germany, the commercial code provides that companies of a specific size are required to keep double-entry books.[213] Fairly detailed rules are provided for how these accounts are to be kept. If an issue is not specifically governed by a written rule, it is to be resolved according to principles of orderly bookkeeping.[214] For tax purposes, determination of taxable income starts with the accounting balance sheet. Specifically, taxable income is determined under the net worth comparison method.[215] The net worth method uses the net worth (assets minus liabilities) in the opening and closing balance sheets for the taxable year.

The basic idea of the net worth method is that taxable income is the difference between closing net worth and opening net worth. It is also, however, necessary to subtract those items that increase closing net worth but that should not be included in taxable income (e.g., tax-exempt receipts and contributions to capital) and to add items that decrease closing net worth but that should not be deductible in determining taxable income (e.g., dividends).

Accordingly, taxable profit for the year is

	(i) the amount of net worth reflected in the closing balance sheet,
less	(ii) the amount of net worth reflected in the opening balance sheet,
less	(iii) contributions to capital and other receipts that are not taxable,
plus	(iv) withdrawals made in favor of the owners and expenses that are not deductible.

---

[213]The discussion in this section is based on Brigitte Knobbe-Keuk, Bilanz- und Unternehmenssteuerrecht (9th ed. 1993).

[214]Handelsrechtliche Grundsätze ordnungsmäßiger Buchführung (GoB).

[215]See vol. 1, ch. 13, for further discussion of the net worth method. The net worth method is set forth clearly in the income tax laws of France and Germany. See FRA CGI § 38; DEU EStG § 4. Under certain circumstances, certain types of income are determined as the difference between income and expenses, instead of being determined by the net worth method. Those familiar with the Haig-Simons concept of income, which also uses a net worth concept, may misunderstand what the net worth method involves. Unlike the Haig-Simons concept, the net worth method generally does not involve mark-to-market taxation, because it uses the book value, rather than the fair market value, of assets on the balance sheet in determining net worth (except in cases where book value is determined according to fair market value).

There are two questions for each item of the balance sheet: (1) should the item be included as an asset (or liability) and (2) if so, how should it be valued? As to both issues, the general rule is that for tax purposes the treatment in the accounting balance sheet applies unless there is a specific rule to the contrary in the tax law. In some cases, the taxpayer has a choice under the accounting rules as to how to treat an item. In these cases, having made an election for accounting purposes, the taxpayer is bound to follow the same treatment for tax purposes. Once the return has been filed, changes to the accounting treatment are permitted only under limited circumstances. If the treatment of an item on the balance sheet is contrary to the accounting rules, then the taxpayer may make the correction. If the treatment results from an option under the accounting rules, the taxpayer may change the treatment for tax and accounting purposes only with the consent of the tax authorities. Even if the tax law specifically authorizes a favorable treatment of an item, it has been provided that the treatment is not available unless the same treatment is applied for commercial accounting purposes.

In a number of specific cases, however, the tax law specifies that the treatment of an item for tax purposes differs from that applicable for accounting purposes. These concern particularly the allowance of deductions. The tax law also contains relatively extensive rules for valuation of property, which apply instead of the accounting norms.

The consequence of this legal structure is that, in the absence of a specific rule in the tax law, the treatment of an item for income tax purposes is governed by the rules in the commercial code. If this does not contain a specific rule, then the principles of orderly bookkeeping apply. It is the principles of accounting practice, rather than specific tax principles, that are consulted in disputes about determining taxable income.

3. France

France also uses the net worth comparison method of determining taxable business income for companies keeping double-entry books.[216] Although tax accounting follows commercial accounting, the application of this principle has been somewhat different from that in Germany. This results from the fact that in France the commercial accounting rules were not codified in the commercial code until relatively recently (1983). Thus, while there was a doctrine that tax and commercial accounting should be the same, absent express provision to the contrary in the tax laws, in practice it was left to the tax laws and to courts interpreting the tax laws to develop accounting principles. Thus, for example, the principle of *créances acquises et dettes certaines* (accrued receiv-

---

[216]The discussion in this section is based on Mémento Pratique Francis Lefebvre Comptable 1991, at 28–30 (1990).

ables and fixed liabilities)[217] was developed as an interpretation of the tax law to govern the timing of accrual.

Now that fairly detailed accounting rules have been codified in the commercial code, France is in approximately the same position as Germany. Future questions about tax accounting will presumably be handled with reference to the rules of commercial accounting. Of course, if the legislature does not like court decisions applying those rules for tax purposes, it is always free to provide specific contrary rules that will apply for tax purposes.

4. United States

The United States represents an example of the opposite extreme from France and Germany. The tax laws of the United States contain no general principle relating commercial accounting and tax accounting. This means that all of the principles of tax accounting must be contained in the Internal Revenue Code and regulations (or must be derived by courts from interpretation of this legislation). There is a separate concept of tax accounting, which is similar to commercial accounting in that it follows the principle of continuity: the taxpayer cannot generally change the method of accounting without the permission of the Internal Revenue Service. In a few special instances, tax provisions have been made applicable on condition that the taxpayer follows the same method of accounting for commercial accounting purposes (e.g., LIFO).[218] And the minimum tax has been based on income as determined for financial accounting.[219] But apart from these special provisions, tax rules are independent.

5. Canada

In Canada, the definition of taxable income by reference to generally accepted accounting principles was proposed but rejected in 1947.[220] Despite the failure to enact this language, the concept of generally accepted accounting principles has been important in the interpretation of the income tax law.[221]

---

[217]This is approximately equivalent to the "all events" test for accrual accounting in the United States. See Treas. Reg. § 1.446-1(c)(1)(ii) ("Generally, under an accrual method, income is to be included for the taxable year when all the events have occurred that fix the right to receive the income and the amount of the income can be determined with reasonable accuracy. Under such a method, a liability is incurred, and generally is taken into account for Federal income tax purposes, in the taxable year in which all the events have occurred that establish the fact of the liability, the amount of the liability can be determined with reasonable accuracy, and economic performance has occurred with respect to the liability").

[218]See USA IRC § 472(c).

[219]See Tax Reform Act of 1986, P.L. 99-514, 100 Stat. 2085, 2326, sec. 701 (1986). The relevant provisions, codified at IRC § 56(f), were subsequently repealed.

[220]See Brian Arnold et al., Canadian Income Tax 290 (19th ed. 1993).

[221]See Brian Arnold, Canada, 10 Tax Notes Int'l 1533 (May 1, 1995); Brian Arnold, Supreme Court of Canada Discusses Financial, Tax Accounting, 16 Tax Notes Int'l 730 (Mar. 9, 1998).

This means that while there is not strict conformity between commercial and tax accounting, there should in practice be a fairly close correlation between the two.

6. Transition Countries

Countries in transition have had to address the relation between tax and commercial accounting rules at a time when both are at an early stage of development. A number of countries have followed the French/German approach. For example, in the Czech Republic, Latvia, the Slovak Republic, and Slovenia, the law explicitly refers to commercial accounting as the basis for tax accounting absent specific provisions to the contrary in the tax law.[222] In Estonia, the statute says nothing about conformity between financial and tax accounting and delegates to the Minister of Finance the specification of the accounting rules.[223] However, the regulations issued under this authority call for income measurement according to the accounting norms, unless otherwise specified by the tax law.[224]

The techniques for linking the definition of taxable income to accounting differ depending on the form of the definition. If taxable income is defined on the basis of net worth comparison, there is a reference to the balance sheet in the definition of taxable income, which can be interpreted without further specification as referring to the accounting balance. In countries where taxable income is defined as the difference between receipts subject to tax and deductible expenses, the usual practice is to state that taxable income is the same as commercial accounting income, with the modifications stated in the tax law.

In Russia, Kazakhstan, and other countries whose tax legislation is influenced by the Russian legislation, the traditional approach has been for the same set of accounting rules to apply for all purposes, including taxation. Thus, under the system that applied in the former Soviet Union, the question of the relation between tax accounting and financial accounting could not even be raised, because there was simply one accounting system. The system was spelled out in detail, leaving little or no room for independent judgment by accountants. When new tax laws were adopted at the time of the split-up of the Soviet Union—and as these were modified thereafter—the tax laws often did contain accounting rules (referring to income being determined as the difference between taxable receipts and deductible expenses), which on their face appeared to make the tax laws independent of the financial accounting norms. However, the new tax rules were by and large interpreted in the light of prior practice, that is, as requiring the accounting norms to be applied for tax purposes. At the same time, financial accounting was undergoing often radical re-

---

[222]*See* CZE ITA § 23(2); SVK ITA § 23(2); LVA EIT § 14; SVN PT § 9.

[223]*See* EST IT § 37(1).

[224]Instructions on the Payment to the Budget of Income Tax on Enterprises, § 5.1.

form to bring it into line with international practice. This reform has proceeded at quite different paces in different countries that were formerly part of the Soviet Union. At the time of writing, there is accordingly some uncertainty as to the current or prospective relationship between tax and financial accounting in these countries. The situation is quite difficult during the transition; in some cases, tax laws have been reformed in advance of accounting reform, so that it is difficult for tax law to refer to accounting practice, which is not fully developed or appropriate for the new tax legislation.[225] Some advisors would in any event prefer to separate tax from accounting. Once accounting reform has been undertaken and accountants have been trained in the new methods, it will be easier to specify a more permanent relationship between tax and financial accounting.

D. Choice Among Different Approaches

As the above review suggests, the relationship between tax and accounting norms differs substantially from one country to the next. It cannot be said that there is one right or best practice for a particular country. The general approach to be pursued in a particular country will be heavily influenced by tradition, and it is usually best to respect the practice with which tax officials and accountants are familiar rather than trying to impose something different because it follows the personal preference of a foreign advisor. Moreover, the state of development of accounting practice is relevant in deciding the extent to which it makes sense to rely on commercial accounting rather than on autonomous tax rules. Within each country's paradigm, however, it is possible to make a number of adjustments so as to assure a solid revenue base. For example, in countries that will be starting with accounting profit, it is important to limit the reserves that are deductible for tax purposes. A number of transition countries have adopted the effective approach of not allowing deductions for reserves unless they are specifically enumerated in the tax law.[226] The reserves allowed can then be limited to those for bad debts (perhaps only for banks) and those for insurance companies. Even these reserves should be carefully circumscribed, but the issues required to do so are beyond the scope of this book.

In addition, in a system that relies generally on the accounting norms, it is possible to provide for any number of deviations from those norms when considered appropriate for tax purposes, although administrative convenience should be taken into account. For example, different rules can be provided for depreciation. To the extent possible, tax and accounting calculations should be on the same basis so as to reduce unnecessary paperwork. In the case of de-

---

[225]This is why the tax codes of Georgia and Kazakhstan, and the enterprise profit tax law of Ukraine, do not refer to accounting norms (unlike the Latvian law, accounting reform in that country having proceeded at a much more rapid pace).

[226]See ROM PT § 4(3); LVA EIT § 6(3); GEO TC § 52(2); KAZ TC § 18(2).

preciation, accounting norms may provide a number of options to the tax-payer. However, from the point of view of tax policy, it is generally considered preferable to have a single set of rules that apply to all taxpayers. Therefore, it may in any event be impossible to achieve total conformity between tax and accounting norms in this regard.

17

Depreciation, Amortization, and Depletion

Richard K. Gordon

> Strictly speaking, the calculation of income demands complete revaluation
> of all assets and obligations at the end of every period. Practically, the
> question is: How shall the requisite value estimates be obtained?
> —Henry Simons

I. Introduction

Henry Simons correctly noted that a comprehensive income tax requires
the revaluation of all assets and obligations to take into account accumulated
gains and losses at the end of every tax period. As a general matter, all income
tax systems have accepted that, in many instances at least, the practical question of valuing property for each relevant period can be very difficult to answer. Changes in the value of property will often not be taken into account
until some particular moment, such as when ownership of the property is
transferred or the property becomes worthless. However, such deferral of accounting for accrued gains and losses may result in either undertaxation, if the
value of the property has increased, or overtaxation, if it has decreased.[1] Most

---

Note: Victor Thuronyi, Leif Mutén, Alvin Warren, Victoria Summers, Philip Dawicki, and
Melinda Milenkovich made numerous helpful comments on earlier drafts. I would like to give
special thanks to Emil Sunley, who took considerable time to disabuse me of many a theoretical
error and who provided particularly close commentary on earlier drafts.

[1]There are other problems. The most important of these is that accounting for accrued gains
only when the property is transferred (or scrapped) turns into, in part, a tax on the act of engaging in transactions. This can result in inefficiencies owing to the so-called lock-in effect, where
taxpayers avoid selling or exchanging their property. On the other hand, if there were no current
accounting for decreases in value, there could be a corresponding "anti-lock-in effect," resulting
in an incentive to sell or transfer the property. *See* Daniel N. Shaviro, *An Efficiency Analysis of
Realization and Recognition Rules Under the Federal Income Tax*, 48 Tax L. Rev. 1, 4–5 (1992).

tax accounting systems allow or require the periodic estimation of gain or loss on certain types of property.[2] Depreciation (often called amortization when involving nonphysical property) is one of the most important instances where the taxpayer is allowed to deduct estimations of loss over time.[3] The decision to accrue estimated declines in value through depreciation is largely predicated on three points: that the property has a "useful life"[4] longer than the taxable year, that absent accrual there would be a substantial likelihood of mismatching current income with unrealized losses, and that reasonable estimates of such losses can be made.

If property has a useful life shorter than the taxable year, its full cost could be completely deducted before the next taxable year, obviating the problem of unaccounted losses.[5] For this reason, most jurisdictions deny a full deduction for the cost of any property with a useful life of greater than one year, while at the same time restricting depreciation allowances to such cost.

Because gain in the value of property is not typically recognized until the property is transferred (or until it is scrapped or otherwise becomes worthless), most tax jurisdictions include a counterbalancing or compensating rule not to recognize accrued but unrealized losses.[6] Also, many jurisdictions do not tax either the gains or the losses on certain property held by individuals. Finally, many tax systems exempt from tax the income generated by some types of property. However, depreciable property usually generates currently taxable income. If deductions were not allowed for losses in the value of such property, there would be a mismatching of income and loss, and therefore overtaxation.[7] For this reason, depreciation deductions are typically limited to property that generates currently taxable income.

---

[2]There are other techniques for taking account of the time value of money when gains or losses are not accrued currently. *See* the discussion *infra* at text accompanying note 12 regarding the application of estimated interest charges on deferral values, and at text accompanying note 13 regarding first year capital recovery.

[3]*See generally* Dale Chua, *Depreciation Schedules, in* Tax Policy Handbook 136 (P. Shome ed. 1995).

[4]The term "useful life" here means the period during which the property would be held for the production of income. At least by the end of the property's useful life, the taxpayer would dispose of it. However, this does not necessarily mean that the property would at that point be completely worthless. It may have a residual value, often referred to as "scrap" value.

[5]If the property has a life greater than the current tax year, a full deduction would result, interest and tax rates remaining equal, in an exemption from tax of any net income, except for economic rents. *See* Institute for Fiscal Studies, The Structure and Reform of Direct Taxation (Report of Committee chaired by J.E. Meade) 231–32 (1978). However, it would be possible to take only a partial deduction. *See infra* note 13 and accompanying text.

[6]*See generally* the discussion of the role of compensating distortions in a comprehensive income tax in Boris I. Bittker, A *"Comprehensive Tax Base" as a Goal of Income Tax Reform*, 80 Harv. L. Rev. 925, 983–84 (1967).

[7]*See* Jeff Strnad, *Taxation of Income from Capital: A Theoretical Reappraisal*, 37 Stan. L. Rev. 1023, 1027–28 (1985). *See also* Example 1 *infra* sec. III(A).

Many types of physical property used to produce income are subject to wear and tear, which reduces the property's value.[8] In addition, technological changes may make the property relatively obsolete and therefore also less valuable. Nonphysical property may also lose value, either because the right to possession or use is limited in time (such as with the case of a lease or patent) or because of technological obsolescence. These factors—wear and tear, obsolescence, and, in the case of nonphysical property, a limited term—all tend to cause the value of certain types of property to decrease over time. Although the rules of different jurisdictions vary, as a general matter it is to the costs of such property that depreciation deductions are normally restricted. The most common, and perhaps most important, method of fixing such a restriction is by limiting deductions to types of property that have predictable useful lives.

Of course, the knowledge that property is losing its value as a result of wear and tear or obsolescence over its useful life does not permit the fixing of the value of each intervening yearly reduction.[9] In addition to yearly fluctuations in the effects of wear and tear and obsolescence, other factors may cause variation in the value of the property. Various market forces, such as changes in supply or demand for the product produced by the property or in the cost of production or availability of replacement property because of technological innovation or other reasons, will likely result in a corresponding increase or decrease in its value. Generally speaking, these effects are less predictable and may result in increases as well as decreases in value. As a result, there is probably no jurisdiction that generally includes such effects when determining allowable depreciation.[10] However, repairs or improvements made to property, or an increase in the term of nonphysical property, may increase its productivity or its productive life and therefore its value. Because these effects are often easier to estimate, they are frequently included in determining depreciation allowances.

There are techniques other than depreciation for compensating for accrued decreases (or increases) in the value of property held for the production

---

[8]The value of the property may decrease for various reasons. One common way is for it to lose efficiency and therefore its productivity. As output drops, so does income; as a result, its value necessarily declines.

[9]Nominal errors in useful lives can be corrected by "recapturing" excess depreciation deductions or by allowing additional deductions when the property is transferred or becomes worthless. See infra sec. III(E). However, even with such corrections, if each yearly allowed depreciation amount varies from the actual, there can be a considerable tax effect owing to the time value of money. See Paul Samuelson, Tax Deductibility of Economic Depreciation to Insure Invariant Valuations, 72 J. Pol. Econ. 604 (1964); Jeff Strnad, Periodicity and Accretion Taxation: Norms and Implications, 99 Yale L. J. 1817, 1822, 1865–79 (1990).

[10]An estimate for depreciation is not necessary if the actual decline in fair market value of the property is known. There may be other instances where actual declines in value can be ascertained without a property transfer. In the majority of instances, jurisdictions do not allow such evaluations outside of the system of depreciation. There are two important exceptions. The first is property held as inventory or trading goods. The other involves the use by certain jurisdictions of "extraordinary provisions." See infra notes 140, 142.

of income. One technique would, instead of allowing current deductions for depreciation, allow a deduction only when the property is transferred (or scrapped), but also give the taxpayer an additional allowance for the time value of the postponement of the deduction.[11] There are a number of problems with this approach. First, whenever interyear tax payments or refunds are involved, circumstances may change, with regard to both the tax system and the taxpayer. Rates may go up or down, taxpayers may go out of business, and, in either case, cash flow is invariably affected. However, as noted, most jurisdictions restrict depreciation in some fashion to property whose decline in value can be predicted through the fixing of a useful life. Nevertheless, property without a known useful life may also depreciate in value. At least in these cases, it might be preferable to allow the taxpayer some allowance for the delay in realizing a tax benefit for incremental reductions in asset value.[12]

It is also possible to go the other way around, and deduct a portion of the full cost of property in the first year in an amount equal to the discounted value of all future deductions, after which no more deductions would be allowed. This technique, proposed by the economists Alan Auerbach and Dale Jorgenson,[13] has a number of advantages, the principal one being that future changes in the inflation rate will not change investment incentives and, therefore, will not create distortions. Again, however, changes in effective tax rates are not automatically compensated for, and it would be necessary to estimate real rates of return and asset lives to determine the discount rate. While the latter is also necessary in other systems of depreciation, errors can be adjusted during the lifetime of the asset.[14] This means that if tax or interest rates change, or if the life of the property is miscalculated, while there may be no distortion, there may still may be windfalls, either for the taxpayer or the government.

The author is not aware of any tax system that employs either of these systems.

II. Definition of Depreciable Property

A. Categories of Property

Although all techniques for accounting for the accrued decrease in the value of business property are related, many jurisdictions have different rules

---

[11]In fact, such a system could be used to compensate for all accrued but unrealized changes in the value of property. *See* Mary L. Fellows, *A Comprehensive Attack on Tax Deferral*, 88 Mich. L. Rev. 722, 728–31 (1990).

[12]The tax administration could construct tables for taxpayers to use in estimating the value of the lost depreciation deductions. *See* David J. Shakow, *Taxation without Realization: A Proposal for Accrual Taxation*, 134 U. Pa. L. Rev. 1111, 1118–23 (1986). Of course, this does not solve the problem of unpredictable annual variations in the value of the property.

[13]Alan Auerbach and Dale Jorgenson, *The First Year Capital Recovery System*, 10 Tax Notes 515 (Apr. 14, 1980).

[14]*See infra* note 140 and accompanying text.

for different types of property. Although methods vary, property may be divided into a number of different categories. For physical property,[15] categories include (1) buildings other than industrial plant, (2) industrial plant and equipment, (3) depletable property (e.g., minerals), (4) land, and (5) inventory. For nonphysical property, they include (1) term-limited rights (e.g., leases, copyrights), and (2) property without specific time limits on use, such as goodwill. In addition, there are sometimes special provisions regarding the self-creation of otherwise depreciable property and incidental expenses, such as repair relating to depreciable physical property. Depending on the jurisdiction, some systems, for example, the accounting-based rules of the French, Germans, and Japanese, tend to rely relatively more on general rules that apply to many categories, while others, particularly those of the Commonwealth, tend to have specific (and sometimes not entirely congruent) rules for each category, or even subcategory, of property.

B. Property the Cost of Which Cannot Be Deducted in One Year

Income tax laws generally allow deductions for the costs of earning or securing current taxable income.[16] Income tax laws should, however, prohibit the taking of a current deduction for the purchase of any property that has a useful lifetime longer than a year.[17] As a corollary, any of the costs of self-creating such property should be treated in the same fashion as the costs of purchasing it.[18] The treatment of the costs of repairing or otherwise extending the life of such property should depend on the effect of the cost. If the effect lasts beyond a taxable year, that cost should also not be deductible. However, if the effect lasts for less than the taxable year, a current deduction is appropriate.[19]

Depreciation deductions should be permitted only for costs relating to a subcategory of such property. Depreciation deductions should be allowed for all of the related costs that had been disallowed as deductions.

---

[15]Although frequently used, the distinction between physical and nonphysical (also referred to as tangible and intangible, or material and nonmaterial) is not always obvious. For example, is computer software physical or nonphysical?

[16]See supra ch. 16.

[17]Except for de minimis rules, which would allow an immediate deduction for relatively small costs. See the discussion at the text accompanying notes 44–48 infra.

[18]See generally Fellows, supra note 11, at 768–70 (1990).

[19]However, it may be difficult to make distinctions among such different costs. When the costs are distinguished, the effect is to divide the property into different pieces, each of which is viewed separately. In theory, this could also be done for the different costs involved in the creation of an asset. Considerations of administrative ease may play the most important role in determining how such costs are treated. See the discussion infra at note 54. See also the discussion concerning de minimis rules below.

Certain systems, typically those found in civil law countries, base their income tax systems directly on financial accounting.[20] The French, German, and Japanese, for example,[21] follow the rules noted above fairly clearly and directly. They have a general provision disallowing a current deduction for expenditures for property, both physical and nonphysical, with a useful life longer than a year.[22] Contained within this accounting rule is the principle that only such property, including any related costs, may be depreciated, provided that other criteria are also satisfied.[23] Indonesia, which adopted a major tax reform in 1984, has a similar rule, although not expressed in terms of financial accounting.[24]

Typically, Commonwealth countries do not have financial accounting-based systems. They often do not have express statutory provisions disallowing current deductions for property with a useful life of more than one year or specifically limiting depreciable property to this category. The result is often a con-

---

[20]*See supra* ch. 16, appendix. There are a number of benefits when financial and tax accounting treatment are equal; these benefits are pointed out throughout the chapter. However, in addition to the obvious benefit of simplicity, the most important benefit may be this: the tax incentive to overstate depreciation so as to minimize tax due can be significantly lessened by the disincentive not to understate income in financial reports. This effect will perhaps be greatest for listed companies, where pressure to report profits, and therefore boost share prices, may be greatest.

[21]This chapter refers to the tax laws of major industrial economies, primarily Australia, France, Germany, Japan, the United Kingdom, and the United States. The chapter also makes frequent reference to the tax laws of a sample of developing and transition economies that have recently undergone major tax reforms (primarily Indonesia, Kazakhstan, and Lesotho). The sample reflects the involvement of either the author or the IMF Legal Department in reforms in these countries and is intended to highlight techniques of adopting rules to developing and transition country circumstances. Finally, the chapter occasionally makes reference to other countries that may have an unusual rule in a particular instance.

[22]Property that has been manufactured by the taxpayer is included in this rule, as in general are any repairs that extend the life or term of the property. *See* FRA CGI art. 39-1-2°, FRA CGI Ann. III art. 38 *quinquies*, FRA Council of State Decision of July 18, 1941; JPN IT art. 31, JPN IT Reg. 21-7 I, II; DEU EStG § 7. The German rule explicitly allows a deduction of costs for maintaining property if the effect of the maintenance lasts for less than one year. DEU Einkommensteuer-Richtlinien (EStR) § 157.

[23]The French statute provides for "write-offs for depreciation actually taken . . . to the extent that such write-offs are generally justified according to the usage of each industry, commerce, or business. . . ." FRA CGI art. 39-1-2°. This rule applies generally to all property both physical and nonphysical with a "predicted life" of more than a year. The cost of property with a life of more than one year cannot be deducted currently, and only assets with a life of more than one year may be depreciated. *See, e.g.,* Decision of the Conseil d'Etat of Feb. 24, 1936 (FRA). The Japanese statute is similar to the French, as is a Japanese regulation. *See* JPN IT arts. 22(3), 31; JPN Rule 7. The German statute more specifically denies a current deduction, and limits depreciation, to property with a use "which extends by experience to a period of more than one year." DEU EStG § 7(1).

[24]The Indonesia statute states that "the cost of earning, collecting, and securing income paid over more than one year may only be deducted through amortization. . . ." *Id.* art. 9(II). "The acquisition price or value . . . shall be adjusted for . . . improvements, alterations, or additions" IDN IT art. 10(II).

fusing set of rules. For example, the British statute denies deductions for costs of "capital."[25] The definition of capital is found not in the statute, but almost entirely in court cases. Unfortunately, the often rather lengthy court definitions are perhaps less clear than the rather succinct accounting system rules. For example, no major British court decision appears to have directly noted that for property to be capital, it must have a useful life of more than a year. Nevertheless, that does seem to be the general implication of existing case law.[26]

Unlike the accounting-based systems, British law does not have a stated statutory rule restricting depreciation to property that is defined as capital in nature. Instead, further statutory language provides allowances for depreciation only for certain limited classes of both physical and nonphysical property. While each class of physical property has its own separate requirement that the expense be capital in nature, there is no general principle that applies to all property or even to all physical property. While the rules for nonphysical property are more general, only listed types of nonphysical property may be depreciated.[27]

As under the accounting system jurisdictions, the cost of property that has been manufactured by the taxpayer is a capital cost. However, in the United Kingdom, the treatment of costs of repairs done to maintain property is neither simple nor particularly logical. The statute specifically disallows as a deductible expense costs to improve structures unless the structures constitute manufacturing plant.[28] There is no such statutory provision for improvement of equipment.

---

[25] The original Income Tax Act 1842, Act 5 & 6 Vict. c. 35(1), S. 100, scheds. A, B, C & D, denied deductions for "capital withdrawn from or any sum employed . . . as capital in [a] trade." The current U.K. statutory provision denying a deduction for capital is found in GBR ICTA § 74(f), (g).

[26] In 1879, a taxpayer coal company attempted to take deductions for depletion. The House of Lords upheld the disallowance of the deduction. "[T]he capital involved in making it would gradually be exhausted and lost; but the *decaying character of the property* would not make it the less subject to be taxed . . . so long as the mineral lasted." Coltness Iron Company v. Black [1881] 6 A.C. 315, 327 (Lord Penzance) (emphasis added). Effectively, this would include as capital any property that lasts for more than a year, in that other property would become "exhausted" in less than a year, and the loss could be realized accordingly. Future cases further defined capital as something that was "not once and for all" but of "enduring benefit." Atherton v. British Insulated and Helsby Cables Ltd. [1926] A.C. 205, 213–14 (Viscount Cave). *Coltness* and its progeny are still relied upon. *See also* Butterworths U.K. Tax Guide 1990–91 § 7:103. The idea of permitting a partial deduction to allow for depreciation was not considered.

[27] The British system did not, in fact, develop to permit deductions for depreciation. Instead, provisions were added to give "allowances" for "capital expenditure" for physical property. These "allowances," in effect, were viewed not as rules essential to determine an accurate picture of actual income, but as a kind of concession. In other words, there was no importation of the rules or, for that matter, the theory, of financial accounting. The current rules providing capital allowances are found in GBR CAA §§ 1(1)(a); 22(1)(a); 35(1); 37(1)(a); 52(1)(a); 60(1)(b); 61(1)(a); 67A(1), (2); 68(1)(b); 159(1)(a). For depletion, *see id.* § 105(1). For certain nonphysical property *see* GBR ICTA § 520(1).

[28] The United Kingdom's Income and Corporation Taxes Act disallows the deduction of "capital employed in improvements of *premises*. . . ." GBR ICTA § 74(g) (emphasis added). Improvements to manufacturing plant would be nondeductible but would be depreciable, given that plant is itself depreciable. GBR CAA § 12.

However, court cases suggest that an improvement would be "part of the cost of the income-earning machine" and therefore not deductible.[29]

Using different logic, court cases have allowed deductions for repairs, with no apparent reference as to how long the repair might last or even to whether the property repaired is itself otherwise eligible for depreciation.[30] Courts have disallowed deductions for renewals of structures, apparently meaning something that transcends mere repairs and comes closer to a replacement.[31] Naturally, this has required the courts to make nice distinctions among repairs, improvements, and renewals,[32] distinctions that are not based on the length of effect of the activity and that therefore do not appear necessary or justified by any theory of depreciation. To add to the confused nature of the system, notwithstanding these cases a deduction will apparently be allowed for renewals if they are of equipment, and apparently even for some plant.[33]

The confusing and patchwork nature of the U.K. rules appears due, at least in part, to the lack of a coherent theory expressed in statutory form, itself the result, most likely, of the incremental fashion in which the system for allowing for depreciation was created.[34] Other Commonwealth countries often rely on British case law, frequently along with their own, often unclear, statutory provisions. The mix may not always be much more systematic than the scheme found in the United Kingdom.[35]

---

[29]*See, e.g.*, Commissioner v. Nchanga Consolidated Copper Mines, Ltd. [1964] A.C. 948, 959 (citing New State Areas Ltd. v. Commissioner for Inland Revenue, S.A.L.R. [1946] A.D. 610, 620, 621 (Watermeyer, C.J.)).

[30]*See, e.g.*, Phillips v. Whieldon Sanitary Properties Ltd. (1952) 33 T.C. 213, 219 (Donovan, J.).

[31]*See id.*

[32]They are discussed in Butterworths U.K. Tax Guide 1990–91 (John Tiley ed., 9th ed. 1990) §§ 7:115–7:119.

[33]This confusing distinction is discussed in *id.* at § 7:119.

[34]*See* Walter W. Brudno & Frank Bower, Taxation in the United Kingdom 192 (Harvard World Tax Series 1957).

[35]For example, the Australian statute denies a deduction for "losses and outgoings of capital, or of a capital . . . nature," AUS ITAA § 51(1) and has case law defining capital predicated on U.K. case law. *See e.g.*, Sun Newspapers Ltd. v. Fed. Comm'r of Taxation (1938) 61 C.L.R. 337, 380 (citing Atherton [1926] A.C. 205). *See also* 1994 Australian Master Tax Guide ¶ 14-060. Unlike the British statute, the Australian statute does not specifically limit depreciation for physical property to capital items. However, for nonphysical property, the statute expressly limits allowances to expenditures of a capital nature. AUS ITAA § 124L(1)(a), (b). Somewhat akin to the British case law, improvement of capital property is generally capital and not deductible, while maintenance and upkeep are not capital and may be deducted; 1994 Australian Master Tax Guide ¶ 14-060. The Lesotho statute is also somewhat unclear on this point. It first denies a deduction for expenses "chargeable to capital account." LSO ITA § 33(3)(c). However, the statute does not explicitly tie depreciation to costs that are so chargeable to "capital account." Instead, it defines "depreciable asset" as "tangible movable property or an industrial building which is wholly or partly used in the production of income subject to tax and which is likely to lose value because of wear and tear, or obsolescence." *Id.* § 3(1). Although implicitly this must refer to property whose usefulness extends beyond the taxable year, this is not stated outright. An "intangible asset," for which depreciation may be allowed, is also not defined with reference to capital. The statute also allows for a deduction for "expenditure (other than expenditure of a capital nature) incurred on repairs to assets used in the production of income. . . ." *Id.* § 42(1).

The U.S. system has two separate, although related, principles. The statute, under a confusingly worded provision entitled "Capital expenditures," denies a current deduction for "[a]ny amount paid out for new buildings or for permanent improvements or betterments made to increase the value of any property or estate."[36] A regulation further states that this means physical property with a life of "substantially" longer than the "tax year," although no such specific rule is applicable to nonphysical property.[37] Another section applies this rule to costs of self-constructed property and includes related and "indirect" costs.[38] While the capital expenditures rule covers improvements, there is no specific rule concerning costs of repair.[39]

In a manner analogous to that of the British experience, therefore, an enormous amount of administrative and judicial attention has been devoted to the distinction between nondeductible improvements and deductible repairs.[40] As with the U.K. cases, the U.S. courts have paid little or no attention to whether the effect of the improvement or repair was to last for longer than a year. There is no specific rule that limits depreciation to that property that cannot be deducted because of its longevity, although this is implied in another regulation.[41] There is also a section that disallows a deduction for costs of property for which a deduction has otherwise been allowed.[42] Kazakhstan, which adopted a major reform in 1995, uses phrasing that is clearer than the American.[43]

---

[36]USA IRC § 263(a)(1).

[37]The regulation reads that the statutory language refers to "a capital expenditure that is taken into account through . . . a charge to capital accounts. . . ." USA Treas. Reg. § 1.263(a)-1(b). Examples of such capital expenditures include "buildings, machinery and equipment, furniture and fixtures, and similar property having a useful life *substantially beyond the taxable year* . . . a copyright . . . [t]he cost of goodwill. . . ." *Id.* § 1.263(a)-2(a), (b), (h) (emphasis added). *See also id.* § 1.446-1(a)(4) (the regulations to the accounting rules under USA IRC § 446).

[38]*See* USA IRC §§ 263A (a), (b).

[39]There used to be a repair allowance as part of the Class Life Asset Depreciation Range System. *See infra* note 50.

[40]*See, e.g.,* USA Treas. Reg. § 1.162-3; Fidelity Storage Corp. v. Burnet, 58 F.2d 526 (1932), *rev'd* 18 BTA 517 (1929) (roof repairs with new material are deductible), Georgia Car & Locomotive Co. v. Helvering, 2 BTA 986 (1925) (new roof not deductible); *see generally* 4 RIA United States Tax Reporter ¶¶ 1625.172–1625.185.

[41]This is buried in a completely different section concerning "methods of accounting." "[A]s a further example . . . a liability that relates to the creation of an asset having a useful life extending substantially beyond the close of the taxable year is taken into account in the taxable year incurred through capitalization . . . and may later affect the computation of taxable income through depreciation. . . ." USA Treas. Reg. § 1.446-1(c)(1)(ii)(A).

[42]*Id.* § 1.161-1.

[43]One article denies deductions to expenses for "fixed assets and other expenses of a capital character. . . ." KAZ TC art. 14(1). Another article defines fixed assets as "assets with a value over 40 minimum wages and a service life of more than one year which are subject to depreciation in accordance with art. 20." *Id.* 5(18). Art. 20 states that assets subject to depreciation do not include "property the value of which is fully deducted in the current year in the determination of taxable income." *Id.* art. 20(2), (3). Two additional articles involve "intangible assets," for which depreciation is allowed under the provisions of art. 20. *See id.* arts. 23, 24. The Kazakh statute also includes a general provision denying more than one deduction to expenses "included in several expenditure categories. . . ." *Id.* art. 14(2). There is a clear-cut rule with regard to costs of repairs: they are deductible, up to a fixed limit. This is discussed *infra* at the text accompanying notes 50–52.

Many jurisdictions have *de minimis* rules, allowing a deduction for costs of acquiring a limited amount of property with a life of longer than a year. The simplification benefits of such a rule depend on the entire system for depreciation. Where a pooling system is used, it is not difficult to depreciate low-cost items: their cost is simply added to the pool in the year they are acquired and there is therefore no need to keep track of the individual assets. In contrast, under a single-asset system, there would be a stronger case for a *de minimis* rule on simplification grounds. The purpose of such rules is to aid administration, but also sometimes to provide relief to small taxpayers. There are various ways in which such rules can be implemented. For example, the German rule permits an immediate deduction for the costs of a unit of movable property with a value of less than DM 800.[44] However, a problem immediately arises as to what constitutes a single unit of property; much property can itself be broken up into smaller pieces. The German solution is to require that the property be "capable of individual use,"[45] which effectively limits costs for creation and for repair. A slightly different tack is taken in the Japanese law, although it uses a test similar to that of the Germans to determine what constitutes a separate piece of property.[46] With a few minor exceptions, physical property that costs less than ¥10,000 is deductible. The U.S. statute takes a rather different approach, allowing small taxpayers a deduction of up to a total yearly limit on the sum of all costs associated with depreciable physical property of US$17,500.[47] Larger taxpayers are not affected by this rule.[48]

Some jurisdictions have rules of thumb regarding deductibility of repair or maintenance expenses. The Japanese, for example, give the taxpayer a choice of capitalizing such costs or of taking an immediate deduction up to limits set by two rules of thumb. The limits for deductibility are set at either 30 percent of an asset's total maintenance expense, or 10 percent of the asset's total acquisition cost, whichever is lower.[49] The United States used to have a *de minimis* rule based on fixed percentages of acquisition costs, but repealed it when accelerated depreciation was introduced in 1981.[50] Kazakhstan defines deductible expenses to include repairs on physical property up

---

[44]DEU EStG § 6(2).

[45]*Id.*

[46]JPN IT Rule 7; JPN IT Basic Circular Notice (195).

[47]USA IRC §§ 179(a), (b), (d)(1).

[48]*Id.*

[49]A number of other methods are also permissible. JPN IT Rule 7. *See generally* Yuji Gomi, Guide to Japanese Taxes 1994–95 ¶ 6-308.

[50]Under that rule, all expenditures for repair and improvement of "repair allowance property" that were not clearly capital expenditures could be treated as deductible to the extent that they did not exceed the repair allowance. The repair allowance was obtained by multiplying the repair allowance percentage by the average basis of the repair allowance property in the ADR (asset depreciation range) class. The repair allowance percentages for the various ADR classes were listed in a number of Revenue Procedures. USA Treas. Reg. §§ 1.167(a)-11(d)(2)(iii), 1.167(a)-11(d)(2)(iii); Rev. Procs. 72-10, 77-10.

to 10 percent of the written-down value of the sum of all depreciable property within a particular category of property.[51] All other repairs must be depreciated.[52]

By and large, the accounting-based jurisdictions appear to have the most transparent and coherent rules concerning what costs for acquiring, creating, and sustaining property cannot be deducted because the effective life of such property extends beyond a year, and limiting depreciation to a subclass of such property. The British and other Commonwealth rules are frequently confusing and inconsistent. Nor are the U.S. rules a model of statutory clarity. Whether or not rules based on accounting are used, the statute should be as clear as possible as to the relationship between asset life, deductibility, and depreciability. First, the statute should deny a current deduction for the costs of any property with a useful life of greater than the current tax year. The German rule provides some guidance.[53]

Another way to do this might be to deny a current deduction for any costs of a capital nature. This could be separately defined to include all property that has a life longer than the current tax year. All costs of self-creation, preparation, repair, or extension that increase the life of the property beyond a single year should be included in "cost."[54] Depreciation allowances should then be limited to those costs for which a deduction was denied. While this can be easily included in accounting-type rules,[55] a separate statement could also be added that restricts depreciation allowances for capital costs.

The German *de minimis* rule makes administrative sense to the extent that it allows taxpayers to avoid keeping separate track of assets with relatively trivial costs. However, if pooling is used to keep track of assets, the argument in favor of such a rule is greatly reduced.[56] Also, as noted, once such *de minimis* rules are adopted, it is necessary to have careful rules regarding what constitutes a single asset. Another possibility would be to adopt the U.S. cumulative *de minimis* rule, which is restricted to small taxpayers and which obviates the need to determine what is a separate piece of property and allows smaller taxpayers to avoid the trouble of depreciating such property. Some combination of these rules—such as allowing deductibility of costs for assets under a certain

---

[51]The phrasing of this rule to apply to cumulative written-down values of classes of property is due to the use of pooling in the Kazakh statute. Pooling is discussed *infra* at sec. III(G).

[52]*See* KAZ TC art. 21.

[53]"In the case of business assets, if the use or exploitation thereof by the taxpayer in the obtaining of income extends by experience to more than one year [the rule describes how much is to be deducted each year]" DEU EStG § 7(1).

[54]*See* the German rule, *supra* note 22. However, an argument could be made that the effective life of each separate repair should be tracked separately, so that each can be depreciated separately. Although theoretically appealing, this would add to administrative inconvenience and would be a highly unusual provision; the author is not aware of any jurisdiction that does so.

[55]*See supra* note 23.

[56]*See infra* sec. III(G).

amount, but with a total limit on costs so deducted, and perhaps limited to small taxpayers—would also be possible.

Rules of thumb regarding the deduction or capitalization of maintenance costs, while not being true to theory, are probably worth the deviations from theory for purposes of improving ease of administration. Variations on the Japanese, old U.S., and new Kazakh rules may all be reasonable guides.

C. Property Held to Generate Current Taxable Income

No deduction should be allowed that represents personal consumption. Therefore, any decrease in the value of any property resulting from personal consumption should not be deductible through depreciation. While perhaps this rule could be subsumed under the general requirement that deductions be limited to the costs of earning current taxable income, the denial of deductions for capital costs found in many laws sometimes appears to require a separate statement of this condition with regard to depreciation.[57] Also, because one of the purposes of depreciation is to prevent mismatching of income and expenses, it should apply only to property that generates *currently* taxable income.[58] As noted above, the French, German, and Japanese rules are closely related to the financial accounting treatment given assets, which means that only property used to generate business income may qualify for depreciation.[59] Indonesia makes a similar provision through a general statutory rule.[60]

Reminiscent of the capital requirement discussed above, the British statute does not include a general rule restricting depreciation to property held to generate currently taxable income. Instead, a separate limit is included for each class of depreciable physical property, while another statutory provision

---

[57]A related issue was raised in Commissioner v. Idaho Power Co., 418 U.S. 1 (1974). That case involved the interrelation between IRC § 263 (which disallows deductions "paid out for new buildings or for permanent improvements or betterments") and IRC § 167(a)(1) (which allows a deduction for depreciation of "property used in a trade or business")(*see also* notes 36 and 64 and accompanying text). The taxpayer contended that § 167 existed independently of § 263, while the Commissioner contended that § 263 took precedence over § 167. The court found for the Commissioner. This is a good example of the need to spell out the interaction between provisions denying deductions and those allowing deductions, particularly the deduction for depreciation. *See supra* ch. 16, sec. II(C). *See also* KAZ TC § 15(3).

[58]This means that even if property is subject to a capital gains tax on sale or transfer, if it is not also held for the generation of taxable income currently, depreciation deductions should not be allowed.

[59]The German rule specifically restricts depreciation to "business" property used "in the obtaining of income" DEU EStG § 7(1). *But see infra* the discussion concerning apportionment at text accompanying notes 65–70.

[60]The Indonesian statute first generally restricts deductions for depreciation or depletion, allowing them only when they are a "cost of earning, collecting, and securing income," and then more specifically restricts depreciation to property "owned and used in a business or owned for the production, recovery, or securing of income." IDN IT § 11(1), (12).

relates to nonphysical property.[61] Other Commonwealth countries, however, may use a smaller number of more general rules, although typically they have separate sections for physical and for nonphysical assets.[62] Kazakhstan does so as well.[63] The U.S. statute, however, includes a general rule that restricts depreciation for both physical and nonphysical property to that "used in the trade or business" or "held for the production of income."[64]

Some jurisdictions with accounting-based systems, such as France and Japan,[65] and the Commonwealth jurisdictions of Australia and Lesotho[66] as well as the United States[67] explicitly allow for apportionment of costs of property used partly for the generation of taxable income and partly not, and allow depreciation attributable to the costs of the former. Other jurisdictions, such as the United Kingdom, do not do so explicitly, but have so allowed through case law.[68] The German rule is quite different. If more than 50 percent of movable depreciable property is used for business purposes, the entire asset is depreciable. If more than 10 percent is not, none of it is. If the business use lies between those two percentages, the taxpayer may choose.[69] Understandably, according to at least one commentary, this rule makes little sense.[70]

It is an essential requirement that to qualify for depreciation, the property, regardless of its type, must be held or used for the production of currently taxable income. While apportionment in the case of "dual use" property seems to make theoretical sense, it may make tax administration that much more difficult. However, the German rule seems unnecessarily favorable to the taxpayer as far as depreciation is concerned.[71]

---

[61]Capital allowances for each separate class are limited to property held "for the purposes of [a] trade." GBR CAA §§ 1(1)(a); 22(1)(a); 35(1); 37(1)(a); 52(1)(a); 60(1)(b); 61(1)(a); 67A(1), (2)(b); 68(1)(b); 159(1)(a). For depletion, the rule is found in id. § 98(1), and for certain nonphysical property in GBR ICTA § 520(1).

[62]For example, the Australian statute includes a general rule limiting depreciation of physical assets to "plant or articles . . . used for the purpose of producing assessable income." AUS ITAA § 54(1). There is also a general rule that applies to depreciable nonphysical property. Id. §§ 124L(1), 124M. Other rules concerning depletion allowances for minerals carry similar restrictions. See, e.g., id. § 122DG(2). Lesotho has similar separate restrictions for physical property and nonphysical property, LSO ITA §§ 3(1), 44(1), and a specific rule for depletion. Id. § 43.

[63]Physical asset depreciation is limited to "capital goods used in production," and intangible asset depreciation to "those utilized over a long period in economic activity." KAZ TC §§ 20(1), 24(1).

[64]USA IRC § 167(a). However, a separate rule exists for depletion, which is restricted as well to a deduction against gross income. Id. § 613.

[65]See Direction général des impôts, Précis de fiscalité ¶ 517 (1994) [hereinafter Précis]; JPN IT § 31.

[66]AUS ITAA § 61; LSO ITA § 41(4).

[67]Treas. Reg. § 1.167(a)-5.

[68]GBR CAA §§ 1, 24(1)(a); G.H. Chambers (Northiam Farms) Ltd. v. Watmouth [1956] 3 All E.R. 485.

[69]DEU EStR § 14.

[70]See Klaus Tipke & Joachim Lang, Steuerrecht 295–97 (13th ed. 1991).

[71]The German rule should be seen in the light of capital gains tax being levied on property labeled business property but not (except for short-term gains) on private (nonbusiness) property.—L.M.

D. Wear, Tear, Obsolescence, and Useful Life

Depreciation is an estimate of a decline in the value of property. There-fore, property that does not decline in value, or whose decline cannot be rea-sonably estimated, should not be eligible for depreciation. Generally speaking, it would be possible to allow depreciation for the costs of any property that de-clines in value. As noted earlier, property can be expected to decline in value for many reasons, including wear and tear, obsolescence, or time-limited rights of use. A number of jurisdictions predicate depreciation first on the existence of these attributes. However, while reductions in value resulting solely from limited terms of use are simple to estimate, it may be quite difficult to do so for those reductions that result from wear and tear and obsolescence. Most juris-dictions therefore greatly restrict how depreciation may be computed. For ex-ample, land may be subject to wear and tear, but because it has no fixed useful life, the decrease in value owing to such wear and tear might be difficult to es-timate, and a deduction for depreciation of land as such is not generally allowed.

Most jurisdictions rely to some extent, either explicitly or implicitly, on the concept of "useful life," to determine whether the costs of a property are eligible for depreciation treatment at all (i.e., it must have a determinable use-ful life), as well as what amount of depreciation will be permitted (i.e., annual rate of depreciation is fixed by reference to that determinable useful life). In essence, a useful life analysis extends the concept of limited term of use (so of-ten applicable for analysis of the decline in value of nonphysical property) to physical property. A variation of the useful life analysis is to assign useful life rules of thumb to property by type. These assume that a particular kind of prop-erty always has an ascertainable useful life and fixes that life. The necessary re-sult of the first function of useful life is that certain types of property are excluded entirely from depreciation. The second function, using useful lives to fix annual depreciation deductions, will be discussed below.[72]

Some systems do not base their analysis for some, or even all, property either on wear and tear or obsolescence or on a useful-life analysis. Instead, they simply provide specific rules for the depreciation of particular properties or classes of properties. Still other systems may provide apparent rules of thumb that are so arbitrary as to suggest that they are not based on any useful-life analysis or on any readily available theory of depreciation. However, two major problems can arise if neither the "subject to wear and tear and obsoles-cence" nor the "determinable useful life" rule exists. First, if the rules refer only to specific properties or classes of property, certain types of property, which ac-cording to theory should be subject to depreciation allowances, may be ex-

---

[72]It should be noted that it may be possible to estimate reductions in a property's value attrib-utable to wear and obsolescence on a current basis without knowing its useful life. However, knowing an asset's useful life allows the mechanical application of a number of techniques for computing depreciation allowances.

cluded, perhaps even unintentionally. Second, if the rules are too general, some property, which according to theory should not be subject to depreciation allowances, may slip through the cracks and be included.

The French accounting-type rule makes no reference to physical wear and tear or to obsolescence. However, only physical and nonphysical property, with reasonably ascertainable useful lives, may be depreciated.[73] However, if the useful life of property cannot be fixed beforehand, and then "extraordinary depreciation" occurs, a deductible provision, similar in effect to depreciation, is allowed.[74] The German rule specifically limits depreciation to property that suffers from wear and tear and depletion, as well as extraordinary technical or financial depreciation.[75] The German regulations also state that only property with a determinable "limited" life may qualify.[76] The Japanese rule is somewhat different, although the effect is largely the same.[77] Under the French rule, depreciation of goodwill is not generally allowed because it has no ascertainable useful life.[78] However, the Germans and Japanese have special rules for the amortization of goodwill.[79] The Indonesian statute has recently switched to an accounting-type model for depreciation. Although the wording is different, the treatment of the costs of physical assets is broadly similar in effect.[80] While the costs of nonphysical property are depreciated, broadly speaking, on the basis of expected useful life, there is no specific restriction requiring that a useful life be ascertainable.[81]

---

[73]The French statutory provision does not expressly state this. See FRA CGI § 39-1-2°. However, decisions of the Council of State make clear that no property can be depreciated unless its useful life can be determined when acquired. See Decision of the Conseil d'Etat of Feb. 24, 1936, Recueil des décisions du Conseil d'Etat [Lebon] 236.

[74]FRA CGI Ann. III, art. 38 sexies.

[75]DEU EStG § 7(1), (6).

[76]DEU EStDV §§ 9a–11d, EStR §§ 42–59c.

[77]The Japanese statute is similar to the French. See JPN IT art. 31. While regulations do not specify that a useful life be determinable, this is implied by the fact that depreciation is based on the determined service life. JPN IT Reg. 21-3. See also JPN IT Basic Circular Notice 191-(3), which states that "since depreciable assets means assets the utility of which decreases gradually, objects of art and curios *the value of which does not decrease despite the lapse of time* are not included (emphasis added)."

[78]However, a provision may be made for extraordinary loss.

[79]See infra sec. II(E)(2).

[80]The previous system (in effect 1984–94) included no general restriction for physical property based on determinable useful lives. However, similar to the U.S. statute, all categories of such property (other than buildings) were assigned to classes based on property life. IDN IT art. 11(III). However, the Minister of Finance was empowered to issue a decree determining what types of property had what useful lives, making the system similar to the Kazakh one. Id. art. 11(XIV). The new law switches to a financial-accounts-based system, predicated on expected useful lives; however, the Minister is to issue a decree fixing the useful lives of (at least some) types of property. IDN IT (1994) arts. 11(10), (11).

[81]IDN IT art. 11(X).

The U.K. statute has no general rule restricting the depreciation of property to wear and tear or obsolescence or to property with determinable useful lives. For certain types of both physical and nonphysical property, there are, however, individual provisions allowing a fixed yearly amount of depreciation for each of a number of different classes. These categories are fixed by type of property and have only two different rates of depreciation; at least in cases other than certain buildings, these categories and rates appear not to be based on useful lives, even as a rule of thumb.[82] A major exception exists in that there is no provision for the depreciation of structures other than industrial buildings or plant and hotels, even if the structure (such as an office building) is used to generate current income.[83] Goodwill is not included as depreciable property.

The Australian statute is in some ways quite similar to the U.K. law, while in others it departs radically. Although it does not specify that a useful life must be determinable, depreciation for the costs of physical property is based on the effective life of the unit.[84] As with the United Kingdom, no depreciation is allowed for the cost of buildings other than plant. Goodwill is also not included. The Lesotho statute starts out by limiting depreciation for physical property to that which "is likely to lose value because of wear and tear or obsolescence."[85] However, the statute makes no reference to useful lives for physical property; there, depreciation is allowed by type of property, although a catchall category allows the depreciation of any depreciable physical property (other than nonindustrial buildings, which are specifically excluded).[86] Intangible assets are depreciated on the basis of useful life.[87]

The U.S. statute begins with a general rule that restricts depreciation for the costs of property, both physical and nonphysical, that is due to "exhaustion, wear, and tear (including a reasonable allowance for obsolescence)."[88] As with the Australian statute, in the case of physical property there is no explicit reference to useful lives.[89] However, also as with the Australian statute, the standard method of determining annual depreciation allowances for the costs of physical property is based on the estimated useful life of that property; there are also a number of rules of thumb that appear to assume consistent useful

---

[82]Costs for industrial buildings, hotels, and dredging are all depreciated at 4 percent a year, GBR CAA §§ 3, 7, 134, and costs for machinery and plant, motor vehicles, mining, patents, and copyrights are all depreciated at 25 percent a year. *Id.* §§ 24, 67, 69, 70–72, 34, 98, 105; GBR ICTA § 520.

[83]*See* Butterworths U.K. Tax Guide 1990–91 §§ 8:12–8:14 (John Tiley ed., 9th ed. 1990).

[84]Depreciation is allowed only for costs of "plant or articles" and a "unit of industrial property," which includes "rights" such as patents, copyrights, or designs. *See* AUS ITAA §§ 54(1), 124K(1), 124L. Depreciation is based on the "effective" life of the property, with six different spans of effective lives from fewer than 3 years to 30 or more. *Id.* §§ 55(1)–(5), 124M(1).

[85]LSO ITA § 3(1).

[86]*Id.* § 43; LSO ITA sixth sched.

[87]*See* LSO ITA § 44(2).

[88]USA IRC § 167(a).

[89]USA Treas. Reg. § 1.167(a)-2.

lives for a few additional classes of property.[90] Regulations permit depreciation for nonphysical property only when its useful life is limited and its length "can be estimated with reasonable accuracy."[91] Explicitly excluded in this rule is goodwill, presumably because it has no accurately determinable useful life.[92] However, a separate statutory provision permits depreciation of purchased goodwill and certain other nonphysical property.[93]

In a manner somewhat similar to the U.S. and Lesotho statutes, the Kazakh statute first limits depreciation to physical property that is liable to wear and tear.[94] It then assigns physical property to a small number of classes, the apparent assumption being that the property in each category has roughly comparable useful lives.[95] However, there is a residual class covering all physical property liable to wear and tear (other than land) that is not listed in the other classes. This means that it is possible for different types of physical property that might have radically different useful lives to be depreciated at the same rate. There is no requirement that nonphysical property be subject to obsolescence, but it must have an ascertainable useful life. Nevertheless, a single depreciation rate is fixed for all nonphysical property.[96]

As noted, a large number of different techniques exist for restricting depreciation to property whose decline in value can be reasonably estimated. For both physical and nonphysical property, either a "subject to wear and tear and obsolescence" or a "determinable useful life" rule would be necessary. In part because a determinable useful life can provide a basis for determining reasonable depreciation allowances, this rule should probably be included.[97] If for administrative reasons it is preferred that various types of property be listed with their assumed useful lives, such lists can be seen as guidelines in specific applications of the general rule. However, in such cases, rather than have catchall rules, it might be better to require the taxpayer to declare a fixed useful life. This would avoid any ambiguity regarding such assets as financial securities.

A French-type rule that allows for a special after-the-fact allowance when a useful life cannot be determined—provided that a reasonable estimate of a reduction in value can be found—makes theoretical sense, although it could prove difficult to administer. One possibility would be to permit such an allowance only if there was clear evidence, such as a recent price for identical property. Another would be to follow the French rule that any additional

---

[90]There are essentially nine property classifications, of which six are based on useful lives, and three—residential rental property, nonresidential real property, and railroad grading or tunnel bores—are based on type; these last three appear to be rules of thumb. USA IRC § 168(c)(1), (e)(1).

[91]USA Treas. Reg. § 1.167(a)-3.

[92]Id. See also X-Pando Corp. v. Commissioner, 7 T.C. 48, 53–54 (1946).

[93]USA IRC § 197.

[94]KAZ TC art. 20(1).

[95]Id. art. 20(3).

[96]Id. arts. 20(3)(3), 24.

[97]See supra sec. II(D).

allowances be reflected in financial statements; however, this would probably be a less effective tool with unquoted companies or in jurisdictions where financial reporting is relatively unimportant. A third possibility would be not to permit deductions or allowances for property without determinable useful lives, but instead, when the property is transferred or is rendered worthless, to impute the time value of the lost deductions. This, however, might be too much of an administrative burden for developing and transition countries.

E. Exclusions of Particular Property

1. Land

As a general matter, costs for acquiring land would be excluded from depreciation through the operation of either the wear-and-tear or determinable-life rule. However, land can be prepared or developed in a way that increases its value, but that preparation or development may itself have a limited useful life. If the value of the preparation or development can be separated from the rest of the land, a reduction in value of this separate amount can be estimated. If the development or preparation is itself part of otherwise depreciable property, those costs can be included and depreciated together.[98] However, if there is a specific statutory exclusion of land, it should be drafted so as not to cover the preparation or development of land that itself may have a determinable useful life. Depletion, an issue related to but different from other matters concerning land, is discussed below.[99]

The French statute does not explicitly exclude the cost of land from depreciation; it only excludes property with no determinable useful life. Therefore, preparations of land that are part of the costs of another depreciable property should not be excluded, nor would other land workings that themselves have a determinable useful life.[100] The German rule is similar,[101] as is the Japanese.[102] Indonesia specifically excludes land and makes no specific reference to whether the workings of land can be depreciated as part of the cost of other property.[103] The same is true of Kazakhstan[104] and the United States.[105] The U.K. law has no specific rule allowing land to be depreciated. As noted earlier, the costs of nonindustrial buildings are generally not subject to depreciation. However, a

---

[98]*See* the discussion *supra* concerning costs regarding self-creation or improvement of property. However, if they are related to depletion, they may not fall in value at the same rate as the mineral property and should have a separate depreciation provision.

[99]*See infra* sec. III(D).

[100]*See* Précis, *supra* note 65, ¶ 1082.

[101]DEU EStDV §§ 9a–11d.

[102]*See* JPN IT Reg. 21(I).

[103]IDN IT art. 11(I).

[104]KAZ TC art. 20(2)(1).

[105]USA Treas. Reg. § 1.167(a)-2.

provision allowing depreciation of certain buildings includes the cost of land preparation.[106] Australia has a more restrictive rule.[107]

If a statute includes a general rule limiting depreciation to property with a fixed useful life, there would appear to be no specific reason to exclude land, nor would there then be a reason to provide a special rule for the workings of land. However, an additional rule, perhaps more appropriate for a regulation than a statute, could spell out that the costs of working land that are related to construction of otherwise depreciable assets must be included as costs and that other workings are depreciable provided that they have a determinable life.

2. Goodwill

What exactly constitutes goodwill may not be entirely self-evident. It is generally thought to include the value, based on reputation, that the relevant public attaches to a particular product or service and the undertaking that provides it. It can be created through the provision of a good product or service and can be enhanced through such things as advertising. It can often be transferred through the sale of a trademark and can constitute part of the value of the transfer of a copyright, a patent, or an entire business.

As noted earlier, some jurisdictions disallow depreciation for goodwill because it has no ascertainable useful life, making it difficult to estimate a decline in its value.[108] Also as noted, it might be possible to impute the value of lost deductions at the point when goodwill is transferred or becomes worthless. However, there are other justifications for disallowing any deductions for a decline in the value of goodwill in certain circumstances. These circumstances exist when costs that relate to the creation or maintenance of goodwill are not disallowed, but are deductible; as a compensating distortion, losses in goodwill itself should not be deducted. As noted, goodwill can be a valuable component of an enterprise, reflected in such things as company trademarks. It derives from many things, perhaps the most important of which are the quality of the enterprise's product and advertising. If the costs of carrying on the business, and of advertising, are generally deductible, losses in the value of goodwill itself should not be.[109] Obviously, a separate and more accurate solution would be to deny a current deduction for at least certain costs, like advertising and promotion, and to

---

[106]GBR CAA § 13.

[107]AUS ITAA § 54(2)(b) limits depreciation for "structural improvements on land" to "(i) fences, dams, and other structural improvements on land which is used for the purposes of agricultural and pastoral pursuits; (ii) structural improvements (not including an improvement that is an access road . . .) . . . on land that is used for the purposes of forest operations."

[108]This is true of both French and U.S. rules, while British and Australian rules do not include goodwill as depreciable property. *Supra* sec. II(D).

[109]At least some evidence would suggest that advertising and promotional expenses have the effect of creating goodwill that lasts longer than a single year. *See* George Mundstock, *Taxation of Business Intangible Capital*, 135 U. Penn. L. Rev. 1179, 1186–89 (1987). Nevertheless, it is common for jurisdictions to permit the deduction of advertising and promotional expenses. *See supra* ch. 16.

either depreciate them independently if a useful life can be estimated or treat them as part of the cost of creating or maintaining goodwill.[110]

This argument works with regard to goodwill that is self-created. However, if goodwill is purchased, rather than created, and deductions for a decline in the value of goodwill are disallowed entirely, there may be a tax incentive for self-created, rather than purchased, goodwill.[111] For example, the German statute permits the amortization of goodwill, but only if it is acquired rather than created; the statute fixes a specific period that is not based on any determinable useful life.[112] The United States also allows depreciation of goodwill over a fixed period and limits such amortization in the case of self-created goodwill to licenses, permits, covenants not to compete, franchises, trademarks, and trade names.[113] Other jurisdictions also allow depreciation or amortization of goodwill over fixed periods, although the provisions themselves are typically not limited to goodwill, but to categories of nonphysical property.[114] The actual periods involved do not appear to be justified by any theory.[115] However, the rules presumably assume that an arbitrary period may better match income and expense than assuming an infinite life and allowing recovery only on sale.

As can be seen, there is little consistency among different jurisdictions concerning how the costs of goodwill should be treated. However, particularly if advertising and promotional costs are deductible, there may be an argument for allowing depreciation of acquired goodwill. As noted earlier, the difficulty in determining useful life might require a special exception to the general rule, as well as a specific rate of depreciation. It may also be possible to deny any depreciation deductions until the goodwill is sold or disposed of and a fair market value of the goodwill is obtained. At the time of the realization, the time value of money of the disallowed depreciation can be imputed.

3. Inventory

Any change in the value of property that is stock or inventory is typically accounted for separately from the depreciation provisions.[116] Thus, inventory should be expressly excluded from the operation of depreciation.[117]

---

[110]*See id.*

[111]Frequently, self-created goodwill is not designated as separate property until an enterprise is sold. Because of this, it is less likely that the issue of depreciating the costs of self-created goodwill would arise.

[112]DEU EStDV §§ 9a–11d; EStR §§ 42–59c. (Note that the seller of goodwill will normally have been taxed.—L.M.)

[113]USA IRC § 197(a), (c)(2), (d)(1)(D), (E), (F).

[114]For a summary of treatment in the EU, *see* Commission of the European Communities, Report of the Committee of Independent Experts on Company Taxation 254 (1992). In Kazakhstan, a single, arbitrary depreciation rate is fixed for all nonphysical property. KAZ TC § 24(2).

[115]*Id.* The Japanese generally allow the depreciation of goodwill, either as a fixed percentage or over a fixed period. Both, however, are determined by the taxpayer. JPN IT Reg. 21-3.

[116]Accounting for inventory is discussed *supra* ch. 16.

[117]*See, e.g.,* KAZ TC art. 20(2)(2); USA Treas. Reg. § 1.167(a)-2(a).

4. Property the Costs of Which Have Already Been Accounted For

If the decline in the value of an asset is already accounted for in some way, no deduction for depreciation is needed. Jurisdictions such as France, Germany, and Japan, which generally rely on accounting-type rules, disallow double deductions through their general accounting rules.[118] Some jurisdictions, such as Kazakhstan, have a general provision denying multiple deductions for the same item of expense, while others, such as the United States, have a rule specifically denying depreciation for property whose cost has been otherwise deducted. Still others, such as Australia, deny deductions for property that has been depreciated.[119] A general rule like that in Kazakhstan could, for the sake of clarity, be supplemented with a more specific statement applying the rule to depreciation.[120]

III. Depreciation Rates and Methods

A. Economic Depreciation

Ideally, allowed depreciation deductions should reflect the actual decrease in the market value of the property. However, absent a yearly sale or exchange of an identical asset, the actual decrease in fair market value will be difficult to determine.

Example
Depreciation Based on Discounted Cash-Flow Analysis

Assume that Taxpayer A purchases the right to use an industrial formula for a period of five years. Assume in this example that there is no inflation and that the formula will produce a cash flow of $1,000 every year until the right to use the formula expires. The market value of the five-year know-how would be equal to the sum of its cash flow. However, $1,000 paid two years from now is worth less than $1,000 paid one year from now. To determine the net

---

[118]See Précis, *supra* note 65, ¶ 517; JPN IT art. 31; JPN IT Rule 3; DEU EStG § 6.

[119]AUS ITAA § 56(3).

[120]There have been instances where double deductions have been allowed. For example, in the United States, an investment credit was allowed for certain property. Originally, the amount of the credit had to be subtracted from the cost of the property for purposes of computing depreciation, but this rule was repealed in 1964. (Strictly speaking, a double deduction was not involved, but the effect of allowing a 100 percent deduction plus a credit is equivalent.) In 1982, Congress required the basis of property to be reduced by one-half the investment tax credit. *See* Staff of the Joint Committee on Taxation, General Explanation of the Revenue Provisions of the Tax Equity and Fiscal Responsibility Act of 1982, JCS-38-82, at 35–37 (1983). Lest the reader consider this an esoteric point, note that the revenue increase from this provision was estimated at US$14 billion over the period 1983–87.

Table 1. Depreciation of Asset Yielding Constant Income

(In units of local currency)

Year	Cash Return	Present Value	Fair Market Value	Depreciation	Taxable Income
0	—	952	4330	—	—
1	1,000	907	3546	784	216
2	1,000	864	2723	823	177
3	1,000	823	1859	864	136
4	1,000	784	952	907	93
5	1,000	—	—	952	48

Cash return: total cash return from investment during the year (as indicated in column 1). Present value: the present value at the beginning of year 1 of $1,000 realized during the year (as indicated in column 1). Fair market value: the value of the investment at the beginning of the year (as indicated in column 1). Depreciation: the accrued capital loss during the previous year (as indicated in column 1) or the change in fair market value during the year. Taxable income: income under a Haig-Simons tax base, or the difference between the cash income of $1,000 and the accrued capital loss listed in the depreciation column.

present value of $1,000 paid each year for five consecutive years, each $1,000 would have to be appropriately discounted.[121]

In this example, the decline in the value of the formula accelerates very slightly over the years. The example assumes that no changes in supply or demand or of obsolescence in the formula will affect its rate of return. Also, at the end of the term during which the taxpayer may exploit the formula, the formula has no residual value.

Now assume that, instead of a formula of limited term, the investment in the example is an item of physical property. The example would then assume that the property produces the same amount of income every year for five years and then abruptly stops producing any. In the real world, it is unlikely that many physical assets would perform in such a manner over the period of their useful life. A number of studies of individual physical properties have been undertaken over the years to estimate how quickly they lose value over their useful lives. On average, it seems that most physical property tends to lose a greater amount of value earlier than the property in the example.[122] Also, at the end of a physical property's useful life, the property often has a residual or scrap value.

---

[121]"[T]he invested capital represents the ability to generate future earnings, and, as an asset with a limited life ages, its value will decline by an amount representing a netting of (a) the loss of the portion of the investment that generated last year's earnings and (b) the increase in value of the remaining investment (i.e., of the future years' earnings that are now nearer on the time horizon)." David S. Davenport, *Depreciation Methods and the Importance of Expectations: Implications for Human Capital*, 54 Tax Notes 1399, 1400 (1992).

[122]*See, e.g.*, Charles R. Hulten & Frank C. Wykoff, *The Measurement of Economic Depreciation*, in Depreciation, Inflation, and the Taxation of Income from Capital 81–125 (Charles R. Hulten ed. 1981).

B. Straight-Line and Accelerated Depreciation

Financial accounting techniques typically use a different method of estimating depreciation deductions.[123] Straight-line depreciation, which is perhaps the most basic type, assumes that the property will lose an equal amount each year during its useful life. In the above example, this would be one-fifth of the cost of $4,330 in each of the five years, or $886 a year. This yearly amount in deductions would be more than that allowed in the example for the first three years and less for the last two. Because of the time value of money, the straight-line deductions are more generous.

Other methods of financial accounting, usually reserved for physical property, allow for greater depreciation deductions in the early years than is found in the straight-line method. Empirical evidence suggests that most physical property declines more rapidly than assumed either in the example or in the slightly faster straight-line depreciation. For this reason, faster depreciation may be provided for such property. There may be another, even faster rate to account for physical property that is subject to unusually rapid technological obsolescence, such as computers, or to other property like cars and trucks, which can continue to operate even when partially broken down.

Even faster depreciation may be allowed to offset the erosion of nominal property value attributable to inflation. This chapter does not specifically address the effects of inflation, which is treated more generally in chapter 13 (see vol. 1). However, it is worth noting here that if there were no other method in place for adjusting for the effects of inflation, increasing the rapidity of depreciation deductions could reflect the faster decrease in nominal value of property attributable to an overall increase in prices.

Another reason for allowing for faster depreciation is that tax rules often seek to provide taxpayers with a schedule of deductions that is more beneficial to them than actual economic depreciation. As a result, effective tax rates are reduced below the apparent or statutory tax rate. This is often justified by the argument that increasing depreciation deductions for an asset in the early years will create an incentive to invest in that asset. This is often known as "accelerated" depreciation, although that term can sometimes be used to refer to any method of depreciation faster than straight-line. Using accelerated depreciation to reduce the rate of taxation on income from a particular asset below that of income from other assets creates an incentive for the taxpayer to invest in that asset, which would distort choices otherwise dictated by the market. Economists would also argue that the incentive effects are heavily biased toward less risky assets.[124]

---

[123]It should be remembered that an important goal of financial accounting is to let the owners know what their income actually is. However, to protect potential investors and creditors in a business, most financial accounting standards have rules built into them to ensure that income estimates are under- rather than overstated. *See* Financial Accounting Standards Board, Statements of Financial Accounting Concepts 60–62 (1994).

[124]I am indebted to Peter Goss for pointing this out to me.

C. Declining-Balance Depreciation

One technique of increasing the proportion of total allowable deductions taken in the early years is called the "declining-balance" method, which is often expressed as a factor of how much more depreciation is to be taken relative to straight-line. If a factor of 2 in a declining-balance method were used in the example (sec. III(A)), in the first year twice the amount of straight-line depreciation would be allowed. Because straight-line allowed one-fifth, or 20 percent, double-declining depreciation would allow 40 percent, or $1,772. However, if depreciation is to reflect a reduction in market value of an asset, 40 percent of cost cannot be allowed each year for five years; the total would add up to more than the cost of the asset, and an asset cannot be worth less than zero. The declining-balance method requires that, for each consecutive year after the first, the percentage allowed as depreciation be taken not of original cost, but of the amount of cost remaining after the previous year's deduction. In this example, the "balance" left for depreciation would be $4,330 minus $1,772, or $2,558. Forty percent of that amount would be $1,023.

Under a pure declining-balance system, not all the depreciation is taken over the predicted useful life of the asset. Instead, the amount of depreciation is extended indefinitely, with ever smaller amounts allowed in each successive year. Indefinite depreciation for each asset would not, however, be practicable. This issue can be resolved in several ways. First, a declining-balance system can be used until the last year of the useful life, at which point the remaining amount can be deducted in the final year. A variation on this rule is to either require or allow the taxpayer to switch over to a straight-line system sometime before the end of the useful life.[125] Second, the depreciation account for the asset could simply be kept open past the end of the asset's useful life. Such depreciation accounts are referred to as "open-ended" because they include assets placed in service in more than one year.

Under the open-ended accounting system, a declining balance can be expressed simply as a yearly percentage deduction of the remaining cost. An estimate of the useful life of an asset can be used to determine which percentage should be allowed; in the above example, one can determine that a 200 percent declining-balance system is equal to a 40 percent annual deduction for those assets with five-year useful lives. But once the 40 percent annual deduction is selected for a particular asset, the useful life is no longer relevant to determining the allowable deductions.[126]

---

[125]For example, in the United States a declining-balance depreciation by a factor of 2 for an asset with a 10-year useful life requires a switch to straight-line at the fifth year. In this way, the amount of cost left to be depreciated (41.2 percent) is deducted in equal portions (6.86 percent) during the final, straight-line period. See USA IRC § 168(b)(1).

[126]Because such a system of open-ended accounts does not depend on a fixed date at which the asset's useful life ends, it is more commonly used to determine allowances not for single assets, but for all similar assets. This allows asset accounting on the basis of "pools," an issue that is discussed at greater length in sec. G infra.

While in the real world some physical property such as computers or cars might actually lose value as rapidly as is estimated in a 200 percent declining-balance system, in the majority of cases it is likely that such a system would vastly overstate economic depreciation.[127] However, a declining-balance system need not "accelerate" depreciation over actual economic depreciation; the net present value to the taxpayer of a declining-balance system depends on the percentage of annual balance allowed. For many physical assets, a declining-balance rule probably reflects economic depreciation more accurately than does straight-line.[128] A system seeking to increase the value of depreciation over straight-line can do so also by reducing the estimated useful life of the asset by a certain percentage. Either a straight-line or a declining-balance system can then be used.

Using a rule of thumb percentage (such as 125 percent) of straight-line over useful lives as a rough estimate of economic depreciation still depends on determining the useful lives of assets, an activity that is hardly an exact science. And, obviously, trying to fix depreciation not on some rule of thumb, but on even more accurate empirical data, is more difficult. There are an enormous number of different assets, and, as noted earlier, technology and markets constantly change. Giving the authority to the taxpayer on her or his own to determine depreciation allowances is clearly an invitation to overestimation; giving the government such authority could easily overburden the tax administration.

Whenever there is great mismeasurement of the depreciation of an asset for tax purposes and the amounts invested in such assets are significant, the effect on tax revenues (and investment incentives) can be substantial. For example, in Indonesia, such sectors as cement, steel, and mineral processing are very important to the economy, employ long-lived assets, and, under their system of depreciation, had been entitled to what empirically appears to have been massively accelerated allowances. As a result, the effective tax rate on income from such assets has been very low. In such circumstances at least, special classes with special depreciation schedules should be fixed.

Certain assets clearly depreciate very rapidly. For example, cars, trucks, and especially computers (as well as other office equipment) may depreciate very rapidly even though their useful lives are rather long. While cars or computers may be used for years, their fair market values may drop precipitously in a short time. For these assets, a rapid declining-balance system would be appropriate. To require slower depreciation would increase the effective tax rate on returns from such equipment, and would create a disincentive to invest in them.

Countries often also provide special depreciation incentives for certain types of preferred property. These choices are not based on any attempt to match economic with tax depreciation. Instead, they are designed to create incentives for the taxpayer to invest in such property by reducing the effective tax rate on

---

[127]See Hulten & Wykoff, *supra* note 122.
[128]See *id.* at 94.

the income it produces. Special tax incentives designed to distort market invest-ment choices are not generally the subject of this chapter. However, when such incentives are adopted, policymakers should make public both the intended ef-fects of such incentives and the justification for adopting them.

As noted earlier, jurisdictions have vastly different basic statutory struc-tures for determining amounts of depreciation deductions. Apart from special incentive provisions, they can be divided into (1) those that base deductions primarily on useful life, (2) those that use somewhat broader rules of thumb, but that are also based primarily on useful life, and (3) those that use rules that appear to be largely arbitrary. Those systems that use (1) may also provide guidance, either mandatory or suggestive, as to what the useful lives of a range of properties are. Those that use (1) and (2) often provide acceleration for properties that appear to decline in value more quickly than straight-line sug-gests. There is also a difference with regard to which jurisdictions include in their estimation the likely scrap value of the property, if any, once it has reached the end of its useful life.

The French and German rules, although somewhat different, provide some of the purest examples of system (1). They are primarily based on the use-ful life of the property, with special provisions for unexpected or exceptional falls in value, though never for increases in value. In France, the useful life of the property is determined by financial accounting principles, although a 20 percent variance is permitted.[129] Straight-line depreciation is then generally required for the property, including all nonphysical property, unless declining balance is specifically allowed.[130] Declining-balance depreciation is allowed, although not required, for certain physical property, including most machinery used in manufacturing and transport, office machines, and buildings used for light industry with a useful life of less than 15 years.[131] The degree of declining balance depends on useful lives: 1.5 for useful lives of 2–4 years, 2.0 for 5–6 years, and 2.5 for 6 years or more.[132] However, because the French system is based on an actual attempt to duplicate real decreases in value of the asset, ex-tra depreciation can be taken on any property to reflect special wear, changes in technology, or even the market for the good.[133] However, the depreciation deductions that are taken for tax purposes also have to be taken for financial reporting purposes.[134] Depletion allowances are uncharacteristically based largely on special provisions that have no apparent relationship to actual de-pletion. In addition, there are many special rules for accelerated depreciation for specially favored property.

---

[129]FRA CGI art. 39-1-2°; Précis, *supra* note 65, ¶ 1083.

[130]*See id.*; FRA CGI Ann. II, art. 24.

[131]FRA CGI art. 39A; FRA CGI Ann. II, art. 22.

[132]FRA CGI Ann. II, art. 24-2.

[133]Although reasonable proof would have to be provided. *See* Précis, *supra* note 65, ¶ 1083. Special deductions can also be taken for property not normally depreciable. *See supra* note 74.

[134]*See* Précis, *supra* note 65, ¶ 1083.

The German rule also bases depreciation primarily on the useful life of the property.[135] However, most useful lives are not determined strictly by financial accounting principles, in that the Ministry of Finance has listed recommended rates by category (machinery, office equipment, office furniture) and then more specifically by individual type.[136] In addition, the statute provides specific rates for certain buildings.[137] However, as in France, a declining-balance system is permitted in some instances for physical property; but in Germany, all movable fixed property is eligible, and up to a factor of 3 over straight-line may be used, but with a limit of 30 percent total deduction a year.[138] Unlike in France, there is also a provision that, for all movable fixed property, allows the taxpayer to fix depreciation as a percentage of output, although the taxpayer must provide "proof."[139] There is also, as in France, a general provision allowing for "extraordinary technical or financial depreciation."[140] There are many special rules for accelerated depreciation for specially favored property.

The Japanese rules have a similar mix of straight-line and declining-balance methods, also based on useful lives for which the Ministry of Finance provides guidance;[141] special deductions can also be taken for most physical property for extra wear or obsolescence.[142] The depletion rules are nearly identical to those in Germany.[143] Accelerated depreciation is also provided for favored property. In both Germany and France, scrap value is not normally taken into account in determining depreciation; however, any value realized from the sale of a depreciated asset would be included in income.[144]

The British rules, not surprisingly, are a fairly good example of system (3) above, where the rules appear to be largely arbitrary. As noted earlier, British depreciation rules are based on neither useful lives nor any other apparent estimation of actual declines in value. With only two rates available for all depreciable physical and nonphysical assets (including depletion), it can be guaranteed that allowances do not approximate reality.[145]

---

[135]DEU EStG § 7.

[136]The tables, with useful lives and rates, are found in Afa-Tabellen, vom Aug. 15, 1957, in der Fassung der ersten bis dreizehnten Ergänzung.

[137]DEU EStG § 7(4).

[138]*Id.* § 7(2).

[139]*Id.* § 7(1).

[140]*Id.*

[141]JPN IT art. 31; Ministry of Finance Ordinance No. 50 (1951).

[142]JPN IT Reg. 21-(2) II, Rule 7-(2).

[143]JPN IT Reg. 21-3.

[144]*See* discussion *infra* at sec. III(E) regarding transfer of property. However, as a matter of accounting conformity, in Germany estimates of scrap value can be included in determining depreciation for depreciable property (e.g., a ship) that normally has a substantial scrap value at the end of its useful life. *See* International Bureau of Fiscal Documentation, Taxation of Companies in Europe, German Federal Republic 53 (1995).

[145]*See supra* note 82.

At least with regard to the limited categories of property that the statute includes as depreciable, Australia is a fairly good example of system (2) above, or those that use somewhat broader rules of thumb, but that are also based primarily on useful lives. Most physical property is put into one of seven categories, based on useful life.[146] A declining-balance system is then used, unless the taxpayer opts for a straight-line system at rates published in the statute.[147] Taxpayers generally determine the useful lives of property, although the Commissioner of Inland Revenue publishes recommended lives, which the taxpayer can use.[148] For most nonphysical property, a straight-line system based on useful life is used.[149]

Lesotho seems to lie somewhere between the British and Australian systems. Its law relies on a broad and rather crude rule of thumb for three different categories of physical property, including depletion, selected by type and not by useful life; these categories allow a 5 percent, 20 percent, or 25 percent annual deduction.[150] However, there is also a catchall category for physical property not otherwise listed (except buildings other than industrial, which may not be depreciated), at the annual rate of 10 percent.[151] However, intangible assets are depreciated over their useful lives in accordance with the straight-line system.[152]

The Kazakh statute is similar to both the British and Lesotho rules.[153] As with Lesotho, there is a residual class covering all property (other than land) not listed in the other classes.[154] Like the U.K. system, a single, arbitrary depreciation rate is fixed for all nonphysical property.[155] These systems do not consider scrap value.

The U.S. statute is similar to the Australian, with most physical property put into one of nine categories based on the property's useful life; three categories are based on rules of thumb without any direct reference to useful lives: residential rental property, nonresidential real property, and railroad grading or tunnel bores.[156] Of course, such reference to useful lives is indirect in that property with similar useful lives was chosen for each class, and the allowable depreciation was based on estimates of those useful lives. Depreciation is allowed using a 200 percent declining balance, switching to straight-line when

---

[146]See AUS ITAA § 55.

[147]Id. §§ 55, 56(1); but see id. § 56(1A). There are special rules for certain other properties, such as certain motor vehicles, works of art, and Australian trading ships.

[148]Id. § 54(A).

[149]Id. §§ 124S, 124M.

[150]Id. sixth sched.

[151]Id. The relatively slow rate of 10 percent is intended to prevent taxpayers from arguing that property is not listed in one of the other classes and therefore falls into the catchall.

[152]Id. § 44(2).

[153]See KAZ TC art. 23(1).

[154]Id. art. 20(3)(3).

[155]Id.

[156]USA IRC § 168(c)(1), (e)(1).

more beneficial to the taxpayer, except for 15- or 20-year property, for which only 150 percent declining balance is allowed, and for immovable property or railroad property, for which straight-line is required.[157] Nonphysical property is depreciated at a straight-line,[158] and depletion is based either on a "reasonable allowance" or on a fixed annual percentage based on a large number of different categories of mineral.[159]

There is an obvious advantage to trying to match tax depreciation to real decreases in value. The accounting-type rules do at least set this as a principal goal. However, there are a number of objections to these systems: they are too complicated, and they give the taxpayer too much of an opportunity either to understate lives or to take unjustified additional depreciation. Therefore, justification can be found for the somewhat simpler rules followed in the United States and in Australia and for the much simplified rules followed in Lesotho and Kazakhstan. However, if administrative considerations permit a somewhat more sophisticated system, compromises can be made to keep the best of the accounting-based systems, without allowing too much latitude to the taxpayer. A compromise might include the following: along the lines of the French, German, and Japanese systems, a general rule could set annual depreciation rates as equal to straight-line over the useful life unless an exception is provided.

The first exception would allow a 150 percent declining balance for all physical property, to take account of the apparently greater speed with which such property actually declines in value. The taxation authority could then publish properties by type, as amended from time to time, along with their useful lives and the yearly depreciation rates. The second exception could allow, where specifically provided in regulations, 200 percent declining balance for physical property that tends to experience more rapid declines in value, as provided by regulation. The taxation authority could then publish properties by type, as amended from time to time, along with their useful lives and the yearly depreciation rates. In addition, any policy to accelerate depreciation for purposes other than ease of administration should be clearly stated and reflected not simply in changes in allowable yearly deductions.

The question of whether scrap value should be taken into account is really one of ease of administration. Certainly, as a matter of theory, scrap values should be included where appropriate, because the existence of a scrap value would mean that the asset does not decline to worthlessness over its useful life. A rule could require that if scrap values are assumed in financial accounts, they should be included in tax depreciation accounts as well. Another possibility would be for the tax administration to provide estimates of scrap values for those items of physical property for which it publishes useful lives,

---

[157]*Id.* § 168(b).

[158]*See* USA Treas. Reg. § 1.167(a)-3.

[159]USA IRC §§ 611(a), 613(a). There are seven different groups of minerals with different allowances. *Id.* § 613(b).

at least those for which scrap value is high. Another would be to use the Japanese rule of thumb method.

D. Depletion

Minerals that are extracted from the land will result in a reduction in the land's value; if the value of the minerals can be separated from the value of the rest of the land, a reduction in value of this separate amount can then be estimated. For a number of reasons, allowances for decreases in the value of mineral or similar property are often conceived of as separate from the accounting for depreciation of other property. One of the most important is that natural resources are often exploited at varying rates over the years. The rate of exploitation directly affects the decline in the value of the natural resource. This is in contrast to the assumption that underlies depreciation allowances for most other property, both physical and nonphysical: the rate of decrease is relatively constant throughout the property's useful life.

To account for the possibility that exploitation may vary over time, depreciation can be fixed on the basis of a reasonable estimate as to how much of each unit extracted reflects a decrease in the amount of total remaining mineral. This is known as "unit-of-production depletion."[160] Of course, this could be expressed as a given useful life, but only assuming a fixed rate of extraction. The second problem is that it is often difficult to determine the exact quantity of a natural resource. Without knowing how much exists, it is difficult to calculate unit-of-production depletion.

Another way to determine depletion allowances is to assume that a certain percentage of the gross income from the exploitation of the resource represents the cost of the depletion of the resource. Unlike with unit-of-production depletion, the amount of cost recovery allowed is reflected in a fixed rule of thumb percentage of gross income, and total deductions may not be limited to the cost of the original investment. This is known as percentage depletion.

The German statute allows depletion allowances to be based either on a useful life analysis or on accurate unit-of-production depletion analysis, the latter of which must be based "according to the portion of the substance consumed."[161] The French and Japanese each have special provisions for depletion. The French statute provides two different fixed annual percentage depletion amounts for hydrocarbons and other minerals; there is no limitation on deductions relative to the total cost of the natural resource.[162] The Japanese allow unit-of-production depletion or the related system based on the esti-

---

[160]The unit-of-production method has also sometimes been used for depreciable assets other than minerals.

[161]DEU EStG § 7(6).

[162]FRA CGI arts. 39 *ter*, 39 *ter* B.

mated life of the mineral or on any other reasonable estimate.[163] The Indonesian rule is similar to the German rule.[164]

The U.K. statute is quite different. It provides a single, and apparently arbitrary, depletion rate for all minerals.[165] Unlike the British provisions, the Australian provisions are based on a useful life analysis.[166] The Lesotho rule is like the British.[167] The U.S. rule gives the taxpayer a choice: it allows depletion based on a reasonable allowance or allows percentage depletion as provided in the statute. The percentage allowed is based on a large number of different categories of mineral.[168] As with France, total allowable depletion is not limited to cost of the mineral. The Kazakh statute is similar to both the British and Lesotho rules.[169]

Because of the relatively greater potential variability of natural resource exploitation, unit-of-production depletion should probably be required. The German phrasing seems adequate. However, because of the difficulty of administering such a rule and the often imperfect science of determining the size of at least some mineral wealth, providing rules of thumb for classes of minerals should also be contemplated. These rules of thumb should be based on empirical evidence of the local jurisdiction.

Probably one of the easiest ways of creating such rules of thumb is through a percentage depletion allowance, as is done in the United States. However, it makes sense to limit the total costs allowed through percentage depletion to the total costs of acquiring the depletable natural resource.

E. Transfer of Property

Depreciation (and depletion) allowances are designed to provide estimates of decreases in the value of property. However, except when they are based on the limited terms of nonphysical property, such decreases are unlikely ever exactly to equal the actual decline in the value of property. Therefore, if such property is transferred (or if it stops being used for the production of currently taxable income) before it becomes worthless, it is likely to have a value either greater or smaller than that predicted by depreciation. Also, in those instances where declining-balance depreciation is used, the property may well become worthless before or after the expiration of its useful life; if declining-balance depreciation is used, the property is nearly certain to become worthless before the balance reaches a trivial amount.

---

[163]JPN Reg. 21-3.

[164]The taxpayer is allowed to use either a single fixed period, or the unit-of-production method, although a rate is not prescribed. IDN art. 11(X), (XII), (XIII).

[165]See GBR CAA § 98(5).

[166]AUS ITAA §§ 122DG, 124ADG.

[167]See LSO ITA § 43.

[168]See supra note 159.

[169]See KAZ TC art. 23(1).

A transfer before the completion of depreciation allowances is therefore likely to result in an actual value at variance with its written-down value. If the actual value is lower, an additional deduction is required; if higher, the difference should be taken into income.

The accounting-type jurisdictions as a general rule take into account gains and losses on the transfer of business assets; this includes those with written-down or depreciated values.[170] The United States has a number of provisions whose net effect is similar.[171] For those assets that are not pooled,[172] the United Kingdom has a number of provisions that generally allow an immediate deduction for a loss and require immediate taxation of gain, although some special rules exist.[173] Australia, which allows pooling for most property, also has specific provisions that tax gains and losses, while permitting the rollover of gains in certain circumstances.[174] Both Kazakhstan and Lesotho include all gains on property as income.[175] Both laws also have specific rules regarding gains and losses on all depreciable physical assets.[176]

In order to ensure that no property, either physical or nonphysical, falls through the cracks, there should be a general provision that includes in income all gains and losses on the disposal of business property, including property subject to any depreciation or depletion allowances.

F. Partial Years

Not all depreciable property is acquired and used on the first day of the tax year; nor may it necessarily be eligible for depreciation allowances for an entire tax year. Therefore, many countries provide a mechanism for ensuring that a full year's depreciation is not deductible when an asset is in use for only part of a year. Again, different systems use different techniques. The accounting-type jurisdictions generally use the accounting rules in their jurisdictions. In France, this means that depreciation is prorated monthly, as of the first day of the month in which it was "acquired" or "built."[177] The Japanese rule is nearly identical.[178]

The general German rule is similar; however, this rule is trumped for movable physical property by an exception that lets the taxpayer round to the

---

[170]*See* FRA CGI art. 38(2); DEU EStG § 6; JPN IT §§ 22, 31(2). The French law, which has a special provision for reduced taxation of long-term capital gains, specifically includes gain up to the amount of depreciation taken as fully taxable short-term gains. FRA CGI art. 39 *duodecies* (b).

[171]*See, e.g.*, USA IRC §§ 168(i), 197(f)(1), 1245(a)(1), (a)(3). This also ensures that "recapture" of depreciation is reflected as a short-term capital gain. Such recapture of depreciation is referred to in some countries as a balancing charge.

[172]For a discussion of pooling, *see infra* sec. III(G).

[173]*See* I.R.C. v. Wood Bros. (Birkenhead) Ltd. [1959] A.C. 487; *but see* GBR CAA §§ 4(2), 60(2), 79.

[174]AUS ITAA § 59(1)–(2), (2A)–(2E). The net effect of rollover is the same as generally found in pooling. *See infra* sec. III(G).

[175]KAZ TC art. 20(6), (7). LSO ITA §§ 41(4), (8), (9), (11), 59.

[176]KAZ TC art. 20(6), (7). LSO ITA §§ 41(4), (8), (9), (11), 59.

[177]*See* Précis, *supra* note 65, ¶ 1100.

[178]International Bureau of Fiscal Documentation, Taxation of Companies: Japan 94 (1992).

nearest half year.[179] The British rule allows a full deduction starting in the tax year in which the taxpayer's "obligation to pay . . . becomes unconditional,"[180] while the Australian and Lesotho rules require an apportionment based on the number of days from the moment the property is "used" or "installed."[181] The United States, on the other hand, generally assumes that physical property was "placed in service" during midyear, allowing for only one-half of the typically allowable deduction.[182]

Which rule is selected will depend on a balance between the relative importance of administrative simplicity and accuracy. There is probably a benefit to requiring consistent treatment among all types of depreciable or depletable property.

G. Pooling

A number of countries, rather than requiring the separate tracking of assets for depreciation purposes, either permit or require certain properties to be "pooled."[183] Pooling can be accomplished using either closed-ended accounts (meaning that only property added in the same tax year is included) or open-ended accounts (meaning that property added in a different tax year is also included). Typically, in a pool, different properties with the same tax depreciation attributes are treated as if they were all one property. In the case of open-ended accounts, whenever a property is created or acquired, the appropriate costs are added to the sum in the appropriate pool, that is, the pool that includes all costs of assets with the same depreciation attributes as defined by the statute.[184]

If a property is sold or exchanged, the value received is subtracted from the pool.[185] If the value of the pool drops below zero, that amount is taken directly into income.[186] At the end of each tax year, a percentage of the entire pool is subtracted as a deduction for depreciation.[187] De minimis rules may provide for a complete deduction if the value of the pool drops below a certain

---

[179]DEU EStDV §§ 9a–11d; DEU EStR §§ 42–59c.

[180]GBR CAA § 159. Kazakhstan, which uses a pooling system, also allows a full deduction for the entire tax year in which the property is "used." KAZ TC art. 20(1), (4), (6). Correspondingly, the full value of sales proceeds from retired property is subtracted from the pool when property is disposed of, thereby denying depreciation for the year of retirement. (Sweden provides another example of allowing full depreciation in year 1.—L.M.)

[181]AUS ITAA § 56(1A)–(1C); LSO ITA §§ 41(3), 43. However, a half-year convention similar to that of the United States applies when pooling is used. LSO ITA § 41(8).

[182]USA IRC § 168(d)(1), (d)(4)(A).

[183]A number of jurisdictions permit or require pooling for different types of assets, including Australia, Canada, Denmark, Finland, Norway, Sweden, and the United Kingdom. See International Bureau of Fiscal Documentation, The Taxation of Companies in Europe (loose-leaf). This discussion will focus primarily on the rules of Kazakhstan and Lesotho, which have recently adopted pooling systems.

[184]See, e.g., KAZ TC arts. 20(4), (6)(2); LSO ITA § 41(5), (8).

[185]KAZ TC art. 20(6); LSO ITA § 41(8).

[186]KAZ TC art. 20(7); LSO ITA § 41(9).

[187]KAZ TC art. 20(6)(1); LSO ITA § 41(7).

amount.[188] A complete deduction for the closing balance is also allowed if all the assets in the pool have been retired or disposed of. As noted earlier, pooling can work only in the case of declining-balance depreciation. This is because no record is kept of the remaining useful life of any individual asset.

The principal difference in economic effect between pooling systems and separate accounting is that, under pooling, if allowable depreciation differs from actual (i.e., economic) depreciation and the asset is transferred before it is scrapped or becomes worthless, the gain or loss cannot be immediately reflected as taxable income (except when the value of the pool drops below zero). For example, under a separate accounting system, if an asset with a cost of $100 and a written-down value (i.e., after depreciation) of 0 were sold for $100, that $100 would be taken into income immediately.[189] Under pooling, however, the written-down value of the asset would not be recorded, so it would be impossible to determine the amount of gain. Instead, the $100 would be subtracted from the pool. This would mean that the taxpayer would not have to take into income $100 immediately, but only over the future in the form of lost allowances.

However, the present value of those future deductions will be less than $100 in immediate income. The extent of the benefit (or detriment) of pooling to a taxpayer over separate accounting will depend on the difference between tax and economic depreciation for each asset and on how often the particular taxpayer disposes of those assets.[190] If all such assets sold were purchased by oth-

---

[188]See, e.g., KAZ TC art. 20(8); LSO ITA § 41(10).

[189]Some tax systems allow a rollover of capital gains reinvested in similar assets or simply other business assets, outside of the context of a pooling system.

[190]For example, assume that the taxpayer purchases two assets, one large and one small. For tax purposes, the taxpayer keeps track of both assets in a 15 percent declining-balance pool. The taxpayer also keeps separate track of the depreciation of each asset for financial accounting purposes. The taxpayer has estimated that a 15 percent declining balance approximates the actual decline in value of the asset.

	Large Asset	Small Asset	Pooling
Year 1	9,000,000	1,000,000	10,000,000
Year 2	7,650,000	850,000	8,500,000
Year 3	6,502,500	722,500	7,225,000
Year 4	5,527,125	614,125	6,141,250
Year 5	4,689,056	522,006	5,220,062
Year 6	3,993,347	443,705	4,437,052

Year 6, sell small asset for $1,000,000
Amount realized: $1,000,000
Basis: $443,705
Gain: $556,295

Under a separate asset accounting system, the $556,295 would be taken into income, and no further deductions would be allowed for the $443,705 left to depreciate. In other words, the taxpayer would lose both the tax due on $556,295 and the present value (in year 6) of $433,705 in declining-balance deductions. Under pooling, this would be subtracted from the pool; that is, the taxpayer would lose the present value (in year 6) of $556,295 plus $443,705 in declining-balance deductions.

Because the present values of the $443,705 are identical, the only question is which is more beneficial to the taxpayer, paying tax currently on $556,295 or losing the present value of declining-balance deductions of $556,295? Current taxation on $556,295 will be greater than the loss of declining-balance deductions whose sum has a nominal value equal to the same number.

ers who were taxed at the same rate, then the net effect of a sale of an asset on state revenues would be nil; the asset would continue to be in use somewhere, and while value would be subtracted from one depreciation pool, it would be added to another pool. However, this may not always be the case. Some purchasers of assets may pay tax at different rates. Others may pay no tax, either because they have offsetting losses, or because they are otherwise tax exempt as governmental or nonprofit entities, or because they are not residents. Some, for example, have reported that oil companies in particular like pooling systems, where different subsidiaries can trade large assets like drilling platforms or other equipment depending on the availability to the subsidiary of other losses and where such assets can be traded out of the pooling jurisdiction entirely.

The economic effects of rolling over the capital gain associated with errors in tax depreciation increase both as the error increases and as the cost of the property increases. Perhaps in part for this reason, jurisdictions that provide for pooling generally require that structures and often other large capital items such as ships, public utilities, or locomotives be depreciated separately.[191] Depending on the wording of the statute, this can be accomplished by requiring either that such property be kept out of the pooling system or that each item of property be kept in its own pool, that is, a separate account.[192]

The oft-stated benefit of pooling is that it encompasses simpler record keeping than single-asset depreciation. However, under typical financial accounting standards, larger taxpayers often must keep separate accounts for assets of any substantial cost. Obviously, for these taxpayers, it may not be particularly onerous to require separate asset accounting for such assets. For taxpayers who are not required to keep separate accounts, the simplicity argument is more compelling. However, for any taxpayer, keeping separate account of assets that are longer lived and of a substantial cost does not seem particularly onerous. How these items of property are identified will depend on earlier choices regarding the structure of the depreciation system. However, as a general matter they could be identified through one or more attributes of cost, type, and length of useful life (or rate of declining-balance depreciation).

For example, all property with total costs in excess of a certain amount, and with a useful life of greater than 10 years or a declining balance of greater than 15 percent, could be required to be depreciated separately. Therefore, while a statutory provision could allow a pooling method for assets with similar depreciation profiles (meaning that they have the same rate of declining-balance depreciation), the tax administration should be permitted to deny its use in certain cases. This would allow both for ease of administration (broad classification of some assets, pooling) and for selective, careful tracking of economic depreciation for important assets.

---

[191]*See, e.g.*, LSO ITA § 41(5), sixth sched.; KAZ TC art. 20.
[192]*See* KAZ TC art. 20.

An additional consideration in deciding whether to use a pooling system is the interaction between the depreciation method used for tax purposes and that used for financial accounting purposes. It is convenient, although not necessary, for tax and financial accounting to be the same in this respect. Although financial accounting is generally done on a single-asset method, pooled methods are often permitted under national accounting standards.[193]

---

[193]*See, e.g.*, Accounting Standard D40, *reprinted in* Financial Accounting Standards Board, Current Text, Accounting Standards 12607 (1994) (unit for depreciation may be an asset or a group of assets); Donald E. Kieso & Jerry J. Weygandt, Intermediate Accounting 528–29 (3rd ed. 1980); Frank Minter, et al., Handbook of Accounting and Auditing C4-11 (1996).

18

International Aspects of Income Tax

Richard J. Vann

> In the long run, the business unit or source will yield more revenue to the public treasury than the individual; and the place where the income is earned will derive larger revenues than the jurisdiction of the person.
> —*T.S. Adams*

I. Introduction

This chapter examines the details of international income tax as an aid to understanding and drafting the parts of the income tax law dealing with international issues. Given the large literature on basic policy issues in international taxation, I deal with general policy matters only in passing.[1] The chapter accepts the general parameters of international income tax law as it is now established without questioning whether the structure provides the best solution to international tax problems.[2] Within that structure, it seeks to provide a detailed discussion of policy, design, and drafting issues. Although the chapter draws on the experience of industrial countries with international taxation, the special concerns of developing and transition countries are emphasized throughout.

Note: The author is grateful for comments from Reuven Avi-Yonah, Michael McIntyre, and Victor Thuronyi. The introductory quote is from the article by Mike Graetz cited in note 8 *infra*.

[1]The usual starting point is Richard Musgrave, United States Taxation of Foreign Investment Income (1969); among more recent works see, for example, Assaf Razin & Joel Slemrod eds., Taxation in the Global Economy (1990) and Organization for Economic Cooperation and Development (OECD), Taxing Profits in a Global Economy (1991). The OECD Committee on Fiscal Affairs, Working Party No. 2 on Tax Policy and Statistics is currently conducting a project on the policy of international taxation.

[2]A good deal has been written in recent years on the need for change in the international tax system, for example, Richard Vann, *A Model Tax Treaty for the Asian-Pacific Region*, 45 Bulletin for International Fiscal Documentation 99, 151 (1991); Sol Picciotto, International Business Taxation (1992); Vito Tanzi, Taxation in an Integrating World (1995).

The major difference between international income tax law and the remainder of the income tax lies in the pervasive importance of treaties.[3] Most countries have entered into one or more bilateral tax treaties that supplement and sometimes replace the income tax law, but only as regards the parties to the tax treaty in question. This chapter gives considerable emphasis to tax treaties and to the work of the Organization for Economic Cooperation and Development (OECD) and the United Nations (UN) in this area.

II. The International Dimension of Taxation

In the development of a country's tax laws, the international dimension plays an increasingly important role that significantly restricts the rules that might be adopted if regard were had only to domestic considerations. The increasing role of international factors is mainly attributable to the globalization of the world economy.

A. Importance of International Taxation

International trade has existed since the birth of nations, but there has been an accelerating growth not only in trade but also in finance and investment since the end of World War II. This growth has far outstripped the general growth in the world economy. One important cause has been the gradual removal of barriers to international trade through the various negotiating rounds of the General Agreement on Tariffs and Trade (the GATT, which as of 1995 is administered by the World Trade Organization, or WTO). For finance, the removal of exchange controls in most industrial countries, commencing from the floating of exchange rates in the early 1970s, has been a notable factor leading to the globalization of world capital and financial markets. The international organizations most involved here have been the IMF and the Bank for International Settlements.

In relation to investment, the main multilateral push is yet to come. In recent years, the foreign direct investment laws of investee countries and the investment rules for various institutional investors in investor countries have been liberalized, and bilateral investment treaties have grown. The Multilateral Agreement on Investment is currently under negotiation in the OECD. When this treaty is concluded in the near future, it is proposed to extend its regime worldwide through the cooperative efforts of the OECD and the WTO, which will see further global relaxation of investment controls. In addition, the end of the cold war has freed up the international transfer of technology, and labor is also becoming more mobile, especially for high-cost services (such as professional, management, and consulting services) and within trade blocs.

---

[3]*See* vol. 1 at 31–33 for a general discussion of the relevance of treaties to tax law.

Overlaying all these developments and substantially contributing to many of them are the great advances in international communications and computer technology.

It is a corollary of this growth in international transactions that international tax laws (along with international trade, finance, and commercial laws) have become more significant to each country's legal system. Moreover, as restrictions in other areas are reduced or removed, taxation is brought increasingly into focus, but there is a significant difference in the tax case. Whereas it may be possible to liberalize or abolish rules in other areas affecting international transactions, taxation needs to be retained in some form for the financing of governments. The international challenge for taxation is the development of a system that does not act as an undue impediment to international transactions while protecting the revenue of each state.

Although this challenge is present for all kinds of taxes, this chapter deals with the income tax.[4] The income tax is usually the major source of revenue and the most complex tax in industrial countries. For both these reasons, the tax causes the most problems in the international arena. In developing and transition countries, the income tax may not be the most important tax in terms of revenue, but it is looked to as serving that role in the future and it will also generally be the tax of greatest concern to foreign investors and expatriate personnel.

B. The Challenge for International Taxation

There are two main categories of case that international tax rules have to deal with. First, there is the taxation of persons from outside a country who work, enter into transactions, or have property or income in the country. Second, there is taxation of persons who belong to a country and work, enter into transactions, or have property or income abroad. The usual term used in international taxation to denote the concept of a person's belonging to a country is "residence" ("resident" and "nonresident" being used to indicate whether a particular person belongs to a country or not); similarly the usual term for income arising in a particular place is "source" ("domestic" and "foreign" being used to indicate whether particular income is sourced inside or outside a country).

The two categories arise in virtually all areas and types of taxation. For the income tax, the issues are the taxation of domestic income of nonresidents and the taxation of foreign income of residents. In both categories of case, the main problem is the potential for double taxation or double nontaxation of the income. That is, more than one country may seek to tax without reference to

---

[4]For a discussion of the international issues for the value-added tax, see vol. 1, at 170–73, 196, 207–08 and 215–16; for excises, see vol. 1, at 248–49; for wealth taxes, see vol. 1, at 310–11 and 314–15; and for social security taxes, see vol. 1, at 384–91.

tax levied in another country, or no country may tax (usually on the assumption that another country is taxing, although often it will be the result of the increased opportunities for tax planning or tax cheating on the part of taxpayers that international transactions offer). Double taxation is likely to act as a barrier to international transactions, and the nations of the world are generally agreed on the desirability of removing such barriers as a means of increasing global welfare.

By similar reasoning, double nontaxation of international transactions will create a bias in favor of international over domestic transactions, leading to a loss of global (and national) welfare, not to mention tax revenue. While, however, there is general agreement among taxpayers and governments on the undesirability of double taxation, double nontaxation is obviously desired by taxpayers and to some extent tolerated or even encouraged by governments. Developing countries often express the view that any increase in global welfare arising from the removal of international barriers accrues mainly to industrial countries. International agreements sometimes contain special regimes to deal with these concerns of developing countries, such as the generalized system of preferences in the GATT, which allows industrial countries to confer tariff privileges on developing countries without being obliged to extend them to all GATT members.

In the income tax field, this developing country view finds expression in the desire to offer tax incentives to international investors in order to attract capital and to ensure that the tax systems of industrial countries do not negate the effect of the incentives by collecting the tax that the developing countries have given up. The desired result of developing countries is generally achieved by tax-sparing provisions in bilateral tax treaties, which effectively sanction double nontaxation and hence create a bias in favor of international investment in developing countries. This particular policy in favor of double nontaxation is dealt with elsewhere in this volume.[5] In this chapter, the general premise is that the basic goal of the international income tax system is to avoid double taxation and double nontaxation.

C. Consensus on International Tax Rules

As the importance of the international dimension of income taxation has grown, an international consensus has emerged about the structure of the international income tax regime. The income tax is typically levied by a country on (1) the domestic and foreign income of its residents and (2) the domestic income of nonresidents. These basic rules are referred to respectively as the residence and source principles of taxation. The tax legislation of a country should in succinct terms state in some suitably conspicuous place (either the general provision levying the income tax, or the beginning of the group of pro-

---

[5]*See infra* ch. 23.

visions dealing with international issues, or both) whether and to what extent it has adopted these rules.

If a resident of one country earns income from a source in another country, double taxation is likely to result because one country will tax that income on a source basis and the other country on a residence basis. In this case, the internationally accepted regime is that the source country has the prior right to tax (although this right may be limited by treaty), and the residence country is responsible for relieving any double taxation that results. Such relief is generally achieved through one of two systems—the exemption system whereby the foreign income is exempted from tax in the residence country, and the foreign tax credit system whereby the tax of the residence country on the foreign income is reduced by the amount of source country tax on the income. Most countries employ some combination of the two systems.

The details of the rules necessary to implement these apparently simple concepts and their interaction with tax treaties will take up the remainder of this chapter. Before embarking on these rules, I will explore briefly the structure, purpose, and effect of tax treaties.

III. Tax Treaties

Tax treaties (also often referred to as double taxation conventions or double tax agreements) are international agreements entered into by countries and hence subject to general international law on treaties as codified in the Vienna Convention on the Law of Treaties.[6] Most tax treaties are bilateral, that is, involve two countries only, and cover income and capital taxes, though there are some examples of multilateral tax treaties. There are well in excess of 1,000 tax treaties and the number is growing rapidly.[7]

A. Structure of Tax Treaties

The history of tax treaties can be traced to the League of Nations, which was pressed to deal with the problem of double taxation after income taxes became important during the First World War and which developed a number of

---

[6]1155 UNTS 331 (1980), *reprinted in* 8 International Legal Materials 679 (1969). Although the convention has not been adopted universally, it is regarded as largely declaratory of customary international law, and so its principles are for the most part applicable to treaties entered into by countries that are not parties to it. *See* Ian Brownlie, Principles of Public International Law 604 (1990).

[7]Because tax treaties are for the most part bilateral, it is difficult to keep track of the number of treaties actually in force; nowadays, research on tax treaties is greatly facilitated by two CD-ROM collections, which are regularly updated: International Bureau of Fiscal Documentation, Tax Treaties Database; and Tax Analysts, Worldwide Tax Treaties. The tax treaties cited in this chapter can be found on these CDs; therefore, only summary citations are given for these treaties below.

models for use in negotiation of bilateral tax treaties.[8] The major modern successor to these models is the OECD Model Tax Convention on Income and on Capital (the OECD Model), which itself has gone through various versions.[9] Of especial interest to developing and transition countries is the 1980 UN Model Double Taxation Convention (the UN Model), which was based on the 1977 OECD Model but designed to take into account the special interests of developing countries.[10]

The typical structure of tax treaties is most easily seen from the chapter and article headings of the OECD Model as follows:

Chapter I	Scope of the Convention
Article 1	Persons covered
Article 2	Taxes covered
Chapter II	Definitions
Article 3	General definitions
Article 4	Resident
Article 5	Permanent establishment
Chapter III	Taxation of income
Article 6	Income from immovable property
Article 7	Business profits
Article 8	Shipping, inland waterways transport, and air transport
Article 9	Associated enterprises
Article 10	Dividends
Article 11	Interest
Article 12	Royalties
Article 13	Capital gains
Article 14	Independent personal services
Article 15	Dependent personal services
Article 16	Directors' fees
Article 17	Artistes and sportsmen
Article 18	Pensions
Article 19	Government service
Article 20	Students
Article 21	Other income

---

[8]The major League of Nations documents are collected in Joint Committee on Internal Revenue Taxation, 4 Legislative History of United States Tax Conventions, Model Tax Conventions (1962). *See also* Michael Graetz & Michael O'Hear, *The "Original Intent" of U.S. International Taxation*, 46 Duke L. J. 1021 (1997).

[9]The current version dates from 1992 and is in loose-leaf format (updated 1994, 1995, and 1997); the earlier versions were the Draft Double Taxation Convention on Income and Capital (1963) and Model Double Taxation Convention on Income and Capital (1977).

[10]United Nations Model Double Taxation Convention Between Developed and Developing Countries (1980) (ST/ESA/102), *reprinted in* Klaus Vogel, Klaus Vogel on Double Taxation Conventions (1991). For documentation of the influence of the UN Model on treaties, *see* Willem Wijnen & Marco Magenta, *The UN Model in Practice*, 51 Bull. Int'l Fiscal Doc. 574 (1997).

This structure (and even the numbering) is followed with only a few variations in nearly all existing tax treaties. The treaties apply to income and capital taxes[11] levied on residents of either of the countries that are parties to the treaty. Chapter III sets out the major substantive rules of the model treaty; they operate by dividing income into classes and setting out rules for each of the classes. These rules generally give the residence country an unlimited right to tax the income and at the same time limit or eliminate the source country's right to tax, with the source-country rights the greatest with respect to active income (business, professions, and employment) and income from immovable property, and the least with respect to passive income from intangibles. The treaty recognizes the source country's prior right to tax by requiring the residence country to relieve double taxation of its residents for taxes levied by the source country in accordance with the treaty. Chapter VI deals with administrative matters, to ensure that the treaty is effective in practice, and with the important issue of nondiscrimination.

On the basis of these models and its own particular policies, each country generally develops its own model that serves as the starting point in negotiations to conclude a tax treaty with another country.[12] A bilateral tax treaty takes

---

[11]Capital taxes as defined in art. 2 of the OECD Model mainly encompass annual wealth taxes, but do not include estate and gift taxes and other wealth transfer taxes for which there is a much smaller network of special bilateral tax treaties based around the OECD 1983 Model Double Tax Convention on Estates and Gifts. The reference in vol. 1, p. 315, to the lack of treaties on annual wealth taxes is to stand-alone treaties on wealth; many countries include the capital (wealth) article from the OECD Model treaty in their bilateral tax treaties.

[12]The model used by the United States has been published: Model Income Tax Convention of September 20, 1996, *reprinted in* Charles Gustafson et al., Taxation of International Transactions (1997).

about two years on average to negotiate and bring into force. In view of this long period of gestation, most treaties fix a minimum time period for their operation (generally about five years), but the expected life of a treaty before replacement by an updated version will usually be of the order of 10–30 years. This long life dictates both that the treaty be expressed in general terms so that it is flexible enough to handle the inevitable changes in the domestic tax laws of the treaty partners that will occur during the life of the treaty, and that the treaty contain mechanisms to deal with issues that arise during its life (primarily through each party keeping the other informed of changes in tax laws and through the consultative mechanisms provided by the mutual agreement procedure).

B. Purpose of Tax Treaties

The purpose of bilateral tax treaties is typically expressed in their preamble to be "the avoidance of double taxation and the prevention of fiscal evasion."[13] As most countries contain within their domestic law provisions to prevent double taxation of their residents in the most common case (where another country taxes the same income on a source basis), the main operation of tax treaties in this respect is for other types of double taxation that can arise as elaborated below. The prevention of fiscal evasion primarily refers to cases where taxpayers fraudulently conceal income in an international setting and rely on the inability of tax administrations to obtain information from abroad. The exchange of information article in tax treaties is the major provision dealing with this problem. Because of the capital flight experienced by many developing and transition countries, exchange of information is important, but in practice there are some considerable hurdles to successful exchange for reasons developed below.

From the perspective of developing and transition countries, there are a number of other purposes of tax treaties that are usually unstated but in many cases are more important. First, there is the division of tax revenues to be derived from income involving the two countries that are parties to the treaty. Where flows of income from business and investment are balanced between two countries, or even among a group of countries, it often does not make a large difference if each country agrees to significantly curtail its source jurisdiction to tax, as its residence taxation of income sourced in the other country is correspondingly increased. Where the flows are substantially unbalanced, the conclusion of a treaty under which each country gives up some of its source jurisdiction to tax generally has the effect of transferring revenue from one country to the other. Typically, developing and transition countries (and many smaller industrial countries) will be in the position vis-à-vis industrial countries of substantial net capital importers and hence will want to preserve source-country tax rights.

---

[13]The OECD and UN Models leave the contents of the preamble to be dealt with in accordance with the constitutional procedure of the negotiating states. The U.S. Model, *supra* note 12, uses this common formulation.

Second, developing and transition countries nowadays generally desire to encourage capital inflows from capital-exporting countries. Tax treaties may facilitate this process in a number of ways. In a very general sense, entering into tax treaties acts as a signal that a country is willing to adopt the international norms. This symbolic function is reinforced by the nondiscrimination article of tax treaties, by which the country undertakes not to discriminate under its tax laws against residents of treaty partners. Many potential investors attach great importance to the nondiscrimination article, in light of the historical antipathy that many developing and transition countries have in the past exhibited to inward investment. It is no coincidence that many tax treaties with transition countries are negotiated alongside investment protection treaties.

In the past, many developing countries took the view that they did not need tax treaties.[14] The countries very often adopted a policy that growth of their economies could best be achieved through domestic production by domestically (often state) owned firms of goods and services for domestic consumption. Hence, foreign investment was not needed and economic policy bolstered the natural human emotional response against ownership by foreigners. As tax treaties involved giving up part of the revenues from source taxation, there seemed little to be gained from them. Likewise, it was a consequence of the domestic focus that investment abroad by residents was not encouraged (a policy often enforced through very strict exchange controls). This situation has now changed, as demonstrated by the rapidly expanding tax treaty networks of many developing countries. Partly, the new attitude is due to a policy shift that accepts the benefits that flow from international trade and, in particular, from export-led growth in the model of the newly industrialized economies of Asia. Another factor has been the practical impossibility of making exchange and investment controls work effectively in a global economy.

Transition economies did enter into tax treaties in the past, but these were mainly political gestures given that there were no significant capital flows from the West.[15] The provisions of the old treaties were often inappropriate for the new situation and they therefore had to be speedily replaced (a phe-

---

[14]This attitude was most noticeable among Latin American countries, while by contrast many Asian countries have extensive tax treaty networks; nowadays, Latin American countries, including Chile, are embarking on active treaty negotiation programs. See Richard Vann, Tax Treaty Policy of Dynamic Non-Member Economies, in Tax Treaties: Linkages between OECD Member Countries and Dynamic Non-Member Economies (Vann ed., 1996). To the extent that countries did encourage foreign investment, tax treaties were necessary for tax sparing in relation to tax incentives; see infra ch. 23. The greater openness in the past of some Asian countries to foreign investment may explain the previous difference in treaty policy between Asia and Latin America.

[15]Tax relations among the transition countries used to be handled by the COMECON treaties (involving Bulgaria, Czechoslovakia, East Germany, Hungary, Mongolia, Poland, Romania, and the Soviet Union): Council for Mutual Economic Assistance Agreement on the Avoidance of Double Taxation on the Income and Property of Bodies Corporate (1979), and Agreement on the Avoidance of Double Taxation on Personal Income and Property (1979). Both of these tax treaties adhere even more strongly to the residence principle than the OECD Model.

nomenon particularly noticeable in the case of the Russian Federation). The need to do so, along with the large needs for capital, has spurred many transition countries to develop their treaty networks in recent years. The tax laws of transition countries are often not sufficiently developed or clear to enable the tax administration to utilize treaty rules. For example, domestic legislation may lack rules for adjusting transfer prices between related parties. This is another matter that the countries are generally remedying.

The remainder of the discussion in this chapter therefore proceeds on the assumption that most developing and transition countries will be actively pursuing the development of a tax treaty network and that, in the case of the transition countries, changes will be made to domestic law to remove the elements that form impediments to this development. What effect does this assumption have on domestic law?

C. Relationship of Tax Treaties and Domestic Law

It is not necessary to incorporate into domestic law the contents of treaties that operate only between states and do not directly affect private persons. A tax treaty, however, is intended to confer enforceable rights on taxpayers against the countries that are parties to the treaty. How this occurs is a matter for the constitutional law of each state, but in many cases it is necessary for each country to carry out some formal law-making process, such as approval of the tax treaty by parliament.

Further, the provisions of tax treaties are intended to have precedence over any inconsistent provisions of domestic tax law. Again, how this is effected is a matter for the constitutional law of the countries concerned. A common practice is to insert such a provision either into the law giving effect to the treaty or into the domestic tax law itself.[16] The usual result of such a provision under the law of most countries is that, apart from the administrative treaty provisions on the mutual agreement procedure and the exchange of information, a treaty sets limits on the operation of domestic law but does not expand its operation.

Thus, if a country taxes business profits arising from sales to residents of the country by a resident of another country without reference to a permanent-establishment concept, the business profits article of a tax treaty will usually prohibit such taxation, unless those profits are attributable to a permanent-establishment in the country. The outcome is the same if the domestic law uses a permanent establishment concept, but the concept is wider than that used in a relevant treaty. Similarly, if the tax applied under domestic law to dividends and interest paid to a resident of the other treaty country exceeds the

---

[16]AUS International Tax Agreements Act § 4(2); GBR ICTA § 788; compare the more equivocal treatment in USA IRC §§ 894(a), 7852(d)(1); Paul McDaniel & Hugh Ault, Introduction to United States International Taxation 174–75 (1989); GEO TC § 4(8); LVA TF § 7; KAZ TC § 1(3).

maximum rates permitted in the treaty, the source state is obliged to reduce its taxation accordingly.

If, however, a country levies no tax on dividends or interest paid to nonresidents, then the fact that a treaty allows such taxation up to a specified limit does not mean that such dividends and interest are taxable. It is possible, however, for domestic law to provide that if a treaty permits taxation that does not otherwise occur under domestic law, then the treaty rule will become the domestic rule for this case. This is the position in France[17] (and many Francophone African countries under their tax legislation) and in Australia with respect to source rules contained in treaties under legislation giving force to tax treaties.[18] Such a result is fairly uncommon, however.

By contrast, the administrative provisions of tax treaties (which may include articles on mutual agreement, exchange of information, and assistance in collection) by their very terms expand domestic law in the sense of giving powers that generally do not exist under domestic law. Thus, the mutual agreement procedure as contained in article 25 of the OECD Model gives an avenue of recourse to challenge assessment to tax in certain cases that does not exist under domestic law and overrides domestic limitation periods. Article 26 gives power to exchange information that does not usually exist under domestic law and modifies the secrecy provisions of domestic law accordingly.

The consequence of this relationship between tax treaties and domestic law suggests an important guideline for drafting the domestic tax rules themselves. If the domestic rules by and large follow the rules typically found in tax treaties, this will simplify the question of the relationship between tax treaties and domestic law and provide transparency to foreign investors as well as indicating (even in the absence of an extensive tax treaty network) the intention of the country to adopt internationally accepted standards.[19] This approach also gives instant access to a substantial body of commentary that is accepted by international consensus as elaborating and explaining the wording in question. The consequences of following—or not following—this guideline will be explored below. Because an international consensus exists on the structure and content of tax treaties, no one country, except perhaps the United States, is able to depart substantially from international norms. Accordingly, having a country tax treaty model that departs radically from the existing international models and following that model in domestic

---

[17]FRA CGI §§ 165 bis, 209 I.

[18]This follows from AUS International Tax Agreements Act s 4(2) and the peculiarly Australian tax treaty article on source of income, for example, Australia-Vietnam art. 22 in sched. 38 to that act.

[19]Even if a country intends to develop an extensive network, in many cases, it will take a significant amount of time to do so (perhaps decades). By following the pattern of tax treaties, a country can quickly achieve a tax regime that mimics what would obtain under a future tax treaty network.

law generally is not a viable option for developing or transition countries.[20] Moreover, no country can sensibly adopt a policy of residence taxation only (i.e., excluding the source principle). Neither would it make sense for developing and transition countries to adopt a policy of source-only taxation.

IV. Definition of Residence

Residence is almost invariably a central concept in the international tax rules of the domestic tax law of a country, with residents taxed on their worldwide income (or at least some categories of income).[21] It is difficult to enter into tax treaties without a concept of residence in domestic tax law because, by the first article of the international models, the tax treaty applies to the residents of each country that is a party to the treaty, and the definition of resident in the treaty refers to a resident under the domestic tax law of the countries. The basic idea behind the residence concept is that a person is a resident of a country if the person has close economic and personal ties to the country. It is possible for a person to be a resident of more than one country.

A. Individuals

Applying this basic policy idea in the case of an individual usually leads in domestic tax legislation to the adoption of one or more of three approaches. First, there is a facts-and-circumstances approach where no criterion is definitive but all the facts are weighed to determine residence. In many countries, this approach is not specifically defined by statute, and it is left to the courts or tax administration to give content to the concept. Tax treaties in the article defining residence give an indication of the factors that are most often used for this purpose: permanent home, personal and economic relations, and habitual abode. The problem with this approach is its uncertainty, which can be ameliorated by combining it with one of the following tests.

Second, the tax legislation may adopt rules for residence that are used for other purposes in the civil law of the country concerned (such as entitlement to work or remain in the country indefinitely under immigration laws, domicile, or citizenship). Many European countries use domicile. The United States is the only major country that uses citizenship as a residence-type test

---

[20]The COMECON treaties, *supra* note 15, did significantly depart from the OECD and UN Models without creating problems as they operated within a closed trading system; such an approach is no longer viable for transition countries. The Andean Model, which adopts exclusive source taxation (in line with the territorial tax systems in effect at the time in the signatory countries), has never received acceptance outside the Latin American countries that sponsored it; Commission of the Cartagena Agreement, Decision No. 40 Annex II (1971) reproduced in 28, No. 8 Bulletin for International Fiscal Documentation Supplement D8 (1974).

[21]Residence is of less significance for countries with a territorial system, but as discussed below, few countries have such a system anymore.

and, in view of the very liberal nationality laws of many countries, the citizenship criterion does not seem appropriate in most cases.[22] The problem with civil law tests is that the policy underlying a test devised for other purposes may not be appropriate for tax purposes, but the advantage is that they are more certain than the facts-and-circumstances approach, unless the civil law concept itself is vague.

Third, a rule of thumb based on the number of days that a person spends in the country during either the tax year or a moving 12-month period may be employed, the usual period being half a year (expressed as 183 days or more). Under this test, physical presence in the country for any part of a day usually counts as one day except when the person is in transit between other destinations and does not pass the customs or immigration barrier.[23] The advantage of using the tax year for this purpose compared with any moving 12-month period that ends or begins in the tax year is that a person can determine residence in relation to a particular tax year at the time of filing the tax return for that year. For example, if the calendar year is the tax year and the due date for filing declarations is March 31, a person who arrived in the country on October 1 will not know until the following October 1 whether the person was a resident from the time of arrival under a moving 12-month test. The disadvantage of a rule that looks solely to the number of days of presence during the tax year is that it effectively allows a person to remain in the country for up to 364 days consecutively spread over two tax years without becoming a resident. An intermediate rule that avoids these problems would look to presence in any consecutive 12-month period ending in the tax year in question.

In either form, the test can be criticized as unfair because it is mechanical—one individual can be treated as a resident despite very short periods of stay in the country (e.g., where a person drives to and from work through a neighboring country each work day),[24] while others can manipulate their period of stay to avoid crossing the 183-day threshold even when they are substantially connected to the country. Most countries use some variation of the

---

[22]The United States taxes residents—defined under USA IRC § 7701(b)—as well as citizens, but citizenship is really an aspect of residence as that term is used in this chapter with the sense of some personal connection to a country. The U.S. jurisdictional rules are stated in the negative rather than in the positive; that is, it is initially provided that all individuals and corporations are taxable on all their income, USA IRC §§ 1, 11(a), and then an exception is noted, USA IRC §§ 2(d), 11(d), 871, 877, and 882, which limits the tax on foreign corporations and nonresident aliens effectively to domestic income.

[23]The Commentary, para. 5 to art. 15 of the OECD Model indicates the way in which the 183-day test is usually counted, although, in the case of the Model, for another purpose. A rule that counted only full days of presence could be avoided by an individual's crossing the border during a sufficient number of days, which might be feasible for an individual living or working close to the country's border. For other possible exceptions and details, see USA IRC § 7701(b).

[24]It is, of course, possible to devise exceptions to cover this sort of case, but this tends to result in a more complex rule (e.g., USA IRC § 7701(b), and some unfairness will persist no matter how many exceptions and qualifications are devised.

183-day test but, because of its problems, often adopt a more substantive test of residence in addition and enact other measures to ameliorate its arbitrary nature, as discussed below.

Often, there is a special residence rule deeming specified government employees stationed abroad to be residents. The main purpose is to ensure that the diplomatic or other government staff of a country who may spend most of their working lives outside the country are nonetheless resident and therefore taxable on their salaries by the country (as they will often not be taxable in other countries, either by virtue of their diplomatic status or by virtue of the government service article in tax treaties).

Under all tests, questions arise as to whether a person can be a resident for tax purposes for part of the tax year and nonresident for part of the year. Most countries permit this possibility mainly to cover the case of migration where a person is moving permanently from one country to another. Where an individual is a resident for only part of a tax year, tax allowances tied to residence are often apportioned.

Some language encompassing these possibilities (other than when reliance is placed on other features of domestic civil law) follows.

(1) Subject to (2) and (3), an individual is a resident of X for the entire tax year if that individual
   (a) has closer social and economic relationships with X during the tax year than to any other country;
   (b) is present in X for 183 days or more in any consecutive period of 12 months ending in the tax year; or
   (c) is an official of the state service of X posted overseas during the tax year.

(2) An individual who was not a resident in the preceding tax year shall not be treated as a resident for the period preceding the day the individual was first present in X during the tax year.

(3) An individual who is not a resident in the following tax year shall not be treated as a resident for the period following the last day on which the individual was present in X during the tax year if during that period the individual had a closer social and economic connection to a foreign country than to X.

(4) For the purposes of (1)(b),
   (a) presence in X for part of a day is counted as a full day, and
   (b) presence in X without immigration clearance in transit between other countries is disregarded.

Some countries distinguish varying degrees of residence, such as residence and permanent residence, for different purposes under domestic tax law.[25] This approach may create confusion in the operation of the law unless the different

---

[25]*See, e.g.*, U. K. Tax Guide 1603–13 (Tiley ed., 1995).

terms are used with care in drafting. It can also cause problems in the application of the tax treaty article defining residence. Countries with a number of residence concepts need to review their model tax treaty to ensure that it is in harmony with the domestic tax law. Generally, it is better to avoid the use of differing residence concepts in the law and to deal with the concerns that give rise to them in other ways (such as special rules for expatriates; see section VI(B) of this chapter).

Because countries use different tests of residence, individuals with dual residence are not uncommon. In fact, even if all countries adopted the most common definition of residence—namely, the 183-day test—it would still be possible for the same individual to be resident in more than one country under each country's tax law at the same time. An example is the frontier worker who lives in one country but works in another and crosses the border between the two countries each work day. Dual residence creates problems of double taxation where each country taxes the worldwide income of its residents. The mechanisms for giving relief for double taxation arising from combined source and residence taxation of the same income are not able to solve this problem (sometimes called residence-residence double taxation). It is difficult for a country to solve this problem on its own, and so tax treaties provide a tie-breaker mechanism to allocate the residence of the individual to one country alone for the purposes of the treaty. This allocation is achieved through a hierarchy of tests involving the individual's permanent home, center of personal and economic relations, habitual abode, and nationality.[26]

For frontier workers, this mechanism may not solve the practical difficulties that average people face in being subject to two tax jurisdictions (either because a taxpayer is resident in one country and receives income sourced in the other country where the taxpayer's employment is conducted, or because the taxpayer is regarded as a resident of both countries). Accordingly, tax treaties between contiguous countries often contain provisions to ensure that frontier workers are taxed on their wages in one of the countries alone.[27]

B. Legal Entities

The residence of other taxpayers besides individuals, that is, corporations and other entities taxed as separate taxpayers, involves similar problems. From a policy perspective, legal entities are ultimately owned by individuals and the

---

[26]OECD Model art. 4(2). This test applies for the purposes of the treaty only and so does not relate to matters not directly covered by tax treaties, such as personal tax allowances; some countries carry the tax treaty tiebreaker rules into domestic tax law more generally, especially in relation to companies, for example, CAN ITA § 250(5); GBR Finance Act 1994 § 249.

[27]Examples are particularly common in Europe, as the following tax treaties show: Austria-Italy art. 15 (1981), Belgium-France art. 11(2)(c) (1974), Germany-Switzerland art. 15 and protocol (1971), Nordic Convention protocol art. VII (1989). Sometimes, special agreements dealing only with frontier workers are negotiated, such as France-Spain (1961).

residence of the owners should determine the residence of the entity. This is not a practical test for a number of reasons: it may be necessary to trace ownership through many tiers of entities, which is not administratively feasible, and in any event the ultimate owners may themselves be resident in different countries. Hence, a number of other tests are used. The first test is the country under whose laws the entity came into existence, commonly referred to as the place-of-incorporation test. Even more than the 183-day rule, this test is quite mechanistic and susceptible to manipulation. Therefore, additional tests and other safeguarding mechanisms are often provided.[28]

The second test is usually based on the place of management of the legal entity. In Anglo-Saxon countries, this is often expressed in the phrase "central management and control," which basically means where the board of directors meets. European countries look to the location of the head office of the legal entity.[29] These tests are based in part on a facts-and-circumstances approach to residence and so are not quite as mechanistic as the place-of-incorporation test, but they are susceptible to manipulation nevertheless.

Tax treaties seek to deal with the problem of dual residence of legal entities as for individuals, but are much less successful in this area mainly because there is no real international consensus on the appropriate tiebreaker, even though the OECD Model uses the place of effective management.[30] Moreover, dual-resident companies can give rise to problems that are not adequately addressed in tax treaties, especially the double claiming of deductions on a residence basis. Hence, a number of countries have enacted rules denying deductions to dual-resident companies in certain cases.[31] For developing and transition countries, it may be better to rely on general antiavoidance rules to deal with this kind of tax planning, as discussed below.[32]

These problems by no means exhaust the issues regarding residence of entities. Most countries have a variety of legal entities, not all of which can be easily fitted into the category of company or corporation for domestic tax law and tax treaty purposes. As exotic entities are being used increasingly in international tax planning,[33] countries should consider the need for special tax res-

---

[28]Some countries, for example, the United States, use this test exclusively in determining the basic jurisdiction to tax.

[29]See DEU AO § 11 ("Sitz" (seat)).

[30]OECD Model art. 4(3); this test seems to be closer to the place of executive management than the central-management-and-control test of Anglo-Saxon countries. The United States will accept only the place of incorporation as a tiebreaker for corporations (since it uses this test under domestic law; see supra note 28), and if the other country is not prepared to agree with this test, dual-resident companies are excluded from the benefits of the treaty; for example, Australia-United States arts. 3(1)(g), 4(1).

[31]AUS ITAA §§ 6F, 80G(6)(ba), 160ZP(7)(ba), and GBR ICTA § 404; see also note 26 supra for more general domestic law provisions dealing with dual residents.

[32]Related problems of double-dipping and treaty-shopping are dealt with infra, sec. VII(G)(5), (6).

[33]Such as limited-liability companies (LLCs) of various states in the United States and the Anstalt and Stiftung of Germanic law.

idence rules for various kinds of entities. Further, if it is not regarded as clear from definitions based on the above criteria that governments (central, regional, or local) and other public bodies of a country are resident in the country, then provision may be made to that effect.

It is common to define both individuals and legal entities that are not resident under the definitions in the domestic law as nonresidents for the purposes of the law,[34] although this may simply be stating the obvious.

V. Definition of Source of Income

Residence establishes a relationship between a country and the taxpayer deriving the income, whereas source concerns the connection between the income itself and a country. The basic policy idea is that income should be sourced in the country with which it has a substantial economic connection. Obviously, income may often have substantial connections with more than one country, in which case it may be appropriate to determine source by apportioning the income between the countries. Source rules have traditionally used differing concepts for active and passive income. In broad terms, active income is usually sourced by a place-of-taxpayer-activity test, while passive income (where the taxpayer often engages in no significant activity in deriving the income) is sourced by the place of activity of the person paying the income. To the extent that a clear distinction can be drawn between active and passive income, the growth of international trade in services raises questions as to whether the place-of-taxpayer-activity test is always appropriate for active income.

A. Geographical Extent of Country

As source involves a geographic connection, it is necessary to define the geographical area in question. For landlocked countries, this definition question does not present a real problem because the land area of the country is the relevant area. For countries with a maritime boundary, the territorial sea is treated under international law as part of the country and the country's jurisdiction also extends to the natural resources of the sea and seabed of the continental shelf. It is customary to extend source tax jurisdiction to the continental shelf. This extension may be effected in a way that reflects the limited rights that a country can exercise over the continental shelf (i.e., the country taxes only those continental-shelf activities over which it has sovereignty) or may be more general and cover all activities on the continental shelf. The resulting difference in tax jurisdiction over the continental shelf is shown by the example of a floating hotel owned by a nonresident and moored on the continental shelf; if the tax jurisdic-

---

[34]E.g., GEO TC § 29(8).

tion of a country is limited by reference to its sovereign powers under international law, the country cannot tax the profits of the hotel, whereas it can tax the profits if the broader formulation is adopted.

It is common to include a similar provision in tax treaties in the definition article. Given the importance of potential oil or gas resources in the continental shelf, oil-producing countries commonly include in tax treaties special provisions on this topic that preserve source-country jurisdiction as far as possible. In the case of other resources of the continental shelf, such as fisheries, some developing countries levy license fees in lieu of income tax, although in either case there are significant enforcement problems.

There is no agreement in international law that countries must limit their taxing jurisdiction for nonresidents to income sourced in the country. Some international lawyers consider that a country can assert the right to tax everybody in the world on their worldwide income,[35] but it will never be able to enforce such a claim and may attract various forms of retaliation from other countries. In other words, the adoption of the residence and source principles of taxation has been very much guided by practical considerations of enforcement and reciprocity. In marginal cases, such as floating hotels moored on the continental shelf, an assertion of tax jurisdiction is not likely to cause any problems practically or in international relations.

B. Structure of Source Rules

Many industrial countries do not have elaborate source rules in their domestic tax laws,[36] instead relying on such general expressions as income arising (from activities) in the country to express the source concept. In these countries, there will usually be a well-developed body of practice as to the detailed application of the general principle,[37] and in any event, there will be an extensive network of tax treaties in place containing explicit and implicit source rules for virtually all types of income. In the past, it was possible for developing countries to elaborate their domestic tax laws without detailed source rules, both because international income tax was not as important for the reasons outlined above and because the countries could usually rely on the body of practice in industrial countries because their tax laws would usually be modeled on the law of one or another industrial country. Transition countries are in all cases actively encouraging foreign investment. However, there is no tax tradition and in most cases no tax treaty network on which they can call to fill

---

[35]*See* Asif Qureshi, The Public International Law of Taxation 22–125 (1994), which deals with the unlimited and limited views.

[36]The United States is usually quoted as the exception, USA IRC §§ 861–865 and regulations thereunder; see also FRA CGI § 164B; JPN Corp TL § 138.

[37]However, even with such a body of practice, uncodified source rules can lead to substantial controversy. For example, a number of judicial decisions in Hong Kong Special Administrative Region (SAR) in recent years have considered the source of income.

in the gaps in their laws on sourcing rules. For both developing and transition countries, fairly detailed source rules will give comfort to foreign investors as to when their income will or will not be taxed.[38]

Tax treaties contain only a few source rules explicitly identified as such, for example, article 11(5) of the OECD Model dealing with interest. Nonetheless, for most kinds of income, there are implicit source rules. The source rule is implied by the way in which a country is given jurisdiction to tax income derived by residents of the other treaty country; for example, in the case of business income, under article 7 a country can tax income only if attributable to a permanent establishment in that country of a resident of the other treaty country. Some countries include a provision in their tax treaties to make clear that these implicit rules are effectively the source rules under the treaty.[39]

Countries can appropriately take these implicit treaty rules as the basic guideline for their source rules, subject to some caveats. First, to give the country negotiating room in the tax treaty process, the source rules in the domestic law should generally be more expansive than those found in treaties. Second (a related point), as the treaty rules operate to divide revenues between source and residence country, the source country will usually want in its domestic law to take full advantage of its taxing powers and have broader rules than those found in treaties. Third, the rules in tax treaties are to some extent shaped by practical considerations of tax administration, with a country giving up taxing rights not because income cannot be regarded as sourced there but because it is simpler for taxpayer and tax administration not to attempt to tax the income. However, it is very helpful if the domestic law generally follows the categorization of income that occurs in tax treaties because this makes the interaction of domestic law and tax treaties easier to understand. It also allows an easy connection between the type of income, and the method of taxation and collection of tax, as outlined below.

Just as it is possible to have residence-source and residence-residence double taxation, so source-source double taxation can arise when more than one country asserts that the same income is sourced in each country.[40] Again, it is difficult for any one country to solve this problem unilaterally, and tax treaties are the usual mechanism for resolving it. The method adopted in treaties is to specify expressly or impliedly for a single source rule to apply between the par-

---

[38] In transition countries whose domestic tax law is very brief, the inclusion of a detailed list of source rules may not be appropriate. These countries can include the detailed rules in regulations or instructions as long as the availability of the rules is made known to nonresident investors. As transition countries develop more detailed statutes, source rules can be included there.

[39]E.g., Canada-Germany art. 23(3) (1986); United Kingdom-Uzbekistan art. 22(3) (1993); see also supra note 18.

[40]For example, one country may have a source rule for services based on the place where the services are performed, while another may base source on the place where the services are utilized or paid for; if services are performed in the first state and utilized in the second, double taxation on a source basis will arise.

ties to the treaty for particular categories of income.[41] In turn, this method creates some impulse for countries to adopt similar rules in their domestic laws as informal harmonization on the same approach will generally overcome source-source double taxation even without tax treaties. Against this background, the various categories of income are now considered basically in the same order as found in tax treaties.

C. Income from Immovable Property

For income from immovable property, such as the rental of buildings or mineral royalties, the income is sourced in the country where the property is situated, whether it is derived as part of a business or otherwise. Under tax treaties, the provisions based on article 6 of the OECD Model include income from agriculture and forestry in this category and have a fairly extensive definition of immovable property that includes reference to the domestic law concept of immovable property. These features can be incorporated in domestic law, although it is probably simpler to omit them. Their effect in practice is not significant.

D. Business Income

For business income, tax treaties start with the permanent-establishment concept, which refers to a relatively enduring presence in a country through either location (e.g., an office) or personnel. The definition article of this term is quite lengthy and can be simplified in domestic law by removing some of the qualifications that limit the concept. Further, some extensions of the concept found in the UN Model may be added, especially as they were designed to increase the taxing reach of developing countries and add negotiating room in the tax treaty process. Special rules on oil and mineral exploration activities may also be appropriate for some countries. A provision with these features could take the following form:

(1) A permanent establishment is a fixed place of business through which the business of a person is wholly or partly carried on.
(2) A permanent establishment also includes
  (a) a building site or construction, installation, or assembly project in the country, or supervisory activities connected therewith; and
  (b) an installation or structure used for the exploration or exploitation of natural resources in the country, or supervisory activities connected therewith.

---

[41]In so-called triangular cases, where more than two countries are involved, the different bilateral treaties involved may produce differing source outcomes; in these kinds of cases, the other income article can often provide the solution if it follows the OECD Model by providing exclusive taxation for the country of residence, but not if the UN Model is used because it allows both residence and source countries to tax other income. *See* Vogel, *supra* note 10, at 916–17.

(3) Where another person is acting on behalf of the person and has, and habitually exercises, in a country an authority to conclude contracts in the name of the person, that person shall be deemed to have a permanent establishment in that country in respect of any activities which that other person undertakes for the person. This paragraph does not apply to an independent agent acting in the ordinary course of business.

The primary sourcing rule for taxing business income will then be through association with a permanent establishment. In addition to the OECD Model and the UN Model tests of connection, many countries also tax technical, administrative, and management fees paid to a nonresident by an enterprise that is resident in the country or that constitutes a permanent establishment of a nonresident in the country. Such a rule deals with cases where persons use deductible service fees to reduce the tax base in the country of the paying enterprise without corresponding taxation by that country of the fees received by the nonresident (which will often be a company that is related to the payer).[42] Alternatively, management and service fees may be taxed as royalties, which will usually be the preferable course. A suggested provision incorporating the UN features, but not technical or other fees, follows:

Business income is sourced in country X if
(1) it is attributable to a permanent establishment of the taxpayer in X;
(2) it arises from sales by the taxpayer in X where the taxpayer has a permanent establishment through which goods of the same or similar kind are sold; or
(3) it arises from other business activities carried on by the taxpayer in X where the taxpayer has a permanent establishment through which activities of the same or similar kind are carried on.

This provision will not exhaust the taxation of business income. First, there will often be special provisions for specific types of business income that take precedence over this general rule. Second, income of certain types that may or may not be income of a business depending on the circumstances (especially passive income, such as dividends, interest, royalties, or capital gains) will generally be taxable if it falls into either the business income rule or into the specific rules for the type of income in question (although the method of taxation will vary for each case as explained below).

---

[42]It is important to notice two different ways of dealing with such services. The position stated in the text uses a rule based on the residence or place of business of the payer to source the income. UN Model art. 5(3)(b) by contrast includes as an addition to the permanent-establishment definition the furnishing of services, including consultancy services, in the country through employees or other personnel engaged for such purpose for a period or periods aggregating more than 6 months in any 12-month period. This method still requires the performance of the services in the country, whereas the rule in the text does not.

Thus, tax treaties have special rules for international transport income, independent professional services, and income from entertainment and sporting activities. Many countries also add income from international communications and insurance. The OECD tax treaty approach for international transport income is premised on the view that the income will be equally balanced between the two countries, so that it is simpler from an administrative point of view to confine taxation to the country of residence of the company carrying out the international transport.[43] In the case of air transport, this assumption will generally be correct because of the restrictions in international airline agreements entered into by governments, which try to share revenues between the airlines of each country, while for shipping very few countries nowadays have substantial shipping industries because of the way that business is organized internationally. While the tax treaty approach thus does little harm, some countries find it easier to use a simple 50/50 rule that divides the income equally between the start and end points of the international transport, an approach also used for international telecommunications income (not separately covered in tax treaties partly because of its recent development and partly because international agreements between countries often share the income between companies in each country).

Professional services income nowadays is generally regarded as the same as business income, and the existence of separate articles in tax treaties is mainly to be explained historically.[44] As the outcome under such articles is similar to that for business income generally, special sourcing rules for such income are not often included in domestic law, except where it is intended to include a time threshold, which is discussed below in relation to employment income.

The taxation of insurance is a very specialized topic. Because of the difficulties involved in calculating the profit of an insurance company, some countries simply levy tax on a percentage of the premium income, either generally or specifically for certain types of insurance or in the international area. The basic sourcing rule adopted is the insuring of risks located in a country.

Business (and employment) income from entertainment and sporting activities is sourced in a country when the activity is carried out there; this is because very high incomes can be earned in short periods within a country that may not be captured under the general business income rules.

When special sourcing rules are adopted for particular types of business income in domestic law, they override the general business income source rule.

---

[43]In fact the OECD Model refers to the place of effective management of the enterprise, but this will usually correspond to the place of residence. The OECD Commentary on art. 8 in para. 2 contemplates the use of residence directly in the treaty article, and many treaties in practice follow this suggestion.

[44]Cf. ch. 14, *supra*, sec. V. The OECD is considering dropping the relevant article from its Model.

In turn, tax treaties will generally overturn the special rules for insurance and telecommunication income and adopt the general business income rule unless the special rules are preserved by provisions inserted for that purpose (which does occur in bilateral treaties and the UN Model for insurance but not for telecommunications). Dividends, interest, and royalties are often regarded as passive income but may be received in a business context, in which event the rules for taxing business income generally apply.

E. Dividends, Interest, and Royalties

Dividends are usually sourced under domestic law, and tax treaties by the residence of the company paying them. Interest under tax treaties also uses as a criterion the basic residence of the payer,[45] but where the interest is borne by the permanent establishment in connection with which the indebtedness is incurred, the interest is sourced by the location of the permanent establishment. Taken together, these rules on interest mean effectively that it is the place where the economic activity giving rise to the payment of the interest occurs that is its source.[46] Interest source rules under domestic laws show some variation from this pattern, most commonly adding the case where the interest relates to a loan that is secured by property situated in the country, but tax treaties generally override this rule. The tax treaty rule for the source of interest differs in one respect from the rule suggested in the text, apparently because of the bilateral nature of tax treaties. Sourcing by a branch rather than by the residence of the debtor occurs only where the branch is in one of the treaty countries; otherwise, the residence of the debtor prevails. This treaty rule can give rise to difficulties and is thus not followed by some countries in their treaties.[47]

Royalties do not have a detailed source rule in the OECD Model, given that taxation is exclusively reserved to the residence country, but almost half of the OECD countries and the UN Model do not follow this pattern. Rather, they replicate the interest-source rule for royalties, that is, residence of the payer with the permanent-establishment qualification. The United States has a sourcing rule of where the property giving rise to the royalties is used[48] and

---

[45]"Payer" in this context does not mean the person who actually hands over the money (which will usually be done by the debtor's bank), but the debtor or obligor; in tax treaties, the OECD Commentary on art. 11 para. 5 also notes that "paid" in this context has the broad meaning of the fulfillment of the obligation to put funds at the disposal of the creditor in the manner required by contract or custom.

[46]Where the debtor is a financial intermediary, it will in turn have loaned the funds to another, but it is not necessary for this purpose to track down the ultimate user of the funds; the branch of the financier that has borrowed the funds will be the determinant of the source of the interest payment. The fact that many interest payments involve financial intermediation creates many problems in the structuring of international tax rules as discussed below.

[47]Australia is the main example; see Australia-Vietnam art. 11(5); the United States in some of its treaties has also taken this approach.

[48]USA IRC § 861(a)(4).

can usually have this accepted in its treaties, but less powerful countries may find it more difficult to go their own way. Certainly, domestic law should contain a clear rule for sourcing royalties, as they are one of the most important forms of income internationally—especially so in a world that is coming to be dominated by trade in technological innovation and services rather than goods.

One of the most important aspects of the source rules for dividends, interest, and royalties is the definition of the terms. Most domestic tax laws will have a definition of dividend in relation to the general rules for taxing distributions by legal entities,[49] and tax treaties effectively adopt this definition. The reliance on the domestic definition of dividend under tax treaties can cause difficulties, as countries have widely differing definitions, which can lead to the consequence that one country regards a payment as a dividend whereas another country regards it as something else. For example, one country may treat a payment on the liquidation of a company to its shareholders, in whole or in part, as a dividend, whereas another country may treat it as a disposal of the shares (and so covered by the capital gain article in tax treaties). Tax treaties do not usually provide any clear resolution of this "conflict-of-qualifications" problem, except the possibility of the mutual agreement procedure. It follows that whatever definition of dividend is adopted for domestic purposes, problem cases can arise internationally under tax treaties. No simple solution is available.

By contrast, the definitions of "interest" and "royalties" in tax treaties do not rely on domestic definitions. The definition of interest in the OECD Model is income from a debt claim (but excluding penalty charges for late payment). While this definition operates clearly in many cases, financial innovation in recent decades has given rise to many instruments that are effectively loans but that do not relate to a debt claim and are therefore outside the definition (e.g., foreign exchange contracts and swaps can be structured to produce interest equivalents). Increasingly, countries are moving in their domestic laws to ensure that such instruments are taxed consistently with interest, but the rules required for such a regime are likely to be very complex. The result is that what is assimilated to interest under domestic laws varies greatly among countries and the definition used will depend on a number of fundamental policy choices in the taxation of interest.[50]

The definition of royalties is more straightforward. The essence of the definition in tax treaties, which is followed in the domestic law of many countries, is a payment for the use of intellectual property, including copyrights, patents, know-how, and secret processes. (The term "royalty" is also commonly used for payments to the owner of land or to the state for the right to extract natural resources, but these are income from immovable property and

---

[49]See supra ch. 19.
[50]See generally OECD, Taxation of New Financial Instruments (1994).

have already been dealt with above.) The OECD Model before 1992 covered equipment rentals in the definition of royalties by including payments for the right to use industrial, commercial, or scientific equipment; the deletion of this item in a bilateral treaty means that equipment rentals come within the business profits article under tax treaties. While the usage covering equipment leasing probably extends beyond the normal understanding of the term royalties, many countries still include equipment rentals in their domestic law definition of royalty.[51] As long as positive tax rates are specified for interest and royalties in tax treaties (not the case in the OECD Model but not uncommon in practice), one justification for this inclusion is that interest can be converted into rental income through the device of the financial lease (i.e., a lease that is the equivalent of a loan), but the treatment under the domestic law and tax treaties will effectively be the same.[52]

One problem of the royalty definition in the OECD Model is the reference to payments "for the use of, or the right to use" patents, etc. This language apparently does not cover disposals of intellectual property and, if so, the royalty definition can be simply avoided as transactions for use can easily be converted into disposal transactions because of the flexibility of patent and copyright law in most countries. For example, a person could be given the right to use a patent in a particular country for a specific period of time in return for payments related to the number of items produced using the patented process, or the patent could be disposed of to the person in respect of that country and time period on the same payment terms. For this reason some countries provide that where some proportion of the payments in relation to intellectual property are contingent on use, then they will be treated as royalties even though the transaction takes the form of a disposal.[53]

In some countries, technical fees are assimilated into the definition of royalties or are taxed similarly to royalties.[54] In the context of tax treaties, similar issues arise. Payments for technical services and the like may be incorporated into the royalties article or subject to a separate but similar article.[55] If no such provision is made, then the domestic rules for taxing such income will be overridden by tax treaties.

---

[51]E.g., AUS ITAA § 6(1) (definition of royalty); JPN Corp TL § 143(7).

[52]One difference is that the rental payment under a finance lease is equivalent to principal and interest on a loan, and so taxation of the full rental payment is more extensive than taxation of interest. To deal with this problem, some countries restrict the tax on a finance lease rental payment to the component equivalent to interest, for example, AUS ITAA § 128AC. This will also be the result when a financial lease is treated as a loan for tax purposes. E.g., GEO TC § 78.

[53]USA IRC § 865(d)(1)(B); alternatively, royalties can be defined to include payments for alienation as well as use, as in JPN Corp TL § 138(7).

[54]E.g., for Malaysia, see Ismail, Experience of Malaysia, in Vann, ed., supra note 14.

[55]All of Brazil's tax treaties, except a very early treaty with Japan, provide for assimilation of technical fees to royalties in protocols to the treaties; a number of treaties and protocols recently negotiated by India, Malaysia, and some African countries have separate articles on technical fees; see Vann, supra note 14.

F. Capital Gains

Capital gains are another area where variation in domestic laws can give rise to problems in their international treatment. Some countries (especially common law countries) have a general conception of capital gains as any gain on an asset other than inventory (and similar property) of a business and personal use assets of an individual (such as consumer durables). Within this group, a number of countries do not tax such capital gains while many others have beneficial rules and tax rates for them. Other countries, especially those based on civil law, have either a much narrower concept of capital gains or no such concept—business profits are taxed with no tax distinction drawn between gains on disposition of inventory and other assets, and individuals are simply taxed on gains on a list of assets without invoking any rubric of capital gain in either case.[56] Hence, the use of the term "capital gains" can cause some confusion in an international setting, and it can be argued that it is better avoided even though it is used in the OECD Model.[57]

Following the tax treaty rules, gains on business assets are generally sourced at the permanent establishment to which the gain is attributable; gains on immovable property are sourced where the property is situated; and gains on other property are sourced where the person disposing of it is resident. A number of countries include special rules in their domestic law and tax treaties for sourcing gains on shares in resident companies in one or more of the following categories: companies whose major assets are immovable property, direct investment interests in companies (usually defined as a certain proportion of the shares, such as 10 percent or 25 percent), and, more rarely, any interest in a closely held company.[58] The first two of these are intended to buttress the rules on taxing gains on business assets and immovable property. A taxpayer can easily avoid those rules by holding the relevant assets in a company and then selling the shares in the company.

While the purpose of the rules on companies is understandable, in practice it is not possible to prevent nonresidents from using variations on the same stratagem to avoid these rules. Rather than selling the shares in the resident company directly holding the relevant assets, a taxpayer can hold the assets through several tiers of companies (usually located in tax havens); it is then possible for one higher-tier nonresident company to sell the shares in the nonresident company below it in the tier and so effectively dispose of assets that may be several tiers below. While domestic law can have rules referring to disposal of shares in companies that amount indirectly to disposal of the relevant

---

[56]*See generally supra* ch. 16.

[57]Although only in the title to art. 13, and not in the text of the article itself, which refers simply to gains; the 1996 U.S. Model, *supra* note 12, uses "Gains" as the title also.

[58]USA IRC § 897 for the first and AUS ITAA § 160T and CAN ITA § 115(1)(b) for the second and third cases.

assets,[59] such rules will be almost impossible to enforce and will usually be overridden to a greater or lesser degree by tax treaties.

G. Employment, Services, and Pension Income

1. Employment Income

Employment income is usually sourced by the place where the employment is carried out (and if it is carried out in several places, the income is apportioned between those places). This is followed in tax treaties, with the exception that the OECD Model contains a 183-day presence threshold before a nonresident employee is taxable, if employed by a nonresident employer that does not deduct the relevant salary as part of the expenses of a permanent establishment in the country. Some short time threshold, such as 30, 60, or 90 days, subject to the same conditions, is a sensible rule for domestic law, as no country can successfully tax such employees who are in the country for very short periods. Especially in the context of developing and transition countries that are seeking to attract foreign investment, this kind of rule allows the important exploratory visits to take place before investment decisions are made without tax impediments so far as the employees of the potential investor are concerned. A monetary threshold can also be used as an addition to the time threshold to eliminate small amounts for ease of administration, or as an alternative to the time threshold to try to capture very high amounts of income earned in a short period.[60] Tax treaties contain time limits for employment income, but not usually monetary limits.

2. Fringe Benefits Tax

Following the lead of Australia and New Zealand, a few developing and transition countries have adopted fringe benefits taxes to deal with the problems of taxing benefits in kind provided by an employer to an employee.[61] The tax is levied directly on the employer at a flat rate and the benefit is then tax exempt in the hands of the employee. Even from a domestic viewpoint, the technical problems of this approach to the fringe benefits problem indicate that the tax should be adopted only when it is politically the only possible way to ensure that the benefits are taxed.[62] Otherwise, the more straightforward

---

[59]The provisions in note 58 refer to shares in resident companies and so can be easily overcome through the use of a nonresident company to hold the relevant asset without a lengthy tier of companies. Canada has recently extended its rules to nonresident companies in certain cases; CAN ITA § 115(1)(b)(v)(D). The UN Model refers to shares in a company whose assets consist "directly or indirectly" principally of immovable property and so is apt to cover such cases if there is a suitable provision in domestic law. In practice, it is rare for tax treaties to cover indirect disposals.

[60]E.g., USA IRC § 861(a)(3).

[61]See supra ch. 14, sec. III(C)

[62]See Vann, Some Lessons from Hussey and Lubick, 7 Tax Notes Int'l 268 (1993). See also supra ch. 14, sec. III(C).

method of treating fringe benefits as the equivalent of cash wages is to be preferred.

From an international perspective, fringe benefits taxes cause significant problems. First, the application of the residence and source principles to the tax is unclear. Does the residence of the employer or the employee count? Is the sourcing rule the same as for wages? If so, one of the claimed advantages of the tax, the avoidance of allocating benefits to individual employees, is lost. Second, how is relief from double taxation effected in domestic law (especially as other countries may not be using the tax, but taxing employees instead)? At the moment, fringe benefits taxes often lack mechanisms to avoid double taxation. Third, no satisfactory tax treaty mechanism has yet been found for dealing with such taxes.[63] Where the traditional approach of taxing fringe benefits to the employee is adopted, tax treaties experience little difficulty because the matter is dealt with by the employment income article.

For developing and transition countries, this fringe benefits tax problem is more than theoretical. As already noted, the taxation of the salaries and benefits of expatriate employees of foreign investors can be a significant factor in investment decisions. If a fringe benefits tax is adopted, it will not be relieved in the country of the expatriate employees' residence if that country applies a foreign tax credit, with resulting double taxation. The foreign investor, rather than the employees, in practice will absorb the fringe benefits tax so that it is simply an additional cost of—and disincentive to—the investment. Given that fringe benefits for good reasons often figure importantly in the remuneration packages of expatriate employees, the cost can become significant. Indeed, even under the traditional approach to fringe benefits, there is an argument for special rules to deal with such employees. Carrying these rules over into a fringe benefits tax will ameliorate but not solve the problem that the fringe benefits tax causes in the international context.

3. Services Income

The employment income source rule is often extended to all forms of services income. This has two effects. First, not only is the employee taxable but also the employer, where the services of the employee are part of the rendering of services of the employer to a third party. Second, in the case of professional services and services with a high value added where no employment is involved, the person rendering the services is taxable without the need for some permanent presence, as is generally true for business income. Because

---

[63]Australia has some provisions in a treaty with Indonesia over exploitation of the Timor Gap and its recent treaty with New Zealand. For all other tax treaties, however, the fringe benefits tax is simply not covered, because treaties are limited to income and capital taxes.

of the increasing significance of high-cost services in international trade, it is sensible for countries to seek to tax such services. They can do this either by adopting a general rule for services based on the place of performance or by including the rendering of services other than as an employee in the definition of permanent establishment. If either is done, it would be sensible to include a short time threshold, for similar reasons as in relation to employment income. Tax treaties based on the OECD Model would eliminate the tax in such a case but the UN Model would allow it, subject to a time threshold.[64] The addition of a monetary threshold in addition to or in lieu of a time threshold raises similar considerations as for employment income. The UN (but not the OECD) Model includes such a threshold for independent personal (i.e., professional) services but not for other services. Consistency across employment, professional, and other high-cost services makes sense from a policy viewpoint, but tax treaties will generally not produce this outcome.

Under domestic law, it is usually necessary (e.g., in relation to withholding on wage income) to draw distinctions between employment and business income.[65] Employers and employees may gain some advantage (in relation not simply to the income tax, but also to payroll-based taxes and even labor law) in converting what is essentially an employment relationship into a business one. One way to achieve this is for the employee to form a company that then contracts the services of the former employee to the former employer (the person is now an employee of the company the person owns but has control over how much income is received from the company in wages and how much in other forms). Domestic tax laws often deal with this problem by expansively defining employment to include such cases or by extending withholding to certain types of business income. As far as the former route is adopted, the rules will generally flow over into tax treaties (tax treaties have a special rule for directors of companies, sourcing directors' fees by the residence of the company, although under the domestic laws of most countries these fees are treated as employment income).

Arrangements designed to convert employment into business income have given rise to particular problems in international situations through manipulation of the time limits for taxing employment income under tax treaties. The OECD has accordingly developed rules for treaty purposes that seek to determine whether there is a genuine employment. These rules can be considered for use in domestic law. The rules address where the responsibility, risk,

---

[64]The UN Model uses "six months within any 12-month period" in the permanent establishment article and "183 days in the fiscal year concerned" in the independent personal services article. It seems preferable to use uniform terminology in both cases. For issues surrounding the counting of days under time-bound tests in a different context, *see supra* sec. II(A) concerning the residence of individuals.

[65]*See supra* ch. 14.

and authority to give instructions lie, where the work is carried out, the method of calculation of remuneration, who provides facilities, and the methods for the conduct of the work.[66]

One form of high-value service that is usually the subject of special rules concerns entertainers and athletes. Their income can be structured, as they desire, as business or employment income (in the latter case through the use of "star" companies similar to the situation just dealt with). Whether the income is employment or business, it is sourced under treaties by reference to the place of performance of the services without time thresholds.[67] Monetary limits may be used to segregate highly paid pop stars from the lower-paid members of, say, a visiting symphony orchestra, although tax treaties usually employ other methods to make this kind of separation (usually based on exceptions for official cultural exchange programs). Tax treaties also usually contain special provisions to look through star companies to the entertainer or athlete and to attribute all the income to that person. A similar rule may be useful in domestic law.

Even with some or all of this panoply of rules to cater to the problems of taxing high-cost services, the growing importance of services in the world economy is going to increase pressure on both source and residence country taxation. A successful computer software company, for example, could locate its programming and management staff in some suitably pleasant tax haven and market its products through mail order solicited by advertisements in computer magazines or on the Internet. Taxing the profits of such a company and the salaries of its employees in the countries where its products are sold is almost impossible, is not provided for in the domestic laws of most countries, and may be prevented by tax treaties. Similarly, much of the income of entertainers and athletes comes from sources not directly related to actual performance, such as video and sound recordings and endorsements. Capturing this indirect income by the country of place of performance entails the same kinds of problems.[68]

As already noted in the discussion of business income and royalties, some countries are responding to this problem by employing a definition of source

---

[66]OECD, Trends in International Taxation: Taxation Issues Relating to International Hiring-Out of Labor (1985) and see the Commentary para. 8 to OECD Model art. 15. Some tax treaties incorporate the tests developed by the OECD, but most countries are content to rely on the Commentary as bringing about the application of the tests. The object of the tests is to determine whether the business that contracts for the services of the company owned by the individual doing the work controls and provides for that person in a similar way as for an actual employee. *Cf. supra* ch. 14, note 60.

[67]For extended treatment of the domestic law and treaty issues arising from the income of entertainers and athletes, *see* Sandler, The Taxation of International Entertainers and Athletes (1995).

[68]Most of the problems under tax treaties in this area arise from the use of the permanent-establishment concept.

based on the residence of the payer.[69] As yet, such a shift does not have general international acceptance. This may, however, be a case where it is wise for domestic law in developing and transition countries to depart from the norms implicit in existing tax treaties and to seek to change their treaty practice accordingly. Considerable resistance will be encountered in tax treaty negotiations with industrial countries if a developing or transition country adopts this course.

4. Pension Income

A form of income often closely related to services income is pension income. Where the pension has been financed by contributions out of services income that have received favorable tax treatment in the country of performance (by exclusion of the contribution from income or a deduction for the contribution), a rule based on the place of performance of the services may be thought suitable for sourcing the pension. This approach will not be practical when the services have been rendered in many countries over a period of many years. For this reason and because pensions can take other forms (such as government benefits, distributions from social security schemes, and purchased annuities), they are often sourced by the residence of the recipient of the pension or by the residence of the payer of the pension. The OECD Model adopts the former while many tax treaties in practice adopt some form of the latter, especially in regard to social security and government benefits. The UN Model adds, in one of its variants, a permanent-establishment sourcing rule as a gloss on the residence-of-the-payer rule. Pensions and similar payments also give rise to some more general problems under international taxation, which are taken up below.

In developing countries, pensions of all kinds are much less common than in industrial countries, whereas they are widespread in transition countries. In both developing and transition countries, pensions tend to be small in amount (especially as a result of recent inflation in transition countries) and are often not taxable either because of an express exemption in the domestic tax law or because they fall entirely within the tax-free zone established by the tax rate scale or by personal allowances. Some developing and transition countries have already experienced immigration of pensioners from industrial countries in part to take advantage of a lower cost of living. It is not advisable therefore to be dogmatic on a source rule for pensions.

As with residence rules, there may be special sourcing-type rules for government employees. Although these rules are not often found in domestic tax laws, tax treaties generally limit taxation of the employee's wages to the gov-

---

[69]E.g., DEU EStG § 49(1)(3), (4) (services performed in Germany, utilized in Germany, or paid for from public funds); COL TC § 24(6) (compensation for personal services paid by the state); id. § 24(8) (income from the rendering of technical services); Price Waterhouse, Individual Taxes: A Worldwide Summary 43 (1997) (for Brazil, source is determined according to place where payer is located); BRA RIR §§ 2, 743, 785; ECU RTI § 8(2) (income derived from residents).

ernment employing the person, except for local employees. A variant of this rule is extended by tax treaties to pensions paid by the government to its former employees.

H. Other Income

For other income,[70] the OECD Model basically adopts a residence-only tax rule. The UN Model allows the country of source to tax the income in accordance with its own source rules without defining such rules. The domestic law of a transition or developing country can sensibly adopt this approach with some generally expressed source rule as a residual.

VI. Taxation of Residents

A. Rate Scale and Personal Allowances

The main reasons for taxing residents on their worldwide income have to do with the fairness of the tax system. When a country adopts a progressive income tax rate scale for individuals, it is usually motivated by the idea that it is fair for higher-income individuals to pay proportionally more of their income as tax. However, unless the individual is taxed on worldwide income, this goal may not be achieved for an individual with income from more than one country. If the progressive tax rates are the same in each country and each taxes only on a source basis, an individual receiving income from each country will pay less tax in total to both countries than an individual who receives the same total amount of income from only one of the countries. This is doubly unfair; not only are two like individuals taxed differently, but individuals are obviously encouraged to split their income between the countries, an avenue that is more likely to be availed of by a high-income taxpayer. There is also a lack of neutrality in such a system because of the splitting incentive that it creates.

Given that it is not practical for a country to tax all individuals in the world on a worldwide basis, the general policy that has been adopted is to tax only residents of a country in this way. A country can generally enforce its tax claims against residents (i.e., persons who have substantial personal contacts with the country), whereas a single-source country is unlikely to know the total income of a nonresident taxpayer and will face enforcement problems in relation to income arising outside the country. From a policy viewpoint, it also seems appropriate for the country taxing on the basis of personal allegiance of the taxpayer to be the one that takes account of the taxpayer's personal attributes. This concept relates not just to the progressive rate scale but also to tax allowances, such as those relating to a zone of tax-free income (which is

---

[70]*See supra* ch. 14, sec. V.

closely related to progressivity), family size and composition, medical costs, and subsidies for home ownership.

Conversely, for nonresidents, this approach implies flat-rate taxation of income sourced in a country and no tax allowances for personal attributes. If residence is changed part way through the tax year, then the taxpayer should change from one regime to the other and allowances should be adjusted to account for the fact that the entitlement is for only part of the year.

In practice, this approach to taxation of residents and nonresidents is often not fully realized. While dividends, interest, and royalties received by nonresidents are generally taxed on a flat-rate basis, the progressive rate scale is often applied to many other forms of income of nonresidents (although the zone of tax-free income is often not applied). Personal allowances (especially those applied by a developing or transition country to an expatriate from an industrial country) are often not significant in revenue terms in relation to nonresidents because of the small number of taxpayers affected. Hence, it is easier from an administrative perspective to apply them to all individual taxpayers and not just to residents or at least to apply them on a whole-year basis to any individual who is resident for part or all of the tax year.

Confining personal reliefs to residents of a country does not infringe on the nondiscrimination rules of tax treaties, which generally seek to ensure that residents and nonresidents are treated alike under the tax law of a country. The reliefs are recognized as part of the residence jurisdiction of the taxing country, so that residents and nonresidents are not treated as being in the same circumstances, which is a threshold condition for the application of the non-discrimination principle.[71] As tax treaties otherwise do not deal with personal reliefs, the tiebreaker rule in the tax treaty that addresses dual residence will not carry over into domestic law for this purpose. Hence, a dual resident will be entitled to the personal reliefs in more than one country, and a special rule in domestic law limiting entitlement to reliefs in such cases is necessary if it is desired to track the tax treaty rule. For developing and transition countries, this qualification seems an unnecessary refinement.

B. Expatriates

There are, however, a number of refinements that need to be considered by developing and transition countries in the taxation of expatriate employees who become residents of the country for a limited time. Expatriate employees will usually be brought into a country where the skills necessary for a particular job are lacking in the country and hence they will usually be very highly paid—especially in comparison with the general level of wages in the country.

---

[71]Words were added to para. 1 of art. 24 of the OECD Model in 1992 to make this point clear, but the addition was regarded as reflecting existing practice, Commentary para. 3 to art. 24; the second sentence of para. 3 of art. 24 also makes this point clear, Commentary para. 22.

They can be employed either by foreign investors or by local employers. While in the past when colonial attitudes prevailed, foreign investors may have been inclined to use expatriate employees for all senior positions whether or not lo-cal skills were available, this position has now generally changed for cost rea-sons and out of greater sensitivity to national sentiment. It will be assumed in what follows that the expatriate employee is providing skills that are in short supply in a country and that the country wishes to encourage—or at least not discourage—the importation of the skills.

For the purposes of the discussion we can distinguish several different sit-uations in which expatriate employees will be used in a country. First, there is the person who comes in to do a specific task and leaves when the task is com-plete; the stay is very short term. Such persons will generally not become res-idents under the domestic law of the country visited and, in the case of employment by a foreign resident investor, will often not be taxable on their employment income by reason of either tax treaties or provisions in domestic law that set time limits on source taxation of employees. Second, there is the person who comes for a more extended stay, say, six months to two years, but who leaves all or part of the person's family and a permanent home behind in the home country. This person will generally become a resident of the country where the work is performed under a 183-day rule while remaining resident in his or her home country, and under tax treaties residence will usually be allo-cated to the home country by the tiebreaker rule. Third, there is the person who comes for a yet more extended stay, but always with the intention of re-turning to the home country (as evidenced by the ownership of property there and the limited period of the assignment). This person may cease to be a resi-dent in the home country for the period of the assignment, but, if not, resi-dence will usually be allocated by tax treaties to the country where the work is being performed. Finally, there is the person who, at the outset, or more usually after an initial period in the country, decides to remain in the country and "go local." This person will usually cease to be a resident of the home country entirely.[72]

Because of the high costs involved with expatriate employees, employers will usually require them to go local after two or three years in the case of placement in an industrial country and after a longer period, say, three to five years, in developing or transition countries; that is, they are thereafter treated in the same way as local employees and do not receive special expatriate allow-ances. The basic structure of the remuneration of employees in the second and third categories above (which are the most common problem cases) will be to provide them with salary and benefits designed to keep their after-tax salary before the assignment intact, compensate them for the additional costs in-curred as a result of the assignment, and provide them with a bonus for under-

---

[72]An exception would be where the person's home country asserts taxing jurisdiction on a cit-izenship basis, as does the United States.

taking the assignment, which will often be viewed as having an element of hardship (such as separation from family, personal security and general living conditions in the country of assignment, and complication of personal affairs).

Typical benefits will thus include free or subsidized accommodation in the country of assignment, payment of private education fees for children, free airfares between the home country and the country of assignment on a regular basis, tax supplements to remove additional tax burdens and free access to specialist tax advice, special pension scheme arrangements, special medical insurance, free car and driver, and general security arrangements, plus a bonus of, say, 25–50 percent of salary.

1. Rate Scale

If an expatriate has become a resident of a developing or transition country under its law, taxation of worldwide income under the progressive rate scale will occur. The appropriateness of the rate scale to the expatriate thus becomes an issue. Generally, it will have been enacted with local incomes in mind. This means in many cases that the maximum tax rate is reached very quickly in comparison with industrial country tax rate scales, because of the generally lower level of local incomes. The result is a greater tax burden on the expatriate than in the home country, even if the maximum tax rates in the countries are the same. There is also a tendency for maximum tax rates in developing and transition countries to be higher than in some major industrial countries.[73] The employer thus will pay a tax supplement to the employee to eliminate the additional taxation, and, because the tax supplement is really just additional salary, it should also be taxable and grossed up for the additional tax accordingly.

To obviate this problem, some countries provide in effect special tax rate scales for expatriates (by giving special additional personal allowances or by stretching the tax brackets) and do not impose tax on tax supplements. Both of these measures represent generous treatment of expatriates. They may be risky in a political sense as favoring wealthy foreigners, but they may send a very positive signal to both foreign investors and to potential expatriate employees. The amount of revenue at stake in terms of overall revenues will usually be small in view of the small numbers of employees involved.

2. Fringe Benefits

The case of fringe benefits given to expatriates is clearer, however. Benefits that are viewed as simply part of a person's working conditions are not generally taxable as fringe benefits (such as pleasant office accommodation,

---

[73]In recent years, the top tax rate has come down in a number of developing and transition countries; however, in transition countries, the combined income and social security taxes can still be very high.

access to labor-saving technology, or payment of costs of work-related travel). It can be argued that although many of the benefits received by expatriates would amount to taxable fringe benefits if received by local employees, in the case of expatriates they are simply part of the conditions of work in the country. Thus, free accommodation in the country of work when the expatriate has left family in a residence in the home country and airfares to return home on a regular basis are little different from payment of the cost of work-related travel. Arrangements to ensure personal security may also be regarded as part of the work conditions.

In addition, taxation of fringe benefits in many countries takes account of disadvantageous work conditions (such as working in remote locations), and, again, the expatriate situation can be assimilated into this thinking. For example, while the expatriate may have sent school-age children to a public school back home, the only realistic option for language and cultural reasons may be to send them to a private school in the country of work to get a comparable education that will allow the children to be absorbed back into the public schools on return home. Free provision of health care up to the standard in the home country can be justified in the same way.

Hence, provided the rules are carefully framed and judiciously enforced by selective audits of expatriates to prevent abuses, nontaxation of such benefits can be justified on the basis of the special position of the expatriate. Indeed, this approach can be generalized for the converse case where residents of the country become expatriates in another country, although in practice legislation on this topic will be much rarer. A provision to this end follows:

(1) A foreign service allowance paid in respect of the additional expenses incurred by reason of employment in X is exempt income [in an amount not exceeding x percent of income (apart from this exemption)].

(2) Paragraph 1 does not apply to any allowance in respect of income tax payable in X. Regulations may further limit the exemption provided under paragraph 1.

(3) This article applies to a taxpayer if
   (a) the taxpayer was a resident of another country under its tax law immediately before undertaking the employment in respect of which the allowance is paid;
   (b) the taxpayer became a resident of X for tax purposes solely as a result of carrying out the duties of the employment; and
   (c) the employment in X lasts no longer than three years.

As indicated by the material in the article in square brackets, the exemption may be limited to a percentage of the taxpayer's income before the exemption is applied, which is a method to limit abuse (e.g., to prevent an employer from paying such an employee a relatively low salary and a substantial foreign service allowance). A limitation is imposed by paragraph 2, which provides that the exemption does not extend to allowances in respect of income tax (tax supplements) that the individual may have to pay in X. Paragraph 3 provides a special test to determine whether the person is entitled to the allowance, based on where the person was resident before moving as a result of the person's employment, and limits eligibility to the allowance to employment in the country for a maximum of three years.

3. Foreign-Source Income

The next problem is the treatment of income of the expatriate derived outside the country where the work is carried out. As already noted, expatriates in the second category referred to above will normally be treated as residents of the home country under the tiebreaker rule in tax treaties, whereas those in the third category will usually be treated as residents of the country where the work is performed. Depending on the precise terms of the treaty, the effect on the second category may be to eliminate taxation by the country where the work is conducted on income derived by the expatriate from sources outside that country and to limit or exclude taxation by that country on dividends, interest, royalties, and other kinds of income derived from sources in that country. For the third category of expatriate, the effect of tax treaties will usually be to permit unlimited taxation of their worldwide income by the country where the work is performed and to limit or eliminate taxation in the home country of income derived by the expatriate from sources in the country of work, the home country, or other countries. Where there is no tax treaty, there will frequently be unrelieved residence-residence double taxation for both the second and third categories. The overall tax position is thus complex and very likely to lead to excessive tax burdens.

If the country where the work is to be done wishes to attract the skills of expatriates, it may seek to deal with the problem in its domestic law. As with fringe benefits, the simplest mechanism is to exempt for a limited time income (other than employment income) derived by the expatriate from sources outside the country. An example of possible statutory language is as follows:

The foreign-source income of a resident of X is exempt income if
(a) it is not employment income;
(b) it does not benefit from a tax reduction under a tax treaty entered into by X;
(c) the taxpayer became a resident solely as a result of employment exercised in X; and
(d) the employment in X lasts no longer than three years.

4. Pensions and Social Security

It is common in many industrial countries for higher-paid employees with special skills to become members of private pension schemes. Under the tax law of industrial countries, the contributions to, income of, and distributions from the pension scheme will usually be subject to favorable tax treatment as a means of encouraging the employee to save for retirement and so not require support from the state in old age. When such a person comes to a developing or transition country as an expatriate employee, it will often be found that the country has no similar provisions in its laws (because of a lack of pension arrangements for old age in developing countries or because of full state provision of pensions in transition countries), or that such provisions as do exist do not apply to foreign pension schemes, or that ceilings on tax-favored contributions to local pension schemes are low by international standards. As entitlements under private pension schemes are often not portable between schemes within a country, let alone across international borders, the expatriate usually has no option but to remain a member of the pension scheme in the home country. The result is an increased tax burden on the employee and employer simply to maintain the existing pension entitlements of the employee, which will not come into effect until many years after the employee leaves the developing or transition country.

Although tax treaties increasingly are seeking to deal with this problem, most existing treaties do not.[74] Hence, countries may wish in their domestic law to recognize the position of foreign pension schemes and to seek to remove the tax problems they and their members currently experience. How this is to be achieved depends on the existing arrangements for domestic pension schemes in the country where the work occurs. If the country has schemes similar to those used in most industrial countries, then it is possible to extend the same preferential treatment to foreign schemes on the basis of reciprocity. Alternatively, if there are no such schemes or if reciprocity is difficult to achieve, a deduction may be provided for contributions from expatriate employees and their employers to pension schemes in the home country of the employee limited by reference to some proportion of salary and employer contributions (say, 10 or 15 percent).

Social security taxes present similar problems, especially in transition countries, where they can amount to up to 50 percent of payroll before tax. Although such taxes are separate from income taxes and are not covered by tax treaties, they are intimately related as far as the employee is concerned, especially as regards provision for retirement. An expatriate employee (or the employer, depending on where the tax is formally levied) will often find that social security contributions must be paid in respect of the employee's salary in both the home country and the country where the employee is working on the basis of residence in each country (the definition of residence under the social

---

[74]*See* OECD, *The Tax Treatment of Employees' Contributions to Foreign Pension Schemes, in Is-sues in International Taxation No. 4, Model Tax Convention: Four Related Studies* (1992) for a discussion of the problems under domestic law and proposals for additional provisions in tax treaties that are now reflected in the Commentary on art. 18 of the OECD Model.

security tax law being in question here, but with similar issues to the income tax).[75] There will generally be no relief from this double taxation, and in addition the expatriate employee or employer will often be insuring privately in respect of some of the matters that may be covered by the social security system (such as medical treatment) because of the difficulties of extracting adequate benefits from the systems of developing or transition countries in such cases. Even if there is no double tax, the local tax may be quite high.

For expatriate employees, the most relevant social security system is that of the home country, because they will avail themselves of very few or no benefits under the system of the country where the work occurs. Hence, it is sensible for the country where the work is carried out not to levy its social security tax on expatriate employees and at the same time to deny benefits under its system. This leaves the matter to be dealt with under the system of the home country or private insurance. Social security totalization agreements are nowadays being entered into between countries to deal with these kinds of problems, but the development of such treaties lags far behind tax treaties.[76]

C. Relief from Double Taxation

In industrial countries, the major residence country tax issue is generally seen as the relief of double taxation on income that has been taxed at source in another country. For developing and transition countries, this issue is less of a problem because residents will derive much less income from foreign sources. So far as there is foreign income, it will frequently be the result of (often illegal) capital flight to low-tax jurisdictions, in which event the problem for the residence country is detection and taxation of the income, not the relief of double taxation. Hence, the discussion of this issue will be fairly abbreviated and will not delve into all the well-known intricacies of credit and exemption systems of industrial countries.

It is necessary to distinguish among four basic methods in this area. The first is for a country not to assert jurisdiction to tax foreign-source income of residents (either at all or for selected types of income). This territorial approach to taxation (taxing only income sourced in the country) means that the country is not following the usual international norm of worldwide taxation of residents and so is not strictly a method for relieving double taxation as residence-source double taxation will simply not arise for its residents.[77]

---

[75]This will not always be the case, as often expatriate employees will not be liable to pay social security tax at home on income earned abroad. *See* vol. 1, ch. 11, at 386–91; USA IRC § 3121(b).

[76]*See* vol. 1, at 391.

[77]The territorial approach used to be common in Latin America, but the major jurisdictions there have moved to a worldwide system. It is still used in some Latin American countries, Hong Kong SAR, and South Africa.

The second method is the exemption system, under which foreign-source income is exempted in the country of residence. If the exemption is unconditional and the exempted income does not affect in any way the taxation of other income, then in substance the result is the same as a purely territorial system. Most exemption systems are not of this kind and so are to be distinguished from territorial systems. Most countries using an exemption system adopt exemption with progression, under which the total tax on all income of a resident is calculated, and then the average rate of tax is applied to the income that does not enjoy the exemption.[78] Exemption systems are also increasingly subject to various conditions to ensure satisfaction of the assumption underlying the system (that the income has been taxed in the source country at its ordinary rates).[79] These conditions can consist of subject-to-tax tests (including the specification of tax rates) or selective application of exemption to foreign countries under domestic law or tax treaties.[80] In particular, the exemption is usually not given where the source tax has been reduced or eliminated by a tax treaty. The result is that there are no countries asserting jurisdiction to tax worldwide income that give an exemption for all kinds of foreign income; where a country is referred to as an exemption country, this generally means that it provides some form of exemption to business income, dividends received from direct investments in foreign companies, and often employment income, with a credit being used in other cases.

The third system is the foreign tax credit system under which a credit against total tax on worldwide income is given for foreign taxes paid on foreign income by a resident up to the amount of domestic tax on that income. This limit is designed to ensure that foreign taxes do not reduce the tax on the domestic income of residents and is calculated by applying the average rate of tax on the worldwide income before the credit to the foreign-source income. In its simplest form, this limit is applied to foreign income in its entirety, without distinguishing the type of income and the country where it is sourced.

The fourth system is to give a deduction for foreign income taxes in the calculation of taxable income. While this system is used in some countries, often as a fallback from a foreign tax credit where the credit may not be of use to the taxpayer,[81] it is not widely accepted as a method for use on its own and, more specifically, is not used in tax treaties.

It can be argued that relief of double taxation in either credit or exemption form involves a number of complexities that are best avoided by developing or transition countries. Pure territorial taxation, however, simply invites tax avoidance through the moving of income offshore, and once qualifications on

---

[78]AUS ITAA § 23AG; FRA CGI § 197C.

[79]AUS ITAA § 23AH in relation to branch profits.

[80]Canada and Germany are two countries that confer exemption only in relation to countries with which they have a tax treaty.

[81]*See* USA IRC §§ 164(a), 901; GBR ICTA § 805.

the pure territorial principle are admitted, such as limiting it to certain kinds of income, it is hard to see that any great simplicity is achieved as problems of characterization of income arise, as well as incentives to convert income from one form to another. Similar difficulties arise when a conditional exemption system is used. For this reason, a simple foreign tax credit system is probably suitable for most such countries—it asserts the worldwide jurisdiction to tax income of residents and does not require significant refinements of calculation. It leaves open the greatest scope for elaboration of the system by domestic law and tax treaties in the future without having to repeal or modify any exemption (often a difficult process politically because of entrenched interests). Given that tax treaties are premised on an item-by-item foreign tax credit limit, rather than on a worldwide limit aggregating all foreign income of the taxpayer, the item-by-item limit is probably easiest to use in domestic law.[82]

Whichever double tax relief system is adopted, some method of apportioning deductions between domestic and foreign income will be necessary. Where deductions allocated to foreign income exceed that income, the loss should not be available for use against domestic income. In practice, most credit countries do end up with some cases of effective exemption for foreign income.[83] One possible example in this context is in relation to the foreign income of expatriates discussed above.

Tax treaties invariably contain an article for relief of residence-source double taxation (they are built on the assumption that each country will assert jurisdiction to tax the worldwide income of residents, which is another reason for asserting this jurisdiction in domestic law). The only methods specified in tax treaties are exemption and credit, but there is no need for the treaty method to follow that used in domestic law. Some countries have no relief method under domestic law, so that the only relief is under treaties,[84] while some countries have the credit method in domestic law but use the exemption

---

[82]This approach is most clear in art. 23A para. 2 of the OECD Model, but also applies to art. 23B. Item-by-item limits can be overcome by using wholly owned subsidiary "mixer" companies in which all foreign income ultimately owned by a resident taxpayer is channeled through an off-shore company so as to average differing foreign tax rates on various kinds of foreign income. To counter this kind of tax planning, elaborate provisions for looking through the mixer company to the underlying income are necessary. It does not seem worthwhile for developing and transition countries to adopt such measures. Alternatively, as suggested in the following text, a country in the early stages of developing its international tax rules may not adopt the underlying or indirect foreign tax credit on which this form of planning depends.

[83]Even the United States, which is generally regarded as the strongest proponent of the credit system, effectively exempts a significant part of foreign employment income of citizens living abroad. See USA IRC § 911(a).

[84]In Switzerland, in the absence of a treaty, double taxation is relieved by the deduction method (i.e., as a cost of earning income), not by credit or exemption, and this occurs even in the case of a few treaties with respect to income where tax is permitted or limited at source. See Xavier Oberson & Howard Hull, Switzerland in International Taxation 128, 130 (1996). Several transition countries lacked relief mechanisms prior to the reform of their tax laws in the transition.

method for selected kinds of income in treaties. Where the country has the credit method in its treaties, this is not generally regarded as preventing it from using the exemption method in domestic law, as exemption is seen as more generous than the credit method and therefore not inconsistent with the treaty obligation. Where the exemption method is adopted by tax treaties, the exemption-with-progression system is usually expressly authorized.

Special double tax relief rules are often provided for foreign direct investment. As already noted, the exemption system is often targeted to foreign-source business income and dividends received by a resident company from a direct investment in a nonresident company. Direct investment in a foreign company is equated with business income to ensure that no bias is created as to the business form used. If an exemption is granted for the business income of a branch in a foreign country, then it should make no difference that the business income is generated by a subsidiary in that country and then repatriated as dividends. By parity of reasoning under a credit system, a resident company should get a foreign tax credit not only for foreign tax paid by a branch but also for foreign tax paid by a subsidiary. This credit, referred to as an underlying or indirect foreign tax credit, in practice involves a number of complexities that most developing or transition countries would do well to avoid. It needs to be recognized, however, that failure to grant an indirect credit creates a bias against investment abroad by residents of the country in the form of subsidiaries. If such investment becomes important to the country, the indirect foreign tax credit issue should be addressed either in tax treaties or in domestic law, or both.

The article in tax treaties on relief from double taxation may also contain special rules for direct investment in a developing or a transition country by a foreign investor to preserve the effect of tax incentives granted by the developing or transition country. This topic is discussed in relation to tax sparing in chapter 23.

D. Capital Flight

The more important residence tax problem for developing and transition countries is capital flight. Many residents, especially those with the greatest wealth, will seek to send their wealth abroad. They may be concerned about devaluation of their own currency and wish to hold foreign currency, which may not be legally possible in their countries; they may be afraid of confiscation (by the state or criminal gangs) or civil unrest; and they may seek not to pay tax on the income produced by the wealth, which itself may have been obtained by illegal means or may represent income that was not declared for tax purposes. Whatever the reasons in any given case, it is clear that capital flight from developing and especially transition countries is a major problem; the need of these countries, on the contrary, is to retain domestic capital for productive local investment.

Most of this fleeing capital finds its way to tax havens, which may be defined for this purpose as low-tax jurisdictions that have bank and other secrecy laws that allow the ownership of assets to be concealed. For transition countries, it is well known that Cyprus is a major destination of nervous capital. For developing countries, there are any number of other tax havens only too willing to assist. Indeed, so lucrative does the business seem that many developing and transition countries actively consider turning themselves into tax havens.

If the money simply finds its way into an anonymous bank account and the income earned thereon is not declared for income tax purposes, then assuming that the residence country asserts jurisdiction to tax the income, this is a case of tax fraud (deliberate nondisclosure). The problem here is one of detection and tax administration. More sophisticated taxpayers may wish to ensure that no tax liability arises in respect of the wealth, and there are a number of stratagems that they can employ. The simplest form is to invest in shares in a tax haven company that in turn simply invests in a very safe form (such as U.S.-dollar-denominated bonds with a high credit rating) and accumulates the interest income for further similar investment. If the shareholder desires the return of the original investment and the income that has accrued in the company, an associate simply buys the shares at a price based on their asset backing. The company is not taxed on the interest that accrues on the bonds (or is taxed at a very low rate) because it is located in a tax haven (from the point of view of the residence country of the investor, it is foreign-source income of a nonresident) and the investor is not taxable on the interest because it accrues to the company and not to the investor.[85] The investor will be taxable in the residence country, if at all, only on the profit on the sale of the shares, but can postpone this tax for many years by not selling. In any event, many developing and transition countries do not tax gains on the sale of shares.

To counter this kind of activity, special rules are required in the domestic tax law of the residence country, in effect to look through the company and tax the resident investor on the underlying income. A number of industrial countries have such laws but they are usually very complex. For developing and transition countries, a simpler provision can be inserted in the tax law to give a discretion to tax and thus to send a signal that such cases will be pursued when detected.[86] A provision may be drafted along the following lines:

(1) Where a resident of X has entered into a transaction that converts income into foreign-source income derived from a tax haven by another person, the tax administration may adjust the income and foreign tax credit position of the resident to reverse the tax effect of the transaction.

---

[85]Even when the company invests in bonds denominated in major currencies, such as the U.S. dollar, there will often be no interest withholding tax in the country of issue because an interest withholding tax exemption is applicable (as to which, see infra sec. VII (C)).

[86]E.g., GEO TC § 66.

(2) The tax administration may treat a foreign country as a tax haven if
that country has
   (a) effective tax rates significantly lower than those of X; or
   (b) laws providing for the secrecy of financial or corporate information that facilitate the concealment of the identity of the real
owner of any asset or income.

This provision is not generally regarded as breaching tax treaty obligations in the unlikely event that there is a treaty with the tax haven. There will
still be an information problem if such a provision is inserted into the law, and
the investor will no doubt be relying on lack of information as much as the in-
terposing of the company to avoid tax. To overcome this problem, it is necessary to have a question in the tax return or tax declaration that requires the
taxpayer to disclose investments in nonresident entities, which will prompt
the tax administration to inquire further. If the resident investor deliberately
answers this question incorrectly, as is likely, the taxpayer's position is back to
tax fraud and problems of detection.

The information problem is almost impossible to solve. The tax haven
will usually not enter into tax treaties, or if it does, it will change the exchange-of-information article so as not to require disclosure in relation to
banks' tax haven operations. As tax treaties generally provide the only way for
tax administrations in different countries to exchange information, cooperation in the disclosure of the information from the tax haven will not be forthcoming. For this reason and many others, developing and transition countries
should be wary of entering into tax treaties with tax havens. The best that developing and transition countries can do for now to deal with capital flight to
tax havens is to try to remove the conditions that give rise to the flight in the
first instance and to apply severe penalties in relation to tax fraud involving
tax havens.

E. Change of Residence for Tax Reasons

One other residence country tax problem can be noted in conclusion.
Some residents who anticipate deriving a substantial amount of foreign-source
income may be tempted to change their residence before the income is received so that it becomes foreign-source income of a nonresident from the
point of view of the former residence country. Obviously the change would be
made to a country that would not tax the income (possibly a tax haven) and
would occur only if there were no substantial source country tax on the income
(because otherwise the residual residence country taxation is likely to be minor). Some industrial countries have special rules to deal with this problem,
but they may be regarded as unnecessary for developing or transition countries.
The main problem for such countries is in fact likely to be the other way
around, that is, the rules of industrial countries in this area may create problems for expatriate taxpayers who become residents. The rules outlined above

to deal with the tax problems of expatriates may also assist in overcoming this problem.[87]

VII. Taxation of Nonresidents

As already noted, general principles suggest that the income of nonresidents should be taxed on a flat-rate basis, as progression is a matter for the residence country. In practice, some taxes on nonresidents are collected on a flat-rate basis, but more for administrative convenience than principle. Because of the general rule found in most legal systems that one country will not assist another in enforcing its tax laws and because of the general administrative difficulties of dealing with persons and assets outside a country, the source country will be well advised to enforce its tax claim on the payer of the income before the payment leaves the country in cases where the recipient does not have any substantial connection with the country, such as a permanent establishment. Hence, it has become accepted as a general principle of international taxation that taxation of passive income unconnected with a business in a country is enforced by flat-rate final withholding taxes, whereas tax on business income arising from a permanent establishment is levied on net income and is collected by the normal assessment system applied to businesses of residents (which may also include some elements of withholding and payment of tax by installments).

For other forms of income, there is less consistency in practice between flat-rate withholding and tax by assessment, although where assessment is used it is normally in accordance with the rate scale applicable to residents, rather than with a special flat-rate scale for nonresidents (although personal allowances including a tax-free amount are often confined to residents). The discussion of taxation of nonresidents will thus start with the related issues of tax rates, method of collection, the use or not of assessments, and the effect of tax treaties, taking the categories of income in turn as for the source area. It will then turn to a number of other issues affecting nonresidents of concern to developing and transition countries.

A. Income from Immovable Property

Income of nonresidents from immovable property is taxed by some countries on a flat-rate final withholding basis on gross rent and by others on an assessment basis. Some countries provide an option to nonresident taxpayers as

---

[87]In a number of industrial countries, for example, USA IRC § 877, the change of residence rules take the form of subjecting the person to tax on gains on the disposal of assets for a period of time after the person ceases to be a resident. If the developing or transition country exempts foreign income of expatriates (other than employment income) from tax for a certain period, the problem of conflicting tax jurisdiction is likely to be avoided.

to the method of taxation[88] since, although final withholding is simple, it can prove very rough and ready because of the wide variation that occurs in the amount of deductions relating to income from immovable property (e.g., the full amount to purchase the property, or none of it, may have been borrowed, leading to very different amounts of interest deductions). As enforcement in this case is not generally a problem (assuming that the tax administration can execute against the immovable property for unpaid tax), tax by assessment on a net basis seems the fairer approach, and requiring private residential tenants to withhold on rental payments is unlikely to be enforced effectively. Tax treaties do not generally constrain domestic law in this case.

B. Business Income

In the case of business income of a nonresident sourced in a country, income attributable to a permanent establishment (or otherwise associated with a permanent establishment and sourced in the country) is generally taxed on a net assessment basis. Tax treaties usually require this approach in the case of income subject to the business profits article but, because of their convoluted drafting, the actual extent of this obligation is not obvious at first sight. The business profits article is usually expressed to be subject to other articles of the treaty, but then other articles either refer the matter back to the business profits article in respect of profits attributable to a permanent establishment (dividends, interest, royalties, and other income) or adopt in effect the same rule as the business profits article (capital gains and implicitly, at least according to the OECD Commentary,[89] income from independent personal services).

Articles that may involve business profits and that override the tax treaty requirement of taxation on a net basis concern income from immovable property (above), international transport, and entertainment and sporting activities. In the case of international transport, source taxation is generally excluded (although the UN Model has a little-used variant for shipping) and in the case of entertainment and sporting activities, taxation on a gross withholding basis is permitted. Taxation by withholding is usually permitted for dividends, interest, and royalties that are not attributable to a permanent establishment.

To the extent that the domestic law provides for taxation, on a net or a withholding basis, of technical fees paid to nonresidents, tax treaties will usually override and prevent the tax levy if the fees are not attributable to a permanent establishment while requiring as a result of the nondiscrimination article that a deduction be given to the permanent establishment or resident company that incurred the expenses, subject to the amount being at arm's length in the case of related parties. Nonresident companies may try to exploit

---

[88]USA IRC § 871(d).
[89]Para. 3 of Commentary on art. 14.

this situation, but depending on the circumstances, it may be possible to find means within the tax treaty to levy tax on both the technical fees and on the salaries of the personnel providing the services.[90] It was noted above that most tax treaties do not deal separately with insurance and telecommunication income, so that the permanent establishment requirement applies, with the result that the profits from these activities in a country are often not taxable. A number of countries nonetheless apply (relatively low, say, 5 percent) flat-rate withholding taxes on insurance premiums, either in the international area specifically or more generally and seek to protect this levy in their tax treaties.

One particular problem that some transition countries experience in the area of business income is the treatment of deductions. In a number of countries, the tax laws, for the purpose of wage control, have denied deductions for wages in excess of a very low threshold. Deductions for other expenses, such as advertising and interest, may also be limited. There has been some debate on the extent to which the requirements of tax treaties that permanent establishments be taxed on a net basis override provisions of domestic law that deny deductions that affect the determination of profit. While it is unlikely that tax treaties will be interpreted to override the denial of deductions in marginal areas where denial is quite common under domestic laws (e.g., entertainment deductions), it is another matter where a fundamental matter of profit determination such as the treatment of wages is concerned.

A number of industrial countries have inserted special provisions in their recent tax treaties with transition countries to attempt to clarify the matter for permanent establishments and to ensure that subsidiaries of direct investors from their countries also get deductions for their full wage costs (because the only tax treaty rule that potentially covers the subsidiary case, the nondiscrimination article, is unlikely to be of assistance).[91] Some transition countries have modified domestic law so that the denial of wage deductions does not apply to branches and subsidiaries of foreign direct investors, and others have repealed the wage deduction denial entirely. For some industrial countries, these rules in the transition country tax systems have raised the more fundamental question of whether their "profit" taxes are income taxes at all in the generally understood sense and have consequently slowed down the development of tax treaty networks.

---

[90]Where, as is common, personnel of a parent company are seconded on a rotating basis to a subsidiary in a developing or transition country, it is possible to apply the hiring out of labor analysis discussed *supra* sec. V(G)(3), or to find that there is a permanent establishment of the parent company on the basis of the use of the subsidiary's facilities, which will mean that the business profits article of tax treaties will apply to the technical fees received by the parent company and the employment article to the employees so that both are taxed in the source country. Alternatively, tax treaties may provide for the taxation of technical fees through extension of the royalties article or addition of a special article on the topic; *see supra* note 55 and text.

[91]United Kingdom–Russia (1994 Exchange of Notes); the features of Russian law causing concern have since been modified but similar problems remain with other transition countries.

C. Dividends, Interest, and Royalties

In the case of dividends, interest, and royalties paid to nonresidents, domestic law usually provides for flat-rate final withholding tax on the gross amount if they are sourced in the country and not attributable to a permanent establishment. The tax rate is typically set at 20–30 percent in developing and transition countries and then is often reduced to 10–20 percent in tax treaties. The rates are set at this level in domestic law to leave negotiating room in the tax treaty process but usually to be below the normal company tax rate in recognition of the fact that the tax is gross and does not take account of expenses. In tax treaty negotiations, developing and transition countries will come under considerable pressure from industrial countries to reduce withholding tax rates on interest and royalties to zero or near zero (special considerations applicable to dividends are discussed further below). The argument used by industrial countries is that the gross tax often wipes out the entire profit, with the result that the price charged to the resident or permanent establishment in the country is increased (i.e., the tax is passed back to the payer) with adverse consequences for the import of capital and technology.

While gross-up for withholding taxes (usually by increase in the interest or royalty rate) undoubtedly occurs and is detrimental to developing and transition countries, reduction of tax rates to zero or near zero likewise produces problems and the appropriate course to take is a matter of judgment. If the treaty tax rate on interest is 10 percent, then banks that lend to residents of the country will find it difficult to make a profit. For example, if the cost of funds of the bank is 9 percent and its lending rate is 10 percent, then on a loan of $1,000 it will make $10 before tax and other expenses besides interest, but the withholding tax will be $10 and so wipe out the profit, forcing the bank to increase the interest rate (assuming that it cannot use the excess foreign tax as a credit against other domestic tax in its residence country). If the OECD Commentary's suggestion to deal with this problem is followed and loans from banks are exempted from tax,[92] this opens the way for simple back-to-back transactions, which will mean that the exemption will be effectively extended to nonbank lenders. If a nonbank nonresident lender deposits money in a nonresident bank and the bank then makes a corresponding loan to a resident (less a small fee), what is effectively a loan from a nonbank becomes for treaty purposes a loan from a bank and is protected accordingly. Some of the problems of this kind can be dealt with better by provisions in domestic law that remove the withholding tax on interest for borrowings in the international capital markets where the debt is widely held (often referred to as Eurocurrency loans). The widely held requirement substantially removes the problem of back-to-back transactions. Many industrial countries have such provisions in

---

[92]Para. 15 of the Commentary on art. 11.

their laws.[93] Nonetheless, in a few cases, reduction of interest withholding to zero under treaties is common for developing and transition countries, especially for concessional loans made by development banks. A general lowering of the interest withholding rate to zero also worsens the thin capitalization problem described below.

Similar considerations apply to royalties, which are also particularly associated with the problem of treaty-shopping discussed below. Hence, there is a good argument for developing and transition countries to have a reasonable positive tax rate on interest and royalties under tax treaties (say, 10–15 percent). If royalties include equipment leasing rentals, there is also a strong argument for uniform tax rates under tax treaties on interest and royalties; indeed, the possibilities for conversion from interest to royalties or vice versa, especially in the case of related parties, extend beyond this area so that equivalence should be a goal in any event. Perhaps more important, because of the problem of treaty shopping, it is imperative to have the rates similar or the same across tax treaties with other countries in the case of interest and royalties. The industrial countries generally (but reluctantly) accept this position in their tax treaties with developing and transition countries; however, they often negotiate most-favored-nation clauses in protocols to the tax treaties in such cases, so that if the developing or transition country grants a more favorable rate or treatment to another industrial country (often defined in terms of membership of the OECD), then either the more favorable treatment is automatically extended to that country or an obligation to renegotiate that tax treaty arises.[94]

D. Capital Gains

Capital gains of nonresidents present a more difficult problem for withholding. While it is possible to have flat-rate withholding based on the sale price either generally or specifically in the case of nonresidents, the gain part of the sale price can vary considerably, and so an option for net taxation should be provided for in domestic law with appropriate administrative safeguards.[95] Enforcement of such withholding is likely to be feasible only in the case of land (because land transactions are usually registered in some way and the collection of tax can be tied in with this procedure) or of a permanent establishment (with the gain taxed on a net basis like most other business profits). Many countries do without withholding in such cases, as it is possible with appropriate administrative mechanisms to deal with the capital

---

[93]Provisions that reach this kind of result, although by various means, are AUS ITAA §128F; CAN ITA § 212(1)(b)(vii); GBR ICTA § 349(3)(c); USA IRC § 871(h)(2)(A).

[94]For example, most of Australia's tax treaties with European countries have such protocols.

[95]As long as inflation is significant and property rights have not been clarified in transition countries, the introduction of a capital gains tax is probably not a high priority generally, let alone in the case of nonresidents.

gains.[96] Attempts to levy capital gains in other cases will generally be over-ridden by tax treaties and any attempt to protect the power to levy tax on gains on shares in resident companies is likely to be futile for reasons already explained.

E. Employment, Services, and Pension Income

Employment income of nonresidents is usually subject to the normal wage withholding and not to any special final withholding, despite the policy arguments that flat-rate withholding is the appropriate method for nonresidents. There are special collection problems where the employer is a nonresident, but tax treaties will usually protect the employee from taxation by the country where the work is performed in this event through the 183-day rule unless a permanent establishment bears the wages (in which event enforcement will not usually be difficult). If the employee is present for 183 days or more, residence will usually arise and the more permanent connection with the country will facilitate withholding, although it is easy for temporarily present employees to slip through the net unless attention is given to this issue by the tax administration. Powers in the domestic law for the tax administration to prevent a person from leaving a country unless taxes are paid can provide some assistance to tax collection depending on how easy or difficult it is to exit the country.

Some transition countries find it difficult to cope with withholding on wages of expatriates because their wages are paid into bank accounts in foreign countries. This is partly a function of some wage taxation laws applying only to wages paid in a country (which should be rectified if necessary, making clear that the law applies to wages sourced in the country, whatever the place of payment) and partly a surrender to the difficulties that the international border creates. Most employers, however, will not use such a device to avoid tax as the penalties on employers for failing to withhold are typically and appropriately severe. Moreover, this is one area where information exchange under tax treaties with the country of the employer can be effective in assisting the tax administration.

Although wage withholding often is not formally final, the way in which obligations to file tax returns are expressed in many developing and transition countries means that many employees are taxed through withholding only, so that in effect the withholding is final.[97] In the case of nonresident taxpayers, returns are not usually required or forthcoming so that the withholding is final in fact. For expatriate taxpayers, adoption of any of the special rules set out

---

[96]For example, Australia has general power in AUS ITAA § 255 to require a person owing money to a nonresident to pay tax owing by the nonresident on receipt of a notice from the tax administration; this procedure can be utilized in the case of substantial capital gains that come to the notice of the tax administration (which may put a watch on land registers for that purpose).

[97]*See generally supra* ch. 15.

above may mean that special attention has to be given by the tax administration to withholding on wages and filing of returns in their case to prevent abuse of the rules.

Some countries extend withholding beyond the employment area (including deemed employments discussed above) to certain services rendered in a business context. As already noted, such income is required by tax treaties generally to be taxed on a net basis, but this obligation can be satisfied by permitting such taxpayers to file returns and to have the withholding credited against the tax liability (with refunds where necessary). The language of tax treaties (although not perhaps the OECD Commentary)[98] suggests that final withholding on professional income is permitted where there is a fixed base (or a presence time limit is exceeded if included in the treaty).

For entertainment and sports-related income, flat-rate final withholding is clearly permitted under tax treaties and provides a simple and effective method of collecting tax via the promoter of the event. Provision for some form of withholding on this income at a reasonably substantial rate, such as 30 percent, should be provided in the domestic law and should apply whether the income accrues to the entertainer or athlete directly, which is very rare, or to some intermediary; that is, the law should permit the tax authorities to look through the intermediaries to the entertainer or athlete.

In the case of pensions, withholding in accordance with the rate scale for individuals is often provided for in domestic law in a similar way as for wage income. Tax treaties may override any tax depending on the source rule adopted (see above). Likewise, wage and pension income of the employees or former employees of foreign governments will usually be subject to withholding under domestic law in the same way as other wages and pensions, but tax treaties may remove the levy of this tax.

F. Company and Shareholder Taxation

The relationship of taxation of company and dividend income in the international setting raises a number of special issues. One major distinction is between direct and portfolio investment. Direct investment refers to the case where the investor in a company has a large enough interest to influence the operations of the company, while portfolio investment is the opposite case of no influence. This distinction often runs throughout the laws and commercial practice of a country (in such areas as takeovers, investment, banking, and accounting, as well as taxation) and may be defined differently for different purposes, although often the taxation definition is affected by treatment in other

---

[98]Commentary art. 14, para. 3 states that taxation under art. 14 should be levied on a similar basis to the net taxation of business profits under art. 7, although there is nothing in the wording of the article to suggest the limitation; the OECD is currently considering whether art. 14 should be dropped from the Model, which would have the result of net taxation under art. 7 applying in such cases.

areas of the law. It is usually defined in terms of owning a certain percentage of the capital or controlling a certain percentage of the votes in a company, with 10 percent and 25 percent or more for direct investment being the most common in taxation laws. The OECD Model uses 25 percent of the capital, while a number of industrial countries use 10 percent of voting power in their tax treaties.[99] The discussion that follows will commence with portfolio investment and then move on to direct investment.

1. Integration Systems

The simplest tax system for companies and shareholders is the separate system; that is, the company is taxed on its income, and then dividends paid by the company are taxed as part of the income of the shareholder without reference to any tax paid by the company. Whatever the method of tax collection under this system in a domestic case (where a resident company pays a dividend to a resident investor), frequently a flat-rate withholding tax is levied on dividends paid by resident companies to nonresidents. Tax treaties will often reduce the rate contained in domestic law, the OECD Model, and most tax treaties specifying 15 percent for portfolio dividends.

In recent years, many countries have moved away from the separate system because of its well-known potential for distorting economic decisions by companies and shareholders in the domestic context. Such "integration" systems may consist of some form of imputation, a split corporate tax rate, or a zero or low tax rate on dividends (in all cases with or without some form of equalization tax on dividends to ensure that corporate tax has been paid on distributions of company profits). Domestic tax laws usually confine the full integration benefits to resident shareholders and often continue to tax nonresident shareholders under a separate system with flat-rate withholding taxes.[100]

Most recently, with the growth of international investment, attention has become focused on the potential for international economic distortions from integration systems of these kinds. This issue has led some countries to extend some of the benefits of integration to nonresident shareholders unilaterally or by tax treaty, for example, by partly removing withholding taxes on nonresidents[101] or by giving imputation credits partly to nonresidents.[102] Some countries have sought to go further and completely equalize the treatment of residents and nonresidents. A simple approach is to align or approxi-

---

[99]For example, Australia, the United Kingdom, and the United States.

[100]For comprehensive treatment of the imputation system in the international setting, see Peter Harris, Corporate/Shareholder Income Taxation and Allocating Taxing Rights Between Countries (1996). *See also infra* ch. 19.

[101]AUS ITAA § 128B(3)(ga); countries with U.K.-style imputation systems simply do not levy withholding taxes on dividends, whether paid to residents or nonresidents, though they may levy equalization taxes, on which see below.

[102]For example, France and United Kingdom.

mate the corporate and maximum individual tax rates and to exempt dividends from further taxation whether paid to resident or nonresident shareholders.[103] From the point of view of the source country (where the company paying the dividend is resident), neutrality may be achieved with such a system. For nonresident portfolio investors, however, neutrality is unlikely because their residence country will almost invariably tax them on the dividends without any benefit of whatever integration system that country has for its resident companies (if any) and with a foreign tax credit only for any withholding tax levied on the dividend by the source country (as distinct from the corporate tax levied on the company paying the dividend).[104]

Hence, there is still a bias in the international tax system for resident shareholders to invest in resident companies that other countries cannot prevent under this or any other form of integration. This bias is now providing policy support for the separate system of company and shareholder taxation, as such a system does treat residents and nonresidents more or less alike if the country of residence of the company taxes shareholders resident there on dividends received and if other countries tax shareholders resident there on the dividends, with a credit for any source country withholding tax.[105] In fact, the position is more complex, as a large proportion of international portfolio investment is made by institutions that are taxed under special regimes in their residence country.

From the point of view of developing and transition countries, a fairly standard treatment of nonresident portfolio shareholders with a flat-rate withholding tax and a tax treaty rate limit of 15 percent is the simplest solution. Any attempt to extend integration benefits to nonresidents generally is likely to produce a transfer of tax revenue to capital-exporting industrial countries without providing any incentive to invest to the nonresident (or rather without removing the disincentive to invest abroad that arises from the residence country tax system).[106] Even if it is decided to extend integration benefits to nonresident portfolio shareholders, it is better to do this unilaterally rather than in tax treaties (even if the domestic law confines the benefit to countries with which there is a tax treaty), because such treaty provisions can lock the country into the form of integration it has adopted. As integration (in the past

---

[103]Ward Hussey & Donald Lubick, Basic World Tax Code and Commentary § 164 (1996).

[104]Some countries seek to overcome the tax credit problem in the residence country of the investor by in effect converting part of the corporate tax into a creditable withholding tax, for example, New Zealand under its domestic law and the United Kingdom in its typical treaties extending imputation benefits to nonresidents.

[105]OECD, Taxing Profits in a Global Economy 195 (1991); the United Kingdom in its 1997 budget effectively abolished its imputation system in the international setting; see Edge, The Last Piece of the Jigsaw, The Tax Journal 2 (Aug. 4, 1997); Harris, supra note 100.

[106]The United Kingdom sought to remove this disincentive from its imputation system with the foreign income dividend scheme introduced in the early 1990s, but this scheme was withdrawn and the whole issue opened up for review in its 1997 budget; see notes 101, 105.

at least) has been primarily a domestic tax policy issue, integration benefits in tax treaties can become the international tail that wags the domestic dog.

A removal of dividend withholding tax on foreign tax-exempt pension funds as part of a regime of reciprocal recognition of the special tax arrangements that many countries use to encourage private pension schemes may be considered. This is usually done outside tax treaties (though note the comments above in relation to tax treaty provisions dealing with contributions to pensions schemes by expatriates) and across all types of investment income, rather than just for dividends.[107]

A country employing an equalization tax as part of its integration arrangements[108] must take care in drafting it to ensure that it does not conflict with tax treaties. Often, such a tax will be effectively at the corporate tax rate and will be triggered by the payment of dividends. It can therefore be viewed as a withholding-type tax on the dividends, in which event there is potential for the tax rate limits in tax treaties to reduce the amount of the tax and so defeat or at least blunt its purpose. There are well-accepted drafting devices to ensure that such a tax is not regarded as a withholding tax on dividends.[109] First, no primary or secondary tax liability can be imposed on the shareholder in relation to the equalization tax, so that it is clearly a tax on the company rather than on the shareholder. Second, it helps to use the dividends simply as a measure for the amount of the tax and not to express the tax as being levied on the dividends as such. Technically, the tax also needs to be at the corporate rate on the amount of the dividend plus the tax, which is most easily done by expressing the tax rate as

$$t/(1-t),$$

where t is the corporate tax rate.

The drafting arrangements for the U.K. advance corporation tax provide a model that can be used to ensure that there is no conflict between the equalization tax and tax treaties (although the basic rate of tax and not the corporate rate is used in the United Kingdom).[110]

---

[107]AUS ITAA §128B(3)(a), referring to § 23(jb).

[108]This tax is designed to ensure that tax credits given under an imputation system to shareholders are in fact supported by tax paid at the corporate level; this can be achieved by levying tax on the company every time it makes a distribution, as in the United Kingdom, or under an accounting mechanism that matches dividends paid with corporate tax and applies the equalization tax only when there is no matching corporate tax; for example, Australia, France, New Zealand, and Singapore.

[109]However, sometimes the tax is purposely structured in the opposite manner, in order to make it a creditable dividend withholding tax in the hands of the shareholders.

[110]GBR ICTA § 14, pt. VI, chs. IV, V, VA. The 1997 U.K. Budget radically altered the U.K. imputation system, but these features initially remained intact; *see supra* note 105. A subsequent Inland Revenue consultative document of Nov. 25, 1997, proposed abolition of the advance corporation tax, which has been a critical part of the system, and gave rise to the issues considered in the text.

2. Reduction of Dividend Withholding Tax on Direct Investment

In the case of dividends generated by direct investment, the international tax position is very different from portfolio investment from a number of perspectives. A foreign direct investor (assumed in what follows to be a company) generally has a choice as to the legal structure of its investment in a country. It can establish a branch (permanent establishment) or a subsidiary (i.e., a separate company).[111] The residence country of the direct investor will grant relief for double taxation by way of a credit or an exemption for corporate tax levied on a branch by the source country (where the branch is situated). It will generally extend this relief to corporate tax levied on a subsidiary when dividends are paid to the direct investor so as not to produce a tax bias in the form of investment.

In its turn, the source country will, by various means, approximate the tax treatment of branch and subsidiary for the same reason. The major likely difference in source country tax treatment in the absence of special provisions in the domestic law or treaties will be that dividends paid by a resident subsidiary to a nonresident parent company are subject to flat-rate dividend withholding tax, while remittances by a branch to its head office (the functional equivalent of dividends) are not subject to any tax. The source country can address this disparity by reducing the tax on direct investment dividends, or by taxing branch remittances, or by a combination of both.

Although it is possible for domestic law to provide a lower tax rate on direct as opposed to portfolio dividends paid to nonresident shareholders, until recently this reduction was most commonly only effected by tax treaties (with 5 percent being the OECD Model norm). Developing and transition countries need not be too concerned with accepting such arrangements for direct investment in treaties, especially where an equalization tax is in place, but it is noticeable that a number of such countries (along with some smaller industrial countries) do not draw the portfolio/direct investment distinction in the dividend article of their tax treaties and apply the same rate of tax to both. Unlike the case of portfolio investment, a lower rate of tax on dividends on direct investment does not usually operate as a transfer of revenues to industrial countries because of the different tax regime in most of them for dividends on direct investment (exemption or underlying foreign tax credit). A small but positive tax treaty rate in the source country also provides some incentive for reinvestment of profits (a major source of investment) by foreign investors without unduly distorting the tax position in the residence country of the investor.

There is now a more general international trend for reducing withholding taxes on dividends paid to nonresident direct investors outside tax treaties.

---

[111]The term "subsidiary" will be used in what follows although it is often used only to refer to the case of control of, rather than influence over, a company; as noted above, direct investment is usually defined in terms of influence rather than control.

One effect of the tax reform that took place in many countries in the late 1980s was to more closely align the tax base and tax rate applied to companies in industrial countries. This meant, for direct investments through subsidiaries, that the corporate tax in the country of the subsidiary would approximate the corporate tax that the same amount of profit would attract in the country of the investor. As that country would relieve double taxation for the corporate tax paid by the subsidiary, the net effect was to wipe out any corporate tax in the residence country of the investor whether a credit or an exemption system was used, but the dividend withholding tax would remain as an additional tax levy above the residence country tax.

A number of major econometric studies in the early 1990s suggested that such withholding taxes were the main factor accounting for a bias against cross-border investment, and hence some pressure has developed for their removal, even though tax treaties typically contain lower tax rates on dividends from direct investment.[112] The fact that the United States typically demands for its resident investors a share of the action in integration systems adopted by foreign countries has also been an influence here. Developing and transition countries that do not have tax treaty networks may therefore wish to consider setting the cross-border dividend withholding tax rate on direct investment at a lower rate (say, 10 percent) than the traditional and typical 20–30 percent tax rate that has been adopted across the board by many countries for dividends, interest, and royalties. There is, however, little reason to adopt a selective zero tax rate on dividends in domestic law as part of regimes of tax incentives for foreign direct investors.[113] As the benefit is only likely to operate long after the initial investment occurs, it has little impact on initial investment decisions and does not encourage reinvestment of profits.

A similar pressure to reduce cross-border dividend taxes may arise when countries form a free trade bloc, given that one of their longer-term objectives is usually to remove not just trade barriers but also investment and other barriers to the creation of a common market. This means that taxes applying only at the border (such as a nonresident dividend withholding tax) become targets of the institutions of the common market. Thus, the EU after many years' debate has adopted a directive that will remove cross-border dividend withholding taxes in the case of direct investment.[114]

This trade bloc reasoning also applies to other income flows within corporate groups, and the EU has a draft directive extending the same treatment to interest and royalties in direct investment cases.[115] However, the reasoning

---

[112]OECD, Taxing Profits in a Global Economy (1991); CEC, Report of the Committee of Independent Experts on Company Taxation (1992). The initial enthusiasm for this analysis, which gave rise to a number of initiatives in the EU, seems to have cooled.

[113]*See infra* ch. 23 for a discussion of such incentives.

[114]Council Directive 90/435/EEC art. 5.

[115]COM (90) 571, OJ C53, 26 (1991).

here is very different from the more general argument in relation to dividends and does not make sense outside a trade bloc. The reasoning is that interest and royalties will be taxed in full in the residence country, which is a member of the bloc, and, as long as investment flows are balanced among the countries in the bloc, the revenues of members do not suffer (alternatively, government-to-government reimbursement mechanisms can be devised if flows are not equal), while at the same time the border impediment is removed.

For developing and transition countries, investment flows are not usually in balance with other countries (even in the Commonwealth of Independent States (CIS), the loose trading bloc formed by most of the countries of the former Soviet Union), and interest and royalties are payments that reduce the tax base (as they are usually deductible in the calculation of taxable profit), with significant potential for causing problems for the taxation of direct investment. Hence, the advice given in relation to these payments above was to maintain reasonable levels of tax at relatively uniform rates in both domestic tax law and treaties. The existence of a trade bloc does not change that advice.[116] More generally, developing and transition countries need to be very cautious in studying the tax arrangements in trading blocs of industrial countries, especially the EU, even where they have ambitions to become members of the bloc. Where a group of developing or transition countries forms a trading bloc, care should be used in extending special free trade arrangements to taxes, as the countries may not have the capacity to deal with the more sophisticated rules often involved. For example, the international value-added tax and excise rules within the CIS have been an ongoing problem.[117]

3. Branch Profits Tax

In the case of direct investment in the form of a branch, the branch profits tax represents a strategy to even up treatment of branches and subsidiaries. To produce precisely the same outcome, it is necessary to define branch remittances that equate to dividends and to tax them at the same rate that applies to dividends on direct investment.

While the statement of the principle is easy enough—the amount of remittance can be determined by comparing the branch's tax balance sheets at the beginning and end of the tax year—in practice, the elaboration of the principle has generally proved very complex, even though to some extent it is

---

[116]From the point of view of the residence country, it is imperative to tax interest and royalty income where source taxation has been reduced or eliminated by tax treaty or trade bloc arrangements and tax treaties and trade blocs assume such a regime; the arguments that can be made for operating an exemption system in relation to dividends on direct investment do not apply to interest and royalties because the underlying assumption is that dividends are not deductible in the source country in determining the taxable profit of the subsidiary.

[117]See Victoria Summers & Emil Sunley, *Analysis of Value Added Taxes in Russia and Other Countries of the Former Soviet Union*, 10 Tax Notes Int'l 2049 (June 19, 1995).

based on the same information used to determine the taxable profit of the branch. Some countries therefore use a simpler but rougher measure, namely, the after-tax taxable profit of the branch. To take account of the fact that subsidiaries typically do not repatriate all of their after-tax profit as dividends, the rate is often set lower than the dividend withholding tax rate based on an assessment of the typical payout ratio of subsidiaries of foreign investors in the country (a tax rate of one-half the dividend rate or less being appropriate in most cases).

Certainly, some rules for calculating the amount subject to branch profits tax need to be set out in domestic law. It is neither sensible nor transparent to introduce the tax through the back door by defining all branches for tax purposes to be subsidiaries so that remittances (presumably) become dividends and, thus, subject to dividend withholding tax. The tax administrations of developing and transition countries will not be able to detect remittances as they occur (the possibilities of method of remittance being infinite and the only practicable measurement device being comparison of tax balance sheets at the beginning and end of the tax year). Although, in some cases of more exotic legal entities, there will be difficult cases of characterization as branch or subsidiary, this is not a reason for the tax law to impose an arbitrary rule that is contrary to generally accepted international norms of taxation in clear cases.

A number of developing and transition countries are considering or have enacted branch profits taxes, in some cases without apparent regard to their tax treaties. Treaties based on the OECD and UN Models override the levy of a branch profits tax,[118] and the treaties in question do not generally contain the necessary modifications to the dividend and nondiscrimination articles to accommodate such a tax. Although new treaties that are negotiated can contain these modifications, the existing treaties will encourage treaty-shopping to short-circuit the effect of the new treaties, and it will be many years before replacement treaties can be put in place.

Further, it is not possible to either tax all effective remittances or achieve in practice the close approximation of the tax treatment of branches and subsidiaries that the branch profits tax is aimed at, because of the interaction of the tax treatment of dividends and capital gains in the context of the branch or subsidiary. Both the dividend withholding tax and a branch profits tax based on remittances can be avoided by not paying dividends or remitting profits, as the case may be—that is, by reinvesting the profits. The gain in each case can then be realized by selling the shares in the company operating the branch or in the subsidiary (or in a holding company in the corporate group). This gain will usually not be taxable in the source country because of either tax treaties or the inability of domestic law to reach sales of holding companies based in other countries (not to mention the lack of the capital gains tax in many developing and transition countries).

---

[118]*See* arts. 10(5) and 23(3) of the OECD Model.

Sale of shares in this way thus achieves an effective remittance of reinvested profits of the branch or subsidiary, but in practice it will be more difficult for a branch to achieve such a sale because the branch will usually be just one part of the operations of the company, with the result that sale of the shares will amount to much more than a realization of the reinvested profits of the branch. Further, as far as capital gains (in excess of those arising from reinvestment of profits) have been made on the investment, the tax treatment of branch and subsidiary will usually differ in practice for the same reason that disposal of the shares in the company operating the branch will often not be a practical possibility. Disposal of the branch will usually be effected by the sale of its assets, which will be subject to the capital gains tax of the country where the branch is situated (if any), while the profits on the sale of the shares in the subsidiary will not be taxed.

Hence, the value of a branch profits tax is doubtful. The tax pales into insignificance when compared with some of the other problems of protecting the tax base of the source country against the base-erosion techniques that are explored below. The main reason why it is sometimes thought to be important for developing and transition countries to have a branch profits tax is to fully tax income from natural resources where many foreign investors typically operate in branch form mainly because of the generous treatment of the early year start-up losses under their home country (especially U.S.) tax law.

4. Branches and Subsidiaries in Transition Countries

The transition countries face a special set of issues in the branch and subsidiary area, which demonstrates once again the problems caused by the lack of clear rules and by departures from international norms in these countries. Under the commercial laws of nontransition countries, there is a generally clear understanding of what is meant by a body corporate (company, corporation) and of when an entity recognized by the law has separate legal personality and when it does not.[119] However, the commercial laws of several transition countries are still in the developmental stage, and it is often not clear when a separate legal person exists or, more important, whether in a particular situation there are two legal persons (parent company and subsidiary) or one legal person with a number of operations (head office and branch).[120]

When a foreign legal person commences operations in a transition country, it is usually required to "register" to do business under the commercial laws of the country. In some of the countries, registration is regarded as the creation of a legal person, because this is how the creation of a legal person is effected in a purely domestic case or, perhaps more accurately, registering to carry on a business in a purely domestic case of itself creates a separate legal person (as

---

[119]See infra ch. 21.

[120]See vol. 1, at 90 n. 55.

the registration is to get approval to do business, and the creation of a separate legal person is a by-product of registration). Representation offices of foreign persons are usually recognized and are not treated as separate legal persons (a separate registration procedure is required in this case), but the functions that such offices can perform under the laws of the transition countries are generally strictly limited, as befits their name.

Before 1989, the question of registering foreign legal persons under domestic procedures did not arise for many transition countries because the only way a foreign legal person could operate a substantial business venture in the country was through the creation of a joint venture with foreign participation, for which special statutes existed. The joint venture in these cases was a separate legal person under the statutes, and the foreign joint venturer a substantial shareholder along with the state-owned enterprise also involved in the venture.

Moreover, in several transition countries (especially members of the CIS), the profits tax is not levied on a legal person as such, but on the separate operational units of the legal person (which may in turn be linked to separate registration of the operational units with the local or regional authority of the area where they are located).[121] Thus, if a state-owned enterprise has a glass factory in one city and a television factory in another city, both the factories will often be taxed separately. This may affect rates of tax because, in many of the countries, there are varying tax rates depending on the nature of the business of an operational unit or the region where it is operating, and, more important, it may affect the treatment of losses, as a loss incurred by one operational unit may not be offset against the profit of another operational unit. This fact makes it less necessary under the systems of some transition countries to distinguish in a particular case whether one legal person is involved or two. Again, this system grew up in the closed days of central planning so that international issues did not intrude. Hence, putting aside the case of the representation office, questions did not arise as to whether a branch of a foreign legal person was taxed in this way (assuming that a branch was possible under the system in question) and as to whether operational units (including those of foreign legal persons) were taxed on their worldwide profits.

These rules have a number of important implications for international taxation and tax treaties in cases of direct investment by industrial country resident companies in transition countries. In many of them, what the industrial country resident regards as a branch (permanent establishment) will often be treated as a subsidiary by the transition country because it is registered in that country. Indeed, in one unusual case, this result was regarded as arising from registration for turnover tax purposes. The "subsidiary" will be taxed as a resident legal person by the transition country, and distributions to the industrial country resident will be treated as dividends and subject to any tax treaty ac-

---

[121]*See infra* ch. 19, sec. VII.

cordingly (although some of the transition countries have no taxes on dividends).

If the legal system of the transition country in question characterizes an operation within its borders as a separate legal person, then the private international law rules applied in most industrial countries will lead to the recognition of this characterization by the general law and usually the tax law of the industrial country in question. However, in many cases, the industrial country resident will not be aware of either the legal intricacies involved or the very different legal structures in some transition countries.

In a number of transition countries, the concept of a branch has become fully accepted for both commercial and tax law purposes, although, even then, exchange controls may make operation in branch form impractical. In most countries, the extension beyond the case of the representation office is piecemeal (e.g., banks and building sites) and seems to require special procedures separate from the business registration procedure. In some countries, the representation office is being put under a lot of pressure as nonresident taxpayers try to establish branches for various reasons. Part of the pressure results from the fact that the transition countries generally find it difficult to deal with cases where the taxpayer breaches the law—in this case, when representation offices engage in activities not legally permitted to them.

If the transition country in question taxes each operational unit separately, then further tax issues arise for the industrial country resident direct investor, whether branches are permitted generally or in special sectors or not at all. In the branch case, the industrial country investor may find that losses on one branch operation will not be offset against profits of another branch operation in the same country, which will be contrary to the expected treatment. This has been a problem in some transition countries, particularly in the oil and mining sector where each drilling rig or mine site is taxed separately.

There does not seem to be anything in article 7 of the OECD Model that precludes this outcome (indeed, the Model seems to follow the approach of treating each permanent establishment separately), and, as the same treatment is applied to domestic enterprises, nondiscrimination is unlikely to be an issue. It is certainly the assumption of industrial countries, however, that legal persons are taxed as a whole and not separately on operational units, although in the source country only profits attributable to the permanent establishment are taxable, and not the worldwide profits of the legal person.[122] A potentially more difficult question arises for the calculation of expenses. Treating each branch separately in the calculation of tax may naturally lead to the disallowance of head office expenses as deductions of the permanent establishment. The separate treatment of the operational

---

[122]U.S. regulations specifically deny a foreign tax credit in this case. *See* Treas. Reg § 1.901-2(b)(4)(ii).

units for tax purposes in transition countries does not seem, however, to produce the consequence that payments between them or to the head office receive dividend treatment.

This range of issues has been the cause of considerable confusion among
industrial country investors, however (the precise legal situation varies from
country to country), and has had an additional chilling effect on foreign direct
investment in a number of transition countries and on the development of tax
treaty networks with industrial countries. One alternative has been for foreign
investors to enter into special tax contracts with the governments of transition
countries that guarantee them a relatively normal tax treatment by market
economy standards. While these contracts solve the problems of the particular
direct investor, they are already complicating tax reform and tax treaty development in a number of transition countries.

In general, it is recommended that transition and developing countries
refrain from entering into special tax contracts or at least limit the effect of the
contracts to a relatively short time before reviewing them. Further, transition
countries should seek to ensure that their commercial and tax laws accord with
the general international distinctions between branches and subsidiaries and
that the tax position of an investor with more than one branch in the country
is aggregated across the branches. Several transition countries have already
taken these steps in recent years.

G. International Tax Avoidance and Evasion

While the source country may be concerned with ensuring that direct
investors are taxed in a way that does not bias the form of the investment
and with collecting its fair share of tax from both direct and portfolio investors, nonresident taxpayers may seek to escape source taxation altogether or
at least to minimize that tax. They may do so through techniques to avoid or
minimize tax—that is, arranging their affairs so that under the law of the
source country the tax is minimized—or through tax evasion—that is, deliberately not complying with the law of the source country even though income is taxable under that law.[123] As with the issues of company and
shareholder taxation discussed above, it is helpful to draw a distinction between direct and portfolio investors; indeed, much of the discussion under
this heading stems from a number of the points already made. The discussion
below initially focuses on nonresident direct investors and then canvasses to
what extent the techniques outlined are available to nonresident portfolio
investors and to resident investors.

Within an international group of companies investing directly in various
countries, what generally matters to the managers and the ultimate shareholders is the after-tax profit of the group; in other words, the corporate group usu-

---

[123]These terms are explained in vol. 1, at 44–46.

ally has an economic incentive to reduce its total tax payments and is economically indifferent as to the countries to which it pays tax. In some cases, especially where the residence country of the parent company in the group operates an imputation system that ties tax credits available to shareholders to the company tax paid in that country by the parent and local subsidiaries, the economic incentive may rather be to pay as much tax as possible in the residence country. In any event, multinational companies investing in developing or transition countries are likely to have an economic incentive to reduce the tax burden in those countries, either as part of reducing tax burdens worldwide (i.e., reducing tax in both residence and source countries) or as part of moving the tax burden to a country that offers the greatest advantages to the ultimate shareholders of the company group.

This economic incentive may not always lead to tax avoidance or evasion. Cultural, ethical, and nontax commercial factors may act as a counterbalance. With the globalization of trade and investment, deregulation in many areas of international business law, and international financial markets that focus on the "bottom line" and are beyond the reach of any single government, the countervailing factors are likely to weaken in influence over time. Most large multinational companies will nevertheless want to conduct their tax planning within the law; that is, they are more likely to practice tax avoidance or tax minimization than tax evasion. Tax evasion internationally and domestically is more of a problem with small or closely held businesses and individual taxpayers (see the discussion of capital flight above for the problem of evasion in relation to resident taxpayers).

The simplest way to minimize tax is to make payments from the branch or resident subsidiary to a related nonresident company that are deductible in determining the amount of profit subject to corporate tax and that are not subject to withholding tax. Alternatively, as a second-best option, payments can be made that are deductible under the corporate tax and are subject to a low rate of withholding tax.

In the past, two basic strategies (which can be combined) have been mainly used to achieve these ends: increasing the prices of payments and changing the type of payments. To take some simple examples, a local subsidiary operating an assembly plant can pay inflated prices for the components and the technical and management services it purchases from related companies; or a nonresident parent company can invest in the subsidiary by way of loan capital rather than share capital and receive interest payments (deductible to the subsidiary) instead of dividends (usually not deductible to the subsidiary). Similar results can be produced by reducing the amount of payments for goods or services to the local branch or subsidiary for goods or services it provides to other (nonresident) members of the group. Recently, international tax planning has become more sophisticated along with the financial markets. The following discussion will start with the simpler methods of tax avoidance and then move to more recent techniques.

1. Transfer Pricing

"Transfer pricing" is the general term used to refer to the problem of allocating profits among the parts of a corporate group. For the group as a whole, all that matters at the end of the day is the after-tax profit of the group rather than of its individual members. The prices charged within the group for goods or services provided and the financing methods used between the members of the group simply serve as means of moving funds around the group and do not in a commercial sense create profits for the group. Hence, there is often no obstacle to charging any price or structuring a transaction in any way within the group, and the fair or proper distribution of the overall group profits among the companies in the group is often a secondary consideration to tax consequences. In financial accounting, which seeks to determine profits for reporting to shareholders and others with financial interests in the group, the response is to require accounts for the enterprise (group) as a whole and to eliminate transactions within the group, as well as (in most countries) accounts for each company in the group.

In taxation, it is necessary to allocate profits among the companies in the group because under international tax norms a country will tax a nonresident only on the profits sourced in that country. While the country can tax a local (resident) subsidiary on its profits worldwide, affairs within a multinational group will usually be arranged so that the subsidiary only has profits sourced in that country. In theory, this allocation of profits can be effected in one of two main ways. A country can take the worldwide profits of the group and allocate some portion of those profits to a source in that country, thus bypassing the need to consider the pricing and nature of transactions within the group. Alternatively, the country can seek to determine the profits of a local branch or subsidiary separately from the rest of the group on the basis of the pricing and nature of the transactions engaged in by the branch or subsidiary with the rest of the group. In the former case, it is necessary to have allocation rules based on formulary criteria like relative assets, revenues, or salaries (and so this method is often referred to as formulary apportionment), while in the latter case rules are needed to deal with the problems arising from the special nature of transactions within the group.

While arguments range back and forth as to which method is preferable, in practical terms countries pursuing a policy of negotiating tax treaties are automatically tied into the separate accounting method because articles 7 and 9 of the OECD and UN Model treaties operate on the basis of taxing each company within the group separately and dealing with problems of pricing and the nature of transactions on the basis of the arm's-length principle. Under this principle, adjustments are made to transactions within the group to reflect the terms and nature of transactions that would have been entered into if the transaction had been made with an independent third party rather than with another part of the group.

A drafting issue for the domestic law is that the arm's-length principle should be provided for both branches and subsidiaries. This is most easily done by using language similar to that found in tax treaties. Such an approach ensures that there is a basis in domestic law for making transfer pricing adjustments. In many countries, it is not clear whether tax treaties on their own would provide a sufficient basis for such adjustments, and, in any event, it is necessary to have the rules in the case of residents of countries with which there is no tax treaty in force. Using statutory language based on treaties has the added advantage of giving a clear signal that the country intends to follow international norms.

Article 7(4) of the OECD and UN Models provides that a country can maintain a customary method of calculating the profits of branches, so long as the result is in accord with the arm's-length principle (a further provision in each case provides for the application of the same method from year to year unless there is good reason to the contrary). Some countries use simplified profit calculation methods for branch cases (such as a specific percentage of turnover of the branch). These methods can be retained in the legislation insofar as they reasonably reflect actual profits and can be used in cases where tax treaties are involved. The application of the arm's-length principle to branches is more complex in one way than in the case of subsidiaries, because the branch and the head office are part of the same legal person, and transactions cannot be sensibly reconstructed in some cases. For example, it is often difficult to allocate notional ownership of property between head office and branch.

Simplified methods in domestic legislation are not generally regarded as consistent with article 9 of the OECD and UN Models in the case of related companies, but this does not mean that countries are confined to making tax adjustments between related companies only in international transactions and on arm's-length principles. Some countries apply their transfer pricing rules in purely domestic cases; where there are different tax rates for different kinds of income or business, taxpayers can use transfer pricing to move profits to categories of income or business with lower tax rates. There are also a number of reasons why countries may wish to have special pricing rules for specific transactions. For example, some countries treat all disposals of property without consideration as having been made for market value—whether between related parties or not—while others treat gifts of property to charities as having been made for the higher of cost or market value. These rules do not directly deal with transfer pricing issues. To the extent that they can apply to international transactions between related parties, they will not generally be contrary to tax treaty arm's-length pricing rules. How all these rules are coordinated within the tax legislation depends on the specific rules adopted and should be reviewed carefully in each country.

To achieve the application of the international arm's-length principle in practice, the tax administration starts with the accounts of the local branch or subsidiary, makes the usual adjustments to reflect differences between financial accounting and tax rules, and then makes such further adjustments in accordance with the arm's-length principle as necessary. Nontax considerations may lead to the group preparing its branch or subsidiary accounts on this basis in any event. For management purposes, the group will wish to know the real profitability of its separate parts, local employees may be remunerated in part on the basis of the local contribution to group profit, and local accounting rules will likely require that the financial accounts give a proper view of the profits of the branch or subsidiary. In practice, the tax administration may use simplified methods and various financial ratios that are similar to formulary apportionment in order to test whether the profits reported by a local branch or subsidiary fall within acceptable boundaries. These methods frequently operate as a means of selecting taxpayers for further checking (audit). The use of such administrative methods will not be contrary to tax treaty rules so long as they are being used as a means to the end of establishing the arm's-length price.

The increasing integration of the activities of corporate groups, the growing importance of unique intragroup intangibles and services, and the sophistication of their financing operations mean, however, that application of the arm's-length standard is becoming more difficult, both conceptually and practically. The problems have been addressed in part by the OECD, which has updated and expanded its guidance on this issue.[124] The OECD standards represent the internationally accepted norms giving content to the arm's-length principle.

Transfer pricing adjustments on the arm's-length principle have traditionally been viewed as involving price only (as the name suggests) and not the reconstruction of transactions in the sense of disregarding the nominal transaction between the related parties and substituting another arrangement for tax purposes. The transfer pricing guidelines,[125] while recognizing that adjusting prices of actual transactions is the norm, do permit tax administrations to recharacterize transactions in two exceptional circumstances: first, "where the economic substance of a transaction differs from the form," and second, where the "arrangements made in relation to the transaction, viewed in their totality, differ from those which would have been adopted by independent enterprises behaving in a commercially rational manner and the actual structure practically impedes the tax administration from determining an appropriate

---

[124]OECD, Attribution of Income to Permanent Establishments (1994); OECD, Transfer Pricing Guidelines for Multinational Enterprises and Tax Administrations (1995, updated 1996, 1997). The problem that transfer pricing currently represents for developing and transition countries is one of administrative capacity. The development of advance pricing arrangements with the encouragement of the OECD (*see infra* note 159) may simplify the administrative task of transition and developing countries in the future by supplying readily applicable formulas for various economic sectors.

[125]*Supra* note 124, paras. 1.36–1.37.

transfer price."[126] The example of thin capitalization is given for the first category (see next heading) and, for the second, the outright transfer of intangible property before its value is fully known when independent parties could have been expected to enter instead into a continuing research agreement (under which payments would not be irrevocably fixed in advance).

Increasingly, countries are enacting general provisions in their tax laws directed against tax avoidance, which give powers to reconstruct transactions.[127] It seems to be increasingly accepted by the OECD that such rules are not in conflict with tax treaty obligations and can be applied to international transactions.[128] While such rules in conjunction with transfer pricing rules expressed in the general terms suggested above can deal with many problem situations, they can leave taxpayers uncertain as to their position. Accordingly, countries are increasingly enacting more specific provisions to deal with particular cases and to spell out the rules in more detail, as shown, for example, under the next heading.

2. Thin Capitalization

Thin capitalization is the practice of excessively funding a branch or subsidiary with interest-bearing loans from related parties rather than with share capital.[129] The fact that interest is usually deductible for the borrower and taxed to the nonresident lender at a low rate of withholding tax (or not at all in some cases) while in most cases company profits funding dividends are fully taxed makes the practice attractive taxwise to a nonresident investor. Although it is possible to deal with these problems under the arm's-length principle, taxpayers and tax administrators often want more guidance on the level of permissible loan funding for a subsidiary than to be told that related-party loans can be made up to the point and on the terms that an independent third-party lender would allow, having regard to the other liabilities of the subsidiary. Thin capitalization rules seek to deal with this problem by denying deductions for interest in defined cases (and possibly recharacterizing the payments of interest as dividends).

Tax law provisions in this area can be drafted in a large variety of ways. One important constraint is the nondiscrimination article in tax treaties. In its typical OECD and UN form, this article overrides thin capitalization rules that apply only to payments of interest to related nonresidents by resident en-

---

[126]*Id.* at para. 1.37.

[127]*See* vol. 1, at 44–53.

[128]*See* OECD, Taxation of New Financial Instruments (1994) and the resulting change to the Commentary on art. 11 of the OECD Model in 1995 para. 21.1; David Ward, *Abuse of Tax Treaties, in* Essays on International Taxation in Honor of Sidney Roberts 397 (Herbert Alpert & Kees van Raad eds. 1993).

[129]*See generally* International Fiscal Association, International Aspects of Thin Capitalization, 81b Cahiers de droit fiscal international (1996).

terprises or by branches of nonresidents unless the rules are applied in accordance with arm's-length principles. Another constraint arises from tax administration concerns. If loans by certain lenders only, such as related nonresidents, are affected by the rules, it is possible to get around this limitation through back-to-back loans.[130] Rules can be drafted to deem such loans to have been made by the parent company—and so subject to the thin capitalization limits—but it is very difficult for the tax administration in the country of the subsidiary to detect such transactions, especially if the bank is located in a country with strict bank secrecy laws. One possible solution to problems of this kind is to make the rules generally applicable to all loans for which interest deductions are claimed. Hence, although the specific problem arises in the context of foreign direct investment, the solution for practical reasons may be across the board for all investment.

Further issues relate to the way in which the denial of interest deductions is calculated. One common approach is to provide express ratios of loan capital to share capital beyond which interest deductions are denied (debt-to-equity rules).[131] Another is to limit interest deductions by reference to a proportion of the income of the taxpayer (earnings-stripping rules).[132] What the appropriate financial ratios are in each case is also an issue (anywhere between 1.5:1 and 3:1 being common for debt-equity rules), as is the application of the rules to financial institutions whose business consists in borrowing and lending and that typically operate at much higher debt levels than other businesses. The following draft suggests a possible approach to these issues.

(1) A taxpayer, other than a bank or a financial institution, is denied a deduction for interest in excess of the product of three times the net income-producing assets of the taxpayer and

    (a) in the case of a loan denominated in the currency of X, 110 percent of the interest rate charged on loans by the Central Bank of X to commercial banks on the last day of the preceding tax year; or

    (b) in the case of a loan denominated in a foreign currency, 110 percent of the interest rate charged by the U.S. Federal Reserve on U.S. dollar loans to U.S. banks on the last day of the preceding tax year.

(2) The net income-producing assets of a taxpayer are assets giving rise to income that is included in the gross income of the taxpayer less liabilities relating to those assets, each averaged between the beginning and end of the tax year.

(3) With the prior written permission of the tax administration, a taxpayer may

---

[130]*See supra* text accompanying notes 92–93.
[131]AUS ITAA § 159GZA (definition of foreign equity product); USA IRC § 163(j)(2)(A)(ii).
[132]USA IRC § 163(j)(2)(a)(I), (B).

> (a) calculate net income-producing assets on an alternative basis; or
> (b) in the case of a loan denominated in a foreign currency other than U.S. dollars, use a different interest rate based on the interbank rate of the central bank responsible for that currency.
>
> (4) Any excess interest that is not allowed as a deduction in a tax year solely as a result of the application of this provision is treated as interest expense of the taxpayer in the following tax year.

Paragraph (1) limits the interest deduction to an amount obtained by multiplying a specified interest rate and three times the net income-producing assets (equity) of the taxpayer. This draft thus provides effectively a 3:1 debt-equity ratio. No limitation in terms of related parties or nonresidents is contained in the provision for reasons already given. Banks and other financial institutions are excluded from the provision altogether, but it would be possible to specify an alternative ratio for this case based on the prudential rules of the central bank for commercial banks. Rather than specifying the amount of loans on which interest is deductible, which is the approach many countries take, the provision directly calculates the amount of interest. This method has two effects. It eliminates the need to calculate the amount of loans, which can be complicated in certain cases, and deals with the problem of excessive interest rates being charged on loans between related parties rather than leaving this as a separate issue for the transfer pricing rules. If an explicit rule is to be provided for thin capitalization, it may as well spell out all the elements.

The interest rate is specified in paragraph (1) using the base rate charged by the central bank at the end of the previous tax year. The provision deals with loans in foreign currency by setting an interest rate based on the international reserve currency, the U.S. dollar, but also permits in paragraph (4) the use of other (major) currencies with the permission of the tax administration. Whether a reference to foreign currency is necessary depends on the rules adopted for dealing with foreign currency in the tax legislation, which are discussed in chapter 16. If, for example, foreign currency conversions are dealt with by recalculating foreign currency assets and obligations at the end of each tax year, giving rise to income or expense accordingly, then no rule for foreign currency is necessary in this provision. The interest rate is set by reference to the end of the previous tax year so that taxpayers know the operative rate at the beginning of the relevant tax year. The central bank rate is marked up by one-tenth on the assumption that most borrowers will not be able to obtain funding at central bank rates.

The net income-producing assets of the taxpayer are defined to include only assets that give rise to income that enters the calculation of taxable income. It is assumed in this draft that interest will be deductible only to the extent that it relates to the production of income included in the calculation of taxable income, which is not the position in all countries. Generally, the calculation is effectively the total assets less liabilities averaged between the beginning and end of the year. For resident companies, the capital and retained profits in the tax balance sheet are effectively equivalent to assets less liabilities (assuming there are no major categories of exempt income for such companies, such as foreign business income). Individuals will often not have a balance sheet as such, and so the calculations of assets less liabilities needs to be made specifically for each case. For nonresidents, only assets giving rise to income sourced in the country and taxed on a net basis after deductions enter the calculation along with their accompanying liabilities. Given that many countries employ final gross withholding taxes on the income of nonresidents, except for income from real property and business (see above), the loans to which the rules apply for nonresidents are likely to be limited.

Where the income-producing assets are shares, the appropriate treatment can be more complicated. Although dividend income is taxed in some countries at a final rate of tax on a gross basis for resident and nonresident shareholders, shares should be included for the purpose of this draft if interest expenses relating to such income will be allowed as a deduction. It is possible, for example, for intercorporate dividends to be exempted so as to eliminate the cascade of company taxation through chains of companies, but for interest expenses relating to the dividend income to be deductible. The rules here need to be coordinated with the interrelationship of the taxation of dividends and the allowance of interest deductions relating to dividend income, but beyond this general caution it is not possible to be specific.

The tax administration may give permission under this draft to vary the calculation of net income-producing assets where the calculations required above are difficult to apply in the particular circumstances of the taxpayer. Interest disallowed as a deduction under this draft is not permanently disallowed, but is carried forward and treated as an interest deduction of the succeeding year. The same calculation is then done for that succeeding year under this draft, and it may turn out that the interest deduction is allowed in that year. The disallowed interest is not treated as a dividend or some other form of payment. Country practices vary widely on this aspect of thin capitalization. Where countries also have general rules relating to characterization of investments as share capital or loans, it will be necessary to consider how those rules should be coordinated with the thin capitalization area. Tax treaties also have standard definitions of interest and dividends that do not provide clear guidance in the thin capitalization area. The OECD Commentaries seem to indicate that it is permitted but not obligatory to recharacterize as dividends interest that is disallowed under thin capitalization rules.[133]

The carryover of interest deductions in the draft will need to be coordinated with the general carryover of losses in the tax legislation, although co-

---

[133]Commentary on art. 10, para. 25 and Commentary on art. 11, para. 19. In the case of rules taking the form of the draft language set out in the text, it would be unusual to recharacterize interest as dividends, since specific debt is not recharacterized under the rule.

ordination is likely to be automatic. The general rule for loss carryover is likely to apply only to deductions that are allowed in a particular tax year and that exceed income; because interest in excess of the permitted amount under this draft for a particular tax year is not allowed as a deduction in that year, it cannot enter such a carryover loss.

While a number of detailed issues would require elaboration in the practical application of the draft (e.g., the identification and valuation of assets and liabilities that are used in the calculation of net income-producing assets), what the draft conspicuously fails to do is to define "interest." The reason is that, with the advent of modern financial instruments, interest is an increasingly difficult concept. We turn now to these instruments.

3. Modern Financial Instruments[134]

The previous heading left open the definition of interest, that is, the characterization of payments as interest or something else. Other issues that have to be considered in the international domain are the source rules, nonresident withholding taxes, and deductions available to the payer for payments under modern financial instruments. The specific focus of the discussion for the moment is direct investment involving related parties.

Because of the complexity of these issues, OECD countries are still searching for solutions. Hence, it is impossible to provide widely accepted methods that may be of use to developing and transition countries, but it is possible to suggest some partial solutions and note the problems that remain. The solutions that are adopted will need to be closely related to the more general question of how modern financial instruments are dealt with in purely domestic cases to ensure that the domestic and international regimes are consistent.

If a narrow definition of interest is adopted in domestic tax law (which is the typical case where new financial instruments have not been specifically addressed in the tax system), then it will be a simple matter for the taxpayer to use some financial instrument that does not generate interest but that is a functional equivalent, so as to avoid rules that refer to interest. For example, an interest swap arrangement can be structured to be the equivalent of a loan, but swap payments are not regarded as interest in many countries. (An interest rate swap is a financial transaction in which two parties agree to make streams of payments to each other calculated by reference to an underlying or notional principal amount; in its simplest form, it involves an agreement between two parties to make each other's interest payments on their respective loans.) In this case, any attempt to deal with thin capitalization will be aborted unless

---

[134]For a general discussion of domestic and international issues, see OECD, Taxation of New Financial Instruments (1994), International Fiscal Association, Tax Aspects of Derivative Financial Instruments 836, Cahiers de droit fiscal international (1995); and Australian Treasury and Australian Taxation Office, Taxation of Financial Arrangements: An Issues Paper (1996).

some general antiavoidance rule is applied to recharacterize the payment as interest in the particular circumstances.

If a broad definition of interest is adopted to deal with this and similar problems (such as any payment or accrual under a financial arrangement widely defined), then it is necessary to adapt the source, withholding, deduction, and related-party rules to the broader scope. One particular problem arises from the fact that tax consequences—inclusions in income or deductions—under regimes dealing with modern financial instruments often occur on an accrual basis (i.e., on an internal-rate-of-return calculation or a mark-to-market rule) without any actual payment. Lack of a payment poses problems for withholding taxes, for example.

Take the relatively straightforward case of a zero-coupon bond where the issuer receives $100,000 on issue and undertakes to pay $161,051 on redemption of the bond in five years. This transaction is the equivalent of a five-year loan of $100,000 at 10 percent annual compound interest with interest payment only on redemption. In a number of countries, this transaction would be treated as giving rise to interest income and deductions in a purely domestic case for the five tax years of $10,000, $11,000, $12,100, $13,310, and $14,641, respectively. If the holder of the bond is a nonresident, it is difficult to collect tax annually because there is no payment to subject to withholding tax, although it is possible to require the issuer to pay tax annually as if a payment had been made. If nonresident withholding tax is postponed until the end of the five-year period, the nonresident may sell the bond to a resident before redemption and avoid the tax (assuming that there is no final interest withholding tax on payments to residents). If tax is collected from the issuer annually and the nonresident sells the bond to another nonresident, the buyer and seller will have to be aware that the issuer has been paying tax and take account of the tax in the pricing of the bond; if the buyer and seller are resident in different countries, the issuer may have to adjust the amount of tax withheld after the sale because of different tax-rate limits in the tax treaties involved.

Mechanical solutions can be devised to deal with the problems of withholding and timing of deductions—for example, levying the nonresident withholding tax only on payment and postponing deduction for the issuer until that time. These solutions usually bring with them practical enforcement problems and borderline issues where different regimes are being applied in different cases. What, for example, is the effect on accrued deductions and inclusions in income in this case where the nonresident transfers the bond to a resident and an accrual system is in place between residents? Not surprisingly, even in the relatively simple case of a zero-coupon bond, there is little agreement as to the appropriate international tax regime and a large amount of diversity in practice. Some countries do not even assimilate such a payment to interest, let alone deal with timing and withholding issues.

For more sophisticated instruments, such as interest rate swaps and currency hedges, withholding tax can make legitimate transactions uncommercial for reasons similar to those discussed above in relation to interest withholding taxes on ordinary loans. Many countries have therefore not extended their interest withholding tax to these cases. This limitation creates a relatively simple way to avoid withholding tax, especially between related parties. If, in response to this problem, withholding taxes on new financial instruments are directed to transactions between related parties, problems arise with back-to-back transactions.[135]

As to source of income, it is possible to create special rules for payments under new financial instruments, even if the payments are not characterized as interest. Without special source rules or recharacterization as interest so that the interest rule applies, the source rules for whatever category the payments are placed in will govern (e.g., business income or capital gains), which may allow nonresident parties to avoid source tax on what is equivalent to interest by manipulating the source rules.

Modern financial instruments may also allow parties, especially by combining different instruments, to make an equity position look like debt and vice versa. In the international context, this could lead to substantial erosion of the corporate tax base in relation to subsidiaries in developing and transition countries for what is essentially equity investment. The thin capitalization discussion above dealt with this problem in the case of related parties, where what is pure debt in a formal sense can be viewed in effect as share capital because no independent third party would have made a loan in the situation. Modern financial instruments open this position up more generally even for portfolio investors (see below) and allow related parties in many cases to escape thin capitalization rules.

Tax treaties further complicate the international situation because they were framed before the era of financial innovation and use traditional categories. The OECD Commentary on the interest article was recently changed to clarify the issue as follows:[136]

> The definition of interest in the first sentence of para. 3 does not normally apply to payments made under certain kinds of nontraditional financial instruments where there is no underlying debt (for example, interest rate swaps). However, the definition will apply to the extent that a loan is considered to exist under a "substance over form" rule, an "abuse of rights" principle, or any similar doctrine.

The import of this paragraph seems to be that hedges and swaps will not be regarded as giving rise to interest, except when a transaction has been deliberately manipulated to substitute a future or a swap for what would otherwise have been a normal borrowing operation and when domestic law has recharacterized the transaction to give rise to interest under an antiavoidance measure. Although the Commentary does not say so, payments of discounts

---

[135]*See supra* text accompanying notes 92–93, 130.
[136]Commentary on art. 11, para. 21.1.

under zero-coupon bonds seem to be accepted as interest for the purposes of tax treaties. The result is that many payments under modern financial instruments to nonresidents will be characterized as business profits, capital gains, or other income, and, for treaties in OECD Model form, the result is that the source country will not be able to levy tax unless the payments are connected with a permanent establishment of the nonresident in the country. To partially address concerns in the related-party area, the OECD Commentary on article 21 has also been revised to include a suggested treaty provision that will allow recharacterization of payments in this kind of case.[137]

Against this complex backgound, what action can a developing or transition country take to protect itself against the sophistication of modern financial markets and multinational enterprises? A number of factors suggest a focus on the deduction area in the form of a general thin capitalization rule, combined with a comprehensive definition of interest for the purposes of the rule to catch all payments under modern financial instruments to the extent they would otherwise be deductible. First, this approach is not contrary to tax treaties, whereas the scope for action in the withholding area is clearly limited by treaties; second, back-to-back problems with related parties can be avoided; and third, the problem of characterization between debt and equity in relation to direct investors is addressed. How the definition of interest is framed for this purpose will depend on whether the country has comprehensive rules dealing with modern financial instruments for general domestic purposes, in which case definitions from that regime can be adopted. Experience to date suggests that a definition framed in general terms is preferable to a list of the kinds of instruments that are covered, given that the number of available instruments increases daily.

As regards withholding tax and source rules, the tax treaty position means that all that can be done directly is to maintain the traditional withholding tax on interest and consider extending it to zero-coupon bonds and similar instruments, although a number of technical problems will arise in doing so, as discussed above. The extract quoted from the OECD Commentary above strengthens the case for including a general antiavoidance provision in domestic law so that it can be applied (especially in the case of related parties) to recharacterize payments under modern financial instruments as interest and can subject them to the interest withholding tax accordingly. Back-to-back transactions may make the involvement of related parties difficult to detect, but the possibility of applying the antiavoidance provision and any resulting penalties may provide an incentive for related parties to fund local branches and subsidiaries by ordinary loans up to the limit permitted by the thin capitalization rules and to pay withholding tax on the resulting interest, thus limiting the problems.

---

[137]Commentary on art. 21, para. 7.

4. Payments to Tax Havens

Where an industrial country resident makes a direct investment in a subsidiary in a developing or transition country, the residence country of the parent will be operating either an exemption system or a foreign tax credit system to relieve double taxation. At first sight it seems, in an exemption system, that there is no residence country concern if income is shifted out of the source country to the residence country, because the income will be exempt. This, however, is not the outcome. If the profit shifting involves transfer pricing, whereby the parent charges inflated prices for the goods or services that it provides to the subsidiary, the increase in the parent's profits will be taxable in the residence country. This result follows because the profits will not usually be regarded as income sourced in the source country that attracts the exemption but rather as an increase of income sourced in the residence country (e.g., increased manufacturing profit) and so taxed there.

Similarly, if thin capitalization of the subsidiary by the parent is used to shift profits out of the source country, the interest received will probably not be exempt to the parent because the exemption usually extends only to business profits of a branch and dividends on direct investments in subsidiaries, and not to interest taxed by low-rate gross withholding in the source country (especially where the tax rate has been limited by a tax treaty). While there may be reasons why a parent company would find it advantageous to shift profits from the source country to the residence country (such as an imputation system in that country that bases tax credits to shareholders on residence country tax paid), often this form of profit shifting will effect little tax saving. In a residence country operating a foreign tax credit system, shifting profits out of the source country to the residence country as a means of lowering tax in the source country will usually lead to a corresponding increase in residence country taxation.

Accordingly, tax planning by multinational company groups is likely to be directed simultaneously to reducing source country and residence country taxation, which means in many cases that a third country needs to be found to which the profits can be shifted. Tax havens will be used for this end. In the transfer-pricing case, one possibility would be for the parent company to sell the goods to a related company in a tax haven for cost plus an artificially small profit (thus shifting part of the profit out of the residence country). The tax haven company then on-sells the goods to the subsidiary in the source country at an inflated price that leaves little profit to that subsidiary and most of the profit with the tax haven company. Similarly, in the thin capitalization case, the parent company may invest in a tax haven company by way of share capital (equity), and that company then lends to the subsidiary. Interest paid to the tax haven company will not be taxed in the tax haven. In each case where the country of the parent company is an exemption country, the tax haven subsidiary may be able to pay a dividend tax free to the parent so that the profits end up with the parent company having suffered very little tax. If the residence country of the parent company is a foreign tax credit country, the profits can often be retained in the tax haven company and used for group operations in other countries without attracting tax in the parent's residence. Again, the overall result is payment of little or no tax in the source or residence country.

Given that both the residence and source countries are suffering from this tax haven activity, action can be expected from both. The source country may deny deductions for payments by resident companies or by branches of nonresident companies to tax havens or may permit deductions subject to special conditions.[138] A rule of this kind has a number of problems. It is necessary to have a list of countries that are treated as tax havens, and, although such lists are readily available, they need frequent updating. The rule reintroduces the problem of the back-to-back transaction, in that the tax-haven-related company in the thin capitalization case above can, for example, route the loan through a bank in a country that is not a tax haven. Such a rule may also affect quite legitimate payments to tax havens (which in a number of cases are major financial and trading centers in their own right). Finally, if a tax treaty is in force with the tax haven, the rule may fall foul of the nondiscrimination provision in the treaty (obviously, great care is needed in negotiating a tax treaty with a tax haven).

Nevertheless, a rule focusing on payments to tax havens should be considered in some form—for example, a tax clearance system for payments that, to the knowledge of the payer, are made directly or indirectly to tax haven entities. Another possibility is to require all companies and branches in the country to report selected information on transactions with tax havens or more broadly on international transactions.[139]

5. Double-Dipping

Alternative techniques for reducing source and residence taxation that have been used in recent times seek to double up on favorable tax rules in both source and residence countries (generally referred to as double-dipping). A variety of methods are used.

One method is to exploit differences in the tax law treatments of the same transaction in the source and residence countries. A common example has been the financial lease of equipment. Some countries recharacterize finance leases for tax purposes as purchases and loans, while other countries treat them in the same way as operating leases (i.e., the lessee is treated as paying rent and the lessor as being the owner of the equipment).[140] The result is

---

[138]*E.g.*, FRA CGI § 238A.

[139]For example, sched. 25A to the Company Income Tax Return in Australia requires extensive reporting of information on international transactions, and a number of countries have special powers for collecting information from foreign persons; AUS ITAA § 264A; USA IRC § 982.

[140]*See supra* ch. 16, sec. VI(A)(4).

that two countries can end up treating two separate taxpayers (one country the lessor and the other country the lessee) as the owner of equipment and entitled to depreciation and interest deductions. Given that rent in economic terms is equivalent to depreciation and interest, the difference in treatment should not produce a substantial tax variance, but many countries have tax incentives for investment in capital equipment in the form of accelerated depreciation, investment credits, or allowances. Where two different taxpayers are treated as the owner of the equipment in different countries and each is entitled to these incentives in one of the countries, the taxpayers effectively double up on the incentives in a way not intended by either country.

It is not clear, however, which country is being disadvantaged in tax terms and which might therefore be expected to take remedial action. One of the affected countries could enact a rule that investment incentives will not be available under its law when similar incentives are being obtained in respect of the equipment under the law of another country, but the rule will lead to circularity if both countries adopt it. Alternatively, a country may limit investment incentives to equipment used in the country, which will work in most cases, although not for mobile equipment like airplanes. Another solution is for each country to do away with or reduce the investment incentives, as in fact happened in many industrial countries during the 1980s (for more general policy reasons having little to do with the problems of international tax avoidance). Where a developing or transition country adopts this kind of investment incentive, a rule limiting the benefit of the incentive to equipment used in the country is probably the easiest way to ensure that it does not suffer unduly from double-dipping of this form.

Another form of double-dipping that has been much exploited involves dual-residence companies. Some countries permit grouping of the income and losses of commonly owned resident companies (often achieved by permitting the transfer of tax losses to related companies). If the same company is resident in two such countries and has borrowed to finance group operations (whether in those countries or elsewhere), it may be able to deduct the interest in each country. If it has little or no current income, a loss will arise from the interest deductions that may be able to offset the income of two related companies, one in each country where the loss company is resident. Again, it is not clear which country is the loser from this transaction. Nevertheless, a number of countries have enacted rules that prevent the losses of dual-residence companies arising from financing transactions being used to offset the income of any other related company in the country; that is, the losses can be used only to offset future income of the dual-residence company.[141] If a developing or transition country does not permit the transfer of losses within a group of compa-

---

[141]See *supra* note 31; because of more general problems involving dual-residence companies, a number of countries are enacting provisions to allocate residence usually in accordance with tax treaty tiebreakers; *supra* note 30.

nies, it is unlikely to suffer from this particular double-dipping problem. It follows that care should be exercised in permitting transfer or consolidation of losses for tax purposes among commonly owned resident companies.

The deduction of the same expense in two countries is not of itself a cause for concern. Where a resident of a foreign tax credit country has a branch in another country, it will typically get deductions for the same expenses in the source and residence countries. These deductions will generally be offset, however, against the same income that each country is taxing, with the residence country giving double tax relief. The double-dipping problem usually involves the offsetting of the same deductions against different income of different taxpayers. As there are probably as many ways for taxpayers to exploit differences in tax systems of different countries as there are differences, and as the outcome is often ambiguous in terms of whether tax avoidance is involved and which country is suffering an unfair reduction in tax, it is likely that double-dipping will continue to be a difficult international tax problem without a clear solution.

6. *Treaty-Shopping*

Tax treaties themselves may become the object of tax avoidance activities, even though they often express the purpose of preventing tax avoidance. This possibility was of course never intended by the original framers of model tax treaties and is not in itself sufficient reason for a country to reject the negotiation of tax treaties as their benefits usually outweigh the detriments. The possibility of abuse arises from two features of the tax treaty network—its incomplete coverage of the world and its bilateral structure. The former feature flows from the latter because it is not possible to negotiate with virtually all of the countries of the world at once (as contrasted, say, to the Uruguay Round of multilateral trade negotiations of the General Agreement on Tariffs and Trade); the latter is regarded as flowing from the wide variations in tax systems around the world, so that it is felt necessary for each country to handcraft a tax treaty accommodation with other countries one by one.

A resident of a country that does not have a tax treaty with a particular developing or transition country can simply incorporate a subsidiary in another country that does (usually one with which the investor's country also has a treaty) and route its investment through that subsidiary, which will be entitled to the reduced tax rates and other protections available under the treaty. Alternatively, a resident of a country with which the developing or transition country does have a treaty may seek what it regards as better tax treatment under another tax treaty by the same route.

For example, the treaty between the investor's country and country X may have a 10 percent rate limit on royalty payments. If that investor can find another country that has a tax treaty with country X that contains a zero tax rate on royalties, then it will be possible to route a licensing transaction through a subsidiary in that country and eliminate the source country royalty tax; if that third country in turn has a treaty with the investor's country containing a zero tax rate on royalties, it will be possible in turn to pay the royalty on to the investor without tax in that country. These examples assume that the royalties are deductible in each country by the person who is paying them. The nondiscrimination article of tax treaties will normally ensure that they are deductible on the same basis as royalties paid domestically, so that the assumption will be correct in most cases.

This kind of practice is known as "treaty-shopping." A country can prevent treaty-shopping by seeking to ensure that its treaties with other countries are uniform in their main elements, especially the tax rate limits on interest and royalties and the definition of permanent establishment. If all treaties to which country X is a party have a 10 percent tax limit on royalties, for example, the planning in the second example in the previous paragraph would not be possible. Many countries have been able to achieve this consistency in their treaty negotiations and have thereby reduced the problems of treaty-shopping. Nonetheless, the possibility remains that residents of nontreaty countries will get treaty benefits through related companies in treaty countries.

One way to deal with the problem is to insert a general provision in tax treaties denying treaty benefits in such cases. The United States is the only country to practice this approach in a comprehensive way[142] although some other countries routinely insert more limited treaty abuse provisions in specific articles of treaties.[143] The Commentary on article 1 of the OECD Model contains a number of possible provisions for this purpose.[144] Developing and transition countries may instead prefer to rely on general antiavoidance provisions in domestic legislation to deal with treaty abuse. While a view is developing that such provisions are not inconsistent with tax treaties, it is probably safer to spell out in the negotiations that the general antiavoidance provision of domestic law will be applied to treaty abuses and to ensure that the general priority rule for tax treaties in domestic law makes this relationship clear.[145]

7. Combinations of Tax Avoidance Techniques

International tax avoidance in many cases will utilize a combination of the techniques outlined above. Thus, treaty-shopping activities will often go hand in hand with the use of tax havens and the interaction of tax treaties and domestic law. For example, and by way of extension of the case of treaty-shopping in the royalties area discussed above, some countries do not in their

---

[142]See U.S. Model Income Tax Convention of Sept. 20, 1996, art. 22, Limitation of Benefits.

[143]The United Kingdom includes special rules in the interest and royalty articles; the beneficial owner rule in arts. 10–12 of the OECD Model also limits treaty-shopping.

[144]Commentary on art. 1, ¶¶ 13, 15, 17, 19, 21.

[145]See supra note 128; Australia makes this relationship clear in International Tax Agreements Act 1953 s 4(2). See also GEO TC § 4(8), (9).

domestic law charge withholding tax on payments of royalties by residents to nonresidents for reasons that have been discussed earlier. If such a country has a treaty with a developing or transition country containing a zero royalty rate, a nonresident investor can incorporate a company there to receive royalties from the developing or transition country and then arrange to have the royalties paid to a tax haven company. If the royalties paid to this company equal the royalties received by the company in the tax treaty country, no tax will be collected in that country because the deduction for the royalties paid will wipe out the royalty income received and no withholding tax will be levied on the outgoing royalties. Hence, the result will be achieved of no tax at all being levied on the royalties (unless the residence country of the ultimate owner of the tax haven company has a controlled foreign company regime of the kind discussed below).

The financing of company groups often involves variations on double-dipping, treaty-shopping, and use of a tax haven. For example, a parent company may borrow to finance investment by way of share capital in a tax haven finance subsidiary, which in turn lends to an operating subsidiary in a developing or transition country through a back-to-back transaction with a bank in a country that has a tax treaty with the developing or transition country, lowering the rate of withholding tax on outgoing interest. If the residence country of the parent is an exemption country but nonetheless permits deduction of the interest paid on the loan taken out to finance the investment in the tax haven subsidiary, it is likely that the dividends received from the tax haven subsidiary (representing the interest received by that subsidiary) will be exempt in the parent's residence country, and yet interest deductions may have been obtained in two countries (that of the parent and the operating subsidiary) for offset against different income of different taxpayers.

Because of the sophistication of international tax planning and its frequent combination of domestic law, tax havens, and tax treaties, the taxation of nonresident direct investors by developing and transition countries is not an easy task. An array of provisions in domestic legislation (such as provisions on transfer pricing, thin capitalization and tax haven payments, and a general antiavoidance rule) and great care in the negotiation of tax treaties will assist in dealing with the differing kinds of tax planning.

A developing or transition country should make clear through explanatory or administrative material that it does not intend to use (the threat of) multiple taxation to penalize taxpayers. If it is felt that the problems of international tax avoidance justify severer penalties than normal, then the tax penalty regime should provide for this directly. Similarly, if higher levels of disclosure of information are required in the international area, the legislation should provide for such disclosure explicitly. Care in drafting such provisions is necessary to ensure that they are not in breach of nondiscrimination provisions in tax treaties. For this reason as well as the considerations raised in relation to residents below, the provisions should apply to both inward and outward investment cases.

Stricter enforcement regimes may be viewed adversely by foreign investors and temper their willingness to invest in the country in question. Each developing and transition country has to judge this issue for itself. The same reluctance may also be triggered by legislation directed at international tax avoidance practices. One possible response (effectively giving in to the difficulties of enforcing international tax rules) is to not include antiavoidance provisions of the kinds outlined above in domestic tax legislation and so to allow nonresident direct investors to determine their tax level for themselves. Alternatively, such provisions can be coupled with special tax regimes for foreign investors conferring tax holidays and other tax privileges on them in specified cases. The alternative approach nominally gives control over the targeting of the tax benefits for foreign investors to the developing or transition country, although in practice, as noted in chapter 23, it generally leads to other forms of tax avoidance.

8. Nonresident Portfolio Investors

The position of nonresident portfolio investors differs substantially from that of direct investors. Because direct investors have control over the transactions undertaken within the company group, they can engage in transfer pricing, thin capitalization, and the like in ways not generally available to the portfolio investor. It is possible for portfolio investors to employ tax havens and treaty-shopping in some of their activities (e.g., using tax treaties to obtain lower withholding tax rates on interest), but generally the scale of the investment in a particular company by a particular investor is unlikely to justify elaborate tax avoidance of the kind that may be practiced by direct investors.

The tax planning of the portfolio investor is likely to consist of portfolio choice. For example, purchasing shares in a company resident in a developing or transition country exposes the investor to the corporate tax and the withholding tax on portfolio dividends, which is probably higher than the tax on dividends paid on direct investment. Some portfolio investors (e.g., tax-exempt pension funds) will be tax privileged in their residence countries and so may not benefit greatly from double tax relief in this case. Failing special provisions in the law of the source or residence country (or both, possibly through a tax treaty) to deal with the international implications of its special tax position, the portfolio investor may adopt a different investment strategy, such as investing in (profit-related) debt of the company resident in the source country and options over the unissued capital of the company. In this way, it benefits from increases in the value of the company's shares and a share in its income stream without being exposed to much if any tax in the source country (interest withholding tax probably being the only tax applicable) while enjoying its tax privileges in the residence country. With the advent of modern financial instruments, more sophisticated strategies are available to the portfolio investor who wishes to be exposed to a particular market or company without the accompanying source tax liabilities.

Often, the influence of the portfolio investor will be felt not directly but indirectly in the source country through the foreign direct investor responding to the needs of the portfolio investor. Since portfolio investment opportunities are often limited in developing and transition countries (because of the lack of a stock exchange or very thin trading in whatever stock market exists), portfolio investors more often than not will invest in the multinational direct investors operating in the countries (and many other countries) as a way of exposing themselves to investment in many countries and at the same time minimizing risk by having multicountry coverage in the investment. As the totality of investment in many multinational companies will be dominated by institutional portfolio investors, such as pension schemes, banks, and insurers, the companies are likely to adapt their tax profile to suit the institutional investors. If the preference of the institutional investors is to have low-taxed returns because of their privileged tax position in their residence countries, the optimal tax strategy for the multinational company may be to reduce its tax liabilities in all countries, which takes us back to the beginning of the discussion in this section of the chapter.

Increasingly in recent times, international investment has developed many tax niches, with offshore funds offering specialized investment products designed to appeal to particular kinds of investors. The discussion of capital flight above dealt with one kind of such fund in the case of resident portfolio investors. Here, the discussion concerns similar funds designed for nonresident portfolio investors. To the extent that the multinationals do not respond to the tax situations of their different classes of portfolio investor, it is often possible to find a fund that consolidates portfolio investors with a similar tax and investment profile and develops investment products that suit that profile. While it often may not be worthwhile for a single portfolio investor to use treaty-shopping and tax havens for its operations, it is for such offshore funds. Hence, the other major effect of portfolio investors in developing and transition countries is being felt through the operations of such funds (with many specializing in investment in (particular) developing or transition countries). To the extent that this investment is highly tax sensitive, there is little that a developing or transition country can do to prevent offshore fund tax planning in which the nonresident portfolio investor decides to invest in a particular fund or to withdraw from the fund.

The major problem that the nonresident portfolio investor poses is the potentially deleterious incentives that the investor's tax position creates for direct investors to reduce source country taxation. Hence, additional anti-avoidance provisions are not necessary in the law to deal with the tax position of the portfolio investor beyond what has been canvassed in earlier discussion. If the source country specifically wants to cater to the tax problems faced by foreign pension funds and the like, some suggestions have already been made.

9. Resident Investors

Although developing and transition countries will most often encounter the forms of tax avoidance outlined above in the case of nonresident direct investors, many of them are equally available to residents of the developing or transition country (resident in the sense that the ultimate investor is a resident of the country and is not foreign owned). It is necessary in this case to distinguish two investment situations: first, where the ultimate investment is made by the resident overseas and, second, where the ultimate investment is made in the developing or transition country itself.

The first case is the more obvious but less frequent in practice from the point of view of the developing or transition country. A resident engaging in direct investment overseas can engage in transfer pricing and the other kinds of activities outlined above for the dual purpose of reducing the tax in the country of source (where the investment is made) and in the country of residence. Avoidance of resident country tax will often involve the diversion of income from the country of residence to tax havens, combined with manipulation of the system of double taxation relief. Avoidance of source country tax in these kinds of cases is not directly the concern of the residence country, its main concern being to protect its own taxing rights. The mechanism to control tax haven use by residents that is increasingly being used in advanced market economies is to tax residents on their share of low-taxed foreign income derived by nonresident companies controlled by the residents. These "controlled foreign company" regimes are usually very complex in operation.[146]

As regards the second case, initially it seems unlikely that a resident of a developing or transition country would get involved in international tax avoidance for investment in that country. In fact, however, a resident direct investor can easily appear as a nonresident direct investor by channeling investment into the country through a nonresident company that the resident owns. By this means, the possibilities of reducing tax in the country through transfer pricing, thin capitalization, tax havens, and treaty-shopping become possible in a similar way as for true nonresident direct investors. In addition, the resident can also by this route seek to enjoy any tax concessions given specifically to nonresident investors.

This possibility of residents assuming the guise of nonresidents is closely linked to the capital flight issue canvassed earlier, at least in transition countries. Capital flight was the first reaction of many wealthy people there to the

---

[146]The seminal comparative work on these regimes is Brian Arnold, The Taxation of Controlled Foreign Corporations: An International Comparison (1986); for a more recent summary of current practice, see OECD, Controlled Foreign Company Legislation (1996).

uncertainty and instability created by the transition. As the situation has clarified to the extent that it is possible to conduct profitable business operations in the countries, it seems likely that a number of these people have reintroduced their capital into businesses as disguised foreign direct investment. While the capital is thus reexposed to the risks that it was originally fleeing, the ownership of the capital is usually hidden (as it often originates in tax havens), tax concessions may be available, and further flight remains possible to the extent that the capital remains mobile. There is some evidence that much of this capital is invested in import-export and similar activities that do not anchor the capital in the same way that investing in large-scale plant and equipment would.[147]

For both kinds of tax avoidance by residents, the provisions discussed above—such as rules on transfer pricing, thin capitalization, tax havens, and general antiavoidance—are available to deal with some of the problems. It was partly because of the need to control circular transactions of residents taking capital offshore and reintroducing it into the country that it has been suggested that many of the rules should not be directed to nonresidents. Eventually, controlled foreign company regimes will be needed, despite the difficulties that they entail. For the time being, the embryonic measure that has been outlined above for the capital flight case can at least be adopted to signal that a developing or transition country is aware of the international tax avoidance techniques that residents may use and proposes to combat them.

VIII. Tax Treaty Issues Not Covered in Domestic Law

A number of provisions found in tax treaties are not usually reflected in domestic law. This section briefly describes these provisions, together with their effect on domestic law, specifically nondiscrimination, exchange of information and assistance in collection, and the mutual agreement procedure.

A. Nondiscrimination

The nondiscrimination article of tax treaties is designed to ensure that foreign investors in a country are not discriminated against by the tax system compared with domestic investors. The OECD Model nondiscrimination provision is narrower, however, than similar provisions found in other areas of international law, such as trade. This difference is necessary because the international tax system operates on the residence and source principles and so necessarily distinguishes the tax position of residents and nonresidents. Hence, it is not usually regarded as discriminatory to collect flat-rate gross

---

[147]*See* OECD, Taxation and Foreign Direct Investment: The Experiences of the Economies in Transition (1995), especially the discussion of Latvia in pt. II.

withholding taxes from a resident of the other state without a permanent establishment when a resident is taxed on the same income on a net assessment basis.

The first paragraph of the nondiscrimination article in the OECD Model provides against discrimination on the basis of nationality, but makes it clear that distinctions on the basis of residence will not be regarded as giving rise to nationality discrimination (in other areas, such as EU law, residence distinctions can amount to nationality discrimination).[148] Hence, to breach this provision it is necessary for a country to treat a resident who is a national of the other state less favorably in the levy of tax or procedural requirements than a resident national, or a nonresident national of the other state less favorably than a nonresident national. Such forms of discrimination are rare in domestic tax laws. The second paragraph of the OECD nondiscrimination article applies a similar rule to stateless persons; this provision rarely appears in actual tax treaties.[149]

The third paragraph of the nondiscrimination article in the OECD Model requires that a permanent establishment of a resident of the other state shall not be less favorably taxed than enterprises of residents carrying on the same activities. This is the most important provision of the article in practice and, combined with the other articles of the Model—especially the business profits article—means that the profits attributable to a permanent establishment have to be taxed on a net basis[150] and that the permanent establishment must otherwise be taxed under the same rules as domestic enterprises. The article deals with the amount of tax liability and not connected requirements so that it is possible, for example, to apply withholding taxes on income derived by a permanent establishment of a nonresident even though such taxes are not applied to a domestic enterprise, so long as the ultimate tax is on a net basis (i.e., any withholding taxes are not final, are credited against the ultimate tax liability, and are refunded if there is an excess). If withholding taxes are applied to income derived by domestic enterprises, there is no question of breach of the nondiscrimination article in applying them to nonresidents, but even if the taxes are final for a resident enterprise, they cannot be for a permanent establishment of a nonresident because of the requirement of the business profits article that taxation be on a net basis.

The exact extent of the nondiscrimination obligation under this paragraph is not clear in all cases, especially as regards application of progressive rate scales to companies, tax relief for intercorporate dividends, and the granting of foreign tax credits to permanent establishments for any foreign tax levied on in-

---

[148]*See* Terra & Wattel, European Tax Law ¶¶ 3.2.1, 3.2.3.1, 3.2.3.2 (1993).

[149]In the 1977 OECD Model and in the UN Model, the second paragraph is a definition of national; this now appears in the definition article of the 1992 OECD Model.

[150]This requirement may have implications for certain forms of presumptive taxation that imposes a tax even in the absence of net income. *See* vol. 1, ch. 12.

come attributable to the permanent establishment. The Commentary to the OECD Model contains a lengthy discussion of these issues.[151] The second sentence of the third paragraph does make clear that it is not necessary to grant personal allowances to a nonresident individual carrying on business through a permanent establishment (this sentence often appears as a separate paragraph in actual treaties). Thin capitalization rules that are applied to a permanent establishment borrowing from related parties but that are not applied to resident enterprises may be contrary to the paragraph, depending on how the rules are framed. The example of thin capitalization rules given above will not be contrary to nondiscrimination rules because they apply to all enterprises. Branch profits taxes may be contrary to the terms of this paragraph, so that its terms need modification if a country wishes to levy a branch profits tax.

The fourth and fifth paragraphs of the OECD nondiscrimination article ensure that resident enterprises whose capital is wholly or partly owned or controlled by a resident of the other state are not subject to discrimination. The fourth paragraph refers specifically to deductions for interest, royalties, and other disbursements and makes clear that deductions can be denied through the application of the arm's-length principle by way of exception to the requirement for the same treatment. If a developing or transition country adopts a rule denying deductions for payments to tax havens, the rule will generally be overridden by the fourth paragraph if a tax treaty is in effect with the tax haven. Hence, the caution above about negotiating tax treaties with tax havens. The fourth paragraph is more general, preventing heavier or different taxation or connected requirements than for other similar enterprises. While it can cover the same ground in part as the fourth paragraph, the fifth is more specific and therefore prevails in the event of overlap. Thin capitalization can be an issue under the fourth paragraph, but not if the rules are applied generally to all enterprises. The fifth paragraph would prevent, for example, a local subsidiary of a parent in the other state from being subjected to a higher tax rate than other companies.

The final paragraph in the OECD Model provides that, unlike the other provisions of a tax treaty, the nondiscrimination article applies to all taxes levied by a state. This provision is often omitted from actual tax treaties or altered to make clear that it applies only to taxes covered by the treaty (which it is not strictly necessary to state).

Because tax treaties are enacted in one way or another as part of domestic law and prevail over other taxing provisions, the nondiscrimination provision is self-executing and overrides domestic rules that conflict with it. Because of the general terms of the nondiscrimination article, it is necessary to be aware of its operation when drafting domestic rules. There is generally little point in devising domestic rules that are contrary to the nondiscrimination rules, except in the case of tax haven provisions.

---

[151]Commentary on art. 24 ¶¶ 19–54.

The nationality paragraph aside, at first sight the nondiscrimination article seems to have a residence state bias because its provisions operate effectively only on the source state (where the permanent establishment or subsidiary operates). This view is not accurate if the structure of tax treaties is looked at broadly. It was noted above that the foreign tax credit system in particular may create an incentive for the source country to increase its taxation on nonresidents (or subsidiaries of foreign parent companies) up to the level of tax in the residence country. While tax treaties impose rate limits on source taxation or exclude source taxation altogether in some cases, for income of a permanent establishment or a subsidiary there are no such limits. Hence, the nondiscrimination article ensures that source countries do not target higher taxes to these cases and prey on the relief system of the residence country.[152] The equivalent undertaking of the residence country is in its treaty obligation to relieve double taxation for source taxes levied in accordance with the treaty. The residence country could not satisfy its obligations under this paragraph by levying tax rates on foreign investment that are higher than those on domestic investment and then purporting to relieve double taxation through a tax credit.[153] The nondiscrimination article does not prevent a country from discriminating in favor of nonresidents (as with tax holidays or other incentives that apply only to foreign investors). Nor does the article prohibit provisions in the domestic law that favor the location of investment in the country; for example, a country can have special tax incentives for research and development conducted in the country or for plant and equipment used in the country, as long as these locational incentives are not confined to residents or locally owned companies.

B. Exchange of Information and Assistance in Collection

Most countries have a domestic law rule that they will not directly or indirectly assist another country in the collection of its taxes.[154] This rule means that exchange of tax information and other forms of assistance in collection of taxes are not possible without a tax treaty that overrides this rule in domestic law. The tax secrecy rules of many countries also prevent the exchange of in-

---

[152]Even in the absence of a treaty, this tactic may not be effective if the resident country denies a credit for so-called soak-up taxes, as does the United States, for example. *See* Treas. Reg. § 1.901–2(c).

[153]This is implicitly recognized in the paragraph in the OECD Model allowing the residence country to apply exemption with progression to income, which it relieves from double taxation by exemption, arts. 23A(3), 23B(2). Exemption with progression takes the foreign income that has been exempted into account in determining the tax payable on domestic income. Usually, an average rate of tax is worked out on the assumption that all the foreign and domestic income of the resident is subject to tax, and this rate is then applied to the domestic income of the resident.

[154]This rule is not found in the tax laws of the country but in the rules of private international law (conflict of laws). Thus, in common law countries, it is simply part of the common law (*see* Government of India v. Taylor [1955] AC 491).

formation. Exchange-of-information provisions are found in virtually all tax treaties, but other forms of assistance are less commonly provided for.

The standard OECD and UN Model exchange-of-information article requires a country to obtain information for its treaty partner where the information is necessary for carrying out the provisions of the treaty or of the country's domestic tax law. Exchanged information is required to be kept secret in accordance with the secrecy rules of domestic law of the recipient country and in accordance with the express treaty rules on this topic. In addition, the standard treaty article provides that information need not be exchanged when it involves commercial or trade secrets. Tax secrecy is often not as strong an institution in developing or transition countries as it is in industrial countries and so can be a very sensitive topic in tax relations between treaty partners. It is implicit in the exchange-of-information article, however, that a country cannot refuse to give information to its treaty partner because of its own tax secrecy laws.

The exchange-of-information article also serves as a test of the lowest common denominator for procedures of collecting information. Information need not be collected if it cannot be obtained under the procedures of either country. For example, the information being sought may be kept at the home of a taxpayer. If the tax procedure law of either treaty country forbids entry of domestic (as opposed to commercial) premises to obtain information, then there is no obligation to obtain the information. If, however, the impediment arises under the law of the country making the request and if the country that has received the request for such information is able to obtain the information under its laws, that country may (but is not obliged to) forward the information to the other country under the exchange-of-information article.

Unlike other articles of tax treaties, the exchange-of-information article is not limited in application to residents of the treaty partners. For example, one country can request the other to obtain information from a permanent establishment in that state of a resident of a third state. Although the Models do not so provide, information is being increasingly extended to taxes other than income taxes for the practical reason that many countries use the same tax officials to enforce a number of different taxes (e.g., income tax and value-added tax), and it is difficult for an official who has received foreign information to use it only in relation to one tax when it is relevant to several taxes.

The OECD provides considerable practical guidance on exchange of information.[155] The use of computers in tax administration is spilling over into this area, and the sophistication of the exchange process has increased rapidly. The OECD has developed a standard computer format for exchange of information.[156] In recent years, the exchange article has given rise to some novel extensions of its use, such as for simultaneous audits of the same or related tax-

---

[155]OECD, Tax Information Exchange: A Survey of Member Countries (1994).

[156]Reproduced in Vann, *supra* note 14.

payers by each party to a treaty (and even by more than two countries through the use of exchange provisions in a number of treaties). The OECD has developed a model agreement for tax administrations to formalize the process.[157] Whether developing or transition countries will be able to participate in these recent developments will depend on their level of computerization and audit capacity.

In addition, provisions for assistance in collection are increasingly being included in tax treaties. Under these provisions, each country undertakes to collect the taxes of the other. As no OECD or UN Model provision currently exists for this purpose, the following text is provided as a sample.

Article 27. Assistance in Collection

(1) The competent authorities of the Contracting States undertake to lend assistance to each other in the collection of taxes, together with interest, costs, and civil penalties relating to such taxes, referred to in this article as a "revenue claim."

(2) Requests for assistance by the competent authority of a Contracting State in the collection of a revenue claim shall include a certification by such authority that, under the laws of that State, the revenue claim has been finally determined. For the purposes of this article, a revenue claim is finally determined when a Contracting State has the right under its internal law to collect the revenue claim and the taxpayer has no further rights to restrain collection.

(3) A revenue claim of a Contracting State that has been accepted for collection by the competent authority of the other Contracting State shall be collected by the other State as though such claim were the other State's own revenue claim as finally determined in accordance with the provisions of its laws relating to the collection of its taxes.

(4) Amounts collected by the competent authority of a Contracting State pursuant to this article shall be forwarded to the competent authority of the other Contracting State. However, except where the competent authorities of the Contracting States otherwise agree, the ordinary costs incurred in providing collection assistance shall be borne by the first-mentioned State, and any extraordinary costs so incurred shall be borne by the other State.

(5) No assistance shall be provided under this article for a revenue claim of a Contracting State in respect of a taxpayer to the extent that the revenue claim relates to a period during which the taxpayer was a resident of the other Contracting State.

(6) Nothing in this article shall be construed as imposing on either Contracting State the obligation to carry out administrative measures of

---

[157]OECD, Transfer Pricing Guidelines, *supra* note 124, ¶¶ 4.78–4.93.

a different nature from those used in the collection of its own taxes or that would be contrary to its public policy (*ordre public*).

(7) Notwithstanding the provisions of article 2 (Taxes Covered), the provisions of this article shall apply to all taxes collected by or on behalf of the Government of a Contracting State.

Whether the last paragraph is included will depend in part on a similar extension being made to the exchange article. On the grounds of administrative capacity, developing and transition countries may not consider such an article appropriate to their circumstances (and, equally, industrial countries may not be willing to agree with them on this article). More elaborate stand-alone treaties dealing with tax administration have been developed, and the Multilateral Treaty on Mutual Administrative Assistance, which covers exchange of information, service of documents, and assistance in collection, is open for signature to those countries that join the Council of Europe or the OECD.[158] It entered into force on April 1, 1995.

C. Mutual Agreement Procedure

The final provision of tax treaties that requires comment is the article on the mutual agreement procedure. Under the Model versions, this article performs three functions: it provides a dispute resolution mechanism in relation to the application of the provisions of tax treaties to specific cases; it allows the countries to settle common interpretations and applications of their tax treaty; and it allows them to resolve cases of double taxation not otherwise dealt with by their treaty. Some countries find that the third function and often the second are difficult to reconcile with their domestic laws and procedures and therefore omit them from their treaties. In practice, it is dispute resolution for the specific case that predominates, whatever the precise form of the article.

The ground on which the taxpayer can invoke this procedure is that the actions of one of the states result or will result in taxation not in accordance with the treaty. The taxpayer has three years to invoke the procedure from the first notification of the act complained of. The states are obliged under the article to consult on the problem raised by the taxpayer if the state with which the problem is raised is unable or unwilling to resolve it unilaterally, but they are not obliged to resolve the case. If a resolution is agreed to by the states, then under the Models it is to be implemented notwithstanding domestic time limits on amending tax assessments. Some countries are unwilling to agree to such overriding of domestic time limits in their tax treaties.

No specific procedure is provided, but it is made clear that the tax administrations can make contact directly and do not need to go through diplomatic channels. The major issue that arises in practice is the relationship between

---

[158]Council of Europe and OECD, Explanatory Report on the Convention on Mutual Administrative Assistance in Tax Matters (1989).

domestic appeal procedures provided for in tax laws and the treaty dispute resolution mechanism. To avoid competition or conflict between domestic appeals and the mutual agreement procedure, some countries provide in their tax laws or procedures that the taxpayer must waive or suspend appeal rights under domestic law, while other countries will not actively pursue the competent authority procedure until domestic appeal periods have expired and the taxpayer has not utilized them.

The mutual agreement procedure has also been the subject of novel uses in recent times. The main development concerns advance pricing arrangements under which the mutual agreement procedure is used to agree to a transfer price in advance, so that taxpayers and tax administration are spared disputes after the event. This is a sophisticated procedure that for the moment is probably relevant only to industrial countries.[159] Taxpayer dissatisfaction with the mutual agreement procedure has led some countries to adopt arbitration procedures in their tax treaties for cases where it is not possible for the competent authorities to resolve disputes. The main purpose of such provisions is to put pressure on the tax administration to resolve international disputes rather than to actually engage in arbitrations.[160]

IX. International Tax Priorities for Developing and Transition Countries

It will be evident from this chapter that the construction of the international elements of the income tax system in domestic law and tax treaties is a complex topic. Among developing and transition countries (as among industrial countries), there will be wide differences in the capability of the tax administration to deal with international tax issues. While priorities will vary from one country to another, this concluding part of the chapter indicates a line of development that should suit many developing and transition countries.

The priority of any tax system will always be to tax the domestic income of resident taxpayers.[161] With the increasing internationalization of economic relations, however, even this goal means that attention must be given to international income tax issues. For better or worse, the globalization of the

---

[159]OECD, Transfer Pricing Guidelines ¶¶ 4.124–4.166. In the medium term, advanced pricing agreements (APAs) developed by industrial countries may help to solve the difficulties for developing and transition countries in enforcing transfer pricing rules.

[160]For a discussion of these issues, see OECD, Transfer Pricing Guidelines paras. 4.167–4.171; the EU has implemented an arbitration procedure in transfer pricing cases, Convention of July 23, 1990, on the Elimination of Double Taxation in connection with the Adjustment of Profits of Associated Enterprises, 90/436/EEC, O.J. No. C304 of Dec. 21, 1976, 4.

[161]With the possible exception of a few countries with small populations and large resource bases exploited by foreign investors.

world economy impinges on developing and transition countries, and it is not possible for a country to isolate itself or its tax system. The interdependence of market economies is a new phenomenon, and transition countries in particular retain a residual belief in the ability of regulation to deal with problems. In some developing countries also the capacity of economic regulation in the current economic environment is overrated. Developing and transition countries face similar problems of international taxation as industrial countries, which means that, whatever may have been the case in the past, it is not possible to adopt the attitude that international issues can wait.

The incentives for capital flight are strong in developing and transition countries even apart from the tax system. If a country operates the source principle only, then it is necessary to have robust rules for the source of income to ensure that the source-based tax is not avoided. Even with such rules, there will be a strong incentive for residents to move income offshore in order to avoid taxation, which will be a relatively simple matter for passive portfolio income (by investment choice). The residence principle should be adopted to prevent this form of tax avoidance. Once the residence principle is adopted, then measures for the relief of double taxation by way of exemption or a simple foreign tax credit are also necessary. At this point of development, the country has satisfied the basic norms for international tax rules on which tax treaties depend.

The ability of residents, again by simple investment choice, to derive foreign-source passive income through nonresident taxpayers (such as offshore mutual funds) indicates that further measures are necessary even for the simple goal of protecting the domestic tax base in the case of residents not engaged in active businesses. A simple provision indicating an intention to levy tax in these cases, together with enforcement efforts directed at tax evasion using foreign bank accounts, is the best that can be achieved to deal with the various kinds of capital flight. Residents involved in purely domestic business activities can also use the international tax system to avoid taxes. In this case, investments will be looped offshore and back into the country, creating the potential for such techniques as transfer pricing, thin capitalization, and profit stripping to move profits out of the country, usually to tax havens. The simplest approach for dealing with such problems is a brief provision levying tax on the resident owners of the offshore entities. Such provisions are necessary today simply to ensure collection of tax on the domestic income of residents.

With provisions in place to secure the domestic tax base, probably the next priority should be tax treaties. These marginally increase the capacity to enforce taxation of the domestic income of residents through exchange of information (although the use of tax havens for much of the offshore activity limits the effectiveness of tax treaties). Most important, they signal to foreign investors the country's intention to play by the generally accepted rules of international taxation and not to discriminate against foreign investors while leaving room (if negotiated in an appropriate form) to extend domestic taxes to foreign investors. Except in the increasingly unusual case of a country deciding not to pursue the negotiation of tax treaties, the contents of tax treaties overshadow the way in which a country should frame its tax laws for the taxation of foreign investors. It has been suggested throughout this chapter that the rules of tax treaties should generally be followed in domestic law for greater transparency and simplicity in the application of the tax law where a tax treaty is operative.

Taxation of foreign investors in developing and transition countries is a politically divisive issue. On the one hand, there is a natural resentment against the economic resources of a country being owned and exploited by foreigners. In the past, this attitude contributed in many developing countries to restrictions on foreign-owned operations. On the other hand, the need for foreign capital, technology, and management skills is increasingly felt as more and more countries compete for what is available, especially since the transition countries have entered the picture. The result is policy and administrative ambivalence to taxation of foreign investment.

Many countries offer tax incentives for foreign direct investors. While the efficacy of these incentives in attracting increased foreign investment may be doubted, any attempt to tax foreign direct investors effectively involves formidable problems of drafting the law and administering it. The basic provisions for taxing nonresidents consist generally of withholding taxes on passive and employment income and collection by assessment on business income. The investment choices for portfolio foreign investors and the tax avoidance techniques available to the foreign direct investor mean that such provisions are not adequate and that rules in domestic law on transfer pricing, thin capitalization, and tax havens are required. These will by no means cover the tax avoidance strategies available. A general antiavoidance provision or doctrine will assist the tax administration to cope with international tax avoidance, but requires considerable effort to implement. In short, any serious attempt to collect tax from foreign direct investors is fraught with drafting and administrative difficulties, while taxation of portfolio investors may simply induce them to move their investment out of the country. For these reasons, the taxation of foreign investors is probably the last international taxation issue that a developing or transition country should seriously tackle.

The number and significance of the international tax problems that confront the income tax are reasons why developing and transition countries do well to rely on alternative tax bases in addition to the income tax as a major source of tax revenue. The value-added tax, excises, social security, and property taxes generally present fewer international difficulties of drafting and enforcement than the income tax.

19

Taxation of Enterprises and Their Owners

Graeme S. Cooper and Richard K. Gordon

> It is also obvious that the type of rules which we have been discussing, although they are unquestionably rules of binding law, have in no way the character of religious commandments, laid down absolutely, obeyed rigidly and integrally. . . . The bundles of fish, the measures of yams, or bunches of taro, can only be roughly assessed, and naturally the quantities exchanged vary according to whether the fishing season or the harvest is more abundant.
>
> —*Branislaw Malinowski*

I. Introduction

A. In General

Two of the perennial issues in tax policy debates are whether a specific tax should be formally imposed on enterprise profits and collected from enterprise earnings, and, if so, how it should be constructed. Levying a separate tax on the earnings of large corporations is almost universal practice,[1] often existing at both national and subnational levels, and in fact predates the imposition of universal income taxes on individuals in some

Note: Victor Thuronyi (who also wrote sec. VII), Alvin Warren, David Brockway, and Melinda Milenkovich provided plentiful, and extraordinarily helpful, comments on earlier drafts. The research for this chapter was supported in part by the Fund for Tax and Fiscal Research, Harvard Law School.

[1]*See supra* Introduction, note 10.

jurisdictions.[2] Yet, the tax is not without its detractors, and suggestions for its reform or even repeal are often heard.

Given the prevalence of a tax on enterprise profits, it may seem curious that there is such a debate, and so this introduction will outline some of the main points of contention before their more detailed examination in the body of the chapter. At the policy level, critics have pointed to the perceived deficiencies of the tax, and their list is indeed long and daunting—the so-called economic double taxation of enterprise income (when enterprise profits are taxed, as are distributions of those taxed profits), the conjectural incidence of the tax (because its effects might be shifted to shareholders, workers, or consumers), the indeterminate and discretionary amount of tax payable (because the amount of tax varies with such factors as the capital structure of the enterprise and the timing and proportion of distributions and retentions), the apparent incentive for business enterprises to finance their activities through debt (because interest is usually deductible while dividends are not) and to retain earnings (because retained earnings are not taxed as dividends but are usually taxed at a lower effective rate as capital gains), and the possible tax-induced distortions of the way economic activities are organized and conducted (avoiding a particular legal form for less transparent but more lightly taxed alternatives).

Despite the shortcomings of the tax—the significance of which is still the subject of much debate—its supporters have pointed to several important benefits. They argue that it could approximate the economist's ideal tax on pure "economic rents"—that is, a tax on the excess of revenue over the enterprise's total input cost, including the cost of capital. Such a tax would have no distortionary effects because it taxes pure profit. Even detractors of the tax acknowledge that there are serious obstacles to removing it, not the least of which is the substantial windfall that would be conferred on holders of equity interests if the tax were removed. Other important obstacles to its removal arise from interdependencies: changing the enterprise tax would also require changing the personal income tax and international tax systems. First, under personal

---

[2]The corporate tax in the United States was first imposed in 1909, four years before the personal income tax was introduced. Historically, the tax was justified as equivalent to a license fee or benefit tax, imposed for the privileges flowing from the creation by the state of a separate person. Those benefits include perpetual life despite changes of investors, limited liability for investors, transferable interests with standardized (but variable) rights for ease of transfer, and the ability to sue (and be sued) in the corporation's own name. That justification has generally been regarded as insufficient because there is little relationship between the value of the privilege and the size of corporate profits.

Another view accepts the legal fiction—that a separate person has been created by the process of incorporation—and the imposition of the separate tax simply affirms this fiction in the tax context. This rationale too is regarded as unsatisfactory today because it conflicts with modern financial theory, which simply regards the enterprise as a group of investors acting collectively under one or more legal structures. The legal fiction of the separate legal person is simply inappropriate in a tax context.

income taxes as they typically currently operate, the enterprise tax is the principal means of preventing deferral of tax and arbitrage of ordinary income into preferentially taxed capital gains. In other words, the enterprise tax is necessary to protect the tax base of the personal income tax. Next, it is an important source of revenue from nonresidents under the existing allocation of taxing rights between countries. The current system allocates rights to tax capital income from equity investments primarily to the source country, and rights to tax capital income from debt investments primarily to the residence country. Unilaterally abandoning the right of the source country by repealing the enterprise tax would confer an unrequited windfall on the residence country.

The other aspect to the debate is more operational—if the tax is to exist, how should it be constructed? At one end of the spectrum, the "separate entity view" would construct and operate the personal and enterprise taxes independently. The other, the "conduit" view discussed below, would adjust the taxes to recognize the existence and operation of both. At present, and on balance, the conduit view has probably emerged in a majority of countries as the most satisfactory theoretical paradigm for imposing tax on income derived from an equity investment in a business enterprise.[3] Ultimately, if the conduit view is accepted, its implementation must lead to one of the three theoretical options—imposing tax at the investor level only, imposing tax at the enterprise level only, or imposing tax at both levels, with the corollary of adjusting one tax for the effects of the other.

This chapter considers these policy and operational questions. Section II examines imposing tax at the investor level only and discusses why a tax imposed at the enterprise level, rather than at the shareholder level only, has generally been regarded as necessary. Section III considers in more detail whether important benefits can be achieved by a tax imposed at the enterprise level only. Section IV examines some possible adverse consequences likely to

---

[3]For example, two successive government reports in Australia—the Asprey Committee in 1972 and the Draft White Paper in 1985—suggested that the ideal treatment for income derived through entities was to approximate the conduit approach: "[the] ideal arrangement . . . would recognize for income tax purposes the shareholder's interest in both the distributed and undistributed earnings of the company and would tax the combined amount at each shareholder's marginal tax rate; the company would be taxed only as a withholding arrangement to collect personal tax on the income." Australia, Reform of the Australian Tax System ¶ 17.9 (1985) [hereinafter Draft White Paper]. In contrast, the United States has always had a completely separate system and continues to do so despite a number of recommendations by the U.S. Treasury Department to the contrary. *See, e.g.*, U.S. Dep't of the Treasury, Blueprints for Basic Tax Reform (January 1977) [hereinafter Blueprints] (arguing for full integration between corporate and personal income taxation); Department of the Treasury, Tax Reform for Fairness, Simplicity, and Economic Growth 117–20 (November 1984) [hereinafter Treasury I] (arguing for partial integration); The President's Tax Proposals to the Congress for Fairness, Growth, and Simplicity (1985) [hereinafter Treasury II]; Department of the Treasury, Integration of Individual and Corporate Tax Systems: Taxing Business Income Once 27–35 (1992) [hereinafter U.S. Treasury Report] (arguing for full integration).

flow from the decision to use an enterprise-level tax that makers of tax policy and tax officials must be aware of and, more important, be prepared to manage. Section V examines systems that have both enterprise-level and investor-level taxes, and some of the options for structuring the interaction between them. Section VI discusses the typology and effect of distributions in their interactions with different enterprise and investor systems. Section VII examines how to define the enterprise taxpayer. Section VIII draws some general conclusions.

B. Relationship Between Enterprise Income and Investor Income

Most countries permit various legal structures for organizing profit-making enterprises. These include sole proprietorships, different types of partnerships, companies, and trusts. Modern financial theory views each form of enterprise as a group of investors acting collectively under one or more legal structures. Those structures are all based on contract law and include partnership law, trust or foundation law, and company law.[4] The traditional forms of organizing an investment include equity, debt, and leases[5] of movable, immovable, and intellectual property. Each different form of investment, whether stock or partnership interest, bank loan or bond, or lease, creates for the investor a different type of claim to the income and property of the joint business enterprise.[6]

Traditionally, equity holders receive their income in the form of a mixture of periodic payments (partnership distributions or dividends) and increases, or perhaps decreases, in the value of their investment (capital gains or losses). Depending on the local law, equity investments in enterprises can take other traditional forms, such as preferred stock.[7] The bondholder or banker is typically entitled both to a fixed rate of return on his or her loan and to repayment of the original amount invested; he or she may sue the enterprise if these

---

[4]The theory that each business enterprise is the product of different contractual relationships among investors was first advanced in the English-speaking world by the economist Ronald Coase. *See* R.H. Coase, *The Nature of the Firm*, 4 Economica 386 (1937).

[5]The term "lease" is used in a broad sense that would include a rental agreement or a licensing agreement as well as finance leases and operating leases.

[6]For example, the typical partner or common stockholder has no right to receive either a fixed rate of partnership distributions or dividends, or a return from the partnership or company of his or her equity contribution. The common stockholder does, however, have other rights: he or she is entitled to what is left of the partnership or company property after other investors have been paid what they are legally entitled to. The partner or stockholder has some direct say in how the company is managed, thereby providing a mechanism for increasing the likelihood of higher rates of return. Limited partners do not participate in the day-to-day running of the partnership, but their liability, as with stockholders in companies, is limited to the amount of their investment. *See* Larry E. Ribstein, *An Applied Theory of Limited Partnership*, 37 Emory L.J. 835 (1988).

[7]Preferred stockholders are paid dividends before other types of equity investors, but those dividends are limited by a cap. *See generally* Richard A. Brealey & Stewart C. Meyers, Principles of Corporate Finance 303–05 (3d ed. 1988).

amounts are not paid.[8] A typical creditor generally has no direct say in managing the enterprise.[9] However, a creditor may also experience increases or decreases in the value of his or her investment depending on changes in the creditworthiness of the enterprise, as well as on changes in interest rates or in rates of inflation.[10]

A lessor is in a legal position similar but superior to that of a creditor whose note is secured by assets. He or she may also see the value of the investment vary on the basis of the value of the security or leased good, as well as the general creditworthiness of the enterprise.[11] A lease can shift the risk of loss from the owner to the person who leases the asset, while the owner may retain the opportunity of increase in value.

Different legitimate market-based reasons exist for packaging investments in different economic forms.[12] Risk is among the most important. As

---

[8]As will be discussed at greater length *infra*, there may be no clear dividing line between "equity" and "debt." *See generally* Franklin Allen, *The Changing Nature of Debt and Equity: A Financial Perspective, in* Are the Distinctions Between Debt and Equity Disappearing? at 12 (Richard W. Kopcke & Eric S. Rosengrew, eds. 1989), and Charles P. Normandin, *The Changing Nature of Debt and Equity: A Legal Perspective, in id.* at 49. However, statues, regulations, and courts have often tried. In the United States, the Court of Appeals in Gilbert v. Commissioner, 248 F.2d 399, 402 (2d Cir. 1957) defined debt as "an unqualified obligation to pay a sum certain at a reasonably close fixed maturity date along with a fixed percentage in interest payable regardless of the debtor's income or the lack thereof." *See also* David Plumb, *The Federal Income Tax Significance of Corporate Debt: A Critical Analysis and a Proposal,* 26 Tax L. Rev. 369, 404 (1971). In the United Kingdom, the Court of Appeal in Lomax v. Peter Dixon & Co., Ltd. [1943] 2 All ER 255, 259–62, noted that each case of whether a payment constitutes interest must be "decided on the facts," and that the relevant factors in making such a determination would be the contract, the term of the loan, the stipulated rate of interest, and the nature of the capital risk. *See also* Butterworths U.K. Tax Guide 1990–91, at 338–90 (John Tiley 9th ed. 1990) [hereinafter Butterworths Guide]. The doctrines developed in case law go beyond "thin capitalization," where equity investors also contribute debt capital.

[9]However, most substantial creditors may, through the terms and conditions of the loan agreement, exercise considerable control over certain aspects of management.

[10]The simple unsecured creditor is only one type of traditional debt investor. There are also secured creditors, who typically have a better chance of getting paid than do unsecured creditors. A secured creditor may also experience increases or decreases in the value of his or her investment depending upon changes in the value of the creditor's security interest. The change in value will be more acute for nonrecourse creditors. A lower debt-to-equity ratio means that there is a greater amount of funds in the business (from the equity capital) to serve as a "cushion" for payment of fixed obligations, which reduces the likelihood of default on the obligations. Other factors affecting the level of risk include the history of payment of the interest and the use of the advanced funds. *See* David V. Ceryak, *Note: Using Risk Analysis to Classify Junk Bonds as Equity for Federal Income Tax Purposes,* 66 Ind. L.J. 273, 283–84 (1990).

[11]Rent compensates the lessor for any accruing capital loss plus the opportunity cost of the asset. *See* George V. Mundstock, *Taxation of Business Rent,* 11 Va. Tax. Rev. 683, 684–85 (1993); George V. Mundstock, *The Mistaxation of Rent: Eliminating the Lease/Loan Distinction,* 53 Tax Notes 353, 353–54 (1991).

[12]*See* Michael C. Jensen & William H. Meckling, *Theory of the Firm: Managerial Behavior, Agency Costs and Ownership Structure,* 3 J. Fin. Econ. 305, 310–11 (1976).

risk increases, investors will demand compensation for assuming that risk. Unsecured loans are riskier than secured loans or leases; partnership interests and common stock may have the greatest risk of all, but also the greatest opportunity for gain.

Changes in the value of the interest of any particular investor should be equal to the investor's share of the change in the total value of the enterprise. In other words, the value of an investor's interest will equal the total change in value of the enterprise minus everyone else's share. However, to make this calculation, one must first determine the income or loss of the enterprise. Forms of investment that have been traditionally referred to as "debt" or "leases" periodically pay or accrue interest, rent, or royalties to the investor. Therefore, the change in the value of the taxpayer's investment in the enterprise can be determined largely from the amount of interest, rent, or royalties that has been paid or accrued to him or her. Debt that is accrued over time, but that is not currently payable, can be recalculated so that the "reinvested" portion of the unpaid interest is included.[13] However, as noted above, the value of the debt or lease investment may not be completely reflected in the stated interest or rent. Even in simple debt relationships, changes in the creditworthiness of the enterprise, or changes in interest rates, will affect the value of the underlying indebtedness.[14]

The legal structures of investments have become increasingly varied and complex and have mixed many of the traditional attributes of equity, debt, and lease.[15] Examples include debt with call options or contingent interest, shared appreciation mortgages, and notional principal contracts. Instruments that allocate risk in different ways are constantly being created.[16] In the more ad-

---

[13]For example, in the United States, original issue discount is accrued over the lifetime of the debt and is compounded semiannually. See USA IRC § 1272(a). See generally David C. Garlock, A Practical Guide to the Original Issue Discount Regulations (1993). A similar regime exists in the United Kingdom. See GBR ICTA § 57, sched. 4; Butterworths Guide, supra note 8, at 397–405. Similar treatment is afforded in Australia; see AUS ITAA Div. 16E. See also Graeme S. Cooper, Tax Accounting for Deductions, 5 Aust. Tax F. 23 (1988).

[14]The difference between pure interest income and gain or loss from interest rate changes is relatively easy to determine. However, unless the debt is an instrument publicly quoted on an exchange, changes in default risk are difficult to determine. See generally David J. Shakow, Taxation Without Realization: A Proposal for Accrual Taxation, 134 U. Pa. L. Rev. 1111, 1164 (1986).

[15]A high-yield high-risk "bond," such as a deeply discounted debt instrument, may more closely resemble traditional equity than a low-yield redeemable cumulative preference share. See generally Jeremy I. Bulow et al., Distinguishing Debt from Equity in the Junk Bond Era, in Debt, Taxes and Corporate Restructuring 135 (John B. Shoven & Joel Waldfogel, eds. 1990). In economic terms, these are all investments, and returns on investments, with different allocations of risk of gain or loss. While the economic realities of investments can be described with some accuracy, it is often difficult to put these realities into clear legal categories.

[16]See the discussion of these forms of investment, and the relationship to risk allocation, in Daniel N. Shaviro, Risk and Accrual: The Tax Treatment of Nonrecourse Debt, 44 Tax L. Rev. 401, 404, 429–31 (1989), and Alvin C. Warren, Jr., Commentary: Financial Contract Innovation and Income Tax Policy, 107 Harv. L. Rev. 460, 483–89 (1993).

vanced economies, these instruments have a long history. However, even in developing markets, there has been a proliferation of forms of financial instruments representing different types of investments in for-profit enterprise. The internationalization of finance and financial advice has resulted in the prompt spreading of those diverse investment forms throughout the world, or at least to those jurisdictions whose legal structure can accommodate them. As investments become more complicated, the difference between the stated "current yield" and the actual net income of the investor can become quite great.[17]

The various types of equity investors are entitled to the income of the enterprise minus the amounts paid or accrued to creditors and lessors. Because of the occasionally bewildering forms of equity participation, exactly how this income is to be divided may be completely clear only to the lawyers who draft the forms of participation. Nevertheless, the earnings of the equity participants are the principal object of the taxation of enterprises.

II. Enterprise Income Taxation as a Withholding Tax on Investors

In principle, it would be possible to tax all income of a business enterprise directly to its equity investors by treating all enterprises as "flow-through" entities and allocating income to investors on a yearly basis.[18] However, treating the enterprise as a separate taxable entity has a number of advantages over flow-through treatment. One problem with flow-through treatment is that it may be difficult to allocate earnings among a large number of increasingly bewildering types of equity holdings. Another is that, as the number of equity investors increases, allocation becomes more difficult.[19] As a result, no country has implemented such an approach.

Some or all of the enterprise earnings may be paid out to the equity investors, often at the option of enterprise managers or the investors themselves.[20]

---

[17]Leif Mutén refers to it as "the floating borderline between capital gain and current yield, which is barely discernable . . . [in] sophisticated financial instruments." Leif Mutén, *International Experience of How Taxes Influence the Movement of Private Capital*, 8 Tax Notes Int'l 743 (1992). However, with regard to fixed-interest debt instruments with a final redemption date, the variation is limited to downside risk over the life of the instrument. Equity, in the form of either securities or direct ownership, constitutes a residual claim to the assets themselves and may fluctuate freely in value; there is no inherent limit on fluctuations. Debt, however, constitutes a finite stream of payments already specified in nominal terms. Debt can decline to zero, but its value cannot exceed the undiscounted sum of nominal payments. With debt, while market value may deviate, the sum of deviations over time will be zero. See Theodore S. Sims, *Long-Term Debt, the Term Structure of Interest and the Case for Accrual Taxation*, 47 Tax L. Rev. 313, 358–59 (1992).

[18]See infra sec. V(B)(6); ch. 21.

[19]These arguments, as well as others, are summarized in U.S. Treasury Report, *supra* note 3, at 27–35.

[20]In the case of preferred stock, payment typically is not optional.

Taxing such distributions does not pose any great difficulty; they can simply be added to the income tax base of the shareholder.[21] A problem arises with the earnings retained by the enterprise. Most of the value of retained earnings is expressed primarily as increases in the value of the interests of those equity investors who have the legal right to the earnings retained by the enterprise.[22] It would, in theory at least, be possible to tax the equity investor on the change in the value of the equity participation.[23] The tax base of such a system would include not only the amount of retained taxable earnings of the enterprise, but total economic income as well, including earnings not typically included in the income tax base, such as unrealized gains in the value of assets.[24] It would also include changes in the value of the equity interest that are not related to the economic income of the enterprise, for example, a systemic shift in stock market prices if the interest is a traded share.[25] Such a change in value would have to be assessed as part of the tax base annually; if not, the taxpayer would benefit from the time value of money on the deferred taxes.[26]

A number of suggestions have been made in favor of such accrual taxation of gains (and losses) on ownership interests in business enterprises. Yet, while such systems might be practicable for equity interests that are regularly traded with enough liquidity to determine a price, they would be difficult indeed for other interests.[27] For other equity interests, it might be possible to

---

[21]See supra ch. 16.

[22]Of course, some of the value can be realized by other investors. An enterprise that retains earnings is likely to be more creditworthy, and the value of its bonds would therefore be likely to increase.

[23]Changes in the value of debt investments could also be taxed on an accrual basis. See Sims, supra note 17, at 336, 338, 356–57. However, valuation problems could be insurmountable, as they may be with equity interests.

[24]This would also include any special tax benefits provided the enterprise, such as the excess of tax depreciation over economic depreciation. See U.S. Treasury Report, supra note 3, at 82, and The American Law Institute, Federal Income Tax Project, Integration of the Individual and Corporate Income Taxes: Reporter's Study of Corporate Tax Integration (Alvin C. Warren, Jr., Reporter: 1993) [hereinafter ALI Integration Report], at 129–32.

[25]See the discussion of "speculative" gains in Michael L. Schler, Taxing Corporate Income Once (Or Hopefully Not at All): A Practitioner's Comparison of the Treasury and ALI Models, 47 Tax L. Rev. 509, 525 (1992).

[26]See Henry Simons, Personal Income Taxation 100 (1938).

[27]Such a system is outlined in David Slawson, Taxing as Ordinary Income the Appreciation of Publicly Held Stock, 76 Yale L.J. 623 (1967). However, there could be strategic selling of traded securities as a way of driving down the price on the valuation date. This could be countered by taking an average price over a limited time period. See also Note: Realizing Appreciation Without Sale: Accrual Taxation of Capital Gains on Marketable Securities, 34 Stan. L. Rev. 857, 871–76 (1982); Victor Thuronyi, The Taxation of Corporate Income—A Proposal for Reform, 2 Am. J. Tax Pol'y 109 (1983). Such proposals have also been made for debt interests. As noted above, in many instances it is difficult to determine whether a particular interest is "equity" or "debt"; it can also be difficult to divide instruments with characteristics of both into their equity and debt parts. See the general discussion of such instruments and how they might be taxed in Warren, supra note 16, at 474–82.

make periodic valuations and to adjust them for errors once the interest is actually traded, or whenever a fair market value can be ascertained with certainty.[28] However, a system of periodic valuation would ignore the possibility that the value of the interest can shift, perhaps even wildly, during the holding period.[29] This can create difficult problems for tax administration.[30]

Even if one could accurately determine changes in the value of equity interests on an annual basis, including these changes in the tax base would still be problematic. First, and perhaps most important, is the problem of collection. Taxes on capital gains are among the more difficult to enforce and collect. Except where there is direct reporting to the tax administration from exchanges or from broker-dealers, each individual taxpayer must voluntarily disclose the amount of gain or loss. The taxpayer must then remit the correct amount of tax. Even in the United States, which has a relatively effective tax administration, taxpayer compliance in reporting capital gains on traded securities and remitting the required tax is low relative to other areas. The most likely reasons are the lack of withholding for such tax and the absence of accurate, easily usable information reporting.[31] And, because there may be a plethora of equity investors, the problem of administration is magnified. Obviously, the less sophisticated the tax administration, or the less likely taxpayers are to report income and pay tax voluntarily, the worse this problem becomes.

A second problem would result from any difference in tax treatment between ownership interests in business enterprise and business income earned directly or through flow-through entities. As noted earlier, accrual taxation of ownership interests would include not only what is commonly accounted for as taxable income, but also accrual taxation of unrealized gains in the value of

---

[28]The correction would have to include the time value of money. This could be done by adjusting the amount of tax due by imputing an interest rate during the time that the taxpayer held the asset. *See* Mary L. Fellows, *A Comprehensive Attack on Tax Deferral*, 88 Mich. L. Rev. 727, 728–31, 733 (1990). *Cf.* USA IRC §§ 1291–1297 (imputed interest rate to account for the benefit of tax deferral).

[29]The more volatile the value of the asset, the more frequently it must be assessed if over- or undertaxation is to be avoided. Because risky assets do not reveal their "value path," there are many possible paths between the starting and ending value and, for each possible path, there is a different continuous tax. Jeff Strnad, *Periodicity and Accretion Taxation: Norms and Implications*, 99 Yale L. J. 1817, 1822, 1865–79 (1990). *See also* Fellows, *supra* note 28, at 744.

[30]*But see* Joseph Bankman & Thomas Griffith, *Is the Debate Between an Income Tax and a Consumption Tax a Debate About Risk? Does It Matter?* 47 Tax L. Rev. 377 (1992), who argue that real value paths might be constructable using computers if the data are available.

[31]*See* Steven Klepper & David Nagin, *The Role of Tax Practitioners in Tax Compliance*, 22 Pol'y Sciences 167 (1989); G.A. Feffer et al., *Proposals to Deter and Detect the Underground Cash Economy*, in Income Tax Compliance: A Report of the ABA Section on Taxation, Invitational Conference on Income Tax Compliance (P. Sawicki, ed. 1983); Steven Klepper et al., *Expert Intermediaries and Legal Compliance: The Case of Tax Preparers*, 34 J.L. & Econ. 205 (1991).

assets held by the enterprise.[32] While proposals have also been made for accrual taxation of all assets used in the course of business,[33] no tax jurisdiction has adopted the rule. If the effective tax rate on the income of business enterprise were substantially different depending on the form of the enterprise (flow-through or non-flow-through), there would be a tax-induced preference to operate in the form that produced the lower effective tax rate. For equity, efficiency, and administrative reasons, such tax incentives should usually be avoided.

The problems inherent in taxing equity interests on an accrual basis can be avoided by levying a tax on the income of the business enterprise as a surrogate for the tax that equity participants would pay if all enterprise income were distributed. In that way, the enterprise would not be able to defer tax simply by not paying dividends. If the enterprise tax were levied at the same effective rate as the tax paid on dividend income by the owners of the enterprise, there would be no deferral benefits. Because most direct equity investors are likely to be taxed either at the top marginal personal rate or at a final schedular rate, business enterprises should also be taxed at this top or schedular rate.[34] A single-rate tax on business income would obviate the need to distinguish among different types of equity holders and, at least initially, to allocate income among such holders.

Income already taxed at the enterprise level may eventually be distributed to physical persons. If the tax system elects to levy a schedular, final tax on income from capital, the tax paid at the enterprise level can serve as that final tax on any distributions. If, instead, such income is taxed at progressive marginal rates, the tax paid at the enterprise level can serve as a withholding tax, for which a credit can be given the investor and for which a refund can be paid if necessary.[35]

---

[32]The Meade Committee in the United Kingdom defined a true profit tax base as "the real current profits of the corporation, whether these be distributed or undistributed. It involves the deduction from gross profits of net interest on debt, an allowance for true economic depreciation . . . a calculation of real accrued capital gains made by the company on its assets [plus inflation adjustment]." Institute for Fiscal Studies, The Structure and Reform of Direct Taxation 229 (1978) (Report of the Meade Committee) [hereinafter Meade Committee Report].

[33]David J. Shakow argues that all business assets should be subject to accrual taxation. David J. Shakow, Taxation Without Realization: A Proposal for Accrual Taxation, 134 U. Pa. L. Rev. 1111, 1119–23 (1986). See also Strnad, supra note 29, at 1903–04, and Fellows, supra note 28, at 741–42.

[34]A detailed discussion on rate relationships can be found in Alvin C. Warren, The Relation and Integration of Individual and Corporate Income Taxes, 94 Harv. L. Rev. 717 (1981). See also 4 Report of the Royal Commission on Taxation [Canada] 51–57 (1966).

[35]The conclusion that a separate company tax should serve as a withholding tax on the earnings of equity investors has recently been advanced in the Ruding Committee Report of the European Union (EU) and in the American Law Institute's Federal Income Tax Project. Commission of the European Communities, Report of the Committee of Independent Experts on Company Taxation [Onno Ruding, Chairman] 31–32 (1992) [hereinafter Ruding Committee Report]; ALI Integration Report, supra note 24. However, the U.S. Treasury recently advanced the theory that a final, separate company tax, without deductions for interest, could serve as a part of a schedular tax on income from capital. See generally U.S. Treasury Report, supra note 3; Nicholas Brady, Letter to Congress, in Department of the Treasury, Treasury Integration Recommendation 2 (1992) [hereinafter U.S. Treasury Recommendation].

Using a separate enterprise tax as either a final schedular tax or a with-holding tax has proved to be an effective way of collecting tax on business in-come. Such a tax is typically levied as a separate legal liability on the enterprise. Because there are fewer enterprises than there are investors, and because they are more easily identifiable, having an enterprise as the principal taxpayer makes administration much easier than having only the investors as legal taxpayers. It also makes it much easier for the tax administration to dis-tribute or collect adjustments resulting from audit.[36]

A number of technical reasons also favor a separate business enterprise tax over flow-through treatment. The first is that losses suffered at the enter-prise level may be prevented from flowing through to equity investors and will then not be set off against other, taxable income.[37] Second, transactions that might not typically be viewed as giving rise to taxable income in the case of flow-through entities can more readily be deemed to do so under a separate en-terprise tax. The most important of these is that the entity may make distribu-tions to its investors of economic income that was not taxed at the enterprise level. For example, income that benefits from tax incentives, or from the in-exact science of tax bookkeeping (such as unintended acceleration of depreci-ation or income from unrealized capital gains), would not normally be taxed currently. However, under a separate system of business enterprise taxation, if such income were distributed as a dividend it might then be subject to tax.[38]

However, treating a business enterprise as a separate taxable entity, even if the tax raised is then treated as a prepayment or withholding of tax on in-come eventually received by the equity investor, can create a number of seri-ous administrative problems. These problems vary depending on (1) whether investors who are physical persons are to be taxed at graduated rates on a glo-bal income basis or at a final schedular rate, and (2) how close a connection is made between the tax on the business enterprise and the tax due at the level of both the equity investor and the nonequity investor. The elaboration of these problems, and how they might be dealt with in an income tax law, con-stitutes the principal subject of this chapter.

Most jurisdictions employ a system of flow-through taxation for certain types of business enterprise and separate taxation for others.[39] The choice of which business enterprises to subject to business entity tax and which to tax on a flow-though basis depends on a number of considerations. The greater the difference in outcome between the separate entity tax and flow-through treat-ment, the greater the incentive for taxpayers to engage in tax planning by se-

---

[36]See George K. Yin, *Corporate Tax Integration and the Search for the Pragmatic Ideal*, 47 Tax L. Rev. 431, 431–33 (1992).

[37]See id.

[38]See infra sec. V(B)(1).

[39]See infra ch. 21. Guidelines as to which entities are subject to company tax are discussed infra sec. VII.

lecting the more favorable form.[40] Such tax planning may make tax administration more difficult and may affect the economy adversely if more efficient legal forms of business enterprise are eschewed in favor of those that are less efficient, but tax preferred. While inefficiencies may result from requiring small partnerships to be treated as separate taxpayers, as a general matter, making the net of inclusion for separate business enterprise tax as wide as possible will, in most instances, ease tax administration. For example, including all legal persons and entities engaged in business or profit-making activities (depending on how such organizations are defined under the applicable law), unless they have a very small number of owners, may be preferable to providing flow-through treatment for all partnerships.

III. Separate Taxation of Business Enterprises and of Distributions to Investors

While theory suggests that, in general, an enterprise income tax should be levied only as a withholding tax or a final schedular tax for business income of enterprises, a number of major income tax systems continue to apply the "classical" system of separate taxes on the income of certain business enterprises, resulting in double taxation of that income.[41] A number of arguments have been advanced in favor of the classical system.

A. Tax on Economic Rents

Some economists have supported the imposition of a separate business enterprise tax in order to capture "economic rents," or pure profits, which an investor earns in excess of the "cost of money"—that is, the given risk-free rate

---

[40]For example, in the United States, where failure to achieve flow-through taxation means not only that losses do not flow through to equity holders, but also that business earnings are subject to a second level of taxation on distribution, there has been a particularly strong incentive for enterprises to organize so as to avoid such double taxation. *See* Francis J. Worth & Kenneth L. Harris, *The Emerging Use of the Limited Liability Company*, 70 Taxes 377 (1992).

[41]For example, the United States has always had a completely separate system and continues to have one despite a number of recommendations by the U.S. Treasury Department to the contrary. *See, e.g.*, Blueprints, *supra* note 3 (arguing for full integration between corporate and personal income taxation); Treasury I, *supra* note 3, at 117–20 (arguing for partial integration); U.S. Treasury Report, *supra* note 3 (arguing for full integration). Although the Japanese moved from a system of integration to a fully separate system in 1990, the general movement has been in the opposite direction—from a separate system to a fully integrated one. For example, France integrated its system in 1965, the United Kingdom in 1973, Germany in 1976, Australia in 1987, and New Zealand a year later. *See* K.C. Messere, Tax Policy in OECD Countries: Choices and Conflicts 346 (1993). Reports from both the OECD and the EU have, although sometimes obliquely, supported full integration over separate income taxation; Meade Committee Report, *supra* note 32; OECD, Taxing Profits in a Global Economy: Domestic and International Issues 25–30 (1991) [hereinafter OECD Report]; Ruding Committee Report, *supra* note 35, at 31–34.

of return to capital.[42] In theory, economic rents can be taxed without adversely affecting investment because they represent a return in excess of that otherwise required to make the investment.[43]

However, taxing both enterprise income and enterprise distributions would not necessarily tax economic rents. Instead, a system of double taxation would more likely result in inaccurate taxation of the amount paid to equity investors. With equity investments, the risk of low dividends or capital losses will largely be offset by the possibility of dividends or capital gains that are higher than the risk-free cost of money. Therefore, over time, earnings will include compensation for that risk. In other words, part of the excess of the return to equity investment over the risk-free average cost of capital is likely to be not economic rents, but risk premium. Taxing this risk premium as economic rent could cause substantial distortions.[44] Methods have been developed to tax such rents; however, these methods appear seriously flawed.[45]

---

[42]Another way of putting it is that economic rents are the part of a return on an investment that exceeds the amount needed to induce the investment in the first place. A patent, for example, can produce economic rents.

[43]For example, if the cost of money is 8 percent, any amount in excess of 8 percent can be taxed away before the investor will select another investment, which, by definition, pays only 8 percent. *See* Ruding Committee Report, *supra* note 35, at 31–32; OECD Report, *supra* note 41, at 21–23 (1991). *See also* Richard Musgrave, The Theory of Public Finance 262–67 (1959); Carl Shoup, Public Finance 266–69 (1969).

[44]For example, if the risk-free cost of capital is 5 percent, then an investor will be willing to put her or his money into a risky investment if the chances are, on average, that she or he will receive 5 percent. Assume that a person at a 40 percent marginal tax rate invests $100 in a company and that income in excess of the cost of capital is taxed away as economic rents. If, in year 1, the company's return on equity were 10 percent, and if it then distributed all of its earnings, the company would pay tax of 5, and the stockholder would pay tax of 2 (40 percent × 5), for a total tax of 7. However, assume that the extra 5 percent earned in year 1 did not constitute economic rents, but a risk premium for investing in equity. The next year the investor would be as likely to earn nothing as she was to earn 10 percent the year before. Therefore, assume that the company had no earnings in year 2. Neither company nor investor would owe any tax. That would mean that, over a two-year period, the investor would have paid tax at a rate of 70 percent. This approach would clearly result in a bias away from risky investments.

[45]One is to permit enterprises to deduct the full cost of all capital investments. The effect of such a deduction would be to eliminate company tax on earnings equal to the risk-free cost of money. In other words, only returns on capital in excess of the cost of money, represented by the present value of a full deduction for capital investment, would be subject to tax. Such a tax on rents would not look like a withholding tax on enterprise income. However, it could be added as a separate tax to a withholding tax on enterprise income. *See* Meade Committee Report *supra* note 32, at 232–33. However, there are a number of caveats: (1) tax rates must remain the same, (2) the tax savings from the expensed asset must be invested at the same rate of return, (3) there must be no preexisting assets on which income can be exempted, (4) all expensed assets must be subject to taxation on disinvestment, (5) the taxpayer must benefit fully from a current deduction, and (6) the investor must be able to borrow any needed funds at a fixed rate of interest. Michael Graetz, *Implementing a Progressive Consumption Tax*, 92 Harv. L. Rev. 1575, 1597–605 (1979).

B. Subsidy Recapture

Some commentators have tried to justify a separate enterprise tax as a surrogate levy for the cost of government goods and services provided to those enterprises.[46] The argument is that all investors operate in an environment deeply affected by free government benefits and that the level of government spending may increase the profitability of economic activity. This additional charge would, it is reasoned, ensure that the government does not distort the market allocation of resources.

It is difficult to see how the cost of government services provided to enterprises can be realistically related to additional income that is attributable to the equity holders of those enterprises. The argument seems to be that the total benefits provided free to the enterprise would equal the total enterprise income tax collected and that a particular enterprise's share of the benefits would equal its share of the tax. This relationship seems highly implausible. Specially designed excise taxes (or, alternatively, charges for the services) would be a more efficient way of compensating for such benefits.

C. Increased Vertical Equity

Some have argued that, because enterprises tend to be owned by the wealthy, enterprise taxes should constitute a separate tax so that the vertical equity or fairness of the overall tax system can thereby be increased. A higher tax on all forms of income from capital would increase overall progressivity. Presumably, the most effective way of increasing the vertical equity of an income tax system is to increase its progressivity on all forms of income. However, under double taxation, only equity investments are subject to a separate tax. Removing existing tax benefits that favor the wealthy or imposing a more progressive income tax rate structure or, perhaps, a wealth tax would be more likely to raise the overall progressivity of the tax system than would taxing the income from equity capital twice.

Even if such a redesigned enterprise tax on rents were added to a withholding tax on income, there could still be an adverse effect on the economy. For innovation to occur, a higher rate of return from innovative ideas may be necessary. This is not just compensation for risk; it is also compensation for the labor that goes into innovation, but for which there has been no other compensation. This theory holds only if the innovators (or those who select them) have an equity participation in their product, something that anecdotal evidence suggests is often the case. The theory can be extended to portfolio equity investors. They are able to pick "winners" only because they apply their own labor to pick them. If these profits were taxed as rents, a decrease in innovation, and the money to finance it, would result.

[46]This argument has been raised directly with the authors by a number of officials in countries in Eastern Europe and Asia.

D. Retention of Existing Double Taxation

Some have argued that, while a separate enterprise tax regime is not preferable in theory, if one is established it should be retained, at least for existing equity.[47] There are two principle arguments: first, eliminating double taxation would reduce revenues,[48] and second, elimination could result in a windfall to current equity holders because the effect of double taxation would already have been capitalized by a reduction in the price of equity.[49] Equity investors will have demanded that other investors compensate them for the double tax burden they bear, so that the after-tax rate of return on equity would equal the after-tax rate of return on other investment forms. If the separate enterprise tax were removed, equity investors would receive a windfall as the value of equity increased.

While these arguments have merit, the effort to preserve a separate tax on old equity is unlikely to be worth avoiding the inequity of potential windfall benefits. First, potential losses in revenue can be made up with higher rates, or by eliminating investment incentives and other tax expenditures; jurisdictions that have recently eliminated double taxation have relied primarily on the latter technique.[50] Second, investors take many forms of risk: one is that the tax system will change in a manner that affects them. If total revenues from capital income do not decrease, then eliminating double taxation will shift wealth from debt investors to equity investors, a risk that both forms of investors would probably have anticipated and for which some discounting may already have occurred. In addition, some have suggested that the burden of the separate enterprise tax is often substantially reduced through tax planning and that the amount of windfall shifting would therefore be small.

---

[47]American Law Institute, Federal Income Tax Project, Reporter's Study Draft—Subchapter C (Proposals on Corporate Acquisitions and Dispositions) 327 (1989).

[48]This is probably one of the most important arguments against eliminating double taxation in industrial countries such as the United States as well as in developing countries. See, e.g., U.S. Treasury Report, supra note 3, at 33. In Ghana, until 1975, the Income Tax Law provided for complete integration of company and personal income taxes. An official tax commission stated in 1977 that it was unable to establish the rationale for adopting the classical system in 1975. However, once enacted, the classical system was difficult to repeal for revenue reasons. See Seth E. Terkper, Ghana, Trends in Tax Reform (1985–93), 8 Tax Notes Int'l 1267 (May 9, 1994). See also Meade Committee Report, supra note 32, at 227–29.

[49]Id. See also American Law Institute, Federal Income Tax Project, Reporter's Study Draft—Subchapter C (Supplemental Study) (1989); Report of the Royal Commission on Taxation to the Federal Government of Canada (Kenneth Le M. Carter, Chairman), Dec. 1966 [hereinafter Carter Commission Report], ch. 19.

[50]See Dale W. Jorgenson, Tax Reform and the Cost of Capital: An International Comparison, 6 Tax Notes Int'l 981 (1993); David R. Tillinghast, Corporate-Shareholder Integration as an Obstacle to the International Flow of Equity Capital, 5 Tax Notes Int'l 509, 510 (1992).

IV. Problems with Retaining Double Taxation of Enterprise Income

A. Aggravation of Tax Planning

A system of double taxation of equity income creates incentives to avoid double taxation through tax planning, and may involve opportunities to avoid tax altogether. Among the techniques are the following:

(1) Choosing business forms that are not subject to double taxation, where feasible. For example, commercial laws may allow taxpayers to set up entities that will be treated as transparent for tax purposes—partnerships or trusts might be available options—and that have enough of the properties investors want, particularly limited liability and free transferability of interests.

(2) Raising capital through legal forms that allow deduction of payments to investors, such as rental payments and interest. As was mentioned above, modern financial instruments give taxpayers opportunities to structure their investment in a form that is classified as debt, so that the return on the investment reduces the corporate tax base, but that has enough of the desired attributes of equity, particularly the opportunity to share in the potential gains from corporate success.

(3) Distributing earnings to equity investors through techniques that do not give rise to the second tax.[51] Corporate law may allow corporations to return amounts to investors through a variety of devices, including the redemption or purchase of stock, and partial reductions of capital. These amounts will be a desirable substitute for a distribution of a similar amount that is labeled a dividend.

(4) Making deductible payments to investors (and their associates) in their capacity as directors or employees. Small businesses in particular will be able to reduce the corporate tax base by paying salaries to owner-managers and to family members, thus achieving two benefits—a reduction in the enterprise tax base and the splitting of income within the family.[52]

(5) Retaining, rather than distributing, profits. The event that triggers imposition of the personal income tax will usually be the payment of a dividend or the sale of shares. Insofar as it is possible for the corporation's managers to delay triggering this event by retaining profits, the shareholder tax can be delayed and thus reduced.

---

[51]See ALI Integration Report, *supra* note 24, at 21; George R. Zodrow, *On the "Traditional" and "New" Views of Dividend Taxation*, 44 Nat'l Tax J. 497, 501 (1991).

[52]See *supra* ch. 14, secs. IX, X.

Such incentives can lead to inefficiencies in the operation of enterprises. How significant these inefficiencies prove to be depends upon the circumstances—a more benign view of these devices regards them as self-help remedies employed by investors to alleviate the problem of double taxation informally.

These issues are symptomatic of the problems that arise whenever one legally defined form of investment is taxed at a higher rate—taxpayers will usually try to recharacterize that investment as a form taxed at a lower rate. This legal recharacterization is time consuming, expensive for the tax administration to prevent, and frequently a losing battle. These problems do not necessarily go away once taxation of equity income is limited to a single level of tax. As long as the final, effective rates of tax on different types of income from business enterprise are different, these problems will exist. While eliminating the second level of tax generally reduces the incentive to recharacterize interests to a preferred type, as long as final effective tax rates differ, the incentives will remain, albeit in a less virulent form.

That is to say, even if a system is formally designed to tax business enterprise income once, the way in which the system is designed may result in income being taxed differently depending on whether capital is in the legal form of equity or debt or lease, or on whether earnings are distributed to equity investors other than through normal distributions.

B. Profit Retention

More generally, two concerns have been expressed about the overall economic impact of the enterprise tax on economic activity. One is that it tempts enterprise managers to retain rather than distribute profits. The other is that it encourages the financing of investment through debt rather than equity.

The effect of the enterprise tax on required rates of return and, by inference, on the cost of capital can be illustrated in the following example. Assume an enterprise tax rate of 30 percent and a personal income tax rate of 40 percent. Assume also that investors have enough other investment opportunities with the same risk profile and that the corporation needs to provide investors with an after-tax return of 6 percent to induce them to part with their savings. In these circumstances, the investment would need to offer a pretax return of 8.5 percent [6/(1 − 0.30)] if it could be financed out of retained earnings and the enterprise did not need to distribute profits, 10 percent [6/(1 − 0.40)] if the investment were to be financed through debt, and more than 14.3 percent [6/(1 − 0.3)(1 − 0.4)] if the enterprise needed to finance the investment with new equity and investors expected to receive dividends.

Not surprisingly, therefore, commentators have tried to assess the consequences of the incentive to retain profits. Insofar as retained earnings are used to finance enterprise expansion, they serve as a substitute for raising that capital through formal borrowing, leasing, or further equity issues. These substitutes are likely to be conducted under the scrutiny of the market—bankers will examine the enterprise's solvency and cash flow before making further loans, underwriters and investment houses will examine the prospectus for a further share or bond issue, and so on. This scrutiny is not applied when the managers of the enterprise can choose how much profit to retain. The fear is that the tax system will encourage managers of existing mature companies to retain funds unnecessarily and invest in projects that are less than optimal in order to use the excess funds. These retained earnings should instead be liberated for the use of fast-growing innovative enterprises.[53] Some argue, however, that retained earnings are a source of additional private savings within an economy.

There is no unequivocal evidence that these outcomes have occurred systematically and that, where they do occur, it is the tax system rather than independent corporate financial policy that is the motivating cause. There are competing visions of the economic effects of these incentives. According to the so-called traditional view, the increased tax cost associated with dividend payouts is likely to be significant, and corporations will therefore tend to rely on retained earnings. When retained earnings prove to be inadequate, and enterprises have to issue further equity, they will have to raise their payout ratios to meet the added tax costs, increasing their cost of capital. But an important qualification to this prognosis is the recognition that systemic factors may prevent excess profit retention from becoming a problem—nonfiscal considerations may outweigh the fiscal advantages. The market may not allow shareholder distributions to be deferred indefinitely, and shareholders may insist on receiving some return as an indication of the ongoing soundness of the enterprise.[54]

An alternate vision, the so-called new view of enterprise taxation, argues that because the tax disadvantages of dividend payouts are well known, enterprises will indeed finance their activities largely through retained earnings. Paradoxically, however, the higher taxation of dividends will be of little consequence.[55] According to this theory, shareholders might save the personal income tax on the dividends they would otherwise have received, but, adopting a longer-term view, they have simply converted the immediate tax on distributions into a deferred capital gains tax liability that will be triggered on the disposal of their investment. If this is so, buyers of the security will discount it to reflect the deferred liability, and so the additional tax is capitalized into the price of the share. The additional tax is a real cost that the original holder of

---

[53]*See generally* OECD Report, *supra* note 41, at 25; Sijbren Cnossen, *Corporation Tax in OECD Countries*, in Company Tax Systems 73–77 (John G. Head & Richard E. Krever eds., 1997).

[54]*See generally* Richard A. Brealey & Stewart C. Meyers, Principles of Corporate Finance, ch. 16 (4th ed. 1991); Frank H. Easterbrook, *Two Agency-Cost Explanations of Corporate Dividends*, 74 Am. Econ. Rev. 650 (1984); Merton H. Miller & Myron C. Scholes, *Dividends and Taxes*, 6 J. Fin. Econ. 333 (1978).

[55]James Poterba & Lawrence Summers, *The Economic Effects of Dividend Taxation*, in E. Altman & M. Subrahmanyan (eds.), Recent Developments in Corporate Finance (1985); Zodrow, *supra* note 51; Leif Mutén, Bolagsbeskattning och kapitalkostnader (1968) (The Corporate Income Tax and the Cost of Capital).

the share will bear regardless of whether the distribution is paid. The buyer of the share recoups the additional tax because he or she has been able to buy the share at a reduced price, reflecting the implicit tax liability. If this new view is correct, the additional tax on distributions becomes almost irrelevant for mature enterprises because the existing shareholders are affected in both cases and the buyer is not affected in either case.

C. Debt and Equity

The final question is whether the enterprise tax system encourages firms to finance their investments excessively through debt. If so, it is feared that firms would be vulnerable to bankruptcy in times of economic downturn and that increased numbers of bankruptcies would exacerbate the destabilization of the national economy during such a period.

Whether there is an incentive to finance new investments through debt or retained earnings, and how significant it is, will depend on the differences between the tax treatment of the investor under the personal income tax and the enterprise tax—that is, the enterprise tax rate on retained earnings must be compared with the personal income tax rate on interest income.

In an international context, the substitution of debt for equity has additional consequences. For an individual country, it implies the diminution of the domestic tax base because the return on enterprise equity is taxed in the source country through the imposition of the enterprise tax on the resident enterprise. The return on enterprise debt, by contrast, is often taxed only in the residence country because the interest reduces the domestic enterprise tax base and there will often be no withholding (or only limited withholding) on interest payments paid to another country. The result is that the investor's country of residence instead of the source country will tax the interest payment.[56]

V. Relationship Between Enterprise Income and Investor Income

A. Single Schedular Tax on Income from Capital

1. Equity Interests

As noted earlier, there are two basic systems for taxing income derived from an equity investment in a business enterprise. The first is to tax the income at a single rate that is applied to all investors and applied on a schedular basis to the net income of the enterprise. The second is to tax the income at different rates (typically graduated) depending on the circumstances of each

---

[56]*See supra* ch. 18.

investor; that is, the particular rate applied is determined by reference to the investor's total net income. Typically, then, the income from the business enterprise is added to the total net income of the investor, and the appropriate rate is applied on the basis of that total net income. Which system is chosen and how the system is implemented are exceptionally important to the operation of the enterprise income tax. A related issue is which system is used to tax income from deductible debt (or lease) investments.

Chapter 14 discusses a number of issues surrounding the choice between taxing income at schedular rates or at multiple (typically graduated) rates applied to a global income base. In addition to those issues, there is often considerable support for exempting not-for-profit organizations and pension funds from income tax. However, it should be noted that the economic and social arguments in favor of such exemptions are often rather less than fully convincing.[57] In addition, existing bilateral double taxation agreements might provide for varying rates of tax depending on the residency of the investor. It is, however, quite possible, and perhaps even advisable, to exempt nonresidents from any withholding tax (in addition, that is, to enterprise-level tax).[58] There have also been a number of concerns that a schedular tax is less equitable than a graduated tax. However, a schedular tax on income from property or capital, with a progressive tax on income from labor, has been advanced as a technique that would combine the added fairness of progressive taxation with the simplicity of schedular taxation.[59] In spite of these arguments, it might still be difficult to fully implement a policy of a single, schedular rate of tax on income from business enterprise.[60]

The main administrative benefit of a single schedular rate is that the tax can largely be levied at the enteprise level, without reference to the investor. As will be discussed later in this chapter, in particular, when a single schedular tax rate is combined with a highly effective enterprise tax and full imputation, problems involving levying taxes on distributions at the shareholder level more or less disappear. As can be imagined, this makes for perhaps the easiest type of enterprise-shareholder tax system to implement. There are two possible exceptions to this rule. The first involves the taxation of capital gains and losses realized by the investor when he or she sells the equity investment. However, as will be discussed, the more effective the enterprise tax, the less important the investor-level capital gains tax. In such cases, one can probably

---

[57]See Richard K. Gordon, *Law Reform and Privatization*, 13 Boston Univ. Int'l L. J. 264 (1995)

[58]See *supra* ch. 18. The elimination of additional withholding tax on distributions to nonresidents is the system used in Singapore, for example.

[59]See, e.g., 4 Carter Commission Report, *supra* note 49, at 51–57; OECD Report, *supra* note 41, at 32; U.S. Treasury Report, *supra* note 3, at 2–4.

[60]For example, the U.S. Treasury recommended a single rate of tax on all business income, primarily because it would aid in the administration of the income tax. Nevertheless, it bows to political reality by failing to recommend one at the present time. *See* U.S. Treasury Report, *supra* note 3, at 2–4.

exempt most investors most of the time from tax on such gains without much loss of revenue or equity.

The second exception is that, if income from each separate business enterprise is taxed on a schedular basis, the losses associated with an investor's share in an unprofitable enterprise will not be used to offset the income of a profitable enterprise. This will raise concerns of tax administration and taxpayer equity, as investors try to accomplish this offset by other means. This problem is, by and large, not completely solvable unless losses of all business enterprises are flowed through along with income. Because levying a tax on business income is designed in part to avoid having to allocate earnings and losses among equity investors, the problem of schedular taxation is shared by all separate enterprise income tax systems.

The most obvious problem with multiple rates is that discussed briefly earlier: to avoid the deferral problems that the enterprise tax is designed to combat, the rate of enterprise income tax must be the highest rate at which investors are taxed. Thus, some investors will be taxed at rates higher than the marginal rate that applies to their other income. The problem does not come up if there is a single rate of tax.[61]

A single rate of tax on all earnings from equity investments is clearly preferable from a tax administration viewpoint. The problems that need to be addressed under a multiple-rate system are discussed later in the chapter.

2. Debt and Lease Interests

Taxing *all* income, including that from debt and leases, at the same schedular rate eases administration markedly. First, one of the more difficult and complex areas in tax administration involves distinguishing equity interests from debt. While limiting taxation of income from equity investments to a single level of tax is an essential step toward equal taxation of equity and debt, it is not the only issue. If income from both equity and debt investments is taxed once, but the income from one or the other is taxed at a different rate, an incentive will still exist to design the legal form of the investment to fit the category of income that is taxed at that reduced rate. It is in part for this reason that the U.S. Treasury Report recommended that the income from both equity and debt investments be taxed identically, at a single schedular rate.[62] The

---

[61]Many systems, particularly transition economies, that subject at least some business enterprise income to double taxation do so by levying a final withholding tax on the amount of the distribution, often at a rate lower than the top marginal rate of individuals. However, the rates of the final withholding tax vary among nonresident taxpayers, and the tax does not generally apply to investors that are legal persons. *See, e.g.,* KAZ TC arts. 31–33. Systems that tax enterprise income only once, at a single schedular rate, do not need to levy an additional withholding tax. *See* McLure et al., Taxation of Income from Business and Capital in Colombia 91–95 (1990). The Dominican Republic imposes a withholding tax that is essentially an advance corporate tax, because the corporation receives a credit for it. *See* DOM TC §§ 297, 299, 308.

[62]*See infra* note 86.

usual administrative response to different tax treatment for income from equity and debt interests is to establish rules of "thin capitalization" or "earnings stripping."[63]

Even if the income from both debt and equity investments is taxed formally at the same rate, the method by which an enterprise income tax is typically levied causes the tax treatment of income from equity and debt investments to differ in some cases. This is because the general treatment of income accruing to a debt investor is to allow the enterprise to deduct the interest accrued or paid.[64] The deduction at the enterprise level ensures that the interest is not subject to tax at that level. Instead, the interest can be taxed as income to the lender.[65] By contrast, income on equity investments is generally taxed at the enterprise level and perhaps also at the shareholder level.

The tax administration problem arises under three circumstances. One of these arises from the mismatching of preference income and deductions: the income of the taxpayer entity is largely tax exempt, while deductible interest (or lease) payments that can be used against income that is not tax exempt are allowed. This issue will be addressed below.[66] The others arise because of the different treatment of income from equity investment and debt investment, shareholder and creditor; even if these categories are taxed formally at the same schedular rate, they are not taxed at the same effective rate.

Deductions are clearly worth more to taxpayers who are in higher tax brackets.[67] If a deduction by one taxpayer is followed by an equivalent inclusion for another, as is generally the case with interest payments, overall taxes will be reduced if the taxpayer paying the deductible amount is in a higher rate bracket than the recipient of the payment. There will then be an incentive for those paying at the higher rate to accrue as many deductions as possible. They can then share the benefits with those paying the lower rate. Of course, if the borrowing can be structured so that a deduction by the borrower is not followed immediately by an inclusion by the lender, a tax benefit will accrue even if the lender is taxed at the same rate.

The borrowing taxpayer can structure investments in a number of ways to increase or accelerate deductions. First, the taxpayer can overstate total amounts of interest. As discussed earlier, payment of interest is directly related to risk.[68] Even if inflation risk is eliminated from taxation through adjust-

---

[63]*See supra* ch. 18.

[64]Where, in the exceptional case, interest on debt is not deducted, it will usually be capitalized into the cost of an appropriate asset, to be subtracted in calculating the gain or loss made on the disposal of the asset.

[65]*See generally* the discussion in chs. 14 and 16 on interest expense.

[66]*See infra* sec. V(A)(3)(A).

[67]For examples, see William D. Andrews, *Personal Deductions in an Ideal Income Tax*, 86 Harv. L. Rev. 309, 337–41 (1972).

[68]*See supra* sec. I.

ment,[69] differences in default risk will result in different interest rates being paid by different borrowers.[70] Therefore, it can be difficult for tax authorities to determine how much of a payment would constitute actual economic interest and how much a return of invested capital.

Debt instruments can also be designed to accelerate interest payments in early years. One way is to structure the instrument so that it pays interest through discount. The payer can then seek to accrue interest on an annual basis without including the compounding effects of the discount. Although both of these avoidance techniques can be countered with proper accounting rules for interest imputation,[71] financial product innovation has made such accounting increasingly difficult.

If, however, both the borrower and the lender are taxed at the same schedular rate on this periodic income, the incentive to shift income is eliminated. Any benefit that the debtor might derive by mischaracterizing interest in order to take a deduction when one is not legitimately due is canceled by the taxation of such income to the creditor.[72] Also, and of great importance, the schedular tax on the creditor can be levied at source.

Identical rates of schedular tax on equity and interest earnings (as well as among different types of interest)[73] would not end all problems of the allocation of payments between interest and principal or of interest over time. This is because it is impossible to effect a single, schedular tax at the enterprise level. Normally under an enterprise-level tax, losses at the enterprise level do not flow through to the investor.[74] Therefore, if the enterprise has no taxable income, and if any carrybacks for current losses do not result in a refund, an interest deduction at the entity level may not be worth any current tax bene-

---

[69]*See* vol. 1, ch. 13.

[70]Some commentators have suggested that, over the past 60 years in the United States, the real risk-free rate of return has been less than 1 percent, with an inflation risk of only 3.1 percent. With nominal interest rates for most borrowers often vastly exceeding this amount, the difference can largely be attributed to default risk. *See* Bankman & Griffith, *supra* note 30, at 337–38, 387–90.

[71]*See* the discussion regarding discounted instruments, *supra* note 13. *See also* the discussion of accrual accounting of interest in ch. 16.

[72]*See* the discussion of mismeasurement and accrual of interest income and its relationship to different effective rates for debtor and creditor, *in* Joseph Bankman & William A. Klein, *Accurate Taxation of Long-Term Debt: Taking into Account the Term Structure of Interest*, 44 Tax L. Rev. 335, 335–37, 348, 367 (1989), and *in* Shaviro, *supra* note 16, at 432–33.

[73]If rates differ among creditors, allocation of payments between interest and principal and temporal allocation of interest will continue to be necessary. *See* U.S. Treasury Report, *supra* note 3, at 53–54.

[74]There are possible exceptions where the equity investor might be able to realize the loss. *See infra* note 79. However, even if losses did flow through, the investor might not have had enough other income against which the loss could be taken, and from which a benefit would accrue for the deduction. Although many tax systems permit taxpayers to carry back losses for a refund if they had paid tax in previous years, or to carry forward losses against income tax due in the future, it is likely that no existing income tax system allows for a refund for business losses if no tax has been paid in the past or if none is paid in the future. Even in the latter case, a deduction that can be taken in the future bears the loss of time value of money. *See* sec. IV(A).

fit.[75] In such cases, there will be an incentive for the creditor to reduce or eliminate interest payments by mischaracterizing interest as principal or by delaying interest deductions.[76]

There are two major reasons that an enterprise may have no taxable income. First, it may be a for-profit business enterprise, but have no taxable income[77] either because it has no economic income or because it benefits from tax preferences—deferral or complete exemption. If the enterprise has no economic income, mischaracterization of interest and principal or delay in accruing interest should not be a significant tax policy concern. The reason that the entity would mischaracterize interest and principal is that the genuine, economic loss resulting from the payment of interest could not be effectively reflected in a reduction in the tax base. Under a Haig-Simons analysis, a decline in wealth should be reflected in a decrease in the taxpayer's tax base.[78] It is only the practical operation of the enterprise-level tax that prevents this loss from being accrued. Therefore, with certain exceptions,[79] the equity owner is unfairly penalized for being unable to realize the value of the deduction for any interest actually accrued or paid. If there is an offsetting reduction in the tax owed by the creditor, there will be no net loss to the exchequer; any shifting of tax benefits between enterprise and creditor can be adjusted by the two actors. If the creditor's tax is collected through withholding at source, the adjustment could be implemented quite easily.[80]

Second, the entity may be a governmental, charitable, or other entity that is statutorily exempt from tax.[81] Pension funds are also typically exempt from income taxation. The problem posed by exempt entities may be reduced by taxing them on their investment income, which may well be advisable from a purely economic perspective as well. Such taxation would create a tax base from which the entity could deduct interest expenses.[82]

---

[75]There may be other reasons for an entity losing the benefit of a current deduction for interest, such as rules for stripping earnings or for "quarantining" interest that govern borrowings used to finance investments in income-preferred assets. See infra sec. V(A)(3)(A).

[76]Of course, the benefit received by the creditor can then be shared with the enterprise.

[77]Including as a result of loss carrybacks. See supra note 74.

[78]See generally Stephen Lewis, Taxation for Development 57–58, 87–90 (1984); David Bradford, Untangling the Income Tax 15–43 (1986).

[79]These exceptions relate to whether the enterprise, or its equity investor, can realize the loss in another way. One way would be for the investor to sell his or her interest at a loss, with the loss being reflected in the interest payment or accrual made at the entity level. If this loss can be used to reduce taxes at the investor level, such as through the application of a capital gains tax at the investor level that permits the deduction of losses, then the value of the interest deduction can, in fact, be used.

[80]This also raises the question of deductibility of interest by the physical person investor or flow-through entity on debt to acquire equity interests in enterprises subject to separate taxation. See supra ch. 16, sec. VI(A).

[81]See infra sec.VII.

It is also possible that there is economic income at the enterprise level, but that this income is "tax preferred," such that no tax is currently due. The preference can be intentional; for example, provisions in the law may exempt some income from tax, tax some income at a lower rate, or delay the inclusion of some income until a later time. Some income may be unavoidably subject to a timing preference because of the deferral of tax on unrealized capital gains. In these instances, there will also be an incentive to understate deductions at the enterprise level, so as to have a mirror understatement of income at the creditor level. Unlike the earlier case, the tax administration should be concerned about understatements of income tax at the creditor level.

These problems can be minimized by reducing or eliminating special tax benefits. However, if a realization system of taxation is retained for most capital gains, the problems will never be eliminated, although this chapter will argue that the distortions caused by the realization event system can be greatly minimized by marking certain financial assets to market, and by taking into income currently total borrowings in excess of the total adjusted cost of assets. However, if these ideas are not implemented or are only partially implemented, the tax administration will have to ensure that interest accrues to the creditor.

As noted earlier, it is difficult to impute interest on debt whenever a risk premium is due. It is also increasingly difficult to impute interest on many financial instruments. One possible solution is to require a minimum imputation of interest on all debt instruments, based on the amount of capital invested. This minimum imputation could be based on a provision in the income tax code that would give the tax administration the authority to impute an interest component on any debt obligation of an enterprise.[83]

One possible technique for more completely equating the tax treatment of income from equity and debt might be to extend deductibility treatment to returns on equity investments. Some proposals have arisen in the past to do so, particularly partially to integrate enterprise and investor taxes.[84] Extending deductibility treatment would not solve the problems discussed above. If the entity had no taxable income, there would still be a benefit to the debt investor and therefore, by extension, to the equity investor who might share the benefit. However, with regard to distributed income, equivalent treatment would certainly prevail. No major income tax system currently affords such treatment, for a number of reasons. Two of the most important are the passing

---

[82]*Id.*

[83]*See, e.g.,* USA IRC §§ 7872, 462(a) and (g). Continental systems such as the French and German have separate, although general, rules for imputation of interest income for legal and for physical persons, as well as specific rules for imputation of interest between or among related parties. *See* chs. 14, 16.

[84]In 1984, the U.S. Treasury recommended a 50 percent deduction for dividends, *see* Treasury I, *supra* note 3, at 136–37, while the White House recommended a 10 percent deduction; *see* Treasury II, *supra* note 3, at 122–26.

along of foreign tax credits to investors and the treatment afforded nonresident equity investors under most double taxation agreements.[85] Dividend deduction models are largely missing from the world tax scene.

Some have suggested that equation of treatment could be reversed; instead of allowing a deduction for payments of earnings on equity investments at the enterprise level, deductions for interest expense could be disallowed. The 1991 U.S. Treasury Report on integrating enterprise and investor taxes recommended taxing income from both equity and debt investments entirely at the enterprise level by denying a deduction for interest payments. This would turn the enterprise tax into a comprehensive business income tax.[86] The problems of understating interest or delaying its payment or accrual would disappear in that the interest deduction would no longer formally be part of the income tax system. However, the net economic result would be the same; the recipient would be able to defer tax on interest income when the entity had economic, but not taxable, income.[87] Once again, the obvious answer is, where possible, to apply a system whereby taxable and economic income most closely approximate each other.

Eliminating deductions for interest could be a technique for ensuring that, at least with regard to interest accrued, such payments would be taxed at the same rate, that is, the entity rate. In this sense, disallowing deductions is analogous to integration schemes that tax enterprise income only and exempt the distribution from tax at the shareholder level. Such treatment would certainly reduce debt-equity and earnings-stripping problems. However, such a system has not yet been attempted in any major tax jurisdiction (except partially, as part of a regime to prevent earnings stripping.)[88] Once again, much of the reason for this may stem from the existence of double taxation agreements and the problems that would arise if all interest income were effectively taxed to nonresidents at the enterprise rate of tax, rather than at the rates specified by those agreements.[89] However, treating interest in this way is logically consistent with taxing equity income only at the entity level and—if a decision is made to tax income from capital at a single rate and if the international

---

[85]See *supra* ch. 18. A deduction for an imputed return on equity is allowed in Croatia. See HRV PT §§ 7–9; Manfred Stöckler and Harald Wissel, *Die Gewinnbesteuerung in der Republik Kroatien*, Internationale Wirtschafts-Briefe 527 (June 14, 1995).

[86]The comprehensive business income tax would levy tax on a schedular basis at the entity level on both debt and equity investments by denying a deduction for interest, levying a single tax on entity income, and exempting from tax at the investor level both equity distributions and interest payments. U.S. Treasury Report, *supra* note 3, at 39–58.

[87]This would be because, without accrual of taxable interest to the creditor, no tax would be levied on that interest.

[88]See the discussion regarding earnings-stripping provisions in chs. 16, 18.

[89]Moreover, problems may arise in applying a foreign tax credit for the creditors. See the discussion of these regimes in ch. 18.

dimensions can be negotiated—may constitute the easiest system of entity taxation to administer.

3. Treatment of Preferred Income

A. DEDUCTIONS FOR INTEREST EXPENSE

As noted earlier, problems arise with regard to the like tax treatment of debt and equity, or of different types of debt and different types of equity, when the entity has tax-preferred income. The tax effect on the equity investor may also be problematic. If the tax on the "preferred" income is deferred or if this income is tax exempt, there will be an incorrect tax result, either a reduction in tax (because of the time value of money) or a complete exemption. However, the taxpayer may be able to finance the investment with borrowed money. Normally, the payment or accrual of interest leads to a real decline in wealth. As noted earlier, under a Haig-Simons analysis, a decline in wealth should be reflected in a decrease in the taxpayer's tax base.[90] However, a taxpayer with no taxable income cannot benefit from the deduction. The benefit of the exclusion afforded the taxpayer on the preferred income would be reduced by the denial of interest deductions. While it is unlikely that denying the interest deduction would have the same effect as the benefit afforded through the preferred income, it would have the effect of a partially compensating disallowance.[91] However, if the taxpayer has other *taxable* income, the taxpayer may use the interest deductions against this income, thereby avoiding tax on this income as well.[92] The effect would be to eliminate the (only partially) compensating distortion caused by the inability to benefit from the deduction of interest, which may compound the problem of having preferred income in the first place.

Tax policy analysts normally recommend, for reasons of economic efficiency and administrative ease, eliminating tax preferences whenever politically possible. If all preferences were eliminated, in theory at least, this mismatching problem would cease to exist. And, although many tax systems have attempted to travel far in the direction of eliminating preferences, the problem of tax deferral under the mixed accrual/realization event system of accounting is unlikely to go away entirely. This means that a taxpayer can borrow against assets that have appreciated in value, but on which the gain has not been taxed, while still being able to deduct interest. This situation has been described as allowing the taxpayer to "realize" the gain (by borrowing against it) without having to pay tax on it.[93]

---

[90]*See supra* note 78.

[91]To do so is "to achieve a second-best state through the creation of compensating distortions." Boris I. Bittker, A *"Comprehensive Tax Base" as a Goal of Income Tax Reform*, 80 Harv. L. Rev. 925, 983–84 (1967).

[92]*See* Shakow, *supra* note 33, at 1165.

[93]Although there is also a shift in risk to the lender. *See* Shaviro, *supra* note 16, at 442–43.

Chapter 16 discusses techniques of quarantining or otherwise disallowing interest deductions when they relate to the financing of tax-preferred income.[94] An alternative approach is to recharacterize not the deduction of interest, but the borrowing itself.

As noted earlier, tax-preferred income can take a number of different forms, the main ones being statutory incentives (which the legislature can avoid enacting) and preferences related to the realization event (which are difficult to avoid). The benefit of the latter is not permanent, but is related to timing. In effect, by delaying the taxation of accrued gains, the taxpayer benefits from the time value of the deferred tax. When the taxpayer realizes the gain by selling or transferring the gain asset, tax is incurred; obviously, if possible, the taxpayer would prefer to avoid such a taxable event.

However, if the taxpayer needs cash, he or she can instead borrow the money. In effect, borrowing the money is analogous to selling or transferring the asset. Instead of quarantining interest by disallowing a deduction in a "compensating distortion," it would be possible to treat the borrowing as a realization event, at least to the extent that the borrowing exceeds the adjusted cost (book value or written-down value) of the asset. If the borrowing is secured by a single asset, the amount of gain can be determined on the basis of that asset alone. To the extent that the borrowing is not secured by a single asset, the amount of the gain can be determined on the basis of all assets held by the taxpayer.

For example, if the taxpayer holds a single asset with an adjusted cost of $10 and borrows $20, he or she would include $10 in taxable income. The asset's cost basis would be increased to $20, and the full amount of interest due on the $20 debt would be deductible. If the taxpayer has a large number of assets, with a total adjusted cost of $100,000, and borrows $200,000, he or she would include $100,000 in income, and the adjusted cost of all assets would be increased by $100,000. However, because each individual asset would have to be adjusted, the $100,000 increase would

---

[94] As chapter 16 discusses, many jurisdictions limit interest deductions for financing tax-preferred income. The U.S. Internal Revenue Code provides for one of the most exhaustive limits on interest deductibility. See USA IRC §§ 56(b)(1)(C) (limitation on interest deduction for purposes of minimum tax); 163(d) (limitation on deduction of interest on investment indebtedness); 170(f)(5) (limitation on deductibility of interest on debt incurred to purchase or carry bond given to charity when interest relates to period during which donor is not taxed on income from bond); 264 (disallowance of deduction for interest on indebtedness related to insurance contracts); 265 (disallowance of deduction for interest on indebtedness related to tax-exempt income); cf. USA IRC §§ 263A(f) (capitalization of construction-period interest); 246A (limitation on dividend-received deduction for debt-financed portfolio stock); 291(e)(1)(B) (partial disallowance as tax preference of interest on debt incurred by financial institutions to purchase or carry tax-exempt bonds); 1277 (deferral of interest deduction allocable to accrued market discount); 1282 (deferral of interest deduction allocable to accrued discount); 7701(f) (regulations to be prescribed to prevent avoidance through related parties of provisions that deal with linking borrowing to investment).

have to be apportioned among all the assets, for example, on a proportional basis.[95]

Although no jurisdiction currently treats borrowing as a realization event, the logic of such an approach seems compelling. It would have additional benefits with regard to taxing economic earnings at the enterprise level that are distributed to the equity investor; this issue will be dealt with at greater length below.

In addition to this technique, other accounting methods can be used to reduce the amount of accrued but unrealized capital gains (and losses as well). The most important of these is to require enterprises to mark assets to market whenever reasonable. In particular, such marking to market could be done for foreign exchange, precious metals, and securities and financial derivatives for which a listed price could be easily obtained.

B. TAXATION OF EQUITY DISTRIBUTIONS FROM PREFERENCE INCOME

Tax-preferred income of flow-through entities can normally be distributed to the investor without any immediate additional tax consequence, although typically there are consequences for the taxation of capital gains and losses when the entity interest is transferred.[96] For investors in entities without flow-through treatment, similar tax rules could apply; all income tax would be levied at the entity level on the preferred income.[97] If the preferred income were of the permanent, or exclusion variety, no tax would ever be paid. If the preferred income were of the deferral type, tax would be paid when the preference expired at the entity level.

---

[95]Using the formula: amount of increase in adjusted cost of a particular asset = adjusted cost of the particular asset/sum of adjusted costs of all assets × total increase of adjusted cost of all assets. Such a formula is used in the United States when a company is purchased through the sale of its shares. To ensure that the adjusted cost of the assets of the company equals the adjusted cost of the shares of the company, the company may "step up" the adjusted cost of its assets. See USA IRC § 338(a) and (b)(1), (4), and (5). See also Treas. Reg. §§ 1.338-3(b), 1.338-4. See also the discussion of related issues in ch. 20. This ensures that gain on the assets is paid only once and results in better correlation of what the Americans call "inside basis" (the adjusted cost of assets held by the enterprise) and "outside basis" (the adjusted cost of the equity interests in the enterprise). Cf. infra ch. 21, sec. II(G). Such a system of comparing total adjusted costs of assets with total borrowings can perhaps be more easily implemented if the balance sheet method of entity taxation is used. See supra ch. 16. In fact, an adjustment for an increase in adjusted cost for each individual asset can be analogized to the balance sheet inflation adjustment described in vol. 1, ch. 13.

[96]Typically, the adjusted cost of the entity equity interest is reduced by the distribution. Once the adjusted cost drops to less than zero, the difference between the cost and zero may be included in income. When the equity interest is transferred, there may be a taxable capital gain (or loss) on the transfer. See ch. 21.

[97]Once again, excluding the issue of taxing capital gains and losses on the transfer of an entity interest.

Such tax treatment of the distribution of preference income to equity investors is extremely rare.[98] In the vast majority of jurisdictions, tax is levied on distributions out of income that was not already fully subject to tax at the entity level. Tax can be levied in various ways, and those variations have considerable effect on the administration of the tax (see discussion below). However, levying tax on such untaxed income has two basic and important effects on tax administration, one somewhat positive and one quite negative. Therefore, before examining the specific effects of different forms of implementation, we discuss why distributions of preference income should be taxed in the first place.

Various arguments have been raised as to why distributions from preference income should be taxed.[99] One reason is that specifically enacted tax preferences may have been designed to encourage investment. Whenever a business entity distributes such income, the implication may be that it is to be used for consumption and not for investment. Therefore, a tax should be levied. Another argument, which applies only to systems that tax all distributions of *economic* income not previously taxed, is that any income arising from timing preferences that can be realized without otherwise incurring entity income tax (primarily through borrowing) should be taxed as if the distribution were a realization event. Finally, if equity holders are taxed at different rates, distributions should always be subject to tax to ensure that a higher-rate investor will pay tax at the higher rate on such distributions.[100]

Again, of course, these problems are reduced, or may disappear entirely, as the amount of preference income is curtailed or eliminated.

B. Multiple Taxes on Income from Capital

A single schedular tax on capital income derived through legal persons may be considered unacceptable for a variety of reasons, not the least of which is the difficulty of finding an acceptable single rate. The conduit view is not fully implemented if the single tax rate imposes higher tax burdens on low-income investors or reduces the tax burden of high-income investors.[101]

Consequently, many countries find it necessary to operate in tandem both the enterprise-level profit tax and the investor-level personal income tax. This

---

[98]One of the few examples is the treatment afforded partnerships (and similar legal forms) in Indonesia. IDN IT § 4(1).

[99]*See* U.S. Treasury Report, *supra* note 3, at 18–21; ALI Integration Report, *supra* note 24, at 58–66.

[100]*Id.*

[101]Although this section focuses on the relationship between individual investors and legal persons, the issues discussed below and the choice of mechanism also arise when the investment is made through the mediation of another legal person. In other words, these kinds of mechanisms are even more necessary to prevent the cascading of corporate taxes and dividend withholding taxes as corporate earnings are passed through a chain of corporations to the individual who is the ultimate investor.

section reviews some of the more commonly used options for reducing or eliminating the double taxation of capital income that these systems can induce. It describes in detail some of the principal interaction mechanisms between the enterprise and personal income tax used in the taxation systems of various countries. Except for one case, the interaction mechanisms attempt to deal only with the double tax on distributions and leave untouched the double tax on retained corporate profits.[102] Given that the issue they try to resolve is the double taxation of equity, they deal only with returns on equity investments, not interest or rent.

Even with these restrictions, it is common to see a wide variety of idiosyncratic mechanisms for integrating the enterprise and individual tax, and so this section will describe the most important features of a few representative types seen in practice.[103] The design of these interaction systems involves many issues, but the most important are the following:

- The level at which the relief is to be provided. The mechanism for reducing double tax on dividends can operate at either the enterprise or the shareholder level.

---

[102]The after-tax return to the shareholder will depend significantly upon the form in which profits are made available to shareholders: cash distribution, distribution of enterprise assets in lieu of cash, allotment of new shares paid for from profits, redemption of existing shares paid for from profits, retention of profits, and so on. In the following discussion, it is assumed that the enterprise's managers choose only the first and last alternatives, distributing some fraction of the enterprise's profits as cash and retaining any balance for reinvestment. It will also be assumed that the cash distribution is not a liquidating distribution (or that, if it is, the distribution is dealt with in an identical manner to a cash distribution).

It is also assumed that all distributions made are taxable so as to prevent managers from recharacterizing detected evasion as the return of capital to shareholders. This assumption accords with the probable wish of the enterprise's managers that shareholders believe that the distribution is from profits, not a return of their investment.

[103]There is a voluminous body of literature on this issue. For descriptions of various methods of interaction and differing taxonomy, see generally 4 Carter Commission Report, *supra* note 49, at ch. 19; Blueprints, *supra* note 3; OECD, Company Tax Systems in OECD Member Countries 9–11 (1973); Alvin C. Warren, *The Relation and Integration of Individual and Corporate Income Taxes*, 94 Harv. L. Rev. 719 (1981); George F. Break, *Integration of the Corporate and Personal Income Taxes*, 22 Nat'l Tax J. 39 (1969); Charles E. McLure Jr., *The Integration of the Personal and Corporate Income Taxes: The Missing Element in Recent Tax Reform Proposals*, 88 Harv. L. Rev. 532 (1975); Charles E. McLure Jr., *Integration of the Income Taxes: How and Why*, 2 J. of Corporate Tax'n 429 (1976); Charles E. McLure Jr., Must Corporate Income Be Taxed Twice? (1979); J. Pechman, Federal Tax Policy 179–89 (5th ed. 1987); Richard M. Bird, Taxing Corporations (1980); Martin Norr, The Taxation of Corporations and Shareholders (1982); OECD, Theoretical and Empirical Aspects of Corporate Taxation, chs. 1, 2 (1973); Martin Feldstein, Capital Taxation, ch. 8 (1983); Congressional Budget Office, Revising the Corporate Income Tax, ch. 8 (R. Lucke ed., 1985); Julian Alworth, *Piecemeal Corporation Tax Reform: A Survey, in* The Political Economy of Taxation 72–73 (Alan Peacock & Francisco Forte eds., 1981); Alan J. Auerbach, *Debt, Equity and the Taxation of Corporate Cash Flows, in* Debt, Taxes and Corporate Restructuring 108–26 (John B. Shoven & Joel Waldfogel, eds. 1990); R.A. Musgrave & P.B. Musgrave, Public Finance in Theory and Practice 395–98 (4th ed., 1984); Richard J. Vann, Eliminating the Double Tax on Dividends: Legal and Practical Issues, chs. 4, 5 (1986); Sijbren Cnossen, *Alternative Forms of Corporation Tax*, 1 Australian Tax Forum 253 (1984); Peter Harris, Corporate/Shareholder Income Taxation (1996).

- The form that the relief is to take. Generally, the options are to use a tax deduction, a tax credit, or an exemption system. A subsidiary issue is whether the application of relief is to be made conditional upon some tracking or verification of other tax payments.
- Whether the relief is to be afforded to nonresident shareholders. The extent to which nonresidents can be further burdened, especially by withholding taxes, will often be controlled by any applicable tax treaties, but the extent to which they may be benefited is largely a matter for domestic law.[104]
- Whether relief is to be afforded to income from equity investments derived by tax-exempt investors.
- Whether different types of shareholders are to be treated differently. These mechanisms often distinguish corporate from individual shareholders, and resident from nonresident shareholders, but other possible distinctions might differentiate holders of controlling interests from holders of portfolio interests.
- The treatment of enterprise tax preferences. Tax preferences can be preserved in full for the benefit of shareholders, be preserved but at a reduced value, or be recaptured entirely at the shareholder level.
- The treatment of foreign-source income. This income can be viewed as raising issues similar to those surrounding enterprise tax preferences. In both cases, domestic enterprise-level tax is not paid on income that is to be distributed or retained (although for foreign-source income, some foreign tax may well have been paid), but the arguments about imposing tax on the distributions are slightly different.

The analysis concentrates on the major aspect of the problem and the topic of this chapter—the treatment of income earned by resident individual shareholders—but is expanded, where relevant, to examine the position of nonresident individual shareholders and income earned by intermediaries, such as other enterprises.[105]

The idiosyncrasies of the mechanisms that countries have adopted (not to mention the peculiarities of nomenclature)[106] make it difficult to generalize.

---

[104]If nonresidents are not to benefit, there may be an issue about whether denying benefits to nonresidents is allowed under the tax treaties of the country. Many tax treaties will contain rules prohibiting discrimination against the nationals of the other treaty partner, and it is a matter of debate whether this denial would breach the nondiscrimination provisions of the treaty. The United Kingdom deliberately chose to implement its interaction mechanism at the enterprise level to avoid this issue.

[105]Many jurisdictions will use a combination of systems—using one for individuals, another for corporations or other intermediaries, and yet another for nonresident shareholders. For example, the United States employs a classical system for individual shareholders and a partial dividend-received deduction system for corporations; Canada employs an imputation system for individual shareholders and a full dividend-received deduction system for corporations; Australia employs an imputation system for individual shareholders and a tax credit system for corporate shareholders.

[106]See Messere, supra note 41, at 342–43 (lamenting the imprecise usage in this area).

Table 1. Interaction Systems

Classical System	Dividend-Relief System for Distributed Profits				Integration System for All Profits
	Corporate level		Shareholder level		
	Dividend-paid deduction system	Split-rate system	Dividend-received exemption/ deduction system	Imputation system	

Nonetheless, once the classical system is abandoned, the mechanisms for recognizing the impact of both enterprise- and shareholder-level income tax can be combined into a few illustrative groups: split-rate systems and dividend-paid deduction systems, dividend-received exemption or dividend-received deduction systems, dividend-imputation systems, and full integration systems (see Table 1).[107] The first three are often referred to as systems for dividend relief—adjusting the combined tax rate on distributions—while the last, integration, is more ambitious—reducing the combined tax rate on all enterprise profits.

There are virtues and vices to each interaction system, which explains why a standard regime has not emerged.[108] To illustrate, systems that reduce the enterprise's primary tax liability (such as dividend-paid deduction systems) will benefit both resident and nonresident shareholders equally, a result the

---

[107]Even the number of interaction mechanisms is a matter for debate. See Pechman, supra note 103, at 175–81 (who says there are five groups but lists six); OECD, Company Tax Systems, supra note 103, at 10 (which lists three). The discussion will not pursue some of the more unusual types of interaction mechanism that have been proposed at various times but not yet implemented.

[108]For example, the U.S. Treasury praised the imputation systems for their "flexibility to respond to different policy judgments on the most important issues of integration." U.S. Treasury Report, supra note 3, at 93. The systems may also be seeking objectives beyond those described above as the defects of the classical system, and possibly also objectives different from each other. For example, it is claimed that imputation systems in Europe were introduced to encourage more people to hold shares, to increase compliance with the corporate tax, and to encourage capital-export and capital-import neutrality within the European Union. See Bird, supra note 103, at 232–35; Harry G. Gourevitch, Corporate Tax Integration: The European Experience, 31 Tax Lawyer 65 (1977); Hugh J. Ault, Introduction, in Imputation Systems—Objectives and Consequences 10 (Hugh J. Ault ed., 1983) ("it was generally hoped that a more favorable treatment of dividend distributions would increase investment in corporate stock, especially on the part of small investors"); Cnossen, The Imputation System in the EEC, in Comparative Tax Studies: Essays in Honor of Richard Goode 85, 105 (S. Cnossen ed. 1983) ("It seems desirable that shareholdings be spread more widely than is the case at present. The imputation system might promote that objective."). The different goals that various interaction mechanisms may be pursuing are most apparent in the more unusual systems suggested, such as the Institute of Fiscal Studies' ACE system, which creates a notional deduction to the corporation for the value of shareholder equity employed by the corporation, with the principal objective of equalizing the return to investors on debt and equity. See Institute for Fiscal Studies, Equity for Companies: A Corporation Tax for the 1990s (1991); see also supra note 85. The U.S. Treasury Report set out with the explicit goals of retaining the implicit tax collected at the corporate level on tax-exempt investors, taxing business income only once (rather than in two offsetting installments). U.S. Treasury Report, supra note 3, at 13.

source country may dislike.[109] Systems that reduce the enterprise's primary tax liability would also reduce the implied tax paid at the enterprise level by tax-exempt investors.[110] Dividend-paid deductions would need to be targeted to deny the tax benefit when distributions are paid to tax-exempt entities or non-residents if the double taxation of dividends is to be sustained for these groups. Dividend-received deduction systems and some imputation systems will not ensure that the enterprise has actually paid any tax on the dividend received by the shareholder although they do preserve the full nominal value of enterprise tax incentives for shareholders.[111] Some systems can result in overtaxation of the enterprise when the tax collected exceeds the enterprise's own tax liability, while others require elaborate record keeping.[112] Integration systems that tax shareholders on the value of retentions can cause solvency problems for individual shareholders when distributions are small but profits are large and are generally considered impractical for large enterprises in part because of the difficulties of administering them[113] and because the substantial inter-

---

[109]Cnossen, *supra* note 108, at 92, for example, notes that "under the imputation system the double tax is mitigated at the level of the shareholder. It would also have been possible, of course, to provide relief at the corporate level by providing a deduction for dividends paid in computing taxable profits. . . . This avenue, which should yield the same result as imputation, has not been followed, however, because governments did not want foreign shareholders to share automatically in the relief." *See also* Bird, *supra* note 103, at 232–35, 239; OECD, Company Tax Systems, *supra* note 103, at 23–30; U.S. Treasury Report, *supra* note 3, at ch. 7.

[110]This latter concern seems to have played a major role in the decision of the U.S. Treasury to suggest a dividend-exemption system, because it collects at least some tax from otherwise exempt investors. U.S. Treasury Report, *supra* note 3, at ch. 6.

[111]Reuven S. Avi-Yonah, *The Treatment of Corporate Preference Items Under an Integrated Tax System: A Comparative Analysis*, 44 Tax Law. 195 (1990); Pechman, *supra* note 103, at 180; U.S. Treasury Report, *supra* note 3, at 93 ("an imputation credit can extend the benefits of integration to tax-exempt and foreign shareholders by allowing refundability of imputation credits or it can deny such benefits by denying refunds").

[112]This is particularly true of the imputation systems in Australia, France, and Germany. *See* Avi-Yonah, *supra* note 111, at 214 ("as the German example shows, however, tracking of income can lead to very complicated account-keeping requirements").

[113]*See* Pechman, *supra* note 103, at 179 ("experts agree that it would not be practical to extend the partnership method to large, publicly held corporations with complex capital structures, frequent changes in ownership, and thousands or millions of stockholders"); Auerbach, *supra* note 103, at 105 (describing proposals for integration as "pure in concept, ambitious in scope, and unadopted in practice"); 4 Carter Commission Report, *supra* note 49, ch. 19 (recommending an optional profit-attribution system because of the solvency and administrative problems); Vann, *supra* note 103, at 30–34.

Some others believe that these administrative difficulties have been overstated. John G. Head & Richard M. Bird, *Tax Policy Options in the 1980s*, in Comparative Tax Studies 16 (Sijbren Cnossen ed., 1983) ("although the difficulties are considerable, there appear to be no insuperable problems"); Anthony P. Polito, *A Proposal for an Integrated Income Tax*, 12 Harv. J. L. & Pub. Pol. 1009 (1989); Peter L. Swan, *An Australian View on Integration*, in Taxation Issues of the 1980s (J.G. Head ed., 1983). It is interesting to note that the U.S. Treasury considered even an imputation system unnecessarily difficult to administer. U.S. Treasury Report, *supra* note 3, at 93.

national treaty network assumes that nonresident shareholders are not currently taxed on retentions.[114]

Not surprisingly, therefore, in a 1993 study, the OECD found representative types of almost all possible systems among the corporate tax systems of its (then) 24 member countries (see Table 2 for a classification of the systems then existing).

The variety of interaction systems that existed in 1993 suggests that the effects of each system on the after-tax returns to shareholders and the cost of enterprise capital will differ. This section analyzes the classical system and four systems of enterprise and shareholder interaction. The models described are stylized to capture the fundamental relationships of the systems discussed, rather than being precise descriptions of the exact rules employed in any particular jurisdiction.

1. Separate (or Classical) System of Enterprise Tax

The pure classical system is declining in industrial countries' tax systems.[115] Among the countries of the EU, Belgium, the Netherlands, Luxembourg, and Sweden[116] retain the classical system for distributions to individual shareholders.[117]

A. RESIDENT INDIVIDUALS

In a pure classical system, there is no formal interaction between the enterprise and individual income taxes, and each is levied without explicit regard for the operation of the other. But even in a classical system, there may be implicit recognition of the dual operation of both taxes in the rate imposed under either tax or in the definition of its base. For example, a lower marginal rate imposed upon an individual's capital income or substantial investment concessions offered to industry may each be a method for recognizing the existence of

---

[114]*See* 4 Carter Commission Report, *supra* note 49, ch. 19.

[115]The United States is the most obvious example of a country that still retains the classical system for individual shareholders, although even it has had a fully integrated system for small corporations in Subchapter S of the Internal Revenue Code 1986. But in respect of larger corporations with more than one class of shares, nonresident shareholders, or passive income, the United States moved clearly against the current trend toward interaction in 1986 by eliminating the $100 dividend-received deduction for individual shareholders. IRC § 116 (repealed). The United States also reduced the size of the deduction for corporate shareholders in some cases from 80 percent to 70 percent of dividends received depending upon the degree of affiliation between the companies. For corporate shareholders, the United States still retains the dividend-received deduction system; IRC § 243. For a discussion of the Netherlands and Luxembourg, *see* J-M Tirard, Corporate Taxation in EC Countries, 1990–91, at 12–13 (1991).

[116]Sweden, inspired by the full imputation systems applied in Finland and Norway, exempted dividend income in the hands of shareholders in 1994, only to restore the full classical system (without the previous partial deduction system) from 1995.—L.M.

[117]*See generally,* OECD Report, *supra* note 41, at 9–41; McLure, Must Corporate Income Be Taxed Twice? *supra* note 103, ch. 3.

Table 2. Degree of Reduction of Economic Double Taxation (Central Government)

None or Very Little	Reduction of Economic Double Taxation				Elimination of Economic Double Taxation	
	Corporate level		Shareholder level		Corporate level	Shareholder level
Classical system	Split-rate system	Partial dividend-deduction system	Partial imputation system	Partial shareholder-relief schemes	Zero-rate system	Full imputation system
Belgium	Germany	Iceland	France	Austria	Greece	Australia
Luxembourg		Spain	Ireland	Canada	Norway	Finland
Netherlands		Sweden		Denmark		Germany
Switzerland				Iceland		Italy
United States				Japan		New Zealand
				Portugal		Turkey

Source: OECD, Taxation in OECD Countries, Table 9, at 67 (1993).

the two layers of tax. The first reduces total tax by encouraging retention of profits by the enterprise and extraction of gain by the individual selling the shares, while the second reduces the total tax collected from the enterprise.[118]

The first option can be seen in the following example.

Example

Assume that the enterprise tax rate is 33⅓ percent, the top marginal rate under the personal income tax is 50 percent, and dividends are taxed at a flat rate of 25 percent imposed on individual shareholders (or perhaps collected by withholding at source). This rate alignment offers a good approximation of the after-tax return [$100*(1 − 0.33)(1 − 0.25) = $50.25] that would be earned if the income from the investment had been earned by a high-income shareholder directly ($50).

Such a system would probably, however, have several serious consequences. First, it might discourage distributions of enterprise profits—indeed, some rule would probably be needed to oblige distributions. If distributions were not obliged, serious strain would be placed on the administration of the capital gains tax as the means of collecting the deferred tax on retained earnings. It would also deliver a sizable benefit to tax-exempt institutions because the enterprise tax is the principal tax that they pay on capital income.

The position of a shareholder in such a system can be expressed algebraically as follows. Under the classical system, the enterprise pays tax (T_c) on its taxable profits (P), and the individual resident shareholder pays income tax (T_i) at progressive marginal rates on the proportion (d) of after-tax profits distributed by the enterprise as dividends. Retained profits $(1 − d)$, reflected as accretions to the value of the shares, are taxed as capital gains (T_g) on a deferred basis when the shares are sold by the shareholder, and are sometimes taxed at a lower nominal rate.[119] Given an enterprise tax system bearing these features, the return (R) to an individual shareholder after payment of enterprise tax on all profits and personal tax on distributions and retentions is[120]

$$R = dP(1 − T_c)(1 − T_i) + (1 − d)P(1 − T_c)(1 − T_g).$$

B. PREFERENCE INCOME

Because the enterprise and the shareholder are taxed separately, this system applies also to distributions of untaxed income, such as income that enjoys tax preferences or foreign-source income that is not subject to tax in the resi-

---

[118]*See* Myron S. Scholes & Mark A. Wolfson, Taxes and Business Strategy 56–57 (1992).

[119]The effect of deferral is the same as formally imposing a lower rate, or as the revenue authority's making an interest-free loan of the unpaid tax to the taxpayer. Hence, the discussion will treat (T_g) as being a rate less than (T_i), even though this may not appear formally to be the case.

[120]Robert R. Officer, *The Australian Imputation System for Company Tax and Its Likely Effect on Shareholders, Financing, and Investment,* 7 Aust. Tax F. 353, 376–77 (1990).

dence country.[121] Earnings that are untaxed or not fully taxed at the enterprise level would, nevertheless, be subject to full shareholder tax:

$$R = dP(1 - T_i) + (1 - d)P(1 - T_g).$$

C. NONRESIDENT SHAREHOLDERS

As the example illustrates, one can achieve the same result as under conduit treatment by reducing the enterprise rate below the top individual rate and imposing a withholding tax on distributions. Another reason for adjusting the personal tax rather than the enterprise tax is the position of nonresident shareholders. For nonresidents, the enterprise tax rate is an important determinant of the total tax that they will pay to the source country, and reducing it will confer a substantial benefit on them. Treaties generally allocate the enterprise tax to the source country and limit its ability to impose substantial withholding taxes on payments to nonresident shareholders.[122] Consequently, a country's treaties and the international norms for taxing enterprise income will most likely make it impossible for the country to impose substantial additional taxes on a nonresident shareholder to compensate for a low enterprise tax rate.

2. Dividend-Paid Deduction System

A dividend-paid deduction system operates at the enterprise level to impose different rates on an enterprise's distributed and undistributed profits. The system achieves this result by giving to the enterprise a tax deduction for distributions made and then imposing tax on the distribution at the shareholder level.[123] A tax deduction for distributed profits means that the profits incur no tax at the enterprise level and are effectively taxed as if they were payments of interest by the enterprise.[124]

---

[121]To facilitate the discussion, foreign income will be called "not taxable" as a shorthand reference to the results of the system for eliminating double tax on foreign-source income. Most countries will have in their domestic laws (and supplemented by international double tax treaties) either a credit system to reduce domestic tax on foreign income or a formal exemption system for foreign income. When foreign income has been comparably taxed at source, and either of these domestic systems applies, the result is that no further residence country tax will be imposed on the income.

[122]See Article 10, Model Tax Convention on Income and on Capital, OECD Committee on Fiscal Affairs, Organization for Economic Cooperation and Development, Paris (updated as of Sept. 1, 1995) [hereinafter OECD Model Treaty]. See supra ch. 18.

[123]See Norr, supra note 103, at ch. 5/C. Before June 1992, Greece, for example, had a dividend-paid deduction system. Tirard, supra note 115, at 102–03. A dividend-paid deduction system is used in Iceland and Hungary and was used in the United States in 1936–37. See Cnossen, supra note 103, at 54–55; Pechman, supra note 103, at 176–77.

[124]See Cnossen, supra note 103, at 92 (noting that the effect of a dividend deduction system is to treat equity as debt, giving the enterprise a deduction for its dividend payments as it does for its interest payments).

A. RESIDENT INDIVIDUALS

Under a dividend-paid deduction system, the enterprise is able to reduce its taxable profits by the amount of any distribution. The enterprise therefore pays no tax on distributed profits, but pays tax at the enterprise rate on retentions. This system has some of the same effects as a split-rate system (discussed below) under which the rate on distributed profits is set at zero. The individual shareholder who is a resident pays income tax at marginal rates on the proportion of profits distributed by the enterprise as dividends, and any retained profits already taxed to the enterprise are taxed as a capital gain on a deferred basis to the shareholder. No deduction or tax credit is given to the shareholder for taxes paid by the enterprise. The after-tax return of an individual shareholder after payment of enterprise tax on all profits and personal tax on distributions and retentions is

$$R = dP(1 - T_i) + (1 - d)P(1 - T_c)(1 - T_g).$$

Again, tax-exempt investors will benefit from the elimination of all tax on distributed earnings.

B. PREFERENCE INCOME

Other forms of untaxed income, such as income enjoying tax preferences or foreign-source income that is not taxable in the residence country, would be subject to enterprise tax only if retained.

Example

Assume a corporation has operating profits in the current year of $30,000, but taxable profits of $24,000 (prior to making any dividend payment) because of a $6,000 enterprise tax preference. Its potential tax liability at a 25 percent rate is thus $6,000 if it makes no distributions. If, in the current year, the company retains $12,000, its tax liability is $3,000 [25 percent of $12,000]. The shareholder will pay tax at personal rates on the $12,000 of taxable profit that is distributed. Tax will thus be collected currently on $24,000, part from the corporation at enterprise tax rates and part from the shareholders at their marginal rates. The other $6,000 of nontaxable operating profit will be taxed as a capital gain to the shareholder when the gain is realized, reducing the value of the tax preference from a permanent to a temporary reduction of tax.

Such a system raises a few stacking and ordering issues, which the example below addresses:

Example

Assume a corporation has operating profits in the current year of $30,000, but taxable profits of $20,000 (prior to making any dividend payment) because of a $10,000 enterprise tax preference. Its potential tax liability at a 25 percent rate is thus $5,000 if it makes no distributions. If the corporation distributes $25,000, two related questions arise: what is the treatment of the $5,000 in the hands of the shareholder, and does the enterprise generate a carryover loss from this transaction? It has an additional deduction of $25,000, which exceeds its taxable profits of $20,000.

The answer should depend on whether the government wishes the enterprise tax preference to be lost. If it is to be recaptured, the shareholder should be taxable on the $25,000, and the enterprise should not recognize a loss from this transaction. If the preference is to be preserved and enjoyed immediately, the shareholder should be exempt from tax, but the enterprise should not have a further deduction. There is an intermediate point, however, that would preserve the preference, but at a reduced value. That position would tax the entire $25,000 distribution to the shareholder under the personal income tax, but allow the enterprise to carry forward the $5,000 as a loss against future income.

A further complication would arise if the enterprise had retained profits from prior years.

Example

Assume a corporation has operating profits in the current year of $30,000, but taxable profits of $20,000 (prior to making any dividend payment) because of a $10,000 enterprise tax preference. Its potential tax liability at a 25 percent rate is thus $5,000 if it makes no distributions. The corporation has $2,000 in retained profits from a prior year. The corporation distributes $32,000.

The same questions would arise: What is the treatment of the $12,000 in the hands of the shareholder, and does the corporation generate a carryover loss from this transaction, given that it has a further deduction of $12,000 that exceeds its taxable profit? The added complication is that the $2,000 of retained earnings was presumably already taxed to the corporation the previous year and perhaps ought not be taxed again if distributed now. An ordering rule would be necessary to resolve this question, one that would identify (and perhaps immunize) the amount paid from taxed retained profits and then identify and deal with the $10,000 paid from the preference income.

C. NONRESIDENT SHAREHOLDERS

One important qualification to the desirability of a dividend-paid deduction system is the position of nonresident shareholders. Current international tax practice is to allocate the enterprise tax to the source country, while a dividend-paid deduction system will effectively abandon any entity-level tax on distributed earnings. Consequently, substantial withholding taxes on a nonresident shareholder would be needed to compensate for the reduction in the enterprise tax. Such an option might be limited by treaties.[125]

---

[125]*See supra* ch. 18.

3. Split-Rate Systems

Split-rate systems reduce the enterprise tax payable on distributed profits or formally impose tax only on retained earnings.[126] The same effect can also be achieved with a tax surcharge on undistributed enterprise profits.[127]

A. Resident Individuals

Under a split-rate system, the enterprise pays tax on its retained profits (T_{cr}), but generally faces a lower rate of tax (T_{cd}) on the proportion of pretax profits distributed as dividends.[128] A resident individual pays income tax at ordinary marginal rates on distributions (T_i), while retained profits are taxed as capital gain (T_g) on a deferred basis to the shareholder, offsetting to some extent the higher rate paid by the enterprise when the profits are earned.[129] The after-tax return to a resident individual shareholder is[130]

$$R = dP(1 - T_{cd})(1 - T_i) + (1 - d)P(1 - T_{cr})(1 - T_g).$$

A lower tax on distributions, combined with an increased personal income tax on distributions, is likely to suffer from some of the same problems alluded to in the discussion of the classical system—it might discourage distributions of enterprise profits. Again, tax-exempt institutions would benefit from the lower tax on distributed capital income.

B. Preference Income

As in a dividend-paid deduction system, distributions of other forms of untaxed income, such as income that enjoys enterprise tax preferences or for-

---

[126]For example, Germany and Hungary apply different rates to distributed and undistributed profits, Germany applying a higher rate on retentions and Hungary a higher rate on distributions. Tirard, *supra* note 115, at 71–72, 87–88; Cnossen, *supra* note 103, at 54–55. This was also the first of many suggested interaction mechanisms proposed for uniform adoption in Europe. Tax Harmonization in the Common Market (Neumark Report) (1963). *See* Bird, *supra* note 103, at 227–28.

[127]*See* Norr, *supra* note 103, ch. 5/B. For example, a further tax was imposed on retained profits in both Australia and the United States. AUS ITAA Div. 7 (repealed). This was not done apparently to formalize the interaction of the enterprise tax and personal income tax although it had the effect of reducing one distortion from the lack of coordination—different rates applying to retained and distributed earnings. The surcharge was imposed to encourage distribution so that there was no gain from sheltering income within the enterprise and the classical system could collect the further tax from the shareholders.

[128]This system is used in France and Germany, although in both countries in combination with an imputation system. There is also a disparity in actual practice, with Germany imposing a lower rate on distributed profits, while France imposes a lower rate on retained profits.

[129]In some cases, $Tg = 0$, for example, in countries like Germany that generally do not tax capital gains of individuals, except for cases of substantial participation.

[130]In the discussion that follows, an issue arises about whether the division of profits (P) occurs before or after the tax is subtracted—that is, does the shareholder receive d percent of after-tax profits or d percent of P, from which tax is taken out? For the purposes of the subsequent presentation, it is assumed that the shareholder receives d percent of P, the pretax profits, and the tax applicable to each share is then taken out at the appropriate rate.

eign-source income that is not taxable in the residence country, would be subject to enterprise tax only if retained. The same stacking and ordering issues would also arise. The after-tax return on preference income would be

$$R = dP(1 - T_i) + (1 - d)P(1 - T_{cr})(1 - T_g).$$

C. NONRESIDENT SHAREHOLDERS

As with a dividend-paid deduction system, split-rate systems can confer benefits on nonresident shareholders that withholding taxes may not be able to offset.[131]

4. Dividend-Received Deduction (or Dividend-Exemption) System

The systems discussed above all reduce the enterprise-level tax paid on distributions. Dividend-exemption or dividend-received deduction systems operate at the shareholder level,[132] by giving the shareholder a deduction from income for some or all of the distributions received or by exempting some or all dividends received from tax.[133] This type of system was in place in the United States until 1986 for a limited amount of dividends received by individuals[134] and is still retained in many countries as the means for adjusting the total tax paid on dividends flowing through chains of enterprise[135] or as a general integration mechanism.[136] Because these systems leave the enterprise's tax liability untouched, they solve some of the problems surrounding tax-exempt and nonresident shareholders mentioned in the prior discussion, but they also raise new issues.

In a dividend-received deduction system, as under the classical system, the enterprise still pays tax on the profits it derives during the year. The shareholder includes in income dividends received. A deduction from income is,

---

[131]Germany found that its split-rate system offered excessive benefits to foreign-owned companies, which could distribute profits taxed at T_{cd}, enjoy reduced withholding tax, and reinvest without being subject to tax in their home countries. For example, keeping up a high enough withholding tax in these cases reportedly cost Germany dearly in its treaty negotiations with the United States.

[132]A version of this system, allowing a deduction for 50 percent of dividends paid, was proposed for the United States in 1984. See Treasury I, supra note 3. It was later revised to a deduction for 10 percent of the amount of dividends paid. See Treasury II, supra note 3. See Bird, supra note 103, at 235–36; Avi-Yonah, supra note 111; U.S. Treasury Report, supra note 3, at ch. 12A.

[133]See Norr, supra note 103, at ch. 6/B. Belgium and the United States, for example, have a dividend-received deduction system for intercorporate dividend distributions; Denmark has an exemption system.

[134]See USA IRC § 116 (repealed).

[135]This is the case in Canada and the United States. In Australia, the deduction of the dividend is replaced by an automatic credit of the amount of tax payable on the dividend. The effect of this credit system is the same as an automatic, full dividend-received deduction.

[136]See, e.g., Charles McLure et al., The Taxation of Income from Business and Capital in Colombia 91–95 (1990).

however, given to resident shareholders for enterprise distributions received, which may be as much as the amount of dividends received but is sometimes limited.[137] In a dividend-exemption system, a percentage of (or all) dividends received are exempt in the hands of the shareholder. In both systems, retained enterprise earnings are taxed to the enterprise and to the shareholder under the capital gains tax, with no adjustment for the enterprise tax already paid.

A. RESIDENT INDIVIDUALS

If the deduction available to the shareholder is for the entire amount of the dividend received, the position of the shareholder after payment of enterprise and personal income tax on the profits is

$$R = dP(1 - T_c) + (1 - d)P(1 - T_c)(1 - T_g).$$

For tax-exempt shareholders, the position now changes from that reached under the systems described above. Because the enterprise tax remains intact and the adjustment occurs under the shareholder's tax, no benefit is conferred on tax-exempt shareholders through the interaction mechanism—the benefit of their exemption is not increased because no tax deduction is available to a tax-exempt entity.

B. PREFERENCE INCOME AND FOREIGN-SOURCE INCOME

When a resident enterprise distributes preference income, the value of the preference is retained and passed through to the shareholders—the enterprise pays no tax on this income because of the incentive, and the investor pays no tax because of the dividend-received deduction.

When a resident enterprise is distributing foreign-source income, the effect of the foreign tax credit system (or system of exemption for foreign income) will in most cases replicate the outcome for preference income; that is, the resident shareholder will receive the dividend income free of further (residence country) enterprise tax and is entitled to a deduction for the amount of the dividend received. The position of the shareholder becomes

$$R = dP + (1 - d)P(1 - T_c)(1 - T_g).$$

But when the shareholder invests directly in a foreign enterprise, there is an added complication. In many countries, dividends received do not qualify for the dividend-received deduction if the paying enterprise is not also a resident. Where this is the rule, and any withholding tax on the dividend is fully creditable in the residence country, the position of the shareholder approximates the position of a shareholder under the classical system, with the important exception that the enterprise tax paid is the foreign enterprise tax (T_{fc}), rather than the domestic enterprise tax. The after-tax position thus becomes

---

[137]*See* USA IRC § 116 (repealed) (which limited the individual's deduction to the lesser of the amount of dividends received or $100).

$$R = dP(1 - T_{fc})(1 - T_i) + (1 - d)P(1 - T_{fc})(1 - T_g).$$

This result need not be the case, of course. The tax system of the residence country might simply include dividends received and then allow a deduction as its means of eliminating double taxation. The effect would be similar to an exemption system for foreign dividends.[138]

C. NONRESIDENT SHAREHOLDERS

When a nonresident shareholder invests in a domestic enterprise, the relationship between the (source country) enterprise tax and the (residence country) investor-level tax is principally a matter for the residence country to resolve because the international norm allocates the enterprise tax exclusively to the source country and limits the ability of the source country to impose withholding taxes on dividends. Indeed, some countries will take that position to its logical conclusion and choose not to impose any withholding taxes on dividends paid to nonresidents.

5. Imputation Systems

The four systems just described adjust the double taxation of distributed earnings by effecting changes at either the enterprise or the shareholder level. Many countries now operate tax credit or tax imputation systems[139] that retain both the separate enterprise tax and the personal tax but treat the payments of one tax as also satisfying a tax liability arising under the other. They achieve this by giving a tax credit of some amount, either to the shareholder or to the enterprise, reflecting more or less accurately the amount of tax that the profits have already borne.[140] This section examines three versions of the wide variety of imputation systems.

---

[138]One important difference would arise, however, if other provisions in the tax system denied a deduction for interest on money used to derive exempt income and if foreign dividends were treated as exempt. In this case, interest on loans used to finance investments that yielded dividends from foreign enterprises would be nondeductible. That result would not necessarily follow if the law contained no similar provision for interest on money used to derive income that was both included and then deducted.

[139]Some of the countries with an imputation system are Australia, Canada, Finland, France, Germany, Ireland, New Zealand, Norway, and the United Kingdom. See generally Cnossen, supra note 103, Table 1.

[140]As will be seen below, some countries, such as Australia, simply impute company taxes paid and then require the shareholder to pay over any additional tax due on untaxed distributions. Other countries apply an additional withholding amount or "compensatory tax" on distributions out of accounting income that have not borne company tax. Called simply withholding in New Zealand, the Advance Corporation Tax (ACT) in the United Kingdom, the précompte mobilier in France, the imposta di conguaglio in Italy, and the Ausschüttungsbelastung in Germany, its principal point is to enforce collection of tax on distributed income not taxed at the company level. There can be ancillary purposes as well. The United Kingdom does not integrate company and investor taxes completely. The ACT serves in part to ensure some double taxation of income.

Imputation systems should not be confused with simple withholding systems in which the enterprise is obliged to withhold tax on distributions and the tax withheld is credited to the shareholder. The difference between imputation and withholding systems is that a pure withholding system is simply a collection mechanism on behalf of the shareholder, and not an attempt to change the consequences of the separate or classical system. For example, most European jurisdictions see the need both to impose a withholding tax at a constant rate on enterprise distributions and to have some other interaction mechanism, such as an imputation system that attributes payments of the enterprise's own tax liability to the shareholders or a dividend deduction system. Even the Netherlands, which retains the classical system, has a withholding system in which tax is collected from the enterprise on distributions. The tax is creditable to the shareholder, but does not further reduce the total tax payable by either the enterprise or the shareholder.

Although all imputation systems have elements in common, within this broad framework, there are also many differences. Common to all systems are the survival of the separate enterprise tax, the attribution to shareholders of at least some enterprise tax paid on distributed profits, and the denial of a credit for enterprise tax paid on retained profits. Differences are manifested, for example, in the accuracy with which imputation systems take account of enterprise tax payments.[141] In some systems, the amount of tax credited to the individual shareholder may not reflect the total tax paid by the enterprise. At one extreme, the Canadian system simply increases the amount of any distribution by a constant amount to represent enterprise tax paid and then gives the shareholder a credit for a portion of the grossed-up amount. The gross-up and credit occur regardless of whether tax has actually been paid at the enterprise level.[142] The United Kingdom's ACT system is slightly more careful to ensure that the tax has been paid, but occasionally at the expense of collecting payments of ACT that exceed the enterprise's own "mainstream" (i.e., enterprise) tax liability.[143] Of the three systems modeled, the most accurate is that used in Australia and New Zealand. It attempts to track the amount of tax an enterprise actually pays on its profits and attributes only those payments to the profits distributed.

Which system a country chooses to put in place will depend upon many factors, but probably the most important are the desired treatment of enterprise-

---

[141]See Avi-Yonah, *supra* note 111.

[142]France and Germany also give a credit to shareholders (for supposed payments of enterprise tax) that is calculated by reference to the enterprise tax rate rather than the enterprise's actual tax payment. *See* Tirard, *supra* note 115.

[143]The ACT is payable at a flat rate on a distribution regardless of whether the profits out of which the distribution is made have already borne tax and regardless of the actual rate of tax that will be imposed upon the enterprise. The payment of ACT discharges the enterprise's primary tax liability to the extent of the ACT payment, and the individual shareholder is credited with the ACT payment against the shareholder's tax liability on the dividend received. *See generally* R. Bramwell et al., Taxation of Companies and Company Reconstructions ch. 9 (4th ed. & Supp., 1988).

level tax preferences,[144] the treatment of exempt shareholders, the preferred treatment of nonresident shareholders, the importance of fairness concerns, the treatment of foreign-source income, and administrative convenience.

A. AUTOMATIC IMPUTATION MODEL

The first imputation system to be described, which is based on the system used in Canada, appears to be the least accurate. It will be seen, however, that except in some unusual circumstances, the alleged accuracy of some systems may be more apparent than real.[145] This system increases the shareholder's distribution by an amount assumed to represent some of the enterprise's tax payment on the distribution and then gives to the shareholder a credit for a proportion of that assumed enterprise tax. For the purposes of this chapter, the automatic operation of the system is the interesting element of the interaction mechanism.[146]

In the Canadian system, the enterprise pays tax on its taxable profits, whether distributed or retained, at the enterprise tax rate.[147] The shareholder must include in income the amount of distributed profits increased by a multiple representing the enterprise tax that is assumed to be paid on the distribution.[148]

---

[144]Enterprise-level tax preferences (and credits for tax paid on foreign income) are an issue under an imputation system that traces actual payments of enterprise tax because the value of the preference (or foreign tax credit) will be recaptured if (untaxed) profits are distributed and even, to a lesser extent, for taxed profits if they are retained. The value of the preference under such a system is reduced from a tax exemption to a tax deferral, which may not be consistent with the level of subsidy intended by the government. It would be possible to solve the problem by specific adjustments to the tax credits offered to shareholders: either to gross up the tax the enterprise actually pays by an amount to represent tax not paid but attributable to preference items or foreign income, or to gross up the shareholder's tax credits. See Avi-Yonah, *supra* note 111.

See, for example, the adjustment made in Australia to the tax liability on trust distributions where part of the distribution represents untaxed profits, reduced because of the building depreciation deduction. AUS ITAA § 160ZM. This same adjustment is not made to distributions from companies with similar deductions.

Even for retained profits, the value of the tax preference is reduced but in this case by less. The value of the preference will possibly be recaptured when profits on the sale of the shares are taxed as capital gains. The size of the recapture depends on how soon the shares are disposed of, the interest discount factor, and the tax rate applicable to capital gains. In the right circumstances, it is possible for the amount of recapture to approach zero.

[145]See U.S. Treasury Report, *supra* note 3, at appendix B2.

[146]See Bird, *supra* note 103, at 236 ("as in Belgium, Italy and Denmark, the amount of the dividend tax credit is completely independent of whether any tax was paid at the corporate level at all"); U.S. Treasury Report, *supra* note 3, at 164 ("because the shareholder credit is not dependent on the actual payment of corporate tax, the Canadian system does not require rules allocating credits to dividends").

[147]See CAN ITA § 123(1).

[148]See CAN ITA § 12(1)(j). The section requires an individual shareholder resident in Canada to include in income any "dividend paid by a corporation resident in Canada on a share of its capital stock," and § 82(1) in effect requires the shareholder to include 125 percent of the amount of any dividend in income.

The factor by which the dividend is increased is set at a constant rate, which is currently 25 percent. The shareholder then pays personal tax on the amount of increased distribution and is given a tax credit against this liability for an amount that is a proportion (currently 66 percent) of the grossed-up amount.[149] Retained earnings are taxed to the enterprise, and the balance after enterprise tax (to the extent reflected in the sales price) is taxable to the shareholder on realization as a capital gain.[150] All the steps involved in making the interaction between enterprise- and investor-level taxes are effected by the operation of the imputation system at the shareholder level.

1. Resident Individuals

Rather than be distracted by the complexities of the system as it actually operates,[151] this section will abstract a little from reality and concentrate on the effect of the automatic interaction mechanism. We therefore treat the imputation process as if the shareholder is given credit under the imputation system at full rates: the gross-up occurs at the full enterprise rate, and the tax credit against the personal income tax occurs in the same amount. If the Canadian system is

---

[149]CAN ITA § 121 provides a credit against tax on the increased dividend of "two-thirds of any amount that is required by paragraph 82(1)(b) to be included in computing his income for the year."

[150]The real possibility that the capital gain may also escape tax under Canada's rather unusual lifetime $100,000 capital gain exemption introduced in 1985 will not be explored. See CAN ITA § 110.6.

[151]The following explanation gives a flavor of the actual complications. When the enterprise reports all of its profits, the balance available for distribution is $[P(1 - T_c)]$. The net amount distributed $[dP(1 - T_c)]$ is then increased by the gross-up amount representing tax that the corporation is assumed to have paid. This step is effected by multiplying the net dividend by a fraction and adding this amount to the net dividend. When all profits are reported, this step becomes $dP(1 - T_c) + dP(1 - T_c)a = dP(1 - T_c)(1 + a)$, where (a) is a gross-up factor applied to dividends received by a resident. The total amount is then subject to personal income tax $[dP(1 - T_c) (1 + a)T_i]$, and the shareholder is entitled to a credit against the personal income tax liability of a proportion (b) of the amount that was included by the grossing-up procedure $[bdP(1 - T_c)a]$. The net tax at the shareholder level on distributed dividends is thus the balance of the liability remaining after subtracting the credit $[dP(1 - T_c)(1 + a)T_i - bdP(1 - T_c)a$, and the shareholder, after paying tax, retains $dP(1 - T_c)(1 + a)(1 - T_i) + bdP(1 - T_c)a$.

Some of the more important adjustments are the current tax surcharge of 3 percent, the provincial tax credit, the small business tax credit (referred to rather confusingly as the "small business deduction"), and the manufacturing and processing tax credit. See CAN ITA, division E, subdivision b. The basic individual rate is currently 29 percent. CAN ITA § 117(2). Each province then imposes further tax on the federal tax payable—the basic rate in Ontario, for example, is a further 52 percent of the federal tax, giving a combined provincial and federal rate of 44 percent. The federal tax rate is also increased by a 5 percent surtax and a further 3 percent "super surtax" on high-income taxpayers. See CAN ITA § 180(1). Given a current corporate tax rate in Canada of 38 percent with a multitude of further tax adjustments, and personal marginal rates approaching 50 percent, it is clear that something less than full integration of the corporate and personal income tax is achieved by this system. Full relief from double taxation for dividends is almost achieved in practice if the average (and marginal) corporate tax rate is about 20 percent. See Bird, supra note 103, at 236.

modeled in this way, and the level of the enterprise tax is lower than the investor-level tax, the after-tax return to the shareholder becomes

$$R = dP(1 - T_i) + (1 - d)P(1 - T_c)(1 - T_g).$$

This treatment comes about from the following steps. The shareholder includes in income the amount of the dividend received increased by an amount set by reference to the enterprise tax rate:

$$dP(1 - T_c) + [dP(1 - T_c) \times T_c/(1 - T_c)],$$

which can be simplified to $dP(1 - T_c) + dPT_c = dP$.

This total is then subject to investor's income tax (dPT_i), and the shareholder is entitled to a credit against the investor income tax liability of the same amount that was included by the grossing-up procedure. The net tax at the shareholder level is thus ($dPT_i - dPT_c$). The procedure operates on the assumption that enterprise tax (dPT_c) was collected from the enterprise and gives effect to the goal of taxing distributed profits (dP) ultimately at the investor's income tax rate (T_i) although the tax is collected at two points. No gross-up and credit system operates for retained profits and they are taxed as under the classical system.

Several interesting design questions arise under such a system. The first is the question of *surplus credits*—what happens when the assumption that the entity-level tax is lower than the investor-level tax is relaxed? That would be the case, for example, with investors who are tax exempt or have carryover losses, and with individuals who are taxed at a low marginal tax rate, most commonly individuals in retirement who are living off the dividend income from their savings. The tax credit is usually conceived as partly satisfying the shareholder's liability for tax on the dividend income, but the shareholder might not have a tax liability on that income. The following example demonstrates the point:

Example

A corporation pays a dividend of $7,500 to a shareholder who is a resident individual. The shareholder has no other income. The enterprise tax rate is 25 percent. The personal income tax has a tax-free zone of $10,000 a year. Income over $10,000 is subject to a 20 percent rate. The shareholder will report income of $10,000 and will be entitled to a tax credit of $2,500, but will still have no tax liability.

Tax credits that exceed the taxpayer's current need for credit can be dealt with in many ways. It would be possible to refund the excess to the investor in cash; deny cash refunds, but allow the taxpayer to carry forward any excess credits to future years; allow the taxpayer to transfer (or perhaps even sell) the credit to another taxpayer, such as a related corporation in a corporate group; or deny any further benefit.

A second, though slightly different, issue is *spillover*—what would happen if the taxpayer had derived other income? Here, the taxpayer could benefit from the tax credit to reduce or eliminate the tax on the other income.

Example

A corporation pays a dividend of $7,500 to a shareholder who is a resident individual. The shareholder has other interest income of $4,000. The enterprise tax rate is 25 percent. The personal income tax has a tax-free zone of $10,000 a year. Income over $10,000 is subject to a 20 percent rate.

The shareholder will report income of $14,000 and will be entitled to a tax credit of $2,500. The shareholder's tax liability is $800 (20 percent of $4,000), which could be fully satisfied by the tax credit with a surplus of $1,700. The interest income would be effectively shielded from tax by the credit for corporate tax paid.

While this transaction may seem innocuous, a variation on this example will show how these enterprise tax credits can be used in tax-sheltering activities.

Example

A corporation pays a dividend of $7,500 to a shareholder who is a resident individual. The taxpayer has a deductible interest expense of $10,000 incurred for the purchase of the shares (the taxpayer obviously assumes capital growth in the value of the shares, which is presently untaxed). The shareholder has employment income of $22,500. The enterprise tax rate is 25 percent. The personal income tax has a tax-free zone of $10,000 a year. Income over $10,000 is subject to a 20 percent rate.

The shareholder will report taxable income of $22,500. The shareholder's tax liability is $2,500 (20 percent of $12,500), and the shareholder will be entitled to a tax credit of $2,500. All the salary income is effectively shielded from tax by the credit for corporate tax paid.

There are several solutions to this problem, assuming it is seen as a problem. One solution, a rule that the tax credits for enterprise tax are quarantined and can be used only to satisfy the tax liability on dividend income, would address both this example and the prior one.[152]

2. Enterprise-Level Tax Preferences

A second series of issues arises from the automatic nature of the process. An automatic gross-up and credit mechanism automatically passes through to shareholders the benefit of preference items offered to enterprises. This is be-

---

[152]Another approach would address the interest deduction claimed by the taxpayer. The United States, for example, has loss limitation rules for passive activities. *See* USA IRC § 469. Rules of this type would defer the interest cost, driving up the taxpayer's income in the current year and generating a tax liability against which the tax credit would be needed. A third possibility would be a dual income tax system as practiced in Finland, Norway, and Sweden. *See* Leif Mutén et al., Towards a Dual Income Tax? (1996).

cause distributions of untaxed preference income come with tax credits attached; the enterprise pays no tax on this income because of the preference and the investor pays no tax because of the automatic tax credit. The following example demonstrates the outcome:

Example

The corporation has pretax financial profits of $30,000. It is entitled to a special tax deduction of $6,000 for making an investment and therefore has taxable profits of $24,000. The enterprise tax rate is 25 percent and so the corporation pays $6,000 in tax. The corporation pays a dividend of $24,000 to a shareholder who is a resident individual. The personal income tax rate is 25 percent on income up to $40,000 and 40 percent thereafter.

The shareholder reports as income $32,000—the sum of the dividend of $24,000 and the gross-up for assumed corporate tax on a dividend of that size of $8,000 ($24,000 × 0.25/0.75). The taxpayer has a tax liability of $8,000 (25 percent of $32,000) and a tax credit of $8,000. The total tax paid is $6,000—one corporate tax payment of $6,000 and no further shareholder tax payment.

In other words, the outcome is just as if the investor, like the company, had faced the following tax rates:

	Amount (In units of domestic currency)	Rate (In percent)	Tax (In units of domestic currency)
Nonpreference income	24,000	25	6,000
Preference income	6,000	0	0
Total	30,000		6,000

The same outcome would have occurred if, instead of being a tax incentive, the difference between commercial profit and taxable income had been brought about because the enterprise earned $6,000 of foreign-source income that was treated as exempt in the residence country. It would also have happened if the $6,000 of foreign-source income had been taxable but the enterprise was entitled to a tax credit of $1,500.

If, as is more common in industrial economies at the moment, the investor's rate is higher than the enterprise rate, the outcome changes in this way:

Example

The corporation has pretax financial profits of $30,000. It is entitled to a special tax deduction of $6,000 for making an investment and therefore has taxable profits of $24,000. The enterprise tax rate is 25 percent and so the corporation pays $6,000 in tax. The corporation pays a dividend of $24,000 to a shareholder who is a resident individual. The personal income tax rate is 30 percent on income up to $40,000 and 40 percent thereafter.

Again, the shareholder reports as income $32,000—the sum of the dividend of $24,000 and the $8,000 gross-up for assumed enterprise tax. The taxpayer now has an initial tax liability of $9,600 (30 percent of $32,000) but still has a tax credit of $8,000. The total tax eventually paid is $7,600—one corporate tax payment of $6,000 and a further shareholder tax payment of $1,600.

In this case, the outcome is just as if the investor had faced the following tax rates:

	Income (In units of domestic currency)	Rate (In percent)	Tax (In units of domestic currency)
Nonpreference income	24,000	30	7,200
Preference income	6,000	6.66	400
Total	30,000		7,600

The outcome in each case occurs because the computation made at the shareholder level is based not on the amount of enterprise tax paid, but on the enterprise tax rate, and occurs automatically. That is, the shareholder must gross up at the rate of

$$T_c/(1 - T_c).$$

There are, of course, other options. One is a nonautomatic tracking system that traces only the amount of tax payments made, a system discussed in more detail below.[153] Automatic systems do have the advantages of simplifying somewhat compliance and administration. However, tying the imputation process to a stipulated rate can lead to a problem, sometimes referred to as *over-integration*. If the gross-up and tax credit are simply a constant proportion of the dividend received, and are not tied to the current enterprise tax rate, the system can become misaligned, for example, when there are multiple enterprise and investor rates:

Example

The corporation has pretax financial profits of $100,000 but has taxable profits of only $94,000. The enterprise tax rate is 10 percent up to $50,000 and 25 percent thereafter. The corporation pays $19,000 in tax ($50,000 × 10 percent plus

---

[153]If only the $6,000 of enterprise tax actually paid had been used in the imputation calculations, the value of the incentive would have been recovered at the investor level. In the first example, the shareholder reports as income $30,000—the sum of the dividend of $24,000 and the enterprise tax paid. The taxpayer has a tax liability of $7,500 (25 percent of $30,000) and a tax credit of $6,000, leaving a net tax payment due of $1,500 and total tax of $9,000. In the second example, the shareholder reports as income $30,000—the sum of the dividend of $24,000 and the corporate tax paid. The taxpayer has a tax liability of $9,000 (30 percent of $30,000) and a tax credit of $6,000, leaving a net tax payment due of $3,000 and total tax of $9,000.

$44,000 × 25 percent). The corporation pays a dividend of $81,000 to a share-holder who is a resident individual. The investor's tax rate is 30 percent on all income up to $40,000 and 40 percent thereafter.

The shareholder reports as income $108,000—the sum of the dividend of $81,000 and the gross-up computed as one-third of the amount of the dividend $27,000 ($81,000 × ⅓). The taxpayer has an initial tax liability of $37,200 ($40,000 × 25 percent plus $68,000 × 40 percent) and a tax credit of $27,000, leaving a net liability of $10,200. The total tax paid is $29,200—one enterprise tax payment of $19,000 and a further shareholder tax payment of $10,200. This is an average tax rate of 29.2 percent.

The alignment of rates in the example may appear bizarre, but common circumstances and plausible arguments can lead to these kinds of situations. The low rate in the enterprise tax might be intended as an incentive or concession for small business. The marginal rates in the investor tax might be intended to reflect government goals about progressivity and wealth redistribution. The choice of a constant ⅓ ratio to represent the gross-up could have been made because it is the right gross-up rate for the higher enterprise rate. The ⅓ ratio is too high a gross-up for the lower enterprise rate—for a 10 percent enterprise rate, the correct gross-up should be ⅑—but it might be a deliberate decision intended to ensure that the benefit of the small business rate is permanent, like the tax incentives discussed above, and is not recovered when the small business distributes its profits to its shareholders. But this benefit is itself subject to the proviso that the progressive rate scales in the investor-level tax will be allowed to operate thereafter to recapture some, though not all, of the benefit delivered to high-income earners. This juxtaposition of policies, each of which may have some merit in isolation, explains how profit of $100,000 can become subject to an average rate of 29.2 percent.

3. The Equalization Tax Variant

The problem highlighted above in relation to untaxed enterprise income and the potential for overintegration can be solved, even within the broad parameters of an automatic tax credit system, with a common European variant of the automatic credit process just described.

Many countries in Western Europe—in particular, France, Germany, and Italy—apply an additional withholding amount or "equalization tax" on distributions out of accounting income that have not borne enterprise tax.[154] Its principal point is to collect tax on distributed income not taxed at the enterprise level. However, while these systems do try to recapture some enterprise preferences, they need not attempt to levy a compensatory tax on *all* distributions of economic income. In particular, foreign-source income distributed by

---

[154]*See generally* International Fiscal Association, Corporate Tax on Distributions (Equalization Tax) (1994); note 140 *supra*.

a resident enterprise to resident shareholders will typically not trigger the equalization tax.

The system in France is typical of this variant.[155] In France, the *précompte* operates within the framework of the basic automatic imputation system. The enterprise pays tax at 33⅓ percent. Every dividend paid by an enterprise carries a tax credit, the *avoir fiscal,* of 50 percent of the amount of the dividend. The shareholder grosses up the dividend by the amount of the tax credit and is taxed on the total with an automatic credit in the manner described above.[156]

Unlike the Canadian variant, however, the automatic process of gross-up and credit is not intended to have the effect of passing enterprise tax preferences through to investors. So, for distributions of untaxed income from domestic sources, and for distributions of profits retained for more than five years, the *précompte* can apply.[157] The rate of *précompte* varies and operates as a supplement to the actual rate of enterprise tax paid, so that the total of enterprise tax and *précompte* equals 33⅓ percent—in other words, the amount needed to fund the *avoir fiscal.*[158] The automatic process is unaffected and functions in the usual way at the shareholder level, but the imposition of the *précompte* at the enterprise level has been interposed to correct for some of the problems noted above.

Example

The corporation has pretax financial profits of $30,000. It is entitled to a special tax deduction of $6,000 for making an investment and therefore has taxable profits of $24,000. The enterprise tax rate is 33⅓ percent and so the corporation pays $8,000 in enterprise tax. The corporation pays a dividend of $20,000. The corporation will be liable to *précompte* of $2,000 (33⅓ percent of $6,000).

The automatic process can now resume at the shareholder level. The personal income tax rate is 40 percent. The shareholder reports as income $30,000—the sum of the dividend of $20,000 and a further one-half of the dividend—the amount of the *avoir fiscal.* The taxpayer has a tax liability of $12,000 (40 percent of $30,000) and has a tax credit of $10,000. The total tax eventually paid is $12,000—$8,000 enterprise tax, *précompte* of $2,000, and the shareholder pays a further $2,000.

---

[155]*See generally* Michael P. Devereux, The Integration of Corporate and Personal Taxes in Europe: The Role of Minimum Taxes on Dividend Payments (Working Paper 96–5) (unpublished paper prepared for Technical Committee on Business Taxation, Canada); Patrick de Fréminet, *Perspective of France, in* International Fiscal Association, Corporate Tax on Distributions (Equalization Tax) 55 (1994).

[156]*See* FRA CGI § 158 *bis.*

[157]Foreign-source income is partially excluded from the *précompte* system by the operation of France's foreign income system. Typically, profits from foreign branches or dividends from foreign subsidiaries are exempt from tax in France, but for the purposes of operating the *précompte* system, foreign taxes are also treated as a credit against French tax, in this case, the *précompte* rather than the mainstream French enterprise tax.

[158]FRA CGI § 223 *sexies.*

In order to operate the *précompte*, the French system requires enterprises to keep accounting records to determine whether the income being distributed has borne enterprise tax at the full rate. However, that process of tracing taxed and untaxed profits raises important administrative questions that recur throughout the remainder of this discussion:

- Because the *précompte* is triggered by payment of a dividend out of untaxed profits, can the enterprise avoid the tax by retaining all profits?
- If it does not want to retain all profits, can the corporation choose which profits are being distributed and to whom, allowing a process generally referred to as "streaming"?
- If not, what are the "stacking" rules; that is, what rules determine the order in which various types of profits are distributed?

These questions also arise in the examination of the remaining systems, and are discussed below.

B. ADVANCE CORPORATION TAX MODEL

An advance corporation tax (ACT) system, modeled on the system used in the United Kingdom, uses a distribution-related tax as both a collection mechanism and the interaction mechanism between the enterprise tax system and the personal income tax.[159] The essence of the ACT mechanism is that a flat-rate tax is imposed on the enterprise making a distribution, and this tax is then credited against both the enterprise's liability for enterprise tax payable on its taxable income and the shareholder's liability for tax on the distribution. While the system used in the United Kingdom is not actually a withholding tax, at least not for the purposes of international tax treaties, an ACT can best be understood as a withholding tax that is credited twice—once for the benefit of the enterprise making the payment and again for the benefit of the investor receiving the payment.

The ACT system described below also abstracts from reality in order to identify more clearly the major policy choices involved. The mechanism of the system operates in these steps. Each dividend distribution made by an enterprise is subject to ACT at a flat rate, and the enterprise subtracts the ACT payment made during the year from its own liability for enterprise tax on its profits.[160] The balance of enterprise tax remaining to be paid after the credit for ACT payment is usually referred to as the mainstream corporation tax (MCT) liability, and it can come about either because the ACT rate on divi-

---

[159]*See generally* S. James & C. Nobes, The Economics of Taxation 287 (3d ed., 1988); U.S. Treasury Report, *supra* note 3, at app. B6.

[160]GBR ICTA § 239(1) provides that "advance corporation tax paid by a company . . . in respect of any distribution made by it in an accounting period shall be set against liability to corporation tax on any profits charged to corporation tax for that accounting period and shall accordingly discharge a corresponding amount of that liability."

dends is less than the adjusted enterprise tax rate on distributed profits or because the enterprise has elected to retain some profits. Where the enterprise retains profits, there is no ACT payment and hence no change to the classical system's consequences for the enterprise and the shareholder. If we assume that the ACT rate (T_a) is less than the enterprise tax rate (T_c), the position of the enterprise after payment of tax is therefore

$$dP[1 - T_a - (T_c - T_a)] + (1 - d)P(1 - T_c) = dP(1 - T_c) + (1 - d)P(1 - T_c).$$

1. Resident Individuals

The shareholder is treated in respect of distributed profits in the same way as under other imputation systems. The shareholder is taxed on the net distribution increased by the amount of ACT and then receives a credit for the ACT.[161] The shareholder includes in income

$$dP[(1 - T_a - (T_c - T_a)] \times [(1 + T_a)/(1 - T_a)].$$

Where (T_a) is set at a lower rate than (T_c), the position for distributions is equal to

$$dP[(1 - T_c)] \times [(1 + T_a)/(1 - T_a)].$$

The shareholder receives a credit equal to the amount of ACT (dPT_a). If the ACT rate (T_a) is set at the same rate as the investor's rate (T_i),[162] and the ACT is lower than the enterprise rate, the after-tax return of the shareholder becomes

$$R = dP(1 - T_c) + (1 - d)P(1 - T_c)(1 - T_g).$$

There is obviously a lot of importance to be attached to the *rate alignments* under such a system; that is, what are to be the relative sizes of the ACT rate, the enterprise rate, and the personal tax rate? At the enterprise level, dividends will effectively be taxed at the higher of the two enterprise rates as the following examples of different rate alignments show:

Example

The corporation has pretax financial profits of $24,000. The enterprise tax rate is 25 percent, and so the corporation is in principle liable to pay $6,000 in mainstream corporate tax. The corporation pays a dividend of $18,000 to a

---

[161]GBR ICTA § 20(1), sched. F. The amount taxed is "the aggregate of the amount or value of [any] distribution and the amount of [any] credit." The credit is provided in GBR ICTA § 231, which states that "where a company resident in the United Kingdom makes a qualifying distribution and the person receiving the distribution is . . . a person resident in the United Kingdom . . . , the recipient of the distribution shall be entitled to a tax credit equal to such proportion of the amount or value of the distribution as corresponds to the rate of advance corporation tax . . . ."

[162]It will be the same rate if T_i is a marginal rate rather than an average rate since income is subject to reliefs, progressive rates, losses, and so on, while T_a is set at a gross rate.

shareholder who is a resident individual. The ACT rate is 15 percent of the amount of dividends paid, and so the corporation is liable to pay $2,700 in ACT. The personal income tax rate is 15 percent on income up to $40,000 and 40 percent thereafter.

The corporation pays ACT of $2,700 and MCT of $3,300 ($6,000 − $2,700). The shareholder reports as income $21,176—the sum of the dividend of $18,000 and the $3,176 gross-up for ACT ($18,000 × 0.15/0.85). The taxpayer has a tax liability of $3,176 (15 percent of $21,176) and has a tax credit of $3,176. The total tax eventually paid is $6,000—ACT of $2,700 and MCT of $3,300, with no further shareholder tax payment.

Where, as here, the enterprise rate is higher than the ACT rate, it is the higher enterprise rate that is collected on distributed profits, but the gross-up occurs at the shareholder level only at the lower ACT rate. Indeed, in the United Kingdom, the ACT rate is approximately the same as the rate charged on taxable enterprise profits under the enterprise tax to avoid some of these problems.[163]

Where the ACT rate is higher than the enterprise rate, the ACT is the amount that is collected before the dividend is received by the shareholder:

Example

The corporation has pretax financial profits of $24,000. The enterprise tax rate is 20 percent, and so the corporation is in principle liable to pay $4,800 in mainstream corporate tax. The corporation pays a dividend of $18,000 to a shareholder who is a resident individual. The ACT rate is 33⅓ percent of the amount of dividends paid, and so the corporation is liable to pay $6,000 in ACT. The personal income tax rate is 33⅓ percent on income up to $40,000 and 40 percent thereafter.

The corporation pays ACT of $6,000 and MCT of 0 ($4,800 − $6,000 = −$1,200). The shareholder reports as income $27,000—the sum of the dividend of $18,000 and the $9,000 gross-up for ACT ($18,000 × 0.33/0.66). The taxpayer has a tax liability of $9,000 (33⅓ percent of $27,000) and has a tax credit of $9,000. The total tax eventually paid is $6,000—an ACT payment of $6,000, no MCT payment, and no further shareholder tax payment.

2. Enterprise-Level Tax Preferences

Because the tax is imposed upon distributions, it is collected whether or not the source of enterprise profits from which the distribution has been paid has borne tax or is even taxable. Nor, usually, does the reduction in the enterprise's tax liability for payments of ACT generate a refund of enterprise tax if the enterprise distributes more than its taxable profits, or if it is taxable at less than the ACT rate on its profits.[164] Effectively, tax is collected from

---

[163]The United Kingdom currently imposes tax at 25 percent on corporations with profits less than £150,000 and 35 percent for other corporations.

the enterprise at the higher of the ACT rate or the enterprise tax rate on distributed profits and at the enterprise tax rate on retentions. An ACT system can thus generate the consequence that all distributions are reduced by an amount of ACT, while some will be reduced by the enterprise tax rate if that is higher. This outcome is especially important for the treatment of tax preferences, which will reduce the enterprise's MCT tax liability by reducing either its taxable income or its tax.[165] Unfortunately, however, under an ACT system fashioned in this way, these items have no effect on the enterprise's ACT liability. This problem is referred to as "surplus ACT"; that is, the enterprise can distribute more profit than its own tax payments would indicate. In such a case, surplus ACT is generated on the difference—the amount by which the ACT on distributions exceeds the enterprise's own MCT liability.

One question that arises is, what should be done with these *surplus ACT credits?* As was discussed above, with all tax credits it is possible to refund them, allow the taxpayer to carry forward any excess credits to future years, allow the taxpayer to transfer (or perhaps even sell) the credit to another taxpayer such as a related corporation in a corporate group, or simply deny any further benefit. Each option will obviously have different consequences under an ACT system. If the excess credits are lost, it means that tax preferences are effectively recaptured at the enterprise level, but are taxed at the ACT rate, not at the personal or the enterprise rate.

If the enterprise reduces its primary enterprise tax liability, for example, by using domestic tax preferences, the after-tax position of the shareholder remains the same for distributions of declared earnings. But lower enterprise tax means that the enterprise's managers can attribute the ACT payment on distributions of undeclared earnings toward the mainstream enterprise tax liability on declared earnings. The gross-up and credit procedure occurs automatically as in the Canadian system, but on the basis that ACT has actually been collected on distributions. No enterprise tax will be collected on retained earnings where tax has been successfully reduced, and no ACT will be collected because profits have been retained. Consequently, only capital gains tax will be collected on the sale of the shares.

---

[164]This consequence is dealt with in the variety of provisions dealing with surplus advance corporation tax. If the corporation has insufficient tax liability, it can carry the credit back and recover tax paid in prior years or forward to use against the tax liability of future years, the liability of other companies in the group, or controlled foreign corporations. *See* GBR ICTA §§ 239, 240. This complication will be ignored.

[165]It also used to be a major problem for the taxation of distributions from foreign income. This issue was resolved in 1994 by the introduction of a special regime, the Foreign Income Dividends system. Under this system, ACT on dividends paid from foreign income, where there is no MCT liability to offset, can be refunded to the corporation. GBR ICTA §§ 246A–246Y.

Example

The corporation has pretax financial profits of $30,000. It is entitled to a special deduction of $6,000 for making an investment and therefore has taxable profits of $24,000. The enterprise tax rate is 25 percent, and so the corporation is in principle liable to pay $6,000 in mainstream tax. The corporation, which could pay a dividend of up to $24,000, decides to pay a dividend of $18,000 to a shareholder who is a resident individual. The ACT rate is 33⅓ percent of the amount of dividends paid, and so the corporation is liable to pay $6,000 in ACT. The personal income tax rate is 33⅓ percent.

The corporation pays ACT of $6,000 and MCT of 0 ($6,000 − $6,000 = 0). The shareholder reports as income $27,000—the sum of the dividend of $18,000 and the $9,000 gross-up for ACT ($18,000 x 0.33/0.66). The taxpayer has a tax liability of $9,000 (33⅓ percent of $27,000) and has a tax credit of $9,000. The total tax eventually paid is $6,000—an ACT payment of $6,000, no MCT payment, and no further shareholder tax payment. The shareholder's shares will have grown in value by an amount related to the $6,000 retained profits.

	Amount (In units of domestic currency)	Rate (In percent)	Tax (In units of domestic currency)
Nonpreference income	24,000	25	6,000
Preference income	6,000	0	0
Total	30,000		6,000

Under an ACT system, there is no problem with allocating tax credits to particular shareholders or groups of shareholders. There is, however, a different allocation question—about the "spillover" of ACT credits to preference income—which this example demonstrates. ACT is collected on distributions, but can ACT payments be used to offset all MCT liabilities, even the MCT on retained earnings? Or are ACT payments to be quarantined, so that they can be used to reduce the MCT only on distributed earnings?

The example above shows how, by retaining the $6,000 in preference income, the enterprise paid ACT only up to the point where the MCT liability was completely eliminated. Thus, the ACT in this case does not ensure that the correct enterprise tax is actually paid when the enterprise enjoys tax preferences but makes distributions. Rather, the ACT simply permits the enterprise's managers to reduce the amount of any final MCT to be paid on declared profits. More enterprise tax will be paid under the ACT mechanism when the enterprise proposes to report less taxable profit than the amount of profit (both taxed and untaxed) that it proposes to distribute. But in the reverse situation—when the enterprise's managers propose to retain the untaxed profits—the ACT system does not recapture preferences.

At the shareholder level, the rate alignment question involves the relationship between the ACT rate and the shareholder's personal rate. Where the amount of ACT is less than the individual shareholder's tax liability, the shareholder can be made to report the deficiency and make a top-up payment, as was shown in prior examples. Where the amount of ACT exceeds an individual shareholder's tax liability, there is a further question about the treatment of the excess ACT paid, as far as the shareholder is concerned. In the United Kingdom, the ACT rate is set at a level equal to the basic personal income tax rate so that the ACT is the effective collection mechanism for the personal tax liability.[166] However, for low-income shareholders who receive dividend income, typically retired individuals, the ACT rate may exceed their own personal income tax rate. When this occurs, there is again the issue of the proper treatment of the surplus credits. It is possible to refund them, allow the taxpayer to carry forward any excess credits to future years, allow the taxpayer to transfer (or perhaps even sell) the credit to another taxpayer, or simply deny any further benefit. In the United Kingdom, the ACT credit, if it exceeds the shareholder's tax liability, is refundable to the shareholder.[167] When the ACT rate is set equal to the highest personal rate rather than the lowest, and there is no intention of refunding "excess" credits to low-rate shareholders, the gross-up and credit procedure achieves nothing, and it is possible to simply exempt dividends received from further tax.[168]

C. Tax-Tracing Model

The final imputation system to be modeled is similar to that used in Australia and New Zealand.[169] Of the three imputation systems discussed, it appears to be the most accurate measure of the interaction of the enterprise and personal income tax, at least on distributed income. The Australian system tries

---

[166]GBR ICTA § 14(1) provides that, "where a company . . . makes a qualifying distribution it shall be liable to pay an amount of corporation tax in accordance with subsection (3)." Section 14(3) formally expresses the ACT rate in the form: $I/(100-I)$, I being "the percentage at which income tax at the basic rate is charged. . . ." Since, at present, the United Kingdom has only two rates of personal income tax (25 percent and 40 percent), this ACT rate is currently 25/75 or 33⅓ percent. The reference to a "qualifying distribution" is the way that returns of capital and certain other distributions are excluded from tax. Distributions from corporations are not subject to further tax because ACT is collected only on the excess of distributions made over distributions received. GBR ICTA § 241.

[167]GBR ICTA § 231(3).

[168]This is done in Estonia and Lesotho. EST ITL § 9(2)(6) ("income of a resident taxpayer does not include . . . dividends taxable under Article 32 of the present Law"). EST ITL § 32 establishes the ACT system for corporate tax. LSO ITA § 87(6) ("a dividend paid by a resident company shall not be included in the gross income of a resident shareholder").

[169]*See generally* R.J. Vann, Company Tax Reform (1988); Richard E. Krever, *Companies, Shareholders and Capital Gains Taxation*, 3 Aust. T. F. 267 (1986); Robert Richards & Ross Doherty, The Imputation System (1987); Robert Officer, *supra* note 120; U.S. Treasury Report, *supra* note 3, at app. B1.

to trace tax payments actually made by the enterprise and to attribute tax credits for those payments to individual shareholders only to the extent that verified tax payments have been made by the enterprise. The stylized Canadian system modeled above assumes that enterprise tax has been paid on all distributions; in other words, it disregards the possibility that distributed profits may not have borne tax. The U.K. system forces the payment of a tax on all distributions through the ACT mechanism, even when no MCT is owed. The Australian system traces the tax actually paid by the enterprise on its profits and attributes only tax actually paid to the profits distributed. It does permit untaxed profits to be distributed, but identifies them as such in the hands of the shareholder.

As under the previous imputation systems, the enterprise still pays tax on its taxable income, whether distributed or retained (PT_c) and will have a balance available for distribution $[P(1 - T_c)]$. The net amount distributed to the shareholder $[dP(1 - T_c)]$ is increased by the gross-up that represents corporate tax, effected by multiplying a fraction of the net dividend[170] by the factor $(T_c/1 - T_c)$ and adding this amount to the net dividend. A resident shareholder pays income tax at marginal rates on the proportion of after-tax profits distributed by the corporation as dividends,[171] and a tax credit is given to the shareholder for the amount of the gross-up.[172] Retained profits are still taxed as a capital gain when the shares are sold by the shareholder; no explicit credit against capital gains tax is given for enterprise tax already paid on retained profits—the tax paid on reported profits that are retained is effectively lost.[173] In this respect, the Australian imputation system, like the other imputation systems discussed, operates in a way similar to the classical system for retained profits.

1. Resident Individuals

The gross-up and credit procedure operates in several steps, which are recorded through entries in a notional account maintained by the enterprise to trace enterprise tax payments made and consumed. First, the enterprise's payment of tax on its taxable profits creates for the enterprise a credit in the enterprise's account (PT_c).[174] The enterprise can then attach a tax credit of that

---

[170]AUS ITAA § 160AQT requires the shareholder to include in income the "franked amount" of the dividend increased by this factor.

[171]See AUS ITAA § 160AQT.

[172]See AUS ITAA § 160AQU.

[173]Generally, no tax credits are attached to retentions. Some minor exceptions to the proposition that tax on retained enterprise profits is not credited to shareholders arise in the case of share buyback arrangements and the attributed income of controlled foreign corporations. See AUS ITAA div. 16J of pt. III, § 461. These exceptions will not be discussed further here.

[174]The amount of the credit is calculated by adjusting the amount of tax paid to express the amount of dividend that can be distributed tax free consequent upon a tax payment of this size. AUS ITAA §§ 160APMA–160APMD. These provisions refer to the amount of the credit as the "adjusted amount" in relation to the payment and § 160APA defines the adjusted amount as the amount multiplied in the manner indicated in the text.

amount to a dividend. When the enterprise declares a dividend of some portion of the after-tax profits (dPT_c), it also reduces the account by this amount, leaving a balance of $[(1 - d)PT_c]$.[175] In contrast to the ACT system, none of these steps affects the enterprise's own tax liability—they merely serve as a record, permitting subsequent calculations to be effected.[176] The shareholder reports the portion distributed increased by the gross-up for enterprise tax (dPT_c).[177] However, this gross-up does not occur as a simple increase of the net dividend by a constant rate. Rather, it is calculated on the amount that has been debited to the enterprise's franking account, which may or may not correspond to the net amount of dividend distributed, as will be shown later. Where the full taxable profits have been declared, this step becomes

$$dP(1 - T_c) + [(1 + T_c)/(1 - T_c)] = dP.$$

This amount is then subject to personal income tax (dPT_i) and the shareholder is entitled to a credit against the personal income tax liability of the same amount that was included by the gross-up procedure (dPT_c).[178] The net tax at the shareholder level on distributed dividends is thus $(dPT_i - dPT_c)$. The after-tax return to the shareholder is

$$R = dP(1 - T_i) + (1 - d)P(1 - T_c)(1 - T_g).$$

The total tax is paid in two parts: enterprise tax (dPT_c) is collected from the enterprise, and when the enterprise rate is less than the personal income tax rate, the deficit $(dPT_i - dPT_c)$ is collected from the shareholder.

Example

The corporation has pretax financial profits of $24,000. The corporate tax rate is 25 percent and so the corporation pays $6,000 in enterprise tax. The corporation pays a dividend of $18,000 to a shareholder who is a resident individual. The payment of $6,000 in enterprise tax will be recorded as a credit in the corporation's tax-paid account, and the payment of the dividend of $18,000 will be a debit of $6,000 to its tax-paid account.

The personal income tax rate is 33⅓ percent. The shareholder reports as income $24,000—the sum of the dividend of $18,000 and the $6,000 debited to the corporation's tax-paid account. The taxpayer has a tax liability of $8,000 (33⅓ percent of $24,000) and a tax credit of $6,000. The total tax eventually paid is $8,000—corporate tax payment of $6,000 and a further shareholder tax payment of $2,000.

---

[175]AUS ITAA § 160AQB prescribes a reduction to the franking account of "the franked amount of the dividend" paid by the enterprise.

[176]However, if the enterprise is found to have overranked a dividend, it must pay further tax to put the account in surplus. This additional tax is treated as a prepayment of the next year's tax.

[177]*See* AUS ITAA § 160AQT.

[178]*See* AUS ITAA § 160AQU.

When the amount of enterprise tax paid is more than the shareholder's own personal liability—for low-income shareholders who receive dividend income, there is again the issue of the proper treatment of the surplus credits—it is possible to refund the surplus results to the shareholder, allow the taxpayer to carry forward any excess credits to future years or to transfer (or perhaps even sell) the credit to another taxpayer, or simply deny any further benefit.

2. Enterprise-Level Tax Preference Income

Even if the two rates are identical, a further shareholder payment also comes about when for some other reason, such as the existence of foreign tax credits or enterprise-level tax preferences, all of the profits distributed by the enterprise's managers have not borne domestic tax at the full enterprise rate.[179] One purpose of the system is to provide tax credits only for enterprise tax actually paid in the country where the enterprise is resident.[180] This has the consequence that enterprise-level tax preferences or foreign tax credits are recaptured at the shareholder level.

Example

The corporation has pretax financial profits of $30,000. It is entitled to a special deduction of $6,000 for making an investment and therefore has taxable profits of $24,000. The enterprise tax rate is 25 percent and so the corporation pays $6,000 in tax. The corporation pays a dividend of $24,000. The payment of $6,000 in enterprise-level tax will be recorded as a credit in the corporation's tax-paid account, and the payment of the dividend of $24,000 will create a debit of $6,000 to its tax-paid account.

The personal income tax rate is 33 percent. The shareholder reports as income $30,000—the sum of the dividend of $24,000 and the $6,000 debited to the corporation's tax-paid account. The taxpayer has a tax liability of $9,900 (33 percent of $30,000) and a tax credit of $6,000. The total tax eventually paid is $9,900—a tax payment of $6,000 and a further shareholder tax payment of $3,300.

	Amount (In units of domestic urrency)	Rate (In percent)	Tax (In units of domestic currency)
Nonpreference income	24,000		
Corporate tax component		25	6,000
Shareholder tax component		(33–25)	1,920
Distributed preference income	6,000		
Shareholder tax		33	1,980
Total	30,000		9,900

---

[179]Any excess that arises—that is, where dPT_c is greater than dPT_r—can be used as a credit against the shareholder's other tax liabilities, but is not refundable.

[180]This is, of course, not consistent with any neutrality principle—either capital-export or capital-import neutrality—and is accordingly open to criticism.—L.M.

This example involves the same problem of the "leakage" of tax benefits that was discussed in relation to the ACT system: Is it possible to use tax credits from taxed but retained profits to immunize untaxed distributed profits from tax? If we relax the assumption that the enterprise distributes all enterprise-level profits, the treatment of untaxed profits distributed as dividends will depend on how the account is debited and how the tax credits are attached to dividends— an issue similar to that raised both in the ACT system and under the equalization tax variant. It is clear that the balance in the account (PT_c) would be insufficient to permit the enterprise's managers to distribute a dividend with full tax credits greater than $[P(1 - T_c)]$. But if the enterprise's managers retain a proportion of the profits $[(1 - d)P(1 - T_c)]$, the "unused" credits in the account (representing tax on taxed but retained profits) can be applied against the undeclared but distributed profits. If so, distributed undeclared profits can also be distributed tax free to shareholders under this system, as they are under an ACT system.

Example

The corporation has pretax financial profits of $30,000. It is entitled to a special deduction of $6,000 for making an investment and therefore has taxable profits of $24,000. The enterprise tax rate is 25 percent, and so the corporation pays $6,000 in tax. The corporation, which could pay a dividend of $24,000, decides to pay a dividend of $18,000 to a shareholder who is a resident individual. The payment of $6,000 enterprise-level tax will be recorded as a credit in the corporation's tax-paid account, and the payment of the dividend of $18,000 will create a debit of $6,000 to its tax-paid account.

The personal income tax rate is 33⅓ percent. The shareholder reports as income $24,000—the sum of the dividend of $18,000 and the $6,000 gross-up for the amount debited to the corporation's tax-paid account. The shareholder has a tax liability of $8,000 (33⅓ percent of $24,000) and a tax credit of $6,000. The total tax eventually paid is $8,000—an enterprise-level tax of $6,000 and a further shareholder tax payment of $2,000. The shareholder's shares will have grown in value by an amount related to the $6,000 retained profits.

	Amount (In units of domestic currency)	Rate (In percent)	Tax (In units of domestic urrency)
Nonpreference income	24,000		
Corporate tax component		25	6,000
Shareholder tax component		(33⅓–25)	2,000
Undistributed preference income	6,000	33⅓	0
Total	30,000		8,000

3. Streaming of Taxed and Untaxed Dividends

The systems in operation actually allow more flexibility than this simple matter of leakage would suggest—hence, the comment above that the accuracy of the crediting mechanism may be more apparent than real. That flexibility raises an issue that is commonly referred to as "streaming"—that is, directing the tax credits to shareholders who can use them most advantageously. The examples above assume that the enterprise's managers will (and must) debit the tax-paid account with its full credit balance if the size of the dividend being paid permits them to do so. But if such a rule does not exist—in other words, if the enterprise's managers have discretion about how much of the credit balance in the account to use and when—the possibility of streaming arises. For example, if the enterprise has shareholders in both high and low tax brackets, it might try to direct the credits predominantly to the former group (and not to the latter, where excess credits at the shareholder level might be unusable). Various devices and techniques would be needed, but having shares with differential rights or declaring successive dividends might be feasible tools, especially in closely held companies.

To reduce this problem, the systems in place try to ensure that all dividends carry the same proportion of credits, where there are insufficient credits to cover all dividends to be declared in a year.[181] But this rule does not apply if the enterprise's managers plan to make distributions from undeclared profits up to the amount of retained declared profits, that is, if the total distribution is less than the balance in the account. This would mean that all dividends, whether out of declared or undeclared profits, up to that amount could effectively be distributed tax free to shareholders. If, however, the enterprise's managers plan to distribute all of the declared profits and some portion of the undeclared profits, the rule does apply and all dividends will carry only fractional credits.[182] The enterprise's managers can effectively attach tax credits to a distribution up to an amount of taxed profits regardless of whether some portion of the amount distributed has actually borne tax. If there are insufficient credits, the gross-up and credit procedure described above will still operate for taxed profits but not for untaxed profits. If the profits are not taxed, they carry no tax credit, and the shareholder simply includes the distributed portion of untaxed profits in income with no gross-up or credit and is taxed in the same way as under a classical system.

---

[181]AUS ITAA § 160AQF provides that all dividends paid under a resolution of the company are taken to be franked to the percentage specified in a declaration made in relation to the dividend. The declaration cannot be varied or revoked. Section 160AQG treats all dividends paid during the year on the same class of shares as being franked to the same percentage declared for the first dividend. The purpose of these sections is to prevent streaming of distributions whereby distributions carrying tax credits are paid to taxpaying entities, while taxable distributions (if any) are directed to tax-exempt bodies. Streaming of this kind would permit the enterprise to increase the after-tax return to both groups of shareholders. The section tries to prevent this practice by insisting on a pro rata attaching of credits rather than a first-in-first-out rule.

[182]The act also offers the enterprise's managers the choice of franking the distribution of untaxed profits to 100 percent, but the enterprise will be obliged at the end of the year to pay additional tax to repay the deficit balance in the franking account. That is, the enterprise effectively prepays the next year's corporate tax.

4. Nonresident Shareholders

The position of nonresident shareholders raises a few novel questions in the context of an account-based imputation system.

One reason for the imputation systems described above is that benefits can be, although they need not be, confined to resident shareholders. But if benefits are so confined, the issue will arise as to whether the tax-paid account must be debited in the case of dividends paid to nonresident shareholders because the shareholders will derive no benefit from the tax credit. Indeed, this is an area where streaming could be expected to occur—allocating all the credits for enterprise tax paid to resident shareholders where the system does not afford any benefit to nonresident shareholders.

International experience in this area is not uniform, although most, but not all, countries choose to confine the benefits of their imputation system to resident shareholders. One interesting exception is Singapore, which levies no additional withholding tax on distributions at all, whether to residents or nonresidents. In addition, some of the treaties negotiated by France, Ireland, and the United Kingdom levy withholding taxes, but allow partial or full credits to flow to nonresidents by refunds in cash.

For example, Australia's tax treaties with France, Ireland, and the United Kingdom allow Australian resident shareholders who are individuals some access to foreign imputation credits. Article 9(6) of the Australia-France treaty provides that an Australian resident who is an individual and receives a dividend from a company resident in France is entitled to a payment from the government of France equal to 85 percent of the tax credit (*avoir fiscal*) that would be attached to the dividend if received by an individual resident of France. Fifteen percent remains in France by way of withholding tax.

6. Full Integration System

The last option to be explored is a full integration system for enterprises.[183] An integration system operates at the shareholder level and attributes the enterprise's income, whether distributed or not, to the shareholders who are taxable on all the enterprise's profits. There are two varieties of full integration systems. One, usually referred to as the partnership version of the integration system, implies that no tax is imposed on the enterprise's profits, unlike the other systems already discussed. Under the other version, where the enterprise remains taxable, the enterprise's tax is then credited to the shareholders as a credit against their liability on the attributed profits.

---

[183]*See generally* Pechman, *supra* note 103, at 178–81; McLure, Must Corporate Income Be Taxed Twice? *supra* note 103, at 2–9; Bradford, *supra* note 78, at 54–56; Blueprints, *supra* note 3, at 63–69; Bird, *supra* note 103, at 235. To add to the complexity, there are also partial integration systems. Under a partial integration system, some (or all) of the corporation's profits are attributed to the shareholders and some (or all) of the corporation's tax is credited to the shareholders. McLure, *supra* note 103, at 15–18.

Schedular integration systems that are not based on a single rate are intended to offset the effect of the enterprise income tax entirely so that all enterprise profits are ultimately taxed at individual marginal rates in the current year, regardless of whether the profits are distributed. This system promises the model treatment to which the other systems aspire, because all profits are taxed at exactly the shareholder's personal income tax rate (although portions of the total tax might be collected from both the enterprise and the shareholder), and there is no gain to the taxpayer from deferring the recognition of income by retaining profits within the enterprise.[184]

The so-called partnership-style integration achieves this result by eliminating the enterprise tax altogether and taxing the shareholders as if they were in partnership—all enterprise profits are included in the individual's taxable income. The United States permits shareholders to elect this treatment under Subchapter S of Chapter I of the Internal Revenue Code for domestically controlled corporations with few shareholders and little foreign-source or passive income.[185] One consequence of the election is that the benefits of corporate losses and tax preference items are passed through to the shareholders.[186] For the reasons discussed in section II above, this style of integration is generally considered unfeasible as a model for all enterprises and will not be considered further in this chapter.

With this exception and for the reasons referred to earlier, no country has adopted a full integration system for the taxation of domestic enterprises and their resident shareholders, despite the support of many commentators and several government reports.[187] But, somewhat surprisingly, a second style of integration system is more common for taxing nonresident enterprises controlled by resident shareholders, where the system is usually referred to as a controlled foreign corporation (CFC) tax system. In this context, the system is used not because it approximates the economist's ideal of eliminating the double taxation of enterprise profits, but rather as an antiavoidance mechanism to prevent the accumulation of untaxed passive or tax-sheltered income offshore.[188] This sec-

---

[184]See Cnossen, supra note 108, at 98; Bird, supra note 103, at 235.

[185]See generally B. Bittker & J. Eustice, Federal Income Taxation of Corporations and Shareholders, ch. 6 (5th ed., 1987).

[186]USA IRC § 1372(b)(1) (corporation not taxable); § 1373(b) (shareholders taxable on all income); § 1374 (corporate losses deductible to shareholders). In this model, the corporation effectively ceases to exist as either a separate taxable entity or a withholding point.

[187]See supra notes 103, 183.

[188]See USA IRC subpt. F, AUS ITAA pt. X. CFC regimes exist in Australia, Canada, France, Germany, Japan, New Zealand, Norway, Sweden, the United Kingdom, and the United States. See B. Arnold, The Taxation of Controlled Foreign Corporations: An International Comparison (1986). Curiously, while CFC systems were originally developed as a means of eliminating the gain from accumulating lightly taxed income offshore, the substantial income tax rate reductions of the 1980s mean that some taxpayers may now benefit from creating a CFC. See Paul McDaniel & Hugh Ault, Introduction to United States International Taxation 118–20 (3d ed. 1989). See also OECD, Controlled Foreign Company Legislation (1996).

tion considers a theoretical CFC-type system, but for domestic enterprises.[189] Such a system is not in use in any domestic tax system, but the one described here would achieve the central element of an integration system, taxing shareholders currently on all declared enterprise profits, but with the innovation of retaining the enterprise tax as a pure withholding mechanism.

A. RESIDENT INDIVIDUALS

For this integration system, it is assumed that the enterprise still pays tax on its profits and that the individual shareholders pay income tax at progressive marginal rates on all the taxable profits of the enterprise, whether or not they are distributed. A tax credit is then given to the shareholders for the entire enterprise tax paid. Again, a decision would have to be made as to whether the tax credit mechanism traces actual payments of enterprise tax or operates automatically. Any retained profits are taxed to the shareholders at the appropriate personal rate when earned (and appropriate credits are also attributed). The shareholder's cost in the shares is increased by the amount of profit taxed to the shareholder, to avoid double taxation when the shares are disposed of.[190] Any further capital gain beyond the value of retained taxed earnings is taxed in the usual way as capital gain. When the enterprise's managers report and pay tax on the enterprise's full profit, the after-tax position of the shareholder is

$$R = P(1 - T_i).$$

This result would be achieved in several steps. First, enterprise tax (PT_c) is collected from the enterprise. The amount of any distribution is included in the shareholder's income together with the usual gross-up for enterprise tax:

$$dP(1 - T_c)[(1 + T_c) / (1 - T_c)] = dP.$$

This approach generates a tax liability at the personal income rate (dPT_i), and the shareholder receives a credit (dPT_c) against this tax liability for the enterprise tax paid. The element that makes this system different from those described earlier is that retained earnings and a further gross-up for enterprise tax

---

[189]*See* Pechman, *supra* note 103, at 178–81. It is one of the prototypes suggested by the U.S. Treasury Report, *supra* note 3.

[190]The result might be prevented in several ways, including, for example, through a further gross-up and credit procedure that increased the basis in the shares by $(T_g/1 - T_g)$ and gave to the shareholder a credit against capital gains tax for the same amount that could be carried forward and used when the shares were sold. Instead, the procedure described here is the one used in the United States to reconcile the capital gains tax and personal income tax on shareholders in S corporations, with appropriate modifications to reflect the fact that the corporate tax has been retained in this discussion. *See also* Blueprints, *supra* note 3, at 64. An alternative procedure—used in Australia for the attributed profits of CFCs—writes down the proceeds of sale by amounts already attributed, permitting shareholders to sell retentions of previously taxed income without further tax. AUS ITAA § 461.

on the earnings would also have to be included in the shareholder's current as-sessable income:

$$(1 - d)P(1 - T_c)[(1 + T_c) / (1 - T_c)] = (1 - d)P.$$

This creates a tax liability of $[(1 - d)PT_i]$ and a credit of $[(1 - d)PT_c]$ is set off against the tax liability.

The capital gains tax is retained to capture items not taxed on a current basis, such as unrealized enterprise profits, tax preferences, or stock market gains.[191] A further adjustment is necessary to reflect the fact that some of the retained profits reflected in the price of the shares will already have been taxed. The adjustment involves annually increasing the shareholder's cost in the shares by the amount of retained earnings taxed in that year.[192] If the tax-payer realizes only the accumulated value of retained taxed profits, the share-holder's basis equals this amount and no capital gain arises.

The annual increase in the shareholder's cost in the shares comes about through a series of steps.[193] Given that the enterprise's managers have distributed some after-tax profits, the enterprise still retains an amount $[(1 - d)P(1 - T_c)]$ on which enterprise tax has already been paid. The shareholder's cost in the total retained earnings is calculated in the following way. First, the share-holder's cost is increased by the amount of taxable profits remaining after en-terprise tax $[P(1 - T_c)]$. Then the shareholder's cost is reduced by the amounts already "liberated" from the enterprise for the benefit of the share-holder—the distributed taxed profits and the tax attaching to all profits. Thus the taxpayer's basis in the earnings is increased by $[(1 - d)P(1 - T_c)]$. The system operates in this fashion:

---

[191]U.S. Treasury Report, *supra* note 3, at 82 ("not all capital gains from increases in the value of corporate equity arise from accumulated retained earnings. Gains from other sources may im-ply different tax consequences than those applicable solely to gains from fully taxed retained earnings"); Head & Bird, *supra* note 113, at 15 note 22 ("a capital gains tax at the personal level would still be needed to tax 'goodwill gains'—those arising from such factors as improved market position, technological developments, and natural resource discoveries").

[192]In the United States, this process occurs in two steps. USA IRC § 1367(a)(1)(A) increases the shareholder's basis in the shareholding by the "items of income described in subparagraph (A) of section 1366(a)(1)." This is the provision that includes in the shareholder's taxable in-come "the shareholder's pro rata share of the corporation's items of income (including tax-exempt income)." USA IRC § 1366(a)(1)(A). A subsequent provision states that this increase in basis occurs "only to the extent such amount is included in the shareholder's gross income on his return." USA IRC § 1367(b)(1). The shareholder's basis is then reduced by "distributions by the corporation which were not includible in the income of the shareholder by reason of section 1368." USA IRC § 1367(a)(2). Section 1368 exempts distributions by an S corporation up to the lower of the shareholder's basis in the shares or the balance in the "accumulated adjustments ac-count." The result of these provisions is that the shareholder will increase his or her basis in the shares by the net of the income actually disclosed by the corporation and distributions up to the amount actually disclosed.

[193]These steps have to be modified from those described in note 192 *supra* because the enter-prise tax still remains in operation, unlike the position of S corporations in the United States.

Example

The corporation has pretax financial profits of $24,000. The enterprise tax rate is 25 percent and the corporation is liable to pay $6,000 in enterprise tax. The corporation pays a dividend of $15,000 to a shareholder who is a resident individual and retains $3,000. The personal income tax rate is 30 percent on income up to $40,000 and 40 percent thereafter.

The corporation pays tax of $6,000. The shareholder reports as income $24,000—the sum of the dividend of $15,000 and a tax credit attached to it of $5,000 ($15,000 × 0.25/0.75) and the retained earnings of $3,000 and the tax credit attached to it of $1,000 ($3,000 × 0.25/0.75). The investor is liable to gross tax of $7,200 and has a total tax credit of $6,000. The shareholder's cost is increased by $3,000.

B. PREFERENCE INCOME

The treatment under such a system of the untaxed enterprise profits, such as enterprise-level tax preferences or foreign income, raises several policy issues. The decision about the crediting mechanism will be the basis for the answer. If the decision is made that preference income is washed out at the shareholder level, then only actual tax payments, rather than an automatic credit, should be used for computing the tax credit. The shareholder's cost is increased by the amount of taxable profits (P) remaining after enterprise tax $[P(1 - T_c)]$ and reduced by the amount of profits distributed without further personal income tax $[dD(1 - T_c) + d(P - D)]$, up to the amount of the taxable profits. Thus, the taxpayer's basis in the earnings is increased by only $[(1 - d)D(1 - T_c) - d(P - D)]$; that is, untaxable but distributed profits effectively reduce the increase in basis by the amount distributed. This means that the capital gains tax calculation becomes

$$\{(1 - d)D(1 - T_c) + (1 - d)(P - D) - [(1 - d)D(1 - T_c) - d(P - D)]\}(1 - T_g),$$

which becomes

$$[(P - D)(1 - T_g)].$$

The eventual after-tax position of the shareholder becomes

$$R = D(1 - T_i) + (P - D)(1 - T_g).$$

Example

The corporation has pretax financial profits of $30,000. Because of a special incentive, it is entitled to a special tax deduction of $6,000. It therefore has taxable profits of $24,000. The enterprise tax rate is 25 percent, and so the corporation is liable to pay $6,000 in tax. The corporation pays a dividend of $15,000 to a shareholder who is a resident individual and retains $3,000 of its taxable profits. The personal income tax rate is 30 percent on income up to $40,000 and 40 percent thereafter.

The corporation pays tax of $6,000. The shareholder reports as income $24,000—the sum of the dividend of $15,000 and a tax credit attached to it of

$5,000 ($15,000 × 0.25/0.75) and the retained earnings of $3,000 and the tax credit attaching to it of $1,000 ($3,000 × 0.25/0.75). The investor is liable to gross tax of $7,200 and has a total tax credit of $6,000. The shareholder's cost is increased by only $3,000.

If the enterprise distributes some of the untaxed profits, the deficiency will be recaptured in the taxation of dividends. But because the tax preference income is not taxable income, it is difficult to see how it could be attributed to shareholders and taxed on a current basis. Therefore, it remains to the capital gains tax to collect tax, albeit deferred, on this income.

Example

The corporation has pretax financial profits of $30,000. Because of a special incentive, it is entitled to a special tax deduction of $10,000. It therefore has taxable profits of $20,000. The enterprise tax rate is 20 percent, and the corporation is liable to pay $4,000 in tax. The corporation pays a dividend of $24,000 to a shareholder who is a resident individual and retains $2,000. The personal income tax rate is 30 percent on income up to $40,000 and 40 percent thereafter.

The corporation pays tax of $4,000. The shareholder reports as income $28,000, the amount of the dividend and the tax credit attached to it of $4,000 (because of the tracing process). The investor is liable to gross tax of $8,400 and has a tax credit of $4,000. The shareholder's cost is not increased so that the retained untaxable earnings of $2,000 will be taxed as capital gain only. Total tax paid is $8,400, $4,000 by the corporation and $4,400 by the investor.

In this case, the outcome is just as if the investor had faced the following tax rates:

	Amount (In units of domesitc currency)	Rate (In percent)	Tax (In units of domesitc currency)
Distributed nonpreference income	20,000	30	6,000
Tax on nonpreference income	4,000	30	1,200
Distributed preference income	4,000	30	1,200
Retained preference income	2,000	0	0
Total	30,000		8,400

C. NONRESIDENT SHAREHOLDERS

Although on the basis of the discussion in previous sections it might be thought that a full integration system is eminently desirable, its apparent virtues are subject to one major and probably insuperable impediment—the difficulties presented in taxing nonresident shareholders.

As has been mentioned already, the general consensus that has developed on the appropriate international allocation for taxing enterprise profits is that the source country is able to tax the enterprise in full and has limited rights to tax dividends paid out of those profits. A system of full integration challenges this consensus by attempting to tax the nonresident shareholder on undistributed profits, an option that tax treaties do not explicitly countenance.[194] It is unclear whether the source country has the right to tax this amount prior to distribution, what rate would be applied, and, correspondingly, whether the shareholder could insist that the tax system in its country of residence give relief for the tax so collected.

Taxing undistributed profits is a challenge not only to the existing tax base orthodoxy, but also to a tax administration. The ability to tax resident shareholders on undistributed income is facilitated by having both the enterprise and the shareholder as residents—any top-up tax on undistributed profits can be collected when the resident files a return. For nonresident shareholders, the tax administration would have to collect both the profit tax and the tax on undistributed profits from the enterprise directly because there is no dividend to tax, and the shareholder is not necessarily within the jurisdiction of the source country's tax administration. While this result is technically feasible, it is not clear what rate should be applied because there is no real information about the marginal tax rate applicable to the nonresident.

Moreover, as a practical matter, in a world where taxes are an important factor in decisions about locating real investments, no country can afford to be the sole country to tax resident enterprises on such a basis.

VI. Distributions

A. Typology of Distributions

For the purpose of this section, distributions are defined as any payment made by an enterprise to its shareholders with respect to the shareholders' capital investment. Distributions can take various forms, the most common of which are amounts paid by companies as dividends and amounts paid either to repurchase company shares or to purchase the shares of a subsidiary of the company. However, inventive finance and tax experts are constantly developing new techniques for making company distributions to shareholders. In addition to assuming various different forms, distributions can have different economic origins. They can be paid out of profits that have been taxed at the company level, out of profits that have not been taxed at the company level, or out of no profits at all (meaning, they constitute a return of capital).

---

[194]This problem already arises when a residence country taxes a resident on the accumulated profits of a foreign controlled corporation under its CFC rules. For a discussion of this problem of the interaction of tax treaties and domestic CFC systems, *see generally* OECD Model Treaty, *supra* note 122, paragraphs 23–26, Commentary to art. 1. *See also* OECD, *supra* note 188.

B. Tax Consequences of Distributions from Different Origins

The tax consequences of a distribution arising from one of these three different origins will vary significantly depending on the type of tax system in place. One constant among income tax systems, however, is that shareholders do not include as income distributions that constitute a return of capital. In addition, shareholders whose tax base includes capital gains and losses on the sale or transfer of their shares must make a downward adjustment to their share cost in an amount equal to such a distribution.[195] Therefore, all tax systems are concerned with whether a distribution constitutes a return of capital.

In addition, fully integrated tax systems are concerned with techniques whereby enterprises may declare taxable bonus shares or with other techniques that allow shareholders whose tax base includes capital gains and losses on the sale or transfer of their shares to, in effect, increase the cost of their shares by the amount retained. In addition, in integrated systems where the enterprise tax is at a higher rate than that of at least some shareholders, these techniques may also allow the shareholder to receive a credit for the difference between the two rates.[196]

The different treatment accorded distributions made from taxed income and from untaxed income will vary depending on a number of factors. The most important is whether there is an integrated enterprise-shareholder tax, where the enterprise rate is equal to or higher than the shareholder rate. In such a system, distributions of income fully taxed at the enterprise level need not be taxed at the shareholder level, although depending on the integration system the shareholder may be entitled to a refund of all or part of the accompanying credit. However, as discussed in the previous section, any distribution from income that was either not taxed at all or not fully taxed at the enterprise level raises the question of whether tax should then be levied.

Obviously, this question can arise only when enterprises are not taxed on a base that closely approximates their economic income or at a rate that is less than the top shareholder rate. As was discussed at length in the previous section, the tax system can either not tax distributions from untaxed income or can tax them in some way. Some of the more common techniques employed to tax distributions from untaxed or partially taxed income include levying a compensatory-type tax on payment at the enterprise level, levying tax on receipt at the shareholder level, or combining the two techniques into a hybrid system.

In jurisdictions without full integration, the issue is different still. These jurisdictions impose tax on distributions from both taxed and untaxed income,

---

[195]From a purely theoretical perspective, it would be possible to require a shareholder who included capital gains and losses on its shares in its tax base to include the return of capital in the tax base, and not require any adjustment of the share's cost. When the shareholder sold or transferred the shares, the shareholder would realize a loss equal to the return of capital previously taxed. If tax rates on income and capital gains and losses were the same, and if the taxpayer could claim the entire loss, the taxpayer would be made whole.

[196]This issue is discussed in greater length *infra* at H.

although typically at the same rate. While the reasoning for imposing double taxation on enterprise income is not particularly compelling, it requires levying a tax on all distributions other than those that constitute returns of capital. Withholding or shareholder-level taxes, or a hybrid of both, can be used to levy this additional tax on the distribution.

C. Implications of Different Tax Consequences for Distributions

As can readily be seen, it would benefit an enterprise's shareholders if it could make distributions of untaxed or partially taxed income without drawing additional tax. For this reason, and depending on the rules the particular jurisdiction has in place, enterprises may attempt to disguise distributions that draw additional tax as distributions that do not draw additional tax. For example, in integrated systems, an enterprise may try to make a dividend look as if it were paid from previously taxed income. In both integrated and unintegrated systems, an enterprise may try to make a dividend or a redemption appear as if it constitutes a return of capital.[197] And, as noted earlier, inventive finance and tax experts are constantly developing new techniques for making enterprise distributions to shareholders, techniques that may not be adequately addressed by existing rules or that may not be sufficiently understood by hard-pressed tax administrators.

D. Simplified Systems

Given these incentives for enterprises to avoid tax, and the inventiveness with which they may try to do so, it would greatly simplify the design and implementation of enterprise-shareholder tax systems if it were unnecessary to tax distributions. If nearly all income were taxed at the enterprise level in a fully integrated system, the question would not arise as to whether any distributions should be taxed because all distributions either would be paid out of taxed income or would represent returns of capital to shareholders. And, if a single-rate schedular tax at the shareholder level equal to and integrated with the tax of the enterprise level were applied, then no distribution would need to be treated as taxable as income by the shareholder.[198] In such a simplified system, the only tax effect a distribution would have would be on those shareholders subject to capital gains tax, who would have to determine whether the distribution were a return of capital; if so, they would be required to adjust downward the cost of the share by the amount of the distribution.

In a nonschedular integration system, it would be necessary to distinguish only between distributions carrying imputation credits (which would be in-

---

[197]With integrated systems, the incentive for the enterprise to find ways to make nontaxable distributions exists only with regard to its untaxed income, while in unintegrated systems the incentive extends to all company income, whether taxed or untaxed at the company level.

[198]This would include nonresident investors, who would be exempt from additional withholding tax.

cluded as income, along with a credit) and those that did not (which would be treated as a return of capital).[199]

E. Rules for Distinguishing Between Distributions of Income and Returns of Capital

In the absence of a schedular system with a single tax rate, it may sometimes be necessary to determine whether a distribution constitutes a return of capital. In addition, in a system where a fair amount of income can escape enterprise tax or where integration is absent or incomplete, there is an incentive to describe distributions as nontaxable returns of capital. However, in a system where substantially all enterprise income is already fully taxed, and where there is complete integration, there is no such incentive. In fact, if anything, there may in some cases be an incentive to disguise distributions of capital so as to avoid reducing the adjusted cost of the share for capital gains purposes. While the latter incentive would presumably be considerably less of a problem than the former, it would still be helpful to have simple techniques for determining what constitutes a return of capital and what does not.

Unfortunately, most jurisdictions have systems in which a fair amount of income can escape enterprise tax, or where integration is nonexistent or incomplete, and are therefore more concerned with proving distributions to be taxable than not to be taxable. One technique for policing distributions is to rely, in effect, on the operations of corporate law.[200] Corporate law governs the circumstances and manner by which a company may make distributions to its shareholders. Under the corporate law of many jurisdictions, distributions to shareholders are subject to a number of restrictions designed to protect the rights of creditors. In the most restrictive company law regimes, distributions are restricted to dividends paid out of company profits (as determined by special corporate accounting rules), and to the redemption of certain limited types of stock (usually preferred);[201] other types of stock redemptions, including the pur-

---

[199]In the former case, distribution plus credit would be added to the shareholder's income, with a credit given against tax due, with only share cost adjustment in the latter case. In these systems, shareholders may be subject to tax at a rate less than the enterprise rate. While it would be one thing to allow small amounts of profits untaxed at the enterprise level also to go untaxed at the shareholder level, it would be another thing to allow these shareholders to claim credits for enterprise tax that was never actually paid. For this reason, it may be advisable to limit the total amount of credits that can be claimed to total amounts of enterprise tax.

[200]Of course, corporate law would not govern enterprises other than corporations. However, most large economic enterprises in most jurisdictions operate in corporate form. In certain cases, it may be possible to apply corporate law to other enterprises that function like corporations.

[201]Such a rule would greatly restrict a company's ability to borrow against appreciated assets and make distributions to a shareholder of the proceeds of the borrowing. If, however, a tax rule were adopted that required such proceeds to be included in income, they should also be treated as income for corporate law purposes.

chase of shares in a subsidiary, are prohibited. In these cases, only the price paid for the redemption of preferred stock would be treated as a return of capital.

However, corporate law rules concerning shareholder distributions, at least in many jurisdictions, are being liberalized. The repurchase of nonredeemable shares is now often permitted, as is, in some jurisdictions, the payment of dividends out of capital. In these cases, it may still be possible to rely on the corporate law rules to define a return of capital for tax purposes. In particular, the rules would have to determine when a dividend is not made out of company income and how much of the purchase price of a share buyback would have to be considered a return of capital.

A helpful modification of this approach may be to combine corporate law rules with special tax rules, particularly with regard to determining a corporation's income. If comprehensive income tax rules are applied, taxable income can, for example, be substituted directly for traditional definitions of corporate "profits."[202] However, the rules concerning what constitutes a repayment of capital in the case of stock redemptions would continue to apply.

In a fully integrated system that effectively taxes nearly all of a company's income, such rules should be relatively easy to apply.

F. Complex Systems

However, it is a different story in systems that do not capture most income through the enterprise tax, or where the shareholder-level tax is equal to and integrated with the tax at the enterprise level. Considerable additional care on the part of tax administrations will be required if they wish effectively to capture distributions from untaxed income (in integrated systems) or from both untaxed and taxed income (classical systems). This is because the incentives to make otherwise taxable distributions look like nontaxable distributions will be greater. In these cases, corporate law rules may be too easily manipulated and may require additional tax rules to prevent tax avoidance. For example, if there is untaxed income at the enterprise level, it will always be preferable to make distributions to shareholders through redemptions if those payments are treated as returns of capital and therefore not taxable.

G. Examples

As described in the previous section, France has a partial imputation system.[203] It levies a compensatory tax on distributions out of income that is not fully taxed at the enterprise level. The tax system does so in what is essentially a two-step process. It determines first if the distribution is from profits

---

[202]*See supra* ch. 16.
[203]This discussion is based on Hugh J. Ault et al., Comparative Income Taxation: A Structural Analysis 304–05 (1997).

(whether taxed or untaxed) and next if the distribution is from income already subject to full tax. If so, the *précompte mobilier* is applied.

Essentially, any distribution to shareholders (other than bonus shares that represent capitalization of reserves or earnings) is deemed to be out of profits unless it qualifies for treatment as a redemption or a liquidation.[204] The enterprise keeps track of what profits it has retained and which have borne full tax, and a stacking rule provides that distributions come first from after-tax profits, and then from untaxed profits.[205]

The French rules on the treatment of redemptions are rather complicated. Where redemptions are permitted, a portion of the distribution may be deemed to be taxable. A number of steps must first be followed to determine what portion. For those shareholders not subject to capital gains tax, the portion of the distribution that exceeds the greater of the shareholder's actual gain or the amount of the share's paid-in capital is taxable as a dividend, up to the extent of the enterprise's accounting profits. All amounts paid out of untaxed profits are subject to the *précompte mobilier*. A different, and more complicated, rule applies to shareholders subject to capital gains tax.

These tax rules appear to allow enterprises to borrow against appreciated assets and then to use the proceeds of the borrowing to pay exempt dividends or to make exempt redemptions. However, French corporate law mitigates these options substantially. It prohibits companies from making distributions of dividends except out of accounting profits, and severely restricts the ability of companies to make redemptions. However, if corporate law were to change, so too might these conclusions.

As described in the previous section, the United Kingdom has only a partial imputation system, and uses the ACT as its primary technique for capturing distributions from untaxed income. Under this system, it is necessary first to determine which distributions are from income (whether taxed or untaxed), for those distributions will attract ACT. Distributions from capital do not attract ACT. Next, it is necessary to determine whether the distribution is from taxed income. This is done by keeping track of total taxes paid and by assuming that distributions are made first from taxed income and then from untaxed income. A partial credit for the ACT is then given against the corporate tax paid. If the ACT credit were given in full, the net effect would be that only those distributions from untaxed income would be subject to tax.

The U.K. law includes in the definition of taxable distribution any dividend allowed under corporate law, as well as any other distribution unless defined as repayment of capital.[206] U.K corporate law allows dividends to be paid

---

[204]Under French law, corporate stock dividends can be received in cash at the choice of the shareholder.

[205]Although a time limit is in effect, after which the after-tax profits can no longer be distributed without bearing the *précompte mobilier*.

[206]GBR ICTA § 209.

from unrealized capital gains, which are taxable. However, a dividend from capital is not permitted. As a general matter, amounts returned to the shareholders in a redemption of capital in excess of the paid-up capital allocable to the shares in question are deemed to be noncapital distributions.[207] There is also a rule that where a company repays share capital and, at any time thereafter, issues any share capital as paid up other than through the receipt of new consideration, then the amount so paid up will be treated as a distribution.[208] A distribution of bonus shares is not treated as a distribution, although the bonus shares may be subject to what is in effect a special tax at the shareholder level.[209]

The U.K. rules do capture borrowings against appreciated assets that are paid out to shareholders as dividends. However, the rules also make it possible for enterprises to turn otherwise taxable distributions into nontaxable returns of capital through share redemptions. While corporate law limits the ability of companies to make redemptions, the opportunities are still greater than under French law.

Canada maintains a partial imputation system without levying additional tax on any distributions. This is due in part to the presumption that distributions to shareholders in the form of dividends have already born enterprise-level tax. Dividends are therefore deemed to have been paid out of taxed income, except those that are deemed to be returns of capital.[210] Because the imputation system is only partial, additional tax may be due at the shareholder level on dividends. However, if the distribution is deemed to be from capital, there will be no additional tax.

The term "dividend" is not defined by statute, but has been interpreted by the courts and the tax administration as meaning any distribution except as an authorized reduction of capital. In addition, the statute defines dividends to include stock dividends. The statute treats all or a portion of distributions made during share redemption or reduction in capital as nontaxable returns of capital. The amount treated as a dividend is the amount distributed in excess of the paid-up capital allocable to the shares in question.

H. Taxable Bonus Shares and Constructive Dividends

Enterprises may wish to retain earnings rather than to distribute them to their shareholders. These retained earnings will be reflected in an increase in the value of the enterprise's shares. If these earnings have been subject to tax, the increase in shareholder value will represent already taxed gains. In a fully

---

[207]*See* Barry Pinson, Pinson on Revenue Law 283 (1981). Generally, the paid-up capital for corporate law purposes is the stated capital of the class of shares in question, as shown in the company's financial statement.

[208]GBR ICTA § 210.

[209]*See* Barry Pinson, *supra* note 207, at 284.

[210]This discussion is based on Brian Arnold et al., Materials on Canadian Income Tax 698 (1993).

integrated tax system, there will be a tax disincentive for retaining these earnings unless the shareholder who is subjected to capital gains taxation is not taxed on these gains. Therefore, such systems typically allow enterprises to take measures to ensure that such shareholders are not so taxed. In addition, in integrated systems where the enterprise tax is at a higher rate than for some shareholders, these techniques may also allow the shareholder to receive a credit for the difference between the two rates.

Two typical methods include allowing enterprises to declare either taxable bonus shares or what has sometimes been termed "constructive dividends." Taxable bonus shares are typically shares paid as dividends that represent capitalized earnings through the issuing of additional shares of stock,[211] although there is no particular tax reason why capitalization under company law should be required. The value of a dividend distributed as a bonus share equals the proportionate amount of capitalized earnings. The result is a decrease in the value of the existing shares equal to the cost of the new shares, which is itself equal to the amount of retained earnings. Systems must ensure only that the bonus share represents after-tax income.[212]

Another technique is to allow enterprises to declare "constructive" dividends.[213] These are notional dividends that are declared but not actually paid and are designed to allow shareholders to increase their share cost by the amount of the retained earnings. This can be effected by an enterprise simply reporting to a shareholder the per share amount of after-tax income the enterprise has retained; a shareholder subject to capital gains taxation can then increase cost by this amount.[214]

VII. Defining Which Business Enterprises Should Be Subject to Separate Corporate Tax

An enterprise tax law must spell out, usually at the beginning of the statute, which entities are subject to tax. As with the individual income tax, a distinction must be drawn between residents and nonresidents, nonresidents typically being taxed only on income sourced in the jurisdiction. The definition of residence is discussed in chapter 18.

---

[211]In a number of countries, taxable bonus shares can be issued only if the company has capitalized the retained earnings. *See* the discussion in Hugh J. Ault et'al., *supra* note 203, at 314–17 (1997).

[212]In some imputation systems, a shareholder taxed at less than the enterprise rate may qualify for a credit for the difference.

[213]The ALI Integration Report describes them in this way, while the U.S. Treasury Department Report refers to them as reinvested dividends. ALI Integration Report, *supra* note 24, at 125–27; U.S. Treasury Report, *supra* note 3, at 87–88, 106–07.

[214]As noted *supra*, in some systems, a shareholder taxed at less than the enterprise rate may qualify for a credit for the difference.

One definitional technique that is often used in civil law countries is to rely on an entity's legal status. Under this approach, if an entity is considered a legal person under the civil code, then it will be subject to enterprise tax. This rule may then be supplemented by listing specific forms of legal persons that are subject to tax, listing as taxpayers certain entities that are not legal persons, and excluding certain legal persons from tax. For example, the German corporate income tax law lists the most common types of commercial companies, adds "any other legal persons under private law," as well as certain entities (such as *Stiftungen*) that may not be legal persons, and also includes enterprises administered by entities that are legal persons under public law (even when the enterprise may not itself be a legal person).[215]

The French approach is broadly similar. The law lists certain forms of company and then refers to "any other legal person carrying out an exploitation or operations of a profit making nature." It then lists certain forms of companies that are subject to corporate tax on an elective basis.[216]

Although, as illustrated in the above examples, corporate tax laws in civil law countries typically start from the status of entities as legal persons, these countries do not uniformly subject entities to corporate tax if and only if they are legal persons.[217]

Common law countries take different approaches. Canada relies on legal personality, imposing the income tax on any "person."[218] The United States imposes the corporate income tax on "every corporation," but corporation is defined as including "associations."[219] In turn, the regulations have adopted a test of corporate resemblance, holding that entities with sufficient corporate characteristics are taxed as associations. Hybrid entities can now elect whether to be treated as a corporation or as a partnership.[220]

In the United Kingdom, corporation tax is imposed on "profits of companies."[221] Company "means . . . any body corporate or unincorporated association but does not include a partnership, a local authority or a local authority association."[222] This differs from the U.S. approach in that partnerships cannot be recharacterized as associations and therefore treated as corporations. In addition, some noncorporate entities such as unit trusts are taxed in essentially the same manner as companies, only at different rates and with more complete integration.

Some transition countries treat as taxpayers under the corporate tax not just legal persons, but separate divisions of legal persons.[223] This practice arises

---

[215]*See* DEU KStG § 1.
[216]*See* FRA CGI § 206.
[217]*See infra* ch. 21, note 18.
[218]CAN ITA § 2.
[219]*See* USA IRC §§ 11, 7701(a)(3).
[220]*See infra* ch. 21, note 38.
[221]GBR ICTA 1988 § 6.
[222]*Id.* § 832(1).

from the treatment of these divisions as separate enterprises under the former command economy. The fact that these enterprises were not separate legal persons may have been of little importance in the past. However, their treatment as separate taxpayers under the profit tax can be problematic. In particular, how can systems designed to tax dividends operate when the dividends are paid not by each separate division but by the legal person? How are transfers of property among divisions to be accounted for? Although taxing divisions separately may not fit very well with a market economy–type corporate tax, there has in some countries been resistance to changing the system of taxing divisions separately. The divisions may be accustomed to keeping separate accounts, and tax officials may also be accustomed to auditing and dealing with divisions separately (corruption may be involved here). Local governments may be used to receiving their share of the revenues from the divisions located in their jurisdictions (they are often entitled to a share on this basis under laws governing the division of revenues from taxes). Eventually, however, as revenue-sharing laws are adjusted, it can be expected that these special rules treating divisions as separate taxpayers will be abandoned.

The opposite issue is consolidation of taxpayers. Consolidation is allowed, for example, in the United States under extremely complicated rules. A few transition countries also allow consolidation.[224] Generally, countries whose tax system is not highly developed should steer clear of allowing consolidation.

Some transition countries impose a tax not on legal persons or corporations but on enterprises, which in some cases can include sole proprietorships. For example, in Latvia, taxpayers of the enterprise income tax are defined as enterprises, with a cross-reference to the Law on Taxes and Fees.[225] That law in turn defines as resident an entity that is "registered" in accordance with the legislation of Latvia.[226] The enterprise income tax excludes from the definition of taxpayer individual enterprises that are not required to submit annual reports in accordance with the Law on Annual Reports of Enterprises. Therefore, sole proprietorships that are required to submit such reports are taxed under the enterprise income tax. And in Vietnam, the new Business Income Tax applies generally both to individuals engaged in production and trade and to business entities. The law itself does not provide for flow-through treatment for partnerships, thereby leading to some confusion when business is carried out in partnership form (particularly when the partners themselves are companies). Who is the taxpayer in that case? The partnership, the partners, or both?

[223]See, e.g., ALB PT § 4; RUS PT § 1(1)(b). Georgia used to tax divisions separately, but has now changed this rule. See GEO TC §§ 12, 44(2).

[224]E.g., KAZ TC § 6(4), second paragraph (allowing consolidation in limited circumstances upon decision of the government); AZE PT § 1(2) (consolidation for certain taxpayers by government decision).

[225]See LVA EIT §§ 1, 2.

[226]See LVA LTF § 14.

The enterprise income tax law of China likewise taxes enterprises, which are defined as state-owned enterprises, collective enterprises, private enterprises, joint-venture enterprises, and "any other organizations deriving income from production and business operations and other income."[227]

Imposing tax on enterprises as described in the preceding paragraph can be faulted for lack of clarity. The basic problem is that "enterprise" is generally not a clear legal concept.[228] It is much better technique for the law to refer to legal persons because it will be clear whether an entity is a legal person.[229] However, one can see the counterargument. If everyone carrying on a business is required to register as an enterprise, it seems an attractive proposition to tax separately each registered enterprise, regardless of its legal status.[230] Again, the same arguments can come up as with corporate divisions. Enterprises may be registered locally. An administrative mechanism may have grown up around the concept of enterprise registration. The basic problems with this approach are that (1) a single legal or physical person may have more than one registered enterprise or branch, and the boundaries around these enterprises may be difficult to draw; and (2) a person may carry on a business without registering it. Using instead the concept of legal person provides for greater certainty because it derives from the legal personality of the taxpayer as defined in the civil code.

---

[227]*See* CHN EIT § 2.

[228]Particularly problematic are enterprises that are operated as partnerships (with greater or lesser degrees of formality) and sole proprietorships. These are generally not legal persons and may or may not be formalized. In China, sole proprietorships are regulated by the Provisional Regulations on the Management of Individual Industrial and Commercial Households in Urban and Rural Areas, promulgated by the State Council on Aug. 5, 1987.

[229]For example, in China, art. 36 of the General Principles of Civil Law of the People's Republic of China, *reprinted in* Robert Guillaumond & Xie Zhao Hua, Code chinois du droit des affaires (Maison Larcier 1995), establishes the concept of a legal person. The Company Law, *reprinted in id.*, establishes two forms of commercial company: limited companies and share companies. Both are legal persons. The law distinguishes between branches of companies, which are not legal persons, and subsidiaries, which are. *See id.* art. 13. Foreign companies are allowed to establish branches in China and must obtain a business license in order for the branch to be allowed to operate in China. *See id.* art. 200. However, such branches are not considered separate legal persons. *See id.* art. 203. The Company Law came into force on July 1, 1994. Companies established before this date are required to take steps to conform to the requirements of this law. *See id.* art. 229. The procedure for registration is governed by the ordinance of June 24, 1994, *reprinted in id.*

[230]For example, in China, the ordinance of June 24, 1994, contemplates the registration of branches, even though branches are not separate legal persons. *See* Ordinance of June 24, 1994, arts. 39–44, *reprinted in* 2 Guillaumond & Hua, *supra* note 229. There is also a registration procedure for permanent representative offices of foreign companies. *See* Detailed Regulations of the Ministry of Foreign Commerce and Economic Cooperation Concerning the Approval and the Administration of Permanent Representative Offices of Foreign Enterprises, *reprinted in id.* The distinction is that representative offices cannot "directly engage in profit-making activities on the territory of the People's Republic of China." *Id.* art. 4.

The definition of taxpayer also needs to specify exemptions. Government agencies, but not government-owned enterprises, are typically exempt. Also typically exempt are various forms of nonprofit organization, whose definition will differ from country to country. When a system of incorporation and registration of such organizations exists outside the tax law, it may be possible to simply make a cross-reference, rather than to put all the necessary qualifications into the tax law. It is necessary to determine which agency (e.g., the tax agency or some other licensing agency) will be responsible for ensuring that the entities in question qualify as nonprofit. While some countries completely exempt certain organizations from tax, others tax nonprofit organizations on their business income if they carry on a business that is not related to their nonprofit purpose. The United States has developed quite detailed rules and practices on what is known as "unrelated business taxable income."[231] A more aggressive approach would be to tax nonprofits not only on their business income but on all their business and investment income. One advantage of such an approach is that it is not necessary to distinguish between business and investment (e.g., how would rental activity be classified?). Whether such an approach is taken is very much a political decision because of possible reluctance to impose tax on entities that are considered to be carrying on good works.

VIII. Concluding Remarks

This chapter began with a discussion of the merits of an income tax system including a separate enterprise tax and continued with recommendations as to how such a tax should be structured. It elaborated a number of arguments in support of a system that taxes enterprise income once, at the highest shareholder marginal rate, and that collects such tax to the greatest extent possible at the enterprise level. In addition, it advocated an enterprise-level tax that sought to capture, as accurately as possible given practical constraints, all income as it accrued and at the same tax rate.

The arguments favoring such a system were primarily rooted in economics, that such a system was likely to result in the fewest distortions and would allow the market to function with greater efficiency. However, an important by-product would be that the system would be far simpler to administer and also considerably less prone to tax avoidance. The primary reasons for this are that, with nearly all economic profits taxed at the enterprise level, there is no need to levy dividend taxes or for rules to determine what consitutes a distribution. Incentives to make nonequity payments would be greatly reduced.

In addition, where there is little untaxed income at the enterprise level, there is a corresponding reduction in the need to tax capital gains at the shareholder level: more of any share's increase in value due to the enterprise's eco-

---

[231]*See* USA IRC §§ 501(b), 511–515.

nomic income will already have been subject to tax at the enterprise level. This reduces the need to administer a capital gains tax at the level of the individual shareholder (including having to provide for the adjustment of the cost of shares for amounts of retained earnings or distributions of capital), a difficult undertaking in industrial countries and correspondingly more difficult in developing or transition economies.[232]

Next, rules providing for the stacking of income or against the streaming of distributions become unnecessary because all income bears the same rate of tax. Finally, the chapter argues that if the enterprise tax is final, meaning that the tax on enterprise income is schedular, there is additional improvement in administrative ease and a reduction in tax avoidance possibilities because the tax system does not need to tax distributions at the shareholder level.

It may be argued that it is impossible to implement a completely effective enterprise-level tax on economic income. Even if this turns out to be the case, to the extent that preference income can be reduced by ending as many intentional enterprise-level tax preferences as possible (such as investment credits, accelerated depreciation, and the like), and deferred capital gains can be reduced by marking to market as many assets as possible for which objective values can easily be ascertained (such as precious metals, foreign exchange, quoted securities, derivatives, and the like), and by including in enterprise income total borrowings net of written-down asset value, the need to capture distributions from untaxed economic income will be reduced. This would mean, in effect, that some or all of the elaborate mechanisms described in section V to capture untaxed income or to allow shareholders to be taxed at marginal rates might raise so little additional revenue as to be necessary only in occasional cases. It would also mean that any of the elaborate rules described in section VI to distinguish among different types of distributions would become similarly less necessary or less important. With significant progress having been made toward such a simplified system, the methods described in those sections can be selectively enacted, or applied, or both, as required.

It may also be argued that it is politically difficult to tax enterprises at the highest shareholder rate. But to the extent that enterprise income and shareholder income were taxed at as close to the same rate as possible, any incentive by enterprises to retain earnings or to make nontaxable distributions to take advantage of the lower enterprise rate would be reduced.

---

[232]In addition, gains and losses of nonresidents are typically exempt either by statute or through bilateral treaties. Of course, this is not to say that there are not benefits to having capital gains taxes, and this chapter argues for the inclusion of gains and losses at the enterprise level. There may in some cases be unleveraged (and therefore untaxed) gains at the enterprise level, and a capital gains tax at the shareholding level would end deferral of tax on those gains when the shares were sold or transferred. Also, there may be gains reflected in the value of shares that are not also reflected at the enterprise level, such as market expectation that an enterprise will earn profits in the future.

Finally, tax designers may also argue that it is unfair to implement a schedular tax on enterprise income. However, to the extent that a nonschedular tax can be limited to the fewest taxpayers possible, the need to file returns, or for enterprises to shift ownership to those taxed at lower rates, would be reduced.

Therefore, even if complete adherence to a simplified system is impossible, there is still considerable merit in designing a tax system with as many features of the simplified system described above as possible.

While these arguments apply in varying degrees to all economies, they have particular relevance to developing countries and to economies in transition. Even in these jurisdictions, many enterprises, particularly larger companies or companies with foreign management, may have developed considerable tax-planning expertise. The globalization of sophisticated tax-planning ability, and therefore tax avoidance, has been a remarkable—and another perhaps unexpected—consequence of the general globalization of markets and financial information. The authors have experienced, in a number of cases, developing and transition countries with complex systems, in which a surprisingly large amount of tax administration resources were dedicated to attempting to prevent sophisticated schemes designed to avoid income tax. However, because of an inadequacy of resources, these tax administrations were less likely to be able to design and implement the rules necessary to operate their complex systems without diverting administrative resources from other tasks. These other tasks, while perhaps more mundane, were also more likely to be productive in the collection of needed revenue.

Therefore, in these circumstances it is perhaps best to design the most effective simple system possible, and to direct limited bureaucratic resources not to trying to capture the relatively meager income that will escape through the tax avoidance net, but to more productive, if less intellectually challenging, activities.

20

Taxation of Corporate Reorganizations

Frans Vanistendael

> You can do anything in Subchapter C. [Subchapter C contains
> reorganization and other corporate provisions.]
>
> —*Martin Ginsburg*

I. Introduction

In designing tax laws for developing or transition countries, drafters often neglect, and sometimes completely forget, provisions for corporate[1] reorganizations.[2] This chapter reviews the forms of corporate reorganization that might be available under company law and the tax consequences of reorganizations

---

Note: Victor Thuronyi contributed to the writing of this chapter.

[1]This chapter assumes that the entities being reorganized are corporations or share companies. As discussed in ch. 21, the tax on legal entities may tax as separate entities various organizations (e.g., forms of partnership) that are not share companies. In countries with such rules, appropriate reference to the legal forms that reorganizations of such organizations take will have to be made in the rules on reorganizations. *E.g.*, FRA CGI § 160 (refers to *droits sociaux* (interests in a company), which is a broader term than *actions* (shares)). There may be substantial differences in the legal form taken by such reorganizations, compared with the reorganization of share companies. To avoid complicating the discussion, we will not address further the necessary adaptations that would have to be made in such cases.

[2]EST IT § 25 provides for nonrecognition treatment for reorganizations in accordance with conditions established by the Minister of Finance. The tax codes of Kazakhstan and the Kyrgyz Republic do not contain provisions concerning reorganization, nor does the income tax decree of Saudi Arabia or the profit tax decree of Romania. In some countries, the absence of provisions relating to reorganization can be explained by the fact that capital gains are not subject to tax. *See also infra* note 45.

in the absence of special tax rules.[3] It then considers the tax treatment of reorganizations if there are special nonrecognition[4] rules and the considerations in designing those tax rules. The discussion supports the desirability of having at least some basic reorganization provisions if policymakers consider that the tax system should not discourage corporate restructuring.

In transition countries, reorganizations can occur as part of the privatization process or thereafter as the ownership of companies changes hands. Even when the top priority is to make existing businesses work rather than to reorganize them through merger or division, it is necessary to think from the start about rules in civil or commercial law that would allow mergers, acquisitions, or divisions, and about their tax implications. It is better not to wait until the first practical cases arise. In developing countries, reorganizations may or may not take place very often. Even if they are not frequent, however, it makes sense to have a set of rules in place so that business reorganizations are not impeded by the tax system. In addition, foreign investors will be more confident when they notice that the legal system in general, and the tax system in particular, provides for such transactions, to which they are used in their own business environment.

Industrial countries generally have specific rules for tax-free reorganizations. In the absence of such rules, business reorganizations could lead to taxable transfers of assets or shares. The resulting tax liabilities could be so large as to obstruct business reorganizations. The general policy view in most countries is that it is economically not efficient to tax corporate reorganizations, because taxation would discourage reorganizations. Where there is a continuation of business activities and of the interest of the shareholders in the company, a corporate reorganization may be considered as tantamount to a legal restructuring of the same business, which does not constitute a sufficient change in economic position to merit taxation.

In developing and transition countries, the basic issues in designing the rules for corporate reorganizations are the same, although these countries will generally want to adopt rules that are as simple as possible given that the volume of reorganizations will be relatively small. In addition, special issues will

---

[3]Further discussion on comparative law can be found in Tax Consequences of International Acquisitions and Business Combinations, 77b Cahiers de droit fiscal international (1992)(since many international acquisitions take the form of *taxable* acquisitions of shares or assets, this work is a good source for discussion of taxable acquisitions; it also deals with tax-free acquisitions and with international business combinations, as well as with related tax planning issues, such as the deductibility of acquisition indebtedness and the impact of imputation systems on acquisition strategies); Peter Begg, Corporate Acquisitions and Mergers (loose-leaf 1997) (covers tax, corporate law, employment law, and regulatory matters in the United Kingdom and the other EU countries); Svetlana Almakaeva, *Effects of Russian Tax Treaties and the EC Parent-Subsidiary Directive on the Tax Planning Strategies of European Multinational Groups Investing in Russia*, 23 Review of Central and East European Law 77 (1997). *See also infra* note 15.

[4]This term is explained *supra* ch. 16, sec. V(B)(7).

be involved in the treatment of investment funds and in privatization, to which we refer in this chapter from time to time.[5]

II. Forms of Corporate Reorganization

Reorganization is used here in a general way to describe transactions involving significant changes in the legal or economic structure of one or more business enterprises. In some countries neither company law nor tax law defines the term, although specific forms of reorganization may be defined,[6] while other countries have a general tax law concept of reorganization.[7]

The forms of reorganization are described below in general terms.[8] Because of differences in company law, the descriptions will not be accurate for some jurisdictions. However, most jurisdictions provide for transactions that more or less correspond to the forms described. In drafting for a specific country, it will of course be necessary to consult the company law, special reorganization law (if any), bankruptcy law, civil law, and other applicable commercial laws of that jurisdiction.

The following parties[9] to a reorganization can be identified: (1) the acquired or transferor[10] company, (2) the shareholders of the transferor, (3) the

---

[5]*See* Yolanda Kodrzycki & Eric Zolt, *Tax Issues Arising from Privatization in the Formerly Socialist Countries*, 25 Law & Policy in Int'l Business 609 (1994). *See* ch. 21 for taxation of investment funds.

[6]Canada has a definition of an amalgamation in sec. 87 (1) ITA, but no overall definition. Council Directive of July 23, 1990 (90/434/EEC) refers separately to "mergers, divisions, transfers of assets, and exchanges of shares" [hereinafter Merger Taxation Directive]. Similarly, the French tax code refers separately to a merger (*fusion*), CGI §§ 160 I ter, 210A, division (*scission*), CGI § 160 I ter, and a transfer of assets (*apport partiel d'actif*), CGI § 210B.

[7]In the United States, reorganizations are defined for tax purposes in IRC § 368. In Germany, for corporate reorganizations in general the word *Umwandlung* is used. Reorganizations are regulated in the *Umwandlungsgesetz* (UmwG) (Reorganization Law) and the Reorganization Tax Law; *see* Klaus Tipke & Joachim Lang, Steuerrecht 432 (1991); Dieter Endres & Karen Pilny, *Germany Releases Draft Regulation on the Reorganization Tax Act*, 14 Tax Notes Int'l 1867 (June 9, 1997).

[8]Other corporation-shareholder transactions relevant to reorganizations—liquidations and redemption of shares—are dealt with in ch. 19. Nonrecognition rules for the incorporation of sole proprietorships, as well as other corporate and partnership formation transactions, are dealt with in ch. 16.

[9]Not all of the listed persons are parties in some reorganizations. For example, the shareholders of the acquiring company may not be parties if their share ownership does not change in the reorganization. The list given in the text is a broad concept of party used in a general sense. A somewhat narrower, more technical concept (which includes only the corporations involved) is defined in USA IRC § 368(b).

[10]Throughout this chapter, we use the term "transferor" to indicate the person or entity transferring assets, shares, securities, or other forms of consideration to another person and the term "transferee" to indicate the person to which such consideration is transferred. The transferor company can also be indicated as the acquired, merged, or divided company, while the transferee company can be indicated as the acquiring, surviving, or newly established company. The terms transferor and transferee are preferred, because they have the same meaning in different kinds of reorganizations.

acquiring or transferee company, (4) the shareholders of the transferee, and (5) all other persons, in particular the creditors, having a contractual or other legal relationship with the transferor or transferee. Reorganizations can be distinguished according to whether or not a legal entity party to the reorganization disappears as part of the transaction. In mergers, consolidations, and corporate divisions, one of the parties may disappear by the mere fact of the transaction. In asset and share[11] acquisitions, the transferor may or may not disappear depending on whether it is liquidated or not. Whether an entity disappears may be relevant for several issues, including the taxation of shareholders and the carryover of tax attributes.

A. Merger

A merger, also called amalgamation,[12] is a transaction in which all or substantially all the assets and liabilities of one or more transferor companies are transferred to a single transferee company, whereby the transferor companies cease to exist by operation of law—that is, not on the basis of a consensual agreement between parties and not through liquidation. In most countries this transfer must take place exclusively or substantially in exchange for shares.[13]

B. Consolidation

A consolidation[14] is a transaction whereby two or more companies transfer their assets and liabilities to a single newly established company. The basic legal mechanism for a consolidation is identical to that of a merger: all or substantially all of the assets are transferred by operation of law in exchange for shares. The only difference is that in a merger the transferee company is a preexisting company, while in a consolidation the transferee is a newly established company.

C. Corporate Divisions

A corporate division is the opposite of a merger or consolidation: all or substantially all the assets of one company are transferred in exchange for shares to at least two or more newly established or preexisting companies, unless these assets are already in the hands of a subsidiary. Three types of divisive

---

[11]This chapter refers to "shares," whose American equivalent is "stock."

[12]CAN ITA § 87. In French this transaction is called *absorption*. In German, either *Verschmelzung* or *Fusion* is used. Directive 78/855/EEC, art. 3 uses the term "merger by acquisition."

[13]In the draft merger directive of the European Union a merger or consolidation is valid only when the transfer of the net value is substantially in exchange for shares, see §§ 2–4 draft directive, referring to Directive 78/855/EEC, which allows a cash payment of up to 10 percent of the nominal value of the shares issued. In the United States, however, there are several states in which a merger in the sense of a legal transfer of all assets and liabilities of a company that immediately ceases to exist is possible without consideration being paid in shares.

[14]In French, this is called a *fusion*. See FRA CGI, Annex II, § 301B. Directive 78/855/EEC, art. 4, uses the term "merger by the formation of a new company."

reorganizations can be identified.[15] In a spin-off, the shares of a subsidiary are distributed to the shareholders of the parent company. In a split-off, the shares of a subsidiary are distributed in exchange for the surrender of shares of the parent company. In a split-up, the parent company distributes its shares in two or more subsidiaries in complete liquidation.

D. Asset Acquisition

An asset acquisition is a transfer of assets and liabilities by one or more companies to a newly established or preexisting company in exchange for any form of consideration (shares, securities, cash, assets in kind, or transfer of liabilities). In an asset acquisition, the transferor company may continue to exist after the transfer or may distribute the proceeds to its shareholders in a complete liquidation. In the latter case, the effect of the transaction will be very close to a formal merger.[16] Since reorganizations deal with substantial and significant structural economic and legal changes, in order to qualify as a reorganization, an asset acquisition will normally have to involve a transfer of substantially all of the transferor's assets. The transfer of a smaller portion of the assets is treated as a sale of these assets, not as a reorganization.

E. Share Acquisition

A share acquisition is the transfer of shares of a company to a newly established or preexisting company in exchange for any form of consideration (shares, securities, cash, assets in kind, or assumption of liabilities). Again, the transaction will be considered to be a reorganization only if the transfer of shares involves a substantial holding, so that the transferee company acquires an important say in the affairs of the acquired company. The transfer of shares may or may not be followed by the liquidation of the acquired company into the transferee company.[17]

---

[15]*See* Boris Bittker & James Eustice, Federal Income Taxation of Corporations and Shareholders ¶ 13.01 (1987); Albert Rädler, General Report, *National and International Consequences of Demergers*, 79b Cahiers de droit fiscal international 557, 558, 565 (1994). (Readers who want to learn more about the comparative tax law of corporate divisions are referred to this work, including the accompanying country reports.)

[16]Under USA IRC § 368 (a)(1) (C), (G), the transferor in an assets acquisition is generally required to liquidate or is treated as if a complete liquidation had taken place. *See* Bittker & Eustice, *supra* note 15, ¶ 14.14. An asset acquisition without liquidation is possible under NLD Vpb § 14(2) (definition of an asset acquisition (*bedrijfsfusie*) for tax purposes) and BEL CIR art. 46 § 1 (contribution of branch or of all assets in exchange for shares).

[17]The share acquisition is the most common form of corporate reorganization in the Netherlands; *see* Van Soest, Inkomstenbelasting 470 (1990); its tax requirements are defined in NLD IB § 14b(2). In France the share acquisition is called *fusion à l'anglaise* (!) and is regulated in CGI Annex II § 301C-I, stating that the acquiring company must acquire at least 75 percent of the shares of the acquired company. In the United States the share acquisition is regulated in IRC § 368 (a)(1)(B), requiring a share of at least 80 percent in the acquired company.

F. Change in Seat or Form

A change in seat is a change in the jurisdiction of incorporation, while a change in form is a change from one type of company to another. Both consist of legal structural changes, but do not necessarily involve economic changes in the way the business of the company is conducted. The assets and liabilities and the economic activity of the company whose seat or form is changed remain unchanged. When the seat of a company is moved from one country to another, or when the form of the company is changed, the company law may provide that the company is liquidated and that a new company is established.[18] Generally speaking, however, when the seat is moved within the same country or when the form is changed, most company laws stipulate that the legal identity of the company remains unchanged.[19]

G. Recapitalization

Recapitalizations are changes in the way a company is financed, that is, structural changes in its share capital or outstanding debt. As with most changes in seat or form, the legal identity of the company remains unchanged.

H. Bankruptcy Reorganizations

Bankruptcy reorganizations may take any of the forms described above, with the distinctive element that one or more companies are declared bankrupt and that as a consequence the outstanding debt of the companies involved is rescheduled. Although the emphasis is on the reorganization of the debt, reorganization of share capital may also be involved, as well as the liquidation of one or more corporate entities.

---

[18]In Switzerland, conversion of a GmbH into an AG is not possible without liquidation. *See* Company Law in Europe: Switzerland § 22 (Peter Meinhardt ed., 3rd ed. 1981). Law No. 66-537 of July 24, 1966, § 154, *reprinted in* Code des Sociétés (Dalloz 1996) provides that a company may change its seat from one country to another if the host country has concluded a treaty with France permitting such a change without disturbing the legal personality of the company. It may not be possible under company law to change the seat of a company to another country. *See, e.g.,* Steven Schuit, *Business Organizations; Corporations, in* Dutch Business Law § 9.10[6] (Schuit, Romyn, and Zevenboom, eds. 1997) (impossible to transfer seat to another country except in extraordinary situations like war). In cases like this, the transfer of seat can be accomplished by forming a new corporation in the target country and merging the existing corporation into the new corporation or by contributing the shares of the existing company to the new company and then liquidating the existing company.

[19]*See, e.g.,* FRA Code civil § 1844-3 (change from one type of company to another does not result in creation of a new legal person); P. Verrucoli, Italian Company Law 205–207 (association of persons can be converted into capital company and vice versa) (1977). *See also* Law No. 66-537, *supra* note 18, §§ 236–238 (providing for change from *société anonyme* to other forms); *id.* § 69 (providing for change from *société à responsabilité limitée* to other forms); Schuit, *supra* note 18, § 9.10[4] (change in form does not affect continued existence of a corporation).

III. Taxable Reorganizations

This section considers the tax consequences of taxable reorganizations. The discussion is relevant in several contexts. First, the tax consequences discussed apply in the absence of special nonrecognition rules for reorganizations. This is relevant to countries that do not have such rules and that are considering whether they should be introduced. Second, even in countries that have nonrecognition rules, some reorganizations will be structured so as to fail to qualify under those rules and will accordingly be considered taxable reorganizations. Why it may be advantageous in certain situations for taxpayers to do so is discussed below. Finally, sometimes taxpayers will seek to structure a transaction so as to qualify for nonrecognition treatment, without meeting the requirements, so that the transaction is treated as taxable. And other transactions simply will not possess the required characteristics of a tax-free reorganization.

A. Tax Position of the Transferor Company

Regardless of how a reorganization is effectuated under company law, income tax systems as a general rule treat reorganizations in which the transferor company disappears as a transfer of assets and liabilities by the transferor to the transferee company. This transfer of assets is treated as a sale, from which any gain is taxable and any loss is deductible.

The amount of gain or loss is calculated in accordance with the normal income tax rules. Assuming that all assets are taxed according to the same rules, the gain or loss is calculated as the difference between the total consideration received by the transferor in the form of shares, securities, cash, or other property and the tax basis of all assets transferred. The consequence of taxing such a transfer is that all profits and gains whose taxation had been deferred before the reorganization will become taxable.

Example

OLDCO TAX BALANCE SHEET[20]

Assets		Liabilities	
Inventory	$20,000	Capital	$30,000
Receivables	$20,000	Reserves	$20,000
Fixed assets	$60,000	Liabilities	$50,000
Total	$100,000		$100,000

Note: Acquisition price: shares of Newco valued at $100,000 plus assumption of all liabilities equals $150,000.

Taxable profit: $150,000 minus $100,000 (tax basis of the assets on the balance sheet) equals $50,000.

---

[20]The value for which assets are recorded in a company's accounts does not always coincide with the tax basis of the assets. This depends on the relationship between commercial accounting and tax accounting, which varies from country to country. See *supra* ch. 16, appendix.

The rate at which the acquired company's gain is taxed depends on the general rules for taxation of profits and capital gains. While in some systems capital gains are taxed at the same rate as ordinary profits, in others there are special arrangements for capital gains. Many countries tax ordinary profits and capital gains of companies at the same rate.[21] Capital gains on business assets are still taxed at preferential rates in Belgium, France, Greece, and Ireland, and recently the capital gains preference has been reintroduced in the United States. When a tax system provides for lower rates on capital assets, it is necessary to allocate the total consideration to the individual assets transferred. The greater the portion of the consideration allocated to capital assets, the lower the amount of tax.

The transferor and the transferee have conflicting interests in allocating the purchase price. The transferor will be interested in minimizing its tax burden by shifting the price to capital assets, whereas the transferee will be interested in recouping the acquisition cost as soon as possible through direct expenses, by shifting the acquisition price to items that are immediately deductible, like the cost of inventory.[22] However, the parties can often reach an agreement to optimize their joint tax situation at the expense of the government, particularly when both companies are members of the same corporate group.[23]

B. Tax Position of the Shareholders of the Transferor

1. Taxability of Shareholders

Whether the shareholders are taxed in a taxable reorganization is determined by the general rules on the taxation of capital gains. These rules vary in many tax systems depending on the category of taxpayer that realizes a capital gain and on the purpose for which the shares are held (business or private investment).[24]

Some countries tax all capital gains on shares regardless of who holds the shares and why the shares are held. Consequently, the transfer of the shares of the acquired company in exchange for the shares of the transferee company,

---

[21]For a survey of the situation in the European Union, see Commission of the European Communities, Report of the Committee of Independent Experts on Company Taxation 243 (1992) (Onno Ruding, Chairman) [hereinafter Ruding Committee Report].

[22]See infra sec. C(1).

[23]In a transaction between unrelated parties, one party can compensate the other party by an adjustment in the purchase price if the latter agrees to bear a greater tax burden. The problem of possible abuse in a transaction between related parties can be addressed through a general rule that gives the tax administration the power to readjust transfer prices between related taxpayers and in some cases (such as tax evasion) even between unrelated taxpayers, so as to reflect the fair market value of the transaction for tax purposes. Such a rule is not specific to reorganizations. See vol. 1, at 53; ch. 18 supra.

[24]See supra ch. 16, sec. VI(B).

bonds, cash, or other forms of compensation is a taxable event, absent special nonrecognition rules.[25]

In many other countries, however (in particular in the European Union, with the exception of the United Kingdom and the Scandinavian countries), individual shareholders are not taxed on the gains resulting from the sale of shares when the shares are held on a long-term basis for private investment.[26] The gains will also be exempt when realized by charities or other exempt organizations. In some countries, however, gains on shares are taxable when the individual shareholder holds a "substantial" share in a company.[27] When an individual shareholder holds shares for business purposes, practically all countries will tax the gain realized on the sale or exchange of the shares.

Shares held by companies are a special case. Many tax systems treat them as assets held for business purposes, and, consequently, any gain on the sale or exchange of shares is a taxable event. However, some countries (e.g., Belgium and Netherlands[28]) consider the gain realized on shares held by a company in a subsidiary company as the expression of the profits that have already been realized and taxed in the hands of the subsidiary. In such countries, capital gains realized on the transfer of shares held by the parent are exempt from tax.

2. Calculation of Taxable Gain

When the gain on the exchange of shares is taxable to the shareholder, the general rules applicable to calculating gains on the disposition of other assets will apply, together with any special rules as to the rate of tax and the deductibility of capital losses.[29] An exchange of shares, or a receipt of a distribution of the proceeds of the corporation's exchange of its assets, may also be treated as a dividend or a liquidating distribution, in which case any special rules applicable to those transactions will come into play.[30]

3. Cost Base of Assets Received in Exchange for Shares

The cost base of the new shares or other forms of consideration (other than cash) received by the shareholders in the exchange is also determined by

---

[25]For example, in the United Kingdom there is a special capital gains tax, which also includes profits on shares held for private investment. *See* GBR TCGA §§ 2, 21.

[26]*See*, for a survey of capital gains tax rates for individual shareholders, Ruding Committee Report, *supra* note 21, at 273.

[27]*See* NLD WIB § 39 (33 percent); BEL CIR § 90/9° (25 percent); FRA CGI § 160 (25 percent); DEU EStG § 17 (25 percent).

[28]*See* BEL CIR § 192; NLD Vpb § 13(1) (minimum 5 percent participation required); Van Soest, Inkomstenbelasting 454 (1990).

[29]*See supra* ch. 16, sec. V, VI(B).

[30]*See supra* ch. 19.

ordinary tax rules. The value they receive for tax purposes is equal to their acquisition cost. The acquisition cost is the price agreed upon between the parties to the reorganization and should be equal to the value of the shares that are surrendered. In the reorganization agreement, that value should reflect the fair market value of the shares, and, if it does not, the value may be subject to correction under a general provision enabling the tax administration to adjust the price agreed upon between the parties.[31]

C. Tax Position of the Transferee

1. Cost Base of the Transferred Assets

After a taxable merger, the assets of the transferor will be valued in the hands of the transferee at the value that has been used to determine the transferor's tax liability in the merger or division, as discussed above in section B. Subsequent profits, depreciation, capital gains, and capital losses on assets will be calculated not on the basis of the old value that the assets had before the reorganization, but on the basis of the new value that was assigned to them in the merger or division. As a consequence, some of the assets of the transferee (assets transferred by the transferor) will be valued for tax purposes at current prices, while others (assets that the transferee owned before the reorganization) will reflect historic and depreciated values. Absent nonrecognition rules, in the case of an assets transfer, the tax law clearly takes a position of discontinuity. It considers the merger or division as a sale of assets for tax purposes, resulting in their revaluation.

A problem that is specific to reorganizations is the allocation of acquisition cost to goodwill. In most cases the total acquisition cost will exceed the total sum of the values of the individual assets. The difference is often accounted for as goodwill. Whether goodwill can be depreciated is determined by the general depreciation rules.[32] When depreciation is disallowed, the transferee company will try to minimize the amount allocated to goodwill; when it is allowed, the transferee will be tempted to inflate goodwill.

2. Transfer of Tax Benefits and Preferential Tax Regimes

In the case of taxable reorganizations in which the transferor company disappears (e.g., mergers and divisions), tax credits, exemptions, and other tax benefits enjoyed by the transferor are commonly canceled. The logic of this rule is apparent in cases of exemption. When an item has been temporarily exempt in the hands of the transferor (i.e., when taxation has been deferred), the logical consequence of taxing a merger is that all exempt items

---

[31]*See supra* note 23.
[32]*See supra* ch. 17, sec. II(E)(2).

become subject to taxation at the time of the reorganization. Tax credits and other tax benefits from which the acquired company may have benefited are typically treated in the same way; that is, they expire with the transferor.[33]

In some cases, however, the benefit may be continued, subject to certain conditions. A typical example is an investment credit. Such a credit is typically recaptured[34] when the asset for which the credit has been granted is sold or transferred, but maintained when the asset continues to be used in the same business.[35] In a merger, the business situation has indeed not changed, because the same asset is still used in the same economic activity, but it is used by the legal entity succeeding the transferor company. However, the continuation of tax benefits in a taxable reorganization might be subject to a continuity-of-interest requirement, similar to the requirement applicable to tax-free reorganizations.[36]

3. Transfer of Tax Loss Carryovers

In the transfer of tax characteristics of the transferor company, tax loss carryovers play a special role.[37] To avoid a situation where profitable companies would chase loss companies to be able to use their tax loss carryovers in a merger or division, tax systems typically limit the carryover of tax losses from one company to another in a corporate reorganization.[38] In the case of a taxable transfer of assets, the transferee would in any event not inherit any loss carryovers of the transferor. In this case, the transferor could offset the loss against any gain realized on the transfer.

4. Transfer of Rights and Obligations in Litigation

The extent to which rights and obligations in tax litigation are transferred from the transferor to the transferee company may be decided by the rules of company law, contract law, or tax law.[39] When there is a formal merger transferring de jure all rights and obligations to the acquiring company, the latter will be entitled to immediately continue all tax protests, appeals, and other forms of litigation of the acquired company. Alternatively, the transferee

---

[33]This rule is very often not explicitly spelled out in the statute, but follows from the general principle that tax characteristics cannot be transferred from one taxpayer to another unless the statute specifically provides for such a transfer. It is stated by negative implication in USA IRC § 381.

[34]When a credit is recaptured, the tax payable is increased by the amount recaptured. Recapture is known as clawback in the United Kingdom.

[35]*E.g.*, USA IRC §§ 50(a)(4), 381.

[36]*See infra* sec. IV.

[37]*See* discussion on tax loss carryovers in the general tax system, *supra* ch. 16.

[38]*E.g.*, USA IRC § 382.

[39]*See* Michael Saltzman, IRS Practice and Procedure ¶ 17.05 (2d ed. 1991).

may be liable on the basis of a contractual agreement or under special trans-feree liability provisions of the tax laws.[40]

5. Methods of Accounting

The transferor and transferee may use different methods of accounting (e.g., one may use cash and the other accrual, or one may use last in, first out (LIFO) and the other first in, first out (FIFO), or the two companies may use different accounting years). After the reorganization, this inconsistency must be resolved. It may be particularly difficult to resolve if there are rules in the tax law that if a company has started to use one method it cannot switch to another. Provision needs to be made to reconcile this rule with the fact that a reorganization will necessarily involve some change in accounting method when the parties use different methods. A purely formal approach would look to continuity of corporate identity: whichever company continues is the one that keeps its methods of accounting. When the successor is a newly formed company, does this mean that the taxpayer has the right to select whatever method it wants?

In addition to dealing with the question of what method of accounting the successor may use, the tax law should deal with the issue of transition. In a taxable reorganization, this is not difficult. For example, in the case of inventory accounting, the successor will typically continue its accounting method and will be treated as having purchased the inventory of the trans-feror. This inventory will be accounted for no differently from inventory purchased in the ordinary course of business. The result in the case of LIFO accounting in an inflationary situation can be harsh, however, in that the difference between the fair market value of the inventory and its historic valuation (which will be artificially low because of the use of LIFO) is taxable.

D. Reorganizations Without Transfer of Assets or Shares

Some forms of reorganization deal with only one company, for example, with changes in corporate seat or form and various forms of recapitalization.

1. Change of Corporate Seat or Form

The change of corporate seat or form is a simple form of reorganization involving a change in the legal structure of the business but not its economic structure. A change in corporate seat should not have any tax consequence as long as the seat of the company stays within the same tax jurisdiction. When the seat changes from one tax jurisdiction to another, however, there may be full taxation of the company, as if it had distributed all its assets in a liquidating

---

[40]E.g., USA IRC § 6901.

distribution.[41] This rule reflects the fact that after the move the company will no longer be subject to the national tax jurisdiction.

A mere change in corporate form (e.g., from a limited-liability company to a share company) should in principle not give rise to any tax liability. All assets and liabilities of the business remain within a single legal entity, albeit a different one, and the shareholders maintain their equity interest unchanged. In a few countries, a change of form may result in tax problems because company law may require a formal liquidation in order to change the company form, so that there is a legal transfer of assets and liabilities from the old company to the new.[42] Typically, however, the transfer is automatic and everything remains unchanged except for the company form. For tax purposes, the mere change of company form should not be considered a taxable event, as long as the change is limited to the legal form of the company and its assets, capital, debt, and outstanding shares remain unchanged.

There may be a problem, however, when, as a result of a change in corporate form, the company changes its taxpayer status from corporate to flow-through treatment or vice versa.[43] It is clear that the tax law should provide for adjustments, when, as a result of a change in the form of the legal entity, its tax regime is also changed from one regime to the other. In such cases a change of form may be treated as a liquidation or an incorporation for tax purposes, resulting in taxation of any untaxed reserves or temporarily exempt profits.[44]

2. Recapitalizations

Increases and decreases in the capital of a company as a rule do not result in any tax liability for the company concerned. The principal tax issue in a recapitalization is whether the receipt of debt by the shareholders has the effect of the distribution of a dividend. If so, it should be taxable as a dividend absent a special rule. A distribution (through a decrease in capital) of what has been

---

[41]Often the transaction is accomplished by forming a new corporation in the state where it is desired to move to and then merging the corporation into this new corporation. *See supra* note 18; Rufus Rhoades & Marshall Langer, 2 Income Taxation of Foreign-related Transactions § 7.02[8] (1996); Notice 94-46, 1994-1 C.B. 356. In some cases, a change in place of incorporation will not be taxable; *e.g.*, Rev. Rul. 87-27, 1987-1 C.B. 134 (liquidation of domestic corporation into a newly formed foreign corporation treated as a change in place of incorporation and hence as a Type F reorganization, which was tax free where the requirements of the regulations under IRC § 367(a) were satisfied).

[42]*See supra* note 18.

[43]*See infra* ch. 21.

[44]In the United States, when a C corporation (taxed as an entity) changes its status to that of S corporation (taxed on a flow-through basis), there is no immediate tax, but a tax is imposed on certain built-in gains of the C corporation if the S corporation realizes those gains within 10 years. *See* IRC § 1374; Bittker & Eustice, *supra* note 15, ¶ 6.07. Germany now allows a tax-free conversion of a corporation into a partnership. *See* Endres & Pilny, *supra* note 7. (This should be seen in the context of Germany having abolished the last remnant of economic double taxation.—L.M.)

effectively paid in by the shareholders will commonly not be taxed as a dividend. Any other distribution should in principle be treated as a taxable dividend or liquidating distribution.

IV. Tax-Free Reorganizations

A. Introduction

Industrial countries typically have specific rules for tax-free reorganizations in their tax laws, and many developing and transition countries do so as well.[45] The objective of these rules is not to grant a tax exemption to the companies or shareholders involved, but rather to "neutralize" the tax consequences of the business reorganization, so that the reorganization involves neither a tax advantage nor a tax disadvantage. The principle of tax neutrality in business reorganization has two aspects. It implies (1) that no tax is levied at the time of the reorganization and (2) that, after the reorganization, the taxable profits of the transferee company and its shareholders are calculated on the basis of tax elements that were present in the transferor company and its shares immediately before the reorganization. The principle is one of deferral of tax on unrealized gains that exist at the time of the reorganization, not exemption of tax on these gains.

B. Conditions for a Tax-Free Reorganization

The detailed rules setting conditions for tax-free reorganizations vary considerably from one country to another, but can be summarized in two basic conditions: (1) continuity of business enterprise and (2) continuity of shareholder interest. Opinions will vary as to the required degree of continuity, but all tax systems allowing tax-free reorganizations will (or should) impose these two basic conditions in one form or another. Doing otherwise would open

---

[45]*See generally* The International Guide to Mergers and Acquisitions (Eric Tomsett et al., eds., IBFD) (loose-leaf 1993–96) (covers most of the OECD countries as well as Argentina, Brazil, Singapore, and South Africa). See the Oct. 13, 1997 issue of Tax Notes International for discussion of rules concerning acquisition of companies in the Netherlands, France, Germany, and the United Kingdom. *See also supra* note 2. In Thailand, reorganizations are taxable. *See* THA RC §§ 72–74. The State Tax Administration of the People's Republic of China has recently issued circulars providing guidance on reorganizations, which provide that certain transactions may be carried out on a tax-free basis. *See* May Huang et al., *China Issues Rules on Tax-Free Corporate Reorganizations,* 15 Tax Notes Int'l 543 (Aug. 18, 1997). In the case of Indonesia, Japan, and Korea, the opportunities for tax-free reorganizations seem to be quite limited. *See* Richard Weisman et al., *Structuring Transactions in Asian Countries: Tax Considerations for Cross-Border Mergers and Acquisitions,* 15 Tax Notes Int'l 215 (1997); Hugh Ault et al., Comparative Income Taxation 330, 339 (1997). Tax-free reorganizations and corporate divisions are allowed in Israel. *See* Arye Lapidoth, *The Israeli 1993 Income Tax Reform Relating to Mergers and Divisions of Companies,* Intertax 202 (1995).

enormous opportunities for tax avoidance, because it would allow the transferor company and its shareholders to finally dispose of all or part of their assets or their equity interest in a company through a tax-exempt merger or division without paying any tax. In some countries, the tax exemption is also made conditional upon the existence of a bona fide commercial or business purpose[46] or on the absence of tax avoidance.[47]

1. Conditions Set in Tax Law or in Company Law

Two different techniques are used in varying degrees to impose conditions on a tax-free reorganization: (1) autonomous conditions provided by tax law and (2) conditions for a reorganization imposed by company law. Sometimes there is a combination of the two.

The advantage of having independent conditions in the tax code is obvious. Regardless of the legal form in which the parties may structure the reorganization, it should benefit from tax exemption only if it meets conditions set in tax law.[48] In addition, as is generally the case when one law refers to another, any reference to company law can be problematic because if there is a change in the conditions of company law there will be a simultaneous change in the conditions for tax exemption. Because the drafters of company law are often not tax experts, changes in company law may lead to unexpected surprises in tax law.

2. Degree of Continuity

The degree of required continuity of shareholder interest determines the degree of flexibility that the parties have in negotiating a tax-free reorganization. When, in an asset acquisition, company law or tax law subjects a tax-free reorganization to the condition that all assets and liabilities must be transferred and that such transfer is compensated exclusively in voting shares, the room for introducing changes in the way of doing business at the occasion of a reorganization is very limited.

Yet there are good business reasons to grant some leeway to the parties to the reorganization to make the necessary changes in the conduct of business or in the distribution of the property interests of the shareholders. As far as the

---

[46]*See* BEL CIR art. 211 §§ 1, 2 al. 3°; GBR TCGA § 137 (1). In the United States, this is the result under the case law.

[47]*E.g.*, Merger Taxation Directive, *supra* note 6, art. 11.

[48]An example of independent conditions in the tax code is the type C reorganization in USA IRC § 368 (a)(1)(C): transfer of substantially all the assets of one company to another company solely in exchange for all or part of the voting stock of the company acquiring the assets. This definition does not refer to any rule in company law, since this differs from state to state. *See infra* note 49. For specific tax conditions for exemption, *see* NLD Vpb § 14; A.J. Van Soest, Belastingen 511 (Arnhem 1995); FRA CGI Annex II § 301B–301F; Merger Taxation Directive, *supra* note 6, art. 2.

transfer of assets is concerned, the transferor company often maintains some assets that are totally unattractive to the transferee company or for which it has no use (e.g., old equipment, dilapidated buildings, or scrap) and for which it is not prepared to pay. If the condition for tax exemption is that all assets need to be transferred, the transferee company will pay a higher price than is economically justified for the transfer and it will try to shed the useless assets after the merger.

A similar problem arises with the continuity of the shareholder's interest. Particularly when a small company is merged into a big one and the shareholders of the former receive only a small fraction of the total shares outstanding in the new company, they may prefer to sell their shares. In other cases, depending on the rules in company law, minority shareholders who are opposed to the merger may wish to exercise their rights to be bought out and receive the fair market value of their shares in cash. When the condition for tax exemption requires compensation of all the shareholders in voting shares of the acquiring company, this means that if the merger goes through, the buyout of the minority shareholders will result in a taxable merger. When this is the situation, the minority shareholders in effect hold a veto power over the merger being tax free. Therefore, the room left in the tax law or the company law for compensation in forms other than voting shares is very important.

An example of a statute that leaves sufficient flexibility with respect to the transfer of assets and the compensation in shares in a merger is the U.S. Internal Revenue Code. The text of the statute does not impose any hard-and-fast conditions, but requires only that the reorganization take the form of a merger under state law.[49] Conditions of continuity of the proprietary interest of the shareholders and of the continuity of business activity have been set by case law and are therefore rather flexible.[50]

---

[49]See USA IRC § 368(a)(1)(A). Under the U.S. federal system, the states are responsible for the general civil law, including company law. This has perhaps contributed to the flexibility of the federal tax law, as it must accommodate differences in company law among the states, and also explains why in the United States the requirements for a merger to be tax free are found in tax law rather than in company law.

[50]See Bittker & Eustice, supra note 15, ¶ 14.11; John A. Nelson Co. v. Helvering, 296 U.S. 374 (1935); Helvering v. Minnesota Tea Co., 296 U.S. 378 (1935); Reilly Oil Co. v. C.I.R., 189 F.2d 382 (5th Cir. 1951). USA IRC § 368 (a)(1)(A) defines a "merger" as a tax-free reorganization. Company law determines what a merger is. However, the United States has many different types of company law, because company law is not federal law but state law. In some states, there is even a valid merger when all or substantially all of the assets are transferred from one company to another, regardless of the form of compensation that is paid for a transfer. This implies that when the major part or even all of the assets of a company are transferred for cash there may be a merger under state law. This is unacceptable for tax purposes, because it would lead to a tax-free sale of most of the assets and the shares in the transferor company and lead to a serious breach in the principle of continuity. Therefore, in addition to the reference made to a "merger" in the sense of the company law, there is an additional condition in the case law, only for tax purposes, that the shareholders must continue a substantial interest in the transferee company. See Cortland Specialty Co. v. C.I.R. 60 F.2d 937 (2d Cir. 1932); Commissioner v. Gilmore's Estate 130 F.2d 791 (3d Cir. 1942); Roebling v. Commissioner, 143 F.2d 810 (3d Cir. 1944).

Generally, a merger will qualify as tax free in the United States if at least half of the net value of the transferor company is remunerated in shares of the acquiring company.[51] As far as the continuity of the business activities of the transferor company is concerned, case law permits nonoperating assets to be excluded from those transferred in the merger and leaves room for changes in business activity.[52] This approach leaves enough room to accommodate the demands of minority shareholders who ask for the redemption of their shares at the time of the merger.

The requirements for other types of reorganizations in the U.S. Internal Revenue Code are more strict and mechanical. For example, in a type C reorganization,[53] the transfer of assets must cover "substantially all" assets, and at least 80 percent of the remuneration for the assets transferred, not taking into account the transfer of liabilities, must consist of voting shares of the acquiring company. Yet, these requirements for a tax-free merger leave room to shed some of the useless assets and to buy out minority shareholders.[54]

An example of a far stricter application of the principle of continuity can be found in the European Union directive on the taxation of cross-border mergers.[55] In defining a merger, the directive refers to a "legal merger." This concept has been developed in the draft directive on cross-border mergers in company law.[56] The directive requires that all assets and liabilities, without exception, be transferred to the acquiring company. This requirement is of course closely linked to the idea that the acquiring company is the universal legal successor to the acquired company and therefore acquires title to all assets and liabilities of the latter without exception. This concept leaves little room for shedding some useless assets or for changing the conduct of business at the time of the merger.

Similar restrictions apply to the continuity of the shareholder's interest. The part of the remuneration that can be paid in a form other than shares of the acquiring company is limited to 10 percent of the nominal value of the capital increase that is necessary to compensate for the transfer of assets.[57] Since the fair market value of the shares is in most cases a multiple of their nominal value, only a small fraction of a few percentage points can typically be paid to the shareholders of the acquired company in a form other than the

---

[51]See Rev. Rul. 66-224, 1966-2 C.B. 114.

[52]Becker v. Commissioner, 221 F.2d. 252 (2d Cir. 1955); Bentsen v. Phinney, 199 F. Supp. 363 (S.D. Tex. 1961); Mary Archer Morris Trust, 42 T.C. 779 (1964).

[53]See supra note 48.

[54]See USA IRC § 368 (a)(1)(C).

[55]Merger Taxation Directive, supra note 6, art. 2.

[56]Commission of the European Communities, Proposal for a Tenth Directive of the Council based on Article 54(3)(g) of the Treaty Concerning Cross-Border Mergers of Public Limited Companies, COM(84) 727 final (Jan. 8, 1985).

[57]See Merger Taxation Directive, supra note 6, art. 2; see also FRA CGI Annex II § 301F. Nominal value is also known in company law as par value.

shares of the acquiring company. The measure in the European Union directive is in most cases just sufficient to compensate in cash shareholders who would receive fractions of a whole share from the acquiring company, thereby eliminating these fractional shares. However, in those countries where minority shareholders have a right to be bought out, the narrow limits imposed by the directive will spell trouble. Paying out a small minority holding in cash would make the merger a taxable one if the holding exceeded the small level stipulated by the directive.

Bankruptcy reorganizations pose a particular problem for continuity of interest, because the shareholders of the bankrupt company may receive few or no shares in the surviving company. Instead, it is typically the creditors who obtain shares in exchange for their debt. To facilitate this type of transaction, it can be provided that no gain or loss is recognized to a transferor company on the transfer of its assets to a new company in a bankruptcy reorganization where creditors of the transferor obtain enough stock to provide continuity of interest.[58] For this purpose, continuity of interest is determined by considering the creditors as owners of the debtor company.

3. Transfer of Liabilities

Another problem related to the continuity of the proprietary interest of shareholders is how to take account of the transfer of the liabilities of the acquired company. Part of the compensation for the assets of the acquired company takes the form of the assumption of its liabilities. To the extent of this compensation, the assets of the acquired company are not transferred in exchange for shares. However, practically all statutes will disregard the transfer of liabilities and apply the criterion of transfer for voting shares only to the net value of the transferor company. Only the transfer of the net value of the assets of the acquired company—that is, after deduction of all liabilities outstanding at the time of the merger—must be compensated for in shares. Thus, the transfer of liabilities is generally disregarded in evaluating the degree of continuity.[59]

4. Nonvoting Shares

Another problem is whether nonvoting shares qualify for the continuity test. In many countries, company law provides for various categories of nonvoting shares. Because most of these types of shares guarantee a minimal fixed return on capital and a payout of the capital value of the shares in priority to common shares, the risk in these categories of shares is much lower. Generally

---

[58]See USA IRC § 368(a)(1)(G).

[59]However, if liabilities exceed the value of assets and only a nominal amount of stock is transferred to the former shareholders, then the continuity of interest requirement might be considered not to be satisfied. See Bittker & Eustice, supra note 15, ¶ 14.14. In such cases, what has occurred in substance is a purchase of the assets by means of an assumption of the liabilities.

speaking, they are very much like long-term bonds. Therefore, nonvoting shares are often not accepted as equivalent to voting shares for a tax-free reorganization.[60] When this rule is applied, a practical problem may arise with some categories of shares, which may be voting or nonvoting from time to time. For example, preferred shares may normally be nonvoting as long as the preferred dividend is paid out, but may become voting when the company fails to pay out the guaranteed preferred dividend. In such a case, the common shares, which are normally voting shares, may become nonvoting. To know whether shares are voting shares, the situation should be judged as it is in fact at the time of the reorganization. If preferred shares are voting at that time, such shares should be considered as voting shares. If common shares are nonvoting at that time, they should be considered as nonvoting shares. However, when these different categories of shares are distributed, it should be taken into account that preferred shareholders may lose control and that common shareholders may gain control some time after the reorganization.[61]

5. Step Transaction Doctrine

When the conditions for a tax-free reorganization are so narrow that, in some cases, unavoidable changes in the business activity or the necessity to buy out shareholders will result in taxation of the reorganization, the question arises as to whether the parties can do after or before the reorganization what the law prohibits them from doing at the time of the reorganization. If the parties can get rid of unwanted assets by selling them or transferring them to a different company before or after the reorganization, the problems in qualifying for a tax-free reorganization are more apparent than real. The same principle applies to the redemption of minority shareholders' interests.

The U.S. reorganization rules, which are rather flexible for changes at the time of the reorganization, are generally rather inflexible before and after; that is, the same restrictions that apply at the time of the reorganization also apply before and after it. This is the result of the application of the "step transaction doctrine" in case law.[62] Under this doctrine, different transactions before and after the reorganization are considered to be "single steps" of the overall transaction if it appears that they were necessary and indispensable steps to reach a

---

[60]*E.g.*, USA IRC § 368(a)(1)(B) (exchange of stock solely for voting stock). *But see* Bittker & Eustice, *supra* note 15, ¶ 14.11 (nonvoting shares are counted in determining continuity of interest in a merger).

[61]The line cannot always be drawn very neatly. *See* Forrest Hotel Corporation v. Fly, 112 Supp. 782 (S.D. Miss. 1953).

[62]U.S. American Potash & Chemical Corporation v. U.S., 399 F.2d 194 (Ct. Cl. 1968); Commissioner v. Gordon, 391 U.S. 83 (1968); Furniss v. Dawson [1984] 2 WLR 226; [1984] AC 474. Similarly, in the Netherlands, tax exemption is subject to the condition that the shares issued by the transferee company in the merger are not sold by the shareholder for three years after the merger, *see* NLD Vpb § 14(1).

general agreement on the reorganization. Therefore, sales of assets or shares before or after the reorganization will be taken into account in determining whether the continuity requirement has been met, when it appears that these sales were implemented as part of the overall reorganization agreement.

Countries with very strict rules on continuity traditionally have not had such a step transaction doctrine.[63] This diversity of experience suggests a choice between, on the one hand, a formalistic system—with strict requirements for qualifying for reorganization treatment—and, on the other hand, a more flexible system policed by antiavoidance rules like the step transaction doctrine. While the latter approach can work in countries such as the United States with its sophisticated system of tax lawyers, tax administrators, and courts, it may be difficult to apply in countries whose tax system is not as developed, except by leaving considerable discretion to the tax administrators. While a formalistic system may therefore be more attractive in developing and transition countries, it also suffers from the potential disadvantage of being open to abuse. If the former choice is adopted, care should be given to defining the transactions eligible for tax-free reorganization treatment.

6. Corporate Divisions

While some countries spell out the requirements for tax-free corporate divisions in their statutes, others allow them by administrative practice, and yet others do not have provisions for tax-free divisions.[64] In some countries, all three techniques of division (spin-off, split-off, and split-up) can qualify for tax-free treatment, while in others only one or two of these can.[65]

There are often requirements concerning which assets can be contributed to a subsidiary that will be divided from the parent, but there are substantial differences in this requirement from country to country.[66] For example, in Germany, the assets of a division must be contributed together, and in the United States both the parent and the subsidiary must hold assets of an active business.

Tax law generally requires that all transferee companies carry on a business activity after a division (not necessarily the same business activity as before the division). If this condition is not imposed either by statute or by case law, it will become possible to split the corporate assets into two parts: one continuing the business and another to be liquidated. Such a transaction should be taxed as a distribution in partial liquidation, rather than as a division.

---

[63]A typical case in point is Belgium before its tax reform of 1989. Tax-free reorganizations were an all-or-nothing affair, whereby all assets had to be transferred exclusively in exchange for voting stock. However, parties to the reorganization were free to dispose of shares and assets before and after the reorganization, making the restrictions at the time of the reorganization a lot less strict.

[64]See Rädler, supra note 15, at 564.

[65]See id. at 565.

[66]See id. at 568–69.

Another typical question is whether the shareholders of the transferor company need to continue their equity interest proportionally in all the transferee companies, or whether it is sufficient that they exchange their shares for voting shares of one or more of the transferee companies. This is an important question, because it determines to a great extent the flexibility of a corporate division. If all shareholders of the transferor are required to acquire the same proportional part in all the transferee companies as the part of the shares they own in the transferor, there is no flexibility at all. Often in a corporate division, some shareholders (group A) of the old company will be interested in continuing part of the business, while other shareholders (group B) will be interested in continuing some other part of the business. Therefore, group A shareholders should receive shares only in company A and group B shareholders, shares only in company B. As long as all, or the largest part, of the shareholders continue their equity interest in one of the transferee companies, the reorganization should maintain its tax-exempt character.

7. Elective Taxable Treatment

Treatment of a proposed transaction as taxable or tax free is often elective in that the taxpayer can change the form of the transaction slightly to make it qualify as tax free or, if the taxpayer considers it more advantageous, to make it fail to qualify. Some countries go beyond this degree of electivity in some cases by allowing the taxpayer to elect for particular transactions whether it will be treated as taxable or as a tax-free reorganization.[67] The theory behind this approach is that it is inefficient to require the taxpayer to manipulate the corporate form of the reorganization to accomplish the particular tax result desired.

8. Requiring Approval

Although there are disadvantages in requiring approval from the tax authorities before a transaction can be engaged in (delays may impede transactions and approval requirements may be invitations for corruption), the technique of requiring a ruling from the tax authority before a reorganization can be carried out on a tax-free basis[68] does have the advantage of simplifying the drafting requirements and alleviating the concern that statutory rules al-

---

[67]Germany allows the transferor company an option to choose between a tax-exempt and a taxable transfer; *see* UmwStG § 11. This choice will of course be agreed upon between the parties to a reorganization. When the transferor company elects a tax-free reorganization, the conditions are such that the continuity of shareholders and business activity is guaranteed so that the tax liability is only deferred. In the United States, a corporation that purchases the stock of a target company may elect to treat the transaction as a taxable purchase of the assets of the target, followed by the contribution of the assets to a new corporation. *See* IRC § 338.

[68]*E.g.*, FRA CGI § 210B (requiring approval for divisions and contributions of part of a corporation's assets). *See* Bernard Chesnais & Yann de Givré, *France, in* 79b Cahiers de droit fiscal international 139, 142–43 (1994).

lowing such transactions might be used for tax avoidance. Approval requirements might be impractical in countries experiencing a large volume of reorganizations, but might be manageable in countries where this is not the case.

C. Tax Consequences of Tax-Free Reorganizations

1. Tax Position of the Transferor Company

The tax exemption of a reorganization in itself is very simple: no tax is levied on the gain that is realized in exchange for shares.[69] When the reorganization rules allow compensation partly in shares and partly in cash and other property, the most common approach is to provide a partial exemption. This means that the gains realized in a reorganization will be tax exempt to the extent that the transfer of assets by the transferor is compensated by voting shares of the transferee, or to the extent that the shares of the acquired company are exchanged for shares in the transferee company.

For problems related to applicable tax rates and differences in tax rates between ordinary profits and capital gains and the allocation of gains to various categories of assets, we refer to the discussion of taxable reorganizations.[70] One problem that is specific to the partially taxable transaction is how the amount of the taxable profit is calculated. Basically there are two approaches. One approach is to allocate the total compensation (shares and taxable compensation) proportionally to all assets.

Examples

EXAMPLE 1

In a merger, OLDCO receives total compensation of $20,000 reflecting its net fair market value. Of this compensation, $15,000 is paid in shares and the balance of $5,000 is paid in cash. The tax basis of the net assets of OLDCO (after deduction of all liabilities) is $6,000. Total gain on the merger realized by OLDCO is $14,000. Of this gain, one-fourth ($5,000 out of $20,000) is taxable, either as an ordinary profit or as a capital gain. The balance of the gain is tax exempt; that is, of the total gain, $3,500 is taxable and $10,500 is tax exempt.

Another approach is to subject to tax all forms of compensation other than shares, but only to the extent that the transferor company realizes an overall profit on the transaction.[71]

---

[69]See BEL CIR § 45; FRA CGI § 210 A. However, the transferor company can elect taxable treatment for the transaction, in which case a concessional rate of 18 percent applies; see FRA CGI § 210 A-4; USA IRC § 354 (a).

[70]See supra sec. III.

[71]E.g., USA IRC § 356.

EXAMPLE 2

The facts are the same as in example 1. Instead of having the total profit proportionally allocated between the compensation in shares and the other forms of compensation, the total gain will be taxed to the extent of the compensation received in a form other than shares (i.e., the total taxable profit will be $5,000).

The amount of taxable profit under the second method will always exceed the amount that is taxable under the method of proportional allocation.

Although most countries will tax the transferor company in a merger to the extent that the transfer of assets is not compensated for in voting shares, some tax systems do not tax the transferor company when, or to the extent that, the nonshare compensation is distributed by that company to its shareholders pursuant to the plan of reorganization. Only the shareholders of the transferor company will be taxed if, and to the extent that, they receive compensation other than voting shares. The basic reason for this approach is that the transferor company is acting only as a conduit to transfer the compensation received in the reorganization to its shareholders, while the transferor itself does not realize a profit and should not be taxed on the compensation transferred to the shareholders.[72] It should be noted, however, that such look-through treatment of the transferor company is inconsistent with the classical system involving double taxation of companies and shareholders.[73]

This rule can be accepted only when it is certain that all shareholders will be taxed on any profits. When individual shareholders are not taxed on their capital gains, this rule should not be applied. In such cases the only place to tax the nonshare compensation is the transferor company.

2. Tax Position of Transferor Shareholders

The same rule should apply to the transferor company and to its shareholders: to the extent that the reorganization is compensated for with voting shares, the gain realized by the shareholders of the transferor should be tax exempt.[74] In many countries, however, gains realized by individual nonbusiness shareholders, nonprofit organizations, or tax-exempt institutions such as pension funds are tax exempt in any case. In these tax systems, it is not necessary to provide a specific exemption for these types of shareholders.

---

[72]See GBR TCGA § 139(1) (applies where the transferor "receives no part of the consideration for the transfer"); USA IRC § 361(b).

[73]This is not to say that the United States has always exhibited great consistency in its approach to the classical system. Up to 1986, corporations could (under the so-called *General Utilities* doctrine) distribute appreciated property to shareholders without incurring tax on the gain, thereby eliminating economic double taxation on these gains. With such inconsistent treatment in the background, it is easy to understand that the merger rule is not always consistent.—L.M.

[74]See FRA CGI §§ 92B, 92J (shares listed on the stock exchange), 160 I *ter* (shares constituting a holding exceeding 25 percent of outstanding capital), 150 A *bis* (shares in real estate companies); DEU UmwStG § 13; GBR TCGA § 135; USA IRC §§ 354(a), 356.

A special case of exemption is the gains realized by holding companies. In some countries, capital gains realized on shares by holding companies are fully tax exempt in order to eliminate double taxation.[75] It follows that even when there is a fully or partially taxable reorganization, the gains realized by a company that is a shareholder in the transferor or acquired company are always tax exempt, even when the latter company is fully or partially taxed on the reorganization.

For business taxpayers, the exchange of shares for consideration other than voting shares should always be a taxable event even within the framework of a "tax-free" reorganization. The reason is that it is easier to partially tax the consideration that has taken a form other than voting shares than it is to transfer the old cost base of the shares surrendered to the assets received. Particularly when the compensation is in cash, it would be awkward to have cash booked with a cost base equal to the value of the old shares surrendered. However, to the extent that compensation is not in cash, it should be possible to exempt the transfer and to defer the tax liability by continuing the cost base of the old assets for the new assets received in exchange.[76]

The taxable profit will be calculated as the difference between the total compensation received and the cost base of the shares surrendered.[77] The alternatives for calculating the amount of profit are the same as those discussed above in connection with taxing the transferor in a partially taxable reorganization. Either the total profit will be proportionally allocated over total compensation in shares and other forms of compensation, or total nonshare compensation will be taxed to the extent that there is an overall profit on the transfer of shares.[78]

Finally, there is the problem of eliminating double taxation between companies and shareholders. As already indicated,[79] this problem has been solved in Belgium and the Netherlands. In other countries, it has not been solved for the simple reason that it is not perceived as a problem. Gain on the exchange of shares in a reorganization is conceptually qualified as a capital gain, which is a category separate from dividends. Therefore, in most countries the concept of double taxation of companies and shareholders is simply not applied to this situation.[80] However, in some countries the gain is considered as a liquidating distribution by the transferor at the time of the reorganization.

---

[75]See supra note 28.

[76]USA IRC § 358(a) provides an adjustment of the tax basis when property is received in exchange for consideration other than stock or securities.

[77]FRA CGI §§ 150 A bis, 160 I ter defer the tax liability until the shares received in exchange are sold.

[78]See supra sec. IV(C)(1).

[79]See supra note 28.

[80]Note, however, the intricate Norwegian "RISK" rules, which allow a step-up of capital gains tax basis for shares with respect to retained, taxed profits, with the purpose of eliminating economic double taxation not just for distributed profits, but for profits the shareholders realize as capital gains.—L.M.

The liquidating distribution is sometimes considered as the equivalent of a dividend, thereby raising the question of relief for double taxation. The shareholders of the transferor company may therefore receive a tax credit or an exemption for dividends received as in an ordinary distribution of a dividend. The problem with these solutions is that in most cases the tax credits or the amount of the exemption for dividends received for the transferor company and its shareholders do not match because, as stated, the gains of the transferor company and its shareholders do not match either. As a consequence, the elimination of double taxation between the transferor company and its shareholders in a partially tax-free reorganization is far from perfect.

The position of the shareholders of the transferor company after the merger is subject to the continuity principle, implying that (1) to the extent that the exchange of shares is free of tax, all the tax attributes of the shares in the transferor company will be carried over to the shares in the transferee company as if the reorganization had not taken place; and (2) to the extent that the exchange of shares has been taxed, the tax basis of the shares in the transferee company will be revalued and all tax attributes of the shares in the transferor company will disappear.

3. Tax Position of the Transferee Company

The transferee company is not taxed in a merger unless it is at the same time a shareholder of the transferor company. This special case will not be discussed here. In a reorganization, the transferee company is mainly interested in what happens after the reorganization. The position of the transferee company is determined by two elements: (1) the tax basis of the assets received from the transferor, and (2) the carryover of other tax attributes of the transferor.

A. TAX BASIS OF THE ASSETS TRANSFERRED

The rules for determining the tax basis to the transferee company after the merger are roughly the same as the rules for determining the tax basis of the new shares on behalf of the shareholders of the transferor company. To the extent that the transfer of assets is taxed to the transferor company there will be a revaluation of these assets for tax purposes; to the extent that the transfer of assets has been tax free, the transferee company will carry over the tax basis that those assets had before the reorganization in the transferor company.[81]

---

[81]*E.g.*, BEL CIR § 212; USA IRC § 362(b). In France, a distinction is made between depreciable and nondepreciable assets. For nondepreciable assets such as land and securities, there is a single carryover of the old tax basis; *see* FRA CGI §§ 40, 151 *octies*. For depreciable assets, the capital gain that has been exempted must be reintegrated in taxable profits over a period of 15 years after the merger; *see* CGI § 210A(3)(d). The argument has been made that in the context of privatized enterprises in transition economies, it may not make much sense to provide for basis carryover, because the basis may bear no relation to reality. The alternative would be to allow such enterprises a fresh start valuation at market value without requiring recognition of gain. *See* Kodrzicki & Zolt, *supra* note 5, at 629–33.

The problems of allocating the amount of taxable profit to various categories of assets (inventory, fixed assets, goodwill) have been discussed in connection with taxable transactions.[82] These problems are exactly the same in a partially tax-free merger. To the extent of the amount taxed, the increase in tax basis has to be allocated over several categories of assets. The valuation of the assets in the reorganization will be decisive in allocating the amount of profit realized by the transferor. When the reorganization is completely tax free, there is no problem of allocation, because the existing tax basis of the assets of the transferor company is carried over.

B. DISPARITY BETWEEN TAX ACCOUNTING AND COMMERCIAL ACCOUNTING

The carryover of the old tax basis of the assets of the transferor company in a tax-free reorganization may result in a disparity between tax accounting and commercial accounting, depending on the accounting rules in the tax jurisdiction. Basically, a reorganization can be accounted for by either pooling accounting or purchase accounting.

Pooling accounting consists in carrying forward without any change all book items of the transferor company as they existed before the reorganization. It is the accounting method that is recommended for tax-free reorganizations in the United States, because the accounting rules coincide with the tax rules.

Purchase accounting treats the transfer of assets in a tax-free reorganization as a sale and results in the revaluation of all assets transferred from the transferor company on the basis of their fair market value. The use of purchase accounting in a tax-free reorganization results in a discrepancy between commercial accounting and tax accounting after the reorganization in respect of the transferee company.

Example

A building that has been completely depreciated is transferred in a tax-free merger. The tax basis of the building is 0. In the merger, the building is valued at $1,000,000. When purchase accounting is used in the merger, the building will be recorded in the accounts of the acquiring company at $1,000,000, and depreciation will be calculated on $1,000,000. For tax purposes, however, the building will be transferred tax free to the acquiring company at a value of 0, and no depreciation will be allowed; hence, a discrepancy arises between depreciation for commercial accounts and depreciation for tax accounts after the merger.

Countries that base tax accounting on commercial accounting will have to use pooling accounting for tax-free reorganizations.[83]

---

[82]*See supra* sec. III.

[83]*E.g.*, DEU UmwStG §§ 4, 12.

c. Carryover of Tax Characteristics from Transferor to Transferee

When a corporation disappears in a merger or its assets are acquired, the question arises as to whether various tax attributes of the corporation are carried over to the transferee. In a formalistic approach, these attributes would disappear, because they are personal to the taxpayer, but the tax laws typically stipulate that they are carried over in a tax-free reorganization, subject to limitations.[84] One difficulty is that there are a number of potential tax attributes whose treatment is not necessarily consistent (in particular, as discussed below, limitations are often placed on the carryover of net operating losses).

The position of the transferee company on the carryover of tax characteristics of the transferor company in general can best be illustrated by the carryover of losses, methods of depreciation, and inventory valuation.

Practically all developed tax systems limit the transfer of loss carryovers from one company to another in tax-free reorganizations.[85] In some systems, loss carryovers are simply prohibited. However, most tax systems apply one of two alternative approaches or, in some cases, may apply both approaches simultaneously.

The first approach is a variation on the substance-over-form approach or the requirement of a specific business purpose for the tax-free reorganization. It is mostly applied by case law or by rulings because it requires some qualitative evaluation of facts. The loss carryover will be permitted only when there is some economic substance to the merger that justifies the compensation of losses from one line of business with profits in another line of business. This approach sometimes leads to surprising results and causes uncertainty for taxpayers. In some cases, tax law allows a tax loss carryover only if there is a business purpose.[86] A variation of this approach requires continuity of business activity.[87]

The second approach is a strict statutory and quantitative approach. The tax law states some hard and fast rules that are based on quantitative restric-

---

[84]*E.g.*, USA IRC § 381; Bittker & Eustice, *supra* note 15, ¶ 16.01.

[85]France requires a preliminary ruling (*agrément préalable*) to carry over tax losses in a corporate reorganization; *see* CGI § 209 II. In Germany, loss carryovers from the company that disappears in a merger are prohibited on the principle that the transferor and the transferee company are two different taxpayers and that losses from one taxpayer cannot be carried over to another taxpayer. Tax practice has applied a self-help method, however, by having the loss company act as the transferee company so that tax losses can be preserved within the entity of the same taxpayer. *See* Brigitte Knobbe-Keuk, Bilanz-und Unternehmenssteuerrecht 598 (1993).

[86]Libson Shops v. Koehler, 353 U.S. 382 (1957); Maxwell Hardware Co. v. Commissioner, 343 F.2d 713 (9th Cir. 1965).

[87]*E.g.*, DEU KStG § 8(4) (denying tax loss carryovers when more than 75 percent of the shares have been transferred and the acquired company has substantially changed its business). This rule puts severe restrictions on the rule that permits the transferee company to carry forward tax losses in a tax-free reorganization.

tions that always apply, even when loss compensation in the tax-free reorganization would be justified on good business grounds.[88] Basically, there are two ways to apply this approach: one is a continuity-of-shareholders test and the other is a comparison-of-assets test.

The continuity-of-shareholders test was used in the United States before the Tax Reform Act of 1986. The rule called for tax loss carryovers to be reduced in proportional amounts when the shareholders of the transferor company did not acquire a certain minimum threshold participation in the transferee company. For example, full loss carryover was permitted only when the shareholders of the loss company obtained at least a 20 percent share participation in the profitable company. For each full percentage point by which the shareholders of the loss company fell short of the 20 percent target, the amount of the loss carryover was reduced by 5 percent. For example, when the shareholders of the loss company acquired only 5 percent of the interest in the profitable company, only 25 percent of the amount of the tax losses could be carried forward.[89]

Another approach is the relative comparison-of-assets test. Losses can be carried forward only to the extent of the percentage share that the assets of the loss company represent in the total assets of the combined company or companies after the reorganization. For example, if the net value of the loss company represents only 5 percent of the total value of the combined companies, only 5 percent of the loss may be carried over.[90]

The United States currently uses a more sophisticated version of this approach, under which the loss carryover is limited to the value of the loss company's shares multiplied by a long-term interest rate.[91] This approach allows the losses to be offset against a notional return on the assets of the loss company.

In a corporate division, loss carryovers should follow the transfer of business activity. That is, when a business is divided in such a way that company A continues the basic business activity, while another company B receives assets and liabilities but carries on a completely new business activity, losses should be transferred exclusively to company A. A net asset test for the division of loss carryovers may result in distortions, because liabilities of the transferor company may be dumped exclusively in the transferee company carrying on the nonprofitable business, thereby reducing its net fair market value almost to zero.

---

[88]In the Netherlands, there is no tax exemption for an asset acquisition when one of the participating companies has a tax loss carryover (combination of Vpb §§ 14 and 20); see also DEU KStG § 8(4).

[89]See USA IRC § 382 (1986); see also AUS ITAA (1936) § 80 DA(A)(d); GBR ICTA § 768 (a major change in ownership and a major change in the nature or conduct of a trade).

[90]See BEL CIR § 206(2).

[91]See USA IRC § 382.

Tax credits should also follow the business activity. To the extent that such credits are related to particular assets, specific investment requirements (e.g., oil exploration), or specific activities (research and development), the credits should follow either the assets or the specific activity to which they are linked.

Another issue is the carryover of depreciation methods, methods of inventory valuation, and other methods of accounting.[92] The basic rule is that the methods of accounting used by the transferor must be continued by the transferee after a tax-free reorganization. However, sometimes the taxpayer is allowed to change these methods when there are good business reasons for such a change. Some, but not all, tax systems also accept a business reorganization as an occasion that justifies such a change, in order to apply the same methods of accounting in the combined company or companies after the reorganization. Such changes may go in both directions. The assets of the transferor company can be valued and depreciated in accordance with practices used before the reorganization by the transferee company, or all assets after the reorganization may be valued or depreciated in accordance with practices formerly used only by the transferor company. In this sense, there may be discontinuity in depreciation practices and valuation practices even after a tax-free reorganization.

Finally, there are the rights of the taxpayer in matters of tax procedure, such as appeals, collection, and litigation. The carryover of all rights and obligations in tax procedures is not so much determined by tax law, which seldom provides that these procedures will be carried forward by the transferee company or that the transferee company will be considered as the general tax successor to the transferor company. The rule imposing a carryover of all procedural aspects of taxation is most often situated in company law or, in some cases, in the code of civil procedure.[93]

In corporate divisions, one way to solve the problem is to make all transferee companies jointly liable for tax obligations, which means that they can also act jointly in tax protests and tax litigation after a corporate division. In practice, collection of tax liabilities should always follow the business activity of the transferee companies. The other transferee companies should be liable only when the tax liability cannot be collected from the transferee company to which it belongs. If a tax liability is specifically linked to a particular asset (e.g., land tax on real estate), the tax liability and ensuing tax protests and tax procedures may appropriately follow the asset.

V. Taxes Other Than Income Tax

The tax consequences of corporate reorganizations are not limited to income tax. There are always the problems of carrying over the tax characteris-

---

[92]*See supra* sec. III(C); USA IRC § 381.

[93]*See also supra* sec. III(C).

tics of any tax from transferor to transferee company and from old to new shares. For two types of taxes, the problems are more pressing than for others because they raise problems of tax exemption: taxes on capital contributions and value-added tax.

Many countries levy taxes on equity contributions to capital or stamp duties on transfers of assets.[94] A corporate reorganization often requires a formal capital contribution, which in some cases may impose a considerable tax burden (e.g., if a newly formed subsidiary is involved). The reasons for exempting reorganizations from tax on capital contribution or stamp taxes are largely the same as the reasons for exemption from income tax. The basic difference between the exemption from these taxes and the exemption from income tax is that the former is final, whereas the latter is temporary. The simplest way to deal with this exemption is to impose the same conditions for exemption as in the income tax.

Finally there is the problem of value-added tax or sales tax.[95] Here too, there is a case for temporary exemption, as long as the transferee who carries on the business also remains responsible for all tax obligations. It will not be appropriate, however, to impose the same conditions for exemption as in the income tax, for the simple reason that the tax fate of the shareholders of the transferor company is irrelevant to the sales tax or value-added tax. Only the transferor and the transferee company are involved as taxpayers. Therefore, the only requirements that should be imposed are (1) that the business activity should be transferred to and continued by the transferee (transfer of all or substantially all assets and liabilities),[96] and (2) that the transferee should be subject to sales tax or value-added tax with the same rights and obligations as the transferor. The type of consideration paid in the reorganization is irrelevant (therefore, sales of a business should qualify for exemption). The type of taxpayer is also irrelevant, so that it should be possible to have a transfer free of value-added tax between a corporation and an individual and vice versa as long as both parties are taxpayers under the value-added tax. The same approach can be applied in the case of the excise tax.

---

[94]Exemptions from these taxes in reorganizations are discussed in Tomsett et al., *supra* note 45.

[95]*See* vol. 1, at 216–17.

[96]In contrast to the requirements for tax-free reorganizations under the income tax, here, substantially all the assets means the assets of a business, not all the assets of the transferor (which may have several businesses).

21

Fiscal Transparency

Alexander Easson and Victor Thuronyi

> Men may put on the habiliments of a partnership whenever it advantages
> them to be treated as partners underneath, although in fact it may be a
> case of "The King has no clothes on" to the sharp eyes of the law.
>
> —*Felix Frankfurter*

I. Introduction

As discussed in chapters 14 and 19, income tax systems invariably draw a
distinction between physical persons and legal persons. In some systems, income tax is imposed by separate laws—an individual income tax law and a corporate (or enterprise) income tax law; in others, physical and legal persons are
taxed under the same law, but are governed by separate rules and rate schedules. Some business or investment income, however, is not earned directly by
such taxpayers, but is earned through entities or arrangements that—depending on the legal system—may or may not be separate persons. In that case, it
is necessary to decide whether to tax the entity as a separate physical or legal
person, or to provide for fiscal transparency, whereby the entity's income flows
through to its owners. Pure transparency would mean disregarding the entity
altogether, which is sometimes done.[1] However, more commonly, the entity is
recognized as existing for tax purposes, but rules are devised so that the entity's
income is taxed not to it but to its owners. This chapter explores the circumstances under which fiscal transparency (also called flow-through treatment)
applies for income tax purposes and the rules by which transparency is given
effect.

---

[1]An example is the treatment of a grantor trust. *See infra* sec. III(D)(1). *See generally* David S.
Miller, *The Tax Nothing*, 74 Tax Notes 619 (Feb. 3, 1997) for a discussion of various cases where
entities are disregarded and the implications thereof.

The topic is a confusing one to investigate on a comparative basis, for two reasons. First, the nature of legal arrangements to which transparency can be applied differs considerably from one legal system to another. In general terms, there is a big difference between common law and civil law countries, although there are also differences within the groups of common and civil law countries. Because tax law must apply to the economic rights that are specified in a country's civil and commercial law, these legal differences have strongly influenced the tax rules in various countries. Given these fundamental differences, it is difficult in this area to generalize and point to an optimal set of rules for the income tax. Second, even laying aside the differences in underlying legal systems, most industrial countries have not formulated rules for transparency in a thorough and consistent fashion. Developing and transition countries that are formulating rules to deal with transparent entities must therefore rethink approaches to the issue that have been employed elsewhere.

A further problem arises from the fact that, while in some countries the tax status of an entity is determined by its status (as a legal person or otherwise) under civil law, in many systems the tax status of an entity is established by the tax law and does not always coincide with its status under private law.[2] In some cases, the entity is a legal person but is not treated as a separate taxpayer for purposes of the income tax on legal persons. In other cases, the converse is true—the entity is not a legal person but is regarded as such for tax purposes.[3] Such a difference in status should not necessarily be considered a defect in the overall legislative scheme; there are perfectly valid reasons why an entity might be regarded as a legal person for purposes of registration or of civil liability, but not for purposes of taxation.

This chapter is primarily concerned with the income tax treatment of those entities that are neither legal nor physical persons, and with entities that are legal persons under the general law but are not treated as such for purposes of the income tax.

There are a great variety of ways in which ownership interests in investment property or in a business may be split up among different participants. In the case of investment property, there can be a pure co-ownership arrangement (such as a joint tenancy), in which two or more persons each own a fraction of the property. In such a case, minimal rules are needed to specify the taxation of the income from the property: each owner is taxed on his or her

---

[2]See vol. 1, at 91–92.

[3]The treatment of an entity may also differ from one tax law to another. For example, a partnership is usually not treated as a separate entity for income tax purposes, but is normally a distinct taxable entity under the value-added tax (see vol. 1, at 175–76) and may also be treated as a taxpayer for other taxes (payroll taxes, property tax, excise taxes). It will generally have an employer identification number and an obligation to withhold PAYE on the same basis as corporate employers. See, e.g., U.S. Treas. Reg. §§ 31.3401(d)-1, 301.6109-1.

fractional share of the income.[4] Such joint-ownership arrangements are not considered further in this chapter.

Arrangements for the joint operation of a business can be referred to generally as partnerships, although the term does not mean precisely the same thing in different legal systems. The tax treatment of partnerships is discussed in section II. Another important joint-ownership arrangement in common law countries is the trust, which has some analogues in civil law countries. Taxation of trusts is considered in section III. Finally, section IV deals with a number of other business entities that are accorded special tax treatment in various countries.

One general approach to taxing such entities is to provide some form of transparent treatment, whereby the income is taxed at the level of the owners rather than at the level of the entity. Precisely how this may be done is considered below. An alternative approach is to accord only partial flow-through treatment to the entity; income that is distributed or allocated to the beneficiaries or owners is taxed to them, with the remainder being taxed at the entity level. This method is commonly adopted for trusts and is designed to ensure that all the income of the entity is taxed once.

II. Partnerships

A. Introduction

1. Legal Nature of Partnerships

The legal concept of partnership exists both in common law legal systems and in civil law countries, although the two concepts are not entirely equivalent.[5] The traditional common law definition holds that "[p]artnership is the relation which subsists between persons carrying on business in common with a view to profit."[6] That is, a partnership is a relationship among persons, essentially contractual in nature rather than a "person" in its own right.

Civil law systems generally do not use the term "partnership" but have the concept of what could be literally translated as an association of persons or company of persons.[7] This concept is distinct from that of a capital company.[8]

---

[4]*E.g.*, LSO ITA § 64. In addition to a rule specifying that each owner is taxed on the owner's share of the income, it may be appropriate to provide for cases where jointly owned property is divided, each owner receiving a portion of the property. In systems where capital gains are taxed, nonrecognition treatment would be appropriate for this kind of transaction.

[5]For an overview of the taxation of partnerships in different countries, with particular emphasis on international aspects, *see* Jean-Pierre Le Gall, *General Report, in* International Tax Problems of Partnerships, 80a Cahiers de droit fiscal international 655 (1995) [hereinafter Cahiers].

[6]Partnership Act, 1890, 53 & 54 Vict., ch. 39, § 1 (GBR).

[7]*Société de personnes, sociedad de personas, Personengesellschaft.*

[8]*Société de capital, sociedad de capital, Kapitalgesellschaft.*

The precise legal nature and form that companies of persons may take differ depending on the civil and commercial laws of each country.[9] In many civil law countries, a distinction is also made between civil law partnerships (governed by the civil code) and commercial partnerships (regulated by the commercial code). Typically, civil law partnerships are those that are engaged in farming or investing in land, or that are carried on by members of the liberal professions—activities not considered to be "commercial."[10] They can also include agreements to split the profits of a business.[11]

Most countries recognize at least two forms of partnership: the general partnership, in which the partners are jointly liable for the debts of the firm, and the limited partnership, in which the liability of some of the partners is limited.[12] In a number of countries, there are more than two forms of partnership, and the tax treatment may vary according to the particular form.[13]

---

[9]See generally S.N. Frommel & J.H. Thompson, Company Law in Europe 16–18 (1975); The International Guide to Partnerships (van Raad and Betten eds., IBFD 1996)[hereinafter Guide]; Cahiers, supra note 5, at 75, 113–14, 294, 337–39, 378–79. For example, in Argentina, the following types of partnerships may be formed: partnerships regulated by the civil code (sociedades civiles), de facto companies (sociedades de hecho), irregular companies (sociedades irregulares), general partnerships (sociedades comerciales colectivas), limited liability companies (sociedades de responsabilidad limitada), limited partnerships (sociedades en comandita simples), partnerships limited by shares (sociedades en comandita por acciones), labor and capital partnerships (sociedades de capital e industria), and associations for particular investments (sociedades accidentales o en participación). See id. at 24.

[10]Cf. supra ch. 14, note 111. In Spain, professional (civil) partnerships are generally taxed on a flow-through basis rather than as legal persons. See ESP IRPF art. 52(1)(B); ESP IS art. 19; Cahiers, supra note 5, at 486.

[11]See infra notes 32–34; DEU Handelsgesetzbuch §§ 230–237 (stille Gesellschaft).

[12]In Germany, the most important forms of commercial partnership are the (general) Offene Handelsgesellschaft (OHG) and the (limited) Kommanditgesellschaft (KG). Under article 105 of the German Commercial Code, an OHG is defined as follows: "A partnership formed for the purpose of running a commercial business under a common firm name is a general commercial partnership where no partner's liability is limited with regard to the partnership's creditors." Martin Peltzer et al., German Commercial Code 95 (1993). The corresponding forms in French law are the société en nom collectif and the société en commandite.

[13]A hybrid corporation/partnership form, the limited partnership with shares, exists in a number of countries, for expample, in Germany (Kommanditgesellschaft auf Aktien—KGaA) and Italy (società in accommandita per azioni), and is taxed as a legal person, unlike other partnerships. However, the share of the general partner of the KGaA is taxed on a flow-through basis. See Brigitte Knobbe-Keuk, Bilanz-und Unternehmensteuerrecht 414 (1993); DEU KStG art. 9(2). A relatively popular business form in Germany is the GmbH u. Co. KG—a type of limited partnership in which the general partner is a limited company; it is taxed on a flow-through basis. In the Netherlands, a distinction is made for tax purposes between an "open" and a "closed" limited partnership (commanditaire venootschap), depending on whether a limited partner's share is freely transferable. Only the closed type receives full flow-through treatment. See Cahiers, supra note 5, at 395, 398–99. The open type is taxed somewhat similarly to the KGaA in Germany—the partnership is subject to corporate tax, but the profit share of the general partners is deductible in computing the taxable profit of the partnership and is taxed in the hands of the general partners. See A.H.M. Daniels, Issues in International Partnership Taxation 18, 32–33 (1991).

In some legal systems, partnerships have legal personality, while in others they do not.[14] In this chapter, the term "partnership" is used not as a term that corresponds precisely to a concept in the legal system of all countries, but as a general one that encompasses a variety of legal forms. This variety and the differences in treatment under civil law, in particular whether the partnership is considered a legal person, make it difficult to generalize about partnerships. To some extent, differences in tax treatment from one country to another may also have been influenced by differences in civil law.

The term "joint venture" may be even more confusing than partnership. In some countries, joint ventures are transparent arrangements that may be less formal than partnerships.[15] The term is also sometimes used in ways that include a number of legal entities, including capital companies.[16]

2. Partnerships as Taxable Entities

The absence of legal personality of partnerships in many countries may have facilitated transparent treatment for tax purposes, although the fact that a partnership is or is not categorized as a legal person is not necessarily determinative of its tax status. Different approaches are possible. In several countries, partnerships are considered legal persons but are not treated as taxable persons.[17] Belgium, Spain, and many Latin American countries treat as taxable persons those forms of partnership that are legal persons, except for specified cases where a fiscal transparency regime applies.[18] In common law countries, partnerships generally are not considered legal persons and are not taxed as corporations, although some partnerships that are considered to resemble corporations are taxed as corporations rather than as partnerships,

---

[14]Generally, in countries with a common law tradition, partnerships do not have legal personality, although in Israel they do, despite the common law origin of the relevant legislation. In civil law countries, partnerships normally have legal personality; for example, they do in Brazil, France (except for *sociétés de fait* and *sociétés en participation*), Mexico, Spain, the Scandinavian countries, Russia (*see* Civil Code arts. 48, 49, 50, 66 (RUS)), Kazakhstan (*see* Civil Code arts. 34, 58 (KAZ)), and the Czech and Slovak Republics (*see* Internationale Wirtschafts-Briefe, Mar. 26, 1997), but do not have legal personality in Belgium, Germany, Indonesia, Japan, the Republic of Korea, the Netherlands, or South Africa. *See* Cahiers, *supra* note 5, at 87, 114, 158, 183, 232, 267, 318, 396, 433, 466, 499, 597, 657.

[15]E.g., Cahiers, *supra* note 5, at 125.

[16]*See* Joint Venture-Strukturen im internationalen Steuer- und Gesellschaftsrecht, Internationale Wirtschafts-Briefe, May 14, 1997; James Dobkin et al., Joint Ventures with International Partners 2-2 to 2-9, 5-1 to 5-20 (1993).

[17]E.g., Argentina, Denmark, Finland, France, Israel, Norway, and Sweden. In the United Kingdom, partnerships in Scotland are legal persons but, as elsewhere in the country, are not taxable persons.

[18]E.g., Brazil and Mexico. *See* Cahiers, *supra* note 5, at 87, 114, 380. In Spain, the general rule is that legal persons are subject to the company tax; however, a transparency regime applies to certain entities. *See* ESP IS §§ 4, 19.

even though they are not legal persons.[19] In Indonesia, partnerships are taxed as separate entities even though they have no legal personality.[20]

In recent years, the civil and commercial laws of many transition countries have undergone changes under which the legal status of various kinds of business entities has been defined or redefined; the tax treatment of such entities has also been in a state of flux. The different patterns that have emerged can be illustrated with some examples. In Kazakhstan and Romania, all legal persons (including partnerships) are subject to income tax as separate entities.[21] In Latvia, the enterprise income tax applies to all enterprises, which are defined according to registration requirements,[22] except that partnerships are taxed on a flow-through basis[23] and physical persons and "individual enterprises" that are not required to submit annual reports under commercial law are taxed on a flow-through basis to the owner.[24] Individual enterprises that are required to submit annual reports are therefore taxed as entities even if they are not legal persons. Similarly, in China, all enterprises are subjected to enterprise income tax as separate entities regardless of whether a given entity is a legal person.[25] In Estonia, the entity-level tax applies to legal persons.[26] General and limited partnerships are taxed under the entity-level tax, except that general partnerships consisting of no more than 10 partners who are all resident physical persons are taxed on a flow-through basis.[27]

Taxing partnerships as entities has the advantage of administrative simplicity, as it is generally easier to collect tax from a single entity than from the individual participants. Income tax returns of partners who are physical persons are kept simple, as they do not include income received through the entity,[28] and complicated rules for the taxation of flow-through entities can be largely avoided. A further advantage of taxing partnerships as entities is that it avoids discrimination between different forms of business organization and

---

[19]See Cahiers, *supra* note 5, at 659. In Australia, limited partnerships formed after 1992 are taxed as companies. In the United States, certain publicly traded partnerships are treated as corporations for income tax purposes, *see* USA IRC § 7704; and limited partnerships may be treated as corporations if they have a predominance of corporate characteristics. *See* Treas. Reg. §§ 301.7701-2, 301.7701-3 (USA).

[20]See Cahiers, *supra* note 5, at 267–68; IDN IT § 2.

[21]ROM PT § 1(1)(a); KAZ TC § 6(3); Civil Code arts. 34, 58 (KAZ).

[22]LVA TF § 14(4).

[23]See LVA EIT § 2(3). In Latvia, partnerships are not legal persons. *See* Law on Partnerships, art. 2 (Feb. 5, 1991)(LVA).

[24]See LVA EIT § 2(4).

[25]CHN EIT § 2.

[26]EST IT § 2(2).

[27]Id. § 4.

[28]Unless the distribution of profits from the partnership to an individual partner is treated as the equivalent of a dividend. This is the case in the Netherlands, where profits of an open limited partnership are distributed to a limited partner. *See* Cahiers, *supra* note 5, at 399.

eliminates "entity shopping."[29] However, the disadvantage is that the income will then normally be taxed at a flat rate rather than at the marginal rates applicable to the individual partners.

If partnerships are taxed as entities, it must also be decided whether they should be treated the same as corporations in all respects. For example, should partnership distributions be treated as dividends, and should all the rules governing transactions between corporations and shareholders apply to partnerships as if partners were shareholders? The answer may depend on what system is used for taxing corporations (classical, imputation, or other).[30]

3. Defining Which Entities Are Subject to Which Regime

A threshold question in designing the income tax on business and other entities is the determination of which entities should be subject to the tax on legal persons[31] and which should be subject to flow-through treatment. As previously noted, this determination does not necessarily depend on whether for other purposes the entity is a legal person. Entities that are not legal persons may still be taxed as if they were, and entities that are legal persons may receive flow-through treatment.

Even in systems that impose a single enterprise tax on business entities or on all legal persons, there are usually some situations where an exception to the general rule is made, and a business arrangement between two or more participants gives rise to income that is allocated and taxed to the participants; that is, it is given flow-through treatment. In civil law countries, such arrangements are usually provided for under the civil or commercial code.[32] They do not normally give rise to a separate registration requirement and are not separate legal persons. A typical example is the arrangement commonly referred to as a joint venture,[33] in which each participant (itself often a legal person) is taxed separately on its share of the venture profits.[34]

Depending on what tax regimes are provided, definitions must be framed to allow distinctions among different entities. For example, the law might provide for three different regimes: (1) entities taxed as corporations, (2) entities taxed on a flow-through basis with income determined at the entity level, and (3) entities or arrangements with full transparency (the distinction between

---

[29]In the United States, for example, many smaller businesses are operated in the form of partnerships or limited liability companies because such forms are taxed less heavily than corporations; *see supra* ch. 19.

[30]*See supra* ch. 19.

[31]*See id.*

[32]*E.g.*, Codul Comercial [Commercial Code] arts. 251, 253 (ROM). In France, *société civile*; in Germany, *bürgerliche Gesellschaft. See* Bürgerliches Gesetzbuch §§ 705–740.

[33]*See infra* sec. IV(A)(1).

[34]For example, in Mexico, although partnerships (which are legal persons) are generally taxable entities, joint ventures (which are not legal persons) are not. *See* Cahiers, *supra* note 5, at 377, 381–82.

(2) and (3) is explained below). How the definitions are framed may depend on the civil and commercial law. For example, it might be provided that all entities that have legal personality under the civil law are taxed as corporations, that all entities (other than legal persons) required to keep books of account under the commercial law are taxed under regime (2), and that all other entities or arrangements are taxed under regime (3).[35] Whether it makes sense to frame the definition in this way depends on the civil law. Sometimes it is difficult to frame the definition in general terms and resort is had to listing types of entities.[36] Whether a list is resorted to or not, the definition is most often framed in terms of the status of the entity under the civil law. Some countries, such as the United States, have adopted an independent definition for tax purposes.[37] Recently, the United States has made the rule elective, so that most foreign entities that are not stock companies can elect whether to be treated as a partnership or as a corporation for U.S. income tax purposes.[38] This raises the possibility of an entity being treated as a taxable person in its country of residence, but obtaining flow-through treatment for U.S. tax purposes, with consequent tax-planning opportunities that exploit the inconsistent treatment by the two countries.[39]

---

[35]On the distinction between partnerships and arrangements that are fully transparent (such as co-ownership of property), see Hugh Ault et al., Comparative Income Taxation 355–56 (1997); Knobbe-Keuk, supra note 13, at 401–02 (a typische stille Gesellschaft (typical silent partnership) is not considered a partnership for purposes of DEU EStG § 15), William McKee et al., Federal Taxation of Partnerships and Partners ¶ 3.03[5] (1997) (distinction between partnership and co-ownership).

[36]E.g., FRA CGI §§ 8, 206, 239 quater, 239 quater C.

[37]The Internal Revenue Code taxes associations as corporations but does not define association. The courts and the Treasury Department gradually evolved a definition that looked at characteristics of the entity being considered, evaluating its resemblance to a corporation on the basis of those characteristics. Eventually, this test was embodied in regulations, but the test included in the regulations was applied in a formalistic manner, so that tax practitioners could, by following the regulations and structuring the entity as appropriate, achieve either partnership or corporate classification. The tax treatment of an entity had therefore become largely elective. This electivity was extended and formalized in 1996. For discussion of the history, see McKee et al., supra note 35, ¶ 3.06. The pre-1996 U.S. approach is unusual, the general approach to classification being explicitly formalistic (i.e., countries generally do not look behind the form of an entity to consider its characteristics under its governing instrument). However, an entity's characteristics do sometimes have to be considered in classifying foreign entities, since the test may be whether the foreign entity resembles entities that are classified as corporations under domestic tax law, and the forms of the foreign entity may not exactly correspond to the local forms. The Netherlands also applies a corporate resemblance test, with the result that it draws distinctions for tax purposes that do not correspond to civil law categorizations. See Daniels, supra note 13, at 18–22.

[38]Treas. Reg. § 301.7701-3.

[39]See Stanley Ruchelman et al., European Approaches to Hybrid Entities and Financing Structures: An Introduction, 14 Tax Notes Int'l 1487 (May 5, 1997). For a discussion of classification of foreign entities in Germany, the Netherlands, and the United States, see Daniels, supra note 13.

4. Partnerships as Flow-Through Entities

With some exceptions noted previously, most countries provide flow-through treatment for partnerships; that is, they do not treat partnerships as taxable entities, but rather tax partnership income only in the hands of the partners themselves according to their respective shares in that income. The remainder of this part of the chapter will assume that partnerships are treated as flow-through entities.

5. Tax Obligations Imposed on Partnerships

The fact that partnership income is flowed through to the partners does not necessarily mean that the tax system entirely ignores the existence of a partnership. In many countries, a partnership is required to file a return of partnership income, even though the tax is imposed on the partners themselves.[40] It may also be appropriate, especially where most personal income is taxed at a flat or standard rate, to have the partnership pay tax at that rate on the total partnership profits;[41] this operates as a form of nonfinal withholding, and the tax is paid on account of the individual partners. This type of system may be useful for taxing the share of a nonresident partner.[42]

B. Allocating Partnership Income to Partners

There are basically two ways of thinking about a partnership. Both imply flow through of partnership income, but the meaning of the flow through is different in each. The first view is that the partnership is an entity separate from the partners. The income of the partnership is therefore to be determined separately, and this income can then be allocated to the partners. This "entity theory" may be particularly strong in jurisdictions where the partnership has independent legal personality.

The second view, which is more consistent with the private law view of partnerships in common law and other jurisdictions where the partnership does not have legal personality, is that the partnership is simply an aggregation of the partners whereby each partner is treated as an owner of a fraction of all the assets of the partnership.[43] This may be called the "aggregate" or "fractional" theory of

---

[40]E.g., Australia, Singapore, South Africa, Sweden, and the United Kingdom. In Canada and the United States, the partnership is not required to file a tax return but must file a periodic "information return."

[41]See GBR ICTA § 111. The individual partners are jointly liable for this tax, not just for the tax on their own shares of the partnership income. Stevens v. Britten [1954] 3 All England Law Reports 385.

[42]In the United States, a partnership must withhold tax from all U.S.-source income allocable to a nonresident partner. See USA IRC §§ 1441, 1446.

[43]Strictly speaking, this interest is not exactly the same as a fractional interest and may be a beneficial interest. See Cahiers, *supra* note 5, at 50, 541–42. See also Tekinalp, *Turkey, in* International Encyclopedia of Laws: Corporations and Partnerships 178 (1994) (*condominium plurium in solidum*).

the partnership. Under this view, the partnership does not exist independently of the partners. There is no need to determine income at the entity level. Rather, each partner is simply allocated the partner's fractional share of partnership receipts and outgoings, and the tax consequences are determined in the hands of each individual partner. Different systems implicitly or explicitly adopt for tax purposes either the entity or the aggregate approach or, more often, a hybrid of the two.[44]

Systems (such as the United States) adopting a hybrid approach can end up with a particularly convoluted set of rules governing partnerships.[45] The reason for this is that either of the polar approaches—entity or aggregate—is internally coherent and allows one to solve new problems through logical application of the approach to the new situation. For example, the aggregate theory holds that when a partner leaves the partnership, the partner disposes of his or her interest in the partnership assets to the other partners. It may be complicated to perform the necessary accounting but there is no conceptual difficulty involved. By contrast, under the entity theory, the partner is treated as disposing not of his or her fractional share of the partnership assets, but of the partner's partnership interest. This leaves the cost base of the partnership assets unaffected.

While appealing from the point of view of logical coherence, strict application of either the entity or the aggregate theory may lead to undesirable consequences. A hybrid approach may be chosen to avoid these, but this loses the benefits of logical coherence and leads to a situation where instead of being able to apply a coherent theory to new situations, each new situation will require an ad hoc response, resulting in an inconsistent and complicated set of rules and little reference point when gaps must be filled in.

Whether a country adopts the entity or the aggregate approach, or some hybrid of the two, a number of general issues can be identified as to the mechanism for allocating partnership income to partners. First, there is the question of elections (including election of accounting methods) in the determination of taxable income (e.g., there may be an election as to whether to claim expensing for certain assets or what method of depreciation to use). These elec-

---

[44]For a discussion of the possibilities along the aggregate-entity continuum, see Cahiers, supra note 5, at 662–63. Denmark and the Netherlands come closest to adopting a pure aggregate view, while Finland and Norway provide examples of an entity approach. Most countries fall in between. See Knobbe-Keuk, supra note 13, at 362–64 for a discussion of the German tax conception of partnerships, which originally favored the aggregate approach (so-called Bilanzbündeltheorie (partnership balance sheet is the aggregation of the balance sheets of the partners)), but has now largely abandoned it in favor of an entity view. See also Daniels, supra note 13, for discussion of the German and Netherlands systems.

[45]See McKee et al., supra note 35, ¶ 1.02[3] (1997); Alfred D. Youngwood & Deborah B. Weiss, Partners and Partnerships—Aggregate vs. Entity Outside of Subchapter K, 48 Tax Lawyer 39 (1995); Kimberly S. Blanchard, IRS Rev. Rul. 91-32: Extrastatutory Attribution of Partnership Activities to Partners, 15 Tax Notes Int'l 859 (Sept. 15, 1997).

tions could be made at the partnership level or by individual partners. It is almost always simpler to require that elections be made at the partnership level. Second, there is the question of whether taxable income is to be determined at the partnership level. The extreme possibilities are (1) to make the determination at the partnership level and then allocate the net amount to individual partners, or (2) to make no determination at the partnership level and to allocate the component elements of the calculation (items of receipt, expense, and credit) to the partners. Third, there is the issue of how to make the allocation to partners (i.e., which partner gets which share? Can different partners get different shares of different items?). Fourth, when income or deductions are allocated to individual partners, how is their character determined? Fifth, if there is a partnership loss, can it also be allocated to individual partners or can it be used only to offset future profits of the partnership? These issues are obviously interrelated, but the number of combinations in the actual practice of countries[46] and the detailed rules sometimes involved are such that a full review is beyond the scope of this chapter. The main possibilities are sketched out below.

1. Allocation According to Partnership Agreement

The first inclination is to follow the allocation of partnership income that is adopted for accounting purposes. Accounting standards will normally provide for the allocation of the income to the partners in accordance with the partnership agreement. This allocation may be directly proportionate to capital contributions or may take into account other factors, such as the amount of expertise or effort that particular partners are expected to bring to the business or the fact that they have contributed different property.[47]

Once the partnership income has been allocated to the partners, each partner includes his, her, or its share in total taxable income and is taxed accordingly. Thus, two partners may pay tax on their shares of partnership income at markedly different rates, such as when one partner has a substantial amount of other income and the other partner does not, or when one partner is a legal person and pays tax at the corporate income tax rate and the second partner is a physical person who pays tax at the individual income tax rate.

It should almost go without saying that, in a flow-through system, partners should be taxed on their share of partnership income regardless of whether the income has been distributed; otherwise, the tax on this income would be deferred. Care should therefore be taken in drafting any rule for the

---

[46]*See* Cahiers, *supra* note 5, at 679–80.

[47]*E.g.*, suppose that two entrepreneurs decide to pool the operation of two restaurants that they previously owned separately. Rather than simply splitting the total income of the partnership between them in proportion to the value of their respective contributions, they may specially allocate a portion of the profit (or any gain on future sale) that is attributable to each separate restaurant to the partner who previously owned that restaurant.

taxation of partners to refer to income "allocated" to the partner rather than to income "distributed" to the partner.

2. Deductions

It would be possible to calculate the share of partnership income attributable to each partner by allocating to the partners an appropriate share of gross receipts and expenditures (the fractional approach). In many flow-through systems, however, the net profits of the business are calculated at the partnership level and are then allocated to the individual partners (the entity approach).[48] Thus, expenses incurred by the partnership for the purposes of earning income will normally have been taken into account in determining a partner's share. For example, interest on money borrowed by the partnership for the purpose of earning income is deducted in computing the partnership profits. Where the money has been borrowed from a partner, the interest paid by the firm is the income of that partner.[49]

In the case of deductions that must be specifically claimed (such as depreciation or capital cost allowances), the entity approach would require that the deductions be taken at the partnership level. That is to say, the partners decide among themselves whether or not to claim the deduction in a particular year. By contrast, under the aggregate approach, each partner would separately choose whether to claim his or her share of the total allowable deduction.[50] Even where the aggregate approach is preferred in general, the entity approach seems much simpler to apply in this type of situation.[51] The same goes for other elections.

Sometimes partnership agreements make provision for a "salary" to be paid to a partner. One view is that the salary should not be deductible in computing the profits of the partnership, given that its true nature is that of an advance share of profits paid to the partner; that is to say, it is received by the partner as a share of partnership profits and is usually characterized as business income. This view is supported by the aggregate theory, on the basis that a partner cannot be his own employee.[52] Alternatively, under the entity theory, the salary could be deducted in determining partnership profits, in the same way as a salary paid to an employee, and be included as a separate component

---

[48]However, the types of partnership income that retain their original character in the hands of the partners must be calculated separately. See *infra* sec. II(C).

[49]In that case, its character is interest income, rather than a share of partnership (business) income. However, interest charged to a partner on an advance has been treated as a reduction in the partner's share of partnership profits. FCT v. Beville, 5 Australian and New Zealand Income Tax Reports 458 (1953).

[50]This approach is followed in Denmark and the Netherlands. See Cahiers, *supra* note 5, at 159, 397; Daniels, *supra* note 13, at 29–32.

[51]This is the method adopted in Australia (ITAA § 90), in Canada (ITA § 96), in the United States, and in Switzerland. See Guide, *supra* note 9, at Switzerland, 70.

[52]See Cahiers, *supra* note 5, at 283.

of the partner's total income. An analogous issue arises in the case of other transactions between the partner and the partnership, such as loans or leases of assets.[53]

Expenses incurred by individual partners on their own accounts do not enter into the computation of partnership profits and should be claimed by the partners themselves. For example, where a partner borrows money in order to buy a share of the partnership, the rules applicable to the deduction of interest expense by individuals will govern the deductibility of the interest.

3. Losses

An important issue is the treatment of partnership losses, in particular whether a partner may deduct a share of a partnership loss against other income for that year. A simple, though harsh, solution would be to treat the partnership in the same way as a legal entity for this purpose and to deny any deduction by the partners themselves; that is to say, a partnership loss could be carried forward (or back) only against partnership profits of other years.[54] Logically, however, under a flow-through system a partnership loss should be allocated proportionately among the partners, and each partner should be entitled to claim a deduction in the same way as for any other business loss, carrying the loss forward or backward against income of other years if necessary.[55] It may nevertheless be appropriate to restrict the amount of loss that may be claimed to the amount of the tax cost of the partner's partnership interest.[56]

---

[53]The former (aggregate) position is taken in Australia and the United Kingdom (*see* Case 81 (1985) 28 CTBR (NS) 609; Stekel v. Ellice [1973] 1 WLR 191) as well as in Denmark and Israel. *See* Cahiers, *supra* note 5, at 160, 283. The United States takes the entity approach, allowing the partnership to claim a deduction for salary paid to a partner for services rendered other than in the capacity of partner (USA IRC § 707(a)) or for payments for a partner's services if those payments are determined without regard to the income of the partnership (USA IRC § 707(c)). The same is true for Italy; *see* Cahiers, *supra* note 5, at 295. In Malaysia, the income of the partnership is computed after deducting salaries or interest paid to a partner, but the salary or interest is treated as business income of the partner (MYS ITA § 55(5)). The same approach is followed in the Netherlands. *See* Guide, *supra* note 9, at Netherlands, 74; Daniels, *supra* note 13, at 30. In France, an employment relation cannot exist between the partnership and a partner, so that the partner's compensation would be treated as part of the partner's profit share (aggregate approach). However, rentals of property or loans are treated under an entity approach. *See* Ault et al., *supra* note 35, at 362–63. In Germany, payments such as rents, interest, or salaries are treated under an aggregate approach: they are characterized as business profits and taxed as part of the partner's profit share. *See* DEU EStG § 15; Daniels, *supra* note 13, at 27; Ault et al., *supra* note 35, at 363; Knobbe-Keuk, *supra* note 13, at 362.

[54]This is the rule in Finland. *See* Cahiers, *supra* note 5, at 185.

[55]*See* AUS ITAA § 92; CAN ITA § 96(1); GBR ICTA §§ 380, 385(5).

[56]This is the situation in Canada and Sweden in the case of a limited partner. *See* CAN ITA § 96(2.1). However, if nonrecourse borrowing is included in the tax cost, this limitation can easily be circumvented. Some countries limit deductions to the amount the partner has at risk. *See* USA IRC § 465; Cahiers, *supra* note 5, at 128 (Canada).

4. Taxable Year

It is customary to specify that partnership income be included in the income of the partner for the partner's taxable year in which the partnership taxable year ends. This makes sense from a practical point of view because it is only when the partnership closes its books for its taxable year that it knows exactly how much income and expenses it had. There is no problem if everyone, including partnerships, must use the same taxable year. But if partnerships are allowed to choose their own taxable year, then they can be used as tools for deferring tax. For example, if the partnership chooses a taxable year ending on January 31, there will be an 11-month deferral of tax. For this reason, some countries have restricted the freedom to select a taxable year that differs from the taxable year of the principal partner or partners.[57] However, given the complexity of such rules, the preferable approach is to require all partnerships and taxpayers to use the same taxable year.

5. Antiavoidance Rules

Partnerships between persons who do not deal at arm's length provide obvious opportunities for tax avoidance. In particular, partnerships between spouses or between parent and child provide opportunities for income splitting. An initial question is whether such an arrangement constitutes a genuine partnership at all; a partnership may exist on paper but not in fact.[58] Even where a true partnership does exist, the tax legislation may specify that the agreed-upon allocation of profits may be disregarded when the parties are related, and a reasonable allocation substituted.[59]

When partners deal at arm's length, it will normally be appropriate to accept for tax purposes the allocation of profits and losses provided for in the partnership agreement.[60] However, special allocations that are not based on capital or work contributed may be used as a tax avoidance device. For example, suppose that, under the income tax, charitable organizations are taxed on business income but not on investment income. A charity that owns a factory used in a manufacturing business, with respect to which it pays tax on the income, could contribute the factory to a partnership that it enters into with an investor who owns an office building. Under the partnership agreement, the rental income is

---

[57]E.g., USA IRC § 706.

[58]See Dickinson v. Gross [1927] 11 Reports of Tax Cases [T.C.] 614 (UK); see also supra ch. 14, note 199.

[59]AUS ITAA § 94; CAN ITA § 103(1.1).

[60]See USA IRC § 704(b). In the United States, reference to the partnership agreement means that special allocations of items of income and deduction under the agreement are possible. By contrast, in Germany, there is also a concept that partnership income or loss is allocated according to the partnership agreement (see, e.g., Knobbe-Keuk, supra note 13, at 427), but apparently what this means is that each year a pro rata share for each partner is determined (so-called Gewinnverteilungsschlüssel). This means that special allocations are not possible. See Ault et al., supra note 35, at 359.

allocated to the charity and the business income to the investor. The result is to convert the charity's taxable income into nontaxable investment income.[61] There are different mechanisms by which this result may be precluded. One is to stipulate that partnership allocations will be accepted for tax purposes only if they have substantial economic effect.[62] In the above example, if the amount of income allocated to the charity is limited to the rental income so that the charity has no economic stake in the performance of the factory, this allocation would have economic effect and would be regarded as legitimate. However, if the agreement requires the investor to reimburse the charity, in one way or another, for deficits in expected rental income, or if the arrangement allows the charity to benefit indirectly from higher manufacturing income, then the allocation of investment income to the charity would be a formal matter only and should not be respected for income tax purposes. An alternative, more strict approach would allow the tax authorities to disregard the parties' allocation of profits—and to substitute what they consider to be a reasonable allocation—even when the arrangements have substantial economic effect, if the principal reason for the arrangements is the reduction of tax.[63]

In addition to antiavoidance rules focusing on the allocation of partnership income and deductions, more general antiavoidance rules may apply to partnerships. For example, the U.S. Treasury Department has promulgated regulations that give the Internal Revenue Service a broad power to attack transactions involving partnerships. One of the rules provides that "the provisions of subchapter K [the subchapter dealing with partnerships] . . . must be applied in a manner that is consistent with the intent of subchapter K. . . . Accordingly, if a partnership is formed or availed of in connection with a transaction a principal purpose of which is to reduce substantially the present value of the partners' aggregate federal tax liability in a manner that is inconsistent with the intent of subchapter K, the Commissioner can recast the transaction for federal tax purposes, as appropriate to achieve tax results that are consistent with the intent of subchapter K. . . ."[64] A second rule allows the Commissioner to treat a partnership under the aggregate theory if entity treatment is being abused: "The Commissioner can treat a partnership as an aggregate of its partners in whole or in part as appropriate to carry out the purpose of any provision of the . . . Code . . ." unless a "provision of the . . . Code . . . prescribes the treatment of a partnership as an entity, in whole or in part, and . . . that treatment

---

[61]The example assumes that charities are taxed on business income but not on investment income. The success of the scheme depends on the rental income retaining its character as investment income. *See infra* sec. II(C).

[62]*See* Treas. Reg. § 1.704-1(b) (USA). Such a rule may relate specifically to partnerships, as in the United States, or be a rule of general application.

[63]*See* CAN ITA § 103(1) (referring specifically to partnerships). A similar result may be achieved by a general antiavoidance rule. The problem does not come up if partnership items are in all cases allocated pro rata to the partners, as in Germany. *See supra* note 60.

[64]U.S. Treas. Reg. § 1.701-2(b).

and the ultimate tax results, taking into account all the relevant facts and circumstances, are clearly contemplated by that provision."[65] These rules are of
uncertain scope and have been criticized as overly broad.[66] They were no
doubt motivated, however, by the difficulty of designing more specific antiavoidance rules in the context of the intricacies of the provisions relating to
partnerships and the ingenuity of tax lawyers and accountants engaged in manipulating those provisions. The fact that such rules were perceived to be
needed may also serve as a warning against imitating the rather detailed statutory scheme for partnership taxation in the United States.

C. Flow Through of the Character of Partnership Income

1. General

The issue of special allocations of partnership income is related to the question of the character of partnership income in the hands of the partners. Almost
all income tax laws classify various types of income in different ways and may
have special rules and limitations depending on the character of the income.
When partnership income is allocated to the partners, there are four main possibilities, corresponding to the aggregate and the entity views of partnership and
points in-between. Under the pure aggregate approach, each item of income or
deduction is treated as if it had been received or incurred by the partner directly.
This means that in certain cases a receipt or expenditure of the partnership will
be treated differently in the hands of different partners, depending on the activity of the partners (e.g., where the partner is a trader in the type of property disposed of by the partnership).[67] Under the second possibility, which is a hybrid
entity-aggregate approach, the character of items of income and deduction is determined at the partnership level, and each item is allocated to the partners and
retains the same character in their hands as it had in the hands of the partnership. Thus, partners may receive their shares of the total partnership income as
business income, dividends, interest, or rental income, as the case may be. Third,
under the pure entity approach, taxable income is determined at the level of the
partnership, with the net amount being allocated among the partners as a single
category of income (most likely, as business income), whatever its original character. Finally, the modified entity approach allows the flow through of specific
items (such as dividends or interest).

The second approach (i.e., partnership-level determination of character
and flowing the character of the income and deductions through to the partners)
is the rule in the United States.[68] It goes hand in hand with a highly complex

---

[65]U.S. Treas. Reg. § 1.701-2(e)(2).

[66]*See* McKee et al., *supra* note 35, ¶ 1.05.

[67]*See* Cahiers, *supra* note 5, at 159–60 (Denmark).

[68]*See* USA IRC § 702; McKee et al., *supra* note 35, ¶ 9.01[4][a]. In a slightly simpler form, it is
also the rule in Canada. *See* CAN ITA § 96(1).

system under which different types of income and expense are subject to special rules and limitations. It is natural under this system to provide for flow through of the character of items of partnership income and expense, because partnerships could otherwise be used as vehicles for avoiding the various limitations.

The alternative, and simpler, entity approach is to treat all partnership income in the hands of the partners as business income, even though it may have been received by the partnership as investment income. This may be justified on the grounds that partnerships are (usually), by definition, business entities;[69] consequently, even income such as dividends and rents received by a partnership may be considered as derived from the carrying on of business by the partners. However, where the tax system treats business income more favorably than investment income, the ability to convert investment income into business income by forming a partnership could open up tax avoidance possibilities.[70] Alternatively, treatment as business income could be disadvantageous such as, for example, when investment income received by individuals is subject to a flat-rate withholding tax. In addition, even a system that generally treats partnership income as business income may still need to make special provision for the flow through of items (e.g., interest, dividends, capital gains, and foreign-source income) that are subject to special regimes (modified entity approach).[71]

2. Capital Gains

Even when a partnership is not a legal entity, it may acquire and dispose of assets in the course of its business, giving rise to the realization of a gain or loss. Because most tax systems treat capital gains differently from other types of income, the question arises as to whether and how a capital gain or loss realized by the partnership flows through to the partners and retains that character in their hands. Flow through may be done in either of two ways. One method measures the gain or loss from disposals at the partnership level, with the resulting net gain or loss being shared among the partners and included in

---

[69]The Australian definition of "partnership" is for tax purposes broader than the general law concept of partnership and does not require a business nature. *See* AUS ITAA § 6; Geoffrey Lehmann & Cynthia Coleman, Taxation Law in Australia 648 (1994). Civil law partnerships may also be formed for the purpose of holding investments. *See supra* sec. II(A)(1).

[70]*E.g.*, where business income is classed as "earned" income, and such income is treated favorably. Contrast the example of the partnership created by a charity, *supra* sec. II(B)(4).

[71]This is generally the approach taken in Germany, *see* DEU EStG § 15; Cahiers, *supra* note 5, at 233; and in most cases in the Netherlands, *see* Betten, *The Netherlands*, *in* Guide, *supra* note 9, at 66–71. According to Knobbe-Keuk, *supra* note 13, at 361, "The partner's profit share belongs to the type of income to which it would belong if the partnership that carries on the business were itself taxable." According to Daniels, *supra* note 13, at 28, "Where the partnership's profits contain items of income subject to a special tax regime, for instance dividends, long-term capital gains, or foreign-source income, these items are taken separately into account, so as to be able to give effect to the special regime at the partner's level."

their income while retaining its character as a capital gain or loss.[72] The other method (the fractional approach), corresponding to a pure aggregate theory, treats each partner as owning a fractional interest in each of the assets of the partnership, so that gains or losses are realized directly by the partners without passing through the hands of the partnership.[73] A problem with the latter approach is that, when there is a change of membership of the partnership, there will often also be a change in the fractional interests of the partners, resulting in a disposal and tax liability or in the need for complex rollover rules.

The problem is avoided with respect to business assets if gains and losses on the disposal of business assets are simply taken into account in determining the profits of the business and receive no preferential treatment. This is the situation in a number of countries, notably Germany and the Netherlands.[74]

3. Foreign-Source Income

A somewhat similar problem arises where a partnership receives foreign-source income. According to the entity theory, that income would simply form a part of the partnership's total income and, in the hands of the partners, would have the character of business income with a source in the country in which the partnership was resident; that is, in most cases, the income would be converted from foreign-source to domestic-source income. One consequence would be that the partners might lose any relief in respect of taxes paid in the original source country. It is true that, when relief from double taxation is provided through the exemption method, the exemption could be taken at the partnership level. But in countries that employ a mixture of the exemption and the credit methods,[75] it would be excessively complex to give relief for some foreign taxes at the partnership level and for others at the level of the individual partners. Consequently, even when there may be a general preference for the entity approach, it seems more appropriate that foreign-source income should retain its character as foreign-source income in the hands of the partners. This in turn raises two problems.

The first is the question of relief for foreign taxes, referred to above. When relief from double taxation is given through a foreign tax credit, the partner should be entitled to claim a proportionate share of the credit. That is, it is not only a share of the foreign-source income that flows through to the partner, but also a share of the foreign tax paid on that income. This procedure involves a certain amount of complexity, in that it requires calculation of the allowable amount of the credit on the tax return of each individual partner.

---

[72]This is the approach taken in Canada. CAN ITA § 96(1)(c)(i).

[73]This approach is taken in Australia; see Lehmann & Coleman, supra note 69, at 329–33 (1994), and in the United Kingdom, GBR CGTA § 60.

[74]See supra ch. 16, sec. IV(B).

[75]See supra ch. 18. There would seem to be no satisfactory way of taking a foreign tax credit at the partnership level.

When relief from double taxation on a particular item of foreign-source income is given through the exemption method, the income should retain its exempt character in the hands of the partner, although the amount of that income may still have to be taken into account in determining the partner's ultimate tax liability if the exemption-with-progression method is used.

The other problem occurs when a member of the partnership is a nonresident. If foreign-source income received by the partnership retains that character in the hands of the partners, the nonresident partner should presumably be exempt from tax on the partner's share of that income.[76] If, however, the income loses its character and becomes converted into business income derived from the partnership, the nonresident partner would be taxable.

D. Disposals of Partnership Interests

A partnership interest is an asset capable of being bought, sold, or otherwise disposed of. Under the aggregate theory of partnership, when a partner disposes of his or her interest in the partnership, the partner is considered to sell a fractional share in all the partnership assets. Gain or loss on the sale of each asset would have to be computed and its character determined separately. Because of its complexity, this approach is followed in only a few countries.[77]

An alternative is to treat the partnership interest as a separate asset.[78] Depending on the rules for taxing capital gains, a gain on the disposal of a partnership interest may or may not be taxable or a loss allowable.[79] If it is, then it will be necessary to provide rules for determining the tax cost of the partnership interest.[80] This amount will not necessarily be the amount originally contributed by the partner, because in the meantime the partnership may have earned income that has not been distributed. Since the partner will already have been taxed on that income, it should be added to the tax cost in order to prevent double taxation. More specifically, the tax cost should be

   (i) the original cost of the partnership interest (including the
       partner's share of partnership debt),

---

[76]To prevent foreign-source income from being allocated to the nonresident partner and domestic-source income to the resident partner, an antiavoidance rule would be needed.

[77]Denmark, *see* Cahiers, *supra* note 5, at 177, and perhaps Japan, *see id.* at 322. *See also supra* note 44. In New Zealand and in the United Kingdom, while the theory is that the partner is considered to dispose of a fraction of all partnership assets, administrative practice has permitted deviations from this strict approach. *See id.* at 420–21, 547.

[78]This is the general rule in the United States, but an exception provides for look-through treatment for certain "hot assets" of the partnership. *See* USA IRC § 751 (the so-called collapsible partnership provision).

[79]*See supra* ch. 16.

[80]For the rules in Canada, which are similar to those proposed here, *see* Cahiers, *supra* note 5, at 127–28.

plus (ii) any additional contributions made by the partner to the partnership,

plus (iii) the partner's total share of partnership income for the period during which he or she was a partner,

less (iv) all partnership income distributed to the partner during that period,

and (v) the partner's share of partnership losses (if a deduction is allowed for such losses).

"Income" in the above formula, should include exempt income of the partnership, because otherwise this income would be taxed in the form of capital gain. The partner's share of debt[81] will depend on whether the partner is a general or a limited partner. Recourse debt is typically allocated to the former and nonrecourse debt to the latter.

It will also be necessary to establish rules for determining the proceeds of disposal of the interest. Although a partnership interest may be sold for a lump sum to some other person who will take the vendor's place in the partnership (usually subject to the agreement of the other partners), it is common for partnership interests to be disposed of in return for a sum payable by installments or for a share of future profits payable over a number of years. Sometimes, it may be specified in the partnership agreement that on the death of a partner the partner's surviving spouse will receive a share of future profits. One possibility is to treat the proceeds of disposal as an amount equal to the present value of the future payments; the payments would then be treated in the same manner as installment payments on the disposition of any other property. The disadvantage, for the continuing partners, is that the payments will presumably be regarded as capital payments for the purchase of the deceased partner's interest and will not be deductible in computing their income from the partnership. Alternatively, the future payments may be taxed as income in the hands of the recipient, in which case the proceeds of disposal must be adjusted accordingly.[82]

E. Formation or Liquidation of a Partnership

Again, depending on the general rules for taxing income and capital gains, there may be a question as to whether contributions of property to a partnership or distributions in liquidation of a partnership give rise to taxable

---

[81]In some countries, liabilities incurred at the partnership level do not affect the basis of the partner in his partnership interest. *See* Ault et al., *supra* note 35, at 360–61. In this case, if partners are allowed to deduct losses in excess of their basis, then negative basis may result.

[82]In Canada, the recipient is treated as though he or she were a partner and is taxed accordingly; CAN ITA § 96(1.1). A hybrid treatment for certain payments to a retired partner, or to a deceased partner's successor in interest, is provided under USA IRC § 736.

gains or allowable losses or to the recapture (or terminal loss) of depreciation allowances. Property contributed by a partner to a partnership may be property previously used by the partner in the partner's own business, in which case any gains might be treated as business gains of the partner. Whether to defer taxation of such gains should probably be resolved in the same way as for formations of legal persons generally. It should be noted that, if a rollover is permitted, one effect may be to transfer potential tax liability for a proportion of any accrued gain to the other partners.[83]

Similarly, when a partnership is liquidated, its property will be disposed of, giving rise to possible capital gains or losses.[84]

In legal systems in which a partnership is not a legal entity, but is merely a relationship between persons, there may be a further problem in that, whenever a partner dies or retires, or a new partner is admitted, the partnership is technically dissolved and replaced by a new one. It would be most inconvenient if every change in membership were to result in a disposal of partnership property and of the interests of all the partners; consequently, it seems advisable to specify that the new partnership should be treated as a continuation of the old one wherever there is a sufficient commonality of membership.

F. Partnership Distributions

Assuming that all partnership income is, in one way or another, taxed to the partners currently, then distributions of cash by the partnership to the partners should not be taxed. They represent either a withdrawal of capital or previously taxed income. As to distributions of property, systems differ substantially on the extent to which gain recognition is required on appreciation of the property. Nonrecognition (rollover) is provided for to varying degrees in Canada, the United Kingdom, and United States.[85] On the other hand, in Germany and other countries that follow a similar conceptual approach, the distribution of partnership property to a partner is treated as a withdrawal of property from the business, which will generally be taxable unless the property is integrated into a business of the partner.[86]

---

[83]For this reason, all the partners should be required to elect for rollover treatment; *see* CAN ITA § 97(2). In the United States, the built-in gain on contribution is allocated to the contributing partner under IRC § 704.

[84]The allocation and flow through of partnership capital gains or losses to the partners have been considered in sec. II, (B) and (C), *supra*. As noted there, some tax systems (e.g., Australia and the United Kingdom) regard partnership property as being owned proportionally by the partners, in which case formation and liquidation of the partnership (and changes in the membership of the partnership) give rise to a change in the proportionate ownership.

[85]*See* Ault et al., *supra* note 35, at 365–66.

[86]*See id.*

G. Adjustment to Cost Base of Partnership Assets

Under a pure aggregate theory, a partner does not have a separate cost base in his or her partnership interest. However, most systems adopt either an entity or a hybrid view under which partners do have such a cost base, which can be referred to as "outside" cost base, the "inside" cost base being the partnership's cost base in its assets. The inside cost base (i.e., the partnership's total cost base in its assets) is initially equal to the total of the "outside" cost bases of all the partners, and remains so if the partnership interests do not change hands.[87] Suppose, however, that the value of the partnership increases and that a partner sells his or her partnership interest to a new partner at a gain. The new partner's cost base will now be greater than that of the old partner, thus upsetting the equality of inside and outside cost base. This can be a problem because it could cause the partners to be taxed on gains realized by the partnership for which the exiting partner has already paid tax. The remedy is conceptually simple but practically difficult. When the new partner is admitted, the cost base of the partnership assets can be increased with respect to the transferee partner to reflect the gain of the retiring partner.[88] Whether to provide such rules depends on the general approach taken to taxing partnerships. If an entity approach is taken, transactions in partnership interests could be considered as unrelated to the inside cost base. Given the complexity of adjustment, an alternative would be to provide for adjustment only upon termination of a partnership. Termination could be provided for in cases where a substantial shift in partnership interests takes place over a specific period.

H. Territorial Application of Partnership Rules

In most jurisdictions, partnerships are not taxable entities and the question of the residence of a partnership does not arise directly.[89] Because partnership income is flowed through to the partners, it is the determination of their residence that is important.[90] As a general rule, a country will assert the

---

[87]*See* McKee et al., *supra* note 35, ¶ 6.01.

[88]*See* USA IRC §§ 743, 754; McKee et al., *supra* note 35, ch. 24. Similar results are achieved in the German system by setting up a separate balance sheet for the transferee partner. *See* Knobbe-Keuk, *supra* note 13, at 899–900.

[89]A partnership appears to come within the definition of "person" ("or other body of persons") in art. 3(1) of the OECD model treaty and is normally entitled to the benefit of provisions of double taxation treaties. *See* OECD, Model Tax Convention on Income and on Capital (looseleaf 1995). The U.S. model expressly includes partnerships in the definition of "person." *See* United States Model Income Tax Convention of September 29, 1996, art. 3(1), *reprinted in* Charles Gustafson et al., Taxation of International Transactions (1997).

[90]Although some countries (e.g., the United Kingdom and the United States) have rules for determining whether a partnership is domestic or foreign, the significance of those rules is limited, *see, e.g.,* USA IRC § 1491 (imposing a tax on the transfer of property to a foreign partnership), except in relation to reporting and withholding requirements.

right to tax a resident partner on worldwide income, which includes both domestic- and foreign-source income from both domestic and foreign partnerships;[91] a nonresident is taxable only on income derived from a source in that country. A variety of situations may exist:

All members of the partnership are resident in country A. In this case, all partnership income allocable to each partner is taxable in country A.

No member of the partnership is resident in country A. In this case, the partners are taxable only in respect of partnership income sourced in country A in the same manner as nonresidents generally.

Some members of the partnership are resident in country A; others are not. In this case, the resident partners are taxable on their entire allocable shares of the partnership's income; the nonresident partners are taxable only on the portion of their shares that is derived from a source in country A.[92]

These rules are simple to state, but may be difficult to apply.[93] Their application depends largely on (1) whether foreign-source income retains that character when flowed through to the partners, and (2) how foreign tax credits are treated. Those questions have been considered in section C above.

In this context, it should also be noted that the taxation of different partners may differ depending on how the partner's country of residence considers the partnership. For example, a partnership doing business in country X may be taxed by this country as a resident business entity. On the other hand, country Y, the country of residence of one of the partners, may treat the partnership on a flow-through basis. In this case, the partner should be able to take a credit in country Y for the tax paid in country X.

I. Conclusion

Several options are available for taxing partnerships. We have already discussed the option of taxing partnerships as separate entities. When this method is not used, some form of flow-through treatment must be prescribed. Given the complexity of this area, one approach for a developing or transition country would be to model its rules on those of another country with a similar legal system. A drawback of doing this is that, as discussed in this chapter, those rules may not be completely coherent, simple, or elaborated. The chief reason for this incoherence is that few countries have adopted a pure aggregate or entity approach to taxing partnerships. The aggregate approach, while coherent, is complex. It is complex from an administrative point of view because it depends on compliance by individual partners; individual compliance com-

---

[91]However, some countries exempt foreign-source business income under certain circumstances, either by statute or by treaty. *See supra* ch. 18.

[92]In this case, it should not matter whether or not the partnership is considered resident in country A. In practice, residency may affect reporting requirements.

[93]For a comprehensive study, *see* Le Gall, in Cahiers, *supra* note 5, and individual country studies, *in* Cahiers, *supra* note 5.

plicates return filing and can lead to enforcement problems that cannot be dealt with by tax administrations that are otherwise weak. The aggregate approach also requires complex calculations for distributions and transfers of partnership interests, because these are considered as involving fractional shares of all the partnership assets. However, somewhat paradoxically, the statutory rules required to implement a pure aggregate rule are not complex. All that would have to be provided is that each partner is considered to be the owner of a fractional share of the partnership assets and income according to the partnership agreement. The partnership itself would not be considered a person for purposes of the income tax. Despite the statutory simplicity, the practical difficulties preclude the adoption of the pure aggregate approach as a general rule in developing and transition countries, although it can be reserved to deal with those forms of co-ownership that are not subject to the general partnership rules.

An alternative to be considered by developing and transition countries therefore would be to adopt as pure an entity approach as possible.[94] This means that income would be determined at the entity level and flowed through to the partners as business income. Limited exceptions might be made for income that receives special income tax treatment. For example, foreign-source income might be broken out separately in order to allow partners to claim the foreign tax credit with respect to such income. Interest and dividends might be flowed through separately if these are subject to special rules (such as being taxed in the hands of individuals through a low-rate final withholding tax). While partners could still manipulate such a system to some extent to minimize tax, the opportunity to do so is limited if the types of income that flow through to the partners are limited. Consideration should also be given to providing for carryover of partnership losses to be used against future income of the partnership, instead of allowing losses to be flowed through to the partners. Such a provision would minimize tax shelter opportunities and is consistent with the taxation of corporations, which also are not allowed to flow losses through to their shareholders. Adoption of an entity approach would solve a number of issues discussed in this chapter. For example, disposition of an interest in a partnership would be treated as disposition of a separate asset, not a disposition of a fraction of the partnership assets. Wages paid to a partner would be deductible by the partnership and taxable as wages to the partner. Under an entity approach, it would be clear that a partnership is a "person" for income tax purposes.[95]

As discussed in section A(3) above, if this modified entity approach is adopted, it will be necessary to specify which entities are subject to this rule. The form of the definition will depend on the legal forms of partnership in the country concerned. There will probably be co-ownership or joint-venture ar-

---

[94]This approach would be along the general lines of the rules applicable in Finland. *See* Cahiers, *supra* note 5, at 183–87.

[95]It is not so treated, for example, in Canada. *See id.* at 124.

rangements that are not legal persons, do not require commercial registration, and would not be subject to this type of entity treatment. For these, a pure aggregate approach may be most appropriate; that is, the joint-ownership arrangement is not treated as a separate person for tax purposes, and the joint owners are treated as directly earning their share of the income.

III. Trusts

A. Introduction

A trust is an arrangement, peculiar to common law systems,[96] whereby legal title to property is vested in a trustee or trustees, but the income from the property (and ultimately the remaining property of the trust, known as the corpus) is or may be distributed to specific beneficiaries. A trust is created by a settlor or a grantor transferring property to the trustee to hold in trust for stipulated purposes and may be created inter vivos or on death, by will (testamentary trust).[97]

Trust arrangements can be very flexible.[98] In the simplest case, sometimes referred to as a "bare" trust, the trust property is held for the sole use and benefit of a single individual, who may terminate the trust at any time and take possession of the property; this is in effect the same as having property held by a nominee. Almost as simple is the case wherein there is a single beneficiary, who is not immediately entitled to end the trust, being a minor or under a legal disability. Under the traditional family trust, the property might be held on trust to pay the income from the property to the settlor's spouse, for life, and then to be divided among the surviving children. In such a case, the spouse would have a present income interest, and the children would have a future capital interest. In other, more elaborate cases, the settlor may direct that the trust income be accumulated (e.g., until a child reaches majority), or the trustee may have discretion as to which of a number of specified beneficiaries should receive the income or capital. Although trusts are most commonly used to hold income-producing property, it is possible for a trust to carry on business, and, in some countries, trusts have been used as a vehicle for family businesses.[99]

---

[96]Roughly equivalent results can sometimes be achieved in civil law systems by other means. *See* William Fratcher & Austin Wakeman Scott, The Law of Trusts 28–31 (4th ed. 1987).

[97]Where executors or administrators hold the deceased's property prior to distribution to the beneficiaries, a situation arises similar to that under a trust, and the tax rules that govern estates in the course of administration generally follow the same principles. *See* USA IRC § 641; Cahiers, *supra* note 5, at 385.

[98]Some special types of trust may be taxed as legal persons, for example, public trading trusts in Australia. In the United States, trusts engaged in active business and possessing the main characteristics of a corporation may be treated as corporations. *See* Treas. Reg. § 301.7701-4(b) (USA).

[99]E.g., in Australia where, until the classical system of taxing corporations was abandoned, a trust had the advantage of avoiding economic double taxation.

Common law jurisdictions will need to include provisions for the taxation of trusts in their income tax laws. Civil law jurisdictions may also provide such rules, given that trust arrangements are also being incorporated into the legal systems of some civil law countries. Developing and transition countries that are civil law jurisdictions probably do not need a detailed set of rules for the taxation of trusts except to cover some of the situations described below. However, even civil law countries whose legal systems do not provide for the existence of trusts should consider providing rules for taxing of income from foreign trusts, because a wealthy individual can easily establish such a trust in a foreign tax haven jurisdiction. Situations may also arise where a person resident in a civil law country is a beneficiary under a trust established in a common law jurisdiction, for example when a person formerly resident in country A (common law) marries and becomes resident in country B (civil law).[100]

B. Flow Through of Trust Income to Beneficiaries

1. General

Trusts raise a similar problem to partnerships in that it is necessary to decide whether to allocate the income of the trust to the beneficiaries for tax purposes and, if so, how. In theory, a trust could be treated as a separate taxable entity and be taxed on the entire amount of the income from the trust property without regard to amounts distributed to beneficiaries, who would presumably receive such amounts free of tax. The objection to that approach is that the rate of tax borne by the trust (whether progressive or flat) would bear no relationship to the income of the beneficiaries. The rate of tax would have to be high (probably equal to the top marginal rate for individuals); otherwise, tax avoidance would be too simple. However, a high rate would be grossly unfair if the income were distributed to a low-income beneficiary. This unfairness can be mitigated by giving the beneficiary a refundable credit for tax paid by the trust, in which case the end result would be much the same as under a flow-through system.[101]

A flow-through system, such as that applicable to partnerships, is an obvious alternative. However, the problem is more difficult than for partnerships in the sense that there is not necessarily an allocation of the trust's current income to the beneficiaries. Some of the income may be accumulated by the trustee for future distribution to beneficiaries at the trustee's discretion, so that the ultimate recipients are not currently known. Consequently, a hybrid system is usually adopted, under which a beneficiary who receives trust income is taxed on that income, while income accumulated by the trustee, to which no beneficiary is currently entitled, is taxed in the

---

[100]See Leif Weizman, *Status of Trusts in Danish Tax Law*, 35 European Taxation 91 (1995).
[101]This is approximately the approach taken in Ireland and the United Kingdom.

hands of the trustee. There may thus be only a partial flow through of trust income.[102]

This system is somewhat artificial and does not necessarily correspond to economic reality. For example, if one beneficiary holds an income interest in a trust and another holds a remainder interest, then in economic terms the holder of the remainder interest has economic income each year because the present value of the remainder interest increases, but is not taxed on that income under generally accepted rules. However, it would be difficult to design rules that more closely correspond to economic reality, and such a goal should in any event not be a matter of priority for developing or transition countries. Accordingly, the generally applied approaches to taxing trusts will be reviewed, because these serve as the most likely models.

2. Method of Taxing Beneficiaries

Beneficiaries may be taxed on their shares of trust income either directly or indirectly. According to one method, a beneficiary includes in his or her income for the year income received (or income to which he or she is entitled) from the trust and pays tax on that income in the normal manner. The trustee is taxed only on the residual undistributed income of the trust.[103] If and when that income is subsequently distributed to a beneficiary, it is received tax free. Under the other system, the trustee is initially taxed on the entire income of the trust. A beneficiary who receives (or is entitled to receive) income from the trust includes that income (grossed up at the rate paid by the trust) in his or her annual return, but is given a credit for the tax already paid on that income in the hands of the trustee. In other words, the system operates as a form of withholding.[104]

3. Allocating Trust Income to Beneficiaries

There are again two alternatives for allocating trust income to beneficiaries: beneficiaries might be taxed only on income actually distributed to them, or they might be taxed on any income that they were entitled to receive,

---

[102]This roughly describes the system adopted in Canada and the United States.

[103]This is the method adopted in Australia, ITAA § 99A; Canada, ITA § 104(13); and the United States, IRC § 652.

[104]This method is used in the United Kingdom, ICTA § 348. *See also* IRL ITA § 154 (providing relief to the beneficiary for tax paid by the trust in the case of income accumulated until the occurrence of a contingency). The method used in New Zealand combines elements of both; if a beneficiary is entitled to income, the trustee is deemed to be his or her agent and is liable for the tax accordingly (NZL ITA § 227). The Singapore treatment is essentially similar (SGP ITA § 35(8)). In the United States, amounts accumulated by a trust are taxed to the trust and may upon distribution be subject to a so-called throwback tax in the hands of the beneficiary to make up the difference between the beneficiary's tax rate and the tax rate of the trust, although there are a number of exceptions and alleviations to this rule. *See* USA IRC § 667.

whether distributed to them or not, in much the same way as partners are taxed.

The first approach has the apparent advantage of simplicity, in that only actual distributions are taxed. However, it opens up the possibility of tax avoidance unless the trust rate is equal to the highest individual tax rate. A beneficiary could simply leave his or her income to accumulate in the trust, withdrawing only what is needed for immediate consumption. Consequently, most countries tax trust beneficiaries on the amounts that they are entitled to receive. For example, in the United States, allocation is on the basis of the amount of the trust's "distributable net income" that is required to be, or is in fact, distributed to beneficiaries during the taxable year (or within 65 days thereafter, at the election of the trustee).[105] Beneficiaries are taxed on the trust's "distributable net income" to the extent of distributions they receive or are legally entitled to receive. This approach calls for taxing beneficiaries on amounts accumulated for their benefit (if they are legally entitled to receive those amounts)[106] in addition to amounts actually distributed to them. The United Kingdom adopts an essentially similar approach.[107]

The difficulty with this approach is that it requires a determination of the entitlement of the beneficiaries under the trust instrument, an exercise that involves interpreting the trust instrument, as opposed to simply observing how much has actually been distributed. It is, however, consistent with the principle that a person should be taxed on income accruing to him or her, whether or not it is actually received.

A trust might direct the trustees to maintain the former family home for the benefit of a surviving spouse and to pay for the upkeep of the home, or to pay for the maintenance or education of a beneficiary. Normally, the value of benefits of this nature will be included in the beneficiary's income.[108]

4. Flow-Through Character of Trust Income

When a trust receives different types of income that are taxed under different rules, the question arises as to whether income flowed through to a beneficiary retains its original character, for example, as a dividend, a capital gain,

---

[105]*See* USA IRC § 663(b).

[106]No beneficiary is currently entitled to amounts accumulated under a discretionary trust or under an express power of accumulation, and such income is taxed to the trust. In Canada, a preferred beneficiary election may be made to have accumulating income treated as if the beneficiary were entitled to receive it; as a result, the income is taxed at the beneficiary's personal rate rather than at the trust rate. *See* CAN ITA § 104(14).

[107]*See* Baker v. Archer-Shee [1927] Appeal Cases [A.C.] 844. It includes amounts actually distributed to a beneficiary under a discretionary trust; the beneficiary is regarded as becoming entitled when the trustees exercise their discretion in his or her favor. For similar rules, *see* AUS ITAA §§ 97, 101; CAN ITA § 104(13); NZL ITA § 227.

[108]*E.g.*, CAN ITA § 105. Other benefits, such as interest-free loans, may also be included.

or foreign-source income. The problem is essentially the same as that encountered with partnerships,[109] and one would expect the legislation to deal with both situations in the same way. However, this is not always the case.

In the United States, the character of distributions is determined on a pro rata basis with reference to the composition of the "distributable net income."[110] Thus, for example, a nonresident beneficiary would pay no tax on foreign-source income deemed distributed to him or her. Although an income beneficiary is normally not entitled to receive a capital gain, the proceeds of a disposal of part of the trust capital may on occasion be paid to a beneficiary (e.g., when there is a power to encroach on capital for the benefit of a beneficiary), and in such a case a capital gain may flow through to the beneficiary.[111] The position is essentially similar in Australia; for example, franked dividends flowed through to a beneficiary retain that character and are consequently free of tax.[112] In Canada, income received by a beneficiary, or to which a beneficiary is entitled, is generally regarded as income from property; thus, income derived by the trust from carrying on business would not be considered earned income in the hands of a beneficiary.[113] However, dividend income, capital gains, and foreign-source income are expressly stated to retain their original character when distributed.[114]

The position is somewhat less clear in the United Kingdom. It appears that foreign-source income retains its character when paid to a nonresident beneficiary.[115] However, in a case in which a trust provided for the payment to a beneficiary of an annuity of a fixed annual amount, and the trust income was insufficient to support the payment with the result that the difference was paid out of capital, the entire amount was held to be income in the hands of the annuitant; that is, the capital nature of the payment did not flow through to the beneficiary.[116]

When a trust is treated as a conduit, to the extent that a beneficiary is entitled to income, all types of income (or capital payments) should in principle retain their original character when flowed through.[117] This is especially important in the cases of tax-exempt income, dividends (if an imputation credit applies), and income that has been subjected to a final withholding tax. It is also necessary to consider whether income from each source should be divided proportionately among the beneficiaries entitled, or whether the trustees, or

---

[109]*See supra* sec. II(C)(1).

[110]*See* USA IRC §§ 661(b), 662(b).

[111]It would seem, however, that a capital loss cannot flow through. *See infra* sec. III(E)(1).

[112]*See* AUS ITAA § 160AQV.

[113]*E.g.*, for the purposes of calculating entitlement to child-care deductions.

[114]CAN ITA § 104(19–22).

[115]Williams v. Singer [1921] 1 A.C. 65.

[116]Brodie's Will Trustees v. IRC [1933] 17 T.C. 432.

[117]An exception might be made in the case of business income, as in Canada, if the business is carried on by the trust but the beneficiary plays no part in the business.

trust instrument, may allocate income from different sources to different beneficiaries.[118]

C. Taxation of the Trust

1. Liability of the Trustee

Whether the entire income of a trust or only the undistributed part is to be taxable in the hands of the trustee, it is necessary to determine in what capacity the trustee is taxable; in particular, it is necessary to indicate whether the trust is to determine its income according to the rules that generally apply to physical persons or to those that generally apply to legal persons. Often hybrid rules may be appropriate, given that all the rules for physical or legal persons, as the case may be, may not be appropriate for trusts.

The usual practice is to tax the trustee (or trustees, jointly) as a separate physical person.[119] This will be the case even if the trustee is a legal person such as a bank or trust company. Thus, the trustee is taxed entirely separately on (1) income accruing to the trustee in the trustee's personal capacity and (2) trust income in respect of which the trustee is taxable. Normally, the trustee is required to file a return of trust income even though no tax may be payable.[120]

2. Income on Which Tax Is Payable

As previously noted, there are basically two systems for taxing trust income. In one (Ireland and the United Kingdom), the trustee is taxed on the entire income of the trust and the beneficiary is entitled to a credit for the tax so paid. In the other, the trustee is liable for tax only on income retained in the trust. This is achieved by allowing the trustee to claim a deduction in respect of income distributed, or required to be distributed, to a beneficiary.[121]

Although the trustee is not generally permitted to claim personal deductions,[122] the usual deductions are normally allowed for expenses incurred in earning trust income—for example, repairs to rental properties or interest on borrowed funds.[123]

---

[118]E.g., can all foreign-source income be allocated to a nonresident beneficiary, or exempt income to a high-income beneficiary?

[119]See, e.g.,CAN ITA § 104(2); USA IRC § 641(b).

[120]E.g., AUS ITAA § 161; USA IRC § 6012.

[121]E.g., CAN ITA § 104(6); USA IRC § 651. Where this method is used, there may nevertheless be circumstances in which the trustee is required to pay tax on behalf of the beneficiary; for example, in Australia, the trustee must pay the tax when the beneficiary is under a legal disability or is nonresident. See AUS ITAA § 98.

[122]E.g., NZL ITA § 228. In the United States, a trust is allowed to deduct a small amount in lieu of a personal exemption. See USA IRC § 642(b). It is not recommended, however, that such a deduction be allowed, and its repeal has been proposed in the United States. See The President's Tax Proposals to the Congress for Fairness, Growth, and Simplicity 92 (May 1985).

3. Rate of Tax

A basic problem with the income taxation of trusts is the rate of tax to be charged. Although trusts are normally treated as separate taxpayers and as physical persons, the application of a graduated rate schedule is inappropriate, because a trust may have a number of beneficiaries (with widely different incomes), and the amount of undistributed income may bear no relationship to the incomes of those beneficiaries.

Trusts provide a variety of opportunities for minimizing taxation, depending very much on the rate or rates at which undistributed income is taxed. If the trust rate is lower than that at which a beneficiary would be taxed, it will be advantageous to accumulate income in the trust, thereby splitting income between trust and beneficiary.[124] If the trust rate is lower than that at which the same income would be taxed to the settlor, there will again be advantages in transferring property to a trust over which the settlor retains some control. In addition, because there are no limits on the number of trusts that a person may create, it becomes advantageous to create multiple trusts if trusts are taxed at progressive rates.

Problems with the use of trusts for tax avoidance can be minimized by specifying that all trust income that is not flowed through to beneficiaries should be taxed at a flat rate equal to the top marginal rate applicable to physical persons.[125] That approach is probably satisfactory if the rate is a moderate one; if it is very high, then it may not be acceptable because it will tax at a high rate income that may be destined for a beneficiary in a much lower rate bracket. Even if rates are moderate, the proposal can be criticized on the basis that it will be unfair in some cases. Inevitably, there will be some trusts accumulating income for the benefit of beneficiaries in low brackets. Some such unfairness is inevitable and is the price of simplicity. The simplicity resulting from such a rule is considerable: there will be no need for multiple trust rules or special rules governing delayed distributions from trusts. The unfairness will be minimal in a country where low-bracket beneficiaries of trusts are likely to be rare.[126]

A suggested general rule, therefore, would be that all accumulated income of a trust be taxed at the top marginal rate for physical persons. Distrib-

---

[123]The treatment of depreciation allowances is problematic, because the benefit of any deduction arguably ought to accrue to the capital beneficiaries rather than to the income beneficiaries. The same is true with capital losses.

[124]Especially if later distributions of accumulated income are tax free.

[125]This is the approach taken in Canada with respect to inter vivos trusts. *See* CAN ITA § 122(1). It is assumed that testamentary trusts are not created principally with a view to tax avoidance. Australia also taxes trusts at the top marginal rate, although the tax commissioner has the discretion to reduce the rate and sometimes does so, especially in the case of testamentary trusts. *See* AUS ITAA § 99A; *see also* LSO IT § 11 (taxation at top marginal rate). In Malaysia and Singapore, trusts are taxed at the same rate as legal persons, but because that rate does not differ greatly from the top individual rate, there is little scope for avoidance.

uted income would be taxed to the individual beneficiaries. However, if certain kinds of investment income are subject to a final flat rate of tax, then it would be unfair to tax that income at the top marginal rate in the hands of a trust where it will ultimately be distributed to beneficiaries who are physical persons. Therefore, the trustee should be allowed to exclude such income as if the trust were a physical person. To prevent abuse, it may be necessary to restrict this rule to cases where the only beneficiaries of the undistributed income are physical persons, as is the case with most trusts. Trusts with corporate beneficiaries do exist, and they should not benefit from a flat withholding tax on investment income if corporations are taxed on such income at the same rate that applies to other corporate income; nor should they be taxed on dividends received through a trust if intercorporate dividends paid directly would be exempt from tax.

An exception to the above rule might also be justified where the trust has only one beneficiary, or where the trustee (or some other person) has the power to vest the corpus or income of the trust in herself or himself.[127] The reason for this rule is that if the trust income is being accumulated for the benefit of a single beneficiary, it makes more sense to tax that income at the possibly lower marginal rate of the beneficiary than at the top marginal rate that would apply to the trust.

In practice, few of the countries that have well-elaborated rules for taxing trusts do impose tax at the top individual rate.[128] In the United States, for example, residual trust income is taxed according to a graduated-rate scale, although the rate scale was compressed by the Tax Reform Act of 1986.[129] In the United Kingdom, where the trustee is taxed on the total income of the trust at the "standard rate," an additional tax is imposed on accumulated income, which reduces—but does not entirely eliminate—the opportunities for tax avoidance.[130] As a consequence, virtually all of the countries in which trusts are common have found it necessary to enact antiavoidance rules of varying complexity.

D. Antiavoidance Legislation

1. Grantor Trusts

In the case of some trusts, it will be appropriate to ignore the existence of the trust for income tax purposes, that is, to treat it as ineffective and to tax its

---

[126]It can also be minimized by providing for qualified beneficiary trusts or preferred beneficiary elections (*see supra* note 106, *infra* note 127), where income is taxed to the beneficiary even though not currently distributed.

[127]*E.g.*, LSO IT § 80.

[128]*See supra* note 125. In Canada, the simplicity of the original system has been undermined by the subsequent introduction of special surtaxes on incomes in excess of stated amounts.

[129]*See* USA IRC § 1(e).

[130]GBR ICTA § 686.

income to the original settlor or grantor. A trust is generally treated as ineffective when the grantor has retained control over the trust or has retained benefits from the trust.

The United States has a rather elaborate and hypertechnical set of rules governing the circumstances under which a trust will be treated as a "grantor trust." These rules were formulated at a time when a substantial tax benefit could be obtained by creating a trust (by taking advantage of the separate taxation of each trust under a progressive rate schedule). They therefore contain a number of safeguard provisions; ironically, they also contain a number of loopholes through which careful estate planners are able to structure arrangements so as to avoid grantor trust treatment. If trust income were taxed at the top marginal rate, as previously suggested, then the definition of grantor trust could be simplified because it would be less critical to catch all possible situations in which grantor trust treatment might be justified, given that the tax benefits from setting up a trust would be minimized.

Under the U.S. rules, the grantor is treated as the owner of a trust in which the grantor has a reversionary interest if, as of the inception of the trust, the value of the interest exceeds 5 percent of the value of the trust.[131] The grantor is also treated as the owner of a trust whose beneficial enjoyment is subject to a power of disposition exercisable by the grantor or a nonadverse party without the approval or consent of an adverse party.[132] "An adverse party" is a person with a beneficial interest in the trust who would be adversely affected by the exercise of the power that the other adverse party possesses.[133] However, a number of exceptions are provided for certain powers that the grantor may hold without running afoul of this rule. These include

- the power to apply income to the support of a dependent, as long as the income is not actually so applied;
- a power the exercise of which can only affect the beneficial enjoyment of the income after the occurrence of an event that is sufficiently remote;
- a power exercisable only by will, with limited exceptions;
- a power to allocate among charitable beneficiaries;
- a power to distribute corpus that is limited by a reasonably definite standard and certain other powers to distribute corpus;
- certain powers to withhold income temporarily;
- a power to withhold income during legal disability or minority of a beneficiary;
- a power to allocate receipts and disbursements between corpus and income;
- certain powers exercisable by independent trustees; and

---

[131]USA IRC § 673. An exception is provided for a reversionary interest taking effect upon the death of the trust beneficiary before age 21 if the beneficiary is a lineal descendant of the grantor. *Id.*
[132]USA IRC § 674.
[133]USA IRC § 672(a).

- a power to distribute, apportion, or accumulate income to or for a beneficiary or beneficiaries, exercisable by trustees who are not the grantor or grantor's spouse, if the power is limited by a reasonably definite external standard.[134]

The grantor is also treated as owner of a trust over which the grantor has certain administrative powers, including

- a power to deal with the trust for less than adequate consideration; and
- a power to borrow from the trust without adequate interest or security.[135]

The grantor is also treated as owner of a trust when

- the grantor has borrowed from the trust and has not completely repaid the loan, unless the loan provides for adequate interest and security and is made by a trustee other than the grantor or a related party;
- a power of administration is exercisable in a nonfiduciary capacity by any person;[136]
- the grantor has the power to revoke the trust, or a nonadverse party has the power to revest title to the property of the trust in the grantor;[137] or
- the income of the trust is—or, at the discretion of the grantor or a nonadverse party, may be— distributed or accumulated for the grantor or the grantor's spouse without the consent of any adverse party.[138]

While the above set of rules can appear daunting (and note that the description is only a simplified summary), it is necessary to have some guidance for when a trust will be treated as a grantor trust. As noted, under a regime that taxes accumulated trust income at the top marginal rate, a simpler set of grantor trust rules can be envisaged. For example, the following set of grantor trust rules for domestic trusts was proposed by the U.S. Treasury Department in 1985:

> The grantor would be treated as the owner of a trust to the extent that (1) payments of property or income are required to be made currently to the grantor or the grantor's spouse; (2) payments of property or income may be made currently to the grantor or the grantor's spouse under a discretionary power held in whole or in part by either one of them; (3) the grantor or the grantor's spouse has any power to amend or revoke the trust and cause distributions of property to be made to either one of them; (4) the grantor or the grantor's spouse has any power to cause the trustee to lend trust income or corpus to either of them; or (5) the grantor or the grantor's spouse has borrowed trust income or corpus and has not completely repaid the loan or any

---

[134]USA IRC § 674(b).

[135]USA IRC § 675.

[136]USA IRC § 675.

[137]USA IRC § 676. An exception is provided for powers the exercise of which can only affect the beneficial enjoyment of the income of the trust after the occurrence of an event that is sufficiently remote. *Id.*

[138]USA IRC § 677.

interest thereon before the beginning of the taxable year. For purposes of these rules, the fact that a power held by the grantor or the grantor's spouse could be exercised only with the consent of another person or persons would be irrelevant, regardless of whether such person or persons would be characterized as "adverse parties" under existing law.[139]

Although the U.S. rules on grantor trusts are considerably more complex than those found in most jurisdictions, more limited rules to similar effect are found in the laws of other countries. For example, where a trust may be revoked, it is commonly provided that the income from the trust is attributed back to the settlor or grantor.[140] Other provisions are found that attribute the trust income back to the settlor if the income is paid or payable to the settlor's spouse or minor children.[141] Provisions of this kind may be found in that part of the legislation that deals with trusts or may be contained in attribution rules of general application. For example, in Canada income and capital gains may be attributed to an individual who "has transferred or lent property . . . either directly or indirectly, by means of a trust or by any other means whatever . . ." to or for the benefit of a spouse or a minor who is a relative.[142]

2. Multiple Trusts

Because there is no limit on the number of trusts that a person may create, there developed in some countries the phenomenon of multiple trusts, whereby property was split among a number of identical or substantially similar trusts so as to take advantage of progressive rate schedules applied to each trust separately. (No advantage will be obtained, of course, if all trusts are taxed at the top marginal tax rate applicable to individuals.)

In Canada,[143] New Zealand,[144] and the United States,[145] the legislative response was to provide rules for aggregating multiple trusts in certain circumstances and to narrow the rate brackets, limiting the amount of income taxed at lower rates.

---

[139]The President's Tax Proposals, *supra* note 122, at 91–92.

[140]*E.g.*, AUS ITAA § 102; GBR ICTA § 672.

[141]*E.g.*, GBR ICTA § 663.

[142]CAN ITA §§ 74.1–74.5, 75.1. An exception is made when the transferee gives full value for the property transferred.

[143]CAN ITA § 104(2).The rule is necessary in Canada because, although inter vivos trusts are taxed at the top marginal rate, testamentary trusts are taxed at progressive rates. It would be possible for a will to create a number of separate trusts for the same beneficiaries.

[144]NZL ITA § 231.

[145]*See* USA IRC § 643(f) (two or more trusts are treated as a single trust if they have substantially the same grantor and beneficiaries and a principal purpose of the trusts is the avoidance of income tax).

E. Disposals of Trust Property and Trust Interests

1. Trust Property

According to usual tax principles, a capital gain or loss may occur (1) when property is transferred to a trust, (2) when the trust itself disposes of property, and (3) when the trust is liquidated.

In the first situation, the principal issue is whether the transferor (e.g., the grantor or settlor) incurs tax liability or can claim an allowable loss.[146] In case (2), assuming that a taxable gain or allowable loss is realized, the question is whether the gain (or loss) accrues to the trust or to the beneficiary. In most circumstances, the benefit of a gain accrues to the ultimate capital beneficiaries and the gain is consequently taxed in the hands of the trust. However, when the trustee encroaches on capital for the benefit of an income beneficiary or makes an advance of capital to a capital beneficiary, it is usually permitted to flow the gain through to that beneficiary, and the gain preserves its character when taxed in the hands of the beneficiary.[147] A capital loss, by contrast, should not flow through because it cannot be distributed. In case (3), if the trust property is sold on liquidation of the trust, the position should be as in (2), except that both gains and losses should flow through to the beneficiaries who receive the proceeds of sale. If, instead, trust property is distributed in specie to a beneficiary, it may be appropriate to provide for a rollover.[148]

2. Trust Interests

An interest in a trust is property that may be alienated. In some cases (e.g., the prospective share of a potential beneficiary under a discretionary trust), it may be difficult to determine the market value, and thus the cost base, of the interest. However, a vested life interest or residuary capital interest can be valued with a reasonable degree of accuracy. For example, if property worth $1 million is settled in trust for person X for life, remainder to person Y, the value (and cost base) of person X's life interest will depend on his or her life expectancy and on the anticipated future earnings from the property. Given that, at the time of the settlement, the combined values of X's and Y's interests must add up to $1 million, the value of Y's interest is also revealed. If X or Y subsequently disposes of an interest, a gain or loss may accrue. However, the calculation of this gain or loss is complicated by the fact that the change in

---

[146]This will normally also establish the cost base of the property in the hands of the trust, although in some cases (e.g., the United States, where the transfer occurs as a result of the death of the grantor), there may be an uplifted cost base without a taxable gain. In other cases (e.g., Canada, where property is transferred to a spousal trust (ITA § 73)), there may be a rollover.

[147]E.g., AUS ITAA § 160; CAN ITA § 104(21).

[148]E.g., CAN ITA § 107(2); USA IRC § 643(e). Before amendment of the latter provision in 1984, a tax-free basis step-up was allowed. *See* Victor Thuronyi, *Tax-Free Step-Up in Basis on Distributions by Trusts and Estates: A Proposal for Reform,* Tax Notes 1461 (June 29, 1981).

value of the individual's interests will be affected by two factors: (1) any change in the value of the underlying trust property, and (2) the fact that X's life interest decreases in value over time (as does his or her life expectancy), and the value of Y's interest increases correspondingly. While it may be legitimate to tax gains attributable to (1),[149] gains or losses attributable to (2) should probably be ignored, because the reduction in the value of X's life interest is offset by the increase in Y's capital interest, and because the calculation would become impossible in more complicated cases involving the trustee's discretion.

F. International Aspects of the Taxation of Trusts

1. General

According to general principles, a country would normally claim the right to tax resident trusts and resident[150] beneficiaries of both resident and foreign trusts on their worldwide income. Nonresident individuals are taxed only on income sourced in the country, and, because trusts are normally taxed as individuals, the same rule should apply to nonresident trusts.[151] In practice, a nonresident trust is likely to be taxed only through the withholding of tax on its investment income.[152]

2. Residence of Trusts

Determining the residence of a trust is obviously important, because residence renders the trust liable to tax on foreign-source income. However, that determination may be a difficult matter because a trust is not a legal person and is not required to register in order to be recognized. Various factors may be taken into account, including

- the residence of the trustee;
- the place of management or administration of the trust;
- the location of the trust assets;
- the residence of the beneficiaries; and
- the residence of the grantor or settlor.

---

[149]In determining the amount of the gain, it is also necessary to take into account that the increase in the value of the underlying trust assets may also be subject to tax in the hands of the trust.

[150]In some countries (e.g., the United States), citizens are taxed on worldwide income even though not resident. *See supra* ch. 18.

[151]*See, e.g.,* AUS ITAA §§ 95(2), 97.

[152]It is possible that a trust is carrying on business in another country and is directly liable to tax.

Generally, the first two factors will be the most important,[153] but it is possible that none of them will be determinative. A trust might have three trustees, each resident in a different country; meetings of the trustees might be held in various locations, as might the trust assets; there might be a large number of beneficiaries, resident in various countries; and the settlor might well be dead. For these reasons, a number of countries have considered it necessary to adopt special rules to prevent tax avoidance through the use of nonresident trusts.[154]

3. Foreign-Source Income

When a resident trust receives foreign-source income, the question arises as to whether the income retains that character when distributed to a beneficiary. For example, investment income from a source in country A, received by a trust resident in country B, and paid to a beneficiary resident in country C might be regarded as sourced in country A (investment income) or in country B (trust income). In the latter case, it will be taxable in country B; in the former, it will not.[155] In the former case, a further question arises as to whether the trustees, or the trust instrument itself, may allocate foreign-source income to nonresident beneficiaries in order to avoid or reduce tax liability. If the foreign-source character is flowed through to a resident beneficiary, then that beneficiary should also be entitled to claim a credit for foreign tax paid.[156]

4. Nonresident Beneficiaries

Apart from the flow-through question discussed in the preceding paragraph, the main concern will be to ensure that tax is paid on trust income distributed to a nonresident beneficiary. When the trustee is taxable on the entire income of the trust, as in Ireland and the United Kingdom, this presents no problem; in those countries in which the trustee is taxed only on the undistributed income of the trust, a nonresident beneficiary's share can be taxed by requiring the trustee to withhold tax.[157]

5. Nonresident Trusts

Foreign trusts (i.e., trusts wherein the trustee is a nonresident) pose a problem because the trustee is beyond the country's taxing jurisdiction. This

---

[153]*See* AUS ITAA § 95(2); Thibodeau Family Trust v. The Queen, [1978] Canada Tax Cases 539, 78 Dominion Tax Cases 6376 (FCTD) (CAN); USA IRC § 7701(a)(31) (defining foreign trust).

[154]*See infra* sec. III(F)(5).

[155]The income apparently retains its foreign character in Australia (ITAA § 97) and the United Kingdom; *see supra* note 115. In Canada, it seems to take on the character of trust income. CAN ITA § 212(11).

[156]*See supra* sec. III (B)(4).

[157]AUS ITAA § 98; CAN ITA § 212(1)(c).

means that a foreign trust (like a foreign company) can be used to defer a country's tax on foreign-source income even though residents of the country are beneficiaries of that income.[158] Provided that foreign-source income is accumulated in the trust, tax is deferred until the accumulated income is either distributed to a resident beneficiary or realized as a capital gain on disposal of the interest in the trust.

Two types of foreign trust may be used to defer tax on foreign-source income. The first is a trust structured as a "roll-up fund," in which beneficiaries purchase an interest (such as units in a unit trust) of a type that carries an entitlement only to capital. A beneficiary can realize his or her interest in the trust either by selling it or by having it redeemed by the trustee. In either case, the beneficiary effectively realizes the income of the trust as a capital gain and, therefore, obtains the benefit of both deferral and the conversion of income into capital gains (which may be concessionally taxed). Because these trusts are structured in essentially the same way as companies, some countries subject such trusts to the same antideferral rules that apply to companies.[159] An alternative approach, adopted in the United Kingdom, is to discourage investment in such trusts by taxing the gain on disposal of the interest in the trust as income rather than as a capital gain.[160]

The second type of trust that may be used to defer tax on foreign-source income is a nonresident discretionary trust. The elimination of deferral for this type of trust poses particular difficulties for tax designers because, in the tax year in which the trust derives the income, it may not be known with any certainty which beneficiaries will ultimately benefit from the income. In other words, there are difficulties in identifying a taxpayer who may be subject to current taxation in respect of foreign income accumulated in such a trust. An initial line of attack against taxpayers transferring property out of the jurisdiction is to tax the transferor on the gain on any appreciated property transferred

---

[158]*See supra* ch. 18 for a discussion of deferral in the context of companies. *See* Lee Burns & Rick Krever, Interests in Non-resident Trusts (1997) for a comparative discussion of the taxation of foreign trusts in Australia, Canada, New Zealand, the United Kingdom, and the United States, on which this section draws.

[159]This is achieved in different ways. In the United States, such a trust is likely to be an "association" and, therefore, a corporation for U.S. tax purposes (IRC § 7701(3)). As such, it will be subject to the controlled foreign corporation and passive foreign investment company regimes (*see supra* ch. 18). In New Zealand, a unit trust is expressly treated as a company for tax purposes (NZL ITA §§ 2 and 211(2)). As such, it will be subject to the controlled foreign companies and foreign investment fund regimes. In Canada, where a resident beneficiary has a 10 percent or greater interest in a foreign nondiscretionary trust, the trust is deemed to be a corporation, the resident beneficiary is deemed to hold shares in proportion to his or her interest in trust income, and the beneficiary is subject to the controlled foreign companies, rules in respect of the trust (CAN ITA § 94). The Canadian offshore investment fund regime (CAN ITA § 94.1) applies to other cases involving foreign nondiscretionary trusts. In Australia, these trusts are still taxed as trusts, but in a way similar to the taxation of foreign companies (AUS ITAA §§ 96A–96C and Part XI).

[160]GBR ICTA §§ 757–764.

to a foreign trust. For example, in the United States, a 35 percent tax is imposed on the unrealized appreciation of property that is transferred by a citizen or resident of the United States to a foreign corporation, partnership, estate, or trust.[161] In Canada, any transfer of property to a trust, other than to a resident "spousal trust,"[162] constitutes a disposal for capital gains purposes. These rules, however, will not act as a deterrent to transferring property to a foreign trust when the property has not appreciated in value, nor will they discourage transfers on death in countries that do not treat death as a taxable event.

Another technique that in effect keeps the trust within the taxing jurisdiction is to treat it as a grantor trust. This means that the grantor will be taxed on the trust's income. This requires applying more expansive grantor trust rules to foreign trusts than to domestic trusts in cases when the grantor is a resident taxpayer. For example, a U.S. citizen or resident who transfers property to a foreign trust is treated as the owner of the portion of the trust attributable to the property, unless no part of the income or corpus of the trust may be paid or accumulated to a U.S. person.[163] For purposes of this rule, a foreign corporation, partnership, trust, or estate is considered a U.S. person if, in the case of a corporation, more than 50 percent of the stock is owned or is considered as owned by a U.S. person; if, in the case of a partnership, a U.S. person is a partner; and if, in the case of an estate or trust, a U.S. person is a beneficiary.

The U.S. grantor trust rule for foreign trusts is a broad one, but it does not cover trusts when the grantor has died or is not a U.S. citizen or resident. In these cases, special rules for foreign trusts may be needed to deal with the problem of tax deferral in cases where the trust is located in a tax haven jurisdiction. While it is possible to tax beneficiaries on their share of distributed income of the foreign trust, they cannot be taxed on trust income accumulated for the benefit of presently unknown beneficiaries. One solution is to impose at the time of a distribution to a resident beneficiary an extra tax, determined by applying an interest rate to the difference between the foreign income tax paid by the trust and the marginal rate that would have applied domestically.[164] Simply taxing the beneficiaries on distributions from the trust as received would not do. The distributions may represent corpus, which should not be taxed at all, or they may represent income that was taxed at a very low rate abroad, so that even full taxation at distribution would confer a substantial tax benefit.

An alternative approach, adopted in Canada, is to simply deem the trust to be a resident and make the trustees and resident beneficiaries (including dis-

---

[161]USA IRC § 1491.

[162]*I.e.*, a trust under which the settlor's spouse is the sole income beneficiary. CAN ITA § 70(7).

[163]USA IRC § 679.

[164]*See* USA IRC §§ 665–668.

cretionary beneficiaries) jointly liable for tax on its income.[165] The rules are complex, can have harsh consequences, and appear to be designed less to ensure that a fair tax burden is imposed on nonresident trusts than to deter the creation of such trusts altogether, it being assumed that the most likely motive for their creation is tax avoidance.

Australia, New Zealand, and the United Kingdom have also introduced grantor trust regimes applicable to nonresident trusts. The Australian and U.K. regimes are broadly similar to the U.S. regime described above.[166] The design of the New Zealand regime is different, although the practical effect is the same. When a New Zealand resident has transferred value to a nonresident trust, the trustee of the trust is liable to New Zealand tax on the foreign-source income of the trust.[167] If the trustee is not a resident, then the trustee is liable for tax as if he or she were a resident. In recognition of the difficulty of enforcing this liability against a nonresident trustee, it is provided that a resident person who has transferred value to the trust is liable to tax as agent of the trustee.[168]

IV. Other Flow-Through Entities

Partnerships and trusts are by far the most common of the entities that are given flow-through treatment, but various other types of business and investment entities that may be taxed in that manner merit a brief mention.[169] A distinction may also be drawn between those entities that are automatically taxed on a flow-through basis and those cases where the flow through is optional and is permitted on an elective basis.

---

[165]CAN ITA § 94(1). However, in the case of a beneficiary, the tax liability may be recovered by the Revenue only out of distributions to the beneficiary or from the proceeds of sale of the interest in the trust (*see* CAN ITA § 94(2)). As a practical matter, therefore, a beneficiary may still obtain the benefit of deferral.

[166]GBR ICTA § 739 and TCGA §§ 86, 91–97; AUS ITAA § 102AAA–102AAZG. The Australian legislation contains a number of exemptions from attribution, including exemptions for testamentary trusts, trusts where the grantor has died, and trusts established before the rules were introduced. Subsequently, the Australian government became concerned that, as a result of these exemptions, a significant amount of income was being accumulated untaxed in foreign trusts for the ultimate benefit of Australian residents. In response, §§ 96B and 96C were introduced with the intention of, inter alia, taxing Australian resident beneficiaries (including discretionary beneficiaries) on income accumulating in nonresident trusts. However, some commentators have strongly argued that the drafting of these sections is inadequate to cover discretionary beneficiaries.

[167]NZL ITA 228(3).

[168]NZL ITA 228(4).

[169]Investment funds, which are sometimes taxed on a flow-through basis, are considered separately in ch. 22 *infra.*

A. Automatic Flow-Through Treatment

1. Joint Ventures

The term "joint venture" can be a confusing one, because it can cover a variety of legal forms. A distinction is commonly made between "equity joint ventures," in which the parties incorporate a separate joint subsidiary corporation, and "contractual joint ventures," which are closer in nature to partnerships and are generally taxed on a flow-through basis. For example, when two companies establish a joint venture for a particular purpose, the normal practice is to tax each of the companies upon its share of the profits from the venture rather than to tax the venture as a separate entity.[170]

A special form of joint venture—the European Economic Interest Grouping (EEIG)—was introduced in the member states in 1985.[171] The EEIG is formed by contract and established by registration, which confers on it legal personality. It is intended as a means of cooperation between individuals or entities that otherwise wish to maintain their independence. The profits from the grouping's activities are treated as the profits of the members themselves and are taxed only in their hands.[172]

2. Other Entities Given Flow-Through Treatment

It is frequently considered appropriate to tax various other types of business or investment entity on a flow-through basis. For example, in Spain, the *impuesto sobre sociedades* (corporate income tax) generally applies to all legal entities, but an exception is made for unquoted portfolio investment entities and for certain family-owned investment-holding companies.[173] In the United States, flow-through treatment is given to investment vehicles such as real estate investment trusts and real estate mortgage investment conduits.[174]

In civil law countries, trust agreements, whereby assets are entrusted to a trustee for the carrying on of business, are typically taxed on a flow-through basis.[175] These are similar to joint ventures and do not involve the complexities of taxing common law trusts because the shares of the beneficiaries are specified.

Certain types of companies are also taxed on a flow-through basis. Sometimes this is done in recognition of their essentially personal nature, as in the

---

[170]*E.g.*, Cahiers, *supra* note 5, at 378–79 (Mexico; *asociación en participación*).

[171]Council Regulation 2137/85 of 25 July 1985 on the European Economic Interest Grouping (EEIG), 1985 O.J. (L 199) 1. The EEIG is based upon the *Groupement d'intérêt économique* (GIE), a business form introduced in France in 1967.

[172]*Id.* arts. 21, 40. The French GIE, which also has legal personality, is similarly taxed on a flow-through basis.

[173]*See supra* note 18.

[174]*See* USA IRC §§ 856–860G.

[175]*See* Cahiers, *supra* note 5, at 379–83.

case of the one-person company (*entreprise unipersonelle à responsabilité limitée*) in France, or their resemblance to a partnership, as with the limited-liability company in the United States.[176] Flow-through taxation of companies may also be adopted as a method of counteracting tax avoidance, for example, when the income of a controlled foreign corporation is allocated among resident shareholders and taxed in their hands whether or not dividends are paid.[177] This treatment may also be appropriate to prevent undue tax deferral through the use of personal holding companies, where the standard corporate tax rate is substantially lower than the top rate of individual income tax.[178]

B. Elective Flow-Through Treatment

Depending on tax rates and the system of taxing corporations, incorporation either may confer a tax advantage (as noted in the preceding paragraph) or may result in a heavier tax burden. The latter is particularly likely to occur when the "classical" system is adopted. Relief from economic double taxation may be given by permitting certain corporations to elect to be taxed on a flow-through basis. For fairly obvious reasons, this solution is appropriate only in the case of relatively small corporations. A well-known example is the U.S. "S Corporation" rules, under which a corporation that has 35 or fewer shareholders, all of whom are individuals resident in or citizens of the United States, may elect to be taxed as a flow-through entity.[179] The flow-through taxation of S corporations is simpler than that of partnerships, in part because S corporations are allowed to have only one class of stock. Thus, allocation of corporate income among the shareholders is straightforward because it can be allocated in proportion to share ownership. Elective flow-through treatment may also be granted to other types of entity that are otherwise normally taxed as legal entities.[180]

In designing appropriate election rules, policymakers should consider the nature of the entity and the rights of its participants. It may be unfair, for ex-

---

[176]*See* McKee et al., *supra* note 35, ¶ 2.01.

[177]The U.S. Subpart F rules are a typical example. *See supra* ch. 18.

[178]*E.g.*, prior to 1989, the undistributed income of a close corporation was apportioned among its shareholders in the United Kingdom. By contrast, in the United States, the problem was addressed by imposing an extra tax on the undistributed income of a personal holding company. *See* USA IRC § 541.

[179]USA IRC §§ 1361, 1362. In addition, as of Jan. 1, 1997, under new "check the box" regulations, *supra* note 38, limited-liability companies and certain other noncorporate entities have been able to elect whether to be taxed on a flow-through basis or to be treated as corporations. For discussion of implications for international tax planning, *see* Ruchelman et al., *supra* note 39; Joni Walser & Robert Culbertson, *Encore Une Fois: Check-the-Box on the International Stage*, 15 Tax Notes Int'l 53 (July 7, 1997).

[180]*E.g.*, in Spain, professional partnerships and certain joint ventures may elect to be taxed as flow-through entities. *See supra* note 18. Elections can also work in the other direction. For example, in France, partnerships, joint ventures, and one-person companies may elect to be subject to corporate income tax. FRA CGI art. 206(3).

ample, to allow the directors of a closely held corporation to elect to have its income taxed in the hands of its shareholders when, as a consequence, a minority shareholder might find himself paying tax on income that he might never receive. In such circumstances, it might be more appropriate to require the election to be made unanimously or by a special majority of the shareholders. Consequently, elective flow-through treatment is normally only appropriate for small businesses or for associations with relatively few participants.

V. Conclusion

Whether and how particular legal entities or arrangements are given flow-through treatment will depend on the precise nature of such entities under the civil and commercial law of a country, as well as on basic income tax policy considerations, such as the desire to simplify individual income taxation. The legal forms differ substantially, particularly between common law and civil law countries. Therefore, one can expect substantial differences in the tax rules from country to country, and a single uniform solution cannot be prescribed. Nevertheless, as this chapter shows, it is possible to identify common approaches that provide guidelines for developing and transition countries, even though the details of the solutions adopted will not be uniform.

22

Taxation of Investment Funds

Eric M. Zolt

> Men will find that they can prepare with mutual aid far more easily what
> they need, and avoid far more easily the perils which beset them on all
> sides, by united forces.
>
> —*Baruch Spinoza*

I. Introduction

This chapter provides an approach for thinking about the income taxation of investment funds and their investors in developing and transition
countries. Although this chapter focuses on investment funds, many of the
same issues and considerations may apply in designing a tax regime for other
investment vehicles, such as special-purpose investment funds, pension funds,
and different types of insurance products.

Basic decisions made in designing the overall tax system for individuals
and enterprises frame the design of a tax regime for investment funds. Decisions are required on such questions as how to tax dividends and interest received by individuals and enterprises, whether to integrate the individual and
enterprise tax regimes, how to tax capital gains and losses, how to tax foreign-
source income, and whether and how to adjust for inflation.

Within the framework defined by these decisions, the choice of tax
rules for investment funds requires balancing three objectives: first, not to
hamper the development of financial intermediaries, such as investment
funds; second, to devise tax rules that are comparable to those that apply to
other investments; and, third, to adopt tax rules that can be administered
and enforced. It is difficult to offer a general blueprint for taxing investment
funds and their investors. This is partly because choices made concerning
the basic tax structure will strongly influence decisions on how to tax investment funds. Another reason is that factors in a particular country influence
the choice of tax regime for investment funds. Given that countries differ

significantly in both their basic tax structure and their administrative capabilities, it is not possible simply to adopt the tax rules that other countries
apply to investment funds.

II. Role of Investment Funds

This chapter uses the term "investment fund" to refer to an entity owned
by many persons and whose primary activity is investing in operating companies. The investment fund acts as an intermediary between the individual investor and the ultimate user of the capital. Several types of investment funds
exist. An "open-end" fund issues and redeems fund units from investors.[1] In
contrast, "closed-end" funds issue a fixed number of units, and investors trade
units with other investors.

The growth of financial intermediaries in developing and transition
countries is not surprising. Market economies require private savings to
provide capital to establish new ventures and to expand existing enterprises.
Financial intermediaries allow small and medium-sized investors to
invest their savings in the market. Such intermediaries may offer investors
the advantages of financial expertise; economies of scale for such items
as market research, portfolio management, and trading activity; and the
opportunity to diversify and pool investments.[2] Diversification enables
investors to reduce the risk inherent in holding a small number of investments without reducing the expected return of the investment. Pooling allows individuals to invest in the more liquid assets of the financial
intermediary, while the intermediary can invest in less liquid and longer-
term investments.

In addition to capital, investment funds may offer privatized businesses
management expertise and expanded access to capital or other business relationships.[3] They may also serve as a check on the actions of managements and
boards of directors to ensure that they remain accountable to the shareholders.[4] This monitoring function may be especially important in Eastern Europe,
where mass privatization schemes have resulted in diffused ownership. Because
of the relatively small ownership stakes distributed in privatization, individual

---

[1]See Richard Gordon & Victoria Summers, *Taxation of Investment Funds in Emerging Capital
Markets: Theory, Problems and Solutions in the Case of Taiwan*, 46 Bull. Int'l Fiscal Documentation
384, 398 (Aug. 1992).

[2]See generally Robert C. Clark, *Federal Income Taxation of Financial Intermediaries*, 84 Yale L.J.
1603 (1975); Gordon & Summers, *supra* note 1, at 384.

[3]See Matthew J. Hagopian, *The Engines of Privatization: Investment Funds and Fund Legislation in
Privatizing Economies*, 15 J. Int'l L. Bus. 75, 81–84 (1975).

[4]See generally Mark J. Roe, Strong Managers, Weak Owners: The Political Roots of American
Corporate Finance 102–23 (1994).

shareholders will probably be unable to exercise effective control over the management of enterprises.[5]

In some countries making the transition to a market economy, investment funds are an integral part of the privatization process.[6] For example, the Polish mass privatization program provided for the government to establish several investment funds to serve as active managers and the primary holders of shares of the newly privatized companies.[7] In other countries, investment funds developed without direct government intervention to act as intermediaries between individual investors and business enterprises. In the Czech Republic, investment funds served the dual purpose of providing liquidity for government-issued investment vouchers and providing active participation in the strategic management of companies in their portfolio.[8]

A. Regulation of Investment Funds

Because of the great variation among countries, this section does not focus on the specifics of the different types of investment funds and the different restrictions and requirements that countries impose. It seeks only to survey the types of restrictions on and requirements for the formation and structure of an investment fund, the types of investments and activities, the operation of a fund, and rules governing distributions to and redemptions by investors.

---

[5]See William C. Philbrick, *The Task of Regulating Investment Funds in the Formerly Centrally Planned Economies*, 8 Emory Int'l L. Rev. 539, 541 (1994).

[6]See Hagopian, *supra* note 3, at 76–81. For an excellent review of the role of investment funds in the Czech Republic, *see* Helena Navratilova, *Czech Republic, in The Taxation of Investment Funds*, 82b Cahiers de droit fiscal international 375, 375–77 (1997)[hereinafter Cahiers].

[7]The 1993 Polish mass privatization program provided for the government to establish 10–20 national investment funds and to choose fund managers from a competitive tender open to international investment and consulting firms. The program further provided for one investment fund to receive 33 percent of the outstanding shares of a privatized enterprise and to act as the lead investor in the enterprise. This structure was intended to allow the lead investment fund to have significant influence on the operation of the enterprise while still requiring the consent of other shareholders for major decisions. *See* Hagopian, *supra* note 3, at 78–79; *see also* Michele Balfour & Cameron Crise, *A Privatization Test: The Czech Republic, Slovakia and Poland*, 17 Fordham Int'l L.J. 84 (1993).

[8]See Navratilova, *supra* note 6, at 375–77. In the former Czechoslovakia, the government issued vouchers to every citizen over the age of 18. The vouchers entitled the holders to purchase shares in state-owned companies participating in the privatization process. Holders had the option of investing their vouchers directly in shares of a specific company or exchanging them for shares in 1 of the approximately 400 investment funds that sprang up to act as intermediaries between the voucher holders and the privatized companies. The investment fund managers used the accumulated vouchers to acquire substantial interests in the companies they believed had the best investment potential. About two-thirds of all vouchers were transferred to investment funds for investment by fund managers. *See* Philbrick, *supra* note 5, at 553, 562.

Countries may have separate securities and tax regulatory regimes for investment funds. Particularly when the tax law conveys tax advantages to investment funds, qualification under the securities law may be necessary, but not sufficient, to qualify for tax purposes.

Countries differ in their approaches to regulating the formation of investment funds.[9] At one extreme, some countries require funds to operate in a specific legal form and adopt model bylaws that specify the rights of investors and the obligations of fund managers.[10] At the other extreme, investment funds have great flexibility in choosing their structure and their relationship with investors. Other issues that arise on formation include the residence of the investment funds (e.g., countries could allow only domestic investment funds or choose to allow foreign funds), the capital structure (e.g., countries could require only equity contributions or choose to allow investment funds to issue debt securities),[11] and disclosure of information about fund managers and officers (e.g., countries could require only names and addresses of fund managers, or they could require managers to make detailed financial disclosure).

Regulations on investment activities can cover the type of investment, the location of investments, and the amount of investments. The regulations share a common objective in seeking to protect investors from the excesses of fund managers.[12] Common restrictions on the type of investment activity include a prohibition on investing in certain types of assets (e.g., partnership interests with unlimited liability, precious metals, commodities, options and futures contracts, and certain types of debt obligations), on holding certain

---

[9]Excellent reviews of several countries' regulatory and tax regimes applicable to investment funds are set forth in Investment Funds: International Guide to the Taxation and Regulation of Mutual Investment Funds and Their Investors (IBFD 1996)[hereinafter International Guide] and in Cahiers, *supra* note 6.

There has been some movement toward standardizing the regulation of investment funds among countries. The European Union has worked on establishing a basic legal framework for investment funds with the aim of liberalizing capital flows among the member countries. It has sought to define the basic qualification requirements for an investment vehicle known as "undertakings for collective investment in transferable securities (UCITS)" and has tried to foster reciprocal agreements among member countries for the operations of these funds. *See* Philbrick, *supra* note 5, at 35.

[10]*See* Hagopian, *supra* note 3, at 88–90 (discussing the rationale for the use of model bylaws for investment funds in Kazakhstan, Poland, and Russia).

[11]*See* Philbrick, *supra* note 5, at 563. For example, the Czech investment funds law prohibits investment funds from issuing debt securities. Law on Investment Companies, Investment Funds (Czech), art. 4.1, *available in* LEXIS, World Library, Law File. For a discussion of the regulatory framework for investment funds in the Czech Republic, *see* Navratilova, *supra* note 6, at 377–85.

[12]A good example of the types of restrictions on the investment activities of investment funds is set forth in guidelines issued by The Federal Commission on Securities and the Capital Market of the Government of the Russian Federation, Interim Regulation on the Composition and Structure of Assets of Unit Investment Funds (Reg. No. 12, Oct. 1995).

nonliquid securities (e.g., the fund's portfolio is required to be substantially, or entirely, invested in publicly traded securities), or on engaging in certain types of activities (e.g., the fund's activities are limited to holding passive investment assets rather than operating assets). Some countries may require that the fund invest all or a substantial percentage of its funds in domestic enterprises. Countries also generally restrict both the percentage of a fund's assets that can be invested in any one issuer and the percentage of an issuer's stock that a fund can own.

To protect and inform investors, countries also generally impose disclosure and auditing requirements on investment funds. Also common are provisions to limit the potential for self-dealing and conflicts of interest between fund managers and the fund.[13]

Finally, depending on the type of investment fund and the applicable tax regime, countries have prescribed rules on distributions to shareholders and redemption requirements. For example, U.S. tax law requires that to obtain favorable tax treatment, an investment fund must distribute to investors 90 percent of certain income received during the year.[14] Russian law requires investment funds to redeem the interests of investors within 15 days of a request for redemption.[15]

B. Goals of Tax Regime for Investment Funds

There are several possible goals of a tax regime for investment funds and investors, and some policymakers may place greater weight on certain goals rather than on others. Some possible goals are discussed in this section.

1. Encourage Development of Investment Funds

General agreement exists that, at a minimum, tax rules should not unduly hamper or prevent development of investment funds or other financial intermediaries. In many countries, the absence of special tax rules governing investment funds would result in an investment fund being treated as a separate taxpayer—with an additional layer of tax imposed on any income or gains rec-

---

[13]See Hagopian, supra note 3, at 93–94 (discussing the use of investment funds legislation to minimize potential conflicts of interest between fund managers and the investment funds).

[14]To qualify for conduit tax treatment under U.S. tax law, an investment fund must distribute annually at least 90 percent of its investment company taxable income (taxable interest, dividends, and the excess of short-term over net long-term capital losses and any capital loss carryforwards, net of expenses) and at least 90 percent of its tax-exempt interest income, net of expenses. Investment funds are not required to distribute any net capital gain income (excess of net long-term capital gains over net short-term capital losses and loss carryforwards). See USA IRC 852(a), (b)(3).

[15]See Decree of the President of the Russian Federation, On Additional Measures to Increase Efficiency of Investment Policy of Russian Federation, ¶ 8 (July 1995).

ognized by the fund.[16] This "double tax" may be substantial enough to stunt the development of investment funds.[17]

Whether tax rules should explicitly favor the development of investment funds is a difficult question. It is part of a larger question of whether tax incentives should be used to encourage saving in general. It also relates to the tax treatment of alternative investment vehicles, such as pension plans and insurance products, and the need to consider comprehensively the tax regimes for all investments and not to address tax rules for specific investments in an ad hoc manner.

Section III(A) presents three variations on tax regimes that provide more favorable tax treatment to investors in investment funds than would be available to taxpayers engaged in direct investments. If a country decides to adopt one of the tax-favored regimes, it may need to consider carefully the qualification requirements for investment fund status so that tax benefits are not available to unintended beneficiaries. Policymakers may also need to estimate the revenue loss from the tax advantages so that they can consider whether the increased incentives justify the lost tax revenue.

2. Market Neutrality

Economists and tax lawyers emphasize that tax rules should be as neutral as possible regarding investment and other decisions. Although almost all taxes distort behavior, policy advisors generally recommend keeping distortions as small as possible. This position rests partly on grounds of market efficiency—that economic resources should be allocated on the basis of market factors that determine the highest return, not on the basis of tax considerations. It also rests on minimizing transaction and tax planning costs. Investors should not spend their resources trying to devise schemes to minimize taxes. To the extent that all investments are taxed similarly, there will be no incentive to try to come within the scope of tax-favored treatment. Finally, if investment funds are accorded tax-favored treatment, it may be difficult to deny tax benefits to other forms of investments; consequently, the tax law will become more complicated, and tax revenue will decline.

---

[16]In Russia, the Ministry of Finance has ruled that investment funds are not "entities" subject to the enterprise profits tax, but rather "asset pools without the creation of a legal person." On Several Tax Issues Arising in Connection with the Creation and Functioning of Unit Investment Funds (Jan. 1996). See also Alexander V. Tolkoushkin & Vladimir N. Zavarnov, Russia, in Cahiers, supra note 6, at 723–26. Similar exemptions from treatment as an entity taxable under the corporate income tax are found in many countries, including France, Germany, and Italy. See International Guide, supra note 9, at 49 (France), 38 (Germany), and 58 (Italy).

[17]For example, assume an operating company earns a rate of return of 10 percent before tax and, after imposition of a 30 percent corporate tax, earns 7 percent after tax. If the income of the company is distributed to an investment fund that is also subject to a 30 percent corporate tax, the after-tax rate of return is further reduced to 4.9 percent.

For purposes of this chapter, market neutrality means that taxpayers should be treated the same whether they invest directly in assets, such as government securities and shares of joint-stock companies, or invest indirectly in such assets through financial intermediaries, such as investment funds.[18] Even if one does not value this goal on independent grounds, it is helpful in examining alternative proposals to determine how the tax consequences for investors of a specific proposal for taxing investment funds differ from the tax consequences of direct investment.

One should also compare the tax rules governing investment funds with the favorable tax rules available to alternative investments. If a country's tax law exempts interest on many government and bank obligations or provides special rules for pensions or life insurance products, then the existence of these tax-favored investments may influence the basic decisions on the tax treatment of investment funds.

3. Administration and Compliance Considerations

As in all areas of tax law, the laws are only as good as the administration. It makes little sense to adopt laws that, while theoretically correct, are difficult or impossible to administer.

The tax regimes for investment funds in many countries rest, on the one hand, on the ability of investment fund managers to process substantial amounts of information and to allocate tax items to individual investors and, on the other hand, on the ability of tax administrators to receive information from investment fund managers and match this information with the individual tax returns of millions of taxpayers.[19] The investment funds are likely to have the computer capability to process the information and allocate the tax items. The ability of the tax administration to develop a system to ensure enforcement and compliance with a tax regime that requires monitoring the tax consequences to many investors is much more problematic and, in many countries, may not be worth the expenditure of substantial administrative resources, given the amount of tax revenue involved.

Another potential compliance problem that may be associated with a special tax regime for investment funds is the ease with which taxpayers can meet the tax and regulatory requirements for investment fund status. If qualification is easy, then adopting a favorable regime for investment funds will create strong incentives for taxpayers to arrange their affairs to obtain favorable tax treatment. If qualification is difficult, then the potential tax motivation for adopting this form of organization is reduced.

---

[18]See Gordon & Summers, supra note 1, at 385.

[19]For example, in 1995, the Internal Revenue Service received over 115 million individual income tax returns and processed over 1 billion information returns. Internal Revenue Service, Pub. No. 55B, 1995 Data Book, tbls. 7, 18 (1995).

4. Revenue Concerns

A complete examination of alternatives for taxing investment funds requires estimating their revenue consequences. To complete this task, one must gather estimates of the number of investment funds, the number of investors, the amount and type of fund investments, the amount and type of income and capital gains of the funds, and the potential capital gains recognized by investors on the redemption of their shares.[20] These estimates may initially be quite speculative; hopefully, over time, the estimates will become more reliable.

III. Taxing Investment Funds in the Context of the Basic Tax Structure

A major difficulty in designing a tax regime for investment funds and their investors is the number of different combinations of components that policymakers may need to consider. This section first reviews the components of a basic tax regime that make up the landscape for examining alternative tax regimes for investment funds. It then seeks to catalogue the different types of investors and the different types of income of an investment fund.

A. Basic Tax Structure

Several components of the basic tax structure may influence the design of a tax regime for investment funds. These include (1) the range of tax rates for individuals and enterprises and the relationship between those rates; (2) whether individuals are taxed on dividends on a flat schedular basis or must combine their income from dividends with other sources of income and incur tax liability on a global basis; (3) the use of either provisional or final withholding for dividends; (4) whether enterprises may exclude dividends received from other enterprises, perhaps tied to the level of share ownership in

---

[20]For example, it is difficult to compare the tax consequences for investors of a tax regime for investment funds with the tax consequences for investors of direct investments without making certain assumptions as to behavior of the enterprises, the investment funds, and the investors. Assumptions that may be important to consider include

(1) the amount of dividends paid by enterprises,
(2) the amount of tax-exempt investment in funds,
(3) the amount and frequency of redemptions,
(4) the amount of capital gains recognized by the funds, and
(5) the mix of individual and enterprise investors.

If, for example, we were confident that enterprises paid little or no dividends and that individual investors could structure their redemptions from the investment funds to pay no capital gains tax, then the choice of tax regime applicable to investment funds may be of little practical significance. Similarly, the value of allowing investment funds effectively to defer paying capital gains tax until an investor redeems the investor's interest may be of little importance if the individual investor can avoid paying any capital gains tax on shares of enterprises held directly.

the enterprise; (5) whether interest is taxed on a schedular or a global basis; (6) the use of provisional or final withholding for interest, and the continuation of the existing tax-exempt status of many types of interest; (7) the treatment of capital gains, in particular whether the same rules apply to individuals and enterprises, the possibility of allowing alternative cost basis approaches for determining gain for individuals, and the possibility of adjusting for inflation; (8) the rules governing tax relief for capital losses; (9) the scheme for integrating the individual and enterprise tax systems—in particular, the type of integration, if any; (10) the rules for taxing foreign-source income, particularly whether foreign income is excluded or whether a deduction or credit for foreign tax paid is allowed; and (11) the rules governing the taxation of nonresident taxpayers—in particular, the rules for individuals and entities that are either passive investors or that receive income in connection with a domestic trade or business.

While it is necessary to reduce the number of alternative combinations from the items listed above before being able to make any definitive comments about the interaction of the basic tax structure and the design of the tax regime for investment funds, two general guidelines can be offered: (1) the more variation in the treatment of different types of income in the hands of different types of investors, the greater the pressure may be to tax the income directly at the investor level; and (2) the less the tax rules vary by type of income in the hands of different types of investors, the stronger is the argument for simply taxing all income at the investment fund level and imposing no further taxes at the investor level.

The tax treatment of capital gains presents perhaps the most complex issue in designing a tax regime for investment funds. Capital gains may arise at the fund level when the investment fund sells shares of its underlying investments, or at the investor level when the investor sells his or her interest in the investment fund, or at both levels. For countries that do not tax capital gains,[21] the potential for two levels of gain raises no additional problems. For a tax system that taxes capital gains, however, the potential exists for the government to collect too much or too little tax. A system can collect too much tax on capital gains if an investment fund realizes a gain on the sale of an enterprise's shares and an investor realizes a gain on the sale of his or her interest in the investment fund unless there exists a mechanism for the investor to receive credit for tax paid at the fund level. A system collects too little tax if an investor can dispose of shares in the investment fund without tax liability and

---

[21]Including those that follow the German/French model of taxing only gains on substantial participations, since the regulatory constraints on investment funds would presumably require sufficient dispersion of investment so that no one investor's share in an investment by the fund would constitute a substantial participation. However, if shares are treated as business assets in the hands of the fund, then an exception would have to be made to provide for their nontaxation.

thus avoid any tax on the unrealized appreciation in the assets of the investment fund.[22]

Several alternatives exist to minimize or eliminate the double taxation of capital gains. One approach imposes capital gains at the fund level, but exempts capital gains at the investor level. Alternatively, a country could choose to tax capital gains only at the investor levels and to exempt fund-level gains. A third alternative imposes tax at the fund level, unless the proceeds of the gain are distributed, in which case the capital gains are taxed to the investors. Finally, a country could choose to tax gains at both levels, but could either give the investors a credit for any tax paid at the fund level or impose tax at both levels at a substantially reduced rate.

The existence of high levels of inflation further complicates the difficulties of designing a rational tax regime. Taxing nominal gains without adjusting for inflation may result in high taxes on what are small or no economic gains, and perhaps even real economic losses. If nominal gains are taxed at both the fund level and the investor level, then the economic return required just to break even after tax may be substantial.

Tax systems can provide for inflation adjustments by allowing investors to index their tax cost for purposes of determining gain on a transaction.[23] Indexation provides a more accurate measure of economic gain than an unindexed tax system, but increases its complexity.[24] The complexity is further increased when inflation adjustments are made at both the fund and the investor level. A system of comprehensive inflation adjustment where gains are taxed at the level of the investment fund only, however, would not be so complex.[25]

B. Types of Investors

Countries generally impose few, if any, restrictions on the types of investors that may invest in investment funds. We can separate domestic individuals by their income level: (1) individuals may have income below the threshold amount for tax liability; or (2) individuals may be subject to tax at low, medium, or high tax brackets, depending on the rate structure under the individual income tax law, the individual's other income, and the rules for aggregating income from different sources.

---

[22]Whether an investor is actually undertaxed depends on whether the market price for the shares of the investment fund reflects the discounted present value of the tax due when the investment fund disposes of the appreciated assets. The relative tax rates of the investor and the fund must also be taken into account. Whether the tax system collects too little tax depends on whether one views the investor's sale of shares of an investment fund as a constructive disposition for tax purposes of the underlying assets.

[23]See vol. 1, ch. 13.

[24]See id. The major complexity arises not from the indexing of the assets for inflation, but rather from the need to index any debt obligations that are related to assets subject to indexation.

[25]See id.

Domestic enterprises may be subject to differing tax rates under the enterprise tax law, although progressive tax rates under an enterprise tax law have little or no theoretical justification. An enterprise with a relatively small ownership position in a particular fund can be classified as a portfolio investor; it can be classified as a substantial investor if it has a relatively large investment position.[26]

There may also exist a group of investors that qualifies for tax-favored or tax-exempt status. In the United States, tax-favored or tax-exempt entities, such as private pension plans and nonprofit institutions, own substantial amounts of shares and securities in enterprises and in investment funds.[27]

Tax rules for nonresident investors may depend on several factors. Different tax rules may apply to foreign individuals and enterprises, and the rules may vary depending on the level of ownership and the nature of the activity of the foreign person within the country. Countries also may consider offering special tax incentives to attract capital from foreign funds or foreign investors.

The tax treatment of income attributable to foreign investment funds raises additional issues, particularly with respect to qualification for relief under a country's double taxation treaties.[28] In many countries, it may be uncertain whether investment funds qualify as a "person" for treaty purposes so that a fund could claim treaty benefits for itself or on behalf of its investors. The decision whether to extend treaty benefits to foreign investment funds is part of the larger policy question concerning the appropriate allocation of tax revenue among the country where the investment is located, the country where the fund is located, and the country where the investors reside.

C. Types of Income

The income of an investment fund must be examined in three parts. The first part involves reviewing the different types of income that an investment fund may receive. The second part entails determining how the different types of income will be categorized for tax purposes. The final part of the analysis focuses on identifying those items that may involve different consequences if the income is allocated and the tax imposed at the investment fund level and at the level of the investors.

---

[26]The classification of an enterprise as a portfolio or a substantial investor takes on great importance in those countries where the tax treatment of intercorporate dividends differs by the level of ownership of the payee corporation.

[27]For example, in the United States in 1990, tax-exempt investors (nonprofit institutions, pension funds, IRAs, and Keogh plans) owned approximately $1.2 trillion or about 37 percent of corporate equity and approximately $750 billion or about 46 percent of corporate debt. *See* U.S. Dep't of Treasury, Integration of Individual and Corporate Tax Systems: Taxing Business Income Once 68, tbl. 6.1 (1992).

[28]The considerations for extending treaty benefits to foreign investment funds are set forth in Lynne J. Ed & Paul J.M. Bongaarts, *General Report, in* Cahiers, *supra* note 6, at 41–57.

1. Possible Types of Income

An investment fund may have the following categories of income:

- dividends from domestic enterprises;
- dividends from foreign enterprises;
- interest income from different domestic sources, with some types of interest income qualifying for tax-exempt status;
- interest income on foreign securities; and
- gains and losses from the sale of investments.

This list assumes that investment funds are limited to holding securities in operating companies and certain government securities. This simple classification also does not reflect the increased use of derivatives and synthetic instruments that makes determination of both the type of income and the source of income more difficult. To the extent that investment funds may engage in other types of activities, such as holding immovable property or direct ownership of operating assets, additional categories of income may need to be added.

2. Categorization for Tax Purposes

The second part of the analysis requires determining how these different types of income will be categorized for tax purposes. For example, a certain type of income may be subject to withholding, some types of income will qualify for tax-exempt treatment or capital gain treatment, and other types of income will be taxed under the rules governing foreign-source income. To the extent that a country changes its basic tax structure, it will be necessary to determine how possible changes in the categorization of different types of income may influence decisions on the design of a tax regime for investment funds.

3. Tax Items That May Require Separate Treatment

The third part of the analysis requires identifying those types of income, deductions, losses, and credits that may be subject to different tax treatment in the hands of different types of investors. These include

- dividends and interest from fund investments, especially if the withholding rates vary by type of investor;
- gains and losses from the sale of property by the investment fund, especially if the calculation of gain differs by type of investor and if restrictions are imposed on the use of capital losses;
- income qualifying for tax-exempt status or subject to other types of preferences;
- certain expenses of the investment fund, the most important of which are management fees and the interest incurred to carry its assets; and

- credits received by the investment fund, such as foreign tax credits attributable to foreign-source income or credits relating to an integration system of individual and corporate taxes.

The purpose of this review is to highlight the consequences of adopting different regimes for investment fund taxation. This allows policymakers to determine how the taxation of investment funds and their investors will differ under the prototypes examined in the next section. It may also provide guidance as to how individual taxpayers may change their behavior when the tax rules for investing through investment funds differ from investing directly in the underlying assets.

IV. Different Prototypes

This section examines several different prototypes that represent different approaches to reducing or eliminating the double—or in some cases, triple—taxation of dividends, interest, and capital gains attributable to investment funds and their underlying investments. They may be useful in revising or designing a tax regime for investment funds.

A. Tax-Advantaged Prototype

Three major alternatives exist to provide tax benefits to investment funds that are not generally available to direct investment. They provide either deferral or exclusion of different types of income at either the fund or the investor level. The first alternative allows deferral of any capital gains recognized by the investment fund by not imposing tax at the investment fund level on any gain realized by the fund on the sale of its investments. The tax is effectively deferred until the investor disposes of the investor's interest in the fund through redemption or sale of shares.

The second alternative goes further and does not impose tax on the investment fund on any dividends, interest, or other income received, or on capital gains. This could be accomplished by allowing receipt of income without any withholding or by providing a refund of any withholding imposed on distributions to the investment fund. This alternative provides for deferral of all income at the investment fund level until investors redeem their shares in the fund.

The third alternative allows a deduction for amounts contributed to the investment fund and then taxes the proceeds upon redemption by the investor.[29]

---

[29]Countries that have adopted approaches similar to the third method generally limit the amount of potential tax benefit by restricting availability to individual investors and by restricting the amount of new investment in the fund each year. See, e.g., the taxation of personal equity plans in the United Kingdom and plans d'épargne en actions in France. International Guide, supra note 9, at 50 (United Kingdom) and 43 (France).

No tax is imposed while the investor holds the shares at either the investor or the investment fund level. Under certain assumptions, this approach is equivalent to excluding from taxation the income from investment in the fund.[30]

B. Pass-Through Prototype

The pass-through prototype treats the investment fund as transparent and allocates all items of income and loss directly to investors. In its purest form, the investment fund acts simply as a reporting mechanism. This approach treats investors as if they earned the income directly and taxes them accordingly, even if the investment fund does not distribute the income to them.

A pass-through prototype requires a system for allocating all items of income and loss to the investors. One alternative provides for each item to be allocated daily over the tax year and assigns to the investors their prorated share each day.[31] A second alternative assigns the tax items for a particular period, for example, for a year or a quarter, to the owners of interest on the last day of the period and allows the market price for the interest to adjust for any tax consequences.[32]

The pass-through prototypes score high on market neutrality. Unfortunately, they score low on administrative and compliance grounds, especially as the number of investors and the number of fund investments become quite large. Therefore, no country uses this system for investment funds.

A variation of this prototype imposes tax on the investment fund on any income it receives at a rate that could be either the highest rate applicable to investors or, alternatively, the one that is most common to investors. This approach allocates to investors their share of the income of the fund and provides a credit for taxes paid by the fund allocable to that income. Investors may then file for a refund if the amount of tax paid exceeds their liability, or they could be assessed additional tax if the amount paid by the investment fund is less than their tax liability. This variation also requires rules for calculating an investor's basis in his or her investment in the fund to determine whether an investor would recognize gain when shares are redeemed.

The third variation is a modified pass-through prototype. This approach aggregates all different types of income at the fund level and requires reporting

---

[30]*See* Michael J. Graetz, *Implementing a Progressive Consumption Tax*, 92 Harv. L. Rev. 1575 (1979).

[31]The United States has adopted such a system for allocating items of income for certain qualifying small business corporations, known as "S" corporations. The shareholders generally take into account their respective prorated shares of income, deductions, and other separately stated items on a prorated, per share daily basis. USA IRC § 1366(a)(1).

[32]*See* U.S. Dep't of Treasury, Blueprints for Basic Tax Reform 70–71 (1977). The allocation proposal in Blueprints used an annual record date for allocating tax items to shareholders and designated the shareholders on the first day of the tax year to be the shareholders of record.

only one, or perhaps two or three, to the investor.[33] Again, this variation could allow for the withholding of taxes at the fund level and for a procedure to provide refunds to investors whose tax rate is below the withholding rate.

The pass-through prototypes come closest to achieving market neutrality between direct investment and investment through investment funds. They do, however, impose substantial administrative burdens on both investors and the taxing authorities to ensure collection of taxes and compliance with the tax rules.

C. Surrogate Prototype

The surrogate prototype changes the focus of taxation from the investor to the investment fund. Surrogate taxation can take many forms. One extreme imposes a tax on the fair market value of the assets of an investment fund in lieu of any income tax at the level of either the investor or the investment fund.[34] A more common surrogate prototype imposes tax on any income received by the investment fund at the fund level and collects tax without regard to the tax characteristics of the investors. It could impose tax on both dividends and interest paid to the investment fund, as well as on any capital gains realized by the fund on the sale of its property.

One variation of this prototype collects no further tax at the investor level on either sale or redemption of the investor's share in the investment fund or, if a fund is allowed to make distributions, on any distributions made by the fund. Another variation imposes a tax on any gains recognized by the investor, but allows the investor a credit for taxes paid by the investment fund with respect to his or her prorated share of the income.

The design of a tax regime for a surrogate model depends largely on the country's rules governing the taxation of dividends and capital gains. A country that imposes schedular taxation of dividends with withholding at the enterprise level requires no special rules for taxing dividends distributed to an intermediary. The tax rules could provide for the funds to be distributed to the individual investors without additional tax liability if they are able to show that tax with respect to the distribution was withheld at the enterprise level.[35]

---

[33]For example, the approach adopted by the United States for separate treatment of only certain types of income of widely held partnerships. See generally U.S. Dep't of Treasury, Widely Held Partnerships: Compliance and Administrative Issues (1990).

[34]For example, Italy imposes a tax on the net asset value of certain types of investment funds in lieu of an income tax. International Guide, supra note 9, at 60–61 (Italy). Sweden imposes tax on 1.5 percent of asset values in lieu of capital gains tax for investment funds; investment companies pay tax on an imputed income of 2 percent of asset values in lieu of capital gains tax. See generally Cecilia Gunne, Sweden, in Cahiers, supra note 6, at 778–79.

[35]The tax regime of the Czech Republic provides a good example of this approach. See Navratilova, supra note 6, at 385–86.

Compared with the other prototypes discussed in this section, the surrogate approach is probably the easiest to administer and the one that will result in the highest level of tax compliance. To the extent that the rate imposed on the income of the investment fund differs from the rate that would be imposed on investors if they received the income directly, then this approach would violate market neutrality. If the tax rate on the investment fund exceeds an investor's tax rate, then investors may be overtaxed on their income.[36] Conversely, if the tax rate on the investment fund is less than an investor's tax rate, then this should encourage the development of these types of funds, perhaps at the cost of lost tax revenue.

D. Distribution-Deduction Prototype

The distribution-deduction prototype taxes the investment fund on any undistributed income and taxes the investors on any income distributed to them. Countries generally achieve this result by treating the investment fund as a taxable entity, but allowing the investment fund to deduct from its income any amounts distributed to investors. The prototype could provide for the investors to receive credit for taxes paid at the fund level with respect to their prorated share of income.

Countries that follow this approach generally require funds to distribute a substantial portion of their income each year. For example, the United States generally requires qualified funds to distribute annually 90 percent of their investment income, other than net long-term capital gains. One reason the United States has adopted this approach is because taxpayers aggregate dividends and interest received with their other income and then pay tax at progressive rates on their total income. The United States also has a sophisticated reporting and matching system that allows taxing authorities to monitor the payment of distributions to investors.

When an investment fund distributes less than its total income for a year, distribution-related prototypes may require rules for determining which income is deemed to be distributed. Such "stacking rules" could, for example, provide for a fund to designate the types of income being distributed, or for income to be deemed distributed in a particular order (e.g., first, dividends and interest received from domestic corporations; second, dividends and interest received from foreign investments; and third, capital gains income) or for a deemed pro rata distribution of the different types of income.

Distribution-related prototypes could also provide for investment funds to treat amounts as being distributed without requiring an actual distribution

---

[36]Whether investors in a low tax bracket are worse off because of the higher tax rate imposed on their share of investment income depends on how the market price of the shares of investment funds under a surrogate tax approach would compare with the market price of the funds under a pass-through approach. Low-bracket taxpayers may be better off under the surrogate approach if there are enough investors in a high tax bracket to bid up the price of the investment funds.

to investors. These deemed distributions would be treated as reinvested by the investors.[37] A "deemed-distribution" option allows for an investment fund to avoid potential double taxation on certain income without requiring the fund to liquidate investments in order to make actual cash distributions.

V. Conclusion

This chapter has set forth a framework for examining issues in the taxation of investment funds and their investors and a survey of the different approaches countries use in taxing income attributable to investment funds. It is not surprising that countries use different approaches in taxing investment funds and their investors. The investment fund tax rules are dictated largely by a country's overall tax regime for individuals and enterprises, and these tax regimes vary substantially among countries. Administrative and compliance considerations also influence the choice of tax rules.

The absence of an ideal structure requires policymakers to balance competing goals. As discussed in section II, these goals could include (1) not discouraging the development of investment funds, (2) achieving market neutrality between direct and indirect investments, (3) designing a regime with low administrative costs and high compliance, and (4) not decreasing, and perhaps increasing, the tax revenue base.

Which prototype for investment fund taxation makes sense in a particular country depends largely on the country's basic tax structure. If a country's tax system has (1) similar tax rates for individuals and corporations, (2) final withholding on dividends and interest (and no variation in withholding rates by taxpayer), (3) no threshold level for excluding capital gains (and similar rules for all taxpayers for taxing capital gains), (4) exclusion of foreign-source income, and (5) no special rules for foreign investors, then the surrogate prototype may be preferable because of the substantial administrative and compliance advantages it offers.

To the extent that a country's basic tax regime differs significantly from the above structure and contains highly differentiated treatment of various types of income for particular types of taxpayers, the surrogate prototype loses much of its attraction. Particularly if substantial weight is given to the goal of market neutrality, then a pass-through prototype or distribution deduction prototype merits serious consideration.

---

[37]Alternatively, funds could stand ready to make distributions upon request but could allow investors to elect to instead reinvest the amount of the distribution in additional fund shares. Many investors would presumably make the election in order to avoid the inconvenience of dealing with distribution payments.

23

Income Tax Incentives for Investment

David Holland and Richard J. Vann

> To lay, with one hand, the power of the government on the property of the
> citizen, and with the other to bestow it upon favored individuals to aid
> private enterprises and build up private fortunes, is none the less a robbery
> because it is done under the forms of law and is called taxation.
>
> —*Justice Samuel F. Miller*

I. Introduction

Many developing and transition countries offer income tax incentives for
investment.[1] The incentives are most often for direct investors as opposed to
portfolio investors, relate to real investment in productive activities rather
than investment in financial assets, and are often directed to foreign investors
on the grounds that there is insufficient domestic capital for the desired level
of economic development and that international investment brings with it
modern technology and management techniques.

Developing and transition countries have introduced investment incentives for varying reasons. In some cases, especially in transition countries that
have not reformed the socialist tax system, the incentives may be seen as a
counterweight to the investment disincentives inherent in the general tax sys-

---

Note: This chapter draws heavily on OECD, Taxation and Foreign Direct Investment: The
Experiences of the Economies in Transition (1995), to which the authors (especially David Holland), along with Alexander Easson, contributed.

[1]Using the tax system to influence economic behavior by granting tax incentives for particular
activities has developed an enormous literature following the lead of Professor Stanley Surrey,
who noted the equivalence of such incentives to direct expenditure programs and coined the
term "tax expenditures" to refer to them. See Stanley Surrey, Pathways to Tax Reform (1973); International Aspects of Tax Expenditures (Stanley Surrey & Paul McDaniel eds., 1985); OECD,
Tax Expenditures: A Review of the Issues and Country Practices (1984); OECD, Tax Expenditures: Recent Experiences (forthcoming). This chapter will not review the many arguments
against tax expenditures generally or the issues involved in costing the revenue forgone from
such measures. For a critique of the tax expenditure concept, see Victor Thuronyi, Tax Expenditures: A Reassessment, 1988 Duke L. J. 1155.

tem. In other countries, the incentives are intended to offset other disadvantages that investors may face, such as a lack of infrastructure, complicated and antiquated laws, and bureaucratic complexities and weak administration, in the tax area or elsewhere. If these are the reasons, the appropriate solution is to reform the existing laws that create the problems and to build the necessary administrative capacities and infrastructure. This solution is often easier said than done, and so tax incentives may provide temporary relief until the more fundamental reforms have been carried out. Countries sometimes introduce incentives to keep up with other countries in competing for international investment. More rarely, tax incentives are introduced after other deficiencies in law and administration are remedied and are directed to areas of economic activity that the country wishes to develop.

Although standard international tax policy advice cautions against the use of tax incentives for investment,[2] many developing and transition countries, as well as many industrial countries, continue to operate or introduce them. Accordingly, this chapter briefly outlines the reasons why such incentives are often found to be unsuccessful and what the more important issues may be for encouraging investment in developing and transition countries. It then considers in more detail the design, drafting, and international taxation issues that such incentives present. Although the discussion considers investment incentives in general, it emphasizes foreign direct investment (FDI). This chapter focuses on the income tax, while also discussing the more important incentives found under other taxes.

II. Relationship Between Taxation and Investment

A. Tax and Nontax Factors Affecting Investment

Investors often emphasize the relative unimportance of the tax system in investment decisions compared with other considerations.[3] Firms first examine a country's basic economic and institutional situation. While they are attracted to the potential markets in developing and transition countries and the relatively low-cost labor, other considerations inhibit large-scale investment, such as uncertainty in the policy stance of governments, political instability, and, in transition economies, the rudimentary state of the legal framework for a market economy. Tax incentives on their own cannot overcome these negative factors.

---

[2]*See* OECD, Taxation and Foreign Direct Investment: The Experiences of the Economies in Transition (1995); Chua, *Tax Incentives, in* Tax Policy Handbook 165–68 (Parthasarathi Shome ed., 1995) and references there cited.

[3]The statements in this section and the next about the views of investors stem from the consultations undertaken in preparing OECD, *supra* note 2. For a survey that gives a somewhat greater importance to taxation in relation to investment decisions, *see* Commission of the European Communities, Report of the Committee of Independent Experts on Company Taxation (1992) (commonly referred to as the Ruding Report after its chair), ch. 5.

To prospective investors, the general features of the tax system (tax base, tax rates, etc.) are more important than tax incentives. In transition countries, many tax laws contain provisions that are held over from the regime that was used under the former socialist economy. These provisions served purposes different from those of a market economy tax regime, for example, controlling the enterprise's budget rather than determining an appropriate tax base. From the point of view of potential foreign investors, these provisions are unfamiliar and anomalous. They can cause the tax base to diverge from market economy norms (especially in relation to depreciation, business expenses, and loss carryovers) and impose taxation that is not consistent with reality from the point of view of business investors. Furthermore, taxpayers expect to be able to predict the tax consequences of their actions, which requires clear laws that are stable over time. In many developing and transition countries, the tax laws are not clearly written and may be subject to frequent revision, which makes long-term planning difficult for businesses and adds to the perceived risk of undertaking major capital-intensive projects. The administration of the law is as important as the law itself, and it is clear that tax administrations in developing and transition countries often have difficulty coping with sophisticated investors, whether in providing timely and consistent interpretations of the law or in enforcing the law appropriately.

Investors may view both income and non-income taxes as potential problems. The latter are payable even if no profits are made and often raise the cost of basic inputs. In particular, social security taxes applied to the wages of expatriates in transition countries and border charges on the importation of capital equipment in developing and transition countries are seen as obstacles to investment.

B. Lack of Success of Investment Tax Incentives

The experience of developing and transition countries with tax incentives has been consistent with that of industrial countries. Tax incentives have not by and large been successful in attracting investment, especially FDI.[4] This underlines the conclusion that tax incentives cannot overcome the other, more fundamental problems that inhibit investment.

At the same time, tax incentives have imposed serious costs on developing and transition countries that need to be considered relative to any modest benefits that they have conveyed. Tax incentives by their nature represent a revenue cost for the government. For the most part, this revenue cost is wasted

---

[4]Some jurisdictions, such as Singapore, Taiwan Province of China, and, more lately, Ireland, have used investment tax incentives and advanced economically, but whether the two matters are connected in these cases has been a matter of dispute. These countries did not suffer from the negative economic, political, and administrative situations that are the major deterrents to investment in many transition economies. Moreover, many more countries have adopted investment tax incentives without any noticeable improvement in investment performance, and a number of countries, such as Chile and Estonia, have advanced economically while eschewing tax incentives.

because the incentives go to investments that would have been made in any event. It is argued that FDI in countries in transition to a market-oriented economy would not occur without the incentive, and so there is no real revenue cost. However, experience has shown that there is investment in short-term, high-profit projects. Because these projects would occur even if there were no tax incentives, the tax incentive is a pure windfall to them. Investment tax incentives have been subject to serious tax avoidance, which has added greatly to their revenue cost. Tax avoidance results, in part, from the design of the incentives and also from the difficulties tax administrations face in auditing taxpayers. The revenue forgone in transition countries as a result of the use of tax incentives to shelter domestic income from taxation may well exceed the incentives earned through legitimate FDI.

Tax incentives introduce complexity into the tax system, because the rules themselves are complex and because tax authorities react to the tax planning that inevitably results from their introduction by putting into place antiavoidance measures. This complexity imposes costs on administrators and taxpayers and increases the uncertainty of tax results. Uncertainty can deter the investment the incentives are intended to attract. Moreover, the introduction of tax incentives creates a clientele for their continuation and spread. The fact that many industrial countries maintain some tax incentives after the tax reforms of the 1980s is less a statement that they are considered to be effective and more a testament to the political difficulty in removing them once they have been introduced. It is because of this tendency that many "temporary" measures, designed to respond to particular perceived disincentives, remain in force long after the conditions that originally led to their introduction have changed.

These costs can be observed fairly directly. What may be the primary cost, however, is much more difficult to observe and measure. The classic argument against the use of incentives is that they distort economic activity by causing the after-tax pattern of returns to diverge from the before-tax pattern, thereby leading to an allocation of resources that differs from the efficient equilibrium the market is assumed to generate. Whether arguments based on advanced markets apply to developing and transition countries may be debated, but there can be no doubt that the more observable costs of tax incentives referred to above do arise in these countries.

Why do countries enact tax incentives despite their drawbacks? There are many factors. Legislators may feel the need to do something to attract investment, but may find it difficult to address the chief reasons that discourage investment; tax incentives are at least something over which they have control and which they can enact relatively easily and quickly. Alternatives to tax incentives may also involve the expenditure of funds, and tax incentives may be seen as a politically easier alternative, since subsidies involving expenditure may undergo closer scrutiny than other public expenditure needs. Further, some countries may feel under pressure from multinational companies, which threaten to locate investment elsewhere if they are not given concessions. Finally, some politicians or their advisors may simply disagree with the analysis presented here. As can be seen, the topic is a complicated one and cannot be resolved here. Therefore, we focus more on the technical tax issues raised by investment incentives and on ways that such incentives can be designed so as to minimize the damage that they can cause.

III. General Tax Incentives

A. Types of General Tax Incentives

Tax incentives can be grouped into a number of categories: tax holidays, investment allowances and tax credits, timing differences, reduced tax rates, and free economic zones. Each type raises different design and drafting issues.

1. Tax Holidays

The tax holiday has often been used by developing and transition countries. It is directed to new firms and is not available to existing operations. With a tax holiday, new firms are allowed a period of time when they are exempt from the burden of income taxation. Sometimes, this grace period is extended to a subsequent period of taxation at a reduced rate.

For transition countries, one advantage of tax holidays is that they provide a simple regime for foreign investors because there is no need to calculate taxes in the early years of operation, at a time when the tax systems are not yet fully developed. This view is certainly not valid for long-term investors, for whom the tax treatment after the holiday has expired is as important as the treatment during the holiday in determining the after-tax profitability of the investment. In addition, the tax treatment of the initial capital expenditures made before and during the holiday period must be determined so that appropriate records will be available for the calculation of depreciation when the holiday ends.

A number of technical issues are important in determining the impact of tax holidays on the return on investments. The first issue is determining when the holiday starts. It could be when production starts, the first year in which the firm makes a profit, or the first year that the firm achieves a positive cumulative profit on its operations. For large projects in particular, losses are usually generated in the early years of production, when the highest capital costs are incurred, including special costs that are linked to the start-up period, training the workforce, and developing the local market. For such projects, a tax holiday that starts when production occurs may actually increase the taxes paid over the life of the project and so act as a disincentive for investment. If losses are experienced during the holiday period, they may not be allowed to be carried forward beyond the holiday period (it would be overly generous to allow losses to be carried forward from a year in which income would not have been subject to tax). Thus, the holiday may occur when no taxes would have been paid in any event and taxes may be increased following the holiday because no losses are available to offset the profits. A similar situation can occur if the holiday starts when profits are first generated. Income may be sheltered that would have been eliminated in any case by the use of the tax losses. This may result in an overall increase in taxation in circumstances when the loss-carryover period is short or the use of losses is restricted in some way. Tax laws usually specify that the holiday commences when profits first occur. However, they are often ambiguous as to whether this means the first year that is in itself profitable or the first year that cumulative net profits are positive.[5]

A related question is the treatment of depreciation during the holiday period. Should it be deducted during the holiday period or can it be deferred until after the holiday has terminated? Depreciation represents a cost in the calculation of income, and so its deduction is necessary to accurately measure the amount of income that should be subject to the holiday. Allowing a deferral of the deduction effectively overestimates the costs associated with the post-holiday period and so leads to a further reduction in tax, which can result in a very generous incentive. The issue is more complicated if some form of accelerated depreciation is also offered with respect to the investment. Forcing the use of the accelerated deductions during the holiday period at the least reduces their value and can actually increase the level of taxation relative to the situation where no incentives are provided. A complete deferral of the deduction, however, can again lead to a generous incentive and an effective tax holiday that is much longer than intended.

Another design question is the length of the holiday. Most of the holidays offered in transition countries have been of short duration and, as discussed below, are of little benefit to long-term capital-intensive projects. Longer holidays would be of greater benefit; for example, there is some evidence in Asia and Hungary that the longer holidays succeeded in attracting some long-term investment.[6] However, the longer the holiday, the higher the revenue cost and the greater the vulnerability to tax-planning schemes.[7]

---

[5]See the appendix for a detailed example of a number of these points.

[6]*See* OECD, *supra* note 2, at 89–101 (Hungary); Easson, *Tax Incentives for Foreign Direct Investment*, 9 Australian Tax Forum 387 (1992).

[7]Because the holidays are limited in time, the typical avoidance scheme involves closing the business when the holiday expires and then forming a new company to carry on the business with the benefit of a new holiday period. The country authorities usually counter this maneuver by providing for recapture of the tax benefits if the business is closed. Such a rule can be avoided by keeping the business in operation, but at a lower level, and at the same time forming a new company. More sophisticated antiavoidance rules can be designed to attack this type of transaction, although enforcement is difficult.

The opposite problem arises when a tax holiday provision providing a lengthy tax-free period is repealed. Because an existing company can continue to take advantage of the holiday for which it qualified, new investment can be structured so as to use the corporate form of these existing companies, sometimes by bringing new investors in or even by selling the holiday company to new investors planning a substantial investment. It is therefore desirable, on repeal of a tax holiday, to stipulate that companies currently taking advantage of a tax holiday will cease to qualify if a substantial change in the ownership of the company takes place. Such a provision would prevent at least the most flagrant abuses.

2. Investment Allowances and Tax Credits

Investment allowances and tax credits are forms of tax relief that are based on the value of expenditures on qualifying investments. They provide tax benefits over and above the depreciation allowed for the asset. A tax allowance is used to reduce the taxable income of the firm. A tax credit is used to directly reduce the amount of taxes to be paid.

The major technical issues are the definition of the eligible expenditures, the choice of the rate of the allowance or credit, restrictions on the use of the credit or allowance, and the treatment of any amounts of incentive that cannot be used in the year in which they are earned as a result of insufficient taxable income. The major problem with determining the eligible expenditures is achieving a precise definition that directs the incentive to the desired activity to minimize revenue "leakage" and, at the same time, provides the taxpayer with certainty as to the applicability of the incentive.

The rate of incentive is directly linked to the amount of incentive that it is intended to provide and the revenue cost to the government. One problem that arises as the rate of the incentive increases is that the benefit to firms of controlling costs is decreased, leading to a "gold plating" of investments, where the most cost-effective techniques are not used. A number of tax avoidance possibilities are encountered when the rate of credit and tax allowance is too high. If a generous investment allowance is provided, firms can flow services through a subsidiary and make money simply by increasing the amounts that the subsidiary charges its parent company for the services rendered. The basic problem is that, because the total amount of tax allowance and depreciation that can be deducted against taxable income exceeds the actual amount spent, the tax benefit to the parent company of spending one dollar exceeds the tax cost to the subsidiary of receiving a dollar of revenue.

The effects of an incentive scheme that is poorly structured and involves excessively high rates of incentive are demonstrated in the following example in which a service subsidiary is used to generate profits out of the tax system.

The real cost to the company is $100. However, it establishes a subsidiary to supply it with the service. The subsidiary pays out the cost of $100 and adds a profit margin of $50 to the amount it charges the parent company. It is assumed that the parent is eligible for a tax credit of 40 percent on its cost of $150 and so earns a credit worth $60. The $150 is fully deductible against other income and thus has a tax value of $60, assuming a 40 percent tax rate. The subsidiary adds the $150 to income and is allowed to deduct its costs of $100, for a net tax on the subsidiary of $20.

Tax Calculation in the Subsidiary		Tax Calculation in the Parent	
Income from parent	$150	Payment to subsidiary	$150
Costs	$100	Value of tax deduction	$60
Taxable income	$50	Value of credit	$60
Tax payable	$20	Total tax benefit	$120

When the results for both companies are added together, washing out the intra-company transactions, the subsidiary has costs of $100 plus the $20 tax. The parent has a tax deduction worth $60 plus a tax credit of the same amount, for a total tax benefit of $120, which just offsets the costs of the subsidiary. The tax system has therefore completely subsidized the company's expenditures.

The use of the incentives can also be constrained to ensure that they do not fully eliminate the tax the firm must pay in the year. For example, an allowance could be restricted to some percentage of taxable income, or a credit could be limited to some percentage of tax otherwise payable. The calculation of these limits can interact with other provisions in a complicated manner and cause firms to enter into arrangements of the type discussed below. They do, however, limit the revenue cost to the government and ensure that firms cannot use incentives to eliminate their tax payable entirely.

An important design issue is what to do if the firm does not have enough taxable income in a given year to take full advantage of an incentive. In some countries the incentive is simply lost. This restrictive access to the incentive operates against firms that do not have other income, which is typical of new foreign investors, and can effectively eliminate the benefits of the incentive for such firms. Additionally, unproductive arrangements may be devised solely to make use of the incentive; for example, an investment allowance can be transferred from a firm benefiting from a tax holiday to a taxable firm through the use of a lease. In effect, the firm obtains both incentives, and government revenues fall by more than the tax that the firm would have paid during the holiday. The use of leasing to transfer incentives is demonstrated in the following example, in which the operator can borrow the funds and purchase the machine directly. Because it cannot benefit from the deductions, it enters into an arrangement where the taxpaying firm borrows the money and purchases the equipment. The equipment is then leased to the operator, who then uses it in his or her business. The difference is that the lessor gets the accelerated deductions.

Table 1 shows that if the lease payment is set as the sum of the interest on the loan plus the principal repayment, the lessor just breaks even before taxes (see section of Table 1 headed "Accounting income"). However, the lessor is better off after tax because it has losses in the early years to shelter other income from tax. In fact, the lease payments would be arranged so that the tax benefits of the arrangement are shared between the private sector parties. The loser in the scheme is the government, which receives less income tax revenue than it otherwise would.

3. Timing Differences

Timing differences can arise through either the acceleration of deductions or the deferral of the recognition of income. The most common form of accelerated deduction is accelerated depreciation, where the cost of an asset may be written off at a rate that is faster than the economic rate of deprecia-

Table 1. Equipment Lease
(*In local currency*)

Year	1	2	3	4	5	6	7	8	9	10
Loan principal	100	90	80	70	60	50	40	30	20	10
Interest	10	9	8	7	6	5	4	3	2	1
Principal repayment	10	10	10	10	10	10	10	10	10	10
Accounting income										
Lease payment	20	19	18	17	16	15	14	13	12	11
Interest	10	9	8	7	6	5	4	3	2	1
Depreciation	10	10	10	10	10	10	10	10	10	10
Accounting income	0	0	0	0	0	0	0	0	0	0
Tax position										
Lease payment	20	19	18	17	16	15	14	13	12	11
Interest	10	9	8	7	6	5	4	3	2	1
Accelerated depreciation	33	33	33	0	0	0	0	0	0	0
Taxable income	−23	−23	−23	10	10	10	10	10	10	10

tion.[8] It can take the form of either a shorter period of depreciation or a special deduction in the first year. The latter has a similar impact to an investment allowance in the first year, but differs in that the amount written off reduces the depreciation base for future years, and so the total amount written off does not exceed the actual cost of the investment. Rather, the deductions occur sooner than otherwise, providing a deferral of tax that is effectively an interest-free loan to the company from the government.

Important timing differences can occur in other, more technical areas. For example, incomes may not be realized until there is a sale of an asset, whereas certain costs are recognized immediately. A typical example is the current deduction of interest on an asset that is held for a period of time. A significant net after-tax rate of return can be realized on an asset whose pretax return equals, but does not exceed, the rate of interest on the funds borrowed for its purchase, simply because of the mismatching of the deductions and the income. These technical timing differences can often be more important than any explicit investment incentives for certain activities (e.g., in the case of timber growing).

The technical issues with accelerated depreciation are similar to the issues of targeting and of carryovers that face investment allowances. However, accelerated depreciation avoids the problem of deductions that exceed the cost of the investment that occurs with an investment allowance.

4. Tax Rate Reductions

General tax rate reductions can be provided for income from certain sources or to firms satisfying certain criteria, for example, to small firms in

---

[8]*See supra* ch. 17.

manufacturing or agriculture. These reductions differ from tax holidays because the tax liability of firms is not entirely eliminated, the benefit is extended beyond new enterprises to include income from existing operations, and the benefit is not time limited. Identifying the qualifying income is the major design issue and may require rules to define eligible taxpayers if the benefit is to be limited to specific types of firms, such as small businesses. If only certain types of income are to qualify, then rules must be defined to measure the income. The rules can rely on separate accounting for different sources of income, but such rules are subject to manipulation and the timing of costs and income to maximize the benefit. The alternative is to use a formula approach, which will be less accurate in directing the benefit. With either approach, the rules tend to be complex and subject to manipulation.

5. Administrative Discretion

A major design issue relevant for different types of incentives is whether incentives should be discretionary and granted only with the preapproval of the authorities.[9] A discretionary approach has a number of potential advantages. As the policy priorities of the government change, it is possible to tailor the incentives to support them, because fewer firms are affected by the changes, and problems of transition can be more easily handled. If there appears to be a risk of tax avoidance under the scheme, then the authorities can deny access to the incentive. Where the extent and the availability of the incentive are determined administratively, it may be possible to provide only that degree of incentive that is required to make the investment economic. This would improve the cost-effectiveness of the program by improving its targeting toward incremental investment.

In practice, however, there is little evidence that these gains are realized. Approval processes can be time-consuming and cumbersome. The authorities can obtain the detailed information necessary for evaluation only from companies that have an incentive to portray it in an advantageous manner. In the real world of politics, it is difficult to deny the incentives to companies that are promising to create employment. Moreover, discretionary incentives are an invitation to corruption. Finally, an approval process undermines the tax system's transparency, which is probably the most important criterion of companies making the investments. For these reasons, the track record of discretionary incentives is not encouraging.

While administrative discretion may not be useful, there are advantages to having a process of vetting and approving investments that do meet the criteria in the relevant legislation before the investor proceeds. Such a process is common in relation to tax holidays and allows governments to keep track of the extent to which the incentive is being used, assure taxpayers of their tax

---

[9]*See* vol. 1 at 62.

position, and amend the legislation where problems in the criteria for the incentive become evident.[10]

B. Comparison of Incentives

General tax incentives can differ markedly in a number of important ways—in particular, in terms of the types of companies and activities that are likely to benefit from them, the time profile of the revenue impact on the government for any given level of incentive, the difficulty of administration, and the possibility of tax avoidance.

1. Beneficiaries

Tax holidays are of greatest value to firms and projects that make substantial profits in the early years of operation. Such enterprises are likely to be engaged in sectors such as trade, short-term construction, and services. Tax holidays are less likely to be of benefit to major capital-intensive projects, which do not normally make a profit in the early years. This has in fact been the experience of transition countries that have introduced tax holidays. Most of the beneficiaries of the tax holidays have been small firms—for example, real estate businesses, restaurants, and firms designed for short-term market exploitation, such as trade and woodcutting.[11] The tax holidays are open-ended in that their value depends upon the amount of profit earned. Arguably, the types of high-profit activities that benefit the most are the least in need of the incentive and would have occurred in the absence of the incentive. Thus, the bulk of the revenue forgone is likely to have had no beneficial impact on investment, and so the ratio of benefits to costs is likely to be low.

The experience of Asian countries with tax holidays directed toward export-oriented industries is also instructive. Low-cost assembly plants that are highly mobile can be the most affected by holidays. In a number of countries, plants were established to take advantage of a tax holiday; when the holiday expired, the plant was disassembled and moved to an adjacent jurisdiction to take advantage of the holiday offered there. The factor that made the project responsive to the incentive also limited the benefit to the country from the investment.[12]

Investment allowances, tax credits, and accelerated depreciation, in contrast, are specifically targeted at capital investment. Their revenue cost is constrained by the amount of capital that the firm is willing to put at risk. As such, they are of little benefit to the quick-profit types of firms that can take best advantage of tax holidays. Tax allowances are of greatest benefit to firms with income from existing operations. These firms can shelter a portion of such

---

[10]*E.g.*, Economic Expansion Incentives (Relief from Income Tax) Act 1985 (Singapore) § 5.

[11]Some countries have excluded services from qualifying for tax holidays.

[12]*See* Easson, *supra* note 6, at 414.

income from tax with the incentives earned on the new investment. Firms with low income and start-up firms cannot begin to take advantage of the incentive until the investment begins to earn income. Provided that a carryover of the incentive is allowed, an investment allowance can operate in a manner similar to a tax holiday in that it can eliminate the tax liability of the firm in the early years of operation. However, the effect of a tax holiday differs, because it is limited in time but normally involves no upper bound on the amount of tax benefit that can be obtained.

General tax rate reductions differ from the other incentives in that they are not specifically directed toward new activity. Income from both existing and new operations is eligible for the incentive. Thus, when rate reductions are viewed as an incentive, they are less likely to be cost-effective than incentives that are related to the amount of new investment.

2. Profile of Revenue Impact

The revenue impact of tax holidays and investment allowances is, in theory, tied to the degree of new activity. Thus, the revenue impact is relatively small in the early years of the program and grows over time as more firms become eligible. A general tax rate reduction, in contrast, has significant up-front revenue costs because it applies to income from existing operations as well.

The pattern of revenue costs of accelerated depreciation is somewhat more complicated. Because accelerated deductions confer a timing benefit only, the government incurs a higher level of up-front cost to achieve the same incentive effect. The revenue cost actually falls over time, because in future years the tax benefits from further new investments are partly offset by the reduced deductions resulting from the acceleration of deductions on the old investments.

For investment allowances and accelerated deductions, the carryover of deductions by firms that cannot fully use them can considerably raise the revenue cost over time. The experience of a number of industrial countries that provided broad-based investment incentives was that over one-half of incentives were earned by firms with no current taxable income. This reduced their cost in the early years of the program. However, there was a significant buildup over time of unused deductions from previous years. As the firms that had these accumulations began to earn income, they used the accumulations to offset income even though they were no longer making expenditures that were eligible for the incentives. The claiming of the deductions was merely delayed, and there was an increasing impact on tax revenues as the deductions from previous years were added to those being earned and used in the current year.[13]

---

[13]*See* Minister of Finance, Canada, The Corporate Income Tax System: A Direction for Change 17–18 (1985).

The buildup of unused deductions and losses also reduced the predictability of the government's revenue stream. Firms that did not expect to be able to use their deductions in time sought ways of transferring them to firms with current taxable income, often in the form of transactions that traded a lower cost of financing for the tax deductions. Thus, the deductions earned in one sector reduced the taxable income of another. Loss-trading mechanisms such as leasing were frequently used in this context.[14]

A number of transition countries have experienced serious unexpected shortfalls in revenues during the transition period, in part because of reduced economic performance and problems of tax administration in the face of a changing economic structure. Tax incentives, particularly holidays, have contributed to this shortfall by providing opportunities for firms to arrange their affairs to avoid paying taxes on income ordinarily subject to taxation.

3. Administration and Tax Avoidance

Auditing incentives provides an extra challenge to tax administrators, who must first verify that the incentive has been applied correctly. Verification can be difficult if complex calculations are involved. Second, administrators must ensure that the activity or firm actually qualifies for the incentive. This process can be complicated if concepts and definitions are vague or ambiguous or, as for foreign-owned firms, the records establishing the eligibility of the firm are in another country. (This problem is compounded by the limited range of tax treaties for many developing and transition countries, which means they do not have access to the exchange-of-information facilities usually contained in treaties.) Third, tax officials must ensure that the amounts eligible for the incentive are correctly reported, for example, that the value of a machine or service has been transferred at its fair market value. If the transaction occurs across borders, particularly among related parties, this task can be difficult. The need to carry out these audits and assessments essentially to verify that no tax, or a reduced amount, is payable diverts resources from other administrative tasks, which can be ill afforded given the shortages of trained staff that exist in most developing and transition countries.

Tax holidays have been particularly susceptible to tax planning, much of which is especially problematic for taxation authorities. Tax planning can lead to considerable revenue leakage, which can exceed the revenue forgone from incentives received by legitimate activities. This outcome further reduces the cost-effectiveness of tax incentives. The tax avoidance strategies, which are often used in combination, include fictive foreign investment. Tax holidays in a number of countries have been directed at firms with a high enough percentage of foreign ownership. Considerable tax revenue seems to have been lost from the creation of fictive foreign-owned companies that carry on what is in

---

[14]See id. at 19–20.

fact a domestically owned business. One way of doing this entails transferring funds from a domestic enterprise to a company incorporated offshore, which in turn reinvests in the home country as if it were a foreign-owned company. The investment thus qualifies for the incentive. It depends upon how the law is written whether this type of transaction is tax avoidance or evasion.[15] In either event, it is difficult for tax authorities to detect such activity on audit, especially if the investment appears to originate in a tax haven with strict secrecy laws.

Furthermore, the existence of a tax holiday introduces the possibility of transferring profits from operations that do not qualify for the holiday to a firm that does. For example, a domestic firm can transfer a small part of its operation to a joint venture with a foreign-owned company; the joint venture qualifies for the incentive; the original domestic company transfers income to the joint venture by manipulating the allocation of costs and the charges made on transactions between the firms, such as the domestically owned company selling intermediate products to the joint venture at a price that ensures that the entire profit from the transaction arises in the joint venture. Other costs, such as financing costs, can be borne on behalf of the joint venture by the domestically owned company. These types of transactions are difficult for tax authorities to detect and even harder to successfully challenge.

Nor is it easy to establish what is a new operation for purposes of qualifying for the tax holiday. A new corporation can be established that then purchases the assets of an existing operation in order to qualify for the incentive, even though no new activity is occurring. This device has occurred in some countries in combination with the above types of tax avoidance. In other areas, such as the construction industry, new firms can be established for each new project, thus maintaining perpetual access to the holiday.

Tax holidays also put the revenues of adjacent jurisdictions at risk. Exporting firms would ordinarily pay tax on their profit from the sale in the country. However, if these firms establish transshipment companies in an adjoining state that provides a tax holiday, so as to purchase the goods from the exporting company and then sell them to the actual purchaser in the destination country, they can avoid taxation through transfer pricing. To accomplish this, the goods are sold at cost to the transshipment company, so that all the profits on the sale are transferred to this company to be sheltered from tax by the tax holiday.

A number of developing and transition countries have attempted to curtail these abuses by stipulating that the foreign investment must exceed a specified value in order to qualify for the incentive. While such restrictions may deter some small operators, they are unlikely to prevent tax avoidance. Firms may contribute overvalued capital goods as part of their initial capital contribution to achieve the threshold. There are usually no restrictions on the use of

---

[15]For a discussion of the meaning of these terms, *see* vol. 1 at 44–45.

the capital contributed under such a restriction, and it would be hard to impose them effectively. Accordingly, firms can effectively repatriate the funds in a number of ways, such as through nonrecourse loans, offshore deposits, and returns of capital. Here, the thresholds impose no effective constraint on tax avoidance.

The other forms of incentive apart from tax holidays are also subject to tax planning. The scope is somewhat more limited for investment-related incentives at moderate rates. The amount of the incentive that can be earned has an upper limit related to the amount of the expenditure and, unlike a tax holiday, is not as exposed to the shifting of large amounts of profits. Problems can occur, however, especially with assets transferred from related offshore companies. There is a motivation to overvalue the purchase price of the asset to maximize the incentive. Clearly, this motivation increases as the rate of the incentive rises. As noted above, at high rates of incentive, this problem can occur even within a country if the rate of incentive leads to a value of tax deductions that exceeds the value of the expenditure. It is possible to increase the benefits to the enterprise on a transfer of assets or services between related companies simply by increasing the price of the item transferred. The other issue that can arise in these circumstances is multiple access to the incentive through progressively moving the asset among a group of companies. Recapture rules and capital gains taxes can address this problem in the case of accelerated depreciation because the increased deductions of the purchaser are offset by the reduced write-offs of the seller. For investment allowances and tax credits, the problem can be dealt with through fairly simple antiavoidance rules, such as providing the incentive only for first use of the asset in the country.[16]

Low tax rates for particular activities suffer from many of the transferring and targeting avoidance problems that arise with tax holidays. For significant rate reductions, taxpayers will make considerable efforts to shift income to the company with lower tax rates, for example, by shifting debt within a corporate group. In addition, firms will attempt to characterize their activity as qualifying for the incentive.

C. Minimizing Problems of Incentives

The overwhelming experience of transition countries and, to a lesser extent, of developing countries with tax holidays has been that they are particularly susceptible to tax avoidance and have been ineffective in attracting FDI. Part of the problem with attracting FDI is that a holiday is only indirectly linked to investment. It is tied to the establishment of a new enterprise, and

---

[16]See CYP IT §12(2)(b) (investment credit for new equipment made in Cyprus or new or secondhand equipment imported from abroad); HUN CIT § 13(4) (incentive allowed only for first use of asset in country).

the amount of the incentive depends not on the size of the investment but on the profits that are made during the initial years of the enterprise. This is at the heart of both the tendency for holidays to be used by firms making short-term investments and the various tax avoidance schemes that have been described. These problems are significantly reduced with investment allowances and credits, and so these types of incentives are likely to perform better if the goal is to promote productive investment.

1. Investment Allowances and Credits

Nonetheless, experience has shown that investment-related incentives have their own set of problems. A number of guidelines should be followed if the incentives are to be as free from abuse as possible. As the examples of tax avoidance activities demonstrate, the problems associated with investment allowances and credits are most evident at higher rates of allowance or credit. Therefore, the rates of benefit offered should be moderate. Moreover, attempts to target the incentives either too finely or at vague objectives are counterproductive because they introduce complexity and uncertainty for both the taxpayer and the tax administrator. If the taxpayer cannot be certain of the eligibility of an expenditure for the incentive, its effect on behavior is reduced significantly or even eliminated. Therefore, the investments eligible for the incentive should be clearly defined and the rules kept as simple as possible.

In many countries, the principal justification for an incentive will be to help create a basic amount of market-oriented activity. As the market develops and foreign firms become familiar with a country, the rationale for an incentive will be reduced. This suggests that incentives should be made valid for a set time with a preannounced expiration date. This automatic expiration is known as "sunsetting" and ensures that the government must review the incentive and take steps to continue to make it available.

With up-front incentives, the same asset is often sold and resold to produce multiple access to the incentive. Appropriate recapture and capital gains rules reduce the problem and should be in place.[17] However, for an incentive such as an investment tax credit, other rules are needed to ensure that an asset receives the incentive only once. One approach is to "claw back" the incentive if the asset is resold, perhaps within a time limit.[18] This approach requires a complex tracking of assets. A simpler approach is to allow the incentive only for the purchase of assets that have not been previously used.[19] To allow for the use of secondhand assets from abroad that might embody technology that

---

[17]*E.g.*, USA IRC § 1245.

[18]Claw-back (known as recapture in the United States) means that the taxpayer must repay the incentive in the form of an increase in tax. *E.g.*, USA IRC §§ 47, 50; HUN CIT § 13(3) (investment credit clawed back if asset transferred or leased within three years).

[19]*E.g.*, USA IRC § 48 (1986).

is unavailable in the country, the rule could be extended to allow the incentive only for the first use of the asset in the country.[20]

The price of assets purchased from abroad from a related person may be inflated to maximize the write-offs for depreciation purposes. Adding an investment incentive on top of depreciation increases the attraction of such tax avoidance. Overcoming this problem is not simple, but there are some guidelines that will help. The law should stipulate that transactions between related parties be conducted at fair market value.[21] Such a provision at least establishes a legal basis for attacking the transaction and will curb somewhat the aggressiveness of major companies. Targeting the incentive to assets, such as machinery and equipment, that have some external secondhand market transaction for comparison also assists. Intangible expenditures like know-how and business services are typically hard to value.

The key to auditing any transaction is information. Typically, the taxpayer has it and the tax administrator does not. This problem is compounded in the case of foreign taxpayers because it is typically more difficult for tax authorities to obtain information from a taxpayer with offices located abroad. This problem is addressed internationally through the exchange-of-information provisions in tax treaties.

2. Tax Holidays

If tax holidays are used, the potential for their abuse can be curtailed in a number of ways. As noted above, holidays are linked more to the establishment of enterprises than to the level of investment. The problems described suggest a number of restrictions that eliminate some of the most obvious abuses and direct the holiday incentives toward the creation of new businesses rather than indirectly attempting to attract new investment. A government may pursue this objective both in attracting foreign firms and in promoting the establishment of new private sector activity domestically.

A frequently encountered problem is the transfer of existing business assets to a new firm that qualifies for the holiday. Firms whose holidays are expiring may transfer assets to refresh the holiday. This practice suggests that the holiday should be restricted to firms the bulk of whose assets has not previously been employed in the country. This ratio of new-to-the-country assets should be quite high, say, 90 percent. The assets so restricted would not include buildings, given that existing buildings may be renovated for a new use. This restriction would also deny the holiday to firms that simply change their form, such as through privatization.

The second restriction would address the problem of transfer pricing and focus the incentive on the objective of creating new enterprises. It would deny

---

[20]See supra note 16.

[21]E.g., USA IRC § 482.

the incentive to any company related to a company operating in the country that did not itself qualify for the holiday. Holidays are frequently targeted to industries that are internationally mobile, such as manufacturing, and denied to firms that are engaged in activities that are more tied to the country, such as distribution and wholesale trade. The question arises as to what happens if a firm is established for manufacturing but carries on ancillary activities that do not qualify for the incentive. A strict targeting to manufacturing could operate in conjunction with the previous restriction to deny the holiday in this situation. Another approach is to allow the holiday, provided that over one-half of the assets or revenues of the company are used in the desired activity. If this is done, the holiday benefits should be restricted to income from the targeted activity. Profits for each activity could be separately accounted for. Alternatively, because separate accounting is complex and subject to manipulation, a simple formula approach can be used to determine the proportion of profits to qualify for the holiday. This proportion can be based on some overall figure, such as wages and salaries employed, total revenues, or assets.

3. Low Tax Rates

Regimes applying reduced tax rates to certain activities or enterprises require a number of rules to minimize tax avoidance. A typical example can be given of low tax rates applied to income earned by small businesses.

The first problem is to define small businesses in relation to a given threshold. The threshold can be measured in terms of assets, capital, number of employees, or total sales. The choice among these criteria, which can be used in combination, will depend in part on the type of business being targeted and on the compliance and administrative costs that are entailed. Seemingly simple concepts such as number of employees can be avoided through the use of employee leasing arrangements, where staff are employed not directly by the company, but rather by a special-purpose employment firm that "leases" the employees to the company. Similarly, businesses can avoid asset restrictions by leasing rather than purchasing assets.

Whatever criteria are chosen, it is crucial to introduce a test that applies to all the companies in a related group. Otherwise, it is a simple matter to break up an operation so that the constituent parts meet the criteria. Unfortunately, applying rules to determine whether companies are related can be very complicated and a constant source of avoidance activity.

Another approach is to simply provide a threshold amount of income that is subject to the lower tax rate, effectively a progressive rate schedule for corporations.[22] A certain amount of the incentive will accordingly be earned

---

[22]While progressive as far as corporations are concerned, the scheme is likely to be quite the opposite as far as the owners of capital go, favoring wealthy individuals who invest in small businesses. Very small businesses owned and operated by low-income individuals are not likely to take corporate form.

by larger corporations. One possibility is to claw back this incentive for income over another threshold.[23] This effectively implies that middle levels of income face a special higher marginal rate of tax. As with size tests, rules are needed to allocate the thresholds among related groups of companies.[24]

Care must be taken to target the low tax rate to appropriate types of activity and to prevent it from being used to avoid taxes that should be paid at the personal level. A low tax rate that applies to all small business income opens an opportunity for individuals to place their investment holdings in a corporation to obtain the benefits of the lower tax rate. Accordingly, rules are required to restrict the incentive to active business income.[25] The distinction between active and passive business is notoriously difficult to maintain, and so arbitrary rules, such as requiring a minimum number of employees to qualify as an active business, may be needed.

IV. Special-Purpose Tax Incentives

A serious disadvantage of offering tax incentives to attract investment is that, to the extent that enterprises that would have invested in any event claim them, tax revenue is lost without any corresponding benefit to the host country. These costs can, in theory, be reduced if means can be found to target the incentives to particular desirable activities or to projects that would not have occurred without the incentive. Countries have employed a number of techniques to achieve this better targeting. These include linking the incentive to specific low-growth regions, tying the incentive to particular objectives—such as employment creation, technology transfer, or export promotion—using free trade or export promotion zones, and providing for administrative discretion. All these approaches have potential advantages, but are likely to give rise to substantial problems in implementation.

One general problem with special incentives is that they inevitably lead to pressure for similar treatment from other deserving sectors. This pressure is much more difficult to withstand once some targeted incentives have been given. In a number of countries, both developing and industrial, the incentives have spread over time to other activities, and removing the incentives once the reason for them is gone has been difficult politically. While any one targeted incentive may not involve a significant revenue cost, the total for all the resulting incentives can sharply erode government revenues from the business sector.

The following discussion focuses on issues peculiar to special-purpose incentives. It should be noted that many of the comments made on general incentives in the preceding section apply here also.

---

[23]E.g., USA IRC § 11(b).

[24]E.g., USA IRC § 1551.

[25]E.g., USA IRC §§ 541–547.

A. Regional Development

Regional development is a common objective of tax incentives in industrial countries and elsewhere. Typically, investors in designated regions— usually the more remote, economically less-developed regions of a country or regions with high levels of unemployment—receive tax holidays, investment allowances, or accelerated depreciation.[26] Experience demonstrates that relatively little new activity is generated in the targeted region relative to the revenue cost. Insofar as the incentives have any effect at all, the chief effect is to divert investment away from its optimum location.[27] The same types of transfer pricing and other avoidance transactions discussed above also typically arise, particularly with firms whose operations are based both in the targeted regions and elsewhere in the country.

B. Employment Creation

Incentives may be directed to promote the establishment of labor-intensive industries or the employment of particular categories of workers, such as young persons, the disabled, or the long-term unemployed.[28] Many of the issues that arise with investment incentives, such as incentives going to employment that would have occurred in any event, are also associated with employment incentives. Moreover, incentives targeted to particular types of employment or increases in the level of employment are subject to manipulation and administrative complexity.

C. Technology Transfer

Many countries have sought to attract investment that would bring in advanced technology, or research and development activities, by granting tax incentives, usually with little success. It is frequently difficult for tax authorities to determine when a particular technology qualifies as "advanced" or "appropriate," and difficult to define precisely what constitutes "research." In most cases, the investor is likely to be receiving a tax break for doing what it would have done in any event, and it is the experience of many developing countries that technology that is introduced is rarely "transferred" to the host country. Because of the generally unsatisfactory experience with tax incentives in this area, a number of countries are turning to nonfiscal inducements, such as the establishment of science parks.

---

[26]*E.g.*, HUN CIT § 13(2); DEU DDR-IG, DEU FGG, DEU InvZulG.

[27]Minister of Finance, Canada, Economic Effects of the Cape Breton Tax Credit (1990).

[28]*E.g.*, USA IRC § 51 (work opportunity credit); RUS PT § 7(2) (tax rate reduction for enterprises where 70 percent of workers are disabled); HUN PIT § 21 (tax deduction for agricultural enterprises employing handicapped persons).

D. Export Promotion

There is evidence, especially from developing countries in Asia, to suggest that incentives to attract export-oriented investment tend to be more effective than most other forms of investment incentives.[29] Certain types of export-oriented enterprises, notably those in the textile and electronics sectors and other labor-intensive assembly industries, are especially sensitive to taxation. Such industries do not rely much on local sources of material supply and do not gear sales to the domestic market. Rather, they are attracted to low-cost environments. While the most important local cost for such industries is labor, taxes may also be a significant component, and so tax reliefs may be especially attractive to such firms. Investment incentives are commonly provided in the form of tax holidays or special investment allowances for firms designated as "export oriented." They may be exempted from tax on a proportion of their profits corresponding to the proportion that export sales bear to total sales, or they may be allowed a generous deduction for expenditures aimed at export promotion. Some of these policies have been successful in attracting foreign investment and have had, at least in the short term, relatively little cost in terms of tax forgone, since much of the investment would not have been attracted without tax exemptions.

The benefits of such investment, however, are questionable. As noted above, many of the enterprises attracted are footloose, and tend to move on as soon as tax holidays expire. There tends to be little in the way of creation of linkages to domestic firms, little transfer of technology, and little sourcing of local raw materials. Moreover, the success of such operations depends to a large extent on the reaction of the countries that provide the sources of capital and the markets for the exports. Many of the incentives that could be offered to attract export-oriented investment may be contrary to the World Trade Organization's subsidy rules;[30] for other operations to succeed, home countries must be prepared to grant "tax-sparing" treatment in their double taxation treaties (see below). With the heightened competition in world markets, these issues are likely to be more important in the future.

E. Free Trade or Export Processing Zones

Export processing zones (EPZs) are closely related to promoting export-oriented investment. These zones, also called customs-free zones, duty-free zones, free trade zones, or special economic zones, have over the past thirty

---

[29]See Easson, *supra* note 6, at 395, 429.

[30]See on this problem, especially for the strengthened subsidy rules flowing from the Uruguay Round of GATT negotiations, Buchs, *Selected WTO Rules and Some Implications for Fund Policy Advice*, IMF Working Paper 96/23; Pearson, *Business Incentives and the GATT Subsidies Agreement*, 23 Australian Business Law Review 368 (1995); Perry, *Taxes, Tax Subsidies and the Impact of Trade Agreements*, 63 Review of Marketing and Agricultural Economics 155 (1995).

years or so been established in more than fifty countries in all parts of the globe, especially in developing and transition countries.

The distinguishing feature of these zones is that they provide a discrete environment in which enterprises (usually both foreign and domestically owned) can import machinery, components, and raw materials free of customs duties and other taxes for assembly, processing, or manufacture, with a view to exporting the finished product. Normally, products from an EPZ sold on the domestic market are treated as imports and are subject to import duties and taxes.

The country establishing an export processing zone is primarily interested in earning foreign exchange from export sales, although it frequently has additional objectives, such as creating employment, attracting technology, or promoting regional policy. Incentives to attract foreign investors to the EPZs commonly take a variety of forms.

Exemption from customs duties and other taxes on importation is the essential feature of EPZs. Such exemptions apply to materials and components that are imported and reexported and are often expanded to capital goods that firms use in the production process. Exemption from such taxes is often one of the more important tax incentives offered to foreign investors because of the immediate impact upon costs. To the extent that zone products are reexported, exemptions appear to be entirely consistent with the provisions of the general Agreement on Tariff and Trade (GATT) and, as far as product taxes are concerned, produce essentially the same result as the zero rating of exports under a value-added tax. The chief advantage of the zonal exemptions is in terms of administration and cash flow. Such measures can be seen as removing impediments rather than providing a special incentive to encourage exports.

Much of the investment attracted to EPZs is highly mobile, cost conscious, and tax sensitive, and additional tax incentives for investment are frequently offered in the zones. In some cases, special incentives such as tax holidays apply for investment in the zone; in others, zone enterprises qualify for the same incentives that are provided—notably for export-oriented investment—elsewhere in the country. The concerns raised above in relation to incentives for export-oriented investment apply equally to zonal incentives of this nature.

It is difficult to evaluate the success or failure of EPZs.[31] In a few countries, they have generated substantial foreign currency earnings, but in other countries they have proved a dismal failure. Between success and failure are instances where it is difficult to say whether the enhanced foreign exchange earnings have been worth the costs of establishing the zones. Real (net) foreign exchange earnings are often but a small proportion of total export sales because most components and raw materials are imported; textile manufac-

---

[31]United Nations, The Challenge of Free Economic Zones in Central and Eastern Europe (1991).

turers in some zones have even imported such items as thread and buttons. Employment creation has been impressive, but has often had little impact on local unemployment because the great majority of jobs have been filled by young women who had not previously been part of the workforce. Technology transfer has usually been negligible and only a few countries have established substantial backward linkages with domestic producers. Attempts to use EPZs as an instrument of regional development policy have mostly failed. Because tax incentives have been the rule in most EPZs, very little tax revenue has been generated directly, although EPZ investors have undoubtedly contributed to revenues through employment creation, in the form of payroll taxes, income tax on salaries, and sales taxes on spending by employees.

It is instructive to note that the countries in which EPZs have tended to be most successful have been those that have concentrated on generating foreign exchange earnings without attempting to pursue ancillary objectives such as regional development and that have emphasized removing obstacles to export processing rather than providing investment incentives as such. They have also tended to be countries in which the general domestic tax climate has been relatively hospitable to investment.

To the extent that tax incentives, other than exemption from taxes and duties on imports, are employed, a potential advantage of EPZs is that they generally localize access to the incentives[32] and so, in theory, allow a closer monitoring of the operation of firms. However, they do not eliminate the problems already referred to. There are various ways to shift profits from operations outside the zone to firms that are based in the zone through intragroup transactions, leading to the effective leakage of zone benefits to ordinary domestic activity.

Finally, the caution recorded in relation to tax incentives for export promotion bears repeating in the context of EPZs. While there would seem to be nothing objectionable in principle in providing exemption from customs duties and taxes on importation,[33] other tax incentives directed specifically at export promotion may run contrary to the GATT and may invite countervailing measures that could negate any advantages obtained from the establishment of the zones.

V. International Aspects of Tax Incentives

Some international issues have already been noted in the previous discussion, for example, transfer pricing and fictive foreign investment. Where FDI

---

[32]They do not always do so—in Cameroon, EPZ benefits are offered to sawmills scattered around the country.—L.M.

[33]There is, however, the problem of smuggling to the domestic market.—L.M.

is involved, however, international tax issues are pervasive.[34] Accordingly, this section first looks at some additional tax incentives that are internationally focused, such as special relief from international withholding taxes. It then discusses the interaction of the tax systems of the investor and the place of investment and concludes with the issue of tax competition.

A. Incentives with an International Focus

1. Incentives for Foreign Investors

Incentives offered in many developing and transition countries are often tied to foreign investment. These can take the form of special tax holidays under the income tax or special relief from customs duties or turnover taxes. The incentives are sometimes directed at firms that are 100 percent owned by foreigners and at other times offered to joint ventures, often with as little as 30 percent foreign ownership.

The attraction for policymakers is that the targeting dramatically reduces the revenue costs of offering the incentives. However, the question arises as to why it would be government policy to favor foreign firms over domestic firms. The discrimination leads to resentment, which is likely to reduce voluntary compliance with the tax system. Domestic firms will lobby, with justification, to have the incentives extended to them. This pressure can be difficult to resist, and so the incentives may spread, leading to a deterioration of the domestic tax system. Moreover, as seen above, the restrictions often do not work. Domestic firms are induced to enter into tax avoidance strategies that have proved difficult for tax authorities to counter.

2. Relief from Cross-Border Withholding Taxes

Among their measures to encourage FDI, many developing countries provide tax relief from withholding taxes on certain interest and royalties and sometimes on dividends on foreign parent companies' investments in subsidiaries. The international chapter of this book explains how interest and royalties can be used for profit stripping. Removal of cross-border withholding taxes on these forms of income can increase the benefits from such tax planning. Such incentives can also be subject to many of the forms of planning outlined above in relation to tax holidays, to which they are closely related (often tax holidays for foreign direct investors and dividend withholding tax relief are applied to the same project).[35]

---

[34]A detailed description of the rules necessary for the international operation of the income tax is provided in ch. 18 *supra*. The discussion here assumes some familiarity with the international chapter.

[35]*See* Easson, *supra* note 6, at 418.

Levying such taxes can also simply increase the cost of funds and technology for local firms. In this case, the argument for relief from withholding tax is stronger, and carefully drafted provisions may be worthwhile. Such measures are not incentives as such, but rather remove barriers where the international tax regime produces more tax than would occur in purely domestic cases. Conversely, relief from withholding tax on dividends for portfolio, as opposed to direct, investment is often effectively eliminated by the tax system of the investor's country of residence. These issues are dealt with in the chapter on international taxation.[36]

Viewed as an incentive, relief from withholding taxes for a direct investment is poorly targeted in that it delivers a benefit to the investor only on repatriation (i.e., at the end of the day, not up front) and encourages repatriation, whereas for the country where the investment occurs, it is better if the income generated is reinvested rather than repatriated.

B. Tax Incentives and Relief from Double Taxation

To determine the tax treatment of FDI, it is necessary to look beyond the country where the activity takes place (the source country). It is also necessary to consider the tax treatment in the country of the foreign investor or parent company (the residence country). There are often further tax consequences in the residence country on income that is earned and taxed in the source country. This can lead to an interaction between the tax systems of the two jurisdictions that modifies the impact of a tax incentive compared with what it would be in the source country alone.[37]

1. Relief from Double Taxation in the Residence Country

An investment can take place in a number of forms. The two basic methods are through a branch and through a subsidiary. A branch is simply a division of the foreign company making the investment, but it is not a separate legal entity. Accordingly, the branch's profits are ordinarily taxed as they are earned in the residence country under the principle of worldwide taxation.[38] Investments can also be channeled through a subsidiary, which is a separate legal entity, and whose income is usually not included in the income of the foreign parent until it is repatriated as a dividend.

Because a subsidiary is the normal form of investment for nonfinancial institutions, the balance of the discussion will focus on the treatment of repatri-

---

[36]See *supra* ch. 18, sec. VI(F).

[37]For a detailed analysis of the relation between tax incentives in developing countries and taxation in capital-exporting countries, see Timo Viherkenttä, Tax Incentives in Developing Countries and International Taxation (1991).

[38]An exception is where the residence country uses the exemption approach for foreign-source business income. See *supra* ch. 18.

ated dividends. Much of the discussion also applies to income earned in branches, except the residence-country tax consequences occur as the income is earned, rather than being deferred until it is repatriated as a dividend. Essentially, two types of tax treatments are applied to dividends paid to the residence country. These have very different implications for the potential effectiveness of tax incentives provided by the source country.

The first type of tax treatment is the foreign tax credit method. Under this method, the residence country applies its tax regime to the income when it is repatriated, but allows a credit for any foreign taxes paid to the extent that they do not exceed the amount of residence-country tax that would be levied on the income. This system effectively means that the source country is allowed the first opportunity to tax the income, but that the residence country will tax the income if it is not fully taxed in the source country. When there is only one source of foreign income, the implications for tax incentives are clearly negative. To the extent that the incentive results in a tax liability that is less than the tax burden that would be applied in the residence country, then the benefit given is taxed back when the income is repatriated to the residence country. There is simply a transfer of tax revenue from the source country to the residence country. A number of important sources of FDI use the foreign tax credit method, for example, Japan, the United Kingdom, and the United States.

The alternative basic system of taxing foreign-source income is the exemption method, employed by countries such as France, Germany, and the Netherlands. Under this method, there is no further tax on the repatriated profits, and so the effective taxing back of the incentive that occurs under the tax crediting method does not occur. In fact, simple categorization of countries is difficult because many countries incorporate aspects of both systems depending upon the type of income and its country of source. A foreign tax credit is applied in some of these countries in certain circumstances, such as when no tax treaty exists. Some exemption systems are structured on the basis of a "subject-to-tax" test or a "comparable-tax" test.[39] This means that if a tax holiday exists, the exemption is not available in the residence country and a credit system applies in its stead. In this event, the comments made in relation to credit systems become relevant.

In examining the extent of the reversal of source-country incentives through foreign tax credits, a number of qualifications need to be made to the simple case outlined. With taxation only on repatriation, to the extent that the earnings are retained in the source country and reinvested, they are not subject to residence-country taxation. Thus, adverse tax consequences can be deferred until the time of repatriation. There has been much theoretical discussion about the true impact of this system. Because the tax on the distribution will occur when the income is repatriated, firms should take it into

---

[39]*E.g.*, AUS ITAA § 23AH.

account in making their investment decisions. However, there is little doubt that firms act as if the deferral inherent in taxation only on repatriation matters to them. Thus, to the extent that the adverse tax consequences can be delayed, they are less problematic to the companies. Levying tax on income only when it is repatriated has implications for the design of tax incentives, namely, that incentives in the income tax of the source country are more likely to be effective than incentives that are provided at the time of repatriation, such as withholding tax relief. These latter incentives are more likely to lead simply to an increase in the other country's tax revenues.

The next qualification is that the tax crediting systems of most countries are generally limited to the amount of tax that would have been paid on the foreign income in the residence country. This limit has two basic methods of calculation: country by country or worldwide (i.e., aggregating all foreign taxes levied on the firm for calculating the limit). Tax reforms in industrial countries over the past decade have, in some countries, lowered the overall domestic tax burden on foreign-source income below that of the amount of tax in the source country. This places many firms, particularly in the United States, in what is known as an excess foreign tax credit position. Taxation in the country of residence has been completely eliminated, and a residual source-country burden remains. In such circumstances, if the residence country operates a worldwide foreign tax credit limit, relief from source-country taxation does not result in a transfer of tax liability to the residence country and so is of benefit to the firm.

For a branch of a foreign company, the foreign tax credit limit can produce worse results for the taxpayer in the presence of incentives. In particular, if the residence country has a credit system without a system of carryback for excess foreign tax credits, reduced taxation in the source country in the early years of the investment may actually result in overall increased source and residence taxation over a number of years, especially for incentives like accelerated depreciation that affect the timing but not the amount of tax deductions. The residence country collects tax on the investment in the early years because of the low source-country tax arising from the acceleration of the depreciation, but may not fully credit the higher source-country tax in later years because of its foreign tax credit limit. A subsidiary can usually overcome this kind of problem by planning the timing of dividend payments.

The final qualification is that foreign tax credit regimes are difficult to operate effectively. In particular, if offshore financing companies are used, taxation in the residence country can be deferred indefinitely. Dividends paid from the source country can be routed to a third country that does not tax them (usually tax havens). Through tax planning, multinational firms can reduce or eliminate both source and residence taxation on FDI in many cases, as discussed in the international tax chapter under the heading of international tax avoidance and evasion, in which event the existence of tax incentives in the source country and the type of relief system in the residence country become largely irrelevant.

Nevertheless, despite these qualifications, many companies do take into account in their tax planning the eventual tax consequences in the residence country.[40] Whether this approach measures the actual impact residence-country taxation will have after all tax planning routes have been exploited or whether it is a simplification used in the evaluation of projects is not clear and certainly varies depending upon the situation of the foreign investor. Overall, this approach by multinational firms does appear to reduce the effectiveness of tax incentives.

2. Tax Treaties and Tax Sparing

One method that avoids the problem of the residence country taxing away the benefit of a source-country tax incentive is "tax sparing." Under tax sparing, the residence country treats the income remitted as if it had been fully taxed and had not benefited from the tax incentive. This method ensures that the full benefit of the tax incentive goes to the investor and is not simply transferred as tax revenue to the residence country. Tax sparing is usually granted under tax treaties. It is traditionally granted by industrial countries, which are most likely to be the residence country in the flow of international investments, to developing countries, which are more likely to be source countries. In more recent times, tax-sparing provisions have appeared in treaties concluded between industrial and transition countries and can also appear in treaties among developing and transition countries.

The main role of tax-sparing provisions is to allow the source country to provide tax incentives without the concern that it is simply transferring tax revenue to the other country and so can be seen as preserving the sovereignty of the source country. This gives the source country more freedom in designing its incentive regime. The fixed-relief method described below can go further and act as an explicit subsidy or foreign aid program to the source country (or more specifically for investors in that country), where credit is provided by the residence country for more tax than is forgone by the source country.

When tax treaties are drafted, the tax-sparing provision is usually inserted in the article that provides for relief from double taxation. Tax sparing comes in two main forms. One form, which is more common and may be referred to as the contingent relief method, gives relief only for source-country tax that has actually been forgiven as a result of the tax incentive. In relation to a residence country that uses the foreign tax credit, it thus becomes necessary to identify the incentive and provide a method of calculation of the amount of tax forgone. This can be done most readily for simple reliefs in the form of tax holidays, low tax rates, and withholding tax reliefs. The true tax benefits of other incentives, such as tax credits, investment allowances, and, in particular,

---

[40]The consultations carried out in writing OECD, *supra* note 2, confirmed this approach by multinational firms.

accelerated depreciation, are more difficult to calculate and so are not covered by this form of tax-sparing relief.

The other form of tax-sparing relief, which is less common and is usually confined to withholding taxes on passive income, may be referred to as the fixed-relief method (or the matching credit). With this method, the taxpayer is usually deemed to have paid tax at a specified rate on a particular form of income. This approach avoids problems of identification of incentives and quantification of tax forgone. However, its operation is not limited to tax forgone under a specific incentive regime, and the effect on residence-country taxation depends on the relative rates of source-country tax on the specified income and the fixed rate of relief. This last feature no doubt explains why the fixed relief is usually confined to passive income. Tax treaties in this area specify an upper limit for source-country taxation and provide relief through a foreign tax credit (even in countries that generally use the exemption method for business income). Thus, it is a relatively easy matter to match the rate of credit with the limit on source-country taxation. Nonetheless, the source country may have lower rates of tax generally on the kind of income specified than the upper limit of the treaty, in which event the fixed relief more than compensates for any tax forgone under a tax incentive. In a few cases, this outcome is created by the treaty itself through specifying a fixed-relief rate above the withholding rate limit on passive income.[41]

While the fixed-relief method has the capacity to deal in a general way with incentives like accelerated depreciation where tax forgone is difficult to identify, it is rarely applied to business income, presumably for reasons just given. The failure of the contingent and fixed-relief measures to deal with such kinds of incentives can produce perverse results. Although the discussion earlier in this chapter suggests that tax holidays and elimination of cross-border withholding taxes are relatively less effective incentives than accelerated depreciation, the international tax system effectively favors the former over the latter, which probably explains why they are common in developing and transition countries.

In specifying the amount of unpaid tax that may be credited under the contingent relief form of tax sparing, the tax treaty usually refers specifically to the incentive legislation by name and section so that the particular incentives and the amount of tax forgone may be calculated. Not all countries, however, are willing to provide tax-sparing provisions, and a number of countries that have offered them in the past are reconsidering their position.[42] The change

---

[41]Brazil is one country that often exhibits this feature in its treaties; Indonesia and Malaysia use the fixed-relief method, but the rate is usually matched to the maximum withholding rate. See Vann, Tax Treaties: Linkages Between OECD Member Countries and Dynamic Non Member-Economies 57–87 (1996); Brazil-Canada income tax treaty, art. 22(3); Brazil-France income tax treaty, art. 22(2)(d); Indonesia-Japan income tax treaty, art. 23(2).

[42]See OECD, Tax Sparing: A Reconsideration (OECD, Paris, 1998).

in attitude is exemplified in part by the now common use of sunset provisions for tax sparing, often containing a five-year life with the possibility of extensions if both countries agree. The recent shift has been brought about partly on policy grounds (based on the failure of incentives to achieve the benefits claimed) and partly on antiavoidance grounds.

For example, in the case of a tax-sparing credit for interest received from a developing or transition country that has a special incentive relief in relation to withholding tax on the loan, it is possible to shop for an appropriate taxsparing treaty and to use the deemed tax-sparing credit to reduce the tax on income derived locally. Thus, a financier based in a third country lends to two subsidiaries in the selected country with the necessary tax-sparing treaty. One of the subsidiaries invests in the other by way of share capital with the loan funds it has received, and that other subsidiary then lends the total funds to the enterprise in the developing or transition country. The on-lending subsidiary receives more interest than it pays (because part of the ultimate loan funds has been routed into it as share capital) and so has a tax liability in the country where the subsidiary is based. The amounts of the loans have been so planned that this tax liability is offset by the deemed tax-sparing credit (no tax having in fact been paid in the developing or transition country on the outgoing interest). The subsidiary that invested the loan funds from the parent in the other subsidiary has no income from the transaction, but can use interest deductions against other income and so reduce tax in the country where the subsidiary is located.[43] Provisions are now being inserted in tax treaties to overcome such tax planning,[44] but the possibilities of misuse of the tax-sparing credit are obvious from this example. In the case of royalties, tax schemes based on tax sparing often rely on the fact that the definition of royalties in most treaties includes payments for equipment leasing[45] so that finance leases can benefit from the same form of tax planning.

The discussion of tax sparing above has been related to situations where a foreign tax credit is operating in the residence country (which generally in-

---

[43]If the ultimate loan is to be $1,000, the parent might lend $750 to subsidiary 1 and $250 to subsidiary 2 at 10 percent interest. Subsidiary 2 invests $250 in shares of subsidiary 1, which then lends $1,000 to the developing or transition country company at 10 percent. Subsidiary 1 thus has interest income of $100 and interest expense of $75, leaving a profit of $25. If the withholding tax rate on interest that is forgone in the developing or transition country under its tax incentive is 10 percent and the corporate tax rate in the country of the subsidiaries is 40 percent, subsidiary 1 has a tax bill of $10 on its income of $25 and a tax-sparing credit of $10 under the treaty, so that it pays no tax. Subsidiary 2 has interest expense of $25, which it can offset against other income.

[44]*See, e.g.,* the protocols to New Zealand's tax treaties with Singapore (1993) and Fiji and Malaysia (1994).

[45]The 1992 change to art. 12 on royalties in OECD, Model Tax Convention on Income and on Capital (OECD, Paris, loose-leaf), which has not to date been reflected in many actual treaties, was based on the nature of this income rather than on considerations relating to tax sparing. *See* OECD, Trends in International Taxation 13 (1985).

cludes all countries in respect of interest, royalties, and portfolio dividends), and the tax-sparing results from treaty provisions. Even when a country uses an exemption system for foreign branch income and FDI dividends, tax-sparing-type issues can arise, for example, when the exemption is predicated on a subject-to-tax or comparable-tax test. The treaty provisions necessary to provide for tax sparing in such cases are usually simpler, specifying that some tax or a comparable tax is deemed to be paid without having necessarily to calculate the amount of tax, as under the contingent relief method. Some countries even structure their domestic tax system so that unilateral tax sparing is possible.[46]

3. International Double Nontaxation

The various tax avoidance devices used internationally to avoid source and residence taxation are catalogued in chapter 18, along with possible legislative responses. The assumption there is that international double nontaxation is a bad thing that both the residence and source countries should seek to prevent. From an economic perspective, double nontaxation favors international investment over domestic investment, which is generally not regarded as desirable.

When a developing or transition country grants a tax incentive to a foreign investor and an industrial country grants a tax-sparing credit in relation to that incentive, the outcome will often be double nontaxation of the income in question (in the source country because of the incentive and in the residence country because of the tax-sparing credit). Here the countries are cooperating to bring about a situation of double nontaxation, rather than cooperating to prevent it. It is no wonder in particular that taxpayers seek to exploit tax-sparing situations and in general that there is a lack of clarity as to whether double nontaxation is good or bad.

In recent years, industrial, developing, and transition countries have moved to create tax niches that attract internationally mobile activities, especially regional headquarters and offshore finance centers. These regimes work by giving tax exemptions or reductions to the activities in question. It is not customary to give tax-sparing relief for such activities, and, indeed, companies that benefit from such regimes are increasingly being excluded from the reliefs under tax treaties. It is often possible nonetheless to achieve double nontaxation through such arrangements, especially if the country of ultimate ownership is an exemption country. These regimes are the subject of further comment in relation to tax competition below.

---

[46]E.g., AUS ITAA § 160AFF (providing for the making of tax-sparing regulations under its unilateral foreign tax credit); Australia has also structured its controlled foreign company regime to permit tax sparing, *Income Tax Regulations* s 152H.

4. Tax Treaty Network

Apart from countries entering into tax treaties specifically for the benefits of tax sparing, a tax treaty network is an important ingredient in the mix of tax policies to attract FDI. Tax treaties are dealt with in more detail in chapter 18. There are two broad groups of tax treaties that require a different policy perspective. The first comprises treaties between countries in a region and countries outside the region that are prospective sources of FDI. From the perspective of the foreign firm, a tax treaty establishes the "rules of the game" for the interaction of the source- and residence-country tax systems. From the perspective of the taxing authority, it provides access to the exchange of information facilities that would allow a better chance to police some of the cross-border tax avoidance schemes that firms might employ.

The second group comprises treaties among countries within a region, which should be designed to facilitate flows of investment and trade within the region, reflecting historic close economic ties. Such treaties often result in provisions on withholding taxes that are less stringent than in treaties with countries from outside the region. They should also be used to allow closer administrative cooperation to help counteract regional tax evasion. This difference in treaty policy within a region is well reflected, for example, in the tax treaties of the Baltic countries (Estonia, Latvia, and Lithuania).

The two groups of treaties have the potential to interact in ways that can hamper a country's ability to ensure that it receives its fair share of tax revenues. This problem can arise if withholding tax rates on certain types of distributions between countries in the region and between countries within and outside the region vary, which is most likely to occur if countries in the region operate separate tax treaty negotiation programs. To counter this problem, countries that maintain close economic links should attempt to develop a coordinated tax treaty strategy and perhaps negotiate in concert. Consideration should also to be given to the problem of treaty shopping in this context and the possible inclusion of provisions to protect the domestic tax base against this practice.

C. Tax Competition

Experience with tax incentives, particularly in Asia,[47] suggests that, when so-called footloose manufacturing plants for export are choosing the location for a new plant, they may be influenced by tax incentives when they are comparing sites in different countries that are otherwise similar. This influence may also occur when a firm targets a region for a strategic investment, but is indifferent as to which country it operates from. For example, it may view any one national market in the region to be inadequate for efficient produc-

---

[47]*See* Easson, *supra* note 6, at 437–38.

tion and may plan to supply the entire region from one plant. Countries may therefore be tempted to try to attract these footloose export industries.

Another reason that policymakers give for offering tax incentives is that they are necessary to maintain their country's competitive position vis-à-vis neighboring countries. They may view another country as having a natural advantage, such as location or raw materials, that makes it more attractive as a destination for foreign investment.

This rationale can be criticized on basic principles. All countries face natural advantages and disadvantages in relation to other countries. A tax incentive merely shifts the private disadvantage from the investor in the particular activity to other economic agents in the country. It does nothing to change the total disadvantage to society because it does not affect the social rate of return, which is the sum of the private after-tax return and the taxes collected from the activity. In fact, the competitive position of the country might be diminished overall as the production in the economy is less efficiently organized than it would have been without the incentive.

It is not necessary to rely on such economic efficiency arguments, however, to see the potential futility of tax competition. A country that views itself as competing for foreign investment will respond to the tax incentives of another country by introducing some form of offsetting incentive. In the end, the tax incentives offered by the two countries do nothing to alter the relative incentive to invest between the two countries. The only result of the competition is that both countries receive lower tax revenues. They would both be better off if they could agree not to compete.

The problem of tax competition is not confined to developing and transition countries. The heightened tax competition among industrial countries in niche areas like headquarters and offshore finance regimes has become an area of concern.[48] Tax incentive regimes for foreign investors in developing and transition countries also give rise to tax competition, not only among these countries but also ultimately with domestic investment in industrial countries. There have been some attempts to reduce tax competition among transition countries.[49] International cooperation in these areas is likely to increase in future years with a view to establishing a narrower range of cases where international double nontaxation is an acceptable policy.

---

[48]Commission of the European Communities, Taxation in the European Union, Brussels, Mar. 20, 1996, Document No. SEC(96) 487 final; Commission of the European Communities, Towards Tax Co-ordination in the European Union (1997) COM(97) final; Commission of the European Communities, A Package to Handle Harmful Tax Competition in the European Union (1997), COM (97) 564 final. The EU in December 1997 and the OECD in January 1998 have approved packages of measures to deal with tax competition. See OECD, Harmful Tax Competition: An Emerging Global Issue (OECD, Paris, 1998).

[49]The Czech Republic, Hungary, Poland, and the Slovak Republic agreed to phase out their tax incentives for foreign investors as of January 1, 1993.

Appendix. Tax Holidays and Loss Carryovers

The following example shows how a poorly designed tax holiday or insufficient loss carryovers can be less beneficial to a start-up company than a good loss-carryover period. In the example, a firm makes an investment of $100 and begins production in the first year. Production is lower than full capacity because markets are just being developed. The firm incurs start-up costs of hiring and training workers and improving production techniques as well as initial marketing costs in the first two years. The net result is losses in the first two years and profit in the next three, with an overall profit of $25 over the period (see Table 2).

Taxes payable are calculated under a variety of assumptions.

In Case 1, there is a loss-carryover period of five years. No taxes are payable until the fifth year, and the total of taxable income is equal to the total amount of profit.

Table 2. Interaction of Loss Carryovers and Tax Holidays

Accounting Income for Firm with Initial Investment of $100

Year	1	2	3	4	5	Total
Revenue	15	25	30	40	50	160
Start-up costs	20	15	0	0	0	35
Income	−5	10	30	40	50	125
Depreciation	20	20	20	20	20	100
Profit	−25	−10	10	20	30	25

Firm's Tax Calculation Under Different Assumptions

1. Multiple-year loss carryover

Year	1	2	3	4	5	Total
Unused prior-year loss	0	25	35	25	5	—
Profit	−25	−10	10	20	30	25
Loss used	0	0	10	20	5	35
Taxable income	0	0	0	0	25	25

2. Two-year loss carryover

Year	1	2	3	4	5	Total
Second prior-year loss	0	0	25	10	0	—
First prior-year loss	0	25	10	0	0	—
Profit	−25	−10	10	20	30	25
Prior-year loss used	0	0	10	10	0	20
Taxable income	0	0	0	10	30	40

3. Holiday, first production

Year	1	2	3	4	5	Total
Taxable income	0	0	10	20	30	60

4. Holiday, first profit two-year loss carryover

Year	1	2	3	4	5	Total
Taxable income	0	0	0	0	30	30

Case 2 shows what can happen if the loss-carryover period is restricted to two years. The losses that had previously been carried over from year two to year five are no longer available, and so taxable income increases by $5 in that year.

In Case 3, a tax holiday of two years starts when production begins, the form of holidays in a number of transition countries (a two-year period is short, but is used here to simplify the example). Unfortunately for the company, it is in the typical position of a large capital project, and it registers losses in the first two years. Not only does it not receive the benefit of the holiday, but it loses the ability to shelter future income from tax with loss carryovers. Accordingly, it begins to pay tax in year three at the expiration of the holiday, and its overall taxable income increases from $25 to $60 over the period.

In Case 4, the tax holiday starts in the first profitable year, year three, and continues for two years. In addition, it is assumed that the loss-carryover period is two years. Both of these features have appeared in tax systems in transition countries. The first year of taxation is the fifth year, as in Case 1. However, the taxable income is greater as losses can no longer be carried over from the second year. Therefore, total taxable income increases from $25 to $60.

These situations could be avoided only if the holiday were to start the first year that there were cumulative profits and if the loss-carryover period were extended. However, this scenario provides a period of six years over which the project does not pay taxes, and the use of a full loss carryover may well be the best targeted way to provide an incentive to invest while maintaining some revenues from taxation.

Comparative Tax Law Bibliography

This is a basic bibliography for the study of comparative tax law. On the assumption that many readers will prefer books in English, for jurisdictions with a language other than English, some books in English have been included, even if outdated. The bibliography is purposely short so as to be manageable; this has required many excellent books to be excluded. Those studying more deeply the tax laws of particular countries will no doubt be able to locate these books without too much difficulty. We do not list separately the *Cahiers de droit fiscal international*, published annually by the International Fiscal Association, which are extremely useful on specialized topics, or the publications of the International Bureau of Fiscal Documentation (see its annual catalogue). See also the annual catalogue of Kluwer, which contains a number of works in comparative tax law and comparative law generally.

Argentina	Enrique J. Reig, Impuesto a las Ganancias (Ediciones Macchi 1991). ISBN: 950-537-182-9.
Australia	Graeme S. Cooper et al., Income Taxation: Commentary and Materials (2d ed., Law Book Co. 1993). ISBN: 0-455-21165-5.
	Geoffrey Lehmann and Cynthia Coleman, Taxation Law in Australia (3rd ed., Butterworths 1994). ISBN: 0-409-30866-8.
	Robin Woellner et al., Australian Taxation Law (8th ed., CCH Australia 1997). ISBN: 1-86264-918-9.
Belgium	Pierre Coppens and André Bailleux, Droit fiscal (2 vols.) (2d ed., Maison Larcier 1992).
	Jacques Malherbe, Droit fiscal international (Maison Larcier 1994). ISBN: 2-8044-0128-6.
	Albert Tiberghien, Belgian Taxation: An Outline (Kluwer 1987). ISBN: 90-6544-342-8.
	Albert Tiberghien, Manuel de droit fiscal (16th ed., Kluwer 1995). ISBN: 2-87377-1879.

Canada
Ernst & Young, The Complete Guide to the Goods and Services Tax (The Canadian Institute of Chartered Accountants 1990). ISBN: 0-88800-248-3.

Vern Krishna, The Fundamentals of Canadian Income Tax (5th ed., Carswell 1995). ISBN: 0-459-57455-8.

France
Maurice Cozian, Précis de fiscalité des enterprises (15th ed., Litec 1991). ISBN: 2-7111-2059-7.

Direction Générale des Impôts, Précis de fiscalité (annual).

Claude Gambier and Jean Ives Mercier, Les Impôts en France (1991).

Guy Gest and Gilbert Tixier, Droit fiscal international (4th ed., Presses Universitaires de France 1986). ISBN: 2-1030-432352.

Harvard Law School, International Program in Taxation: Taxation in France (Commerce Clearing House 1966).

Thierry Lambert, Contrôle fiscal: Droit et pratique (Presses Universitaires de France 1991). ISBN: 2-13-044018-5.

Gilbert Tixier and Guy Gest, Droit fiscal international (2d ed., Presses Universitaires de France 1990). ISBN: 2-13-043235-2.

Germany
Harvard Law School, International Program in Taxation: Taxation in the Federal Republic of Germany (Commerce Clearing House 1963).

Brigitte Knobbe-Keuk, Bilanz- und Unternehmenssteuerrecht (9th ed., O. Schmidt 1993). ISBN: 3504-2066.

Joachim Lange and Klaus Tipke, Steuerrecht: Ein systematischer Grundriss (13th ed., O. Schmidt 1991). ISBN: 3-504-20046-4.

Klaus Tipke, Die Steuerrechtsordnung (O. Schmidt 1993). ISBN: 3-504-201010.

Klaus Vogel, Klaus Vogel on Double Taxation Conventions (Kluwer Law and Taxation Publishers 1991). ISBN: 90-6544-447-5.

Italy
Augusto Fantozzi, Diritto Tributario (1994). ISBN: 88-02-4454-6.

Raffaello Lupi, Diritto Tributario (2 vols.) (4th ed., Giuffrè 1996). ISBN: 88-14-06224-2, 88-14-06281-1.

Memento Pratico, IPSOA-Francis Lefebvre Fiscale, 1997. ISBN: 88-217-0958-2.

Japan   Yuji Gomi, Guide to Japanese Taxes 1994–95 (Zaikei Shôhô Sha) (annual). ISBN: 4-88177-136-1.

Hiromitsu Ishi, The Japanese Tax System (Clarendon Press 1993). ISBN: 0-19-828616-3.

Ministry of Finance, Tax Bureau, An Outline of Japanese Taxes (Printing Bureau, Ministry of Finance) (issued annually; obtainable from Seifu Kankobutso Service Center, 1-2-1 Kasumigaseki, Chitoda-ku, Tokyo 100).

Mexico   Emilio Margáin Manautou, Introducción al Estudio de Derecho Tributario Mexicano (Editorial Porrúa 1996).

Netherlands   Gerrit te Spenke, Taxation in the Netherlands (3rd ed., Kluwer Law and Taxation Publishers 1995). ISBN: 9-0654-5994.

South Africa   Costa Divaris and Michael L. Stein, Silke on South African Income Tax (1989 with loose-leaf updates). ISBN: 0-7021-1336-0.

Spain   César Albiñana, Sistema Tributario Español y Comparado (2d ed., Editorial Tecnos 1992). ISBN: 84-309-2118-4.

Sweden   Harvard Law School, International Program in Taxation: Taxation in Sweden (Little, Brown and Co. 1959).

Switzerland   Harvard Law School, International Program in Taxation: Taxation in Switzerland (Commerce Clearing House 1976).

Ernst Höhn, Ein Grundriss des Schweizerischen Steuerrechts für Unterricht und Selbststudium (7th ed., Paul Haupt 1993). ISBN: 3-25804-7375.

Jean-Marc Rivier, Droit fiscal suisse: L'imposition du revenu et de la fortune (Editions Ides et Calendes 1980).

Walter Ryser and Bernard Rolli, Précis de droit fiscal suisse (3d ed., Editions Staempfli 1994). ISBN: 3-7272-0956-9.

United Kingdom	Butterworths U.K. Tax Guide (John Tiley ed.) (annual).
	Chris Whitehouse et al., Revenue Law—Principles and Practice (15th ed., Butterworths 1997). ISBN: 0-40689-4949.
United States	Boris I. Bittker and James S. Eustice, Federal Income Taxation of Corporations and Shareholders (6th ed., Warren, Gorham & Lamont 1994). ISBN: 0-79131-8656.
	Boris I. Bittker and Lawrence Lokken, Federal Taxation of Income, Estates and Gifts (5 vols.) (2d ed., 1989).
	Bruce Hopkins, The Law of Tax-Exempt Organizations (6th ed., Wiley 1992). ISBN: 0-471-555-101.
	Joseph Isenbergh, International Taxation: U.S. Taxation of Foreign Persons and Foreign Income (2d ed., loose-leaf, Little, Brown, and Co. 1996). ISBN: 0-31643-2903 (v. 1); 0-31643-2938 (v. 2); 0-31643-2512 (v. 3).
	William S. McKee, William F. Nelson, and Robert L. Whitmire, Federal Taxation of Partnerships and Partners (2d ed., Warren, Gorham, & Lamont 1990, with annual supplements). ISBN: 0-7913-2970-4.
	Michael I. Saltzman, IRS Practice and Procedure (2d ed., Warren, Gorham & Lamont 1991, with supplements). ISBN: 0-7913-2019-7.
	Stanley S. Surrey et al., Federal Income Taxation: Cases and Materials (Foundation Press 1986). ISBN: 0-88277-3275.
General	Hugh Ault et al., Comparative Income Taxation: A Structural Analysis (Kluwer 1997). ISBN: 90-411-0605-7.
	Sijbren Cnossen, Excise Systems: A Global Study of the Selective Taxation of Goods and Services (Johns Hopkins 1977). ISBN: 0-8018-1962-8.
	Organization for Economic Cooperation and Development, Taxpayers' Rights and Obligations: A Survey of the Legal Situation in OECD Countries (1990). ISBN: 92-64-13390.
	Alan A. Tait, Value-Added Tax: International Practice and Problems (IMF 1988). ISBN: 1-55775-012-2.
	Ben Terra and Peter Wattel, European Tax Law (Kluwer Law and Taxation Publishers 1993). ISBN: 90-6544-784-9.

Tax Policy for Developing Countries

There are many books, but by consulting the following, which have been published in the past few years, and the references listed in these, the reader should be able to locate most of the literature.

Ehtisham Ahmad and Nicholas Stern, The Theory and Practice of Tax Reform in Developing Countries (Cambridge University Press 1991). ISBN: 0-521-39742.

Richard M. Bird and Oliver Oldman, eds., Taxation in Developing Countries (4th ed., Johns Hopkins 1990). ISBN: 0-8018-4265-4.

Richard M. Bird, Tax Policy and Economic Development (Johns Hopkins 1992). ISBN: 0-801-842239.

Malcolm Gillis, ed., Tax Reform in Developing Countries (Duke University Press 1989). ISBN: 0-82230-8983.

Malcolm Gillis, Carl S. Shoup, and Gerardo P. Sicat, eds., Value Added Taxation in Developing Countries (World Bank 1990).

Richard Goode, Government Finance in Developing Countries (Brookings 1984). ISBN: 0-815731-965.

Richard Goode, *Tax Advice to Developing Countries: An Historical Survey*, 21 World Development 37 (1993).

Javad Khalilzadeh-Shirazi and Anwar Shah, eds., Tax Policy in Developing Countries (World Bank 1991). ISBN: 0-8213-1990-6.

Charles E. McLure et al., The Taxation of Income from Business and Capital in Colombia (Duke University Press 1990). ISBN: 0-8223-0925-4.

David Newbery and Nicholas Stern, eds., The Theory of Taxation for Developing Countries (Oxford 1987). ISBN: 1-55775-490.

Parthasarathi Shome, ed., Tax Policy Handbook (IMF 1995). ISBN: 1-55775-490-X.

Alan Tait, ed., Value-Added Tax: Administrative and Policy Issues, Occasional Paper No. 88 (IMF 1991). ISBN: 1-55775-184-6.

Vito Tanzi, Public Finance in Developing Countries (Edward Elgar 1991). ISBN: 1-85278-374-5.

Wayne Thirsk, ed., Tax Reform in Developing Countries (1997). ISBN: 0-8213-3999-0.

Bibliography of National Tax Laws of IMF Member Countries

A number of publications provide summaries of the tax laws of the world's countries.[1] The full text of the laws, however, is not available in one place. Nor is there a bibliography that lists the tax laws of each country and where the full text may be obtained. This bibliography seeks to fill this gap. It should be of use to those interested in obtaining the text of the tax laws of a particular country or in getting a sense of the structure of the tax legislation. Its panoramic aspect should make it of interest to those studying comparative tax law. For those engaged in tax law reform internationally, the laws listed in this bibliography represent the raw material for such an effort.

This bibliography is believed to be the most comprehensive currently available in one book. Yet, given resource constraints, it has not been possible on this first attempt to produce a complete list of tax laws.[2] We have, however, listed sources for the principal tax laws for virtually all IMF member countries.

---

[1]Summaries for most countries of the world can be found in the various publications of the International Bureau of Fiscal Documentation (IBFD). Recently, the country chapters tend to include a bibliography of legislation. A one-volume summary covering 123 countries is Coopers & Lybrand, 1997 International Tax Summaries. This work is revised annually. Francophone Africa is covered by Fiscalite africaine, an annual three-volume set published by Editions Fiduciaire France Afrique (Ernst & Young International), Paris. Price Waterhouse publishes annually Individual Taxes: A Worldwide Summary and Corporate Taxes: A Worldwide Summary. Ernst & Young publishes guides entitled "Doing Business in [name of country]." Deloitte Touche Tohmatsu International publishes International Tax and Business Guide for numerous countries. These contain a list of the major tax laws of each country covered. The European Commission periodically publishes an Inventory of Taxes, which summarizes all the taxes of the European Union (EU) member countries. It contains in most cases the citations for the tax laws, although not their full text. We draw on this publication in this bibliography. European Commission: Inventory of Taxes Levied in the Member States of the European Communities (16th ed. 1996). This publication contains a survey of the duties and taxes in force in Belgium, Denmark, France, Germany, Greece, Ireland, Italy, Luxembourg, Netherlands, Portugal, Spain, and the United Kingdom on Jan. 1, 1994. Tax Management publishes quite useful summaries of the tax laws of a limited number of countries.

[2]Not all the laws listed are up to date, not all tax laws are included, and not all available sources are listed. Given the multiplicity of sources and languages involved, some typographical errors may lurk somewhere in this bibliography despite our efforts to weed them out, so caveat lector.

In the case of laws, primarily for minor taxes, where we have not identified sources, we have tried to list the taxes or tax laws in force.[3]

Even as a matter of theory, a comprehensive listing of tax laws is elusive, as the concept of a tax law is an elastic one. We have generally excluded customs laws, although these are relevant for some taxes, such as the value-added tax and excises. Although similar to taxes, customs duties are traditionally thought of separately from taxes, largely for institutional reasons, and, given that this book does not cover customs, they are not included here. We have also not included laws on social security contributions in a systematic way, except when these are included in collections of tax laws.[4] Moreover, besides the laws that impose taxes, there are often tax provisions in other laws (usually relieving some deserving industry or group from tax), such as laws on investment or specialized laws for particular industries. To understand the tax laws, reference will often have to be made to provisions of other laws that are not specific to tax, such as the constitution, the civil or commercial code, the criminal code, the code of civil procedure, labor laws, and others. To identify all the relevant provisions would be a significant effort, requiring experts in each country to be consulted, and this task has not been attempted. Tax treaties are also not included in our listing, because comprehensive collections of tax treaties are available.[5]

The distinction between taxes and tax laws should be kept in mind. A tax law may impose more than one tax. Some tax laws do not impose a tax; for example, a tax law may govern procedure, or exemptions, or certain aspects of a tax, so that several laws must be considered together in order to understand the rules applicable to a single tax. This bibliography generally lists the tax laws, not the taxes.

The bibliography is limited to national tax laws; thus, taxes of political subdivisions of a country are generally not included. Moreover, only the basic laws themselves are included, and not the regulations and other secondary legislation. Only the most recently available texts that have been located by the compilers are included in this list. For countries that have codified all their tax laws in one tax code, this bibliography contains only one entry, namely, for the tax code. Reference to the tax code itself will be sufficient for most cases; however, practitioners in these countries also consult the amending laws because not all amendments, particularly those that are transitional or those with a narrow scope of application, take the form of textual amendment to the code. No attempt is made here, however, to list all the amending laws, both because this would be a laborious exercise and because those with a sufficient interest can be expected to have access to these laws already.

---

[3]Unless otherwise indicated, these lists rely on the sources cited in note 1 *supra*.

[4]*See* vol. 1, at 345–48 for discussion of whether social security contributions should be considered taxes.

[5]*See supra* ch. 18, note 7.

The bibliography also sets forth complete citations for the laws cited in the footnotes in this volume. For example, in the footnotes, the Profit Tax Law of Albania is cited as ALB PT. The abbreviations used in the footnotes are noted in the relevant entry for the law.

Notes to the Bibliography

The format is generally as follows: number of law, title of law (in original language), translation of title, date of enactment, and citation to official gazette or the source where the law is reprinted.

For laws that have been consolidated, the amending acts are not listed. Only the date of the last amendment or the date of the consolidation is indicated. Where amending acts are listed, they are indented.

Where laws have been obtained from a commercial publisher, the publisher's name (and, if available, contact details) is indicated. Presumably, the most up-to-date revision will be available from these publishers.

Where the original language of the legislation is not English, the language of the law or of the translation available is indicated.[6]

For some countries, a brief explanatory note precedes the entry.

Tax Law Compendia That Cover Multiple Jurisdictions

Tax Laws of the World

In a multivolume loose-leaf series called *Tax Laws of the World*, Foreign Tax Law Publishers produces an English translation of the major tax laws of many countries, cited in this bibliography as TLW. The current list of available laws is available on the Internet (http://www.foreignlaw.com).

Latin America

A collection of tax legislation, limited to Latin American countries, can be found on a compact disk published by the International Bureau of Fiscal Documentation (IBFD), which is updated annually. The laws contained in this collection are cited here. The IBFD collection does not include all the tax laws of the countries covered, but it does include the major tax laws. They are in full text in the original language only (Spanish or Portuguese). Some regulations are also included.

---

[6]In some cases, we can only cite an unpublished English translation. We nevertheless added these to the list with the intent to give the most complete picture of a country's tax legislation.

Tax Analysts

Electronic databases are becoming increasingly important. TaxBase, which is published in conjunction with *Tax Notes International*, makes available the full text of an increasing number of tax laws, and this bibliography indicates when the source as of the time of publication is TaxBase. TaxBase is available on the Internet by subscription. In most cases, what is available is an English translation. TaxBase also contains articles and other information besides the text of laws. Tax Analysts also publishes on a CD, called the North American OneDisc, the tax laws of Canada (in French and English), Mexico (in Spanish and English), and the United States.

Lexis

Although Lexis contains an astounding amount of material, collections of non-U.S. law are limited. Extensive collections exist for a few countries, but there is little or nothing for most countries. Instead of indicating in this list all the countries represented in Lexis, we have assumed that subscribers to Lexis will consult the annual catalogue for what is available.

Central and Eastern European Legal Texts

This is a series of translations published by Columbia University, which we cite as CEEL (also available on Lexis). These cover only a fraction of the legislation of the region, and most of the tax laws are out of date although the translations are generally of high quality.

Other Internet Sites

The information superhighway contains a number of seductive billboards promising various things, including foreign laws. However, when one gets to the relevant site it often seems to be "in development." This is not the place to give a guide to such sites, which in any event are constantly changing. We include a few citations. So far, not many tax laws are available in full text on the Internet, although this is likely to change over the coming years.

Foreign Law: Current Sources of Codes and Basic Legislation

For a general guide to finding legislation, a multivolume work published in 1989 provides a guide to obtaining laws of the world's countries.[7] It contains some references to tax laws, but because it is a general work those references are less detailed than the ones found here.

---

[7] Tomás Reynolds & Arturo Flores, Foreign Law: Current Sources of Codes and Basic Legislation in Jurisdictions of the World (1989, with loose-leaf updates).

Finding a Country's Tax Laws

To find the tax laws of a particular country, besides consulting the listing in this bibliography, readers may find it helpful to consult the sources described in the section Notes to the Bibliography, above, and the summaries described in note one above. These sources are periodically updated, and a law for a particular country might subsequently be found in one of these places even if it is not listed in this bibliography. Because amendments to tax laws are made every year in most countries, the listing in this bibliography will not be up to date at the time it is consulted. However, one can generally obtain a current version by asking for the latest edition of the works cited.

Tax laws are, of course, enactments of the legislature, and one can therefore always find them by consulting the session laws of the particular country. The session laws are a chronological publication of the enactments of the legislature. They may be published in the official gazette or in a separate publication reserved for acts of the legislature.[8] The session laws will have to be consulted to update any consolidated text of the law.

While it is possible to rely solely on the session laws, this is not usually desirable in the tax area. The reason is that, unless the tax law in question is a new one, there will usually have been a number of amending laws. If one can locate all of these, then it is possible to ascertain the text of the law as amended by consolidating all the amendments. This work being somewhat tedious, it normally does not make sense to do it if someone else has already done so.

There are several different types of sources for consolidations. Commercial publications are normally timely and for many countries are not very expensive. In a number of countries, commercial publishers have put together a consolidated collection of the tax laws in one or more volumes. In countries for which we have located a commercial publisher, a listing is included in this bibliography. We have not, however, tried to list all available commercial publishers in countries where there is more than one. In addition to paper copies of legislation, electronic versions of tax legislation are increasingly becoming available. Often, regulations, cases, and other materials are included. We have not included these sources here; they will presumably be known to practitioners in the country concerned.

A second type of source for consolidations is the ministry of finance or the tax authority. Often, one of these agencies publishes a consolidation, particularly in countries where no commercial publisher has done so.

---

[8]See Reynolds & Flores, *supra* note 7, for a discussion of sources for session laws in particular countries. The Bluebook also has citations for the session laws of many countries. In some countries, particularly in the former Soviet Union, we have cited to newspapers in which a particular law was published, rather than to the official session laws. This is because in some countries newspapers are a more timely source, given delays in official publications. (At the time of writing, the session laws of Russia are coming out in quite a timely and efficient manner, however.)

Finally, in a number of countries, particularly English-speaking ones, the consolidated laws are periodically published by the government printer.[9] Usually the consolidation is done pursuant to authority of a law and has legal effect. In some cases, a consolidation is done every decade or so. In others, the consolidation is kept up to date with loose-leaf inserts. Where such a consolidation is cited, we have also tried to include citations to the laws passed after the date of the consolidation.

Recognizing that many readers will need translations of the laws rather than the laws in the original language, we have listed translations in the bibliography, although not on a comprehensive basis. Multijurisdictional sources for translations are listed in the section Notes to the Bibliography. In addition, the bibliography lists commercial publishers in specific countries that have published translations.

Abbreviations Used in Bibliography

TLW	Tax Laws of the World
IBFD-CIAT	CD-ROM published by the International Bureau of Fiscal Documentation
TaxBase	database found at http://www.taxbase.tax.org
EU Inventory	Inventory of Taxes in the European Union
CEEL	Central and Eastern European Legal Texts
NTIS	National Technical Information Service, U.S. Department of Commerce
GLIN	Global Legal Information Network, a Library of Congress website

Tax Laws

Afghanistan, Islamic State of (AFG)

Income Tax Law, *reprinted in* TLW (as amended to May 1978) [in English].

Foreign and Domestic Private Investment Law (as amended to May 1978), *id.*

Albania (ALB)

The official gazette (in Albanian) is called Fletorja zyrtare. We have relied on Compilation of Legal Acts of Albania as Amended: Taxation, by The Albania Law Report, Tirana, Albania, published by ALBAL SH.P.K.

Ligj nr. 7676, Për tatimin mbi qarkullimin (Law on Turnover Tax), Mar. 2, 1993, *reprinted in* The Albania Law Report (Albal SH.P.K. Tirana), Compilation of Legal Acts of Albania as amended as of Apr. 1996 [in Albanian, English].

---

[9]*See id.* for discussion of consolidation in particular jurisdictions.

PT—Ligj nr. 7677, Për tatimin mbi fitimin (Law on Profit Tax), Mar. 3, 1993 [in Albanian, English], id.

Ligj nr. 7678, Për akcizat në Republikën e Shqipërisë (Law on Excise Tax in the Republic of Albania), Mar. 9, 1993 [in Albanian, English], id.

Ligj nr. 7679, Për tatimin mbi biznesin e vogël (Law on Small Business Tax), Mar. 3, 1993 [in Albanian, English], id.

Ligj nr. 7681, Për administrimin e tatimeve dhe taksave në Republikën e Shqipërisë (Law on the Administration of Taxes in the Republic of Albania) [in Albanian, English], id.

Ligj nr. 7758, Për dokumentimin dhe mbajtjen e llogarive për tatiment (Law for Documentation and Keeping Documents for Taxes), Oct. 12, 1993 [in Albanian, English], id.

Ligj nr. 7777, Për sistemin e taksave në Republikën e Shqipërisë (Law for the Fee System in the Republic of Albania), Dec. 22, 1993 [in Albanian, English], id.

Ligj nr. 7786, Për tatimin mbi të ardhurat personale (Law for Personal Income Tax), Jan. 27, 1994 [in Albanian, English], id.

Ligj nr. 7805, Për tatimin mbi pasurinë (Law for Property Tax in the Republic of Albania), Mar. 16, 1994 [in Albanian, English], id.

Ligj nr. 7928, Për tatimin mbi vlerën e shtuar (Law for Value Added Tax), Apr. 27, 1995 [in Albanian, English], id.

Law N° 7680 on the Tax System in the Republic of Albania, Mar. 9, 1993 [in English].

Algeria (DZA)

Codes des impôts directs (Code of Direct Taxes), reprinted in Direction générale des impôts, Code des impôts directs et taxes assimilées (Office des publications universitaires 1992) [in French].

Tax on Global Income and Tax on Company Profits, reprinted in TLW (as amended up to Oct. 1993) [in English].

Value Added Tax, reprinted in TLW (as amended to Oct. 1993) [in English].

Ordonnance N° 95-27, Dec. 30, 1995, portant loi de finances pour 1996, Journal officiel, Dec. 31, 1995 [in French].

Angola (AGO)

As of 1993–94, the following taxes were in effect in Angola: imposto sobre os rendimentos do trabalho (tax on earned income), imposto sobre o aplicação de capitais *(tax on capital income)*, imposto industrial *(industrial tax)*, imposto de produção de petróleo *(oil production tax)*, imposto de rendimento de petróleo *(oil income tax)*, imposto de transações sobre o petróleo *(tax on petroleum transactions)*, imposto de consumo *(consumption tax)*, imposto predial urbano *(urban real estate tax)*, imposto sobre as sucessões e doações *(inheritance and gift tax)*, sisa sobre a transmissção de imobiliários por título oneroso *(real estate transfer tax)*, and imposto de selo *(stamp tax)*. *Royalties and other special regimes apply to mining companies. In terms of legislation, the only reliable source we have found thus far is the official gazette (* Diário da república*).*

Legislative Decree N° 3868, General Tax Code and Income Tax Law, *reprinted in* 1 TLW (as amended to Aug. 1984) [in English].

Lei N° 14/96 de Alteração ao código geral tributário (Amendment to the General Tax Code) Diário da república, May 31, 1996 [in Portuguese].

Codigo do imposto industrial (actualizado) (Industrial Tax Code) (mimeo publication by Direcção Nacional de Impostos) [in Portuguese].

Lei N° 12/92 que aprova o novo código de imposto sobre os rendimentos do trabalho (Law Approving the New Code of the Tax on Labor Income), Diário da república, June 19, 1992 [in Portuguese].

Lei N° 9/89 dos crimes contra a economia (Law on Economic Crime), Diário da república, Dec. 11, 1989 (see art. 38 on tax fraud) [in Portuguese].

Imposto de selo (Stamp tax), amended by Decree N° 67/91, Diário da república, Nov. 15, 1991 [in Portuguese].

Lei N° 4/96 dá nova redacção ao artigo 114-A da tabela geral do imposto do selo (Law on the New Wording of Art. 114-A of the General Table on Stamp Tax), Diário da república, April 12, 1996 [in Portuguese].

Lei N° 6/96 dá nova redacção aos artigos 17 e 28 do código do imposto predial urbano, (Law on the New Wording of Arts. 17 and 28 of the Urban Property Tax Code), Diário da república, Apr. 19, 1996 [in Portuguese].

Lei N° 7/96 dá nova redacção ao artigo 32 do código do imposto industrial (Law on New Wording of Art. 32 of the Industrial Tax Code), Diário da república, Apr. 19, 1996 [in Portuguese].

Lei N° 12/96 que cria a unidade de correção fiscal (Law Creating Unit of Fiscal Adjustment) [i.e., inflation adjustment], Diário da república, May 24, 1996 [in Portuguese].

Antigua and Barbuda (ATG)

A consolidated index of statutes and subsidiary legislation (as of Jan. 1, 1996) has been published by the Faculty of Law Library, University of the West Indies, Barba-

dos. This lists the amending laws, and so they will not be listed here. The tax laws are listed below. The following taxes also apply: education levy (Board of Education Act 1994), social security levy, medical benefits levy (Medical Benefits Act 1978), telecommunications tax, insurance premium levy, casino tax, lottery and betting tax, and foreign currency levy.

Business Tax Act (Cap. 65).

Consumption Tax Act 1993.

Cruise Passenger Tax Act (Cap. 122).

Customs Service Tax Act (Cap. 128).

Customs Service Tax (Continuation) Act (Cap. 129).

Embarkation Tax Act (Cap. 146).

Entertainment Duty Act (Cap. 154).

Excise Act (Cap. 158).

Fiscal Incentives Act (Cap. 172).

Football Pool Betting Tax Act (Cap. 174).

Hotel Guest (Levy) Act (Cap. 202).

Hotels Tax Act (Cap. 205).

Income Tax Act (Cap. 212).

Income Tax (Federal Endowments) Act (Cap. 151).

Land Sales Duty Act (Cap. 236).

Property Tax Act (Cap. 348).

Provisional Collection of Taxes Act (Cap. 351).

Rum Duty Act (Cap. 388).

Stamp Act (Cap. 410).

Timesharing Tax Act (Cap. 428).

Travel Tax Act (Cap. 438).

Argentina (ARG)

Cites to B.O. are to the official gazette: Boletín oficial de la República Argentina; for the compilation of amendments, we have relied on a private publisher: La Ley. It issues annually a thick two-volume set of tax legislation (Legislación impositiva). This is more comprehensive than IBFD-CIAT.

Ley N° 11.683, Procedimiento para la aplicación, percepción y fiscalización de impuestos (Procedures for the Application, Collection and Inspection of Taxes), B.O., Dec. 11, 1978 (as amended to Dec. 1996), *reprinted in* Legislación impositiva, La Ley [in Spanish], *and in* IBFD-CIAT [in Spanish].

Ley N° 23.771, Régimen penal tributario (Criminal Legislation as Relating to Tax), B.O., Feb. 27, 1990 (as amended by Law N° 23.871, B.O., Oct. 31, 1990), *reprinted in* Legislación impositiva, *supra* [in Spanish].

Ley N° 19.549, Procedimientos administrativos (Administrative Procedures), B.O., Apr. 27, 1972 (as amended by Law N° 21.686, B.O., Nov. 25, 1977), *id.* [in Spanish].

Ley N° 22.610, Tasa de actuación ante el tribunal fiscal de la nación (Proceedings in the National Taxation Court), B.O., June 24, 1982 (as amended by Ley N° 23.871, B.O., Oct. 31, 1990), *id.* [in Spanish].

Ley N° 23.548, Régimen transitorio de distribución de recursos fiscales (Transitional System Governing the Distribution of Fiscal Resources), B.O., Jan. 26, 1988, *id.* [in Spanish].

Ley N° 23.614, Promoción industrial (Industrial Promotion), B.O., Oct. 17, 1988 (as amended by Ley N° 1174/89, B.O., Sept. 26, 1989), *id.* [in Spanish].

Ley N° 23.658, Bono de crédito fiscal para promoción industrial (Tax Credit Vouchers for Industrial Promotion), B.O., Jan. 10, 1989, *id.* [in Spanish].

IT—Ley N° 20.628, Impuesto a las ganancias (Income Tax), B.O., Sept. 1, 1986 (as amended to Dec. 1996), *id.*, *reprinted in* IBFD-CIAT [in Spanish]; *and in* TLW (as amended to Mar. 27, 1996) [in English].

Ley N° 23.905, Impuesto sobre los activos (Tax on Assets), B.O., Dec. 18, 1990 (as amended by Ley N° 23.905, B.O., Feb. 18, 1991), *reprinted in* Legislación impositiva, *supra* [in Spanish]; also *reprinted in* TLW (as amended to Jan. 1, 1996) [in English].

Ley N° 23.427, Fondo para educación y promoción cooperativa (Fund for Education and Cooperative Activities), B.O., Dec. 3, 1986 (as amended by Ley N° 23.760, B.O., Dec. 18, 1989), *reprinted in* Legislación impositiva, *supra* [in Spanish].

Ley N° 20.630, Impuesto de emergencia a los premios de determinados juegos de sorteos y concursos deportivos (Emergency Tax on Specified Lotteries and Sporting Competitions), B.O., Jan. 22, 1974 (as amended by Ley N° 23.497, B.O., Feb. 19, 1987), *id.* [in Spanish].

Ley N° 21.280, Impuesto sobre las transferencias de títulos valores (Tax on Security Transfers), B.O., July 28, 1986 (as amended by Ley N° 23.469, B.O., Dec. 5, 1986), *id.* [in Spanish].

Ley N° 18.526, Impuesto sobre las ventas, compras, cambios o permutas de divisas (Tax on the Sale, Purchase, Exchange or Transfer of Foreign Exchange), B.O., Jan. 13, 1978 (as amended by Ley N° 23.905, B.O., Feb. 8, 1991), id. [in Spanish].

Ley N° 23.760, Gravamen sobre servicios financieros (Levy on Financial Services), B.O., Dec. 18, 1989, id. [in Spanish].

Ley N° 23.658, Impuesto sobre intereses y ajustes en depósitos a plazo fijo (Tax on Interest and Adjustments Relating to Fixed-Term Deposits), B.O., Jan. 10, 1989 (as amended to Dec. 31, 1991), id. [in Spanish].

Ley N° 23.760, Impuesto sobre los débitos bancarios en cuenta corriente y otras operatorias (Tax on Current Account Deposits, Debts and Other Bank Operations), B.O., Dec. 18, 1989 (as amended by Ley N° 23.905, B.O., Feb. 18, 1991), id. [in Spanish].

Ley N° 18.524, Impuesto de sellos (Stamp Tax), B.O., Sept. 3, 1986 (as amended by Ley N° 23.905, B.O., Feb. 18, 1991), id. [in Spanish].

Ley N° 23.898, Tasas judiciales (Court Fees), B.O., Oct. 20, 1990, id. [in Spanish].

Decreto 1547/78, Tasas de constitución e inspección de sociedades por acciones (Fees on the Incorporation and Inspection of Joint Stock Companies), id. [in Spanish].

Ley N° 23.349, Impuesto al valor agregado (Value Added Tax), B.O., Aug. 25, 1986 (as amended to Dec. 1996), id. [in Spanish], reprinted in IBFD-CIAT [in Spanish].

Ley N° 3.764, Impuestos internos (Internal Taxes), B.O., Oct. 30, 1979 (as amended by Ley N° 23.871 B.O., Oct. 31, 1990), reprinted in Legislación impositiva, supra [in Spanish].

Ley N° 19.408, Fondo nacional de autopistas (National Highway Fund), B.O., Jan. 3, 1972 (as amended by Ley N° 22.408, B.O., Feb. 26, 1981), id. [in Spanish].

Ley N° 14.574, Impuesto a los pasajes aéreos al exterior (Tax on Overseas Air Trips), B.O., July 14, 1988, id. [in Spanish].

Ley N° 23.905, Impuesto a la transferencia de inmuebles de personas físicas y sucesiones indivisas (Tax on Real Estate Transfers by Natural Persons and Estates), B.O., Feb. 18, 1991, id. [in Spanish].

Decreto 2.733, Impuesto sobre los combustibles líquidos y otros derivados de hidrocarburos y gas natural (Tax on Liquid Fuels, Other Hydrocarbon Products and Natural Gas), B.O., Jan. 7, 1991, id. [in Spanish].

Ley N⁰ 23.562, Fondo transitorio para financiar desequilibrios fiscales provinciales (Transitional Fund for Financing Fiscal Imbalances in the Provinces), B.O., June 1, 1988 (as amended by Ley N⁰ 23.763, B.O., Jan. 4, 1990), *id*. [in Spanish].

Ley N⁰ 23.966, Impuesto sobre los bienes personales no incorporados al proceso económico (Tax on Personal Goods not Incorporated into an Economic Process), Título VI, *reprinted in* Separatas Errepar (Errepar S.A., Av. San Juan 960, 1147 Buenos Aires) [in Spanish], *amended by* Law N⁰ 24.468, Mar. 23, 1995, *reprinted in* TLW [in English].

Armenia (ARM)

Law on Taxes (entered into force May 31, 1997).

Law of the Republic of Armenia on Income Tax, Feb. 8, 1995 [in English].

Law Regarding the Introduction of Changes and Amendments to the Republic of Armenia Law on the Income Tax, June 14, 1994 [in Armenian].

Law on the Granting of Tax Exemptions for Specific Economic Activities that Are Taxed on the Basis of Documented Payments of the Income and Profit Taxes as well as Documented Payments of the Income Tax, June 14, 1994 [in Armenian].

Law on Exempting Tax Paying Legal and Physical Persons (Entities) in the Republic of Armenia from Paying Taxes Assigned to Other Payers, Fines and Payments to Out-of-Budget State Funds, as well as Fines, Penalties and Other Obligations for Transgressions Against Tax Laws, Apr. 26, 1994 [in Armenian].

Excise Law of the Republic of Armenia, June 6, 1992, NTIS [in English].

Law of the Republic of Armenia on Amendments and Additions to Excise Tax of the Republic of Armenia, Mar. 18, 1993 [in English].

Law of the Republic of Armenia on Amendments in the Law of the Republic of Armenia on Excise Tax, Nov. 30, 1994 [in English].

Law of the Republic of Armenia on Land Tax, Apr. 27, 1994 [in English].

Profit Tax Law, Dec. 19, 1994 [in English].

Law of the Republic of Armenia on Foreign Investment, July 31, 1994.

Law of the Republic of Armenia on the Amendments to the Law of the Republic of Armenia on Profit Tax, June 14, 1994 [in Russian].

Law of the Republic of Armenia on Property Tax, Feb. 3, 1995 [in English].

Republic of Armenia Law on Value-Added Tax, June 16, 1997 [in English].

Australia (AUS)

At the federal level, Australia imposes the income tax and related taxes and the sales tax. For the income tax legislation, we have cited to an annual multivolume paperback set published by CCH. Australia is in the process of income tax law simplification, involving piecemeal replacement of the 1936 Act, so we cite both this law (which remains in force in part) and the 1997 Act that has replaced it in part.

ITAA (1936)—Income Tax Assessment Act 1936, *reprinted in* 1A and 1B 1996 Australian Income Tax Legislation (as amended to Jan. 1, 1996) (CCH Australia Limited 1996).

ITAA (1997)—Income Tax Assessment Act, *id.*

Income Tax Act 1986, *reprinted in* 2, 1996 Australian Income Tax Legislation (as amended to Jan. 1, 1996) (CCH Australia Limited 1996).

FBTAA—Fringe Benefits Tax Assessment Act 1986, *id.*

Fringe Benefits Tax Act 1986, *id.*

Fringe Benefits Tax (Application to the Commonwealth) Act 1986, *id.*

Income Tax (Bearer Debentures) Act 1971, *id.*

Income Tax (Deferred Interest Securities) (Tax File Number Withholding Tax) Act 1991, *id.*

Income Tax (Deficit Deferral) Act 1994, *id.*

Income Tax (Diverted Income) Act 1981, *id.*

Income Tax (Dividends, Interest and Royalties Withholding Tax) Act 1974, *id.*

Income Tax (former Complying Superannuation Funds) Act 1994, *id.*

Income Tax (former Nonresident Superannuation Funds) Act 1994, *id.*

Income Tax (Franking Deficit) Act 1987, *id.*

Income Tax (Fund Contributions) Act 1989, *id.*

Income Tax (Mining Withholding Tax) Act 1979, *id.*

Income Tax (Offshore Banking Units) (Withholding Tax Recoupment) Act 1988, *id.*

ITRA—Income Tax Rates Act 1986, *id.*

Income Tax (Securities and Agreements) (Withholding Tax Recoupment) Act 1986, *id.*

Income Tax (Withholding Tax Recoupment) Act 1971, *id.*

Infrastructure Certificate Cancellation Tax Act 1994, *id.*

Medicare Levy Act 1986, *id.*

Taxation (Interest on Nonresident Trust Distributions) Act 1990, *id.*

Taxation (Unpaid Company Tax—Promoters) Act 1982, *id.*

Taxation (Unpaid Company Tax—Vendors) Act 1982, *id.*

Trust Recoupment Tax Act 1985, *id.*

Taxation Administration Act 1953, *id.*

Administrative Decisions (Judicial Review) Act 1977, *id.*

Insurance and Superannuation Commissioner Act 1987, *reprinted in* 3 Australian Income Tax Legislation (as amended to Jan. 1, 1996) (CCH Australia Limited 1996).

Small Superannuation Accounts Act 1995, *id.*

Superannuation Entities (Taxation) Act 1987 (formerly Occupational Superannuation Standards Act 1987), *id.*

Superannuation (Financial Assistance Funding) Levy Act 1993, *id.*

Superannuation Guarantee (Administration) Act 1992, *id.*

Superannuation Guarantee Charge Act 1992, *id.*

Superannuation Industry (Supervision) Act 1993, *id.*

Superannuation (Resolution of Complaints) Act 1993, *id.*

Superannuation Supervisory Levy Act 1991, *id.*

Crimes (Taxation Offences) Act 1980, *id.*

Taxation (Interest on Overpayments and Early Payments) Act 1983, *id.*

Taxation (Interest on Underpayments) Act 1986, *id.*

Taxation (Unpaid Company Tax) Assessment Act 1982, *id.*

Trust Recoupment Tax Assessment Act 1985, *id.*

The sales tax legislation is available on the website of the Australian Legal Information Institute (www.austlii.edu.au) and includes the following laws: Sales Tax Assessment Act 1992, Nº 114 of 1992; Sales Tax Imposition (Excise) Act 1992, Nº 115 of 1992; Sales Tax Imposition (Customs) Act 1992, Nº 116 of 1992; Sales Tax Imposition (General) Act 1992, Nº 117 of 1992; Sales Tax Amendment (Transitional) Act 1992, Nº 118 of 1992; Sales

Tax (Exemptions and Classifications) Act 1992, N° 119 of 1992; Sales Tax (Exemptions and Classifications) Amendment Act 1992, N° 131 of 1992; Sales Tax Imposition (In Situ Pools) Act, N° 148 of 1992; Sales Tax Laws Amendment Act (N° 2) 1992, N° 150 of 1992; Sales Tax Assessment Amendment (Deficit Reduction) Act 1993, N° 44 of 1993; Sales Tax (World Trade Organization Amendments) Act 1994, N° 155 of 1994; Sales Tax (Low-Alcohol Wine) Amendment Act 1994, N° 95 of 1994; Sales Tax Laws Amendment Act (N° 1) 1996, N° 68 of 1996.

Austria (AUT)

We cite to an annual paperback compilation of tax legislation, published by Linde Verlag (Vienna). The official gazette cites are to the Bundesgesetzblatt (BGBl.). The structure of the Austrian tax laws closely resembles that of Germany, but substantial differences have developed in the details over the years.

EStG—Einkommensteuergesetz 1988 (Income Tax Law), BGBl. 1988/400, *reprinted in* Kodex des Österreichischen Rechts: Steuergesetze (Christoph Ritz ed., 20th ed., Linde Verlag, Wien, 1995) (as amended to Nov. 1, 1995) [in German].

Familienbesteuerungsgesetz 1992 (Household Taxation Law), *id.*

Endbesteuerungsgesetz (Law on a Withholding Tax on Income from Capital), BGBl. 1993, *id.*

Bundesgesetz über steuerliche Sondermaßnahmen zur Förderung des Wohnbaus (Special Tax Measures for the Promotion of Apartment Construction), *id.*

KStG—Körperschaftsteuergesetz 1988 (Corporation Tax Law), BGBl. 1988/401, *id.*

Umgründungssteuergesetz (Reorganization tax law), BGBl. 1991/699, *id.*

Bundesgesetz vom 7. Juli 1954 über die Umwandlung von Handelsgesellschaften (Federal Law Governing Changes to Commercial Companies), *id.*

Bundesgesetz über die Besteuerung der Umsätze (Umsatzsteuergesetz 1994) (Turnover Tax Law) (as of Jan. 1, 1995, UStG 1994, BGBl. 663), *id.*

Umsatzsteuergesetz 1972 (Turnover Tax Law), BGBl. 1972/223, *id.*

Bundesgesetz über die Einführung des UStG 1972 (Federal Law on the Introduction of the Turnover Tax Law 1972), *id.*

Mietrechtsgesetz (Law on Leases), BGBl. 1981/520, *id.*

Bewertungsgesetz 1955 (Valuation Law), *id.*

Bewertungsgesetznovelle 1972, über die Erhöhung der Einheitswerte ab 1.1. 1997 und 1.1. 1980 (Amendment to the Valuation Law) BGBl. 1972/447, *id.*

Bodenschätzungsgesetz 1970 (Law governing Mineral Resources), *id.*

Grundsteuergesetz 1955 (Real Estate Tax Law) BGBl. 1955/149, *id.*

Abgabe von land-und forstwirtschaftlichen Betrieben (Levy on Land and Forest Management Businesses), *id.*

Bodenwertabgabegesetz 1960 (Underdeveloped Real Estate Tax Law), *id.*

Gebührengesetz 1957 (Fees Law), *id.*

Gebührengesetznovelle 1976, (Fees Law Amendments), *id.*

Stempelmarkengesetz, BGBl. 1964/24, (Stamp Duty), *id.*

Erbschafts-und Schenkungssteuergesetz 1955 (Inheritance and Gift Taxes Law), *id.*

Grunderwerbsteuergesetz 1987 (Tax Law Concerning the Transfer of Real Estate), *id.*

Kapitalverkehrsteuergesetz (Tax Law Concerning Capital Transfers), *id.*

Versicherungssteuergesetz 1953 (Tax Law on Insurance), *id.*

Pensionskassengesetz (Law on Pension Funds), *id.*

Feuerschutzsteuergesetz 1952 (Law Governing Fire Insurance Coverage), *id.*

Straßenverkehrsbeitragsgesetz 1978 (Road Traffic Tax Law), *id.*

Kraftfahrzeugsteuergesetz 1952 (Law on Motor Vehicle Taxation), *id.*

Kraftfahrzeugsteuergesetz 1992 (Law on Motor Vehicle Taxation), *id.*

Straßenbenützungsabgabegesetz (Law on Road Use Fee), *id.*

Abgabe von Zuwendungen (Tax Contributions), *id.*

Bundesgesetz mit dem eine Sonderabgabe von Banken erhoben wird (Federal Law by Which a Special Duty Is Levied on Banks), *id.*

Bundesgesetz, mit dem eine Sonderabgabe von Erdöl erhoben wird (Federal Law by Which a Special Levy Is Charged on Petroleum), *id.*

Investmentfondsgesetz (Investment Funds Law), *id.*

Altlastensanierungsgesetz (Law on Soil Decontamination—Rehabilitation of Contaminated Soil Law), *id.*

Normverbrauchsabgabegesetz (Tax on Motor Vehicles), *id.*

Konsulargebührengesetz 1992 (Consular Fees Law), *id.*

BGBl. 1992/824 (Sicherheitsbeitrag) (Airport Security Contribution), *id.*

Kommunalsteuergesetz 1993 (Law on Local Taxes) BGBl. 1993/819.

Karenzurlaubszuschußgesetz (Repayment of Certain Benefits for Children), *id.*

Familienlastenausgleichsgesetz 1967 (Law Governing Government Allowances Payable to Families), *id.*

Bundesabgabenordnung (Federal Fiscal Code), BGBl. 1961/194, *id.*

Abgabenverwaltungsorganisationsgesetz (Tax Administration Organization Law), *id.*

Zustellgesetz (Law on Delivery of Official Documents), *id.*

Auskunftspflichtgesetz (Information Disclosure Law), *id.*

Finanzstrafgesetz 1958 (Law Governing Criminal Acts in Financial Activities), *id.*

Kreditwesengesetz 1993, § 38 (2) (Banking Law) (excerpt on bank secrecy), *id.*

Azerbaijan (AZE)

Law of the Republic of Azerbaijan on the Taxation of Income of Natural Persons in the Republic of Azerbaijan, June 24, 1992, *reprinted in* Bulletin of a Businessman (Baku) (as amended to Dec. 24, 1996) [in English].

PT—Law of the Republic of Azerbaijan on Profit Tax for Enterprises and Organizations, Nº 221-1G, Dec. 24, 1996, *reprinted in* Bulletin of a Businessman (Baku) [in English].

Law of the Republic of Azerbaijan on Value Added Tax, *reprinted in* Bulletin of a Businessman (Baku) (as amended to Dec. 24, 1996) [in English].

Law of the Republic of Azerbaijan on Excises, Nº 43, Dec. 31, 1991, *reprinted in* Bulletin of a Businessman (Baku) (as amended to June 24, 1996) [in English] (list of excisable goods and rates have been modified several times by decrees of the national assembly and of the cabinet of ministers).

Zakon Azerbaydzhanskoy Respubliki o zemel'nom naloge (Law of the Republic of Azerbaijan on Land Tax), Nº 490, Feb. 2, 1993 [in Russian].

Law Nº 222, on the State Revenue Service, July 21, 1992 [in English].

Law Nº 992 on Property Tax, *reprinted in* Bulletin of a Businessman (Baku) (as amended to Dec. 24, 1996) [in English].

Law Nº 995, on Mining Tax, Mar. 24, 1995 [in English].

Law on the State Road Fund, Feb. 16, 1994, Vedomosti Azerbaijan, 1994, Nº 5–6, item 49.

Law Nº 997 on State Duty, Apr. 24, 1995 [in Azerbaijani].

Bahamas, The (BHS)

We have cited to the official codification of all the laws of The Bahamas, a nine-volume text. This does not contain enactments after 1987. There is no income tax, sales tax, or inheritance and gift tax. Copies of Acts of The Bahamas may be obtained from Government Publications, P.O. Box N-7147, Nassau, The Bahamas. Amending acts and other laws passed subsequently to this codification are listed in The Commonwealth of The Bahamas: Consolidated Index of Statutes and Subsidiary Legislation (1996).

Fiscal Reform and Tax Relief Act 1990, Nº 16 of 1990.

Registrar General Act, Cap. 174, *reprinted in* The Statute Law of The Bahamas (rev. ed. 1987).

Passports Act, Cap. 180, *id.*

Real Property Tax Act, Cap. 339, *id.*

Business Licenses Act, Cap. 302, *id.*

Passenger Tax Act, Cap. 343, *id.*

Casino Taxation Act, Cap. 335, *id.*

Stamp Tax Act, Cap. 334, *id.*

Harbour Dues Act, Cap. 251, *id.*

Bahrain (BHR)

The following citations are from William Ballantyne, Register of Laws of the Arabian Gulf (loose-leaf).

Petrol Tax Law of 1968, Notice 10/68.

Decree Law 22/79 on Income Tax.

Decree Law 12/93 on Zakat Fund.

Ministerial Resolution 4/94 on Hotel Service Charges (imposes a tax on hotel prices).

Bangladesh (BGD)

In addition to those listed below, the following taxes are imposed in Bangladesh: stamp duties, entertainment tax, motor vehicle tax, irrigation tax, tax on transfer of immovable property, wealth tax (Wealth Tax Act, XV of 1963), gift tax (Gift Tax Act, 1963), land development tax, VAT (Value Added Tax Ordinance, 1991), excise duty (Excise and Salt Tax Act, 1944, as amended by VAT), foreign travel tax, advertisement tax, insurance premium tax, and electric duty (Electric Duty Act, 1935).

The Income Tax Ordinance 1984, Bangladesh Gazette, Extraordinary, June 4, 1984, *reprinted in* National Board of Revenue, Income Tax Manual, Part I (Bangladesh Government Press). (This has subsequently been amended by annual finance acts.)

Act N⁰ 12 of 1995, Finance Act 1995 (Dhaka, Government Printer).

Barbados (BRB)

A consolidated index of statutes and subsidiary legislation (as of Jan. 1, 1997) has been published by the Faculty of Law Library, University of the West Indies, Barbados. This lists the amending laws, and so they will not be listed here. The tax laws listed are as follows:

Banks (Tax on Assets) Act 1983 (Cap. 59B).

Betting and Gaming Duties Act 1977 (Cap. 60).

Betting and Gaming Duties (Validation) Act 1992.

Consumption Tax (Validation) Act, 1995, N⁰ 11 of 1995.

Duties, Taxes, and Other Payments (Exemption) Act 1981 (Cap. 67B).

Environmental Levy Act 1996, N⁰ 8 of 1996.

Excise Tax Act 1996, N⁰ 29 of 1996.

Fiscal Incentives Act 1974 (Cap. 71A).

Fiscal Incentives (Validation of Benefits) Act (Cap. 71AA).

Income Tax Act (Cap. 73), *reprinted in* TLW (as amended to 1992).

Income Tax (Federal Endowments) Act 1960 (Cap. 151).

Land Development Duty Act (Cap. 78).

Land Tax Act 1973 (Cap. 78A).

Land Tax Validation Act 1980 (Cap. 78B).

Retail Sales Tax Act 1974 (Cap. 86).

Road Traffic (Road Tax, Reg. Fee and Permits) (Validation) Act 1992.

Service Tax Act 1980 (Cap. 90).

Stamp Duty Act (Cap. 91).

Tax on Remittances Act 1983 (Cap. 91A).

Technical Assistance (Taxation Relief) Act (Cap. 92).

Travel Ticket Tax Act 1984 (Cap. 92B).

Treasury Bills and Tax Certificates Act 1987 (Cap. 106).

Value Added Tax Act 1996, Nº 15 of 1996.

Belarus (BLR)

In the former Soviet Union, newspapers are an important source, so some of the cites are to newspapers. The cites to Vedomosti Verkhovnogo Sovyeta Respubliki Belarus are to the official session laws. There is also a worldwide website, http://belarus.net.softinfo (cited as website).

Zakon Respubliki Belarus o Nalogakh na Dokhody i Pribyl Predpriyatiy, Obedineniy, Organizatsiy (Law on Taxing the Income and Profits of Enterprises, Associations, and Organizations), Vedomosti Verkhovnogo Soveta Respubliki Belarus, 1992, Nº 4, Article 77 [in Belarussian], *reprinted in* Sovetskaya Belorussiya, Jan. 24, 1992 [in Russian] and same law dated Feb. 1993 [in Russian], *translated in* FBIS-USR-92-049, Apr. 28, 1992 [in English](also on website).

Zakon Respubliki Belarus o Vnesenii Izmeneniy i Dopolneniy v Zakon Respubliki Belarus O Nalogakh na Dokhody i Pribyl Predpriyatiy, Obedineniy, Organiztsiy (Amendment to the Law on Taxing the Income and Profits of Enterprises, Associations, and Organizations), Apr. 19, 1996, Vedomosti Verkhovnogo Soveta Respubliki Belarus Nº 12 (194), Apr. 1996 [in Russian].

Law Nº 780-XIII, Zakon Respubliki Belarus o Vnesenii Izmeneniya v Zakon Respubliki Belarus O Nalogakh na Dokhody i Pribyl Predpriyatiy, Obedineniy, Organiztsiy (Amendent to the Law on Taxing the Income and Profits of Enterprises, Associations, and Organizations), Nov. 13, 1996, Vedomosti Verkhovnogo Soveta Respubliki Belarus Nº 35 (217), Dec. 15, 1996 [in Russian].

Zakon Respubliki Belarus' o Podojodnom Naloge s Grazhdan (Law on Payment of Income Tax by Citizens), Vedomosti Verkhovnogo Soveta Respubliki Belarus, Feb. 15, 1992, Nº 5, Art. 79 [in Russian], *reprinted in* Sovetskaya Belorussiya, Jan. 23, 1992 [in Russian], *translated in* FBIS-USR-92-049, Apr. 28, 1992 [in English] (also on website).

Zakon Respubliki Belarus o Naloge na Dobavlennuyu Stoimost (Law on the Value Added Tax), Vedomosti Verkhovnogo Soveta Respubliki Belarus, 1992, Nº 3, Art. 51. Law on Changes in Taxation, *reprinted in* Sovetskaya Belorussiya, Apr. 2, 1992, at 3 [in Russian], *translated in* FBIS-USR-92-054, May 5, 1992, at 55–57 (also on website); Zakon Respubliki Belarus o Vnesenii Dopolneniya v Zakon Respubliki Belarus o Naloge na Dobavlennuyu Stoimost (Amendment to the Law on Value Added Tax), May 16, 1996, Vedomosti Verkhovnogo Soveta Respubliki Belarus Nº 16 (198), June 5, 1996 [in Russian].

Law Concerning Taxes and Duties in the Republic of Belarus, Jan. 1, 1992 (on website) [in English].

Zakon Respubliki Byelarus o Vnesenii Dopolneniya v Zakon Respubliki Byelarus o Nalogakh i Sborakh, Vzimaemykh v Byudzhet Respubliki Byelarus (Amendment to the Law on Taxes and Duties in the Republic of Belarus), June 20, 1996, Vedomosti Verkhovnogo Soveta Respubliki Belarus № 23 (205), Aug. 15, 1996 [in Russian].

Law Concerning Excise Taxes, Jan. 1, 1992 (on website) [in English].

Law Concerning the Tax on Exports and Imports, Jan. 1, 1992 [in Belarussian, English].

Law on Taxation of the Use of Natural Resources (ecology tax), Feb. 1993 (on website) [in English].

Law on Immovable Property Tax, Dec. 23, 1991 (on website) [in English]; Zakon Respubliki Byelarus o Vnesenii Dopolneniya v Zakon Respubliki Byelarus o Naloge na Nedvizhimost (Amendment to the Law on Immovable Property), June 20, 1996, Vedomosti Verkhovnogo Soveta Respubliki Belarus № 23 (205), Aug. 15, 1996 [in Russian].

Law on Payments for Land (on website) [in English].

Law Concerning a Tax on the Use of Automotive Fuel, Jan. 1, 1992 [in English].

Law Concerning the Transit Tax, July 1, 1992, Vedamastsi Vyarkhownaga Saveta Respubliki Byelarus, Feb. 25, 1992 [in Belarussian, English].

Law of April 13, 1995 on Dues for Driving Means of Motor Transportation on Motor-Roads of Common Use in the Republic of Belarus (on website) [in English].

Law on the Introduction of Amendments and Additions to Belarus Law on Taxation, Mar. 17, 1992, Narodnaya Gazeta [in Belarussian].

Zakon Respubliki Belarus' o Vnesenii Izmeneniy i Dopolneniy v Zakony Respubliki Belarus' Po Voprosam Nalogooblozheniya (Law on Amending Certain Tax Laws), May 1, 1995 [in Belarussian].

Law on the State Duty, Jan. 10, 1992 (on website) [in English].

Belgium (BEL)

Maison Larcier publishes the laws of Belgium in five large volumes in the French language. Volume 4 is economic and fiscal law (Droit économique et fiscal) and contains all the tax laws. These are organized into several codes, but there are also laws and royal decrees, too numerous to list here, that are not codified but are included in the above-referenced volume. We list below the major tax laws (other than local taxes) contained in this volume as of the 1995 edition:

Arrêté royal portant coordination des dispositions générales relatives aux douanes et accises (Royal Decree on the Coordination of General Provisions Relating to Customs Duties and Excise Taxes), July 18, 1977 (the general customs law; also has some provisions relevant to excise).

Arrêté royal relatif au régime général, à la détention, à la circulation et aux contrôles des produits soumis à accise (general rules for excise; we omit the laws and decrees containing the rules for specific excises, for which see Maison Larcier *supra*), Dec. 29, 1992.

Arrêté royal N° 64, contenant le code des droits d'enregistrement, d'hypotèque et de greffe (Code of Registration Duties, Mortgage Duty, and Court Fees) (this is the general law; again, we omit several specific laws and decrees that can be found in Maison Larcier *supra*), Nov. 30, 1939.

Arrêté royal N° 308, établissant le code des droits de succession (Inheritance Duty Code), Mar. 31, 1936.

Arrêté du Régent contenant le code des droits de timbre (Stamp Duty Code), June 26, 1947.

Loi ordinaire, visant à achever la structure fédérale de l'état, Livre III, Écotaxes (environmental taxes), July 16, 1993.

CIR—Arrêté royal portant coordination des dispositions légales relatives aux impôts sur les revenus, July 30, 1992 (Code des impôts sur les revenus 1992) (Income Tax Code of 1992) (we omit a number of laws and decrees relating to income tax that have not been codified, for which see Maison Larcier, *supra*).

Arrêté royal portant codification des dispositions légales relatives aux taxes assimilées aux impôts sur les revenus (Code of Taxes Assimilated to the Income Tax) (motor vehicles, gambling, automatic entertainment devices), Nov. 23, 1965.

Arrêté royal approuvant la coordination des dispositions législatives sur les taxes assimilées au timbre, qui porteront le nom de «Code des taxes assimilées au timbre» (Code of Taxes Assimilated to Stamp Duty), Mar. 2, 1927.

Loi créant le code de la taxe sur la valeur ajoutée (VAT Code), July 3, 1969 (we omit a number of decrees relating to VAT that have not been codified, for which see Maison Larcier, *supra*).

Arrêté royal coordonnant les dispositions légales concernant les débits de boissons fermentées, Apr. 3, 1953 (Tax on the Sale of Fermented Beverages) (we omit some other laws and decrees relating to this tax, for which see Maison Larcier, *supra*).

Belize (BLZ)

Amending acts for tax laws listed below may be found in Belize: Consolidated Index of Statutes and Subsidiary Legislation (1996).

Income Tax Act, Cap. 46, *reprinted in* TLW (as amended to Apr. 1997).

Gross Receipts Tax Act Nº 15 of 1994, Official Gazette of July 23, 1994, *id.*

Entertainment Tax Act, Cap. 41 (as amended to 1990), available on TaxBase.

Estate Duty Act, Cap. 42 (as amended to 1990), available on TaxBase.

Fiscal Incentives Act, Cap. 45, Apr. 17, 1990, available on TaxBase.

Land Tax Act, Cap. 47 (as amended to 1990), available on TaxBase.

Stamp Duties Act, Cap. 51 (as amended to 1990), available on TaxBase.

Towns Property Tax Act, Cap. 52 (as amended to 1990), available on TaxBase.

Departure Tax Act, Cap. 53A (as amended to 1990), available on TaxBase.

Act Nº 16 of 1995, Value Added Tax Act, 1995, Jan. 18, 1996, *reprinted in* TLW (as amended through May 31, 1997).

Benin (BEN)

Code général des impôts (General Tax Code), *reprinted in* République Populaire du Bénin, Ministère des finances, Code général des impôts (Graphic Ouest Africa 1983) [in French].

Taxe sur la valeur ajoutée (Value Added Tax), Loi 91-005, Feb. 22, 1991, *reprinted in* Ce que vous devez savoir sur la taxe sur la valeur ajoutée, Ministère des finances, Mar. 1991.

Loi Nº 91-014, portant loi de finances pour la gestion 1991, Apr. 12, 1991.

Loi Nº 95-013, portant loi de finances rectificative pour la gestion 1995, Sept. 26, 1995.

Ordonnance Nº 96-02, portant loi de finances pour la gestion 1996, Jan. 31, 1996, Journal officiel de la République du Bénin, Feb. 1, 1996.

Bhutan (BTN)

According to Revised Taxation Policy 1992, published by the Ministry of Finance, Royal Government of Bhutan, the following taxes were in effect at the time: corporate income tax, business income tax, sales tax, amusement tax, excise duty, contractors tax, salary tax, health contribution, industrial registration and license fees, trade license fees, company registration fees, motor vehicle tax, rural taxes, municipal taxes. The best information we have (which is sketchy) indicates that these taxes are imposed according to royal orders and that tax laws (in the sense of a comprehensive set of written norms imposing the tax) are either nonexistent or unavailable.

Bolivia (BOL)

In 1986, the specific tax laws of Bolivia were revised and consolidated into a single law (Law Nº 843). In addition to this law, the tax code (Law Nº 1340) provides the general rules of procedure. We cite to a compilation published by the tax authority (Dirección general de impuestos internos), as well as to the IBFD CD-ROM.

Ley Nº 843, Ley de reforma tributaria (Tax Reform Law), May 20, 1986, *reprinted in* Recopilación tributaria al 31 de diciembre de 1992 (Dirección general de impuestos internos 1993) (as amended to May 1995) [in Spanish] *reprinted in* IBFD-CIAT [in Spanish].

Ley Nº 1340, Código tributario (Tax Code), May 28, 1992, as amended to Dec. 1994, *reprinted in* IBFD-CIAT [in Spanish].

Bosnia and Herzegovina (BIH)

Law on the Corporate Income Tax, Official Gazette, Feb. 10, 1995 [in English].

Law on the Tax for Reconstruction of the Republic of Bosnia and Herzegovina [in English].

Law on the Personal Income Tax, Official Gazette, Feb. 10, 1995 [in English].

Law on Social Security Contributions, Feb. 3, 1995 [in English].

Law on the Sales Tax on Products and Services, Oct. 14, 1995, and Law on the Sales Tax on Products and Services, Official Gazette Nº 6, Nov. 8, 1995 [in English].

Porez' Na Dobit (Law on Profit Taxes), *reprinted in* Narodni List Hravatske Republike Herceg-Bosne, Jan. 1994 Nº 2 at 55 [in Serbo-Croatian, English].

Law on Federal Tax Administration (Aug. 27, 1996) [in English].

Botswana (BWA)

In addition to the taxes listed below, Botswana imposes a capital transfer tax, mineral royalties, and real estate transfer duty.

Act Nº 12, Income Tax Act, 1995, Botswana Government Extraordinary Gazette, Supplement A, July 1, 1995, Government Printer, amended by Act Nº 11 of 1996, Income Tax (Amendment) Act, 1996.

Sales Tax Act, 1993, Botswana Government Gazette, Supplement A, Feb. 26, 1993.

Capital Transfer Tax (Amendment) Act, 1996.

Brazil (BRA)

The Brazilian Constitution distinguishes different sorts of laws. The lei complementar requires a special majority and is required to govern certain matters specified in the Constitution. For example, the National Tax Code (which contains the general rules applicable to the specific taxes) is a lei complementar. An ordinary law (lei) is promulgated by the Congress. A decree-law (decreto lei) also has the force of law; it is promulgated by the President. A decree is also promulgated by the President, but it has a rank below that of a law or decree-law and therefore is not included in this bibliography. The exception is the Regulamento do Imposto de Renda. This is a decree that consolidates the laws relating to income tax. As a consolidation, it has the force of law.

RIR—Regulamento de Imposto sobre a renda (Income Tax Regulations) approved by Decree Nº 1.041 of Jan. 11, 1994, Diario oficial, Jan. 12, 1994 (as amended by Lei Nº 8.981 of Jan. 20, 1995) (Decree Consolidating the Various Laws Relating to Income Taxation), *reprinted in* IBFD-CIAT [in Portuguese] *and* (as amended to end-1995) *in* TLW [in English].

Lei Nº 8.981 Altera a legislaçao tributaria federal e dá outras providências (Law Amending the Federal Tax Legislation and Other Matters), Jan. 20, 1995, *reprinted in* IBFD-CIAT [in Portuguese].

Lei Nº 5.172 Código tributário nacional (National Tax Code), Oct. 25, 1966, *reprinted in* Código tributário nacional, Editora Saraiva 21 (1990) [in Portuguese].

Lei complementar—estabelece normas integrantes do estatuto da microempresa, relativas a isenção do Imposto sobre circulação de mercadorias (ICM) e Imposto sobre Serviços (ISS) (Supplementary Law Regulating the Exemption of Small Enterprises from the Tax on the Circulation of Goods and the Service Tax), Dec. 10, 1984, *id.*

Lei Nº 4.320, Estatui normas gerais de direito financeiro para elaboração e controle dos orçamentos e balanços da união, dos estados, dos municípios e do distrito federal (Law Establishing General Regulations Under Financial Legislation for the Preparation and Inspection of the Budgets and Balance Sheets of the Federal Government, States, Municipalities and the Federal District), Mar. 17, 1964, *id.*

Lei Nº 4.504, dispõe sobre o estatuto da terra e dá outras providências (Law Governing Land Tenure and Other Related Matters), Nov. 30, 1964, *id.*

Lei Nº 4.729, define o crime de sonegação fiscal e dá outras providências (Law Defining the Crime of Tax Evasion and Governing Related Matters), July 14, 1965, *id.*

Lei Nº 5.143, Institui o imposto sobre operações financeiras, regula a respectiva cobrança, dispõe sobre a aplicação das reservas monetárias oriundas da sua receita, e dá outras providências (Law Establishing the Tax on Financial Transactions and Regulating the Collection and Application of Financial Reserves Resulting from the Income Derived Therefrom and Other Related Matters), Oct. 20, 1966, *id.*

Lei Nº 6.099, dispõe sobre o tratamento tributário das operações de arrendamento mercantil, e dá outras providências (Law Governing the Treatment for Taxation Purposes of Commercial Leasing and Other Related Matters), Sept. 12, 1974, *id.*

Lei Nº 6.830, dispõe sobre a cobrança judicial da dívida ativa da fazenda pública e dá outras providências (Law Governing the Court-Ordered Collection of Debts Due for Payment by the Treasury and Other Related Matters), Sept. 22, 1980, *id.*

Lei Nº 7.256, estabelece normas integrantes do estatuto da microempresa, relativas ao tratamento diferenciado, simplificado e favorecido, nos campos administrativo, tributário, previdenciário, trabalhista, creditício e de desenvolvimento empresarial (Law Regulating the Status of Small Enterprises as Regards the Special, Simplified and Favorable Treatment to Be Afforded Them with Respect to Administration, Taxation, Social Security, Labor Legislation, Credit and Enterprise Development), Nov. 27, 1984, *id.*

Lei Nº 7.505, dispõe sobre benefícios fiscais na área do imposto sobre a renda concedidos a operações de caráter cultural ou artístico (Law Governing Income Tax Benefits Applicable to Cultural and Artistic Operations), July 2, 1986, *id.*

Lei Nº 7.680, altera valores das taxas de fiscalização da instalação dos serviços de telecomunicações, constantes do Anexo I à Lei Nº 5.070, de 7 de julho de 1966 (Law Amending the Rates of Inspection Fees for the Installation of Telecommunication Services Referred to in Law Nº 5,070 of July 7, 1966, Annex I), Dec. 2, 1988, *id.*

Lei Nº 7.689, institui contribuição social sobre o lucro das pessoas jurídicas, e dá outras providências (Law Establishing a Profits Tax on Juristic Persons (corporations) and Governing Other Related Matters), Dec. 15, 1988, *id.*

Lei Nº 7.700, cria o adicional de tarifa portuária (ATP) e dá outras providências (Law Establishing a Supplementary Levy on Port Charges and Governing Other Related Matters), Dec. 21, 1988, *id.*

Lei Nº 7.711, dispõe sobre formas de melhoria da administração tributária, e dá outras providências (Law Introducing Improvements in Tax Administration and Governing Other Related Matters), Dec. 22, 1988, *id.*

Lei Nº 7.712, dispõe sobre a cobrança do pedágio nas rodovias federais, e dá outras providências (Law Governing the Collection of Federal Highway Tolls, and Other Related Matters), Dec. 22, 1988, *id.*

Lei Nº 7.713, altera a legislação do imposto sobre a renda, e dá outras providências (Law Amending Income Tax Legislation and Governing Other Related Matters), Dec. 22, 1988, id.

Lei Nº 7.714, altera a legislação dos incentivos fiscais relacionados com o imposto sobre a renda (Law Amending Legislation on Tax Incentives Relating to Income Tax), Dec. 29, 1988, id.

Lei Nº 7.730, institui o cruzado novo, determina congelamento de preços, estabelece regras de desindexação da economia, e dá outras providências (Law Establishing the New Cruzado, Freezing Prices, Establishing Rules for Eliminating Indexation, and Governing Other Related Matters), Jan. 31, 1989, id.

Lei Nº 7.751, dispõe sobre a incidência do imposto sobre a renda na fonte sobre rendimentos decorrentes de aplicações financeiras, e dá outras providências (Law Governing the Applicability of Income Tax Withheld on Income Derived from Applications of Funds, and Other Related Matters), Apr. 14, 1989, id.

Lei Nº 7.752, dispõe sobre benefícios fiscais na área do imposto de renda e outros tributos, concedidos ao desporto amador (Law Governing Income Tax Benefits, and Other Tax Benefits, Granted to Amateur Sporting), Apr. 14, 1989, id.

Lei Nº 7.766, dispõe sobre o ouro, ativo financeiro e sobre seu tratamento tributário (Law Governing Gold and Financial Assets and Their Treatment for Tax Purposes), May 11, 1989, id.

Lei Nº 7.772, dispõe sobre a compensação, com imposto sobre a renda da pessoa jurídica, da diferença resultante da correção monetária incidente sobre empréstimos concedidos com recursos da caderneta de poupança, e dá outras providências (Law Governing Compensation—with the Corporate Income Tax—for Differences Resulting from the Monetary Correction Applied to Passbook Loans, and Other Related Matters), June 8, 1989, id.

Lei Nº 7.777, expede normas de ajustamento do programa de estabilização econômica de que trata a Lei Nº 7.730, de 31 de janeiro de 1989, e dá outras providências (Law Establishing Regulations for the Adjustment of the Economic Stabilization Program Defined in Law Nº 7.730, and Governing Other Related Matters), June 19, 1989, id.

Lei Nº 7.782, dispõe sobre a incidência do imposto sobre a renda na fonte em aplicações de renda fixa, e dá outras providências (Law Governing Income Tax Deducted at Source from Fixed-income Investments, and Other Related Matters), June 27, 1989, id.

Lei Nº 7.799, altera a legislação tributária federal e dá outras providências (Law Amending Federal Tax Legislation, and Other Related Matters), July 10, 1989, id.

Lei N° 7.827, regulamenta o art. 159, c, da constituição federal, institui o fundo constitucional de financiamento do norte (FNO), o fundo constitucional e financiamento do nordeste (FNE) e o fundo constitucional de financiamento do centro-oeste (FCO) e dá outras providências (Law regulating Article 159 (c) of the Federal Constitution, establishing FNO (the Constitutional Fund for Financing the North), FNE (the Constitutional Fund for Financing the Northeast), and FCO (the Constitutional Fund for Financing the Center-West), and other related matters), Sept. 27, 1989, *id.*

Lei N° 9.249, altera a legislação do imposto sobre a renda das pessoas jurídicas, bem como da contribuição social sobre o lucro liquido, e dá outras providências (Law Amending the Legislation on Corporate Income Tax , and Also Social Tax on Net Profits Together with Other Provisions) available on TaxBase [in Portuguese].

Lei Complementar N° 84, da seguridade social—fonte de costeiro—instituição na forma do sect. 4 do art. 195 da Constituição Federal (Supplementary Law on Social Security—Cost Center—in Accordance with Section 4 of Article 195 of the Federal Constitution), Jan. 18, 1996, available on TaxBase.

Decreto-Lei N° 37, dispõe sobre o imposto de importação, reorganiza os serviços aduaneiros e dá outras providências (Decree-Law Governing Import Tax, Reorganizing Customs Services, and Other Related Matters), Nov. 18, 1966, *reprinted in* Código tributário nacional, *supra.*

Decreto-Lei N° 57, altera dispositivos sobre lançamento e cobrança do imposto sobre a propriedade territorial rural, institui normas sobre arrecadação da dívida ativa correspondente e dá outras providências (Decree-Law Amending Regulations Governing the Recording and Collection of Rural Property Tax, Establishing Rules for the Collection of Debts Due on Such Property, and Governing Other Related Matters), Nov. 18, 1966, *id.*

Decreto-Lei N° 195, dispõe sobre a cobrança da contribuição de melhoria (Decree-Law Governing the Collection of Special Assessment Tax), Feb. 24, 1967, *id.*

Decreto-Lei N° 406, estabelece normas gerais de direito financeiro, aplicáveis aos impostos sobre operações relativas à circulação de mercadorias e sobre serviços de qualquer natureza, e dá outras providências (Decree-Law Establishing General Regulations Under Financial Law Applicable to Taxation on the Circulation of Goods and All Types of Services, and Other Related Matters), Dec. 31, 1968, *id.*

Decreto-Lei N° 822, extingue a garantia de instância nos recursos de decisão administrativa fiscal, e dá outras providências (Decree-Law Eliminating Guaranteed Hearings in the Case of Appeals Against Tax Administration Decisions, and Governing Other Related Matters), Sept. 5, 1969, *id.*

Decreto-Lei Nº 858, dispõe sobre a cobrança e a correção monetária dos débitos fiscais nos casos de falência e dá outras providências (Decree-Law Governing Collection and Monetary Correction as Applied to Tax Debts in Cases of Insolvency, and Other Related Matters), Sept. 11, 1969, *id.*

Decreto-Lei Nº 1.438, altera o Decreto-Lei Nº 284, de 28 de fevereiro de 1967, estende a incidência do imposto sobre transportes, e dá outras Providências (Decree-Law Amending Decree-Law Nº 284, (1967), Increasing the Scope of Application of the Transportation Tax, and Governing Other Related Matters), Dec. 26, 1975, *id.*

Decreto-Lei Nº 1.578, dispõe sobre o imposto sobre a exportação, e dá outras providências (Decree-Law Governing Export Tax, and Other Related Matters), Oct. 11, 1977, *id.*

Decreto-Lei Nº 1.705, dispõe quanto à obrigatoriedade de recolhimento antecipado, pelas pessoas físicas, do imposto sobre a renda sobre os rendimentos que especifica (Decree-Law Governing Compulsory Advance Collection by Natural Persons of Income Tax Payable on Specified Items), Oct. 23, 1979, *id.*

Decreto-Lei Nº 1.715, regula a expedição de certidão de quitação de tributos federais e extingue a declaração de devedor remisso (Decree-Law Governing the Issue of Receipts for Federal Taxes and Eliminating the Declaration of "Debtor in Arrears"), Nov. 22, 1979, *id.*

Decreto-Lei Nº 1.755, dispõe sobre a arrecadação e restituição das receitas federais, e dá outras providências (Decree-Law Governing the Collection and Refund of Federal Income and Other Related Matters), Dec. 31, 1979, *id.*

Decreto-Lei Nº 1.780, concede isenção do imposto sobre a renda às empresas de pequeno porte e dispensa obrigações acessórias (Decree-Law Granting Exemption from Income Tax and Related Obligations to Small Enterprises), Apr. 14, 1980, *id.*

Decreto-Lei Nº 1.783, dispõe sobre o imposto sobre operações de crédito, câmbio e seguro, e sobre operações relativas a títulos e valores mobiliários (Decree-Law Governing the Tax on Credit, Exchange, and Insurance Operations and on Securities Operations), Apr. 18, 1980, *id.*

Decreto-Lei Nº 1.793, autoriza o poder executivo a não ajuizar as ações que menciona e dá outras providências (Decree-Law Authorizing the Executive Branch Not to Undertake Legal Proceedings in Specified Cases, and Governing Other Related Matters), June 23, 1980, *id.*

Decreto-Lei Nº 1.804, dispõe sobre tributação simplificada das remessas postais internacionais (Decree-Law Governing Simplified Taxation Procedures in the Case of International Postal Remittances), Sept. 3, 1980, *id.*

Decreto-Lei N° 1.852, regula a distribuição aos municípios da parcela do imposto sobre transmissão de bens imóveis e de direitos a eles relativos (Decree-Law Governing the Distribution to Municipalities of a Portion of the Tax on the Conveyance of Real Estate and Related Rights), Jan. 27, 1981, id.

Decreto-Lei N° 1.875, dispõe sobre a simplificação de normas gerais de direito financeiro aplicáveis a municípios com população inferior a 50.000 (cinqüenta mil) Habitantes (Decree-Law Governing the Simplification of General Regulations of Financial Law Applicable to Municipalities with Fewer than 50,000 Inhabitants), July 15, 1981, id.

Decreto-Lei N° 1.881, altera a Lei N° 5.172, de 25 de outubro de 1966, cria a reserva do fundo de participação dos municípios (FPM), e dá outras providências (Decree-Law amending Law 5.172 of 1966 Establishing the Reserve Fund for the FPM (Municipalities' Participation Fund), and Governing Other Related Matters), Aug. 27, 1981, id.

Decreto-Lei N° 1.940, Institui contribuição social, cria o fundo de investimento social-FINSOCIAL, e dá outras providências (Decree-Law Establishing the Social Security Tax and FINSOCIAL (the Social Investment Fund), and Governing Other Related Matters), May 25, 1982, id.

Decreto-Lei N° 2.108, concede isenção dos impostos de importação e sobre produtos industrializados nos casos que especifica (Decree-Law Granting Exemption from Taxes on Imports and Processed Products in Specified Cases), Feb. 27, 1984, id.

Decreto-Lei N° 2.120, dispõe sobre o tratamento tributário relativo a bagagem (Decree-Law Governing Tax Treatment of Baggage), May 14, 1984, id.

Decreto-Lei N° 2.186, institui o imposto sobre serviços de comunicações, e dá outras providências (Decree-Law Establishing the Tax on Communications Services, and Governing Other Related Matters), Dec. 20, 1984, id.

Decreto-Lei N° 2.227, dispõe sobre processo de consulta e dá outras providências (Decree-Law Governing The Consultation Process, and Other Related Matters), Jan. 16, 1985, id.

Decreto-Lei N° 2.446, dispõe sobre o pagamento dos tributos relativos ao ingresso de bens de procedência estrangeira, nas condições que menciona, e dá outras providências (Decree-Law Governing the Payment of Taxes on the Entry of Goods from Abroad Under Specified Conditions, and Other Related Matters), June 30, 1988, id.

Decreto-Lei N° 2.450, altera a legislação do imposto sobre produtos industrializados (Decree-Law Amending Legislation Governing the Tax on Processed Goods), July 29, 1988, id.

Decreto-Lei N° 2.452, dispõe sobre o regime tributário, cambial e administrativo das zonas de processamento de exportação (ZPE) e dá outras providências (Decree-Law Governing the Taxation, Exchange and Administrative Regimes to be Applied in Export Processing Zones, and Other Related Matters), July 29, 1988, *id.*

Decreto-Lei N° 2.472, Altera disposições da legislação aduaneira, consubstanciada no Decreto-Lei N° 37, de 18 de novembro de 1966, e dá outras providências (Decree-Law Amending the Customs Legislation Contained in Decree-Law N° 37 of 1966, and Governing Other Related Matters), Sept. 1, 1988, *id.*

Decreto-Lei N° 2.479, dispõe sobre a redução de impostos de importação de bens, e dá outras providências (Decree-Law Governing the Reduction of Taxes on the Importation of Goods, and Other Related Matters), Oct. 3, 1988, *id.*

Value-Added Tax (Tax on Industrialized Products) excerpts from The New Regulation, approved by Decree 87.981, Dec. 23, 1982, *reprinted in* TLW [in English].

Brunei Darussalam (BRN)

Income Tax Act, Laws of Brunei, Cap. 35 (rev. ed. 1984), *reprinted in* TLW (as amended to Sept. 19, 1987).

Stamp Act, Laws of Brunei, Cap. 34 (rev. ed. 1984).

Excise Act, Laws of Brunei, Cap. 37 (rev. ed. 1984).

Investment Incentives Act, Laws of Brunei, Cap. 97 (rev. ed. 1984).

Income Tax (Petroleum) Act, Laws of Brunei, Cap. 119 (rev. ed. 1984).

Bulgaria (BGR)

We have cited to a multivolume compilation of the tax laws by Trud I Pravo (in Bulgarian). In addition, Collection of Bulgarian Laws [hereinafter Collection], published by Legis Bulgarian News, Sofia (fax: 3592-9433058) is an annual publication of English translations of selected Bulgarian laws and regulations. In addition to taxes cited below, a tax on buildings and an inheritance tax are imposed, and companies with more than 50 percent state ownership must pay an irrigation contribution and a tax on excess wage increases.

Zakon za Danak vorkhu Obshtya Dokhod (Law on Income Tax), *reprinted in* Danachno Oblagane za 1994 Godina 120 (IK Trud i Pravo 1995) (as amended to Dec. 31, 1994) [in Bulgarian].

Profit Tax Law, Official Gazette N° 59 (July 12, 1996), *reprinted in* 1997 Collection, *supra.*

Zakon za Danak varkhu Dobavenata Stoynost (Law on Value Added Tax), Official Gazette, N° 90 of 1993, reprinted in Danachno Oblagane za 1994 Godina 202 (IK Trud i Pravo 1995) [in Bulgarian], and in 1994 Collection, supra [in English]; amendments reprinted in 1997 Collection, supra.

Zakon za Danachnata Administratsiya (Law on Tax Administration), Official Gazette, N° 59 of 1993, reprinted in Danak Varkhu Dobavenata Stoynost 82 (IK Trud i Pravo 1994) [in Bulgarian], reprinted in CEEL [in English] and in 1994 Collection, supra [in English].

Zakon za Danachnoto Proizvodstvo (Law on Taxable Production), Official Gazette, N° 61 of 1993, id. [in English].

Zakon za Aktsizite (Law on Excise Tax), Official Gazette, N° 19 of 1994, reprinted in Aktsizi: Zakon i prilagane 12 (IK Trud i Pravo 1994) [in Bulgarian] and in 1997 Collection, supra.

Durzhaven Vestnik N° 61, (1993), Law on Tax Procedures, July 1, 1993, reprinted in CEEL and in 1994 Collection, supra [in English].

Regulations on Road Taxes on Motor Vehicles (Govt. decree of Feb. 10, 1992), reprinted in 1993 Collection, supra [in English].

Burkina Faso (BFA)

Code des impôts, reprinted in Ministre de l'économie et des finances, Direction générale des impôts, recueil de textes relatifs à la fiscalité interieure (Oct. 1996).

Code de l'enregistrement, du timbre, et de l'impôt sur les valeurs mobilières, reprinted in id.

Burundi (BDI)

Code général des impôts et taxes (General Tax Code), reprinted in Burundi, Ministère des finances, Departement des impôts, (l'INABU 1985) (as amended to Nov. 1, 1985) [in French].

Décret-Loi N° 1/04 portant reforme de la taxe sur les transactions (Decree-Law Governing the Reform of Tax on Transactions), Jan. 31, 1989 [in French].

Décret-Loi N° 1/039 portant modification de la Loi du 17 février 1964 relative à l'impôt réel (Decree-Law of Dec. 31, 1990 amending the Law of Feb. 17, 1964 on Property Tax), Dec. 31, 1990 [in French].

Décret-Loi N° 1/012 portant révision de certains dispositions de la loi du 21 septembre 1963 relative a l'impôt sur les revenus (Law N° 1/012 revising provisions in the Law of September 21, 1963 Governing Income Tax), Feb. 23, 1993 [in French].

Décret-Loi N⁰ 1/013 portant revision de certaines dispositions du code général des impôts et taxes (Decree-Law N⁰ 1/013 Revising Provisions in the General Tax Code), Feb. 23, 1993 [in French].

Loi N⁰ 1/005 portant fixation du taux de la taxe ad valorem a percevoir sur la cigarette (Law Setting the Rate for the Ad Valorem Tax on Cigarettes), Oct. 14, 1993 [in French].

Loi N⁰ 1/005 portant modification des articles 14 et 15 du Décret-Loi N⁰ 1/04 du janvier 31 1989 portant reforme de la taxe sur les transactions (Law Amending Articles 14 and 15 of Decree-Law N⁰ 1/04 of Jan. 31, 1989, Reforming Tax on Transactions), Mar. 31, 1994 [in French].

Loi N⁰ 1/006 portant abrogation du Decret-Loi N⁰ 1/10 du 3 mai 1978 portant institution d'une taxe touristique (Law Repealing Decree-Law N⁰ 1/10 of May 1978 Establishing the Tourist Tax), Mar. 31, 1994 [in French].

Cambodia (KHM)

Obviously, the decree listed below is outdated. According to the IBFD supplement on Cambodia dated Apr. 1996 (in Taxes and Investment in Asia and the Pacific), applicable taxes included profits tax, income tax, turnover tax, tax on renting of houses and land, undeveloped land tax, registration tax, stamp duty, and sales tax (imposed on petroleum products, beverages, and cigarettes).

Royal Decree of Sept. 13, 1954, Tax on Industrial, Commercial, Non-Commercial, Agriculture and Real Estate Profits, *reprinted in* TLW [in English].

Cameroon (CMR)

CGI—Code général des impôts (General Tax Code), *reprinted in* Code général des impôts remis à jour au 1 juillet 1996 (Alpha Conseil Formation, B.P. 14670 Yaoundé; Tel. 221258) [in French], *reprinted in* TLW (as amended to Feb. 1988).

Code de l'enregistrement du timbre et de la curatelle, mis à jour au 1 juillet 1995: Législation harmonisée en UDEAC, et Législation non harmonisée (Registration Stamp Tax and Fee), *reprinted in* Collection des Codes DIN [in French].

Canada (CAN)

For the income tax and goods and services tax (GST), we cite to one of several compilations published by commercial publishers. Note that the GST is part of the Excise Act. The Excise Act has been used to implement a number of federal taxes, including the sales tax. As of 1991, the sales tax portions of the Excise Act have been replaced by the GST provisions. Other parts of the Excise Act remain in effect. Incidentally, it is frightening to note that although the GST has been in effect for only a few years, it is already the subject of a seven-volume loose-leaf service.

ITA—Income Tax Act, R.S.C. 1985, *reprinted in* H. Stikeman, Stikeman Income Tax Act, Annotated (23rd ed., Carswell Thomson Professional Publishing 1994) (as amended to July 31, 1994).

Goods and Services Tax provisions contained in the Excise Tax Act, R.S.C. 1985, *reprinted in* The Practitioner's Goods and Services Tax, Annotated (David M. Sherman, ed., 6th ed., Carswell Thomson Professional Publishing 1996) (as amended to June 1, 1996).

Excise Act, Revised Statutes of Canada 1985; amendments may be found in Canada Statute Citator (Canada Law Book Inc., loose-leaf 1997).

Cape Verde (CPV)

Regulamento do imposto profissional (Regulation on Professional Tax), 1963, *reprinted in* Ministério das Finanças do Planeamento, Regulamentos Tributários 5 (Grafedito 1992) (as amended to 1992) [in Portuguese].

Regulamento da contribuição industrial (Business Tax Regulation), 1963, *id.*

Decree-Law 126/85 of Sept. 25, 1985, Boletim oficial, Nov. 9, 1985 (approves table of consumption tax rates).

Decree-Law 27/88, Boletim oficial, Apr. 2, 1988 (exemption from customs duties, consumption tax, and general fees for imports financed by IDA project).

Central African Republic (CAF)

Code général des impôts directs (General Code on Direct Taxes) (Direction générale des impôts, 1983) [in French].

Code des impôts de l'enregistrement, sur le revenu des valeurs mobilières et du timbre (Oct. 1, 1970: G.I.R.C.A., Bangui) [in French].

Ordonnance Nº 74-013, Jan. 24, 1974, Journal officiel, Mar.15, 1974 [in French].

Loi Nº 88-008, May 19, 1988 [in French].

Loi Nº 94.003, Mar. 22, 1994, arrêtant le budget pour l'année 1994 (established turnover tax and excise) [in French].

Chad (TCD)

The tax legislation is codified in the Code Général des Impôts. Recent amendments are made by Ordonnance Nº 1/PR/96, portant budget général pour 1997 [in French].

Chile (CHL)

We cite to a compilation published by the internal revenue authority (Servicio de Impuestos Internos), as well as to the IBFD CD-ROM.

Decreto Ley N° 830 sobre código tributario (Tax Code) D.O., 31 de diciembre de 1974 y actualizado hasta el 31 de julio de 1994, *reprinted in* Textos Legales, Servicio de Impuestos Internos, Arrayan ed. (1995) [in Spanish], as amended by Ley N° 19.398, Aug. 4, 1995, *reprinted in* IBFD-CIAT [in Spanish].

IR—Decreto Ley N° 824 de Impuesto a la Renta (Income Tax), D.O., 31 de diciembre de 1974 y actualizado hasta el 4 de febrero de 1995, *reprinted in* Textos Legales, *supra*, as amended to Nov. 1996, *reprinted in* IBFD-CIAT [in Spanish].

Decreto Ley N° 825 sobre impuesto a las ventas y servicios (Law on Sales and Services Tax), D.O. 31 de diciembre de 1987 y actualizado hasta el 31 de diciembre de 1994, *reprinted in* Textos Legales, *supra*, as amended by Ley N° 19.398 of Aug. 4, 1995, *reprinted in* IBFD-CIAT [in Spanish] *and in* TLW (as amended to May 1991) [in English].

Ley N° 16.271, de impuesto a las herencias, asignaciones y donaciones (Inheritance and Gift Tax Law) D.O., 10 de julio de 1965 y actualizado hasta el 31 de diciembre de 1994, *reprinted in* Textos Legales [in Spanish].

Decreto Ley N° 3.475 de impuesto de timbres y estampillas (Stamp Tax Law) D.O. 4 de septiembre de 1980, *reprinted in* Información Tributaria (Servicio de Impuestos Internos 1988) (as amended to Aug. 31, 1987) [in Spanish].

Ley N° 17.235 sobre impuesto territorial (Land Tenure Tax) D.O., 24 de diciembre de 1969 y actualizada hasta el 31 de agosto de 1994, *id.*

Decreto Ley N° 600 de 1974, sobre estatuto de la inversión extranjera (Foreign Investment Law) D.O., 18 de marzo de 1977, *reprinted in* Información Tributaria (Servicio de Impuestos Internos 1988) (as amended to Aug. 31, 1987) [in Spanish].

Decreto Ley N° 889 de 1975 modifica el régimen aduanero, tributario y de incentivos a la I, II, III, XI y XII Regiones y a la actual provincia de Chile (Regional Tax Provisions), D.O., 21 de febrero de 1975, *reprinted in* Información Tributaria (Servicio de Impuestos Internos 1988) (as amended to Aug. 31, 1987) [in Spanish].

Decreto Supremo N° 341 de 1977, aprueba el texto refundido y coordinado de los Decretos Leyes N°s 1.055 y 1.233 (1975), 1.611 (1976) y 1.698 (1977) sobre zonas y depósitos francos (Free Zones and Deposits), D.C., 8 de junio de 1977, *reprinted in* Información Tributaria (Servicio de Impuestos Internos 1988) (as amended to Aug. 31, 1987) [in Spanish].

Texto del D.F.L. N° 2 de 1959 sobre plan habitacional, D.O., 31 de julio de 1959 y actualizado al 31 de agosto de 1994, *id*.

China (CHN)

In addition to those listed below, an urban real property tax and a tax on vehicles and ships are imposed.

Income Tax Law of the People's Republic of China for Enterprises with Foreign Investment and Foreign Enterprises, enacted by the National People's Congress on Apr. 9, 1991, *reprinted in* National Taxation Bureau—Foreign Taxation Administration Department, a Collection of Tax Laws and Regulations of the People's Republic of China, at 184 (State Statistics Bureau 1994) [in Chinese, English].

EIT—Provisional Regulations of the People's Republic of China on Enterprise Income Tax, enacted by the State Council on Dec. 13, 1993, *id*.

Provisional Regulations of the People's Republic of China on Consumption Tax, enacted by the State Council on Dec. 13, 1993, *id*.

Provisional Regulations of the People's Republic of China on Business Tax, enacted by the State Council on Dec. 13, 1993, *id*.

Individual Income Tax Law of the People's Republic of China, enacted by the Standing Committee, National People's Congress, Oct. 31, 1993, *id*.

Provisional Regulations of the People's Republic of China on Value-Added Tax, enacted by the State Council, Dec. 13, 1993, *id*.

Provisional Regulations of the People's Republic of China on Resource Tax, enacted by the State Council, Dec. 13, 1993, *id*.

Provisional Regulations of the People's Republic of China on Land Appreciation Tax, enacted by the State Council, Dec. 13, 1993, *id*.

Provisional Regulations of the People's Republic of China Concerning Stamp Tax, enacted by the State Council, Oct. 1, 1988, *id*.

Supplementary Provisions [to the Criminal Law] Concerning the Imposition of Punishments in Respect of Offenses of Tax Evasion and Refusal to Pay Tax, enacted by the Standing Committee, National People's Congress, Sept. 4, 1992, *id*.

The Law of the People's Republic of China Concerning the Administration of Tax Collection, enacted by the Standing Committee, National People's Congress, Sept. 4, 1992, *id*. at 236. Amendment of the People's Republic of China Tax Collection Administration Law based on the Feb. 28, 1995 Decisions Regarding Revision of the People's Republic of China Tax Collection Administration Law of the Eleventh Meeting of the Eighth National People's Congress Standing Committee, FBIS Database, FBIS-CHI-95-069 [in English].

Colombia (COL)

The tax laws of Colombia have, since 1989, been codified in the Tax Code (Estatuto Tributario). Most provisions of tax laws (e.g., Law N° 49 of 1990, cited below) consist of amendments to the code. However, certain provisions, largely of a transitional nature, do not amend the code and hence someone who needs to know all the tax laws of Colombia must consult these provisions in addition to the code. We cite to a commercial publisher of the Code as well as to the IBFD-CIAT.

TC—Decreto N° 624, Estatuto Tributario (Taxation Statute), Mar. 30, 1989, as amended to Dec. 1995, *reprinted in* IBFD-CIAT *and in* Rodrigo Monsalve T., Impuestos 1991 (renta, ventas e indirectos) (Centro Interamericano Jurídico-Financiero 1991) (as amended to 1991) [in Spanish] *and in* TLW (art. 1-364, as of Mar. 30, 1989) [in English].

Ley N° 49 de 1990, reforma tributaria 1990 (Law on Tax Reform), D.O., 31 diciembre de 1990, *reprinted* in IBFD.

Comoros (COM)

Loi N° 85-018/AF du 24 décembre 1985, Code générale des impôts (General Tax Code), *reprinted in* Comoros, Administration générale des impôts, Code général des impôts (1985) [in French].

Congo, Democratic Republic of the (ZAR)

(Formerly known as Zaïre.)

CDC—Code des contributions (General Tax Code) (as amended to June 1989).

Congo, Republic of (COG)

CGI—Code générale des impôts (General Tax Code), tome 1 et 2 (ed. 1990), Brazzaville, République populaire du Congo (author not identified but presumably an official publication).

Amending acts:
Loi de finances N° 5.92, Mar. 10, 1992.
Loi de finances N° 14.94 du 17 juin 1994 pour l'année 1994.
Loi de finances N° 15.94 du 15 juillet 1994 portant modification du budget de l'état pour 1994.
Loi de finances portant modification du budget de l'État pour 1995.
Loi de finances N° 5.96 du 2 mars 1996 pour l'année 1996.
Loi de finances N° 2.97 du 29 mars 1997 pour l'année 1997.

Costa Rica (CRI)

In addition to the taxes listed below, Costa Rica imposes mineral royalties, real estate tax, real estate transfer tax, stamp taxes, and assets tax.

Decreto Nº 4755, Código de Normas y Procedimientos Tributarios (Code of Tax Regulations and Procedures), May 3, 1971, as amended to Feb. 1996, *reprinted in* IBFD-CIAT [in Spanish].

Ley Nº 7092, Impuesto sobre la Renta (Income Tax Law), Apr. 21, 1988, as amended by Law Nº 7551 of Sept. 22, 1995, *reprinted in* IBFD-CIAT [in Spanish] *and in* TLW (as amended to Sept. 1991) [in English].

Ley Nº 6826, Impuesto General sobre las Ventas (General Sales Tax Act, Act), Nov. 8, 1982, as amended by Law Nº 7543 of Sept. 14, 1995, *reprinted in* IBFD-CIAT [in Spanish] *and in* TLW (as amended to Sept. 1991) [in English].

Ley Nº 7535 de Justicia Tributaria, July 31, 1995, *reprinted in* IBFD-CIAT [in Spanish].

Ley Nº 7543, Ajuste Tributario (Tax Adjustment Law), Sept. 12, 1995 available on TaxBase [in Spanish].

Côte d'Ivoire (CIV)

Code général des impôts 1981 (General Tax Code), *reprinted in* République de la Côte d'Ivoire, Code général des impôts (Impr. Nationale 1981) (as amended to Dec. 31, 1980), *also in* Codes et Lois Usuelles de Côte d'Ivoire (A. Aggrey ed.) (as amended to 1985) [in French].

Croatia (HRV)

Zakon o Porezu na Dohodak (Income Tax Law), Narodne Novine Nº 109, Dec. 7, 1993 [in Serbo-Croatian].

PT—Zakon o Porezu na Dobit (Profit Tax Law), Narodne Novine Nº 109, Dec. 7, 1993 [in Serbo-Croatian], *translated in* Croatian Income Tax & Profit Tax Acts (Institut za Javne Financije, Zagreb, 1994) [in English].

Income and Profit Tax Amendments, Narodne Novine Nº 95, Dec. 27, 1994, *reprinted in* Income Tax Act, Profit Tax Act (Institut za Javne Financije, Zagreb 1995).

Value Added Tax Act, Narodne Novine, Nº 47, July 12, 1995 (Institut za Javne Financije, Zagreb 1995) [in Croatian, German, English].

Cyprus (CYP)

In addition to those listed below, the Assessment and Collection of Taxes Law of 1978, as amended, applies. VAT applies as of July 1, 1992.

IT—The Income Tax Laws, 1961–1988 (N⁰ 3), *reprinted in* TLW (as amended to Dec. 1990) [in English].

Law N⁰ 52 of 1980, Capital Gains Tax, 1980, Printing Office of the Republic of Cyprus [in English].

Estate Duty Law (as amended to 1985) [in English], *id.*

The Immovable Property Tax Law (as amended up to Feb. 26, 1981) [in English], *id.*

The Imposition of Tax on Certain Services Law, 1984 [in English], *id.*

The Stamp Law (as amended to 1984) [in English], *id.*

The Special Contribution (Temporary Provisions) Law, 1974 (as amended to 1984) [in English], *id.*

Czech Republic (CZE)

We cite to the session laws (Sbírka zákonů) as well as to a commercially prepared translation of up-to-date tax laws published by Trade Links. The latter comes out about once a year and so will not always be completely up to date. Moreover, it does not contain all the laws. České zakony, edited by P. Bohata and H. Valkova (Beck: Munich) is a loose-leaf service that will contain an up-to-date compilation in Czech; see also Danove a finančni pravo by the same editors, which focuses on tax and financial laws.

ITA—N⁰ 586/1992, Zákon o daních z příjmů (Income Taxes Act), *reprinted in* Czech Taxation in 1997 (Z. Pošustová et al. trans., Trade Links Prague) (as amended to Feb. 1997) [in English].

N⁰ 593/1992, Zákon o rezervách pro zjištění základu daně z příjmů (Act on Reserves for the Purposes of Determining Income Tax Base), *id.*

N⁰ 588/1992, Zákon o dani z přidané hodnoty (Value Added Tax Act), *id.*

N⁰ 587/1992, Zákon o spotřebních daních (Excise Duties Act), *id.*

N⁰ 357/1992, Zákon o dani z převodu nemovitostí (Real Estate Transfer Tax) (excerpts), *id.*

N⁰ 338/1992, Zákon o dani z nemovitostí (Real Estate Tax Act), *id.*

N⁰ 337/1992, Zákon o správě daní a poplaktů (Law on the Administration of Taxes and Fees), *id.*

N⁰ 119/1992, Zákon o cestovních náhradách (Travel Expense Reimbursement Act), *id.*

N⁰ 16/1993, Zákon o dani silniční (Road Tax Act), *id.*

Zákon české národní rady o dani dědické, dani darovací a dani z převodu nemovitostí (Law on Inheritance Tax, Gift Tax, and Real Estate Transfer Tax) N⁰ 357/1992 Coll., Sbírka zákonů, July 7, 1992 [in Czech].

Zákon N⁰ 322 kterým se mění a doplňuje zákon české národní rady N⁰ 357/ 1992 Sb., o dani dědické, dani darovací a dani z převodu nemovitostí, ve znění zákona české národní rady N⁰ 18/1993 Sb. (Amendments to Law N⁰ 357 on Inheritance Tax, Gift Tax, and Real Estate Transfer Tax), Sbírka zákonů, Dec. 30, 1993 [in Czech].

N⁰ 85/1994 Zákon který m se doplňuje zákon české národní rady N⁰ 357/1992 Sb., o dani dědické, dani darovací a dani z převodu nemovitostí, ve znění zákona české národní rady N⁰ 18/1993 Sb., zákona N⁰ 322/1993 Sb., zákona N⁰ 42/1994 Sb., a zákona N⁰ 85/1994 Sb. (Amendments to Law N⁰ 357 on Inheritance Tax, Gift Tax, and Real Estate Transfer Tax) (Amendments to Law N⁰ 357), Sbírka zákonů, at 1162, July 8, 1994.

Denmark (DEN)

We cite to a commercial compilation (Dankse Skattelove) that comes out annually. In addition to the listed taxes, the following taxes are imposed: church tax, tax on lottery winnings, tax on hunting licenses, excise duty on petrol, excise tax on certain petroleum products, tax on gas, tax on electricity, registration tax on motor vehicles, excise duty on tobacco, excise tax on spirits, excise duty on wine and fruit wine, excise duty on beer, excise duty on mineral waters and the like, excise duty on tea and tea extracts, excise duty on coffee, coffee extracts, and coffee substitute, excise duty on chocolate and sweets, tax on ice cream, tax on incandescent lamps and electric fuses, sundry consumption tax, tax on certain retail packaging, tax on totalizator betting, tax on rents released from Landlord's Investment Fund, weight tax on motor vehicles, tax on pleasure-craft insurance, levy on banks and savings banks, levy on insurance businesses, fund income tax, legal action tax, tax on coal, lignite, and coke, environmental tax, tax on certain chlorofluorocarbons and halons, tax on waste and certain raw materials, tax on gramophone records and compact discs, tax on casino games, flight transportation tax, tax on football-pool betting and lotto, tax on labor costs, energy tax on mineral oil, excise duty on cigarette paper, chewing tobacco and snuff, carbon dioxide tax on certain energy products, excise duty on water pipelines, taxation of pension schemes, real-interest tax on certain pension capitals, etc. References to the respective laws imposing these taxes are found in EU Inventory. The Tax Ministry has published an English summary of the tax system, Direct Taxation in Denmark (Jan. 1995).

Afskrivningsloven (Act on Fiscal Depreciation) Lovbekendtgørelse nr. 205 af 23. Marts 1990 om skattemæssige afskrivninger, *reprinted in* Danske Skattelove 1990/1991 med henvisninger (Peter Taarnhoj ed., A/S Skattekartoteket Informationskontor 1990) (as amended through July 1990) [in Danish].

Aktieafgiftsloven (The Share Duty Act) Lov nr. 228 af 22. Apr. 1987 om afgift ved overdragelse af aktier m.v., *id.*

Aktieavancebeskatningsloven (Act on Taxation of Share Profits) Lovbekendtgørelse nr. 698 af 5. Nov. 1987 om beskatning af fortjeneste ved aftåelse af aktier m.v., *id.*

Amtskommuneskatteloven (County Authority Income Tax) Lovbekendt-gørelse nr. 534 af 30. Oktober 1974 om udskrivning af skat til amtskommu-nen, id.

Arve-og gaveafgiftsloven (Act on Inheritance and Gift Tax) Lovbekendt-gørelse nr. 62 af 6. Februar 1987 om afgift af arv og gave [in Danish], id. Also reprinted in TLW (as amended to Nov. 1988) [in English].

Bunden opsparing (Act on Compulsory Saving) Lov nr. 137 af 6. Apr. 1985 om bunden opsparing, reprinted in Danske Skattelove, supra [in Danish].

Børnefamilieydelsesloven (Act on Child Benefits) Lovbekendtgørelse nr. 163 af 4. Marts. 1990 om en børnefamilieydelse, id. [in Danish].

Dobbeltbeskatningsloven (Act on Double Taxation) Lov nr. 74 af 31. Marts. 1953 om indgåelse af overenskomster med fremmede stater til undgåelse af dobbeltbeskatning m.v., id. [in Danish].

Ejendomsavancebeskatningloven (Act on Taxation of Real Estate Profits) Lovbekendtgørelse nr. 558 af 16. Sept. 1988 om beskatning af fortjeneste ved afståelse af fast ejendom [in Danish], id. Also reprinted in TLW (as amended to Nov. 1988) [in English].

Ejerlejlighedsbeskatningsloven (Act on Duty on First-Time Transfer of Cer-tain Freehold Flats) Lov nr. 193 af 9. Apr. 1986 om beskatning af fortjeneste ved førstengangsafståelse af visse ejerlejligheder m.v., reprinted in Danske Skat-telove, supra.

Etableringskontoloven (Act on Establishment Accounts) Lovbekendtgørelse nr. 240 af 17. Apr. 1990 om indskud på etableringskonto, id.

Fondsbeskatningsloven (The Foundation Tax Act) Lovbekendtgørelse nr. 528 af 2. Aug. 1989 om beskatning af fonde, visse foreninger og institutter m.v., id.

Forhåndsbeskedloven (Act on Advance Notice) Lov nr. 143 af 13. Apr. 1983 om bindende forhåndsbesked om skattespørgsmål m.v., id.

Forsvarerbistandsloven Lovbekendtgørelse nr. 489, Sept. 19, 1984, om adgang til forsvarerbistand under en administrativ skatte-eller afgiftsstraffesag (Act on Defendant Benefits, Sept. 19, 1984, on access to defendant assistance during a tax or fine administrative proceeding), id.

Frigørelsesafgiftsloven (Act on Property Release Tax) Lovbekendtgørelse nr. 441 af 26. Sept. 1985 om frigørelsesaftgift m.v. af fast ejendom [in Danish], id.

Fusionsloven (The Merger Act) Lovbekendtgørelse nr. 527 af 2. Aug. 1989 om beskatning ved fusion af aktieselskaber m.v. [in Danish], id.

Gensidig bistandslov (Act on Mutual Assistance) Lov nr. 635 af 13. Dec. 978 om gensidig bistand inden for området direkte skatter mellem stater, der er medlem af De europæiske Fællesskaber [in Danish], id.

Husdyrbesætningsloven (Act on Livestock) Lovbekendtgørelse nr. 526 af 2. Aug. 1989 om den skattemæssige behandling af husdyrbesætninger, *id.*

Inddrivelsesloven (Act on Tax Collection) Lov nr. 278 af 26. Maj 1976 om fremgangsmåden ved inddrivelse af skatter og afgifter m.v., *id.*

Indexkontraktloven (Act on Indexed Savings Accounts) Lovbekendtgørelse nr. 16 af 12. Januar 1972 om pristalsreguleret alderdomsforsikring og alderdomsopsparing, *id.*

Investeringsfondsloven (Act on Investment Funds) Lovbekendtgørelse nr. 241 af 17. April 1990 om investeringsfonds, *id.*

Investeringsforeningsloven (Act on Unit Trust (Mutual Funds)) Lovbekendtgørelse nr. 654 af 8. Oktober 1987 om beskatning af medlemmer af investeringsforeninger, *id.*

Kapitaltilførselsaffgiftsloven (Duty on the Raising of Capital Act) Lovbekendtgørelse nr. 761 af 12. Dec. 1988 om kapitaltilførselsafgift, *id.*

Kildeskatteloven (Act on Withholding Tax) Lovbekendtgørelse nr. 662 af 19. Oktober 1989 om opkrævning af indkomst—og formueskat for personer m.v., *id.*

Kommuneskatteloven (Local Authority Income Tax Act) Lovbekendtgørelse nr. 620 af 25. Sept. 1987 om kommunal indkomstskat, *id.*

Kulbrinteskatteloven (The Hydrocarbon Tax Act) Lovbekendtgørelse nr. 739 af 20. Nov. 1987 om beskatning af indkomst i forbindelse med kulabrinteindvinding i Danmark, *id.*; also [in English] *reprinted in* 9 TLW, at 115 (as amended to Nov. 1988) [in English].

Kulbrinteopkrævningsloven (Act on Collection of Hydrocarbon Tax) Lovbekendtgørelse nr. 740 af 20. Nov. 1987 om ansættelse og opkrævning m.v. af skat ved kulbrinteindvinding, *id.* also [in English] *reprinted in* 9 TLW, at 125 (as amended to Nov. 1988) [in English].

Kursgevinstloven (Act on Gains from Bonds and Securities) Lovbekendtgørelse nr. 627 af 29. Sept. 1987 om skattemæssig behandling af gevinst og tab på fordringer og gæld, *id.*

Ligningsloven (Act on Tax Assessment) Lovbekendtgørelse nr. 660 af 10. Oktober 1989 om påligningen af indkomst—og formueskat til staten, *id.*

Pensionsbeskatningsloven (Act on Taxation of Pension Schemes) Lovbekendtgørelse nr. 569 af 26. Aug. 1987 om beskatning af pensionsordninger m.v., *id.*

Personskatteloven (The Personal Tax Act), Lovbekendtgørelse nr. 661 af 19. Oktober 1989 om indkomstskat og formueskat for personer m.v., *id.*

Realrenteafgitsloven (Act on Real Interest Tax) Lovbekendtgørelse nr. 762 af 12. Dec. 1988 om en realrenteafgift af visse pensionskapitaler m.v., *id.*

Rentenedslagsloven (Act on Interest Abatement) Lov nr. 343 af 4. Juni 1986 om nedslag i skatteansættelsen for renteindtægter m.v., *id.*

Sagkyndig bistandsloven (Act on Expert Advice) Bekendtgørelse nr. 518 af 8. Aug. 1986 af lov om omkostningsdækning af udgifter til sagkyndig bistand i skattesager, *id.*

Særlig Indkomstskat (Act on Special Income Tax) Lovbekendtgørelse nr. 900 af 21. Dec. 1987 om særlig indkomstskat m.v., *id.*

Selskabsskatteloven (The Corporation Tax Act), Lovbekendtgørelse nr. 593 af 30. Sept. 1988 om indkomstbeskatning af aktielskaber m.v., *id.*

Skattekontrolloven (Act on Tax Inspection) Bekendtgørelse nr. 28 af 11. Januar 1988 af skattekontrolloven, *id.*

Skattestyrelsesloven (The Tax Administration Act), Lov nr. 824 af 19. Dec. 1989 om skattemyndighedernes organisation og opgaver m.v., *id.*

Sømænd, særlige fradrag (Act on Special Allowances for Seamen) Lov nr. 362 af 1. Juli 1988 om særlige fradrag til sømænd m.v., *id.*

Statsskatteloven (Act on Income Tax to the Government) Lov nr. 149 af 10. April 1922 om indkomst—og formueskat til staten, *id.*

Varelagerloven (Act on Stock-in-Trade) Lovbekendtgørelse nr. 564 af 21. Aug. 1987 om skattemæssig opgørelse af varelagre m.v., *id.*

Virksomhedsomdannelsesloven (Business Conversion Act) Lovbekendtgørelse nr. 594 af 4. Sept. 1986 om skattefri virksomhedsomdannelse, *id.*

Virksomhedsskatteloven (Act on Business Taxation) Lovbekendtgørelse nr. 575 af 22. Aug. 1989 om indkomstbeskatning af selvstændige erhvervsdrivende, *id.*

Djibouti (DJI)

Code général des impôts (General Tax Code), tome 1: Contributions directs (Direct Taxation); tome 2: Fiscalité indirecte (Indirect Taxation) (no author or date indicated, but seems to be an official publication dating from 1991).

Dominica (DMA)

We cite to the official gazette and to a 12-volume consolidation, called The Laws of Dominica in Force on the 31st Day of December 1990, prepared by the Law Revision Commission, Ministry of Legal Affairs, 1991. The laws in effect as of Jan. 1, 1996 are listed in Commonwealth of Dominica: Consolidated Index of Statutes and

Subsidiary Legislation (Faculty of Law Library, University of the West Indies, Barbados 1996). The amending acts can be found in that index and are not listed here.

Income Tax Act, ch. 67:01, Laws of Dominica.

Tax Information Exchange Act, Laws of Dominica, ch. 67:02.

Sales Tax Act, Laws of Dominica, ch. 67:06.

Development Levy Act, Laws of Dominica, ch. 67:10.

Stamp Act, Laws of Dominica, ch. 68:01.

Hotel Occupancy Tax Act of April 1971, Laws of Dominica, ch. 70:06.

Fiscal Incentives Act, Laws of Dominica, ch. 84:51.

Rum Duty Act, ch. 70:02.

Income Tax (Federal Emoluments) Act 1960 (Cap. 151).

Provisional Collection of Taxes Act, ch. 66:02.

Collection of Taxes Act, Laws of Dominica, ch. 66:01.

Caribbean Free Trade Association Act, ch. 80:01.

Consumption Tax Order, 1984, Statutory Rules and Orders (S.R.O.) Nº 23 of 1984, Official Gazette of June 28, 1984 (Government Printer).

Consumption Tax (Amendment) Order of 1987, S.R.O. Nº 62 of 1987, Official Gazette of Nov. 19, 1987 (Government Printer).

Consumption Tax (Amendment) Order of 1989, S.R.O. Nº 57 of 1989, Official Gazette of Dec. 28, 1989 (Government Printer).

Consumption Tax (Amendment) Order of 1990, S.R.O. Nº 27 of 1990, Official Gazette of Aug. 23, 1990 (Government Printer).

Consumption Tax (Amendment) Order of 1991, S.R.O. Nº 18 of 1991, Official Gazette of Apr. 25, 1991 (Government Printer).

Consumption Tax (Amendment) Order of 1991, S.R.O. Nº 19 of 1991, Official Gazette of Apr. 4, 1991 (Government Printer).

Consumption Tax (Amendment) Order of 1992, S.R.O. Nº 26 of 1992, Official Gazette of Aug. 6, 1992 (Government Printer).

Consumption Tax (Amendment) Order of 1993, S.R.O. Nº 36 of 1993, Official Gazette of Aug. 26, 1993 (Government Printer).

Consumption Tax (Amendment) Order of 1993, S.R.O. Nº 53 of 1993, Official Gazette of Dec. 2, 1993 (Government Printer).

Consumption Tax (Amendment) Order of 1994, S.R.O. Nº 8 of 1994, Official Gazette of Mar. 3, 1994 (Government Printer).

Foreign Currency Levy Act, Laws of Dominica, ch. 70:04.

Dominican Republic (DOM)

The Dominican Republic consolidated its tax legislation in a Tax Code in 1992, at the same time carrying out a tax reform. Mineral royalties are imposed under separate legislation (Mineral Law N° 146, June 4, 1971).

TC—Código tributario de la República Dominicana (Tax Code of the Dominican Republic) Ley N° 11–92, May 16, 1992, *reprinted in* Código Tributario de la República Dominicana (1992), Government Publisher [in Spanish], *in* Francisco Canahuate, Ley N° 11–92 de Código tributario de la República Dominicana (1992) *and in* IBFD-CIAT [in Spanish]; *also reprinted in* TLW (as amended to Nov. 1993) [in English].

Ecuador (ECU)

In contrast to Colombia and the Dominican Republic, Ecuador's tax code is not a consolidation of all the tax laws, but rather constitutes the general provisions applicable to the various taxes. In addition to the sources listed below, the Ediciones Legales, S.A., Apartado 1703–186, Pasaje Donoso 131 y Whymper, Quito, publishes loose-leaf services [in Spanish] for tax and other areas of commercial law (fax 5932-507-729, or 554-954). The tax service is called Regimen Tributario Ecuatoriano, in three volumes.

Decreto Ley N° 1015-A, Codigo Tributario, Dec. 6, 1977 (as amended to Jan. 1996), *reprinted in* IBFD-CIAT [in Spanish].

RTI—Ley de Régimen Tributario Interno, Función Legislativa N° 56, Dec. 14, 1989, as amended to March 1997, *reprinted in* IBFD-CIAT [in Spanish].

Impuesto al Valor Agregado (Value Added Tax), Ley de Régimen Tributario Interno, Función Legislativa N° 56, Título II of Dec. 14, 1989 (as amended to Dec. 1996), *reprinted in* IBFD-CIAT [in Spanish] Official Gazette, Dec. 22 1989, *reprinted in* TLW (as amended to June 1991) [in English].

Régimen Tributario de las Empresas Petroleras Mineras y Turísticas (Tax Regime Applicable to Petroleum, Mining and Tourism Enterprises), Función Legislativa N° 56, Título IV of Dec. 14, 1989, *reprinted* in IBFD-CIAT [in Spanish].

Ley de Impuesto a la Renta (Income Tax Law), RO 305:8-IX-71, *reprinted in* Ley de Impuesto a la Renta y Reglamento (Corporación de Estudios y Publicaciones 1988) (as amended to Aug. 1988) [in Spanish], *reprinted in* IBFD-CIAT [in Spanish].

D.S. N° 87, Ley de Timbres y Tasas Postales Telegráficas (Law on Stamps and Telegraphic Postal Rates) (as amended to July 1988), *reprinted in* Corporación de Estudios y Publicaciones [in Spanish].

Egypt (EGY)

Income Tax Law, N° 157 of 1981, Official Journal N° 37, Sept. 10, 1981, *reprinted in* TLW (as amended by Law N° 187 of 1993) [in English], amended by Law N° 90 of 1996, Official Journal, N° 25 bis, June 30, 1996; Law N° 226 of 1996, Official Journal, N° 26 bis, July 14, 1996.

Law N° 147 of 1984, imposing a duty for the development of the financial resources of the state.

Sales Tax Law of 1991, Apr. 23, 1991.

Fiscal Stamp Law N° 111 of 1980, amended by Law 155 of 1980 (imposes stamp duty).

El Salvador (SLV)

Decreto Legislativo N° 134, Ley de Impuesto sobre la Renta, Dec. 18, 1991, as amended to Oct. 1994, *reprinted in* IBFD-CIAT [in Spanish].

Decreto Legislativo N° 296, Impuesto a la Transferencia de Bienes Muebles y a la Prestación de Servicios (Tax on Transfers of Personal Property and the Provision of Services) of July 24, 1992, as amended by Decreto N° 406 of July 13, 1995, *reprinted in* IBFD-CIAT [in Spanish] .

Equatorial Guinea (GNQ)

The tax laws of Equatorial Guinea have been consolidated into one law, cited below, which is therefore effectively a tax code.

Decreto-Ley N° 1/1986 por el que se aprueba el sistema tributario de la República de Guinea Ecuatorial (Law Approving the Tax System), B.O.E., 24 de febrero de 1986 [in Spanish].

Decreto-Ley N° 7/1988, por el que se modifican ciertos artículos del Decreto Ley N° 1/1986, Aug. 17, 1988 (amending the above).

Eritrea (ERT)

ITP—Proclamation N° 62/1994, Income Tax Proclamation, 4 Gazette of Eritrean Laws N° 7, Oct. 5, 1994 [in English].

Proclamation N° 63/1994, Rural Agricultural Income Tax and Cattle Tax Proclamation, 4 Gazette of Eritrean Laws N° 7, Oct. 5, 1994 [in English].

Proclamation N° 64/1994, Sales and Excise Tax Proclamation, 4 Gazette of Eritrean Laws N° 8, Oct. 5, 1994 [in English].

Proclamation N° 65/1994, Stamp Duty Proclamation, 4 Gazette of Eritrean Laws N° 9, Oct. 5, 1994 [in English].

Proclamation Nº 67/1995, Income Tax on Eritreans Working Abroad, Feb. 10, 1995.

Estonia (EST)

The tax laws of Estonia were substantially reformed in 1993. We cite a commercially published book constituting a compilation of the tax laws, translated into English (Estonian Taxes). Updated versions in English are available from IMG Konsultant, Liivalaia 12, Tallinn, EE0001, Estonia. Fax: 372-6461153. Cites to RT are to the official gazette (Riigi Teataja). Some cites are to a Russian translation of the official gazette called Pravovye Akti Estonii (PAE) (e.g., PAE 1997, 41, 808 means item 808 of issue Nº 41 of 1997). In addition to those listed below, an excise tax on packaging and a tax on natural resources (under the law on environmental protection) are imposed.

Law on Taxation, RT 1996, 57, 714 (as amended to Apr. 10, 1996), *reprinted in* PAE, Oct. 15, 1996 [in Russian]. Law on Taxation, RT 1994, 30, 5 (as amended to March 16, 1994), *reprinted in* Estonian Taxes (Piret Joalaid ed., Marje Einre trans., AS Vaba Maa 1994) [in English].

Amended by PAE 1996, 57, 714; 1996 50/51, 953; 1996, 60, 1379; 1996, 62/63, 1447; 1997, 22, 363; 1997, 30, 447; 1997, 40, 778.

Zakon o Vnesenii Dopolneniya v Zakon o Nalogooblozhenii (Amendment to the Law on Taxation), Mar. 11, 1997, *reprinted in* PAE, Mar. 27, 1997 [in Russian].

IT—Income Tax Law, PAE, 1994 3/4, 1184, Dec. 8, 1993 (as amended to Jan. 1, 1996), *reprinted in* PAE, Feb. 20, 1996 [in Russian], *and in* Estonian Taxes, *supra* [in English].

Amended by PAE 1996, 11/12, 171; 1996, 19, 292; 1996, 27, 527; 1996, 56, 1240; 1996, 72/73, 1542; 1997, 21, 307; 1997, 30, 536; 1997, 35, 572; 1997, 41, 808.

Amendment to the Income Tax Law, Law on the Compensation Fund, Article 56, Sept. 11, 1996, *reprinted in* PAE, Nº 56, Oct. 10, 1996 [in Russian].

Zakon o Vnesenii Izmeneniy v statyiu 5 Zakona o Pododokhodnom Naloge (Amendment to Article 5 of the Income Tax Law), Feb. 27, 1997, *reprinted in* PAE, Mar. 26, 1997 [in Russian].

Income Tax Amendment Law, *reprinted in* PAE, Nº 31, May 12, 1997 [in Russian].

Law on Value-Added Tax, RT 1996, 54, 1149 (as amended to Aug. 15, 1996), *reprinted in* PAE, Sept. 30, 1996 [in Russian]. Law on Value-Added Tax, RT I 1993, 60, 84, Aug. 25, 1993 (as amended to Dec. 9, 1993); *reprinted in* Estonian Taxes, *supra* [in English].

Law on Amendments to the Law on Value-Added Tax, RT 1996, 60, 1344, *reprinted in* PAE, Nov. 15, 1996 [in Russian].

Also amended by PAE 1996, 62/63, 1447; 1997, 12, 96; 1997, 35, 621; 1997, 40, 773; 1997, 41, 776.

Law on Social Tax, RT 1990, 9, 102 (as amended to Dec. 7, 1993), *reprinted in* Estonian Taxes, *supra* [in English].

Amendment to the Law on Social Tax, RT 1996, 59, 1307, *reprinted in* PAE, Oct. 25, 1996 [in Russian].

Law on Land Tax, May 6, 1993, *reprinted in* PAE, June 21, 1993 [in Russian], *and in* Estonian Taxes, *supra* [in English]; amended by Zakon o Zemelnom Naloge (Land Law on Land Tax), RT I, 1996, 41, 797, *in* PAE, Dec. 23, 1996 [in Russian] and by Zakon o Vnesenii Izmeneniy v Zakon o Zemelnom Naloge, Dec. 10, 1996, *in* PAE, Jan. 10, 1997 [in Russian].

Zakon o Vnesenii Izmeneniy v statyiu 5 Zakona o Zemelnom Naloge (Amendment to Article 5 of the Land Tax Law), Dec. 9, 1996, *reprinted in* PAE, Jan. 10, 1997 [in Russian].

Zakona o Naloge c Azartnych igr (Law on Gambling Tax), Aug. 26, 1992, Vedomosti Estonskoy Respubliki 35, 458, Sept. 18, 1992 [in Russian], *reprinted in* Estonian Taxes, *supra*; Zakon o Vnesenii Izmeneniy v Zakon o Provedenii Lotereiy I v Statiy 7 Zakona o Naloge c Azartnych igr (Amendment to the Law on the Lottery and to Article 7 of the Law on Gambling Tax), Dec. 18, 1996, *reprinted in* PAE, Feb. 5, 1997 [in Russian].

Law on Fur Excise Tax, RT 1991, 40, 492 (as amended to Aug. 24, 1992), *reprinted in* Estonian Taxes, *supra* [in English].

Law on Tobacco Excise Tax, RT 1992, 31, 409, *reprinted in* Estonian Taxes, *supra* [in English]; amended by RT 1, 1996, 87, 1543, PAE, Dec. 23, 1996 [in Russian].

Law on Motor Fuel Excise Tax, RT 1993, 38, 563, *reprinted in* Estonian Taxes, *supra* [in English]; Zakon o Vnesenii Izmeneiy v Zakon ob Aktsize na Motornoe Toplivo (Amendment to the Law on Motor Fuel Excise Tax), RT I, 1996, 74, 1308, *reprinted in* PAE, Oct. 25, 1996 [in Russian] ; Amendment to the Law on Motor Fuel Excise Tax, RT 1, 1996, 80, 1436, *reprinted in* PAE, Nov. 22, 1996 [in Russian].

Law on Alcohol Excise Tax, RT 1992, 11, 170 (as amended to Jan. 27, 1994), *reprinted in* Estonian Taxes, *supra* (as amended to Mar. 15, 1994) [in English], amended by RT 1, 1996, 87, 1544, PAE, Dec. 23, 1996 [in Russian].

Law on State Duty, RT 1995, 22, 328 (as amended to Feb. 15. 1995), *reprinted in* PAE, Sept. 23, 1996 [in Russian]; Law on State Duty, RT 1990, 11, 118 (as amended to Feb. 9, 1994), *reprinted in* Estonian Taxes, *supra* [in English]; Amendment to the Law on State Duty, RT 1996, 52, 969, *reprinted in* PAE, Sept. 19, 1996 [in Russian].

Ethiopia (ETH)

Income Tax Proclamation, 1961, as amended through Proclamation N⁰ 36/ 1996, Federal Negarit Gazeta, N⁰ 2, N⁰ 24 (May 14, 1996), *reprinted in* TLW [in English].

Act N⁰ 68/1993, Sales and Excise Tax Proclamation, *id.*

Act N⁰ 53/1993, Mining Income Tax Proclamation, as amended by Proclamation 23/1996, Federal Negarit Gazeta, N⁰ 2, N⁰ 11 (Feb. 15, 1996), *id.*

Act N⁰ 296/1986, Petroleum Operations Income Tax Proclamation, *id.*

Proclamation N⁰ 37/1996, Investment Proclamation, *id.*

Proclamation N⁰ 77/1976, Rural Land Use Fee and Agricultural Activities Income Tax, *id.*

Act N⁰ 334/1987, Stamp Duty Proclamation, *id.*

Act N⁰ 108/1994, Payment of Tax on Gains from Capital Proclamation, *id.*

Fiji (FJI)

In addition to those listed below, Fiji imposes natural resource royalty, urban land tax, and land sales tax.

Income Tax Act, *reprinted in* Laws of Fiji: ch. 201, rev. 1985, Income Tax (Government Printer). Amended by

> Act N⁰ 9 of 1995, Income Tax (Amendment) Act, 1995 (Suva, Govt. Printer)
> Act N⁰ 18 of 1995, Income Tax (Amendment) (N⁰ 2) Act, 1995 (Suva, Govt. Printer)
> Act N⁰ 2 of 1996, Income Tax (Amendment) Act, 1996 (Suva, Govt. Printer)

Hotel Turnover Tax, *id*, ch. 202.

Excise Tax, *id*, ch. 199, amended by Act N⁰ 22, Excise (Amendment) Act, 1996; Act N⁰ 29, Excise (Amendment) (N⁰ 2) Act, 1996.

Value Added Tax Decree 1991, Decree N⁰ 45, 5 Fiji Republic Gazette 913 (extraordinary ed. Nov. 22, 1991), amended by Value Added Tax (Amendment) Act, 1995; Act N⁰ 29 of 1995, Value Added Tax (Amendment) (N⁰ 2) Act, 1995.

Stamp Duties Act, *reprinted in* Laws of Fiji, ch. 205, rev. 1985.

Finland (FIN)

In addition to those listed below, Finland imposes payroll tax, church tax, net wealth tax, excise, motor vehicle tax, stamp duty, and real estate tax. The tax laws (and other legal publications) are available [in Finnish] from Lakimiesliiton Kustannus, Uudenmaankatu 4–6 A, 00120 Helsinki, Finland.

Income Tax, *reprinted in* TLW (as amended to Mar. 1989) [in English]; Act on Amendments to the Income Tax Law, Jan. 1, 1996, available on microfiche and on TaxBase [in Finnish].

Laki Perinto—Ja Lahjaverlolain Muuttamisesta (Law of Amendments to Inheritance and Gift Tax Law) Dec. 1995, available on TaxBase [in Finnish].

Laki Arvonlisaverolain Muuttamisesta (Law of Amendments to VAT Law), Jan. 1996, available on TaxBase [in Finnish].

France (FRA)

The tax laws of France are consolidated into the Code général des impôts. In 1981, the procedural provisions were moved to a separate volume, called the book of tax procedures. Taxes that have their legal basis outside the general tax code and the finance laws are Departmental Tax to Preserve Sensitive Natural Areas (Loi N° 85-729 sur la taxe départementale des espaces naturels sensibles) and Levy for Failure to Provide Parking Places (art. 69, Loi du 31 décembre 1976). See EU Inventory.

CGI—Code général des impôts 1996 (General Tax Code), *reprinted in* Code général des impôts (Dalloz 1996) (as amended to Dec. 11, 1995) [in French].

Livre de procédures fiscales 1992, Ministère du budget, Imprimerie nationale 1992 [in French].

Gabon (GAB)

Code général des impôts directs et indirects (General Code of Direct and Indirect Taxes), *reprinted in* Gabon, Ministère de l'économie et des finances—direction générale des contributions directes et indirectes, Code général des impôts directs et indirects (Multipress-Gabon S.A., Sept. 1, 1997) [in French].

Gambia, The (GMB)

We cite to the codification as of 1990 (Laws of The Gambia), as well as to individual laws obtained from the government printer.

Income Tax Act N° 26 of 1948, as amended through Act N° 5 of 1990, Act N° 17 of 1992, Income Tax (Amendment) Act of 1992, Act N° 6 of 1994, Income Tax (Amendment) Act of 1993, Act N° 7 of 1994, Taxpayer Identification Number Act of 1993, *reprinted in* Laws of The Gambia (1990), Cap. 81, amended by Decree N⁰ 63, Income Tax Act (Amendment) Decree, 1995 (Banjul, Govt. Printer).

Stamp Act N⁰ 12 of 1931 (as amended to 1985), *id.*, at Cap. 82.

National Sales Tax Act N⁰ 9 of 1988, *id.*, at Cap. 83:01.

Taxes Act N⁰ 11 of 1984 (as amended to 1988), *id,.* at Cap. 83:02.

Private Practitioners Tax Act N⁰ 10 of 1983, *id.*, at Cap. 83:03.

National Development Levy Act N⁰ 26 of 1976, *id.*, at Cap. 83:04.

Payroll Tax Act N⁰ 22 of 1976, as amended to 1984, *id.*, at Cap. 83:05.

Groundnuts Sales Tax Act N⁰ 1 of 1963, *id.*, at Cap. 83:06.

Medical Services (Financial Contributions) Act N⁰ 11 of 1983, *id.*, at Cap. 83:07.

Parastatal Corporations (Payment of Royalties) Act N⁰ 14 of 1984, *id.*, at Cap. 83:08.

Taxpayer Identification Number Act N⁰ 7 of 1994, the Government Printer.

Georgia (GEO)

Georgia has adopted a tax code, the provisions of which come into effect on various dates between July 24, 1997 and Jan. 1, 1998. As of Jan. 1, 1998, the tax code replaces all the existing tax legislation of Georgia, with the exception of certain provisions of the road fund. Accordingly, we list below only the tax code and the road fund law.

TC—Tax Code of Georgia, July 9, 1997. Amendments passed September 1997. English translation will probably become available on the website of the Georgian Parliament (www.parliament.ge).

Zakon Respubliki Gruziya N⁰ 802 O Dorozhnom Fonde v Respubliki Gruziya (Law N⁰ 802 of the Republic of Georgia on the Road Fund), Sept. 2, 1995, *reprinted in* Nalogi v Gruzii, Kodifitsirovannyy Tekst Nalogovogo Zakonodatel'stva po Sostoyaniyu na 1996 g., Sagadasakhado Matsne, Tbilisi [in Russian] *and in* Georgian Taxes (Mar. 1, 1996), Sagadasakhado Matsne Publishers 1996 [in English].

Germany (DEU)

All cites are to the official gazette: Bundesgesetzblatt (BGBl.). A comprehensive list of German tax legislation with the official gazette cites and amendments can be found on the internet at http://www.jura.uni-sb.de/BGBl/SYS610.HTML. The full text of the laws, however, is available only for acts adopted after 1995. There are also several commercial compilations of German tax law that are published annually; we cite Deutsche Steuergesetze 1996, 8th ed. IDW-Verlag GmbH, Düsseldorf, which contains, according to its publisher, the text of the more important tax legislation. Beck Verlag (München) publishes a one-volume loose-leaf collection of the tax laws (it is called Steuergesetze). The tax laws and regulations are also available [in German] on CD, published by Verlag Neue Wirtschafts-Briefe, Postfach 101849, 44629 Herne, Germany. In addition to the listed taxes, the following taxes are imposed: tax on dogs, hunting and fishing tax, excise duty on mineral oils, duty on tobacco, duty on spirits, excise duty on beer, duty on beverages, excise duty on sparkling wines, tax on licenses to sell beverages, duty on intermediate products, excise duty on coffee. References to the laws imposing these taxes are found in EU Inventory.

AO—Abgabenordnung 1977 (Fiscal Code), BGBl. I S. 613, ber. BGBl. 1977 I S. 269, *reprinted in* Deutsche Steuergesetze 1996 (8th ed., IDW-Verlag GmBH 1996) (as amended to 1996) [in German].

Europäischen Gemeinschaften (EG)—Amtshilfe-Gesetz (Law on Assistance to Authorities Within the European Union), Dec. 19, 1985, BGBl. I S.2441, *reprinted in id.*

Gesetz zur Entlastung des BFH (Bundesfinanzhofs) (Law on Streamlining for the Federal Tax Court), Sept. 15, 1975, BGBl. I S.1861, *reprinted in id.*

Gesetz über die Finanzverwaltung (FVG) (Law on Tax Administration), Aug. 30, 1971, BGBl. I S. 1426, *id.*

EStG—Einkommensteuergesetz 1990 (Income Tax Law), Sept. 7, 1990, BGBl. I S. 1898, *id.*, *reprinted in* TLW (as amended to Dec. 21, 1992).

Eigenheimzulagengesetz (Law Governing the Capital Gains on Residences), Dec. 15, 1995 (BGBl. I S.1783), *reprinted in* Deutsche Steuergesetze, *supra.*

Solidaritätszuschlaggesetz (Solidarity Contribution Law), June 23, 1993, BGBl. I S. 975, *id.*

Gesetz über die Besteuerung bei Auslandsbeziehungen (Außensteuergesetz) (Foreign Tax Law), Sept. 8, 1972, BGBl. 1972 I S. 1713, BStBl. I S. 450, *id.*

Auslandsinvestitionsgesetz (Foreign Investment Tax Law), Aug. 18, 1969, BGBl. 1969 I S. 1211, 1214, *id.*

Berlinförderungsgesetz (BerlinFG) (Berlin Incentives Law), Feb. 2, 1990, BGBl. I S.174, *id.*

DDR-IG—Investitionsgesetz (DDR Investment Law), June 26, 1990, BGBl. I S. 1143, *id.*

FGG—Fördergebietsgesetz (Regional Promotion Law), Sept. 23, 1993, BGBl. I S. 1655, *id.*

InvZulG—Investitionszulagengesetz 1996 (Investment Additions Law 1996), Jan. 22, 1996, BGBl. I S. 61, *id.*

Steuerliches Kapitalerhöhungsgesetz (Capital Increase Tax Law), Oct. 10, 1967, BGBl. I S. 977, *id.*

Umwandlungssteuergesetz (Reorganization Tax Law), Oct. 28, 1994, BGBl. I S. 3267, *id.*

Fünftes Vermögensbildungsgesetz (Fifth Capital Formation Law), Mar. 4, 1994, BGBl. I S. 407, *id.*

Wohnungsbau-Prämiengesetz (Law on Premium for Residential Construction), July 30, 1992, BGBl. I S. 1405, *id.*

Zonenrandförderungsgesetz (Zonal Area Promotion Law), Aug. 5, 1971, BGBl. I S. 1237, *id.*

KStG—Körperschaftsteuergesetz 1991 (Corporation Tax Law), Mar. 11, 1991, BGBl. I, 639, *id.*, *reprinted in* TLW (as amended through Feb. 25, 1992).

Gewerbesteuergesetz (Business Tax Law), Mar. 21, 1991, BGBl. I S. 815, *reprinted in* Deutsche Steuergesetze, *supra.*

UmwStg—Umsatzsteuergesetz 1991 (Turnover Tax Law), Apr. 27, 1993, BGBl. I S. 566, ber. S. 1160, *id.*

BewG—Bewertungsgesetz (Valuation Tax Law), Feb. 1, 1991, BGBl. I S. 231, *id.*

Vermögensteuergesetz (Wealth Tax Law), Nov. 14, 1990, BGBl. I S. 2467, *id.*

Erbschaftsteuergesetz (Inheritance Tax Law), Feb. 19, 1991, BGBl. I S. 469, *id.*

Grundsteuergesetz (Land Tax Law), Aug. 7, 1973, BGBl. I S. 965, *id.*

Grunderwerbsteuergesetz (Land Transfer Tax Law), Dec. 17, 1982, BGBl. I S. 1777, *id.*

Feuerschutzsteuergesetz (Fire Protection Tax Law), Jan. 10, 1996, BGBl. I S. 19, *id.*

Kraftfahrzeugsteuergesetz (Motor Vehicle Tax Law), May 24, 1994, BGBl. I S. 1103, *id.*

Rennwett-und Lotteriegesetz (Racing and Lottery Law), Apr. 8, 1922, RGBl. S. 393, *id.*

Versicherungsteuergesetz 1996 (Insurance Tax Law), Jan. 10, 1996, BGBl. I S. 23, *id.*

Steuerberatungsgesetz (Tax Advising Law), Nov. 4, 1975, BGBl. I S. 2735, *id.*

Ghana (GHA)

In addition to those listed below, Ghana imposes gift tax (in limited circumstances), payroll tax, wealth tax, stamp duty, commercial passenger vehicle tax, casino revenue tax, service tax, and motor vehicle purchase tax.

Income Tax Decree, 1975, S.M.C.D. 5, Gazette of Dec. 24, 1975, *reprinted in* Income Tax Decree, 1975: Consolidated up to June 1996 (Commissioner of Internal Revenue), *reprinted in* TLW (as amended to Dec.1991).

Income Tax (Delivery of Returns) Law of 1988, *reprinted in* TLW.

Act Nº 514, Income Tax (Amendment) Act, 1996.

Act Nº 515, Income Tax (Amendment) (Nº 2) Act, 1996, June 26, 1996, available on TaxBase.

Capital Gains Tax Decree, 1975, N.R.C.D. 347, Gazette of Aug. 29, 1975.

Capital Gains Tax (Amendment) Decree, 1976, S.M.C.D. 46, Gazette of July 30, 1976.

Capital Gains Tax (Amendment) Law, 1988, P.N.D.C.L. 198, Gazette of July 8, 1988.

Capital Gains Tax (Amendment) Law, 1990, P.N.D.C.L. 302, Gazette of June 22, 1990.

Capital Gains Tax (Amendment) Law, 1991, P.N.D.C.L. 267, Gazette of Nov. 1, 1991.

Act Nº 513 of 1996, Capital Gains Tax (Amendment) Act, 1996.

Value Added Tax Act, 1994, Act Nº 486.

Internal Revenue Service Law 1986 (P.N.D.C.L. 143).

Additional Profit Tax Law 1985, *reprinted in* TLW (as amended to Dec. 1991).

Petroleum Income Tax Law, 1986, P.N.D.C.L. 185, Aug. 7, 1987. *id.*

Selective Alien Employment Tax (Amendment) Law, 1991, Nov. 1, 1991. *id.*

Act Nº 502, Customs and Excise (Duties and Other Taxes) Act, 1995, P.N.D.C.L. 330.

Act Nº 512, Customs and Excise (Duties and Other Taxes) Act, 1996, P.N.D.C.L. 330.

Act Nº 496, Customs and Excise (Petroleum Taxes and Petroleum-Related Levies) Act, 1995.

Act Nº 509, Customs and Excise (Petroleum Taxes and Petroleum-Related Levies) (Amendment) Act, 1996.

Act Nº 311 of 1965, Stamp Act, 1965, amended by Act Nº 510, the Stamp (Amendment) Act, 1996.

Greece (GRC)

In addition to those listed below, Greece imposes inheritance and gift tax, payroll tax, stamp duty on wages, real estate transfer tax, tax on corporate capital contributions, capital gains tax, turnover tax, stamp duties, tax on movement of capital, special tax on bank transactions, duty on tobacco products, duty on purchases of manufacturing tobacco in leaf form, excise duty on cigarette paper, road tax on motor vehicles, single-payment additional duty on motor vehicles, special passenger vehicle tax, special tax on petroleum products, duty on alcohol and alcoholic products, tax on television advertisements, duty on malt, duty on isopropyl alcohol, income tax levy on behalf of the Agricultural Insurance Organization, additional 0.5 percent tax on the value of all imported goods, port use tax on petroleum products (including imported products), central bank levy, levy on behalf of the Merchant Marine Pensions Fund, duty on alcoholic beverages, special duty on bananas, special levy under Legislative Decree Nº 49/1968 (private goods vehicles), special levy under Law Nº 383/1976 (public goods vehicles), charge on heavy plant and machinery, and levy in favor of ELGA (Greek Agricultural Insurance Organization). References to the laws imposing these taxes are found in EU Inventory.

Income Tax, *reprinted in* TLW (as amended to Mar. 1988) [in English].

Value Added Tax, *reprinted in* TLW (as amended to Mar. 1988) [in English].

Grenada (GRD)

Grenada: Consolidated Index of Statutes and Subsidiary Legislation (as of Jan. 1, 1997) has been published by the Faculty of Law Library, University of the West Indies, Barbados. This lists the amending laws, and so they will not be listed here. The tax laws listed are as follows:

Excise Act (Cap. 94).

General Consumption Tax Act 1995.

Income Tax Act 1994, amended by Act Nº 5 of 1996, Income Tax (Amendment) Act, 1996; Act Nº 33, Income Tax (Amendment) (Nº 2) Act, 1996.

Land Transfer Tax Act (Cap. 163).

Motor Vehicles Tax Act 1994.

Petrol Tax Act 1986.

Provisional Collection of Taxes Act (Cap. 261).

Purchase Tax Act 1978.

Stamp Act (Cap. 309).

Ticket Tax Act (Cap. 319).

Guatemala (GTM)

In addition to those listed, Guatemala imposes inheritance and gift tax, payroll tax, natural resource royalties, mercantile tax (net asset tax), and solidarity tax (for 1997; based on income and net assets).

Decreto Nº 26-92, Impuesto sobre la renta (Income Tax Law), May 7, 1992, (as amended to Oct. 13, 1995), *reprinted in* IBFD-CIAT [in Spanish] *and in* TLW [in English].

Decreto Nº 27-92, Impuesto al valor agregado (Value Added Tax Law), May 7, 1992 (as amended by Decree Nº 60-94 of Nov. 30, 1994), *reprinted in* IBFD-CIAT [in Spanish] *and in* TLW (as amended to Nov. 1993) [in English].

Decreto Nº 6-91, Codigo tributario (Tax Code) Mar. 25, 1991 (as amended to 1996), *reprinted in* IBFD-CIAT [in Spanish].

Decreto Nº 61-87, Ley del impuesto del papel sellado y timbres fiscales (stamp tax), *reprinted in* Luís Emilio Barrios Pérez, Leyes y Reglamentos de la Reforma Tributaria (Ediciones Legales Comercio e Industria 1991).

Decreto Nº 64-87, Ley del impuesto sobre circulación de vehiculos (vehicle tax), *id.*

Decreto Nº 62-87, Ley del impuesto unico sobre inmuebles (tax on immovable property), *id.*

Decreto Nº 63-87, Ley de fomento avícola (poultry development incentives), *id.*

Guinea (GIN)

Ordonnance 91-018 portant code des impôts directs d'état (Code on Direct State Taxes) Feb. 8, 1991 [in French].

Ordonnance 92-013 portant loi de finances pour 1992 (Finance Law), Feb. 7, 1992, Secretariat Général du Gouvernement [in French].

Loi L/95/009/AN, portant loi de finances pour 1996, Dec. 28, 1995 [in French].

Guinea-Bissau (GNB)

We cite to the official gazette (Boletim oficial).

Decreto Nº 20/80 Aprova o Regulamento do Imposto do Selo (Stamp Tax Regulations), B.O. 10 de maio de 1980 [in Portuguese].

Decreto Nº 23/83 Aprova o Código do Imposto Profissional (Professional Tax Code), B.O. 6 de agosto de 1983 [in Portuguese].

Decreto Nº 39/83 Aprova o Código da Contribuição Industria, (Industrial Tax Code), B.O. 30 de decembro de 1983 [in Portuguese].

Decreto Nº 5/84 Aprova o Código da Contribuição Predial Urbana (Urban Tax Code), B.O. 3 de março de 1984 [in Portuguese].

Guyana (GUY)

We cite to the official codification (Laws of Guyana) (cited as 1973 rev.), the last update for which was issued in 1977, and to individual laws from the government printer subsequent to that time. For amending acts, see also Guyana: Consolidated Index of Statutes and Subsidiary Legislation (1996).

Acreage Tax Act (Cap. 81:22), 1973 rev.

Excise Regulations Act (Cap. 82:03), 1973 rev.

Provisional Collection of Taxes Act (Cap. 79:03), 1973 rev.

Revenue Protection Act (Cap. 79:01), 1973 rev.

Rice (Cess) Act (Cap. 80:05), 1973 rev.

Stamp Duties (Management) Act (Cap. 80:03), 1973 rev.

Sugar Levy Act 1974 (Cap. 83:01), 1973 rev.

Act Nº 43 of 1939, Tax Act (an act to consolidate the enactments relating to the imposition of taxes for the public use in Guyana), Cap 80:01, L.R.O. 1/ 1977, *reprinted in* Laws of Guyana, as amended through Act Nº 46 of 1974, amended by

> Act Nº 8 of 1978 Tax Amendment Act 1978.
> Act Nº 13 of 1978 Tax Amendment Act (Nº 2) 1978.
> Act Nº 4 of 1981 (Tax Amendment Act 1981).
> Act Nº 5 of 1981 (Tax Amendment (Nº 2) Act 1981).
> Act Nº 7 of 1981 (Miscellaneous Enactments (Amendment) (Nº 2) Act 1981).
> Act Nº 12 of 1981 (Guyana Gold Board Act 1981).
> Act Nº 3 of 1982 (Miscellaneous Enactments (Amendment) Act 1982).
> Act Nº 5 of 1982 (Miscellaneous Enactments (Amendment) (Nº 2) Act 1982).
> Act Nº 14 of 1982 (Fiscal Enactments (Amendments) Act 1982).
> Act Nº 6 of 1983 (Tax (Amendment) Act 1983).
> Act Nº 11 of 1983 (Fiscal Enactments (Amendment) Act 1983).
> Act Nº 8 of 1984 (Tax (Amendment) Act 1984).
> Act Nº 4 of 1985 (Miscellaneous Enactments (Amendment) Act 1985).
> Act Nº 9 of 1986 (Cinematograph (Amendment) Act 1986).
> Act Nº 5 of 1987 (Fiscal Enactments (Amendment) Act 1987).
> Act Nº 23 of 1988 (Fiscal Enactments (Amendment) Act 1988).

Act N° 7 of 1989 (Tax (Amendment) Act 1989).

Act N° 8 of 1989 (Tax (Amendment) (N° 2) Act 1989).

Act N° 13 of 1989 (Fiscal Enactments (Amendment) (N° 2) Act 1989).

Act N° 6 of 1991 (Taxation Laws (Relief) Act 1991).

Act N° 20 of 1991 (Tax (Amendment) Act 1991).

Act N° 7 of 1992 (Tax (Amendment) Act 1992).

Act N° 26 of 1992 (Tax (Amendment) (N° 2) Act 1992).

Act N° 3 of 1993 (Tax (Amendment) Act 1993).

Act N° 11 of 1993 (Miscellaneous Enactments (Amendments) Act 1993).

Act N° 10 of 1994 (Tax (Amendment and Miscellaneous Provisions) Act 1994).

Act N° 3 of 1995 (Fiscal Enactments (Amendment) Act 1995).

Act N° 3 Fiscal Enactments (Amendment) Act 1996, Feb. 29, 1996, available on TaxBase.

Act N° 13 of 1969, Consumption Tax Act, Cap. 80:02, L.R.O. 1/1977, *reprinted in* Laws of Guyana, as amended through Act N° 4 of 1972, amended by

Act N° 6 of 1980 Consumption Tax (Amendment) Act 1980,
Act N° 7 of 1985 Consumption Tax (Amendment) Act 1985,
Act N° 8 of 1986 Export and Import (Special Provisions) Act 1986, and
Act N° 8 of 1993 Consumption Tax (Amendment) Act 1993.

Act N° 22 of 1927, Entertainments Duty Act, Cap. 80:06, L.R.O. 1/1973, *reprinted in* Laws of Guyana, as amended by

Act N° 12 of 1977 Cinematograph (Amendment) Act 1977, and
Act N° 6 of 1991 Taxation Laws (Relief) Act 1991.

Act N° 10 of 1973, Travel Voucher Tax Act, Cap. 80:09, L.R.O. 1/1975, *reprinted in* Laws of Guyana, as amended by

Act N° 14 of 1982 Fiscal Enactments (Amendment) Act 1982, and
Act N° 11 of 1983 Fiscal Enactments (Amendment) Act 1983.

Act N° 17 of 1929, Income Tax Act, Cap. 81:01, L.R.O. 1/1977, amended through Act N° 3 of 1976, *reprinted in* Laws of Guyana, *and in* TLW (as amended to Apr. 1988), amended by

Act N° 2 of 1978 Income Tax (Amendment) Act 1978,
Act N° 18 of 1980 Income Tax (Amendment) Act 1980,
Act N° 3 of 1982 Miscellaneous Enactments (Amendment) Act 1982,
Act N° 14 of 1982 Fiscal Enactments (Amendment) Act 1982,
Act N° 11, 1983 Fiscal Enactments (Amendment) Act 1983,
Act N° 17, 1983 Savings Schemes Act 1983,
Act N° 10 of 1985 Income Tax (Amendment) Act 1985,
Act N° 2 of 1986 Income Tax (Amendment) Act 1986,
Act N° 4 of 1986 Taxation Laws (Amendment) Act 1986,

Act Nº 5 of 1987 Fiscal Enactments (Amendment) Act 1987,
Act Nº 11 of 1988 Income Tax (Amendment) Act 1988,
Act Nº 23 of 1988 Fiscal Enactments (Amendment) Act,
Act Nº 6 of 1989 Fiscal Enactments (Amendment) Act 1989,
Act Nº 14 of 1989 Taxation Laws (Amendment) Act 1989,
Act Nº 6 of 1990 Income Tax (Amendment) Act 1990,
Act Nº 9 of 1991 Income Tax (Amendment) Act 1991,
Act Nº 28 of 1991 Fiscal Enactments (Amendment) Act 1991,
Act Nº 8 of 1992 Fiscal Enactments (Amendment) Act 1992,
Act Nº 13 of 1993 Fiscal Enactments (Amendment) Act 1993,
Act Nº 14 of 1993 Hotel Accommodation Tax Act 1993, and
Act Nº 3 of 1995 Fiscal Enactments (Amendment) Act 1995.

Act Nº 16 of 1951, Income Tax (in Aid of Industry) Act, Cap. 81:02, L.R.O. 1/1973, as amended through Act Nº 47 of 1969, *reprinted in* Laws of Guyana, amended by

Act Nº 4 of 1986 Taxation Laws (Amendment) Act 1986,
Act Nº 14 of 1992 Fiscal Enactments (Amendment) (Nº 2) Act 1992,
Act Nº 13 of 1993 Fiscal Enactments (Amendment) Act 1993, and
Act Nº 16 of 1994 Fiscal Enactments (Amendment) Act 1994.

Act Nº 30 of 1970, Corporation Tax Act, Cap. 81:03, L.R.O. 1/1977, as amended by Act Nº 25 of 1971, *reprinted in* Laws of Guyana, amended by

Act Nº 14 of 1989 Taxation Laws (Amendment) Act 1989,
Act Nº 28 of 1991 Fiscal Enactments (Amendment) Act 1991,
Act Nº 14 of 1992 Fiscal Enactments (Amendment) (Nº 2) Act 1992,
Act Nº 13 of 1993 Fiscal Enactments (Amendment) Act 1993, and
Act Nº 16 of 1994 Fiscal Enactments (Amendment) Act 1994.

Act Nº 13 of 1966, Capital Gains Tax Act, Cap. 81:20, L.R.O. 1/1975, as amended through Act Nº 33 of 1970, *reprinted in* Laws of Guyana, amended by

Act Nº 11 of 1983 Fiscal Enactments (Amendment) Act 1983,
Act Nº 5 of 1987 Fiscal Enactments (Amendment) Act 1987,
Act Nº 6 of 1989 Fiscal Enactments (Amendment) Act 1989,
Act Nº 14 of 1989 Taxation Laws (Amendment) Act 1989,
Act Nº 6 of 1991 Taxation Laws (Relief) Act 1991,
Act Nº 8 of 1992 Fiscal Enactments (Amendment) Act 1992, and
Act Nº 16 of 1994 Fiscal Enactments (Amendment) Act 1994.

Act Nº 19 of 1962, Property Tax Act, Cap. 81:21, L.R.O. 1/1977, as amended through Act Nº 6 of 1975, *reprinted in* Laws of Guyana, amended by

Act Nº 11 of 1983 Fiscal Enactments (Amendment) Act 1983,
Act Nº 5 of 1987 Fiscal Enactments (Amendment) Act 1987,
Act Nº 23 of 1988 Fiscal Enactments (Amendment) Act 1988,

Act Nº 6 of 1989 Fiscal Enactments (Amendment) Act 1989,
Act Nº 14 of 1989 Taxation Laws (Amendment) Act 1989,
Act Nº 8 of 1992 Fiscal Enactments (Amendment) Act 1992.

Act Nº 14 of 1993, Hotel Accommodations Tax Act, *reprinted in* Laws of Guyana, Guyana National Printers, 1993.

Haiti (HTI)

Joseph Paillant, Code fiscal mis à jour 1994 (Imprimerie Henri Deschamps 1994) is a one-volume collection of tax laws and decrees and selected economic legislation. The legislative references to the Official Monitor are given in this book and so are omitted here.

Impôt sur le revenu (income tax), *reprinted in* Paillant, *supra* [in French] *and in* TLW (as amended to Oct. 1994) [in English].

Carte d'identité fiscale (tax identification card), Paillant, *supra*.

Carte d'identité professionnelle (professional identity card), *id*.

Droit de fonctionnement (fee for operation), *id*.

Droit de non fonctionnement (fee for nonoperation), *id*.

Droit de timbre proportionnel sur capital social (stamp duty in proportion to social capital), *id*.

Droit de transmission des titres et taxe sur actions (fee for passage of title and tax on stock), *id*.

Taxe sur masse salariale (tax on wages), *id*.

Droit de licence (license duty), *id*.

Droit pour l'obtention du quitus fiscal (tax clearance duty), *id*.

Patente (license), *id*.

Contribution foncière des propriétés bâties (tax on improved real estate), *id*.

Droit d'alignement (fee for certifying boundary), *id*.

Taxe pour numérotage des maisons (tax on house numbers), *id*.

Taxe d'étalonnage (stamping fee), *id*.

Taxe sur matériaux et denrées sur la voie publique (tax on materials on the public roads), *id*.

Taxe sur le chiffre d'affaires (turnover tax), *id*.

Droit d'accise (excise duty), *id*.

Droit de timbre (stamp duty), *id.*

Taxe sur les spectacles publics (tax on public shows), *id.*

Taxe sur appels téléphoniques (tax on telephone calls), *id.*

Taxe sur primes d'assurance (tax on insurance premiums), *id.*

Taxe pour la légalisation des pièces (tax for the legalization of documents), *id.*

Droit de péages sur les routes (road tolls), *id.*

Taxe pour laisser passer (tax on free passage), *id.*

Taxe frontalière (border tax), *id.*

Taxe irrigation Fleuve Artibonite (Artibonite River irrigation tax), *id.*

Taxe irrigation (irrigation tax), *id.*

Taxe pour l'obtention de passeport (passport fee), *id.*

Contribution à la construction d'un aéroport (contribution for construction of an airport), *id.*

Taxe d'aéroport sur les passagers et marchandises (airport tax on passengers and merchandise), *id.*

Taxe sur ticket de voyage (travel ticket tax), *id.*

Inspection des véhicules (vehicle inspection), *id.*

Immatriculation des véhicules (vehicle registration), *id.*

Taxe de première immatriculation (tax on initial registration), *id.*

Taxe pour permis de conduire (tax for driver's license), *id.*

Droit spécial sur bordereaux DGI, AGD, ED'H, TELECO (special duty on notes), *id.*

Droit spécial sur police d'assurance véhicules contre-tiers (special duty on third-party vehicle insurance), *id.*

Honduras (HND)

Decreto-Ley N⁰ 25, Impuesto sobre la renta (Income Tax Law), Dec. 20, 1963, Gaceta N⁰ 18.161, *reprinted in* Secretaría de Hacienda y Crédito Público, Dirección General de Tributación, Ley de Impuesto sobre la Renta y sus Reformas (Secretaría de Hacienda y Crédito Público, Dirección General de Tributación 1987) (as amended to Aug. 1, 1987) [in Spanish], as amended to Apr. 1996, *reprinted in* IBFD-CIAT [in Spanish] *and in* TLW (as amended through June 1991) [in English].

Decreto-Ley N° 24 Impuesto sobre ventas (Sales Tax Law), Jan. 1, 1964, Gaceta N° 18.161, *reprinted in* Secretaría de Hacienda *supra*, as amended by Decree N° 135-94 of Oct. 12, 1994, *and in* IBFD-CIAT [in Spanish].

Decree N° 76, Gaceta, June 20, 1957, Tax on Transfer of Real Property, *reprinted in* TLW (as amended through 1979).

Hungary (HUN)

We cite to The Hungarian Rules of Law in Force [hereinafter HRLF]. This is a three-language version (Hungarian, German, and English) of selected Hungarian legislation, published by Verzál Ltd., Budapest (in the United States, distributed by Int'l Info. Services, Inc., P.O. Box 3490, Silver Spring, MD 20918). The Ministry of Finance also publishes translations of tax laws in a pamphlet series (Perfekt Publishing Company: Budapest). In addition to those listed below, Hungary imposes inheritance and gift tax, payroll tax, and real estate transfer tax.

CTDT—Törvény a Társasági Adóról és az osztalékodóról (Corporate and Dividend Tax Law), Act LXXXI of 1996, *reprinted in* 8 HRLF 1 (Jan. 1, 1997).

Törvény az Altalános Forgalmi Adóról (Value Added Tax Law), Act 74 of 1992, Magyar Közlöny N° 128, Dec. 19, 1992, *consolidated text reprinted in* 8 HRLF 269 (Feb. 15, 1997).

Act XCI of 1990 on the Rules of Taxation, *consolidated text reprinted in* 7 HRLF 453 (Apr. 1–15, 1996).

PIT—Törvény a személyi jövedeemadóról (Act CXVII of 1995) on Personal Income Tax, *consolidated text reprinted in* 8 HRLF 73 (Jan. 15–Feb. 1, 1997).

Act CXXVI of 1996 on the Use of a Specified Amount of Personal Income Tax for Public Purposes in Accordance with the Taxpayer's Instruction, *reprinted in* 8 HRLF 731 (May 15, 1997).

Act N° 78 of 1991 on Consumption Tax and Consumption Price Subsidy, *consolidated text reprinted in* 7 HRLF 1184 (Sept. 15, 1996).

Act LVIII of 1993 on the Regulation and Control of Excise and Subcontract Distillation Spirits Tax, *reprinted in* HRLF, N° 1995/21, amended by

Act XXXIII of 1996, *reprinted in* 1996 HRLF 158.

Act LXXXII of 1991 on the Motor Vehicle Tax, *reprinted in* HRLF N° 1995/9, amended by

Act XCVIII of 1995, *reprinted in* 1996 HRLF 73.

Act C of 1990 on Local Taxes, *reprinted in* HRLF 1993/8, amended by

Act XCVIII of 1995, *reprinted in* 1996 HRLF 76.

Iceland (ISL)

The following taxes are imposed in Iceland: corporate income tax, turnover tax (market charge, industrial loan fund contribution, and industrial charge), property tax, payroll tax, value added tax, excise, national income tax, net wealth tax.

Lög nr. 75/1981 um Tekjuskatt og Eignarskatt (Law Nº 75/1981 on Income Tax), *reprinted in* Lög nr. 75/1981 um tekjuskatt og eignarskatt, med sidari breytingum (Fjármáláráduneytid 1987) (as amended to Law Nº 72 of Dec. 31, 1986) [in Icelandic].

India (IND)

The tax laws, rules, explanations, indexes to judicial decisions, and other materials are published in a series of publications by Taxman, 59/32 New Rohtak Road, New Delhi 110 005 (fax 91-11-5725041).

The Income Tax Act, 1961, *reprinted in* J.P. Bhatnagar, All India Taxation Manual (Central Law Agency, Allahabad, 28th ed., 1992); *reprinted in* TLW (as amended through Finance Act, 1992), *and in* Taxman's Income Tax Act (published annually by Taxman).

The Expenditure Tax Act, 1987, *reprinted in* All India Taxation Manual, *supra*.

The Interest Tax Act, 1974, *id*.

The Wealth Tax Act, 1957, *id*.

The Gift Tax Act, 1958, *id*.

The Central Excise Tariff Act, 1985, *reprinted in* Central Excise Tariff 1991–92 ed. (Cen-Cus Publications: New Delhi 1991).

The Central Excises and Salt Act 1944, *reprinted in* Central Excise: Law, Practice and Procedure (Acharya Shuklendra ed., Modern Law Publications, Allahabad 1987) (as amended to Sept. 1987).

Indonesia (IDN)

Taxation Laws of Indonesia (prepared by Dr. S. Sutanto) [hereinafter Tax'n Laws] is a multivolume loose-leaf set published by Asian-Pacific Tax and Investment Research Centre, Singapore, and IBFD Publications BV, Amsterdam. Besides the laws, it also contains regulations, decrees, and treaties [in English]. Besides those listed below, exit tax (on residents) and excise are imposed.

Law Nº 6 of 1983, General Tax Provisions and Procedures, State Gazette of the Republic of Indonesia Year 1983 Nº 49, *reprinted in* Tax Laws of the Republic of Indonesia 1 (Ministry of Finance, Directorate General of Taxation

1991)[*hereinafter* MOF] [in English] *and in* Tax'n Laws, *supra* (as amended through 1994).

IT—Law Nº 7 of 1983 Income Tax Law, State Gazette of the Republic of Indonesia Year 1983 Nº 50, *reprinted in* MOF *and in* Tax'n Laws, *supra* (as amended through 1994), *reprinted in* Indonesia, National Development Information Office, Law on Income Tax (B. Wiwoho ed., Jakarta 1996).

Law Nº 8 of 1983 on Value Added Tax on Goods and Services and Sales Tax on Luxury Goods, State Gazette of the Republic of Indonesia Year 1983 Nº 51, *reprinted in* MOF *and in* Tax'n Laws, *supra* (as amended through 1994), *reprinted in* Indonesia, National Development Information Office, Law on Value Added Tax and Sales Tax (B. Wiwoho ed., Jakarta 1996).

Law Nº 12 of 1985 Land and Building Tax, State Gazette of the Republic of Indonesia Year 1985 Nº 68, *reprinted in* MOF *and in* Tax'n Laws, *supra* (as amended through 1994).

Law Nº 13 of 1985 Stamp Duty, State Gazette of the Republic of Indonesia Year 1985 Nº 69, *reprinted in* MOF *and in* Tax'n Laws, *supra* (as amended through 1994).

Iran, Islamic Republic of (IRN)

Law Nº 113, Income Tax Law, Nov. 22, 1982, *reprinted in* TLW (as amended through 1971) [in English].

Iraq (IRQ)

Law Nº 113, Income Tax Law, Nov. 22, 1982, *reprinted in* TLW (as amended to July 6, 1988) [in English].

Ireland (IRL)

As in the United Kingdom, the tax legislation of Ireland consists of periodic consolidations, together with annual finance acts that contain nontextual amendments.[10] *Little point would be served in listing each of these here. The tax laws are collected in three volumes published annually by Butterworth Ireland: The Tax Acts, the VAT Acts, and the Capital Tax Acts. In addition to those listed, the following taxes are imposed: excise duty on hydrocarbons, excise duty on tobacco products, excise duty on ethyl alcohol, excise duty on wine, excise duty on made-wine, excise duty on beer, excise duty on cider and perry, betting duty, residential property tax, excise duty on certain licenses, orders and authorizations, and excise duty on foreign travel. References to the laws imposing these taxes are found in EU Inventory.*

ITA—Income Tax Act 1967, *reprinted in* The Tax Acts, *supra*.

---

[10]*See* vol. 1, at 81–82.

Capital Gains Tax Act 1975, *id.*

Corporation Tax Act 1976, *id.*

Value Added Tax Act 1972, *reprinted in* The VAT Acts, *supra.*

Stamp Act 1891, *reprinted in* The Capital Tax Acts, *supra.*

Stamp Duty Management Act 1891, *id.*

Capital Acquisitions Tax Act 1976, *id.*

Imposition of Duties (No 221) (Excise Duties) Order, 1975, as amended.

Imposition of Duties (No 236) (Excise Duties on Motor Vehicles, Televisions, and Gramophone Records) Order, 1979, as amended.

Imposition of Duties (No 273) (Excise Duty on Motorcycles) Order, 1984, as amended.

Imposition of Duties (No 260) (Excise Duty on Video Players) Order, 1982, as amended.

Israel (ISR)

We cite to a commercially published loose-leaf compilation and translation. In addition to those listed below, payroll tax, petroleum royalties, property tax, real estate acquisition tax, and stamp duty are imposed.

Income Tax Ordinance, *reprinted in* Income Tax Ordinance (Aryeh Green-field-A.G. Publications 8th ed., Haifa, 1996) (as amended to March 1996) [in English].

Income Tax (Inflationary Adjustments) Law. 5745-1985 (A.G. Publications, July 1990) [in English].

Property Tax and Compensation Fund Law 5721-1961, *reprinted in* Property Tax and Compensation Fund Law (A.G. Publications, 3rd ed., 1992).

Value Added Tax, *reprinted in* TLW (as amended to Apr. 1989) [in English] *and in* Value Added Tax 1997 (A.G. Publications, Jan. 1997) [in English].

Taxes (Collection) Ordinance (consolidated and updated English translation) (A.G. Publications, Sept. 1994).

Italy (ITA)

In addition to those listed, the following taxes are imposed: duty on betting, tax on dogs, succession and gift duty, duty on mineral oils, duty on liquefied petroleum gases, duty on methane, consumption tax on manufactured tobacco, duty on mechanical lighters, duty on matches, duty on spirits, duty on beer, duty on electricity, entertainment tax, lottery duties, duty on official concessions, insurance tax, stock exchange turnover tax, registration tax, mortgage tax, cadastral duty, tax on motor vehicles, excise duty on plastic bags, tax on net assets, inheritance and gift tax, stamp duty, and corporate franchise tax. References to the laws imposing these taxes are found in EU Inventory.

ISR—Istituzione e disciplina dell'imposta sul reddito delle persone fisiche (Personal Income Tax), Dec. 1986, *reprinted in* Italian Income Taxes Consolidated Text 30 (Peter C. Alegi trans., 2nd ed., Alegi & Associates, 1993) (as amended to Oct. 31, 1993) [in Italian, English] *and in* TLW (as amended to Apr. 28, 1993) D.P.R. N° 917.

Istituzione e disciplina dell'imposta sul reddito delle persone giuridiche (Corporate Income Tax), D.P.R. N° 917 of Dec. 1986, *reprinted in* Alegi, *supra, and in* TLW (as amended to Apr. 28, 1993).

Imposta locale sui redditi (Local Income Tax), *reprinted in* Alegi, *supra.*

Imposta sul valore aggiunto (Value Added Tax), D.P.R. 26 ottobre 1972, n. 633, *reprinted in* Imposta sul Valore Aggiunto (2nd ed., Banco di Roma, ed., Collana Tributaria Edita, 1984) (as amended to 1984) [in Italian] *and in* TLW (as amended to Apr. 28, 1993).

Disposizioni in materia di imposta sul valore aggiunto e di imposte sul reddito e disposizioni relative all'Amministrazione finanziaria, *reprinted in* Codice delle Imposte Dirette 121 (Edoardo Cintolesi & Mauro Longo, 8th ed., Buffetti Editore, 1987) (as amended to Jan. 1987) [in Italian] D.L. 19 diciembre 1984, n. 853, as amended to Feb. 1985.

Legge n. 649 disposizioni relative ad alcune ritenute alla fonte sugli interessi ed altri proventi di capitale (Law Establishing Provisions Relating to Certain Withholdings from Interest Payments and Other Capital Earnings), Nov. 25, 1993, *id.*

Decreto Legge 10 iuglio 1982, n. 429, Norme per la repressione dell'evasione in materia di imposte sui redditi e sull'IVA e per agevolare la definizione delle pendenze in materia tributaria (Decree-Law Providing Regulations for the Elimination of Income Tax Evasion and the Evasion of VAT and for Facilitating the Definition of Outstanding Tax Balances), *id.*

Decreto del Presidente de la Republica 29 settembre 1973, n. 601, Disciplina delle agevolazioni tributarie (Decree governing tax payment facilities), *id.*

Legge 4 maggio 1983, n. 169, Agevolazioni fiscali per l'ampliamento del mercato azionario e modifiche al D.P.R. 31 marzo 1975, n. 136 (Law providing for tax facilities for the development of the stock market and amending D.P.R. N° 136 of March 1975), *id.*

Legge 30 aprile 1985, n. 163, Agevolazioni per reinvestimenti nel settore dello spettacolo (Law Granting Facilities for Reinvestment in the entertainment industry), *id.*

Decreto Ministeriale 4 giugno 1985, Modalità di applicazione delle agevolazioni fiscali concesse nel settore dello spettacolo (Law Defining the Manners in Which the Tax Concessions Granted to the Entertainment Industry Are to Be Applied), *id.*

Decreto del Presidente de la Republica 29 settembre 1973, n. 602, Disposizioni sulla riscossione delle imposte sul reddito (Decree governing the collection of income tax), *id.*

Decreto del Presidente de la Republica 26 ottobre 1972, n. 636, Revisione della disciplina del contenzioso tributario (Order Governing the Procedure for Tax Litigation), *id.*

Jamaica (JAM)

Jamaica: Consolidated Index of Statutes and Subsidiary Legislation (as of Jan. 1, 1996) has been published by the Faculty of Law Library, University of the West Indies, Barbados. This lists the amending laws, and so they will not be listed here. The tax laws listed are as follows:

Contractors Levy Act 1985.

Education Tax Act 1987.

Estate Duty Law 1954.

Excise Duty Act.

General Consumption Tax Act 1991.

Hotels (Accommodation Tax) Act.

Income Tax Act, *reprinted in* TLW (as amended to March 1993).

International Finance Companies (Income Tax Relief) Act 1971.

Land Development Duty Act.

Land Improvement Tax Act.

Land Taxation (Relief) Act .

Property (Rates and Taxes)(Relief) Act.

Property Tax Act.

Provisional Collection of Tax Act.

Revenue Administration Act 1985.

Revenue Board Act 1981.

Rifle Clubs Tax Relief Law 1908.

Stamp Duty Act.

Tax Collection Act.

Technical Assistance (Immunities and Privileges) Act 1982.

Transfer Tax Act.

Travel Tax Act.

University of the West Indies (Tax Exemption) Act 1963.

Urban Renewal (Tax Relief) Act 1995, N⁹ 14 of 1995.

Japan (JPN)

To get an overview of the tax system, it is helpful to consult An Outline of Japanese Taxes, published annually by the Ministry of Finance. This publication includes a table listing the national tax laws and regulations. As of 1995, besides the laws listed in the paragraphs below, the national tax laws included the following: Special Corporation Surtax Law, Law N⁹ 15 of Mar. 31, 1992; Land Value Tax Law of May 2, 1991; Registration and License Tax Law, Law N⁹ 35 of June 12, 1967; Liquor Tax Law, Law N⁹ 6 of Feb. 28, 1953; Tobacco Tax Law, Law N⁹ 72 of Aug. 10, 1984; Gasoline Tax Law, Law N⁹ 55 of Apr. 6, 1957; Aviation Fuel Tax Law, Law N⁹ 7 of Mar. 31, 1972; Petroleum Tax Law, Law N⁹ 25 of Apr. 18, 1978; Motor Vehicle Tonnage Tax Law, Law N⁹ 89 of May 31, 1971; Local Road Tax Law, Law N⁹ 104 of July 30, 1955; Securities Transaction Tax Law, Law N⁹ 102 of July 31, 1953; Liquefied Petroleum Gas Tax Law, Law N⁹ 156 of Dec. 29, 1965; Bourse Tax Law, Law N⁹ 23 of March 31, 1914; Tonnage Due Law, Law N⁹ 37 of Mar. 31, 1957; Special Tonnage Due Law, Law N⁹ 38 of Mar. 31, 1957; The Bank of Japan Law, Law N⁹ 67 of Feb. 24, 1942 (Bank of Japan Note Issue Tax); Promotion of Power-Resources Development Tax Law, Law N⁹ 79 of June 6, 1974; General Law of National Tax, Law N⁹ 66 of Apr. 2, 1962; Administrative Appellate Law, Law N⁹ 160 of Sept. 15, 1962; Law of Exemption, Reduction or Deferment of Collection of Taxes for Those Who Suffered from Disasters, Law N⁹ 175 of Dec. 13, 1947; National Tax Violations Control Law, Law N⁹ 67 of Mar. 17, 1900; National Tax Collection Law, Law N⁹ 147 of Apr. 20, 1959.

IT—Law N⁹ 33, The Income Tax Law, Mar. 31, 1965, *reprinted in* TLW (as amended to May 1990) [in English], *also reprinted in* The Income Tax Law of Japan, IV EHS Law Bulletin Series, Eibun-Horei-Sha, ed. (as amended to Dec. 1988) (1989) [*hereinafter EHS*] [in English].

Consumption Tax Law, *reprinted in* Japan—National Consumption Tax Law: An English Translation with Cabinet Orders as of Apr. 1, 1989 (CCH International 1989) [in English].

Law N⁹ 28, The Corporation Tax Law, Mar. 31, 1947, *reprinted in* EHS (as amended to June 1992) *and in* 21 TLW (as amended to 1990) [in English] *and in* translation by Yugi Gomi (1995).

Law N° 73, The Inheritance Tax Law, Mar. 31, 1950, *reprinted in* EHS (as amended to Mar. 1975) [in English].

Law N° 110, The Assets Revaluation Law, Apr. 25, 1950, *reprinted in* EHS (as amended to Dec. 1986) [in English].

Law N° 23, The Stamp Tax Law, Mar. 31, 1967, *reprinted in* EHS (as amended to May 1993) [in English].

Law N° 26, Special Taxation Measures Law, Mar. 31, 1957, *reprinted in* EHS (as amended to 1963) [in English].

Jordan (JOR)

Law N° 57 of 1985 Income Tax Law of the Hashemite Kingdom of Jordan, *reprinted in* Income Tax Law of the Hashemite Kingdom of Jordan (as amended to 1995) [in English].

Real Estate Sales Tax Law of 1974, *reprinted in* TLW [in English].

Amended Sales Tax Law, 1995 (Ali and Sarif Law Office, Amman, 1996).

Kazakhstan (KAZ)

Most of the tax legislation of Kazakhstan was reformed and consolidated in a presidential decree issued in 1995, informally referred to as the tax code.

TC—Ukaz o Nalogakh i Drugikh Obyazatel'nykh Platezhakh v Byudzhet, Apr. 16, 1995, *reprinted in* The Gazette of the Supreme Soviet of the Republic of Kazakhstan, 1995, N° 5, p. 4, *and in* Decree on Taxes and Other Mandatory Payments to Revenue (Tax Code) (Ministry of Finance Informational Bulletin Bureau and International Tax and Investment Center 1997) (as amended to Mar. 1, 1997) [in Russian, English].

Decree by the Government of the Republic of Kazakhstan, N° 1747, Dec. 31, 1996, on Excise Rates for Goods Produced in the Republic of Kazakhstan and Subject to Excise Taxation, and for Gambling Business (this decree sets the excise tax rates, as authorized by the tax code).

Zakon Respubliki Kazakhstan o Gosudarstvennoi poshline (Law of Republic of Kazakhstan on State Duty), Dec. 31, 1996, *reprinted in* Zakoni i Normativnie Akti "UG," N° 4 (1997) [in Russian].

Kenya (KEN)

Laws of Kenya is a multivolume loose-leaf service containing the consolidated text of laws, published by the Government Printer, Nairobi.

ITA—The Income Tax Act, ch. 470, *reprinted in* TLW (as amended to Dec. 1994).

The Customs and Excise Act, Laws of Kenya, ch. 472 (rev. 1984).

The Telecommunications Tax Act, *id.*, ch. 473 (rev. 1981).

The Refinery Throughput Tax Act, *id.*, ch. 474 (rev. 1983).

The Air Passenger Service Act, *id.*, ch. 475 (rev. 1989).

The Value Added Tax Act, *id.*, ch. 476 (rev. 1993), *reprinted in* The Kenya Value Added Tax Act (cap. 476) (Deloitte Touche Tohmatsu International 1997) (as amended to Jan. 1997).

The Hotel Accommodation Tax Act, *id.*, ch. 478 (rev. 1989).

The Entertainments Tax Act, *id.*, ch. 479 (rev. 1990).

The Local Manufactures (Export Compensation) Act, *id.*, ch. 482 (rev. 1987).

The Second-Hand Motor Vehicles Purchase Tax Act, *id.*, ch. 484 (rev. 1991).

Act Nº 13 of 1995, Finance Act, 1995 (Nairobi, Govt. Printer).

Kiribati (KIT)

Income Tax Act 1990.

Income Tax Amendment Act 1992.

Korea (KOR)

Besides the tax laws listed in the paragraphs below, the following national tax laws are listed in Ministry of Finance, Korea, Korean Taxation 1994 (this work provides a summary of the tax system and is updated annually): Excessively Increased Value of Land Law, Excess Profits Tax Law, Special Excise Tax Law, Liquor Tax Law, Telephone Tax Law, Stamp Tax Law, Transportation Tax Law, Education Tax Law, and Tax Evasion Punishment Law. Current Laws of the Republic of Korea is a multivolume loose-leaf set of English translations published by the Korea Legislation Research Institute [hereinafter Current Laws]. The tax laws are contained in Part IX: Tax, Tobacco and Ginseng Laws. In addition, where indicated, some of the cites below were obtained from GLIN, an online database hosted by the Library of Congress. These laws are available online in Korean only.

Basic National Tax Act, *reprinted in* Current Laws, *supra* (as amended through Dec. 6, 1995) [in English].

National Tax Collection Act, *reprinted in id.* (as amended through Dec. 6, 1995).

Tax Accountant Act, *reprinted in id.* (as amended through Dec. 6, 1995).

Tax Reduction and Exemption Control Act, *reprinted in id.* (as amended through Dec. 29, 1995).

Corporation Tax Act, *reprinted in id.* (as amended through Dec. 29, 1995), amended by Law 5192, Dec. 30, 1996 [GLIN].

Income Tax Act, *reprinted in id.* (as amended through Dec. 29, 1995), amended by Law 5155, Kwanbo, Aug. 14, 1996; Law 5191, Kwanbo Dec. 30, 1996 [GLIN].

Securities Transaction Tax Act, *reprinted in id.* (as amended through Dec. 5, 1978).

Value Added Tax Act, *reprinted in id.* (as amended through Dec. 29, 1995).

Law for Coordination of International Tax Affairs (LCITA) and Presidential Enforcement Decree, Jan. 1996, available on TaxBase [in English].

Inheritance Tax Law, *reprinted in* TLW (as amended through June 1991) [in English].

Assets Revaluation Law, *reprinted in* TLW (as amended through June 1991) [in English].

Law 5037, amends the Education Tax Act, Kwanbo, Dec. 29, 1995 [GLIN].

Law 5026, amends the Special Accounting Act on Traffic Facilities, Kwanbo, Dec. 6, 1995 [GLIN].

Law 5277, amends the Tourism Promotion Development Fund Act, Kwanbo, Jan. 13, 1997 [GLIN].

Law 5034, amends the Special Consumption [excise], Kwanbo, Dec. 29, 1995 [GLIN].

Law 5035, amends the Transportation Tax Act, Kwanbo, Dec. 29, 1995 [GLIN].

Law 5163, amends the Tax Reduction and Exemption Control Act, Kwanbo, Oct. 2, 1996 [GLIN].

Law 5193, amends the Inheritance Tax Act and changes the name of the Act to the Inheritance and Gift Tax, Kwanbo, Dec. 30, 1996 [GLIN].

Law 5285, amends the Development Gain Collection Act, Kwanbo, Jan. 13, 1997 [GLIN].

Law 5173, amends the Act Concerning the Adjustment of National and Local Tax, Kwanbo, Dec. 12, 1996 [GLIN].

Kuwait (KWT)

See also Ballantyne, Register of Laws of the Arabian Gulf (loose-leaf).

Imposition of Tax [Corporations], *reprinted in* TLW (as amended to 1985) [in English].

Kyrgyz Republic (KGZ)

The Kyrgyz Republic consolidated and reformed its tax legislation in 1996 in a tax code modeled on that of Kazakhstan. Amendments to the code were made on Dec. 27, 1996.

Zakon Respubliki Kyrgyzstan N⁰ 25, Nalogovi Kodeks, June 26, 1996 (Tax Code), *reprinted in* Nalogovi Kodeks (publisher not indicated, but presumably Ministry of Finance) (as amended through 1996) [in Russian].

Lao People's Democratic Republic (LAO)

The following taxes are levied (as of May 1997): profit tax, income tax, real estate transfer tax, land tax, turnover tax, excises, business and professional licenses, road tax, air travel fees, transit tax, timber royalties, taxes on natural resources.

Latvia (LVA)

Latvia reformed its major tax laws in early 1995.

TF—Law on Taxes and Fees, Feb. 2, 1995, 95 TNI 70-20, doc. 95-2044 [in English].

Law on Excise Tax of Dec. 1990 (as amended to Mar. 1995) [in English].

Izmeneniya v Zakone ob aktsiznom naloge (Amendments to Excise Tax Law), May 23, 1996, Diena, May 29, 1996 [in Russian].

Izmeneniye v Zakone "Ob Aktsiznom Naloge" (Amendments to Excise Tax Law), June 20, 1996, Sreda, June 26, 1996 [in Russian].

EIT—Law on Enterprise Income Tax, Feb. 9, 1995, 95 TNI 64-26, doc. 95-20442 [in English].

Izmeneniye v Zakone "O Podokhodnom Naloge v Predpriyatiy" (Amendments to Enterprise Income Tax), June 21, 1996, Sreda, June 26, 1996 [in Russian].

Zakon Latviyskoy Respubliki O Podokhodnom Naloge s Naseleniya (Law of the Latvian Republic on Income Tax on Population), Dec. 12, 1990, *reprinted in* Vedomosti Verkhovnogo Soveta i Pravitelstva Latviyskoy Respubliki 1991 N⁰ 1/2, item 7 [in Russian] (as amended to July 20, 1995) [English trans.].

Law on the Property Tax, Dec. 18, 1990 [in English].

Law on the Value Added Tax, Mar. 9, 1995 [in English].

Izmeneniya v Zakone "O Naloge na Dobavlennuyu Stoimost" (Amendments to the Value Added Tax Law), May 10, 1996, Sreda, May 15, 1996 [in Russian].

Law N⁰ 66 on Land Tax of Dec. 20, 1990 (as amended to 1993), Official Documents of the Supreme Soviet and the Council of Minister of the Republic of Latvia, June 4, 1993 [in Russian, English].

Law N° 352 on the insertion of Amendments into the Latvian Code of Civil Procedure relating to matters of recovery of tax delinquencies, Proceedings of the Supreme Soviet and Government of the Latvian Republic, Sept. 12, 1991, N° 35/36 [in Russian].

Law N° 182 on Social Security Tax Amendments of Mar. 27, 1991, Proceedings of the Supreme Soviet and Government of the Latvian Republic, June 6, 1991, N° 21/22 [in Russian].

Laws N°s 249 and 250 on Social Security Tax Amendments of May 28, 1991, Proceedings of the Supreme Soviet and Government of the Latvian Republic, Aug. 1, 1991, N° 29/30 [in Russian].

Izmeneniye v Zakone "O Sotsial'nom Naloge" (Amendments to Social Tax Law) June 21, 1996, Sreda, June 26, 1996 [in Russian].

Law on Natural Resource Tax of Dec. 12, 1990 [in English] and Law N°s 196 and 197 on Natural Resources Tax Amendments of Apr. 23, 1991, Proceedings of the Supreme Soviet and Government of the Latvian Republic, June 20, 1991, N° 23/24 [in Russian].

Izmenenie v Zakone o Lgotakh po Podokhodnomu Nalogu s Predpriyatiy dlya Predpriyatiy (predprinimatelskikh obshchestv) obshchestv invalidov, predpriyatiy (predprinimatelskikh obshchestv) Meditsinskogo Kharaktera, a takzhe dlya Predpriyatiy (predprinimatelskikh obshchestv) drugikh Blagatvoritelnykh Fondov v 1995, 1996 i 1997 godakh (Amendment to the Law on Tax Privileges for Charitable Institutions), Sept. 10, 1996 *reprinted in* V Saeyme i Kabinete Ministrov, Sept. 25, 1996 [in Russian].

Law on Amendments to the Law of the Republic of Latvia on Foreign Investments in the Republic of Latvia, Mar. 2, 1995.

Lebanon (LBN)

In addition to income tax, Lebanon imposes inheritance and gift duty, payroll tax, built property tax, amusement tax, stamp duty, and tax on movable property gains.

Income Tax, Legislative Decree N° 144 of July 12, 1959, *reprinted in* TLW (as amended to 1991), *and in* Income Tax Law (Beirut, Bureau of Lebanese and Arab Documentation, P.O. Box 165403, Beirut, Lebanon) (as amended to Feb. 1995).

Lesotho (LSO)

ITA—Income Tax Order 1993, 38 Lesotho Government Gazette Extraordinary N° 33, at 403, amended by Act N° 2 of 1994, Income Tax (Amendment) Act 1994, 39 Lesotho Government Gazette Extraordinary N° 54, at 552; Act

Nº 10 of 1996, Income Tax (Amendment) Act, 1996, Sept. 20, 1996, 41 Lesotho Government Gazette Extraordinary Nº 88, at 1119.

Sales Tax Act, 1995, 41 Lesotho Government Gazette Extraordinary 423 (Apr. 29, 1996).

The Casino Act, Nº 26 of 1969; Legal Order Nº 42 of 1971; Casino Order Nº 4 of 1989 (impose gambling levy).

Valuation and Rating Act 1980; Urban Government Act 1993; Legal Notice Nº 10 of 1997 (tax on urban real property).

Proclamation Nº 20 of 1935 as amended (estate duty and succession duty).

Transfer Duty Act, 1965, Nº 7 of 1966; Transfer Duty Order, Nº 1 of 1972.

Customs and Excise Consolidated Act, Nº 10 of 1982.

Trading Enterprise Order, 1993; Order Nº 11 of 1997 (trade licenses).

Fuel and Service Control Act 1983, Nº 23 of 1983; Legal Notice Nº 63 of 1988 (petrol levy).

Precious Stones Order 1970, Nº 24 of 1970 (diamond export tax).

Proclamation 16/07 as amended; Stamp Duties (Amendment) Order Nº 20 of 1972; Legal Notice Nº 58 of 1988 (stamp duty).

Toll Gate Act of 1976; Legal Notice Nº 18 of 1988; Legal Notice Nº 1 of 1992 (tax on vehicles leaving Lesotho).

Liberia (LBR)

Revenue and Finance Law, Title 37 Liberian Code of Laws, *reprinted in* TLW (as amended to June 1991).

Libya (LBY)

In addition to the taxes listed below, a tax is imposed on gasoline, diesel, cigarettes, airline tickets, foreign currency transfers, and letters of credit.[11]

The Income Tax Law, Law Nº 64 of 1973, *reprinted in* TLW [in English].

Zakat (Charity Tax) Law, *reprinted in* TLW [in English].

Entertainment Tax Law, *reprinted in* TLW [in English].

Jihad Tax Law, *reprinted in* TLW [in English].

Social Security Contributions Law, *reprinted in* TLW [in English].

Stamp Duty Law Nº 65 of 1973.

---

[11]See 1977 Tax Summaries, *supra* note 1, at L-28.

Lithuania (LTU)

According to the law on the administration of taxes, the following 15 taxes apply in Lithuania: VAT, excise, individual income tax, tax on profits of legal persons, tax on immovable property of enterprises, land tax, tax on state natural resources, tax on oil and gas resources, tax on environmental pollution, consular fee, stamp duty, tax on places of commerce, surcharge on revenues from sales in accordance with law on road fund, tax on gifts and inheritances, and contributions for mandatory health insurance. We cite to the session laws (Vedomosti Litovskoy Respubliki). The laws are available (in Lithuanian) on the home page of the Parliament of Lithuania: http://www.lrs.lt or on GLIN.

Zakon Litovskoy Respubliki ob Administrirovanii Nalogov (Law on Tax Administration), Law N° I-974, June 28, 1995, Vedomosti Litovskoy Respubliki N° 33, November 30, 1995 [in Russian], amended by

Zakon N° I-1321 O Vnesenii Izmeneniy v Statyu 2 Zakona Litovskoy Respubliki "O Vvedenii v Deystviye Zakona Litovskoy Respubliki ob Administrirovanii Nalogov" (Amendments to Article 2 of the Law on Bringing into Force the Law on Administration of Taxes) Apr. 30, 1996, Vedomosti Litovskoy Respubliki N° 19, July 10, 1996 [in Russian].

Zakon N° I-1370 O Vnesenii Dopolneniya v Statyu 5 Zakona Litovskoy Respubliki ob Administrirovanii Nalogov (Law on Making Additions to Article 5 of the Law on Administration of Taxes) Vedomosti Litovskoy Respubliki 1995, N° 33-580 Vedomosti N° 21, July 31, 1996 [in Russian].

Zakon N° I-1382 O Dopolnenii Zakona Litovskoy Respubliki ob Administrirovanii Nalogov Statey 26 (Addition of Article 26 to Law on Administration of Taxes), June 13, 1996, Vedomosti N° 22, Aug. 10, 1996 [in Russian].

Zakon N° I-1416 O Vnesenii Izmeneiy v Stati 5, 8, 11, 17, 25, 50, 52, 55, 56 Zakona Litovskoy Respubliki ob Administrirovanii Nalogov (Amendment to Articles 5, 8, 11, 17, 25, 50, 52, 55, 56 of the Law on the Administration of Taxes), July 2, 1996, Vedomosti Litovskoy Respubliki N° 28, Oct. 10, 1996 [in Russian].

Zakon N° VIII-107 O Vnesenii Izmeneiy v Stati 25, 39, 49, 50, 52, 54, 55, 56 Zakona Litovskoy Respubliki ob Administrirovanii Nalogov I dopolnenii zakona statei 39[1] (Amendment to Articles 25, 39, 49, 50, 52, 54, 55, 56 of the Law on the Administration of Taxes and Addition of Article 39[1]), Feb. 13, 1997, Vedomosti Litovskoy Respubliki N° 17, June 20, 1997 [in Russian].

Zakon N° VIII-146 O Vnesenii Izmeneiy v Stati 49 i 50 Zakona Litovskoy Respubliki ob Administrirovanii Nalogov (Amendment to Articles

49 and 50 of the Law on the Administration of Taxes), Mar. 13, 1997, Vedomosti Litovskoy Respubliki № 17, June 20, 1997 [in Russian].

Zakon № VIII-164 O Vnesenii Izmeneiy v Statyu 26¹ Zakona Litovskoy Respubliki ob Administrirovanii Nalogov (Amendment to Article 26¹ of the Law on the Administration of Taxes), Mar. 27, 1997, Vedomosti Litovskoy Respubliki № 17, June 20, 1997 [in Russian].

Law on State Tax Inspectorate of June 26, 1990, *reprinted in* CEEL [in English].

Zakon № I-1365 O Mestnikh Sborakh (Law on Local Fees) June 6, 1996, Vedomosti № 21, July 31, 1996 [in Russian].

Law on Excise Taxes of May 1, 1994 [in English], amended by

Postanovleniye № 158 O Chastichnom Izmenenii Postanovleniya Pravitelstva Litovskoy Respubliki ot 25 Aprelya 1994 g. № 302 "Ob Aktsizakh" (Amendments to the Decree on Excises), Jan. 31, 1996, Vedomosti Litovskoy Respubliki № 10, Apr. 10, 1996 [in Russian].

Postanovleniye № 582 Pravitelstva O Chastichnom Izmenenii Postanovleniya Pravitelstva Litovskoy Respubliki ot 25 Aprelya 1994 g. № 302 "Ob Aktsizakh" (Amendments of Decree on Excises), May 17, 1996, Vedomosti № 17, June 20, 1996 [in Russian].

Zakon № I-1307 O Vnesenii Izmeneniy v Statyi 8¹,8²,9 Zakona Litovskoy Respubliki ob Aktsizakh (Amendments to Excise Tax Law) Apr. 30, 1996, Vedomosti № 19, July 10, 1996 [in Russian].

Postanovleniye № 815 O Chastichnom Izmenenii Postanovleniya Pravitel'stva Litovskoy Respubliki ot 25 Aprelya 1994 g. № 302 "Ob Aktsizakh" (Amendments to Government Decree on Excises), July 10, 1996, Vedomosti № 25 Sept. 10, 1996 [in Russian].

Law on Charity and Sponsorship, June 4, 1993, *reprinted in* Lithuania. Seimas. Parliamentary Record, 1993 [in English].

Zakon № I-1320 O Vnesenii Izmeneniy v Zakon Litovskoy Respubliki o Naloge s Imushchestva, Perekhodyashchego v Poryadke Nasleldovaniya ili Dareniya (Amendments to the Law on the Tax on Property Transferred by Gift or Inheritance), Apr. 30, 1996, Vedomosti № 19, July 10, 1996 [in Russian].

Zakon № I-1394 O Vnesenii Izmeneniy v Statyu 11 Zakona Litovskoy Respubliki o Naloge s Imushchestva, Prekhodyashchego v Poryadke Nasledovaniya ili Dareniya (Amendments to Law on Tax on Property Transferred by Gift or Inheritance), June 20, 1996, Vedomosti № 22 Apr. 10, 1996 [in Russian].

Provisional Law on Income Tax of Natural Persons, № I-644, Oct. 9, 1990 (as amended to May 16, 1995) [in English].

Zakon O Vnesenii Izmeneniy i Dopolneniy vo Vremenniy Zakon Litovskoy Respubliki o Podokhodnom Naloge s Fizicheskikh Lits (Law of the Lithuanian Republic on Amendments and Additions to the Provisional Law of the Lithuanian Republic on Income Tax of Natural Persons), July 13, 1993, *reprinted in* Ekho Litvy, July 30, 1993 [in Russian].

Zakon № I-1184 O Vnesenii Izmeneniy i Dopolneniy vo Vremenniy Zakon Litovskoy Respubliki o Podokhodnom Naloge s Fizicheskikh Lits (Amendments to Individual Income Tax Law), Jan. 23, 1996, Vedomosti № 11, Apr. 20, 1996 [in Russian].

Zakon № I-1265 O Lgotakh po Podokhodnomu Nalogu s Fizicheskikh Lits Proizvodyashchim Selskokhozyaystvennuyu Produktsiyu i Predostavlyayushchim Uslugi Selskomu Khozyaystvu Khozyaystvennim Tovarishchestvam i Individualnim (Lichnim) Predpriyatiyam (Law on Individual Income Tax Exemptions for Farm Producers), Apr. 2, 1996, Vedomosti № 13, May 10, 1996 [in Russian].

Zakon № I-1309 O Vnesenii Izmeneniy v Stati Vremennogo Zakona Litovskoy Respubliki o Podokhodnom Naloge s Fizicheskikh Lits (Individual Income Tax Law Amendments), Apr. 30, 1996, Vedomosti № 19, July 1996 [in Russian].

Zakon № I-1400 O Vnesenii Izmeneniy I Dopolneniy v Stati 7, 15, 16, 24, 35 Vremennogo Zakona Litovskoy Respubliki o Podokhodnom Naloge s Fizicheskikh Lits (Individual Income Tax Law Amendments), June 25, 1996, Vedomosti № 30, Oct. 31, 1996 [in Russian].

Zakon № I-1461 O Vnesenii Izmeneniy v Statyu 7 Vremennogo Zakona Litovskoy Respubliki o Podokhodnom Naloge s Fizicheskikh Lits (Individual Income Tax Law Amendments), July 10, 1996, Vedomosti № 30, Oct. 31, 1996 [in Russian].

Zakon № I-1483 O Vnesenii Izmeneniy v Statyu 24 Vremennogo Zakona Litovskoy Respubliki o Podokhodnom Naloge s Fizicheskikh Lits (Individual Income Tax Law Amendments), July 11, 1996, Vedomosti № 29, Oct. 19, 1996 [in Russian].

Zakon № I-1338 O Deklarirovanii Imushchestva i Dokhodov Naseleniya (Law on Declaration of Property and Incomes of the Population), May 16, 1996, Vedomosti № 18, June 28, 1996 [in Russian].

Law on Taxes on Profits of Legal Persons, № I-442, July 31, 1990 (as amended to Apr. 11, 1995) [in English].

Zakon № I-1516 O Vnesenii Dopolneniy v Stati 5,6 i 8 Zakona Litovskoy Respubliki o Naloge na Pribil yuridicheskikh Lits (Corporate Income Tax Amendments), June 27, 1991, June 20, 1991, Vedomosti № 20, July 20, 1991 [in Russian].

Izmeneniya v Zakone O Podokhodnom Naloge s Predpriyatiy (Amendments to Enterprise Income Tax), Mar. 13, 1996, Sazitie, Mar. 20, 1996 [in Russian].

Zakon № I-1266 O Lgotakh po Nalogu na Pribyl Selskokhozyaystvennym Predpriyatiyam (Law on Exemption of Agricultural Enterprises from Profit Tax), Apr. 2, 1996, Vedomosti № 13, May 10, 1996 [in Russian]

Zakon № I-399 O Vnesenii Izmeneniy i Dopolneniy v Stati 1,3, 5, 6, 7, 8 Zakona Litovskoy Respubliki o Naloge na Pribyl Yuridicheskikh Lits (Amendment to Articles 1, 3, 5, 6, 7, 8 of the Law on Taxes on Profits of Legal Persons), June 25, 1996, Vedomosti № 29, Oct. 19, 1996 [in Russian].

Zakon № I-1310 O Vnesenii Izmeneniy v Stati 14, 15, 16 Zakona Litovskoy Respubliki o Naloge na Pribyl Yuridicheskikh Lits (Amendments to Law on Profit Tax for Legal Persons), Apr. 30, 1996, Vedomosti № 19, July 10, 1996 [in Russian].

Zakon № I-1426 O Vnesenii Izmeneniy i Dopolneniy v Stayu 3 Zakona Litovskoy Respubliki o Naloge na Pribyl Yuridicheskikh Lits (Amendment to Article 3 of the Law on Profit Tax for Legal Persons), July 2, 1996, Vedomosti № 29, Oct. 19, 1996 [in Russian].

Zakon № I-1460 O Vnesenii Izmeneniy i Dopolneniy v Stati 3, 5, 6 Zakona Litovskoy Respubliki o Naloge na Pribyl Yuridicheskikh Lits (Amendments to Articles 3, 5, 6 of the Law on Profit Tax for Legal Persons), July 10, 1996, Vedomosti № 29, Oct. 19, 1996 [in Russian].

Law № I-345 on Value-Added Tax, Dec. 22, 1993, as amended on Oct. 1994 and Jan. 1995 [in English].

Zakon № I-1185 O Vnesenii Izmeneniy i Dopolneniy v Zakon Litovskoy Respubliki o Naloge na Dobavlennuyu Stoimost (Law on VAT Amendments), Jan. 23, 1996, Vedmosti Litovskoy Respubliki № 12, Apr. 30, 1996 [in Russian].

Zakon № I-1339 O Vnesenii Izmeneniy v Statyu 38 Zakona Litovskoy Respubliki o Naloge na Dobavlennuyu Stoimost (Amendments to Article 38 of VAT Law), May 16, 1996, Vedomosti Litovskoy Respubliki № 17, June 20, 1996 [in Russian].

Zakon № I-1346 O Vnesenii Izmeneniy v Statyu 38 Zakona Litovskoy Respubliki o Naloge na Dobavlennuyu Stoimost (Amendments to Article 38 of VAT Law), May 21, 1996, Vedomosti Litovskoy Respubliki № 17, June 20, 1996 in Russian].

Zakon № I-11402 O Vnesenii Izmeneniy v Statyu 23 Zakona Litovskoy Respubliki o Naloge na Dobavlennyu Stoimost (Amendments to Article

23 of VAT Law), June 25, 1996, Vedomosti Litovskoy Respubliki Nº 29, Oct. 19, 1996 [in Russian].

Zakon Nº I-1308 O Vnesenii Izmeneniy v Stati 35 i 36 Zakona Litovskoy Respubliki o Naloge na Dobavlennuyu Stoimost' (Amendments to Articles 35 and 36 of VAT Law), Apr. 30, 1996, Vedomosti Nº 19, July 10, 1996 [in Russian].

Law Nº I-565 on the Tax Imposed on Immovable Property of Enterprises and Organizations, July 20, 1994 [in English].

Zakon Nº I-1311 O Vnesenii Izmeneniy v Stati 7 i 9 Zakona Litovskoy Respubliki o Naloge na Nedvizhimoye Imushchestvo Predpriyatiy i Organizatsiy (Amendments to Articles 7 and 9 of Law on Tax on Immovable Property of Enterprises and Organizations), Apr. 30, 1996, Vedomosti Nº 19, July 10, 1996 [in Russian].

Zakon Nº I-1436 O Vnesenii Izmeneniy v Stati 1, 2, 3, 4, 5, i 11 Zakona Litovskoy Respubliki o Naloge na Nedvizhimoye Imushchestvo Predpriyatiy i Organizatsiy (Amendments to Articles 1, 2, 3, 4, 5, and 11 of Law on Tax on Immovable Property of Enterprises and Organizations), July 4, 1996, Vedomosti Nº 29, Oct. 19, 1996 [in Russian].

Law on Land Tax, Valstybes Zinios, 1992, Nº 21-612, amended by Law Nº I-992, Valstybes Zinios, July 19, 1995 [in Lithuanian] [available on website].

Zakon Nº I-1312 O Vnesenii Izmeneniy v Stati 12 i 13 Zakona Litovskoy Respubliki o Zemel'nom Naloge (Amendments to Articles 12 and 13 of Law on Land Tax), Apr. 30, 1996, Vedomosti Nº 19, July 10, 1996 [in Russian].

Zakon Nº I-1163 O Nalogakh na Gosudarstvennye Prirodnye Resursy (Law on Taxes on State Natural Resources), Mar. 31, 1991, Vedomosti Nº 11, Apr. 11, 1991 [in Russian].

Zakon Nº I-1313 O Vnesenii Izmeneniy v Stati 7, 9, 10 Zakona Litovskoy Respubliki o Nalogakh na Gosudarstvennye Priorodnye Resursy (Amendments to Article 7, 9, and 10 of Law on Taxes on State Natural Resources), Apr. 30, 1996, Vedomosti Nº 19, July 10, 1996 [in Russian].

Zakon Nº I-1314 O Vnesenii Izmeneniy v Stati 5, 8, 9, 12 Zakona Litovskoy Respubliki o Naloge na Resursy Nefti i Gaza (Amendments to Articles 5, 8, 9 and 12 of Law on Tax on Oil and Gas), Apr. 30, 1996, Vedomosti Nº 19, July 10, 1996 [in Russian].

Zakon Nº I-1205 O Nalogakh Za Zagryaznenie Okruzhayushchey Sredy (Law on Taxes on Environmental Pollution), Apr. 9, 1991,Vedomosti Nº 12, Apr. 30, 1991 [in Russian].

Zakon Nº I-1315 O Vnesenii Izmeneniy v Zakon Litovskoy Respubliki o Nalogakh za Zagryazneniye Okruzhayushchey Sredy (Amendments to

Law on Taxes on Pollution of the Environment) Apr. 30, 1996, Vedomosti N⁰ 19, July 10, 1996 [in Russian].

Zakon o Gosudarstvennom Sotsialnom Strakhovanie (Law on State Social Insurance), Vedomosti N⁰ 17, June 20, 1991 [in Russian].

Zakon N⁰ I-1319 O Vnesenii Izmeneniy v Statyu 2 Zakona Litovskoy Respubliki o Dorozhnom Fonde (Law on Amendments to Law on the Road Fund), Apr. 30, 1996, Vedomosti Litovskoy Respubliki N⁰ 19, July 10, 1996 [in Russian].

Zakon N⁰ I-1318 O Vnesenii Izmeneniy v Stati 7 i 10 Zakona Litovskoy Respubliki o Naloge na Mesta Torgovli (Amendments to Law on Tax on the Place of Trading), Apr. 30, 1996, Vedomosti Litovskoy Respubliki N⁰ 19, July 10, 1996 [in Russian].

Law on Stamp Tax, Valstybes Zinios, 1994, N⁰ 51-950, N⁰ 89-1712; 1995, N⁰ 47-1135; 1996, N⁰ 18-462, N⁰ 46-1112, N⁰ 116-2691; 1997, N⁰ 33-810 [available on website] [in Lithuanian].

Law on Alcohol Control, Valstybes Zinios, 1995, N⁰ 44-1073, N⁰ 61-1527; 1996, N⁰ 8-195, N⁰ 53-1247; 1997, N⁰ 33-809 [available on website] [in Lithuanian].

Luxembourg (LUX)

In addition to income tax, Luxembourg imposes inheritance and gift duty, payroll tax, real property transfer tax, capital tax, tax on betting on sporting events, tax on lotto, wealth tax, estate duty, value-added tax, excise duty on mineral oils, excise tax on road fuel, excise duty on manufactured tobacco, excise duty and consumption tax on ethyl alcohol, excise duty on wines and other nonsparkling and sparkling fermented beverages, excise duty on beer, fire service tax, tax on land and buildings, stamp duty, mortgage tax, tax on motor vehicles, trade tax, tax on licensed premises, entertainment tax, tax on gross proceeds from casino gambling, excise duties on intermediate products. References to the laws imposing these taxes are found in EU Inventory.

Income Tax Law of Dec. 4, 1967, *reprinted in* TLW (as amended to Dec. 24, 1996) [in English].

Macedonia, former Yugoslav Republic of (MKD)

Citations to Sluzben vesnik na Republika Makedonija (Official Gazette of the Republic of Macedonia (SVRM)) and to Sluzben vesnik na Sociajalisticka Republika Makedonija (Official Gazette of the Socialist Republic of Macedonia (SVSRM)) are taken from IBFD, Macedonia, in Taxation and Investment in Central and East European Countries (Dec. 1996, supp.).

Law on the Personal Income Tax, Ministry of Finance, updated to Dec. 30, 1993 [in English], SVRM N⁰ 80/1993, amended by SVRM N⁰ 70/1994.

Law on Property Tax, Ministry of Finance, as updated to Dec. 30, 1993 [in English], SVRM Nº 80/1993.

Law on Profit Tax, Ministry of Finance, as updated to Dec. 30, 1993 [in English], SVRM Nº 90/1993, amended by SVRM Nº 43/1995.

Sales Taxes on Products and Services Law, SVRM Nº 34/1992, amended by SVRM Nº 62/1992, Nº 3/1991, Nº 4/1993, Nº 80/1993, and Nº 42/1992.

Amendments to the Sales Tax Law, Jan. 16, 1996 [in Macedonian] available on Microfiche and from the Tax Analysts' Access Service/TaxBase.

Law on the Temporary Lodgings Tax, Apr. 1996 [in Macedonian] available on Microfiche and from the Tax Analysts' Access Service/TaxBase.

Excise Tax Law, SVRM Nº 78/1993, amended by SVRM Nº 42/1995.

Public Revenue Office Law, SVRM Nº 80/1993.

Taxes Imposed on Foreigners Law, SVRM Nº 4/1993.

Taxes on Transfer of Property, Copyrights and Other Rights Law, SVSRM Nº 40/1984, amended by SVSRM Nº 51/1988, Nº 29/1989, and SVRM Nº 4/1993.

Madagascar (MGD)

Code Général des Impôts (General Tax Code), *reprinted in* Code Général des Impôts (Imprimerie d'Ouvrage Educatifs 1986) (as amended to 1986) [in French].

Law Nº 91-020, Aug. 12, 1991, to institute a regime of industrial free zones, Journal oficiel, Aug. 13, 1991.

Malawi (MWI)

In addition to those listed below, real estate transfer duty and fringe benefits tax apply. Laws of Malawi is a 10-volume loose-leaf service issued by the government printer.

ITA—An Act to Provide for the Taxation of Income and for Purposes Ancillary Thereto, ch. 41:02 of the Laws, *reprinted in* TLW (as amended to June 1992) amended by

> Act Nº 1 of 1995, Taxation (Amendment) Act, 1995, Malawi Gazette Supplement, Apr. 1, 1995.
> Act Nº 2 of 1996, Taxation (Amendment) Act, 1996, Malawi Gazette Supplement, Mar. 22, 1996.
> Act Nº 5 of 1997, Taxation (Amendment) Act, 1997, Malawi Gazette Supplement, Apr. 1997.

Customs and Excise Act, Laws of Malawi, ch. 42:01 (rev. 1974).

Tobacco Cess Act, *id.*, ch. 42:02 (rev. 1968).

Tea Cess Act, *id.*, ch. 42:03 (rev. 1981).

Hides and Skins (Cess) Act, *id.*, ch. 42:04 (rev. 1968).

Stamp Duties Act, *id.*, ch. 43:01 (rev. 1986).

Estate Duty Act, *id.*, ch. 43:02 (rev. 1970), amended by Estate Duty (Amendment) Act, 1997.

Malaysia (MYS)

Besides those listed below, contractors' levy, stamp duty, film-hire duty, and excise are imposed.

ITA—Income Tax Act, 1967, *reprinted in* TLW (as amended to Finance Act 1997).

Service Tax Act Nº 151 of 1975, *reprinted in* Laws of Malaysia.

Promotion of Investments Act of 1986.

Excise Tax Act Nº 176 Official Gazette (P.U.) of June 24, 1976, *reprinted in* Laws of Malaysia.

Sales Tax Act Nº 64 of 1972, as amended to July 1987, Official Gazette (P.U.) (B) 72/72, *reprinted in* International Law Book Services, ed. (1987).

Petroleum Income Tax Act 1967.

Maldives (MDV)

The Maldives has no general income tax, although there is a tax on bank profits. There are customs duties, an airport departure tax, a tourism (bed) tax, stamp duty (on registration of mortagages), and company registration fee.

Mali (MLI)

We cite to a compilation published by Cabinet SEAG Conseil (address: B.P. 18, Bamako; tel./fax: 230672).

Code général des impôts (General Tax Code), *reprinted in* Code général des impôts (Cabinet SEAG Conseil) (as amended to Dec. 31, 1995) [in French].

Malta (MLT)

Act Nº LIV of 1948, Income Tax Act, *reprinted in* Income Tax Act, Cap. 123 (as amended to 1994), Ippubblikat mid-Dipartiment ta' l-Informazzjoni—Kastilja (Department of Information) [in Maltese], *reprinted in* TLW (as amended through Aug. 20 1996) [in English].

Act № XXII of 1995 to amend the Income Tax Act, Cap. 123, July 24, 1995, Ippubblikat mid-Dipartiment ta' l-Informazzjoni—Kastilja (Department of Information) [in Maltese].

Act № XVIII of 1994, Income Tax Management, Sept. 13, 1994, Ippubblikat mid-Dipartiment ta' l-Informazzjoni—Kastilja (Department of Information) [in Maltese], available on TaxBase [in English], reprinted in TLW (as amended through July 28, 1995) [in English].

Act № XVII Income Tax of 1994, Income Tax (Amendment) (№ 2) Act, 1994, Sept. 13, 1994 [in English].

Act № XVII Duty on Documents and Transfers Act, 1993, Ippubblikat mid-Dipartiment ta' l-Informazzjoni—Kastilja (Department of Information) [in Maltese, English], available on TaxBase.

Act № XVI of 1994 Duty on Documents and Transfers (Amendment) Act, 1994 to regulate the collection of income tax and to provide the administrative machinery for such collection, Sept. 13, 1994 [in English], available on TaxBase.

Act № XIII of 1994 Malta Financial Services Centre Act, 1994, available on TaxBase [in English].

Act № XII of 1997, Customs and Excise Tax Act, 1997, reprinted in TLW.

Marshall Islands (MHL)

Citations are to the official code of the Marshall Islands (Marshall Islands Revised Code (1988) [hereinafter MIRC]).

Income Tax Act 1989, MIRC, Title 11, ch. 1A (rev. 1992).

Firearms Control Tax Act 1978, MIRC, Title 11, ch. 2.

Import Duties Act, MIRC, Title 11, ch. 5A (rev. 1992).

Tax Collection Act, MIRC, Title 11, ch. 7 (rev. 1989).

Financial Management Act 1990, MIRC, Title 11, ch. 8A (rev. 1992).

Mauritania (MRT)

Code Général des Impôts (General Tax Code), reprinted in Mauritania, Ministère des Finances, Loi de Finances, 1990 [in French], amended by Ordinance № 91-06, Apr. 22, 1991, Journal officiel, May 15, 1991.

Mauritius (MUS)

Act № 16 of 1995 on Income Tax, Aug. 3, 1995, Legal Supplement to Government Gazette of Mauritius, Aug. 12, 1995, reprinted in TLW (as amended through July 1, 1997), also available on TaxBase.

Act № 9 of 1997, Finance Act 1997, July 28, 1997 reprinted in TLW.

Mexico (MEX)

We cite to Legislación Fiscal, an annual two-volume loose-leaf compilation of the tax laws by the Ministry of Finance (in Spanish); the IBFD CD; Tax Laws of the World, and TaxBase. CCH publishes Mexican tax and related legislation, as well as explanatory guides, in English. Tax Analysts includes the Mexican tax legislation in its North American OneDisc (CD) (cited as Tax Analysts OneDisc); Ediciones Andrade, Colime N° 213, Col. Roma, 06700 Mexico, D.F., Mexico (fax: 511-7047) publishes tax as well as other legal material.

Ley del Impuesto sobre la Renta 1997(Income Tax Law), *reprinted in* Secretaría de Hacienda y Crédito Público, Legislación Fiscal, *also reprinted in* IBFD-CIAT [in Spanish] *and in* Tax Analysts OneDisc [in Spanish and English].

Código Fiscal de la Federación 1997 (Federal Tax Code), *reprinted in* TLW, Legislación Fiscal, *supra, and in* IBFD-CIAT [in Spanish] *and in* Tax Analysts OneDisc [in Spanish and English].

Ley del Servicio de Administración Tributaria, *reprinted in* Legislación Fiscal, *supra, and in* Tax Analysts OneDisc [in Spanish and English].

Ley Orgánica del Tribunal Fiscal de la Federación, *reprinted in* Legislación Fiscal, *supra, and in* Tax Analysts OneDisc [in Spanish and English].

Ley del Impuesto al Activo (Assets Tax Law), Diario Oficial (hereinafter D.O.), Dec. 31, 1988, Ca 5, art. 10 de la ley que establece, reforma, adiciona y deroga diversas disposiciones fiscales, vigente a partir del 1° de enero 1989, *reprinted in* Legislación Fiscal, *supra,* TLW (as amended through Dec. 31, 1996), *and in* Tax Analysts OneDisc [in Spanish and English].

Ley del Impuesto al Valor Agregado 1997 (Value Added Tax Law), *reprinted in* IBFD-CIAT [in Spanish], *reprinted in* Legislación Fiscal, *supra, and in* Tax Analysts OneDisc [in Spanish and English]; *also reprinted in* TLW (as amended to Apr. 24, 1997) [in English].

Ley del Impuesto Especial sobre Producción y Servicios (Special Tax on Production and Services Law (excise tax)), *reprinted in* Legislación Fiscal, *supra, and in* Tax Analysts OneDisc [in Spanish and English].

Ley del Impuesto Sobre Tenencia o Uso de Vehículos (Law on Tax on Ownership or Use of Vehicles), *id.*

Ley de Contribución de Mejoras por Obras Públicas Federales de Infraestructura Hidráulica, (Special Assessment Taxes on Federal Public Works Relating to Water Infrastructure), *id.*

Ley del Impuesto Sobre Automóviles Nuevos (Tax on New Automobiles), Dec. 30, 1996, available on TaxBase [in Spanish].

General Import Tax Law, Dec. 18, 1995, available on Microfiche and from the Tax Analysts' Access Service/TaxBase [in Spanish].

General Export Tax Law, Dec. 22, 1995, available on Microfiche and from the Tax Analysts' Access Service/TaxBase [in Spanish].

Social Security Law, published in D. O., Dec. 21, 1995, *reprinted in* TLW [in English].

Micronesia, Federated States of (FSM)

Federated States of Micronesia Income Tax Law, Federated States of Micronesia Code Annotated, Title 54, ch. 1 (Pacific Island Planning Consultants: Kolonia, Pohnpei 1995, with 1996 annual update).

Import and Export Taxes, *id.*, Title 54, ch. 2.

Revenue and Administration, *id.* Title 54, chs. 8, 9.

Moldova (MDA)

The following national taxes are in effect in Moldova: VAT, enterprise income tax, excise, privatization tax, tax on incomes of banks, securities transaction tax, insurance income tax, state duty, and customs. In addition, there are numerous local taxes. The Parliament has under consideration legislation that would reform and consolidate the legislation in a tax code. See Nikolai Golovchenko, Nalogi Moldovi: sevodnia i zavtra (Taxes of Moldova: Today and Tomorrow), Nezavisimaya Moldova, May 7, 1997.

Zakon Respubliki Moldova o Podokhodnom Naloge s Fizicheskikh Lits (Law of the Republic of Moldova on Income Tax on Natural Persons), Dec. 3, 1992, *reprinted in* Nezavisimaya Moldova, Mar. 10, 1993 [in Russian], *and in* FBIS-USR-93-062, May 14, 1993, at 96–100 [in English].

Zakon Respubliki Moldova ob Osnovakh Nalogovoy Sistemy (Law of the Republic of Moldova on the Foundation of the Tax System), Nov. 17, 1992, *reprinted in* Nezavisimaya Moldova, Dec. 24, 1992 [in Russian].

Law Nº 968-XIII of July 24, 1996, amending several legislative acts, *Monitorul Oficial*, item Nº 681, Oct. 31, 1996 [Russian edition] (amends law on foundation of the tax system).

Zakon Respubliki Moldova O Gosudarstvennoy Nalogovoy Sluzhbe (Law of the Republic of Moldova on State Tax Service), Jan. 22, 1992, Nº 876-XII [in Russian], amended by Zakon 367 o Vnesenii izmeneniy i Dopolneniy v Nekotorye Zakonodatelnye Akty, Statya IX, Monitorul Oficial Al Republicii Nº 40–41, June 20, 1996 [in Russian].

Zakon o Vnesenii Izmeneniy v Zakon o Gosudarstvennoy Nalogovoy Sluzhbe i v Zakon ob Osnovakh Nalogovoy Sistemy (Amendment to the Law on the Tax

Service and to the Law on the Foundation of the Tax System), Feb. 6, 1997, Monitorul Oficial Al Republicii № 15, Mar. 6, 1997, item № 160 [in Russian].

Zakon Respubliki Moldova o Naloge na Pribyl' Predpriyatiy (Law of the Republic of Moldova on Income Tax of Enterprises), Dec. 2, 1992, № 1214-XII, *reprinted in* Nezavisimaya Moldova, Jan. 23, 1993 [in Russian], *and in* Law on Taxes on Business, Associations and Organizations (1992) [in English].

Law on Banks and Other Credit Institutions Profit Tax (Bank Income Tax Law) of June 1995 [in English], amended by Zakon № 850-XIII o Vensenii Dopolneniya v Statyu 5 Zakona o Nalogooblozhenii Pribyli Bankov i Drugikh Kreditnykh Uchrezhdeniy (Amendment to the Law on Banks and Other Credit Institutions Profit Tax), May 29, 1996, Monitorul Oficial Al Republicii № 40–41, June 20, 1996 [in Russian].

Law on Tax on Securities Transactions, May 10, 1993, *reprinted in* Nezavisimaya Gazeta, July 17, 1993 [in Russian], *and in* FBIS-USR-93-113, Aug. 30, 1993, at 78–79 [in English].

Zakon № 802-XIII o Vnesenii Izmeneniy i Dopolneniy V Zakon o Naloge na Operatsii c Tsennymi Bumagami (Amendment to the Law on Tax on Securities Transactions), Apr. 5, 1996, Monitorul Oficial Al Republicii № 28, May 9, 1996 [in Russian].

Law on the Land Tax and the Taxation Procedure, Dec. 22, 1992, *reprinted in* Nezavisimaya Moldova, Mar. 16, 1993 [in Russian], *and in* FBIS-USR-93-062, May 14, 1993, at 100–102 [in English].

Zakon o Naloge na Dobavlennuyu Stoimost' (Law on Value-Added Tax) (as amended through Dec. 5, 1995 by Law № 675-XIII) [in Russian].

Zakon № 633-XII o Poryadke Vzyskaniya Nalogov, Sborov i Drugick Platezhey v Byudzhet i vo Bnebyudzhetnye Fondy, ne Vnesennykh v Ustanovlenye Sroki (Law № 633-XII on the procedure for the imposition of duties, taxes and other payments to the budget and to nonbudgetary funds not paid on time), Nov. 10, 1995, Monitorul Oficial Al Republicii, № 8–9, Feb. 8, 1996 [in Russian].

Zakon № 869-XIII o Vensenii Izmeneniy i Dopolneniy v Zakon o Poryadke Vzyckaniya Nalogov, Sborov i Drugikh Platezhey v Byudzhet i vo Bnebyudzhetnye Fondy, ne Vnesennykh v Ustanovlenye Sroki (Amendments and Additions to the Law on the Procedure for the imposition of duties, taxes, and other payments to the budget and to nonbudgetary funds not paid on time), June 7, 1996, Monitorul Oficial Al Republicii № 46–47, July 11, 1996 [in Russian].

Zakon № 78-XIII o Vnesenii Izmeneniy i Dopolneniy v Nekotorye Zakonodatelnye Akty, Staya XIII, v Zakon o Gosudarstvennoy Poshline № 1216-XII ot 3 Dekabrya 1992 goda (Amendment to the Law on State Fees of Dec. 3, 1992), Monitorul Oficial Al Republicii № 40–41, June 20, 1996 [in Russian].

Zakon № 736-XIII o Vnesenii Izmeneniy i Dopolneniy v Statyu 8 Zakona o Zemelnom Naloge i Poryadke Nalogooblozheniya (Amendment to Article 8 of the Law on Real Estate Tax), Feb. 20, 1996, Monitorul Oficial Al Republicii № 17–18, Mar. 21, 1996 [in Russian].

Zakon № 744-XIII o Vnesenii Dopolneniy v Statyu 4 Zakona o Gosudarstvennoy Poshline (Addition to Article 4 of the Law on State Fees), Feb. 20, 1996, Monitorul Oficial Al Republicii № 16, Mar. 14, 1996 [in Russian].

Zakon № 691-XIII o Byudzhete Gosudarstvennogo Sozialnogo Strakhovaniya na 1996 God, Tarify Vznosov na Obyazatelnoe Gosudarstvennoe Sozialnoe Strakhovanie na 1996 God i Racpredelenie Poluchennyck Sredstv (Law on the State Social Security Budget for 1996, Rate for the Mandatory Social Security Dues), Dec. 19, 1995, Monitorul Oficial Al Republicii № 4, Jan. 18, 1996 [in Russian].

Zakon № 926-XIII o Vnesenii Izmeneniya i Dopolneniya v Prilozhenie k Zakony o Byudzhete Gosudarstvennogo Sotsialnogo Strakhovaniya na 1996 God (Amendment to the Law on the State Social Security Budget for 1996) July 12, 1996, Monitorul Oficial Al Republicii № 56, Aug. 22, 1996 [in Russian].

Postanovlenie Parlamenta № 402 o Kontseptsii Nalogovoi Reforme (Resolution of Parliament on the concept of tax reform), Apr. 24, 1997, Monitorul Oficial, № 46–47, July 17, 1997 [in Russian].

Mongolia (MNG)

General Law of Taxation, Nov. 23, 1992 (as amended through 1997) (unpublished) [in English].

Personal Income Tax Law, Nov. 23, 1992 (as amended through 1997) (unpublished) [in English].

Income Tax Law on Self-Employed Persons Whose Income Is Impossible to Define, 1993, reprinted in Ministry of Finance [in English].

BEIT—Business Entity and Organization Income Tax Law, Dec. 14, 1992 (as amended through 1997) (unpublished) [in English].

Transport Facilities and Vehicles Tax Law, Dec. 1, 1992, reprinted in Ministry of Finance (as amended through June 1996) [in English].

Hunter's Gun Tax Law, May 11, 1993, reprinted in Ministry of Finance (as amended through June 1996) [in English].

Sales Tax Law, reprinted in Ministry of Finance (as amended through June 1996) [in English].

Excise Tax Law, Jan. 21, 1993 (as amended through the law of Apr. 11, 1997) (unpublished) [in English].

Law of Mongolia Concerning Tax Assessments, Auditing of Tax Payments, and Tax Collections, 1996, *reprinted in* Ministry of Finance [in English].

Law of Mongolia on State Stamp Duties, July 15, 1993, *reprinted in* Ministry of Justice of Mongolia, Commercial Laws of Mongolia (Brookers Limited, Wellington, New Zealand 1997) [in English].

Morocco (MAR)

Impôt sur les societés (Corporation Tax), B.O. N° 3873, Jan. 21, 1987, *reprinted in* Morocco, Ministère des finances, Direction des impôts, Impôt sur les societés (SONIR 1987) [in French].

Taxe sur la valeur ajoutée (Value Added Tax), B.O. N° 3818, Jan. 1, 1986, *reprinted in* Ministry of Finance Tax Office, Sales Tax Division, Taxe sur la Valeur Ajoutée (SONIR 1986) [in French].

Mozambique (MDZ)

Código dos Impostos sobre o Rendimento (Income Tax Code), *reprinted in* Direcção Nacional de Impostos e Auditoria, Ministério das Finanças, Código dos Impostos sobre o Rendimento (CEGRAF 1992) [in Portuguese].

Decree N° 43/96, Oct. 22, 1996, Actualização do código do imposto de consumo (Consumption tax code) [in Portuguese].

Law N° 3/87 of Jan. 19, 1987 (establishes fundamentals of tax system and delegates authority to Council of Ministers to establish taxes by decree), Boletim da república, Suplemento, Jan. 30, 1987 [in Portuguese].

Decree N° 1/87 of Council of Ministers (establishing turnover tax code: Código do Imposto de Circulação), Jan. 30, 1987, Boletim da República, Suplemento, Jan. 30, 1987 [in Portuguese], amended by

> Decree 13/91, Boletim da República, June 19, 1991.
> Decree 44/96, Boletim da República, Oct. 22, 1996.

Decree N° 2/87 of Council of Ministers (miscellaneous tax provisions), Jan. 30, 1987, Boletim da República, Suplemento, Jan. 30, 1987 [in Portuguese].

Decree N° 3/87 of Council of Ministers (establishing income tax code: Código do Impostos sobre o Rendimento), Jan. 30, 1987, Boletim da República, Suplemento, Jan. 30, 1987 [in Portuguese].

Decree N° 4/87 of Council of Ministers (establishing national reconstruction tax code: Código do Imposto de Reconstrução Nacional), Jan. 30, 1987, Boletim da República, Suplemento, Jan. 30, 1987 [in Portuguese].

Decree Nº 30/90, tax on professionals, Boletim da República, Dec. 7, 1990 [in Portuguese].

Decree Nº 18/87, alters the tax rates on low tension use of electricity, Boletim da República, July 20, 1987 [in Portuguese].

Decree Nº 31/90, income taxation, Boletim da República, Dec. 7, 1990 [in Portuguese].

Decree Nº 10/87, approves the scheme of incentives to be offered to national investors, Boletim da República, Jan. 30, 1987 [in Portuguese].

Decree Nº 12/93, approves the Code of Tax Benefits, Boletim da República, July 21, 1993 [in Portuguese].

Decree Nº 13/88, revaluation of fixed assets, Boletim da República, Nov. 11, 1988 [in Portuguese].

Myanmar (MMR)

In addition to income tax, commercial tax, payroll tax, natural resource royalty, stamp duty, property tax, land tax, and excise are imposed.

Income Tax Act (India Act XI of 1922), *reprinted in* TLW (as amended to Mar. 1989) [in English].

Namibia (NAM)

Income Tax Act, Nº 24 of 1981, *reprinted in* Legiserve—Namibia—Legislation (Butterworths) (as amended through Aug. 8, 1996).

Sales Tax Act, 1992, Act 5 of 1992, Government Gazette, Nº 386 (Apr. 4, 1992), amended by

Act 31 of 1992.

Sales Tax Amendment Act, 1993, Act 12 of 1993, Government Gazette, Nº 695, Aug. 24, 1993.

Sales Tax Amendment Act, 1994, Act 13 of 1994, Government Gazette, Nº 927, Sept. 23, 1994.

Additional Sales Duties Act, 1993, Act 11 of 1993, Government Gazette, Nº 694, Aug. 23, 1993.

Stamp Duties Act, 1993, Act 15 of 1993, Government Gazette, Nº 698, Aug. 25, 1993, amended by

Moratorium on the Payment of Stamp Duty or Transfer Duty in Respect of Rationalization Schemes Act, 1993, Act 13 of 1993, Government Gazette, Nº 696, Aug. 24, 1993.

Stamp Duties Amendment Act, 1994, Act 12 of 1994, Government Gazette, Nº 924, Sept. 22, 1994.

Transfer Duty Act, 1993, Act 14 of 1993, Government Gazette, Nº 697, Aug. 25, 1993.

Petroleum (Taxation) Act, 1991, Act 3 of 1991, Government Gazette, Nº 179, Apr. 10, 1991.

Act Nº 9 of 1995, Export Processing Zones Act, 1995, Government Gazette, Nº 1069 (Apr. 1995).

Nepal (NPL)

The laws listed below are published in mimeo by Nepal Press Digest (Private) Ltd., Lazimpat, Katmandu. Citations are to the official gazette (Nepal Rajapatra, hereinafter N.R.).

Income Tax Act, 1974, as amended through Act of June 24, 1993, 43 N.R. (Extraordinary).

Value Added Tax Act, 1996, 45 N.R. Nº 49 (E) (March 20, 1996).

Excise Act, 1958, as amended through Act of Apr. 20, 1992, 41 N.R. Nº 73 (E).

Land Tax Act, 1978, as amended through Act of Dec. 23, 1992, 42 N.R. Nº 51 (E).

Wealth Tax Act, 1991, 40 N.R. Nº 58 (E) (Mar. 4, 1991).

Vehicles Tax Act, 1974, as amended through Act of Dec. 13, 1990, 40 N.R. Nº 44 (E).

Houses and Compounds Tax Act, 1963, as amended through Act of Apr. 2, 1974, 23 N.R. Nº 75 (E) (Apr. 2, 1974).

Houses and Compounds Rent Tax Act, 1966, as amended through Act of Apr. 2, 1974, 23 N.R. Nº 75 (E) (Apr. 2, 1974).

Netherlands (NLD)

We cite to one of the available annual commercial compilations. In addition to those listed, the following taxes are imposed: excise duties on mineral oils, tobacco, wine, sparkling beverages, nonalcoholic beverages, beer, and spirits, tax on passenger cars and motor bicycles, fuel tax, "waterschappen" (public corporations responsible for drainage, dykes, roads, bridges, etc. in particular areas), levies, tax on dogs, tax on the pollution of surface waters, tax on noise pollution caused by civilian aircraft, tax on ground water, tax on stocks of petroleum products, tax on manure surplus, tax on the right of user, tax on building land, tax on public advertisements, tax on tour-

ists, parking tax, duty on intermediate products. References to the laws imposing these taxes are found in EU Inventory.

WIB—Wet op de Inkomstenbelasting 1964 (Individual Income Tax Law), Stb. 519, *reprinted in* Verzameling Nederlandse Belastingwetgeving 1995/96 (Koninklijke Vermande bv-Lelystad) (as amended to Jan. 1, 1995) [in Dutch].

Wet op de Loonbelasting 1964 (Wage Tax Law), *id.*

VpB—Wet op de Vennootschapsbelasting 1969 (Corporation Income Tax Law), *id.*

Wet op de Dividendbelasting 1965 (Dividend Withholding Tax), Stb. 621, *id.*

Wet op de Vermogensbelasting 1964 (Net Wealth Tax), Stb. 520, *id.*

Successiewet 1956 (Inheritance Tax), *id.*

Wet op de Belastingen van Rechtsverkeer 1970 (Legal Transfer Tax), Stb. 611, *id.*

Wet op de Omzetbelasting 1968 (Turnover Tax), Stb. 329, *id.*

Wet op de Belasting van Personenauto's en Motorrijwielen 1992 (Motor Vehicle Tax), Stb. 709, *id.*

Wet op de kansspelbelasting 1961 (Lottery Tax Law), Stb. 313, *id.*

Gemeentewet 1992 (Municipal Law), Stb. 96, *id.*

Algemene wet Bestuursrecht 1992 (General Law on Public Administration), Stb. 315, *id.*

Algemene wet Inzake Rijksbelastingen 1959 (General Tax Code), Stb. 301, *id.*

Wet Administratieve Rechtspraak Belastingzaken 1956 (Administrative Judicial Proceedings), Stb. 323, *id.*

Invorderingswet 1990 (Tax Collection Law), Stb. 221, *id.*

New Zealand (NZL)

We cite to one of the available annual commercial compilations. In addition to the taxes listed below, stamp duty is imposed. In addition to the CCH publications cited below, Butterworths publishes a three-volume loose-leaf (Butterworths Taxation Library), which contains the text of the major tax laws.

ITA—Income Tax Act, 1994, *reprinted in* Income Tax Legislation (Commerce Clearing House (CCH) New Zealand Limited 1996).

Tax Administration Act 1994, *reprinted in id.*

Taxation Review Authorities Act 1994, *reprinted in id.*

Goods and Services Tax, *reprinted in* Goods and Services Tax Legislation (5th ed., CCH New Zealand Limited 1990) (as amended to Sept. 1, 1990).

Act Nº 35 Estate and Gift Duties, Nov. 25, 1968, *reprinted in* Statutes of New Zealand, New Zealand Government, 1979. [Note: estate duty was repealed as of Dec. 17, 1993, but gift duty is still in effect.]

Inland Revenue Department Act 1974.

Nicaragua (NIC)

We cite to the CD-ROM published by the IBFD (IBFD-CIAT) and Théodulo Báez Cortéz and Julio Francisco Báez Cortéz, Todo Sobre Impuestos en Nicaragua (1995) (TSIN), which is a compilation in Spanish of the national and municipal tax legislation of Nicaragua and a commentary thereon. TSIN sets forth the consolidated text of the laws and regulations as amended to August 1995.

Decreto Nº 243, Ley Creadora de la Dirección General de Ingresos (Decree Establishing the General Directorate for Revenue), La Gaceta D.O. Nº 144 del 29 de junio de 1957, *reprinted in* TSIN.

Decreto Nº 713 Legislación Tributaria Común (Common Tax Legislation), June 22, 1962, as amended to Jan. 1993, *reprinted in* TSIN and IBFD-CIAT [in Spanish].

Decreto Nº 662, Impuesto sobra la Renta (Income Tax Law), Nov. 25, 1974, as amended to Sept. 1993, *reprinted in* IBFD-CIAT [in Spanish] *and in* TLW (as amended to May 15, 1997).

Decreto Nº 1357, Ley para el Control de las Facturaciones (Law Governing Invoices), La Gaceta, D.O. Nº 280 del 13 de diciembre de 1983, *reprinted in* TSIN.

Decreto Nº 55-92, Exclusividad de Competencia en lo Tributario, La Gaceta, D.O., Nº 188, Oct. 1, 1992, *reprinted in id.*

Decreto Nº 32-90, Exoneraciones Fiscales las Autoriza el Ministerio de Finanzas, la Gaceta, D.O., Nº 149, Aug. 1990, *reprinted in id.*

Decreto Nº 4-93, Eliminación de Exenciones y Exoneraciones Tributarias, La Gaceta, D.O., Nº 7, Jan. 11, 1993, *reprinted in id.*

Decreto Nº 20-94, Publicación de Decretos y Disposiciones de Caracter Fiscal, La Gaceta, D.O., Nº 113, June 17, 1994, *reprinted in id.*

Decreto Nº 850, Ley Creadora Registro Unico del Ministerio de Finanzas, La Gaceta, D.O., Nº 246, Oct. 30, 1981, *reprinted in id.*

Decreto Nº 41-91, Sanciones y cierre de negocios por actos vinculados con la evasion tributaria, La Gaceta, D.O., Nº 182, Sept. 30, 1991, *reprinted in id.*

Decreto Nº 1369, Ley del Recibo Fiscal (Law Governing Receipt for Taxes), La Gaceta, D.O., Nº 286, Dec. 21, 1983, *reprinted in id.*

Decreto Nº 839, Reformas a la Ley del Delito de Defraudación Fiscal (Decree Reforming the Law on Tax Evasion), La Gaceta, D.O., Nº 239, Oct. 22, 1981, *reprinted in id.*

Decreto Nº 68-90, Ley de Renta Presuntiva Minima (Decree-Law on Minimum Presumptive Income), La Gaceta, D.O., Nº 247, Dec. 24, 1990, *reprinted in* TSIN.

Decreto Nº 1534, Ley de Rentas Presuntivas (Law on Presumptive Income), La Gaceta, D.O., Nº 249, Dec. 27, 1984, *reprinted in id.*

Decreto Nº 523, Impuesto sobre Actuaciones de Artistas Extranjeros (Tax on Performances by Foreign Artists), La Gaceta, D.O., Nº 78, Apr. 23, 1990, *reprinted in id.*

Decreto Nº 567, Ley de Impuestos a la Carne de Ganado Vacuno (Law Governing the Taxation of Beef), La Gaceta, D.O., Nº 270, Nov. 22, 1980, *reprinted in id.*

Decreto Nº 3-95, Impuesto sobre Bienes Inmeubles (Tax on Immovables), La Gaceta, D.O., Nº 21, Jan. 31, 1995, *reprinted in id.*

Decreto Nº 36-91, Impuesto sobre Bienes Inmuebles (Tax on Immovables), La Gaceta, D.O., Nº 158, Aug. 26, 1991, *reprinted in id.*

Decreto Nº 1531, Ley de Impuesto General al Valor Agregado (Value Added Tax), La Gaceta, D.O., Nº 248, Dec. 26, 1984, *reprinted in* TSIN *and in* IBFD-CIAT [in Spanish].

Decree Nº 12-92 to amend the general value added tax, Feb. 28, 1992, *reprinted in* TLW.

Decree Nº 14-92 to exempt certain imports from value added, Feb. 28, 1992, *reprinted in* TLW.

Decree Nº 16-92 amending the rates of income tax withholding at the source, Feb. 28, 1992, *reprinted in* TLW.

Decree Nº 17-92 repeal of net wealth tax and substitution by a tax on immovable assets, Feb. 28, 1992, *reprinted in* TLW.

Decreto Nº 23-94, Impuesto Específico de Consumo (Special Consumption Tax), La Gaceta, D.O., Nº 113, June 17, 1994, *reprinted in* TSIN.

Decreto Nº 8-92, Impuesto Unico al Consumo Nacional del Azucar (Tax on the Consumption of Sugar), La Gaceta, D.O., Nº 40, Feb. 28, 1992, *reprinted in id.*

Decreto N⁰ 40-91, Ley de Aranceles del Registro Público (Fees on Public Register), La Gaceta, D.O., N⁰ 182, Sept. 30, 1991, *reprinted in id.*

Decreto N⁰ 276, Ley sobre Aranceles de Tránsito (Law on Transit Fees), La Gaceta, D.O., N⁰ 200, Sept. 7, 1987, *reprinted in id.*

Decreto N⁰ 637, Ley de Comercialización, Impuesto y Excedentes sobre el Oro y la Plata (Tax on Gold and Silver), La Gaceta, D.O., Feb. 17, 1981, *reprinted in id.*

Decreto N⁰ 956, Ley de Impuesto para el Servicio de la Deuda Pública (Law on Tax for the Service of the Public Debt), La Gaceta, D.O., N⁰ 37, Feb. 15, 1982, *reprinted in* TSIN (tax on foreign exchange transactions).

Decreto N⁰ 1553, Ley de Exclusión de Exenciones (Decree/Law Governing Exclusions from Exemptions), La Gaceta, D.O., N⁰ 5, Jan. 7, 1985, *reprinted in id.*

Decreto N⁰ 703, Ley de Impuesto sobre el Consumo de Cemento (Decree/Law Governing the Tax on Cement Consumption), La Gaceta, D.O., N⁰ 151 July 6, 1962, *reprinted in id.*

Decreto N⁰ 136, Ley de Impuesto de Timbres (Stamp Tax Law), La Gaceta, D.O., N⁰ 229, Nov. 28, 1985, *reprinted in id.*

Decreto N⁰ 559, Ley de Licencias Comerciales (Law Governing Commercial Licenses), La Gaceta, D.O., N⁰ 39, Feb. 15, 1961, *reprinted in id.*

Decreto N⁰ 539, Ley Creadora de Licencias de Comercio (Law Instituting Business Licenses), *reprinted in id.*

Decreto N⁰ 362, Ley de Patentes de Licores (Law Governing Alcoholic Beverage Licenses), La Gaceta, D.O., N⁰ 136, June 30, 1945, *reprinted in id.*

Decreto N⁰ 277, Ley sobre Aranceles de Migración y Extranjería (Governing Levies Applied to Migrants and Aliens), La Gaceta, D.O., N⁰ 200, Sept. 7, 1987, *reprinted in id.*

Decreto N⁰ 49-93, Régimen de Circulación de Vehículos, La Gaceta, D.O., N⁰ 216, Nov. 15, 1993, *reprinted in id.*

Ley N⁰ 127 de Inversiones Extranjeras (Foreign Investment Law), June 19, 1991, *reprinted in* Ministerio de Economia y Desarrollo, Ley de Inversiones Extranjeras [in Spanish, English].

Law N⁰ 257-97, Tax and Commercial Justice Law, May 25, 1997 *reprinted in* TLW.

Niger (NER)

The tax laws of Niger as of 1981 have been published as a single code in Régime fiscal de la République du Niger (Imprimerie Nationale).

Ordonnance sur le péage routier, *reprinted in* Recueil de lois et règlements (République du Niger, 2d ed. 1994).

Nigeria (NGA)

We cite to the Laws of the Federation of Nigeria, a multivolume consolidation of the laws in force on Jan. 1, 1990.

Capital Gains Tax Act, Laws of the Federation of Nigeria, Cap. 42.

Casino Taxation Act, *id.*, Cap. 45.

Companies Income Tax Act, *id.*, Cap. 60.

Customs and Excise Management Act, *id.*, Cap. 84.

Customs and Excise Management (Disposal of Goods) Act, *id.*, Cap. 85.

Customs and Excise (Special Penal and Other Provisions) Act, *id.*, Cap. 86.

Income Tax Management Act, *id.*, Cap. 173.

Income Tax (Armed Forces and Other Persons) (Special Provisions) Act, *id.*, Cap. 174.

Income Tax (Authorized Communications) Act, *id.*, Cap. 175.

Industrial Development (Income Tax Relief) Act, *id.*, Cap. 179.

Petroleum Profits Tax Act, *id.*, Cap. 354.

Stamp Duties Act, *id.*, Cap. 411.

Value-Added Tax Decree 1993, Supplement to Official Gazette Nº 27, vol. 80, item 102, at A1203, Sept. 1, 1993.

Norway (NOR)

The laws of Norway are available [in Norwegian] over the internet or on CD-ROM from The Lovdata Foundation, Oslo, Norway. Its homepage is http://www.lovdata.no. A list of the current tax laws is available at this site.

Oman (OMN)

See also Ballantyne, Register of Laws of the Arabian Gulf (loose-leaf). Amendments were published in the Official Gazette on Nov. 2, 1996. See 14 Tax Notes Int'l 19 (Jan. 6, 1997).

Company Income Tax Law, 1979 [in English].

Royal Decree 46/87 (June 1987).

Royal Decree 39/96 (reorganizing Ministry of Finance).

Pakistan (PAK)

In addition to the taxes listed below, zakat applies to Muslim citizens and corporations the majority of whose shares are owned by such citizens.

Income Tax Ordinance, 1979, *reprinted in* Central Board of Revenue, Income Tax Manual: Part I, Income Tax Ordinance 1979 (Printing Corporation of Pakistan Press 1984) 5th ed. (as amended to July 1993) *and in* Tax Code (P.L.D. Publishers, Nabha Road, Lahore) (1990–91) *and in* TLW (as amended through Finance Act 1996).

Act Nº XV of 1963, Wealth Tax Act, *reprinted in* Tax Code, *supra* (as amended to 1990–91).

The Sales Tax Act, 1990, *reprinted in* Tariq Najib Choudhry, Sales Tax Act 1990 (as amended to Aug. 1, 1995) (Tariq Najib Corp., Lahore).

Act Nº XII of 1994, The Finance Act, The Gazette of Pakistan, June 30, 1994.

The Central Excises and Salt Act, 1944, *reprinted in* The Central Excises and Salt Act, 1944, M. Farani, Lahore Law Times Publications (as amended to 1985), *and in* Najib Choudhry, Manual of Central Excise Laws (Tariq Najib Corp., Lahore) (as amended through Feb. 1, 1995) (also contains rules and orders).

The Central Board of Revenue Act Nº IV of 1924, *reprinted in* Farani, *supra*.

Provisional Collection of Taxes Act Nº VIII of 1931, *id.*

The Oilseeds Cesses Act, Nº IX of 1946, *id.*

The Chemical Fertilizers (Development Surcharge) Act Nº XLI of 1973, *id.*

The Excise Duty on Minerals (Labour Welfare) Act Nº VIII of 1967, *id.*

The Stamp Act, Nº 2 of 1899, *reprinted in* M. Farani, Manual of Stamp Laws (Lahore Law Times Publications, undated).

Finance Act 1996, The Gazette of Pakistan, Extraordinary, July 1, 1996.

Palau (PLW)

Unified Tax Act, Title 40, Palau National Code Annotated (Palau National Code Commission) (published by Orakiruu Corp., Koror, Palau) (loose-leaf).

Panama (PAN)

Fiscal Code, *reprinted in* TLW (as amended to July 2, 1997).

Ley Nº 8 Impuesto sobre la Renta (Income Tax), Jan. 27, 1956 (as amended to June 1996), *reprinted in* IBFD-CIAT [in Spanish], *reprinted in* TLW (as amended to Jan. 17, 1996).

Ley N° 75 of 1976, Impuesto a la Transferencia de Bienes Muebles con Crédito Fiscal (Tax on the Transfer of Movable Goods with Fiscal Credit) (as amended by Law N° 17 of July 15, 1992), *reprinted in* IBFD-CIAT [in Spanish].

Law N° 45, Nov. 14, 1995, creating Selective Tax on Consumption of Carbonated and Alcoholic Beverages and Cigarettes, *reprinted in* TLW.

Papua New Guinea (PNG)

Excise Act, Revised Edition of the Laws of Papua New Guinea, ch. 105 (1983).

Excise (Beer) Act, *id.*, ch. 106 (1983).

Excise Tariff Act, *id.*, ch. 107 (1984).

Income Tax and Dividend (Withholding) Tax Rates Act, *id.*, ch. 111 (1985).

Income Tax Act 1959, *reprinted in* Papua New Guinea Income Tax Legislation (CCH Australia Limited) (as amended to 1995).

Industrial Development (Incentives to Pioneer) Industries Act, Revised Edition of the Laws of Papua New Guinea, ch. 119.

Licenses Act, *id.*, ch. 112 (1980).

Personal Tax Act, *id.*, ch. 113.

Provisional Collection of Taxes Act, *id.*, ch. 115.

Stamp Duties Act, *id.*, ch. 117.

Paraguay (PRY)

The 1992 law simplified the tax system and consolidated the tax legislation.

Ley N° 125/91 que establece el nuevo régimen tributario (Law Establishing a New Tax System), Jan. 9, 1992, as amended to June 1993, *reprinted in* TLW *and in* IBFD-CIAT [in Spanish].

Peru (PER)

In addition to the taxes listed below, selective consumption tax (excise), real estate, and real estate transfer tax apply. Editorial Economía y Finanzas, Las Orquídeas 435, San Isidro, Lima; fax: 442-1356 publishes a loose-leaf service for tax [in Spanish]: Manual del Impuesto a la Renta (two vols.), Manual del Código Tributario (two vols.), Impuesto a las Ventas, and Tributos Municipales.

Decreto Legislativo N° 774, Impuesto a la Renta (Income Tax Law), Dec. 30, 1993, as amended to Nov. 1996, *reprinted in* IBFD-CIAT [in Spanish], and Unified Consolidated Text of the Income Tax Law, originally Legislative Decree N° 200 of June 12, 1981, now Supreme Decree N° 185-87-EF of Sept. 28, 1987; *also reprinted in* 33 TLW (as amended to Mar. 1989).

Decreto Legislativo N° 773, Código Tributario (Tax Code), Dec. 30, 1993 (as amended to Dec. 1996), *reprinted in* IBFD-CIAT [in Spanish].

Decreto Legislativo N° 775, Impuesto General a las Ventas (General Sales Tax), Dec. 30, 1993 (as amended to May 1996), *reprinted in* IBFD-CIAT [in Spanish].

Decreto Ley N° 19654 del 12 de diciembre de 1972 Impuesto al Patrimonio Empresarial (Corporate Property Tax), *reprinted in* Impuesto al Patrimonio Empresarial, Ministerio de Economía, Finanzas y Comercio (1984).

Philippines (PHL)

We cite to one of the available annual commercial compilations.

NIRC—National Internal Revenue Code of 1977, *reprinted in* The National Internal Revenue Code of the Philippines Annotated (Jose N. Nolledo ed., National Bookstore, Inc. 1993) *and in* TLW (as amended to June 10, 1993).

Poland (POL)

There are a number of sources for the consolidated text of Polish tax laws, both in Polish and in English. For English translations, we cite to Polish Taxation and Customs Duties 1993 and Polish Taxation 1993, Part II (with 1994 supp.). This work has now been superseded by a loose-leaf entitled Polish Law Collection (hereinafter Collection), published by TEPIS and edited by Danuta Kierzkowska, and available from International Information Services, Inc., P.O. Box 3490, Silver Spring, Md., tel. 301-565-2975, fax 301-565-2973. There are also a couple of collections in Polish dated 1993, but presumably updates have been or will be published periodically. These are more complete in that they contain not only all the tax laws, but also the regulations. One is called VAT (Tadeusz Fijałkowski ed., Evan: Warsaw 1993) and the other is Podatki: Zbior Przepisow (Lex: Gdansk 1994). In addition to the taxes listed below, motor vehicle tax and payroll tax are imposed.

Tax Obligations Act, Dziennik Ustaw (Dz. U.) 1980, N° 27, item 111 (Excerpts), *reprinted in* Polish Taxation and Customs Duties 1993, TEPIS, Ministry of Privatization (as amended to 1992) [in English] *reprinted in* Collection, *supra* (as amended through 1996) [in English] [Note: on Aug. 29, 1997 a new version of this law was passed, to be effective Jan. 1, 1998. Presumably the new version will be included in Collection, *supra*.]

Fiscal Penal Act, Dziennik Ustaw (Dz. U.) 1984, N° 22, item 103, *id.*

Fiscal Control Act, Dz. U. 1991, N° 100, item 442, *id.*, *reprinted in* Collection, *supra* (as amended through 1992) [in English].

Ustawa ó podatku dochodowym od osób fizycznych (Natural Persons' Income Tax Act), Dz. U. 1991, Nº 80, item 350, *reprinted in* Polish Taxation 1993 Part II, with amending supplement 1994 (Danuta Kierzkowska, ed., Irena Gratkowska et al. trans., TEPIS 1993) (as amended to Dec. 16, 1993) [in English], *reprinted in* Collection, *supra* (as amended through 1996) [in English].

Ustawa ó podatku dochodowym od osób prawnych (Legal Persons' Income Tax Act), *reprinted in* Collection, *supra* (as amended through 1996) [in English].

Remuneration Increase Tax Act, Dz. U. 1991, Nº 1, item 1, *reprinted in* Polish Taxation and Customs Duties 1993, at 56, TEPIS, Ministry of Privatization (as amended to 1992) [in English].

Agricultural Tax Act, Dz. U. 1984, Nº 52, item 268, *id.*

Inheritance and Donation Tax Act, Dz. U. 1983, Nº 45, item 207, *id.* (amended version in Dz. U. 1997, Nº 16).

Taxes and Local Charges Act, Dz. U. 1991, Nº 9, item 31, *id.*

Stamp Duty Act, Dz. U. 1989, Nº 4, item 23, *id.*

Ustawa o podatku od towarów i usług oraz o podatku akcyzowym (Tax on Goods and Services and Excise Duty), Dz. U. 1993, Nº 11, item 50, *reprinted in* Collection, *supra* (as amended through 1996) [in English].

Turnover Tax Act, Dz. U. 1983, Nº 43, item 191, *reprinted in* Polish Taxation and Customs Duties 1993, at 20, TEPIS, Ministry of Privatization (as amended to 1992) [in English].

Ordinance Governing the Income Tax on Certain Kinds of Income of Foreign Individuals and Legal Entities Domiciled or Headquartered Abroad, of Apr. 3, 1992, Dz. U. Nº 32 (1992), item 137, *reprinted in* CEEL [in English].

Portugal (PRT)

We cite to a compilation published by the tax authority. In addition to those listed, the following taxes are imposed: consumption duty on tobacco, domestic consumption duty on coffee, motor vehicle tax, tax on petroleum products, road license and road hauling taxes, gaming tax, tax on the use, carrying, and possession of weapons, entertainment tax, special consumption duty on alcoholic beverages, excise duty on alcohol, and tax on insurance premiums. References to the laws imposing these taxes are found in EU Inventory.

Decreto-Lei Nº 442-A/88, Código do Imposto sobre o Rendimento das Pessoas Singulares (Individual Income Tax Code), Nov. 30, 1988, *reprinted in* Código do Imposto sobre o Rendimento das Pessoas Singulares (IRS): Comentado e Anotado (2nd ed., Direcção-Geral das Contribuições e Impostos 1990) (as amended to 1990) [in Portuguese] *and in* TLW.

Decreto-Lei Nº 442-B/88, Código do Imposto sobre o Rendimento das Pessoas Colectivas (Corporation Tax Code), Nov. 11, 1988, *reprinted in* Código do Imposto sobre o Rendimento das Pessoas Colectivas (IRC): Comentado e Anotado (Direcção-Geral das Contribuições e Impostos 1990) (as amended to 1990) [in Portuguese] *and in* TLW (as amended to Mar. 10, 1993).

Decreto-Lei Nº 290/92, Código do Imposto sobre o Valor Acrescentado (Value Added Tax Code), as amended to Apr. 1994, *reprinted in* Código do Imposto sobre o Valor Acrescentado (Rei dos Livros 11th ed. 1994) [in Portuguese].

Decreto Nº 45 760, Código do Imposto de Transações (Transaction Tax Code), June 5, 1964, *reprinted in* Código do Imposto de Transações (as amended to 1985) (Rei dos Livros 1985) [in Portuguese].

Decreto-Lei Nº 44 561, Código do Imposto de Capitais (Capital (Wealth) Tax Code) of Sept. 10, 1962, *reprinted in* Código do Imposto de Capitais, Rei dos Livros, 6ª ed. (as amended to 1987) [in Portuguese].

Decreto-Lei Nº 45 103, Código da Contribuição Industrial (Industrial Contribution Code) of July 1, 1963, *reprinted in* Código da Contribuição Industrial, Rei dos Livros 12ª ed. (as amended to 1987) [in Portuguese].

Decreto-Lei Nº 46 373, Código do Imposto de Mais-Valias (Capital Gains Tax Code), June 9, 1965, *reprinted in* Código do Imposto de Mais-Valias, Rei dos Livros 5ª ed. (as amended to 1987) [in Portuguese].

Decreto-Lei Nº 41 969, Código da Sisa e do Imposto sobre as Sucessões e Doações (Transfer, Succession and Gift Tax Code), Nov. 24, 1958, *reprinted in* Código da Sisa e do Imposto sobre as Sucessões e Doações, Rei dos Livros 5ª ed. (as amended to 1987) [in Portuguese].

Código da Contribuição Predial e do Imposto sobre a Indústria Agrícola (Code Governing the Urban Property Tax and the Agricultural Industrial Tax), Decreto-Lei Nº 45 104, de 1 de junho de 1963, *reprinted in* Código da Contribuição Predial e do Imposto sobre a Indústria Agrícola, Rei dos Livros 5ª ed. (as amended to 1988) [in Portuguese].

Decreto-Lei Nº 44 305, Código do Imposto Profissional (Occupational Tax Code), Apr. 27, 1962, *reprinted in* Código do Imposto Profissional, Rei dos Livros 10ª ed. (as amended to 1988) [in Portuguese].

Decreto-Lei Nº 45 399, Código do Imposto Complementar (Code of Complementary Tax), Nov. 30, 1963, *reprinted in* Código do Imposto Complementar, Rei dos Livros 9ª ed. (as amended to 1988) [in Portuguese].

Decreto-Lei Nº 12 700, Imposto do Selo, Regulamento e Tabela Geral (Stamp Tax: Regulations and General Schedule), Nov. 20, 1926, *reprinted in* Imposto do Selo, Regulamento e Tabela Geral, Rei dos Livros 7ª ed. (as amended to 1988) [in Portuguese].

Decreto-Lei Nº 154/91, Código de Processo Tributário (Code of Taxation Procedure), Apr. 23, 1991, *reprinted in* Código de Processo Tributário, Rei dos Livros 3ª ed. (as amended to 1993) [in Portuguese].

Qatar (QAT)

See also Ballantyne, Register of Laws of the Arabian Gulf (loose-leaf).

Decree-Law Nº 11 of 1993 concerning the Income Tax, Official Gazette Nº 12 of 1993 [in English].

Romania (ROM)

We have been unable to locate a published collection of tax legislation. Therefore, we cite to the official Gazette (Monitorul Oficial al României, hereinafter M. Of.). The tax legislation is summarized in şaguna, Drept Financiar şi Fiscal (Oscar Print: Bucharest 1997). A general citator to the legislation of Romania, consisting of a chronological list of laws and other norms, a citator to amendments, and an index, is Ioan Vida and Clara Melinte, Repertoriul Legislatiei Romaniei 1989–1996 (Lumina Lex: Bucharest 1997). We abbreviate Lege (Law) as L. and Ordonanţa ale Guvernului (Government Ordinance) as O.G. A few commercial and tax laws are available in English on the RDA website (http://www.rda.ro).

Lege privind Impozitul pe Salarii Nr. 32/1991 (Tax on Salaries), M. Of., June 29, 1993 [in Romanian] (as amended), *reprinted in* JPRS-EER-94-006-S, Feb. 18, 1994, at 4 [in English], amended or affected by

> L. Nº 46, July 4, 1994, M. Of., July 6, 1994.
> O.G. Nº 17, Aug. 17, 1995, M. Of., Aug. 17, 1995.
> O.G. Nº 8/1996, M. Of., Jan. 30, 1996.
> L. Nº 42/1990, M. Of., Aug. 21, 1992.
> L. Nº 9, May 25, 1992, M. Of., May 25, 1992.
> O.G. Nº 23, Aug. 21, 1992, M. Of., Aug. 28, 1992.
> O.G. Nº 22, Aug. 25, 1993, M. Of., Aug. 30, 1993.
> L. Nº 61, Sept. 22, 1993, M. Of., Sept. 28, 1993.
> L. Nº 44, July 1, 1994, M. Of., July 7, 1994.
> L. Nº 4, Jan. 10, 1995, M. Of., Jan. 19, 1995.
> O.G. Nº 13, Jan. 31, 1995, M. Of., Feb. 3, 1995.

Decret-Lege privind organizarea şi desfăşurarea unor activitaţi economice pe baza liberei iniţiative Nr. 54/1990 (Decree-Law on the organization and carrying out of certain economic activities on the basis of free initiative) [in Romanian].

O.G. 44, Imbunatatirea impunerii activitatilor producatoare de venit din exerciturea unei profesii libere şi din lucrari literare, de arta şi ştiinaţific (taxation of income-producing activities in the exercise of liberal professions and literary, artistic, and scientific work), M. Of., Sept. 1, 1995, amended and approved by L. 125, M. Of., Dec. 27, 1995 [in Romanian].

Lege privind Impozitul pe Venitul Agricol Nr. 34/1994 (Law on Tax on Income from Agriculture), M. Of., June 2, 1994 [in Romanian and in English], FBIS-EEU-95-005, Jan. 9, 1995.

Decretul Nr. 153 privitor la impozitul pe veniturile populaţiei (Decree on taxing the incomes of the population) Buletinul Oficial al Marii Adunari Naţionale a R.P.R. Nr. 22, May 11, 1954 [in Romanian].

Decree Nr. 394/1973 Privitor la impunerea veniturilor realizate din îmchirieri de imobile (Decree on the taxation of incomes realized from the lease of immovable property), July 10, 1973.

PT—Ordonanţa Guvernului privind Impozitul pe Profit (Profit Tax), Nr. 70/ 1994, M. Of., Aug. 31, 1994, approved and amended by Law Nº 73/1996, M. Of., Aug. 2, 1996, republished as amended, M. Of., March 12, 1997 [in Romanian], affected by

> L. 29/1996 (Bugetrul de stat pe anul 1996), M. Of., May 6, 1996.
> L. 109/1996, Organizarea şi functionarea cooperatiei de consum şi a cooperatiei de credit, M. Of., Oct. 18, 1996.
> L. 52/1992, depunerea unor sume in contul "Moldova", M. Of., June 2, 1992.
> L. 71/1994 (foreign investment), M. Of., July 22, 1994.
> O.G. 31/1997 (foreign investment), M. Of., June 16, 1997 (available in English on RDA website).
> L. 134/1995 (oil production), M. Of., Dec. 29, 1995.

Ordonanţa Guvernului Nr. 3/1992 privind Taxa pe Valoarea Adaugata (Value Added Tax Law), republished as amended, M. Of., Jan. 11, 1995 [in Romanian], modified or affected by

> O.G. 9, Jan. 27, 1995, M. Of., Jan. 31, 1995.
> Ordin al Ministrului de stat, Ministrul finanţelor, Nº 350, Feb. 27, 1995, M. Of., May 19, 1995.
> L. 130/1992, M. Of., Dec. 30, 1992.
> O.G. 2/1996, M. Of., Jan. 26, 1996.
> O.G. 21, July 24, 1996, M. Of., July 30, 1996.

O.G. 26, Aug. 18, 1995 privind impozitul pe dividende (tax on dividends), M. Of., Aug. 30, 1995, approved by L. 101, M. Of., Nov. 21, 1995.

O.G. 47, privind impunerea unor venituri, realizate din România, de persoanele fizice şi juridice nerezidente (taxation of incomes realized in Romania by nonresident physical and legal persons), M. Of., Aug. 30, 1997 [in Romanian].

O.G. 11/1996, executarea creanţelor bugetare, M. Of., Jan. 31, 1996, corrected in M. Of., June 25, 1996, amended and approved by L. 108, M. Of., Oct. 17, 1996.

Legea Nº 42/1993, privind accizele la produsele din import şi din ţară precum şi impozitul la ţiţeiul din producţia intern şi gazele naturale, M. Of., July 1, 1993, republished as amended, M. Of., Dec. 11, 1995, amended by O.G. 20, M. Of., July 30, 1996.

Hortărârea Guv., Nr. 679, Oct. 1, 1991, M. Of., Nov. 12, 1991, impozitul pe spectacole.

L. 12/1990 (tax equal to value of illegal commercial activities), M. Of., Aug. 8, 1990.

L. 54, M. Of., June 4, 1992, impozitul pe sumele obţinute din vânzarea activelor societăţilor comerciale cu capital de stat, amended by O.G. 14, Aug. 26, 1992; O.G. 70, M. Of., Aug. 31, 1994.

O.G. 24, M. Of., Aug. 5, 1996, impozitul pe venitul reprezentaţelor din România ale societăţilor comerciale şi organizaţiilor economice straine.

L. 29, May 3, 1996, Law on the State Budget for 1996, M. Of., May 6, 1996 (contains various tax provisions).

Various tax preferences are provided by the following:

> L. 84/1992 (free zones), M. Of., July 30, 1992.
> L. 18/1991 (agricultural lands), M. Of., Feb. 20, 1991.
> L. 134/1995 (foreign investors in petroleum sector), M. Of., Dec. 29, 1995.
> H.G. 566/1993 (obligations of TAROM).
> L. 27/1994 (local taxes), M. Of., May 24, 1994.
> D.-L. 118/1990 (exemption for persons persecuted for political reasons), M. Of., Apr. 9, 1990.
> L. 47/1991 (insurance), M. Of., July 19, 1991.
> L. 34/1991 (National Bank), M. Of., Apr. 3, 1991.
> L. 54/1991 (real property of trade unions), M. Of., Aug. 7, 1991.
> L. 42/1990 (veterans, etc.), republished, M. Of., Aug. 23, 1996.
> L. 57/1992 (handicapped persons), June 12, 1992.

Russia (RUS)

Russia suffers from a plethora of tax legislation, which is especially complex because of the number of levels of government and administrative agencies issuing orders, cir-

culars, etc., with varying degrees of legal effect. If one restricts the examination to federal laws, however, the situation is manageable. Amendments are frequent, but they are not so numerous that it is impossible to keep track of them. The federal laws are identified by FZ number (FZ is the Russian abbreviation for federal law) and are published in the Sobranie Zakonodatelstva Rossiskoi Federatsii (Collection of Legislation of the Russian Federation) [hereinafter Sobranie]. This comes out every few weeks and (as of early 1997) has been arriving to subscribers within a few weeks of publication, so that it is not difficult to keep up to date by consulting this publication. The most recent amendment of a federal law contains a list of all the previous amendments. Of course, as with the tax laws of any other country, it becomes tedious to consolidate the amendments once they start piling up. The consolidated text is published by various publishers. We cite a CD-ROM called Kodeks [in Russian], published by Computer Software Development Center, Isakievskaya pl. 6, 190107 St. Petersburg (e-mail: ask@kodd.spb.ru). See its website at http://www.dux.ru/kodex/ engkodexhome. English translations are published by Ernst & Young, including periodic consolidated texts. The tax legislation of Russia in English (as amended through 1995) is also reprinted with commentary in the taxation chapter of Business and Commercial Laws of Russia (Mark C. Swords ed., McGraw-Hill 1995). This publication contains decrees, circulars, and other material in addition to the text of the basic laws and is therefore quite useful for the English reader. A website with laws in Russian can be found at http://www.inforis.nnov.su/infobase.

Law № 2118-1 of the Russian Federation of Dec. 27, 1991, Concerning the Fundamental Principles of the Taxation System in the Russian Federation (as amended through Federal Law № 9-FZ of the Russian Federation of July 1, 1994) [in English by Ernst & Young].

Zakon № 188-FZ O Vnesenii Izmeneniy i Dopolneniy v Otdel'nye Zakony Rossiyskoy Federatsii o Nalogakh (Law on Making Amendments and Additions to the Various Tax Laws of the Russian Federation), Nov. 30, 1995, Sobranie, Dec. 4, 1995 [in Russian].

Zakon № 5238-1 O Federal'nykh Organakh Nalogovoy Politsii i Ugolovno-Protsessual'nyy Kodekx RSFSR (S Izmeneniyami na 17 dekabrya 1995 goda) (Law of the RF on the Federal Organs of Tax Police), June 24, 1993 (as amended to Dec. 17, 1995), CD Legal Information System "Kodeks" 1992–96 [in Russian].

Zakon № 943-1 O Gosudarstvennoy Nalogovoy Sluzhbe RSFSR (s Izmeneniyami i Dopolneniyami na 25 febralya 1993 goda) (Law on The State Tax Service of the RSFSR), Mar. 21, 1991 (as amended to Feb. 25, 1993), CD Legal Information System "Kodeks" 1992–96 [in Russian], amended by Law № 67-FZ of June 13, 1996, Sobranie, June 17, 1996, № 25, art. 2958.

Zakon № 2025-1 Rossiyskoy Federatsii O Nalogooblozhenii Dokhodov Bankov (Law on the Taxation of Income on Banks), Dec. 12, 1991, Delovoy mir June 3, 1993 [in Russian] [in English by Ernst & Young] (as amended through the Law of the Russian Federation of Dec. 22, 1992, Concerning Amendments and Additions to Certain Tax Laws of the Russian Federation).

Law Nº 29-FZ of the Russian Federation, Oct. 27, 1994, Concerning the Introduction of Amendments and Additions to Certain Laws of the Russian Federation, and Concerning Special Considerations Relating to the Procedure for Contributions to Certain State Non-Budgetary Funds [in English by Ernst & Young].

Law Nº 37-FZ of the Russian Federation, Nov. 11, 1994, Concerning the Introduction of Amendments and Additions to Certain Tax Laws of the Russian Federation and Concerning the Establishment of Exemptions in Relation to Compulsory Payments to State Non-Budgetary Funds [in English by Ernst & Young].

PT—Law Nº 2116-1 of the Russian Federation, Dec. 27, 1991, Concerning Tax on the Profit of Enterprises and Organizations [in English by Ernst & Young] (as amended through Law Nº 54-FZ of the Russian Federation of Dec. 3, 1994).

> The amending acts since 1995 are Law Nº 64-FZ of Apr. 25, 1995, Sobraniye, May 1, Zakon Nº 25 o Spetsialnom Naloge s Predpriyatiy, Uchrezhdeniy i Organizatsiy dlya Finansovoy Podderzhki Vazhneyshikh Otrasley Narodnogo Khozyaystva, Feb. 23, 1995, Sobranie Zakonodatelstva Feb. 27, 1995 [in Russian], Law Nº 25-FZ of the Russian Federation of Feb. 23, 1995, Concerning Special Tax on Enterprises, Institutions, and Organizations for the Financial Support of Major Sectors of the National Economy of the Russian Federation and Provision for the Stable Activity of Enterprises of those Sectors [in English by Ernst & Young].

Zakon Nº 2030-1 O Naloge na Imushchestvo Predpriyatiy (S Izmeneniyami i Dopolneniyami na 22 Avgusta 1995 goda) (Law on the Taxation of Property of Enterprises) Dec. 13, 1991, as amended to Aug. 22, 1995), CD Legal Information System "Kodeks" 1992–96 [in Russian] and [in English by Ernst & Young] (as amended through Nov. 11, 1994), amended by Law Nº 1-FZ, Sobranie, Nº 2, art. 217 (Jan. 12, 1998).

Law Nº 2-17 Concerning Rates and Exemptions Relating to Tax on the Assets of Enterprises, Mar. 2, 1994 [in English by Ernst & Young].

Zakon Nº 222-FZ Ob Uproshchennoy Sisteme Nalogooblozheniya, Ucheta i Otchetnosti Dlya Sub'ektov Malogo Predprinimatel'stva (Law on Simplifying the System of Taxation, Organization and Accounting for Subjects of Small Enterprises) Dec. 29, 1995, CD Legal Information System "Kodeks" 1992–96 [in Russian and English], available on Microfiche and from the Tax Analysts' Access Service/TaxBase.

Law of the Russian Federation of Dec. 6, 1991, Concerning Excise Duty [in English by Ernst & Young] (as amended by Law Nº 4229-1 of Dec. 25, 1992). The consolidated text of the excise tax law as amended by Law Nº 23-FZ of Mar. 7, 1996, was published in Sobraniye, Mar. 11, 1996, Nº 11, art. 1016, *reprinted in* Rossiyskaya Gazeta March 13, 1996 [in Russian], FBIS-SOV-96-068-S, FBIS-Database, Mar. 13, 1996 [in English]. It was amended by Law Nº 12-FZ of Jan. 10, 1997, Sobranie, Jan. 20, 1997, Nº 3, art. 356.

IT—Zakon Nº 1998-1 RSFSR O Podokhodnom Naloge s Fizicheskikh Lits (s Izmeneniyami i Dopolneniyami na 5 marta 1996 goda) (Law on Income Tax of Physical Persons of Dec. 7, 1991, as amended to Mar. 5, 1996), CD Legal Information System "Kodeks" 1992–96 [in Russian] and [in English by Ernst & Young] (as amended through July 16, 1992). The amending acts since 1995 are Law Nº 10-FZ of Jan. 27, 1995, Sobranie, Jan. 30, 1995, Nº 5, art. 346; Law Nº 95-FZ of June 26, 1995, Sobranie, June 26, 1995, Nº 26, art. 2403; Law Nº 211-FZ of Dec. 27, 1995, Sobranie, Jan. 1, 1996, Nº 1, art. 4; Law Nº 22-FZ of March 5, 1996, Sobranie, March 11, 1996, Nº 11, art. 1015, *reprinted in* Rossiyskaya Gazeta Mar. 7, 1996, also available on Microfiche and from the Tax Analysts' Access Service/TaxBase; Law Nº 83-FZ of June 21, 1996, Sobranie, June 24, 1996, Nº 26, art. 3035; Law Nº 11-FZ of Jan. 10, 1997, Sobranie, Jan. 20, 1997, Nº 3, art. 355; Law Nº 94-FZ of June 28, 1997, Sobranie, Nº 26, art. 2955; Law Nº 159-FZ of Dec. 31, 1997, Sobranie, Nº 1, art. 6.

Zakon Nº 2020-1 O Naloge s Imushchestva, Perekhodyashchego v Poryadke Nasledovaniya Ili Dareniya (S Izmeneniyami i Dopolneniyami na 27 Yanvarya 1995 goda) (Law of the RF on Inheritance and Gift Tax), Dec. 12, 1991 (as amended to Jan. 27, 1995) CD Legal Information System "Kodeks" 1992–96 [in Russian] *reprinted in* 2 Business and Commercial Laws of Russia: Business Enterprises, Privatization, Commercial Trade, McGraw-Hill [in English] (original law without amendments).

Zakon Nº 2071-1 Ob Investitsionnom Nalogovom Kredite (V Redaktsii Zakona Rossiyskoy Federatsii og 16 Iulya 1992 goda) (Law on Investment Tax Credit), Dec. 20, 1991 (as amended to July 16, 1992), CD Legal Information System "Kodeks" 1992–96 [in Russian].

Law Nº 31-FZ of the Russian Federation of Mar. 13, 1995, Concerning Certain Issues Relating to the Granting of Exemptions to Participants in Foreign Economic Activity [in English by Ernst & Young].

Zakon Nº 2003-1 O Nalogakh na Imushchestvo Fizicheskikh Lits (S Izmeneniyami i Dopolneniyami na 27 yanvarya 1995 goda) (Law on the Taxation of Property of Physical Persons) Dec. 9, 1991 (as amended to Jan. 27, 1995), Rossiyskaya Gazeta Feb. 14, 1991 [in Russian] and CD Legal Information System "Kodeks" 1992–96 [in Russian] and [in English] by Ernst & Young] (as amended through Law Nº 25-FZ of the Russian Federation of Aug. 9, 1994).

Zakon № 1759-1 O Dorozhnykh Fondakh v Rossiyskoy Federatsii (S Izme-neniyami i Dopolneniyami na 27 Dekabrya 1995 goda) (Law on the Road Fund), Oct. 18, 1991 (as amended to Dec. 27, 1995), CD Legal Information System "Kodeks" 1992–96 [in Russian], amended by Law № 82-FZ of May 26, 1997, Sobranie, № 22, June 2, 1997, item 2545.

Zakon № 2023-1 O Naloge na Operatsii S Tsennymi Bumagami (V Redaktsii, Vvedennoy v Deystviye s 23 Octyabrya 1995 goda (Law on Taxing Securities Transactions, as amended to Oct. 23, 1995), CD Legal Information System "Kodeks" 1992–96 [in Russian].

Zakon № 2005-1 O Gosudarstvennoy Poshline (Law on State Duty) (this is like a stamp tax in some respects and like a fee (such as court filing fees and passport fees) in other respects), Dec. 9, 1991, *reprinted in* Ekonomicheskaya Gazeta № 16 Apr. 1992 [in Russian], amended by Law № 4499-1, On Changes and Additions to the Law of the RF on the State Stamp Tax, Feb. 17, 1993 [in English] and Law № 118-FZ o Vnesenii Dopolneniya v Zakon Rossiyskoy Federatsii o gosudarstvennoy Poshline, Aug. 20, 1996, *reprinted in* Ekonomika i Zhizn № 36 [in Russian], and Law № 105-FZ, Sobranie, July 21, 1997, № 29, art. 3506.

Zakon № 1992-1 O Naloge na Dobavlennuyu Stoimost (S Izmeneniyami i Doppolneniyami na 1 Aprelya 1996 goda) (Law Concerning Value Added Tax) Dec. 6, 1991 (as amended to Apr. 1, 1996) in CD Legal Information System "Kodeks" 1992–96 [in Russian, in English] available in TaxBase (translation of text as amended through Apr. 1, 1996). Amendments after Apr. 1, 1996: Law № 45-FZ of May 22, 1996, Sobranie, May 27, 1996, № 22, art. 2582, available in TaxBase [in English]; Law № 54-FZ, Sobranie, Mar. 24, 1997, № 12, art. 1377; Law № 73-FZ, Sobranie, May 5, 1997.

Act № 2019-I, Dec. 12, 1991, RSFSR Health Resort Charge on Natural Persons Act, *reprinted in* Business and Commercial Laws of Russia, *supra* § 4.52 [in English].

Act № 2000-I, RSFSR Natural Persons Business Registration and Fee Act, *reprinted in* Business and Commercial Laws of Russia, *supra* § 4.54 [in English].

Law № 5238-1, On the Federal Organs of the Tax Police, June 24, 1993, CD Legal Information System "Kodeks" 1992–96 [in Russian].

Rwanda (RWA)

Loi du 2 juin 1964 relative aux impôts sur les revenus, J.O. № 12 du 15.6.1964, as amended through 1984, *reprinted in* Ministère des finances et de l'économie, Code des impots directs, tome 1 (Imprimerie nationale).

Impôt personnel, Decree-Law of Dec. 28, 1973, *reprinted in* Codes et lois de Rwanda (Rejntjens and Gorus eds., 1983) (as of Dec. 31, 1978).

Contribution personnelle minimum, Law of Feb. 28, 1968, *reprinted in id.*

Code des investissements, Decree-Law Nº 30-77 of Sept. 21, 1977, *reprinted in id.*

Taxe de consommation à percevoir sur les bières de fabrication locale, Law of Mar. 5, 1968, *reprinted in id.*

Taxe de consommation à percevoir sur les limonades, eaux gaseuses et autres boissons non alcooliques de fabrication industrielle locale, Decree-Law of Dec. 31, 1974, *reprinted in id.*

Law Nº 29/91, June 28, 1991, Business Income Tax, Journal officiel, July 1, 1991 [in French].

St. Kitts and Nevis (KNA)

Auctioneers Ordinance Nº 4 of 1947, Government Printery.

Act Nº 6 of 1972, The Licenses on Businesses and Occupations Act, 1972, Government Printery.

Act Nº 13 of 1973, Licenses on Business and Occupations Act (Reduced License Fees Order), 1973, Government Printery.

Order Nº 5A of 1987, The Cable Television (Fee) Order, Government Printery.

Act Nº 5 of 1980, Companies (Amendment) Act [providing for Tax Exempt Certificate Fee], Government Printery.

Act Nº 5 of 1982, Companies (Amendment) Act (exempting certain offshore companies from income tax), Government Printery.

Act Nº 5 of 1974, Consumption Tax Act, 1974, amended by

> Consumption Tax Order Nº 19 of 1976.
> Consumption Tax Amendment Order Nº 38 of 1980, Government Printery.

Act Nº 17 of 1972 to amend the Dog Tax Ordinance, Government Printery.

Act Nº 15 of 1968, Public Entertainments and Lotteries Tax Act, Government Printery.

Act Nº 9 of 1990, The Finance Act, Government Printery.

Act Nº 17 of 1969, The Betting and Gaming Act, amended by

> Act Nº 10 of 1977, The Betting and Gaming (Amendment) Act, Government Printery.
> Act Nº 17 of 1974, The Fiscal Incentives Act, Government Printery.

Act Nº 12 of 1976, Hotel Accommodation Tax Act, amended by

Act Nº 6 of 1979, Hotel Accommodation Tax (Amendment) Act,
Act Nº 11 of 1980, Hotel Accommodation Tax (Amendment) Act,
Act Nº 1 of 1982, Hotel Accommodation Tax (Amendment) Act,
Act Nº 8 of 1983, Hotel Accommodation Tax (Amendment) Act,
Act Nº 2 of 1990, Hotel Accommodation Tax (Amendment) Act,
Act Nº 2 of 1994, Hotel Accommodation Tax (Amendment) Act, Government Printery.

Income Tax Ordinance Nº 17 of 1966, amended by

Act Nº 20, Income Tax (Amendment) Ordinance, 1966.
Statutory Rules and Orders Nº 41 of 1966, The Income Tax (Evasion of Tax Payment) (Prevention) Rules.
Act Nº 12 of 1970, Income Tax Ordinance (Amendment) Act.
Act Nº 5 of 1972, Income Tax Ordinance (Amendment) Act.
Act Nº 19 of 1972, Income Tax Ordinance (Amendment Nº 2) Act.
Statutory Rules and Orders Nº 28 of 1972, The Income Tax (Approved Mortgages) Regulations.
Act Nº 13 of 1974, Income Tax Ordinance (Amendment) Act.
Act Nº 13 of 1976, Income Tax Ordinance (Amendment) Act.
Act Nº 63, The Income Tax (Evasion of Tax Payment) (Prevention) (Amendment) Rules 1976.
Act Nº 17 of 1979, The Income Tax (Approved Institutions) Order, 1979.
Act Nº 14 of 1980, The Income Tax Ordinance (Amendment) Act (Witholding Tax).
Act Nº 3 of 1982, Income Tax (Amendment) Act, 1982.
Act Nº 3 of 1988, Income Tax (Amendment) Act, 1988.
Act Nº 2 of 1989, Income Tax (Amendment) Act, 1989, Government Printery.

Act Nº 14 of 1986, Exempt Insurance Companies Act, Government Printery.

Land and House Tax Ordinance, *reprinted in* The Revised Laws of St. Christopher, Nevis, and Anguilla, Cap. 251, Waterlow & Sons Ltd. 1964, amended by

Ordinance Nº 4 of 1964, Land and House Tax (Amendment) Ordinance, Government Printery.
Act Nº 4 of 1972, Land and House Tax Ordinance (Amendment) Act, Government Printery.
Act Nº 6 of 1988, Land and House Tax (Amendment) Act of 1988, Government Printery.
Nº 14 of 1996, Land and House Tax (Amendment) Act Cap. 251, available on TaxBase.

Liquor License Ordinance, *reprinted in* The Revised Laws of St. Christopher, Nevis, and Anguilla, Cap. 252, Waterlow & Sons Ltd. 1964, amended by

> Act Nº 3 of 1972, Liquor Licenses Ordinance (Amendment) Act.
> Act Nº 3 of 1975, Liquor Licenses Ordinance (Amendment) Act.

Act Nº 15 of 1982, The Mercantile Tax Act, Government Printery.

Act Nº 13 of 1985, The Social Services Levy Act, Government Printery.

Stamp Act, *reprinted in* The Revised Laws of St. Christopher, Nevis, and Anguilla, Cap. 257, Waterlow & Sons Ltd. 1964, amended by Act Nº 4 of 1982 Stamp (Amendment) Act.

The Telecommunications (Licenses and Fees) (Amendment) Order of 1983, Government Printery.

Act Nº 12 of 1980 Traders Tax Act, Government Printery, amended by

> Act Nº 10 of 1985, Traders Tax (Amendment) Act.
> Act Nº 1 of 1988, Traders Tax (Amendment) Act.
> Act Nº 3 of 1989, Traders Tax (Amendment) Act.

Travelling Agents and Pedlars Licenses Ordinance, Cap. 260, *reprinted in* The Revised Laws of St. Christopher, Nevis, and Anguilla, Cap. 260, Waterlow & Sons Ltd. 1964, amended by

> Act Nº 1 of 1970, Travelling Agents and Pedlars Licences Ordinance (Amendment) Act.
> Act Nº 27 of 1976, Fees, (Miscellaneous Amendments) Act.

Act Nº 2 of 1981, Travel Tax Act, Government Printery.

Vehicles and Road Traffic (Fees), Order Nº 10 of 1987, Government Printery.

Act Nº 14 of 1980, Income Tax Ordinance (Amendment) Act, Government Printery.

St. Lucia (LCA)

Saint Lucia: Consolidated Index of Statutes and Subsidiary Legislation to 1st January 1996 has been published by the Faculty of Law Library, University of the West Indies, Barbados. This lists the amending laws, and so they will not be listed here. The tax laws listed are as follows:

Consumption Tax Act 1968.

Excise Ordinance (Cap. 203).

Fiscal Incentives Act 1974.

Foreign Currency Export Tax 1982.

Hotel Accomodation Tax Act 1973.

Income Tax Act, 1989, *reprinted in* TLW (as amended through Income Tax (Amendment) (Nº 2) Act, 1994), amended by Act Nº 8 of 1996, Income Tax (Amendment) Act, 1996.

Income Tax (Federal Endowments) Act 1960 (Cap. 151).

Insurance Premium Tax Act 1980.

Land and House Tax Ordinance (Cap. 217).

Stamp Duty Ordinance (Cap. 219).

Succession Duty (War Deaths) Ordinance (Cap. 221).

Travel Tax Act 1982.

St. Vincent and the Grenadines (VCT)

We cite to the 1990 Revised Edition of The Laws of St. Vincent and the Grenadines, a consolidation of the laws in force on Jan. 1, 1991. The tax laws are mostly in volume 7, Title XXIV, Revenue and Currency. Amending acts are listed in Saint Vincent and the Grenadines: Consolidated Index of Statutes and Subsidiary Legislation (1997).

Bay Rum and Perfumed Spirits Act, The Laws of St. Vincent and the Grenadines, ch. 299.

Consumption Tax Act, *id.*, ch. 301.

Cotton Tax Act, *id.*, ch. 38.

Duties and Taxes (Exemption in the Public Interest) Act, *id.*, ch. 305.

Excise Act, *id.*, ch. 307.

Excise Equalisation Duty Act, *id.*, ch. 308.

Export Tax Act, *id.*, ch. 309.

Finance (Provision for Payment of Taxes) Act, *id.*, ch. 310.

Fiscal Incentives Act, *id.*, ch. 336.

Hotel Tax Act, *id.*, ch. 338.

Income Tax Act, *id.*, ch. 312, as amended by Act Nº 41 of 1988, Income Tax (Amendment) Act, 1988, available on TaxBase; amended by Act Nº 10 of 1993, Income Tax (Amendment) Act, 1993; Act Nº 38 of 1993, Income Tax (Amendment) (Nº 2) Act, 1993.

Insurance Business Tax Act, *id.*, ch. 313.

Interest Levy Act, *id.*, ch. 314.

International Communications Service Surcharge Act, *id.*, ch. 315.

Land Tax Act, *id.*, ch. 316.

Provisional Collection of Taxes Act, *id.*, ch. 317.

Stamp Act, *id.*, ch. 318.

Travel Tax Act, *id.*, ch. 319.

Currency Export Tax Act, *id.*, ch. 321.

Samoa (WSM)

The taxes imposed in Samoa include income tax, VAT (Value-Added Goods and Services Tax Act 1992/93), payroll taxes, business license, airport departure tax, import and export duties, and stamp duty. (Note: Samoa recently changed its name from Western Samoa.) The laws as of Jan. 1, 1978, are set forth in Reprint of the Statutes of Western Samoa (N. Slade, Attorney-General, ed.). Subsequent enactments through June 1, 1989, are listed in Patrick Fepulea'i and Rosemary Gordon, Western Samoa Legislation Lists (3d ed. 1989).

San Marino (SMR)

The following laws were obtained from the official gazette:

Legge sulle imposte de successione (Inheritance Tax), Oct. 29, 1981.

Legge sulle imposte di registro (Registration Tax), Oct. 29, 1981.

Legge sulle imposte di bollo (Stamp Tax), Oct. 29, 1981.

Legge N° 91 Istituzione dell'imposta generale sui redditi (income tax), Oct. 13, 1984.

> Legge N° 155 (Dec. 30, 1986) Modifiche alle leggi 13 ottobre 1984 N° 91 "Istituzione dell'Imposta Generale sui Redditi" e 22 marzo 1986 N° 38 "Provvedimenti in materia Fiscale" (income tax and tax provisions amendments).

> Legge N° 9 (Jan. 22, 1993) Modifiche alla legge 13 ottobre 1984 N° 91 "imposta Generale sui Redditi" (income tax amendments).

Legge N° 9 Aggiornamento imposte e diritti catastali (revises land tax rates), Jan. 25, 1984.

Legge N° 27 Tassa di circolazione per i veicoli (car tax), Feb. 20, 1991.

São Tomé and Principe (STP)

Decree-Law 42/93, May 18, 1993, amends taxes on inheritance, gifts, and transfer, Diario da república, Aug. 10, 1993 [in Portuguese].

Decree-Law 11/88, May 14, 1988, Airport Taxes, Diario da república, May 25, 1988 [in Portuguese].

Decree-Law 40/88, April 9, 1988, approves the general table of stamp tax, Diario da república, Dec. 20, 1988 [in Portuguese].

Decree-Law 20/88, June 14, 1988, specifies amounts of travel tax for passengers on international flights, Diario da república, June 22, 1988 [in Portuguese].

Saudi Arabia (SAU)

The income tax regulations and the zakat regulations are issued by royal decree, but much of the operative rules are contained in resolutions, circulars, etc. An English translation of many of these is contained in Regulations for Income Tax, Road Tax, and Zakat (1978) and in Regulations for Income Tax (1981), both published by the Zakat and Income Tax Department of the Ministry of Finance and National Economy. See also Ballantyne, Register of Laws of the Arabian Gulf (loose-leaf).

Income Tax Regulations, *reprinted in* Ministry of Finance and National Economy, Zakat and Income Tax Department, Regulations for Income Tax, Road Tax, and Zakat (Safir Bureau: Riyadh), *and in* TLW (as amended to Mar. 1993).

Zakat Regulations, *reprinted in* Ministry of Finance, *supra* [in English].

Senegal (SEN)

Code général des impôts annoté (Editions juridiques africaines 1990).

Loi N⁰ 92-40 du 9 juillet 1992 portant Code générale des impôts.

Seychelles (SYC)

The Business Tax Act, 1987, Supplement to Official Gazette, Jan. 1, 1988.

Decree N⁰ 11 of 1978, The Income Tax Assessment Decree, as amended by Act N⁰ 1 of 1979, *reprinted in* 35 TLW.

Trades Tax Act N⁰ 19 of 1985, Supplement to Official Gazette of Jan. 6, 1986.

Sierra Leone (SLE)

Income Tax Act, N⁰ 1 of 1943, ch. 273, *reprinted in* The Income Tax Act (as amended to Dec. 31, 1992) (unofficial consolidation).

The Sales Tax Decree, 1995, N.P.R.C. Decree N⁰ 5, Supplement to the Sierra Leone Gazette, vol. CXXVI, N⁰ 16, Apr. 13, 1995.

Singapore (SGP)

CCH International publishes a one-volume loose-leaf service (Singapore Revenue Legislation) containing the tax laws of Singapore.

ITA—Act Nº 39 Income Tax Act of 1947, as amended through Act Nº 20 of 1991, Cap. 134, *reprinted in* The Statutes of the Republic of Singapore, Singapore Ministry of Finance, Revenue Division 1992, Government Printers (rev. ed. 1992), *reprinted in* Peter Owyoung, Gim Hong, and Laurence Chan, Handbook of Singapore Tax Statutes (Butterworths) (Malayan Law Journal 1989) [hereinafter Handbook] *and in* TLW (as amended through Act Nº 32 of 1995).

Act Nº 2 of 1992 Income Tax (Amendment) Act 1992, *reprinted in* Republic of Singapore, Government Gazette Acts Supplement, Mar. 13, 1992.

Act Nº 32 of 1995, Income Tax (Amendment) Act 1995, Government Gazette Nº 34 (Oct. 1995).

Act Nº 19 of 1931, Estate Duty Act, as amended through Act Nº 14 of 1984, Cap. 96, *reprinted in* The Statutes of the Republic of Singapore, Government Printer, 1985 revised ed., *and in* Handbook, *supra.*

Act Nº 31 of 1993, The Goods and Services Tax Act 1993, *reprinted in* Singapore, Government Gazette Acts Supplement, Nº 28, 1993.

Act Nº 16 of 1929, Stamp Duties Act, Cap. 312 of 1985 ed., *reprinted in* The Statutes of the Republic of Singapore, Government Printer 1986, *and in* Handbook, *supra.*

Act Nº 36 of 1967, Economic Expansion Incentives (Relief from Income Tax) Act, as amended through Act Nº 37 of 1984, Cap. 86, *reprinted in* The Statutes of the Republic of Singapore, (Government Printers), 1985 revised ed., *and in* Handbook, *supra.*

Act Nº 2 of 1965, Payroll Tax Act, Cap. 223 of 1985 ed., *id.*

Ordinance Nº 40 of 1950, Betting and Sweepstake Duties Act, as amended through Act Nº 10 of 1981, Cap. 22 of 1986 ed., *id.*

Act Nº 8 of 1966, Cinematograph Film Hire Duty Act, Cap. 40 of 1985 rev. ed., *id.*

Ordinance Nº 39 of 1950, Entertainments Duty Act, Cap. 94 of 1985 rev. ed., *id.*

Ordinance Nº 36 of 1952, Private Lotteries Act, as amended through Act Nº 31 of 1961, Cap. 250 of 1985 rev. ed., *id.*

Act Nº 39 of 1968, Statutory Boards (Taxable Services) Act, as amended through Act Nº 1 of 1984, Cap. 318 of 1985 rev. ed., *id.*, *reprinted in* Handbook, *supra.*

Property Tax Act (ch. 254, 1985 rev. ed.), reprinted in Handbook, supra.

Property Tax (Surcharge) Act (ch. 255, 1985 rev. ed.).

Slovak Republic (SVK)

ITA—Zákon o Daniach z Príjmov (Income Tax Law), Zákon Federalneho zhromazdenia CSFR c.286/1992 Zb. of Apr. 28, 1992, as amended by Zákon c.626/1992 Zb., Dec. 15, 1992, reprinted in Sústava Daní a Poplatkov od roku 1993 (Ing. Jozef Troják, CSc. a kolektív 1993) [in Slovak].

Zákon o Dani z Pridanej Hodnoty (Value Added Tax Law), Zákon Federalneho zhromazdenia CSFR c.222/1992 Zb Apr. 16, 1992, as amended by Zákon c.595/1992 Zb., Nov. 26, 1992, id.

Zákon o Spotrebných Daniach (Excise Tax Law), Zákon Federalneho zhromazdenia CFSR c.213/1992 Zb. of Apr. 16, 1992, as amended by Zákon c.595/1992 Zb., Nov. 26, 1992, id.

Zákon O Správe Daní a Poplatkov a O Zmenách v Sústave územnych Finančnych Orgánov (Law on the Administration of Taxes and Fees and on Financial Organs), Zakon SNR c. 511/1992 Zb., Sept. 30, 1992, id.

Zákon O Dani Nehnutel'ností (Law on Real Estate Tax), Zákon Slovenskej narodnej rady c 317/1992 Zb., Apr. 29, 1992, id.

Zákon O Dani z Dedičstva, Dani z Darovania a Dani z Prevodu a Prechodu Nehnutel'ností (Law on Inheritance Tax, Gift Tax, and the Tax on the Transfer of Real Property), Zákon Slovenskej narodnej rady c.318/1992 Zb., May 4, 1992, id.

Zákon o daňovych poradcoch a Slovenskej Komore daňovych poradcov (Law on Tax Advisers and the Slovak Chamber of Tax Advisers), Nº 78, Jan. 29, 1992, 1992 zb. částka 20, strana 507.

Slovenia (SVN)

In addition to income tax, sales tax, payroll taxes, property tax, and inheritance and gift tax are imposed.

Zakon o Dohodnini (Income Tax Law), Uradni List Republike Slovenije Nº 71, Dec. 30, 1993 [in Slovenian].

PT—Zakon o Davku od Dobička Pravnih Oseb (Law on the Profit Tax of Legal Persons), Uradni List Republike Slovenije Nº 72, Dec. 31, 1993 [in Slovenian, in English].

Zakon o davkih občanov (Law of Tax on Citizens) Sept. 28, 1988, Official Gazette Uradni List Nº 36 of Oct. 21, 1988, as amended by Law Nº 343 Official Gazette Nº 8, Mar. 3, 1989, and Law Nº 300 Official Gazette Nº 7 of Feb. 4, 1993 [in Slovenian].

Solomon Islands (SLB)

The Acts of Parliament 1982 of the Solomon Islands, Government Printing Works, Honiara, Solomon Islands, contains an index of legislation in force as of the end of 1982. The following tax laws are included (we do not list the amending acts):

Customs and Excise (Cap. 58).

Income Tax (Cap. 61).

Stamp Duties (Cap. 64).

Sales Tax Act 1990, amended by Act Nº 16 of 1995, The Sales Tax (Amendment) Act 1995 (Honiara, Govt. Printer).

The Goods Tax Act 1992, Nº 9 of 1992, Government Printer, amended by The Goods Tax (Amendment) Order 1996, Legal Notice Nº 84, Government Printer.

Somalia (SOM)

Trattamento fiscale degli atti da prodursi al Pubblico Registro Automobilistico (tax treatment of the documents required to be presented to the Motor Vehicles Registry), Law of Jan. 1, 1960, n. 1 rep., *reprinted in* Abdullahi Darman Ali, Raccolta Delle Disposizioni Legislative Vigenti in Somalia in Materia Fiscale at 95 (as amended to July 31, 1985) [in Italian].

Trattamento fiscale delle concessioni di pubblici servizi (tax treatment applicable to public service contracts), Law of Jan. 1, 1960, n. 2 rep, *id.*

Legge relativa all'imposta sugli spettacoli (Law Governing the Entertainment Tax), Dec. 21, 1965, n. 23, *id.*

Imposta sulla circolazione degli autoveicoli (Tax on the Use of Motor Vehicles on Public Roads), Decreto Legislativo, Dec. 28, 1965, n. 4, *id.*

Imposta di Bollo (Stamp Tax), Decreto Legislativo, Dec. 7, 1966, n. 6, *id.*

Testo Unico delle leggi sulle Imposte Dirette, Decreto Legislativo, Nov. 5, 1966, n. 5 (Body of Laws on Direct Taxation 1966), *id.* at 165, *reprinted in* TLW (as amended to 1986) [in English].

Decreto Legge Ordinamento delle tasse sulle Assicurazioni in Libia e nell'Africa Orientale Italiana (Taxation System Applicable to Insurance in Libya and Italian East Africa), Mar. 9, 1939, XVII, n. 1935), *id.*

Decreto Legge Determinazione delle Tasse di licenza dei generi di monopolio (Law Concerning Taxes on Monopoly Goods Licenses), Feb. 23, 1959, n. 3, *id.*

Decreto Legge, Determinazione delle tasse di concessione governativa per il rilascio di passaporti ordinari e di lasciapassare per l'estero, nonché di carte di frontiere (Decree/Law Concerning Taxes on Government Concessions for the Issuance of Ordinary Passports and International Laissez-Passer Documents and Identity Cards), Oct. 25, 1960, *id.*

Legge, Determinazione di una nuova tariffa delle tasse di concessione governativa sulle autorizzazioni per la detenzione e porto di armi in genere, sulle licenze di vendita di armi e relativo munizionamento (Law Concerning the Setting of New Tax Rates for Government Concessions for Authorizations to Possess and Bear Arms in General and for Licenses to Sell Arms and Ammunition), Dec. 10, 1960, *id.*

Legge, Determinazione di nuove aliquote delle tasse di concessione governativi per il rilascio di certificati di idoneità alla conduzione di autoveicoli in genere (Law Setting New Tax Rates for Government Concessions for the Issuance of Certificates of Proficiency for Drivers of Vehicles in General), Jan. 27, 1961, *id.*

Legge, Norme sull'immigrazione (Immigration Law/Regulations), Jun. 27, 1966, *id.*

Diritti e tasse del Decreto Legge, n. 7 [Estensione e modificazione del "Codice Marittimo"] (Fees and Taxes Imposed Under Decree-Law N° 7 of Nov. 1, 1966: Extensions and Amendments to the Maritime Code), Nov. 1, 1966, *id.*

Legge, Tasse governative sulle concessioni di licenze di caccia delle tabelle 19–24 e 25 annesse alla legge sulla protezione della fauna (caccia) e del patrimonio forestale (Government Taxes on the Granting of Hunting Licenses under Schedules 19–24 and 25, Annexed to the Law Governing the Protection of Animals and Forest Land), Jan. 25, 1969, *id.*

Legge, Unificazione delle tasse scolastiche (Unification of School Taxes), Apr. 8, 1971, n. 31, *id.*

Legge, Norme sulla documentazione amministrativa, sulla legalizzazione e autentificazione di firme—Ministero Affari Esteri (Regulations Governing Administrative Documentation and the Authentication of Signatures: Ministry of Foreign Affairs), Nov. 14, 1972, *id.*

Decreto Legge Facilitazioni fiscali a favore delle società a partecipazione statale (Tax Facilities for Government and Parastatal Enterprises), Mar. 4, 1963, *id.*

Decreto Legislativo Limiti massimi delle imposte delle tasse e dei diritti indicati nell'art. 30 della Legge 14 Agosto 1963, n. 19, sulle Amministrazioni Municipali (Upper Limits to the Taxes and Charges Imposed Pursuant to Article 30 of Law N° 19 of Aug. 14, 1963 on Municipal Authorities), Jun. 9, 1965, *id.*

Legge Norme sull'accertamento e sulla repressione di violazioni delle leggi finanziarie (Regulations Governing the Investigation and Suppression of Violations of Financial Laws), Aug. 1, 1966, *id.*

Legge Concessioni di agevolazioni fiscali alla S.P.A. Somali Airlines (Concession of Tax Facilities to SPA (Somali Airlines)), July 24, 1970, *id.*

Legge N. 58, Gestione finanziaria di imprese ed enti pubblici (Financial Management of Public Enterprises and Agencies), July 31, 1972, *id.*

Legge N. 67, Norme sul trasferimento del diritto di proprietà immobiliarie (Regulations Governing the Transfer of Real Estate Property Rights), July 27, 1972, *id.*

Legge sulla definizione dei contesti fiscali delle Imposte e tasse indirette (Law Governing the Settlement of Fiscal Issues Arising from Indirect Taxation), Sep. 21, 1972, *id.*

South Africa (ZAF)

In addition to the taxes listed below, stamp duty and company duties apply.

ITA—Income Tax Act Nº 58 of 1962, as amended by Income Tax Act Nº 21 of July 1995, *reprinted in* Tax Handbook 1995–96 (E Damziger. EM Stack, Digma 5th ed. 1996) (published by Butterworths), *and in* TLW (as amended through Act 49 of 1996).

Act Nº 89 Value-Added Tax Act, 1991, Government Gazette Nº 13307 of June 12, 1991, as amended by Taxation Laws Amendment Act Nº 20 of 1994 *reprinted in* Tax Handbook 1995–96 (E Damziger. EM Stack, Digma 5th Ed. 1996).

Estate Duty Act Nº 45 of 1955, as amended by Taxation Laws Amendment Act Nº 37 of 1995, *id.*

Transfer Duty Act Nº 40 of 1949, as amended by Taxation Laws Amendment Act Nº 37 of 1995, *id.*

Spain (ESP)

In addition to the sources cited below, the tax laws and regulations are collected in a thick one-volume paperback, G. Casado Ollero et al., Código Tributario (Aranzadi 1995) with 1996 supp. The publication Leyes Tributarias, cited below, is supplemented periodically.

Ley General Tributaria (General Tax Law), B.O.E. de 31 de diciembre de 1963, *reprinted in* 1 Leyes Tributarias, Legislación Básica 27 (5th ed., Spain, Ministerio de Economía y Hacienda 1993) (as amended to Dec. 30, 1992) [in Spanish].

Ley Orgánica 1/1985, de reforma del Código Penal en materia de delitos contra la Hacienda Pública (Organic Law Reforming those Provisions of the Criminal Code Relating to Offenses Against the Treasury), Apr. 29, 1995, B.O.E. Nº 103, de 30 de abril de 1985, *id.* at 425.

Ley Orgánica 7/1982, de 13 de julio, que modifica la legislación vigente en materia de contrabando y regula los delitos e infracciones administrativas en la materia (Organic Law Amending Current Legislation on Contraband and Regulating Related Administrative and Other Offenses), July 13, 1982, B.O.E., 14 de mayo, 1 de agosto y 2 de octubre de 1982, *id.* at 429.

IRPF—Ley 18/1991, del impuesto sobre la renta de las personas físicas (Personal Income Tax Law), June 6, 1991, B.O.E., 7 de junio y 2 de octubre de 1991, *id.* at 469.

IS—Ley 61/1978, del impuesto sobre sociedades (Corporation Tax Law), Dec. 27, 1978, B.O.E. de 30 de diciembre de 1978, *id.* at 655.

Law 43/1995 on Corporate Income Tax, Dec. 27, 1995 [in Spanish] available on TaxBase.

Ley 19/1991, del Impuesto sobre el Patrimonio (Law Governing Wealth/ Property Tax), June 6, 1991, B.O.E., 7 de junio y 2 de octubre de 1991, *id.* at 883.

Ley 29/1987, del impuesto sobre sucesiones y donaciones (Law Governing the Tax on Bequests and Gifts), Dec. 18, 1987, B.O.E., 19 de diciembre de 1987, *id.* at 911.

Real Decreto Legislativo 3.050/1980, por el que se aprueba el texto refundido de la ley del Impuesto sobre transmisiones patrimoniales y actos jurídicos documentados (Royal Legislative Decree Approving the Revised Law Governing Transfer Tax for Cases Where No Sales Tax Applies), Dec. 30, 1980, B.O.E., 3 de febrero y 17 de marzo de 1981, *reprinted in* 2 Leyes Tributarias, Legislación Básica 1025 (5th ed., Spain, Ministerio de Economía y Hacienda 1993) (as amended to Dec. 30, 1992) [in Spanish].

Ley 37/1992, del Impuesto sobre el Valor Añadido (Value Added Tax), Dec. 28, 1992, B.O.E. de 29 diciembre de 1992, B.O.E., 8 de febrero de 1993, *id.*

Ley 38/1992, de Impuestos Especiales (Law Governing Special Taxes), Dec. 28, 1992, B.O.E. de 29 de diciembre de 1992 y 19 de enero de 1993, *id.*

Ley 8/1989, de Tasas y Precios Públicos (Law Concerning Government Pricing of Goods and Services), Apr. 13, 1989, B.O.E., de 15 de abril de 1989, *id.*

Ley Orgánica 8/1980, de Financiación de las Comunidades Autónomas (Organic Law Governing the Financing of the Autonomous Regions of Spain), Sept. 22, 1980, B.O.E., 1 octubre de 1980, *id.*

Ley 30/1983, reguladora de la cesión de Tributos del Estado a las Comunidades Autónomas (Law Regulating the Transfer of Central Government Tax Revenue to the Autonomous Regional Authorities), Dec. 28, 1983, B.O.E., 29 de diciembre de 1983, *id.*

Ley 39/1988, reguladora de las Haciendas Locales (extracto) (Law Regulating Local Branches of the Treasury), Dec. 28, 1988, B.O.E., 30 de diciembre de 1988 y 14 de agosto de 1989, *id.*

Ley 46/1984, reguladora de las Instituciones de Inversión Colectiva (Law Regulating Undertakings for Collective Investment), Dec. 26, 1984, B.O.E., 27 de diciembre de 1984, *id.*

Ley 14/1985, de Régimen Fiscal de Determinados Activos Financieros (Law Governing the Taxation System Applicable to Certain Financial Assets), May 29, 1985, B.O.E. Nº 129, 30 de mayo de 1985, *id.*

Ley 8/1987, de regulación de los Planes y Fondos de Pensiones (Law Regulating Pension Plans and Funds), June 8, 1987, B.O.E. Nº 137, 9 de junio de 1987, *id.*

Real Decreto Legislativo 1.091/1988, por el que se aprueba el Texto Refundido de la Ley General Presupuestaria (Royal Legislative Decree Approving the Revised Text of the General Budget Law), Sept. 23, 1988, B.O.E. Nº 234, 29 de septiembre de 1988, *id.*

Ley 20/1990, sobre Régimen Fiscal de las Cooperativas (Law Governing the Taxation System Applicable to Cooperatives), Dec. 19, 1990, B.O.E. Nº 304, 20 de diciembre de 1990, *id.*

Ley 29/1991, de Adecuación de Determinados Conceptos Impositivos a las Directivas y Reglamentos de las Comunidades Europeas (Law Adapting Certain Categories of Taxation to the Regulations of the European Union), Dec. 16, 1991, B.O.E. Nos. 301, 17 de diciembre de 1991, y 34, 8 de febrero de 1992, *id.*

Real Decreto-Ley 5/1994, por el que se regula la obligación de comunicación de determinados datos a requerimiento de las Comisiones Parlamentarias de Investigación (Royal Decree-Law Regulating the Requirement for the Submission of Certain Items of Information to Parliamentary Commissions of Inquiry), Apr. 29, 1994, B.O.E. n. 103, 30 de abril, 1994, *reprinted in* Leyes Tributarias, Legislación Básica, Boletín Informativo Nº 2 abril-mayo-junio 1994, at 247, Ministerio de Economía y Hacienda [in Spanish].

Real Decreto-Ley 7/1996 sobre medidas urgentes de carácter fiscal y de fomento y liberalización de la actividad económica (Law Concerning Urgent Measures for the Promotion and Liberalization of Economic Activities), June 7, 1996 available on TaxBase.

Real Decreto-Ley 8/1996, de medidas fiscales urgentes sobre corrección de la doble imposición interna intersocietaria y sobre incentivos a la internacionalización de las empresas (Law on Urgent Fiscal Measures Regarding the Adjustment of Intercompany Double Taxation at Domestic Level and Incentives to Enterprises to Enter the Global Economy), June 7, 1996, available on TaxBase.

Sri Lanka (LKA)

In addition to the taxes listed, stamp duties apply, as well as a 100 percent tax on the value of land transferred to a nonresident.[12]

Act N⁰ 28 of 1979 Inland Revenue Act, *reprinted in* Inland Revenue Act of 1979 (as amended to Dec. 31, 1988), Department of Government Printing, 1990.

Act N⁰ 11 of 1989, Inland Revenue (Amendment) Act, Gazette of the Democratic Socialist Republic of Sri Lanka (Supp. May 19, 1989), Department of Government Printing (1990).

Act N⁰ 22 of 1990, Inland Revenue (Amendment) Act, Gazette of the Democratic Socialist Republic of Sri Lanka (Supp. June 15, 1990), Department of Government Printing (1990).

Act N⁰ 42 of 1990, Inland Revenue (Amendment) Act, Gazette of the Democratic Socialist Republic of Sri Lanka (Supp. Nov. 30, 1990), Department of Government Printing (1990).

Act N⁰ 49 of 1991, Inland Revenue (Amendment) Act, Gazette of the Democratic Socialist Republic of Sri Lanka (Supp. Dec. 27, 1991), Department of Government Printing (1991).

Act N⁰ 27 of 1995 Inland Revenue (Amendment) Act, Nov. 22, 1995, available on TaxBase.

Act N⁰ 13 of 1995, Surcharge on Income Tax (Amendment) Act.

Act N⁰ 45 of 1990, Specified Certificate of Deposits (Tax and Other Concessions) Act, Gazette of the Democratic Socialist Republic of Sri Lanka (Supp. Dec. 7, 1990), Department of Government Printing (1990).

Act N⁰ 52 of 1991, Defence Levy Act, Gazette of the Democratic Socialist Republic of Sri Lanka (Supp. Dec. 27, 1991), Department of Government Printing (1992).

Act N⁰ 36 of 1992, Defence Levy (Amendment) Act, Gazette of the Democratic Socialist Republic of Sri Lanka (Supp. Aug. 7, 1992), Department of Government Printing (1992).

---

[12]*See* 1977 Tax Summaries at S-115.

Act N° 40 of 1988, Betting and Gaming Levy Act, Gazette of the Democratic Socialist Republic of Sri Lanka (Supp. Nov. 25, 1988), Department of Government Printing (1988).

Act N° 5 of 1989, Tax Amnesty Act, Gazette of the Democratic Socialist Republic of Sri Lanka (Supp. May 12, 1989), Department of Government Printing (1989).

Act N° 13 of 1989, Excise (Special Provisions) Act, Gazette of the Democratic Socialist Republic of Sri Lanka (Supp. Oct. 12, 1989), Department of Government Printing (1989).

Act N° 5 of 1996, "Save the Nation" Contribution Act, Mar. 20, 1996 [available on TaxBase], amended by Act N° 37 of 1996, Save the Nation Contribution (Amendment) Act.

Act N° 34 of 1996, Goods and Services Tax Act.

Sudan (SDN)

In addition to income tax, payroll tax (under the Social Security Act of 1974) and a sales tax of limited scope apply.

Income Tax Law, 1971, *reprinted in* TLW (as amended to Sept. 1986) [in English].

Zakat and Taxation Act 1984 (mimeo by Hassabo & Company, Certified Accountant, Khartoum) [in English].

Suriname (SUR)

Income tax, profit tax, net wealth tax, inheritance tax, excises, entertainment tax, lottery tax, tax on alumina production, motor vehicle license, wood export tax, and payroll taxes are imposed.

Income Tax Law 1922, and Wage Tax Law *reprinted in* Surinaamse Belastingwetgeving: Wetten Dividendbelasting, Huurwaardebelasting, Inkomstenbelasting, Loonbelasting en AOV, 1996 (dividend tax, income tax, wage tax, old-age pensions fund), Ministerie van Financien, Directoraat der Belastingen, Paramaribo, 1996 [in Dutch] *and in* TLW (as amended to 1960).

Swaziland (SWZ)

In addition to those listed below, mineral rights tax, real estate transfer tax, and stamp duty are imposed.

Income Tax Order N° 21 of 1975, as amended by Income Tax Amendment Act N° 6 of 1994, *reprinted in* The Income Tax Order 1975 amended by Act N° 6 of 1996, Income Tax (Amendment) Act 1996.

The Sales Tax Act N° 12 of 1983, *reprinted in* The Kingdom of Swaziland, The Sales Tax Act, 1983, Webster Print (as amended to 1991).

Sweden (SWE)

All cites are to the Swedish Statute Book (Svensk Författningssamling (SFS)). The Swedish tax laws are reprinted in several sources, including Skatte-och taxering-författningarna, Skatteförvaltningen, Riksskatteverket, 1998 [in Swedish published annually]. The principal laws currently in effect are set forth below, arranged according to subject matter.

1. Kommunal inkomstskatt—Municipal income tax

Kommunalskattelag (1928:370)—Municipal income tax act.

Lag (1979:417) om utdebitering och utbetalning av skatt vid ändring i rikets indelning i kommuner, landstingskommuner och församlingar—Act on charging and payment of tax when the division of municipalities and assemblies is altered.

2. Kommunal inkomstskatt; kompletterande lagar—Municipal income tax; supplementary laws

Lag (1993:1539) om avdrag för underskott av näringsverksamhet—Act on deductibility of losses incurred in business activity.

Lag (1993:1536) om räntefördelning vid beskattning—Act on interest allocation for tax purposes.

Lag (1982:60) om beräkning av avdrag på grund av avyttring av skog i vissa fall—Act on calculating deductions based on disposal of forests.

Lag (1992:1643) om särskilda regler för beskattning av inkomst från handelsbolag i vissa fall—Act on certain deductions after sale of forests in certain cases.

Lag (1993:1538) om periodiseringsfonder—Act on profit periodization reserves.

Lag (1993:1537) om expansionsmedel—Act on expansion fund.

Lag (1955:257) om inventering av varulager för inkomsttaxeringen—Act on physical counting of inventory for income tax purposes.

Lag (1990:663) om ersättningsfonder—Act on replacement reserves.

Lag (1979:611) om upphovsmannakonto—Act on originator account.

Skogskontolag (1954:142)—Forest account act.

Lag (1990:676) om skatt på ränta på skogskontomedel m.m.—Act on tax on interest from funds placed on forest account etc.

Lag (1963:173) om avdrag för avgifter till stiftelsen svenska filminstitutet—Act on deduction for fees to Swedish Film Institute.

Lag (1990:696) om avdrag för bidrag till stiftelsen Sveriges tekniska museum—Act on deductions for contributions to the foundation Sveriges tekniska museum.

Lag (1970:599) om avdrag vid inkomsttaxeringen för avgifter till Värdepapperscentralen VPC Aktiebolag—Act on deductibility of fees to the Securities Register Centre VPC Ltd.

3. Statlig inkomstskatt—National income tax

SIL—Lag om statlig inkomstskatt (1947:596)—National income tax act.

4. Statlig inkomstskatt; kompletterande lagar—National income tax; supplementary laws

Lag (1994:1852) om beräkning av beskattningsbar inkomst på förvärvsinkomster vid 1996–1999 års taxeringar—Act on 5 percent national income surtax on earned incomes for the assessment years 1996–99.

Lag (1996:761) om inkomstskatteregler m.m. med anledning av ändrade bestämmelser om aktiekapitalets storlek—Act on income tax rules due to changed rules on paid-in capital.

Lag (1994:775) om beräkning av kapitalunderlaget vid beskattning av ägare i fåmansaktiebolag—Act on calculation of the capital base for tax purposes of shareholders in closely held limited companies.

Lag (1951:733) om statlig inkomstskatt på ackumulerad inkomst—Act on national income tax on accumulated income.

Lag (1993:1469) om uppskovsavdrag vid byte av bostad—Act on tax deferral when changing dwelling or permanent home.

Lag (1993:1540) om återföring av skatteutjämningsreserv—Act on cancellation of tax deferral reserves.

Lag (1990:655) om återföring av obeskattade reserver—Act on cancellation of equalization reserves.

Lag (1992:1352) om återföring av allmän investeringsfond—Act on cancellation of general investment fund.

Lag (1996:725) om skattereduktion för utgifter för byggnadsarbete på bostadshus—Act on tax reduction for construction expenditures concerning dwellings.

Lag (1992:702) om inkomstskatteregler med anledning av vissa omstruktureringar inom den finansiella sektorn—Act on income tax rules concerning certain reorganizations within the financial sector.

Lag (1993:5) om inkomstskatteregler vid statligt stöd till vissa kreditinstitut—Act on income tax rules concerning governmental support to certain financial institutes.

Lag (1993:541) om inkomstbeskattning vid ombildning av värdepappersfond—Act on income taxation of reorganizations of investment funds.

Lag (1994:760) om inkomstskatteregler vid ombildning av Landshypoteksinstitutionen—Act on income tax rules concerning reorganization of Landshypoteksinstitutionen.

Lag (1992:1061) om inkomstskatteregler vid ombildning av föreningsbank till bankaktiebolag—Act on income tax rules concerning reorganization of an agricultural cooperative bank to a stock-corporation bank.

Lag (1995:1623) om skattereduktion för riskkapitalinvesteringar—Act on tax reduction for risk capital investments.

Lag (1992:1091) om inkomstskatteregler vid utskiftning av aktier i vissa fall—Act on income tax rules on distribution of stock in certain cases.

Lag (1990:912) om nedsättning av socialavgifter—Act on reduction of social security fees.

Lag (1990:659) om särskild löneskatt på vissa förvärvsinkomster—Act on special wage tax on certain earned incomes.

Lag (1978:188) om avdrag vid inkomsttaxeringen för avgift för kostnadsutjämning enligt allmän pensionsplan m.m.—Act on tax deductions for fees for equalization of expenses according to general pension plans.

Lag (1990:1427) om särskild premieskatt för grupplivförsäkring, m.m.—Act on special wage tax on group life insurances etc.

Lag (1990:661) om avkastningsskatt på pensionsmedel—Act on tax on the yield from pension funds.

5. Intern internationell skatterätt—Internal international tax law

Lag (1996:161) med vissa bestämmelser om tillämpningen av dubbelbeskattningsavtal—Act containing certain rules on the application of double taxation treaties.

Kupongskattelag (1970:624)—Dividend Withholding tax act (coupon tax).

Lag (1994:1854) om beskattning vid gränsöverskridande omstruktureringar inom EG—EC cross-border reorganization tax act.

Lag (1994:1853) om beskattning av europeiska ekonomiska intressegrupper—Act on taxation of European Economic Interest Groups.

Lag (1984:974) om beskattning av utländska forskare vid tillfälligt arbete i Sverige—Act on taxation of foreign scientists temporarily working in Sweden.

Lag (1986:468) om avräkning av utländsk skatt—Foreign tax credit act.

Lag (1990:314) om ömsesidig handräckning i skatteärenden—Act on mutual assistance in tax cases.

Lag (1991:586) om särskild inkomstskatt för utomlands bosatta—Act on special income tax for foreign residents.

Lag (1991:591) om särskild inkomstskatt för utomlands bosatta artister m.fl.— Act on special income tax for nonresident artists and athletes.

Lag (1976:661) om immunitet och privilegier i vissa fall—Act on privileges and immunities in certain cases.

Lag (1988:1461) om skattefrihet för vissa ersättningar från Österrike—Act on tax exemption on certain compensations from Austria.

6. Socialavgifter—Social security fees

Lag (1962:381) om allmän försäkring—Act on social insurance.

Lag (1981:691) socialavgifter—Act on social security fees.

Lag (1994:1920) om allmän löneavgift—Act on general salary fees.

Lag (1994:1744) om allmänna egenavgifter—Act on general payroll tax.

Lag (1991:687) om särskild löneskatt på pensionskostnader—Act on special wage tax on pension costs.

Lag (1993:931) om individuellt pensionssparande—Act on individual pension plans.

Lag (1967:531) om tryggande av pensionsutfästelse m.m.—Act on safeguarding pension commitments etc.

Lag (1991:1047) om sjuklön—Act on sick pay.

7. Mervärdesskatt—Value added tax

Mervärdesskattelag (1994:200)—Value added tax act.

Mervärdesskatteförordning (1994:223)—Value added tax decree.

8. Punktskatter—Excise taxes.

Lag (1984:151) om punktskatter och prisregleringsavgifter—Act on excise duties and price regulation fees.

Lag (1984:404) om stämpelskatt vid inskrivningsmyndigheter—Act on stamp duty to land registration administration.

Lag (1994:1776) om skatt på energi—Energy tax act.

Lag (1994:1564) om alkoholskatt—Alcohol tax act.

Lag (1972:266) om skatt på annonser och reklam—Advertisement and advertising tax act.

Lag (1991:1482) om lotteriskatt—Lottery tax act.

Lag (1991:1483) om skatt på vinstsparande m.m.—Act on tax on profit savings.

Lag (1972:280) om skatt på spel—Act on tax on gambling.

9. Fastigheter—Real Estate

Lag (1984:1052) om statlig fastighetsskatt—Act on national real estate tax.

Lag (1997:441) om omräkningstal för 1998 års taxeringsvärden—Act on recalculation figures for the tax assessment value for 1998.

Lag (1996:1231) om skattereduktion för fastighetsskatt i vissa fall vid 1997–2001 års taxeringar—Act on tax credits concerning national tax on real estate in certain cases on the assessment of tax of 1997–2001.

Fastighetstaxeringslag (1979:1152)—Tax assessment value act.

Lag (1994:1850) om direktavdrag för byggnader m.m.—Act on accelerated depreciation for buildings etc.

10. Förmögenhet, arv och gåva—Wealth, inheritance and gift taxes

Lag (1997:323) om förmögenhetsskatt—National wealth tax act.

Lag (1997:324) om begränsning av skatt i vissa fall—Act on limitation of tax in certain cases.

Lag (1941:416) om arvsskatt och gåvoskatt—Inheritance and gift tax act.

11. Taxering, process—Assessment and procedure

Skattebetalningslag (1997:843)—Tax payment act.

Lag (1997:484) om dröjsmålsavgift—Act on fee for delay.

Uppbördslag (1953:272)—Tax collection act.

Lag (1984:668) om uppbörd av socialavgifter från arbetsgivare—Act on collection of social fees from employers.

Taxeringslag (1990:324)—Tax assessment act.

Lag (1990:325) om självdeklaration och kontrolluppgifter—Act on income tax returns and statements of earnings and tax deductions.

Lag (1951:442) om förhandsbesked i taxeringsfrågor—Act on advance rulings in tax matters.

Lag (1989:479) om ersättning för kostnader i ärenden och mål om skatt m.m.—Act on compensation for costs in tax cases.

Lag (1995:575) mot skatteflykt—Tax avoidance act.

Lag (1994:466) om särskilda tvångsåtgärder i beskattningsförfarandet—Act on certain measures in tax assessment procedure.

Lag (1978:880) om betalningssäkring för skatter, tullar och avgifter—Act on distraint order for securing payment for taxes, customs and fees.

Lag (1982:188) om preskription av skattefordringar m.m.—Act on statute of limitations of tax claims.

Lag (1957:686) om taxeringsväsendet under krigsförhållanden—Act on assessment authorities during war.

Lag (1971:289) om allmänna förvaltningsdomstolar—Act on general administrative courts.

Skatteregisterlag (1980:343)—Tax register act.

Utsökningsregisterlag (1986:617)—Debt recovery register act.

12. Övriga—other

Lag (1995:1592) om skatteregler för ersättning från insättningsgaranti—Act on tax rules on compensation from deposit guarantee.

Stiftelselagen (1994:1220); transumt ur—Act on foundations (excerpt from).

Lag (1971:118) om skattefrihet för ersättning till neurosedynskadade—Act on freedom of taxation for compensation to people suffering from thalidomide injuries.

Lag (1978:401) om exportkreditstöd—Act on export credit subventions.

Lag (1958:295) om sjömansskatt—Seamen's tax act,

Lag (1970:912) med anledning av riksskatteverkets inrättande—Act concerning the establishment of the National Tax Board,

Lag (1985:354) om förbud mot yrkesmässig rådgivning i vissa fall, m.m.—Act on prohibition against professional advising in certain cases etc.

Lag (1930:173) om beräkning av lagstadgad tid—Act on calculation of statutory time.

Skattebrottslag (1971:69)—Tax penal code.

Lag (1972:78) om skatt för gemensamt kommunalt ändamål—Act on tax for joint municipal purpose.

Switzerland (CHE)

The official citations are parallel citations to the official collection of federal law published in German, French, and Italian: Systematische Sammlung des Bundesrechts (SR) [in German], Recueil systématique du droit fédéral (RS) [in French], Raccolta sistematica del diritto federale (RS) [in Italian]. The index to the official collection with a list of all tax statutes can be found on the internet.

Loi fédéral sur les droits de timbre (Stamp Taxes), June 27, 1973, RS/SR 641.10.

Loi fédéral sur l'harmonisation des impôts directs des cantons et des communes (Federal Law Governing the Harmonization of Direct Taxation in Cantons and Communes), Dec. 14, 1990, RS/SR 642.14, amended by Law of Oct. 7, 1994.

LIFD—Loi fédéral sur l'impôt fédéral direct (Federal Law Governing Direct Taxation), Dec. 14, 1990, RS/SR 642.11, *reprinted in* Ferdinand Zuppinger, Rebecca Brunner-Peters and Robert Umbricht, The Direct Federal Tax Law 1995 (Schulthess Polygraphischer Verlag, Zürich 1993) [in German, French, English, and Italian]. .

Ordonnance sur l'imposition des personnes physiques domiciliées à l'étranger et exerçant une activité pour le compte de la Confédération ou d'autres corporations ou établissements de droit public suisse (Taxation of Foreigners), Oct. 20, 1993, RS/SR 642.110.8, *reprinted in* TLW at 39.

Loi fédéral sur l'impôt anticipé (Federal Law Governing Estimated Taxation), Oct. 13, 1965, RS/SR 642.21.

Ordonnance régissant la taxe sur la valeur ajoutée (Value Added Tax), June 22, 1994, RS/SR 641.201.

Loi fédéral sur la taxe d'exemption du service militaire (Federal Law Governing the Tax on Exemption from Military Service), June 12, 1959, RS/SR 611.

Loi fédérale sur l'imposition du tabac (Tax on Tobacco), Mar. 21, 1969, RS/SR 641.31.

Arrêté du conseil fédéral concernant un impôt fédéral sur les boissons (Federal Tax on Drinks), Aug. 4, 1934, RS/SR 641.411.

Syrian Arab Republic (SYR)

Law N° 112, Lump Sum Income Taxation, Aug. 11, 1958 (as amended to June 30, 1989) [in Arabic].

Legislative Decree N° 85, Income Tax Law, May 21, 1949 (as amended to Dec. 31, 1988) [in Arabic].

Law N° 19, Expatriates' Fees, June 3, 1990, *reprinted in* Ministry of Finance, 2 Collection of Tax Legislation [in Arabic].

Law № 18, Consumption Expenditure Fee, Apr. 2, 1987, *reprinted in id.* [in Arabic].

Legislative Edict № 117(1), Automobile Fees, Nov. 26, 1961, *reprinted in id.* [in Arabic].

Law № 223(1) Fees on Equipment to Receive Television Broadcasts, July 17, 1960, *reprinted in id.* [in Arabic].

Legislative Edict № 103(1), Cement Fee Statute, Aug. 18, 1940, *reprinted in id.* [in Arabic].

Resolution № 125, Flammable Materials Tax Law, May 8, 1928, *reprinted in id.* [in Arabic].

Law № 114, Sugar Restriction Statute, Dec. 19, 1944, *reprinted in id.* [in Arabic].

Law № 165(1), Statute on Fees for Substances Containing Alcohol, May 8, 1945, *reprinted in id.* [in Arabic].

Law № 203, Imposing a Computation Fee on Imported Goods, July 4, 1960, *reprinted in id.* [in Arabic].

Legislative Edict № 151(1), Corporations and Commercial Establishments Outside the Territory of the United Arab Republic Which Have a Branch or an Agent Inside Syria, Mar. 3, 1952, *reprinted in id.* [in Arabic].

Entertainment Statute, Jan. 8, 1938, *reprinted in id.* [in Arabic].

Law № 80(1), Salt Exploitation Statute, Jan. 4, 1939, *reprinted in id.* [in Arabic].

Law № 16/L.R.(1), Tobacco Monopoly Law, Jan. 30, 1935, *reprinted in id.* [in Arabic].

Custom Revenues, Mar. 31, 1983, *reprinted in id.* [in Arabic].

Law № 449(1), Army Fee on Electrical Power Allotment Bills, Jan. 15, 1949, *reprinted in id.* [in Arabic].

Tajikistan (TJK)

Zakon Respubliki Tadzhikistan ob Osnovakh Nalogovoy Sistemy (Law of the Republic of Tajikistan on the Fundamentals of the Tax System), *reprinted in* 500 Voprosov i Otvetov po Nalogam i Tsenam (NPMP "Amri Iln" 1994), July 20, 1994 [in Russian].

Ukaz Prezidenta Respubliki Tadzhikistan ob obrazovanii Glavnogo Nalogovogo upravleniya Respubliki Tadzhikistan (Decree of the President of Tajikistan on the Creation of the Main Tax Bureau of the Republic of Tajikistan), Glavnoe Gosudarstvennoe Nalogovoe Upravlenie Respubliki Tadzhikistan (Main State Tax Authority of the Republic of Tajikistan), *reprinted in* Zakonodatelnye i Normativnye Akty po Nalogam i Nalogooblozheniyu 1994 [in Russian].

Zakon № 590, Respubliki Tadzhikistan o gosudarstvennykh nalogovykh orga-nakh Respubliki Tadkzhikistan (Law of the Republic of Tajikistan on State Tax Organizations of the Republic of Tajikistan), Mar. 14, 1992, *id.*

Zakon № 977, Respubliki Tadzhikistan ob osnovakh nalogovoy sistemy (Law of the Republic of Tajikistan on the Basis of the Tax System), June 20, 1994, *id.*

Zakon № 226, Respubliki Tadzhikistan o gosudarstvennoy registratsii pred-priyatiy v Respublike Tadzhikistan i vzimanii platy za nee (Law of the Republic of Tajikistan on Government Registration of Enterprises in the Republic of Tajikistan and the Registration Fee), Feb. 21, 1991, *id.*

Zakon № 498, Respubliki Tadzhikistan o naloge na dobavlennuyu stoimost (Law of the Republic of Tajikistan on the Value Added Tax), Jan. 6, 1992, *id.*

Zakon № 500, Respubliki Tadzhikistan ob aktsizakh (Law of the Republic of Tajikistan on Excises), Jan. 6, 1992, *id.*

Zakon № 502, Respubliki Tadzhikistan o podokhodnom naloge s grazhdan Respubliki Tadzhikistan, inostrannikh grazhdan i lits bez grazhdanstva (Law of the Republic of Tajikistan on Individual Income Tax for Citizens of the Re-public of Tajikistan, Foreigners, and Those Without Citizenship), Jan. 6, 1992, *id.*

Zakon № 494, Respubliki Tadzhikistan o nalogooblozhenii vladel'tsev trans-portnykh sredstv i drugikh samokhodrykh mashin i mekhanizmov (Law of the Republic of Tajikistan on Taxes for Owners of Means of Transportation and Other Vehicles), Jan. 6, 1992, *id.*

Zakon Respubliki Tadzhikistan o plate za zemlyu (Law of the Republic of Tajikistan on Payments for Land), Mar. 8, 1992, *id.*

Zakon № 710, Respubliki Tadzhikistan o tamozhennoy tarife (Law of the Re-public of Tajikistan on Customs Tariffs), Nov. 25, 1992, *id.*

Zakon № 877, Respubliki Tadzhikistan nalogoblozheniya dokhodov ot stra-khovoy deyatel'nosti (Law of the Republic of Tajikistan on the Taxation of Profits from Insurance Activities), Dec. 27, 1993, *id.*

Zakon № 889, Respubliki Tadzhikistan o nalogakh na imushestvo fiz-icheskikh lits (Law of the Republic of Tajikistan Relating to Property Taxes on Physical Persons), Dec. 27, 1993, *id.*

Zakon № 895, Respubliki Tadzhikistan o dorozhom fonde (Law of the Repub-lic of Tajikistan on the Road Fund), Dec. 27, 1993, *id.*

Ukaz Nº 278, Prezidiuma Verkhovnogo Soveta Respubliki Tadzhikistan o vvedenim spetsialnogo naloga (Decree of the Supreme Soviet of the Republic of Tajikistan on the Implementation of Special Taxes), June 18, 1994, *id.*

Zakon Nº 1001, Respubliki Tadzhikistan o naloge na pribyl' predpriyatiy i organizatsiy (Law of the Republic of Tajikistan on the Taxation of Corporations and Organizations), July 21, 1994, *id.*

Tanzania (TZA)

The annual finance acts have made amendments to the tax laws listed below.

Income Tax Act Nº 33 of 1973 (as amended to Jan. 28, 1991), *reprinted in* TLW.

The Sales Tax Act, 1976, Nº 13 of 1976, Nov. 12, 1976.

The Stamp Duty Act, 1972, Nº 20 of 1972, Aug. 18, 1972.

The Hotel Levy Act, 1972, Nº 23 of 1972, Aug. 18, 1972.

The Business Licensing Act, 1972, Nº 25 of 1972.

The Training Levy (Imposition) Act, 1972.

The Road Tolls Act, 1985, Nº 13 of 1985, Oct. 21, 1985.

The Foreign Commercial Vehicles (licensing) Act, 1970, Nº 23 of 1970, June 29, 1970.

The Motor Vehicles (Tax on Registration and Transfer) Act, 1972, Nº 21 of 1972, Aug. 18, 1972.

The Port Service Charge Act, 1973, Nº 11 of 1973, July 23, 1973.

The Video Business Regulation Act, 1988, Nº 6 of 1988, Nov. 23, 1988, Gazette of the United Republic of Tanzania, Nº 13, Vol. 70 (March 31, 1989) (Act Supplement).

The Payroll Levy Act, 1985, Nº 12 of 1985, Oct. 21, 1985.

The Airport Service Charge Act, 1962, Nº 26 of 1962, July 11, 1962.

The Car Benefit Tax Act, 1991, Nº 19 of 1991, Dec. 30, 1992.

Act Nº 1 of 1996, Finance Act, 1996, Acts Supplement to the Gazette of the United Republic of Tanzania, Vol. 77, Nº 21 (May 1996) (Dar es Salaam, Govt. Printer).

Thailand (THA)

In Thailand, the tax legislation is contained in one Revenue Code. The taxes included are income tax, VAT, specific business tax, and stamp duty. Excises are governed by separate legislation.

RC—The Act Promulgating the Revenue Code, B.E. 2481, *reprinted in* The Revenue Code as amended up to February 1995 (V.T. Associates trans., ACREV, Lawyers, Auditors and Tax Consultants: Bangkok, 1995) [in English].

Excise Tax Act, B.E. 2527, *reprinted in* Technical Services Division, Excise Dept., Excise Tax Act (Aug. 1985).

Emergency Decree Amending the Excise Tariff Tax, B.E. 2527, *reprinted in* Technical Services Division, Excise Dept., Emergency Decree Amending the Excise Tariff Act (Aug. 1985).

Togo (TGO)

Code général des impôts (General Tax Code), *reprinted in* Code général des impôts 1985, Ministère de l'economie et des finances [in French], as amended by the following laws and ordinances:

Loi de Finances Nº 86-01 portant modifications du Code général des impôts (Appropriation and Finance Law amending the General Tax Code), Jan. 6, 1986, Ministère de l'Economie et des Finances [in French].

Loi Nº 87-01 portant Loi de finances pour la gestion 1987 (Budget Law for FY 1987), Journal Officiel, numéro spécial du 29 janvier 1987 [in French].

Loi Nº 88-01 portant Loi de finances pour la gestion 1988 (Budget Law for FY 1988), Ministère de l'Economie et des Finances [in French].

Loi Nº 89-10 portant modification du Code général des impôts (Law Amending the General Tax Code), May 5, 1989, Ministère de l'Economie et des Finances [in French].

Loi Nº 89-26 portant modification du Code général des impôts du 7 novembre 1989 (Law Amending the General Tax Code), Ministère de l'Economie et des Finances [in French].

Loi Nº 89-32 complétant les articles 186, 252, 539 de la Loi Nº 83/22 du 30 décembre 1983 portant Code général des impôts (Law Supplementing Articles 186, 252, and 539 of Law Nº 83/22 of Dec. 30, 1983 Establishing the General Tax Code), Nov. 30, 1989, Ministère de l'Economie et des Finances [in French].

Loi Nº 90/01 portant Loi de finances pour la gestion 1990 (Law Nº 90/01, the Budget Law for FY 1990), Ministère de l'Economie et des Finances [in French].

Ordonnance Nº 90-07 portant modification de la Loi Nº 89-26 du 7 novembre 1989 ayant modifié le Code général des impôts (Order Amending Law Nº 89/26 of Nov. 1989 amending the General Tax Code), Ministère de l'Economie et des Finances [in French].

Loi N° 91/01 portant Loi de finances pour la gestion 1991 (Law N° 91/01, the Budget Law for FY 1991), Ministère de l'Economie et des Finances [in French].

Ordonnance N° 93/005 portant Loi de finances pour la gestion 1993 (Budget Law for FY 1993), Ministère de l'Economie et des Finances [in French].

Loi N° 94/001 portant Loi de finances pour la gestion 1994 (Budget Law for FY 1994), Ministère de l'Economie et des Finances [in French].

Loi N° 95-011 portant Loi de finances pour la gestion 1995 (Budget Law for FY 1995), Ministère de l'Economie et des Finances [in French].

Loi N° 96-005 portant Loi de finances pour la gestion 1996 (Budget Law for FY 1996), Ministère de l'Economie et des Finances [in French].

Loi N° 96-015 portant Loi de finances pour la gestion 1997 (Budget Law for FY 1997), Ministère de l'Economie et des Finances [in French].

Tonga (TON)

Income Tax Act N° 17 of 1976, Cap. 68 (as amended to 1988), Nov. 8, 1976, V.V. Misi Government Printer, 1976.

Income Tax (Amendment) Act N° 4 of 1990.
Income Tax (Amendment) Act N° 7 of 1992.

Sales Tax Act N° 3 of 1986, Cap. 69, Government Publisher (1988 Ed.).

Act N° 6 of 1990 (to amend the Sales Tax Act 1986).

Port and Service Tax of 1949 (as amended to 1954), Cap. 95 V.V. Misi Government Printer, 1949.

Port and Service Tax Act of 1976, Tonga Government Gazette Extraordinary, June 14, 1976.

Fuel Sales Tax Act N° 6 of 1964, Cap. 97 V.V. Misi Government Printer, 1964.

Act N° 3 of 1985 to Amend the Fuel Sales Tax Act, Government Publisher, Sept. 27, 1985.

Act N° 4 of 1985 to impose an Accomodation and Entertainment Sales Tax, V.V. Misi Government Printer, Sept. 27, 1985.

Trinidad and Tobago (TTP)

Trinidad and Tobago: Consolidated Index of Statues and Subsidiary Legislation (as of Jan. 1, 1996) has been published by the Faculty of Law Library, University of the West Indies, Barbados. This lists the amending laws, and so they will not be listed here. The tax laws are as follows:

Corporation Tax Act (ch. 75:02), *reprinted in* Taxation, Vol. 1: Principal Legislation (Ernst & Young, 1995 and revised periodically) (as amended).

Excise (General Provisions) Act (ch. 78:50).

Fiscal Incentives Act 1979 (ch. 85:01), *reprinted in* Taxation, Vol. II: Supplementary Legislation (Ernst & Young, 1995 and revised periodically) (as amended).

Hotel Development Act (ch. 85:02), *reprinted in id.*

Housing Act (ch. 33:01), *reprinted in id.*

Income Tax Act (ch. 75:01), *reprinted in* TLW (as amended to Mar. 1995), *and in* Taxation, Vol. I: Principal Legislation (Ernst & Young, 1995 and revised periodically) (as amended).

Income Tax (Federal Endowments) Act 1960 (ch. 151).

Income Tax (in Aid of Industry) Act (ch. 85:04), *reprinted in* Taxation, Vol. II: Supplementary Legislation (Ernst & Young, 1995 and revised periodically)(as amended).

Lands and Buildings Taxes Act (ch. 76:04).

Miscellaneous Taxes Act (ch. 77:01).

Petroleum Production Levy and Subsidy Act (ch. 62:02), *reprinted in* Taxation, Vol. II: Supplementary Legislation (Ernst & Young, 1995 and revised periodically) (as amended).

Petroleum Taxes Act (ch. 75:04), *reprinted in id.*

Provisional Collection of Taxes Act (ch. 74:01).

Rates, Taxes, and Licenses (Payments by Cheque) Act (ch. 74:02).

Stamp Duty Act (ch. 76:01).

Tax Appeal Board Act (ch. 4:50).

Tax Information Exchange Agreements Act 1989, N° 30/1989.

Taxes Exemption Act (ch. 76:50).

Unemployment Levy Act (ch. 75:03), *reprinted in* Taxation Vol. II: Supplementary Legislation (Ernst & Young, 1995 and revised periodically) (as amended).

Value Added Tax Act 1989, as amended to Feb. 1994, *reprinted in* VAT Administration Centre, Inland Revenue, Value Added Tax Act 1989 (Government Printery 1994), *and in* Value Added Tax (Ernst & Young, 1995 and revised periodically) (as amended).

Tunisia (TUN)

Income Tax Code 1990, Official Journal Nº 88 of Dec. 31, 1989, *reprinted in* TLW (as amended to March 1995); Loi Nº 89-114 du 30 décembre 1989 portant promulgation du code de l'impôt sur le revenu des personnes physiques et de l'impôt sur les sociétés, *reprinted in* Ministère des finances, Direction générale des études et de la legislation fiscales, Recueil des textes relatifs aux impôts directs (as amended to Sept. 1, 1994) [in French].

Law Nº 61, June 2, 1988, Code de la taxe sur la valeur ajoutée (Value Added Tax Code), Journal officiel de la République Tunisienne Nº 39 of June 10, 1988 [in French].

Law Nº 62, June 2, 1988, Revising Consumption [Excise] Tax System, Official Journal, June 10, 1988 [in Arabic].

Code de l'impôt de la patente et de l'impôt sur les bénéfices des professions non commerciales (Code Governing the Tax on Business Profits and the Tax on Earnings from Noncommercial Occupations), *reprinted in* 1 Textes fiscaux, Ministère des finances, Direction générale des impôts (as amended to Mar. 31, 1984).

La Contribution personnelle d'Etat et impôt sur les traitements et salaires (Personal Income Tax and the Tax on Earned Income), *reprinted in* 2 Textes fiscaux, Ministère des finances, Direction générale des impôts (as amended to Mar. 31, 1984).

Taxes sur les chiffres d'affaires (Turnover Tax), Dec. 29, 1955, *reprinted in* 3 Textes fiscaux, Ministère des finances, Direction générale des impôts (as amended to Apr. 15, 1984).

Impôts sur les revenus des valeurs mobilières (Taxes on Income Derived from Transferable Securities), Dec. 23, 1918, *reprinted in* 4 Textes fiscaux, Ministère des finances, Direction générale des impôts (as amended to Dec. 31, 1985).

Loi Nº 62-71, Impôt agricole (Agricultural Tax), Dec. 31, 1962, *reprinted in* 5 Textes fiscaux, Ministère des finances, Direction générale des impôts (as amended to Dec. 31, 1985).

Loi Nº 62-72 La Déclaration unique des revenus (Single Income Tax Return), Dec. 31, 1962, *id.*

Loi Nº 93-53 Code des droits d'enregistrement et de timbre, May 17, 1993, Journal officiel Nº 39, May 25, 1993, *reprinted in* Code des droits d'enregistrement et de la timbre (Imprimerie officielle de la République Tunisienne, 1993).

Loi Nº 95-109, Dec. 25, 1995, portant loi de finances pour la gestion 1996, 138 Journal Officiel, Nº 104 (Dec. 1995).

Loi Nº 96-113, Dec. 30, 1996, portant loi de finances pour la gestion 1997, 139 Journal Officiel, Nº 105 (Dec. 1996).

Turkey (TUR)

In addition to the taxes listed below, inheritance and gift tax, payroll tax, property tax, and stamp duty are imposed.

Income Tax Law, *reprinted in* 42 TLW (as amended to Aug. 1989) [in English].

Corporation Tax Law, *id.*

Value-Added Tax Law, *id.*

Turkmenistan (TKM)

For a list of presidential decrees on taxation in addition to the laws and decrees listed below, see IBFD, Turkmenistan in Taxation and Investment in Central and East European Countries (May 1996 supp.). In addition to those listed below, tax on income of small-scale enterprises, tax on security transactions, excises, tax on vehicle owners, natural resource tax, property tax, excess wage tax, state insurance contributions, state duty, and business licenses are imposed.

Statute on Income Taxation of the Citizens of Turkmenistan, Foreign Citizens, and Persons Without Citizenship, Confirmed by Decree of the President, Jan. 6, 1992. Nº VII-252 [in English].

Decree on Amendments and Additions to the Statute on Personal Income Tax on Citizens of Turkmenistan, Foreign Citizens, and Stateless Persons, Nov. 22, 1993 [in English].

Law Nº 895-XII of Turkmenistan on the Profit Tax, Oct. 8, 1993 [in English].

Law Nº 894-XII of Turkmenistan on Value-Added Tax, Oct. 8, 1993 [in English].

Statute Nº VII-250 on the State Tax Service, Jan. 6, 1992 [in English].

Decree of the President of Turkmenistan Nº 1613 on Amendments and Additions to Decree Nº 513 of the President of Turkmenistan of Jan. 1, 1992 on Excise Taxes, Dec. 1993 [in English].

Statute on the Procedure for Levying and the Rates of the Tax on Owners of Means of Transportation [in English].

Statute Nº VII-250 on the State Tax Service, confirmed by Decree of the President of Turkmenistan, Jan. 6, 1992 [in English].

Uganda (UGA)

ITA—The Income Tax Act, 1997, Nº 11 of 1997, 90 Uganda Gazette Nº 81, Acts Supplement Nº 8 (Dec. 31, 1997).

The Stamps Act of 1915, as amended to 1965, Cap. 172, Stamps, Laws of Uganda, Government Printer, Entebbe.

The East African Excise Management Act (Cap. 28, rev. 1970).

The Excise Tariff Act of 1954 (as amended to 1962), Cap. 174, Excise Tariff, Laws of Uganda, Government Printer, Entebbe.

Value Added Tax Statute, 1996, *reprinted in* Statutes Supplement N° 5 to the Uganda Gazette, N° 21, Vol. 89, Apr. 4, 1996.

The Uganda Revenue Authority Statute, 1991, Statutes Supplement N° 5 to the Uganda Gazette N° 36, Aug. 16, 1991.

The Tax Appeals Tribunals Act, 1997, N° 12 of 1997, 90 Uganda Gazette N° 81, Acts Supplement N° 1 (Dec. 31, 1997).

The Investment Code 1991.

The Finance Statute, 1988 (June 23, 1988) (Statute N° 4: 1988) (amends various tax laws).

The Finance Statute, 1993 (July 20, 1994) (Statute N° 9: 1994) (amends various tax laws).

The Finance Statute, 1994 (Nov. 15, 1994) (Statute N° 17: 1994), Uganda Gazette, Statutes Supplement, Dec. 2, 1994 (amends various tax laws).

Ukraine (UKR)

We cite to a newspaper source (Golos Ukrainy) and to the session laws (Vidomosti, or Vedomosti in Russian). The list below is reasonably complete, except that it does not list the amending laws in all cases. At the moment, the tax laws of Ukraine do not seem to have been published in one book in an up-to-date version; they can be found in periodicals (for example, the weekly Vse o Buchgalterskom Uchete, published in Russian by the Association of Professional Accountants of Ukraine).

Law of Ukraine on the System of Taxation, Journal of the Supreme Council of Ukraine, 1997, N° 16, Art. 119, amended by Law N° 221/97-VR, Apr. 19, 1997; Law N° 303/97-VR, June 4, 1997.

Decree of the Supreme Soviet of Ukraine on the Fundamental Provisions of Tax Policy and Tax Reform in Ukraine, Dec. 13, 1995, FBIS-SOV-96-023-S.

Edict of the Cabinet of Ministers of Ukraine on Collection of Overdue Taxes, Non-Tax Payments, *reprinted in* Pravda Ukrayiny, Feb. [in English], FBIS-Database, FBIS-USR-93-027, Mar. 10, 1993.

Law N° 314/97-BP, June 5, 1997, On cancelling and restructuring taxpayers' tax liabilities as of March 31, 1997.

Edict of the Cabinet of Ministers on Local Taxes and Tax Collection, *reprinted in* Golos Ukrainy, June 11, 1993 [in Ukrainian] *and in* FBIS-USR-93-083, July 6, 1993.

Law Nº 283/97 Pro opodatkuvania pributku pidpriemstv (Law of the Ukraine on Taxation of the Profits of Enterprises) May 22, 1997, *reprinted in* Vse o Buchgalterskom Uchete (Feb. 4, 1998) (as amended) [in Russian].

Law Nº 168/97-BP on Value Added Tax, Apr. 3, 1997, amended by Law Nº 403/97-BP (June 27, 1997), Law Nº 460/97-BP (July 16, 1997), Law Nº 535/97-BP (Sept. 19, 1997), Law Nº 550/97-BP (Sept. 26, 1997), Law Nº 573/97-BP (Oct. 15, 1997), Law Nº 644/97-BP (Nov. 19, 1997), Law Nº 698/97-BP (Dec. 5, 1997), Law Nº 770/97-BP (Dec. 23, 1997), Law Nº 794/97-BP (Dec. 30, 1997), Law Nº 799/97-BP (Dec. 30, 1997) (published in Feb. 4, 1998 issue of Vse o Buchgalterskom Uchete as amended) [in Russian].

Cabinet of Ministers Edict on Personal Income Tax (Dec. 26, 1992), *reprinted in* Golos Ukrayiny (Voice of Ukraine), Jan 11, 1993, at 9–12 [in Ukrainian], *translated in* FBIS-USR-93-020, Feb. 25, 1993 [in English].

Decree of Cabinet of Ministers Nº 18-92 On Excise Duty (Dec. 26, 1992).

Law Nº 30/96-BP On Rates of Excise and Customs Duty on Imported Cigarette Products (Feb. 6, 1996).

Law Nº 178/96-BP, On Rates of Excise and Customs Duty on Ethyl Alcohol and Alcoholic Beverages (May 7, 1996).

Law Nº 216/96-BP Rates of Excise and Customs Duty on Automobiles and Tires (May 24, 1996).

Law Nº 313/96-BP On Rates of Excise and Customs Duty on Several Goods (Products) (July 11, 1996)

Law Nº 527/97-BP On Excise Duty on Alcoholic Beverages and Cigarette Products (Sept. 11, 1997)

Law Nº 1963-XII, Zakon o naloge c vladel'tsev transpornykh sredstv i drugikh samokhodnykh mashin i mekhanizmov (Law on Taxation of Automobile Owners), Dec. 11, 1991, Vedomosti Ukrainy, Mar. 17, 1992, Nº 11, item 150 [in Russian], amended by Law Nº 75/97-BP, Feb. 18, 1997.

Edict on Export Tax: Addendum 1993, *reprinted in* Golos Ukrayiny, Jan. 28, 1993, FBIS-Database, FBIS-USR-93-027, Mar. 10, 1993 [in English].

Decret Cabinetu Ministriv Ukrainiy Pro Dershavne Meto (Decree of the Ukrainian Cabinet of Ministers on State Duty, Feb. 12, 1993, Golos Ukrainiy, Nº 27, Feb. 12, 1993 [in Ukrainian], FBIS-USR-93-033 [in English].

Law Nº 2535-XII On Payment for Land (July 3, 1992).

Presidential Decree Nº 78594 On Establishment of Royalty Payments for Oil and Gas Extracted in Ukraine (Dec. 21, 1994).

Decree of Cabinet of Ministers Nº 24-93 On Tax on Trade (Mar. 17, 1993).

Geological Fee: Resolution of Cabinet of Ministers Nº 645 of Aug. 11, 1995 on Payment for Geological Works Carried out at the Expense of the State Budget. Minerals Code of Ukraine, Law Nº 132/94-BP (July 27, 1994).

Fee on Natural Resource Use: Minerals Code, Law Nº 132/94-BP, Water Code, Law Nº 213/95-BP (June 6, 1995), Forest Code, Law Nº 3852-XII (Jan. 21, 1994).

Environmental Pollution Fee: Law Nº 1264-XII (June 25, 1991).

Chernobyl Fund contributions: Law Nº 386/97-BP (June 20, 1997).

Law Nº 402/97-BP On Fee for Obligatory Social Insurance (June 26, 1997).

Law Nº 400/97 On Fee for Obligatory State Pension Insurance (June 26, 1997).

Resolution of Cabinet of Ministers On Formation of State Innovation Fund (Feb. 18, 1992).

Law Nº 98/96-BP On Licensing for Certain Kinds of Entrepreneurial Activity (Mar. 23, 1996).

Decree of Cabinet of Ministers Nº 56-93 On Local Taxes and Fees (May 20, 1993).

United Arab Emirates (ARE)

According to Taxes and Investment in the Middle East (IBFD, 1990), "the only tax imposed in the United Arab Emirates is the tax on the income of corporate bodies. Each emirate has its own income tax decree. . . ." Coopers Lybrand, 1997 International Tax Summaries adds: "In practice, however, no income or other tax is levied on companies. The main exceptions are taxes on the profits of oil companies and foreign banks. . . ."

United Kingdom (GBR)

It has historically been frustrating to deal with the tax legislation of the United Kingdom because of the practice of enacting freestanding provisions in finance acts, rather than consolidating all the relevant provisions into one law and making textual amendments to that law. Parliament has responded to this problem by enacting some massive consolidations over the past decade, including the Income and Corporation Taxes Act 1988, the Taxation of Chargeable Gains Act 1992, and the Value Added Tax Act 1994. The problem has not completely gone away because there are still nontextual amendments, but these consolidations have made it much easier to navigate through the relevant statutes.

All the tax laws (together with statutory instruments, extrastatutory concessions, and other official pronouncements) are published in a two-volume set by CCH International (1996–97 U.K. Tax Statutes and Statutory Instruments). Butterworths pub-

lishes the Orange Tax Handbook and the Yellow Tax Handbook, which between them contain all the tax laws. The Taxes Acts is a multivolume set (six volumes for the 1994 edition) covering income tax, corporation tax, and capital gains tax, published annually by Inland Revenue and available from HMSO. The Taxes Acts includes provisions of various annual Finance Acts that have not been codified into the principal tax acts, as well as miscellaneous enactments that contain provisions relevant to taxation. These are not listed below. The Taxes Acts also includes the text of the regulations relevant to the tax laws it covers.

Taxes Management Act 1970, *reprinted in* Great Britain, Board of Inland Revenue, The Taxes Acts: Income Tax, Corporation Tax and Capital Gains Tax (HMSO 1994) (as amended to 1994).

ICTA—Income and Corporation Taxes Act 1988, *reprinted in id.*

CAA—Capital Allowances Act 1990, *reprinted in id.*

TCGA—Taxation of Chargeable Gains Act 1992, *reprinted in id.*

Value Added Tax Act 1994, *reprinted in* The Law Reports Statutes 1994, pt. 5, The Incorporated Council of Law Reporting for England and Wales, Cap. 23 at 1393, and Orange Tax Handbook, Butterworths, 1995–96.

Inheritance Tax Act of 1984, *reprinted in* 43 Halsbury's 1068 and Orange Tax Handbook, Butterworths, 1995–96.

Stamp Duties, *reprinted in* Orange Tax Handbook, Butterworths, 1995–96.

National Insurance Contributions, *reprinted in* Orange Tax Handbook, Butterworths, 1995–96.

Insurance Premium Tax, *reprinted in* Orange Tax Handbook, Butterworths, 1995–96.

Hydrocarbon Oil Duties Act 1979, as amended by Finance (No. 2) Act 1979 and subsequent Finance Acts. *See* European Commission, Inventory of Taxes Levied in the Member States of the European Communities (16th ed. 1996).

TA—Tobacco Products Duty Act 1979, as amended by the Finance Acts 1981 and 1988. *See id.*

Matches and Mechanical Lighters Duties Act 1979, as amended by the Finance Act 1981. *See id.*

Alcoholic Liquor Duties Act 1979, as amended by subsequent Finance Acts and the Alcoholic Liquors (Amendment of Enactments Relating to Strength and to Units of Measurement) Order 1979 and the Isle of Man Act 1979 and the Customs and Excise Management Act 1979. *See id.*

Oil Taxation Act 1975, Petroleum Revenue Tax Act 1980 and Oil Taxation Act 1983, as amended by annual Finance Acts. *See id.*

Betting and Gaming Duties Act 1981, as amended by the Finance Acts 1982, 1986, 1987, and 1990. *See id.*

Bingo and Gaming Duties Act 1981, as amended by the Finance Acts 1982, 1983, and 1986. *See id.*

Vehicles (Excise) Act 1971, as amended by subsequent Finance Acts. *See id.*

Car Tax Act, 1983. *See id.*

United States (USA)

IRC—Internal Revenue Code, *reprinted in* The Complete Internal Revenue Code: All the Income, Estate, Gift, Employment, Excise, Procedure and Administrative Provisions (Research Institute of America, Inc., 1995) (as amended to Dec. 31, 1994).

Uruguay (URY)

The tax laws of Uruguay have been consolidated into a single tax code, most recently by Decree 338/96 (Sept. 1996). The full text is available at www.parlamento.gub.uy.

Código Tributario (Tax Code), Texto Ordenado 1996, *reprinted in* IBFD-CIAT [in Spanish].

Uzbekistan (UZB)

Tax laws, regulations, and other materials are published in the Nalogovy Vestnik Uzbekistana (in Russian), which is published by the State Tax Committee of the Republic of Uzbekistan, Tashkent. There is also a private publisher (Fund, Alleya Paradov Street 2, Tashkent, Uzbekistan 700000; fax: 394268 or 442021) of a series called Nalogovoye Zakonodatelstvo Respubliki Uzbekistan (Tax Legislation of the Republic of Uzbekistan), also in Russian. There is also an English translation of various legislation, including tax legislation, published by Uzbekiston, Tashkent (1992), ISBN: 5-640-01410-5. This translation includes the law on taxes from enterprises, associations, and organizations (as amended through 1992).

In April 1997, the Parliament adopted a tax code that replaced the existing tax laws. The new code is heavily influenced by the codes of Kazakhstan and the Kyrgyz Republic. While the existing laws continue to apply until the new code comes into effect, we have not listed the precode laws here since they are now presumably transitory (those with a particular interest should check the resolution putting the new code into effect to ascertain the effect on existing laws).

Nalogovii Kodeks Respubliki Uzbekistan (Tax Code of the Republic of Uzbekistan) (presumably will be published by one or more of the sources cited above, as well as in the official gazette and in newspapers) [in Russian].

Law on Payment of Fees for State Services, Documents and Privileges (State Duty), *reprinted in* Khalq Sozi, Jan. 15, 1993 [in Uzbek, English], FBIS-USR-93-042, Apr. 5, 1993.

Vanuatu (VUT)

The Business Licence Act Nº 25 of 1983, Official Gazette of Oct. 17, 1983 (as amended to 1985), Ministry of Finance.

The Hotel and Licensed Premises Tax Act Nº 2 of 1982, Ministry of Finance.

Venezuela (VEN)

In addition to the citations below, the tax legislation and commentary (as well as other economic legislation) are available in a series of publications in loose-leaf, CD-ROM, or Internet format from Legis Editores, C.A., Zona Industrial La Urbina, Calle 8, Edificio Ródano, Piso 3, Caracas; fax: 242-5547 or 241-6451.

Código Orgánico Tributario (General Tax Code), Texto Ordenado of Aug. 4, 1992, as amended by Decreto Nº 189 of May 25, 1994, *reprinted in* IBFD-CIAT [in Spanish] *and in* G.O. Nº 2.992 Extraordinario del 3 de agosto de 1982 [in Spanish].

Ley de Impuesto sobre la Renta (Income Tax Law), Gaceta Oficial de la República de Venezuela of Sept. 9, 1993 [in Spanish], as amended by Decreto Ley Nº 188 of May 25, 1994, *reprinted in* IBFD-CIAT [in Spanish] *and reprinted in* 45 TLW (as amended to Dec. 1993).

Decreto Nº 3113 Ley de Reforma Parcial de la Ley de Impuesto sobre la Renta (Law on the Partial Reform of the Income Tax Law), Aug. 26, 1993, Gaceta Oficial Nº 4.628 Extraordinario del 9 de septiembre de 1993 [in Spanish].

Decreto Nº 3.266 Ley de Impuesto a los Activos Empresariales (Law on the Taxation of Business Assets), Nov. 26, 1993, Gaceta Oficial de la República de Venezuela Nº 4.654 of Dec. 1, 1993 [in Spanish].

Decreto que Establece el Impuesto al Consumo Suntuario y a las Ventas al Mayor (Decree Establishing a Tax on Luxury Consumption and Wholesale Sales), Gaceta Oficial de la República de Venezuela of May 27, 1994 [in Spanish] (as amended up to Sept. 9, 1994), *reprinted in* IBFD-CIAT [in Spanish].

Value Added Tax Law *reprinted in* 45 TLW (as amended to Dec. 1993) [in English].

Vietnam (VNM)

We cite to two sources, both in English. Selection of Fundamental Laws and Regulations of Vietnam [hereinafter FLRV] is a paperback; Foreign Investment Laws of Vietnam [hereinafter FIL] is a multivolume loose-leaf published by Phillips Fox So-

licitors, Melbourne, Australia. Some laws are also available on a website (http://coombs.edu.au) [hereinafter website].

Law on Corporate Income Tax passed by the National Assembly on June 30, 1990 and amended and added to on June 6, 1993, *reprinted in* FLRV, 2nd ed., THÊ GIOI Publishers, Hanoi, 1995, p. 344 [in English] .

Law on Export and Import Duties passed by the National Assembly in Dec. 1991, amended and added to on July 5, 1993, *reprinted in* FIL, FLRV.

Ordinance on Natural Resources Tax passed on Mar. 30, 1990 (excerpts), *reprinted in* FIL, FLRV.

Law on Turnover Tax, passed by the National Assembly on June 30, 1990, amended and added to on July 5, 1993, *reprinted in* FIL, FLRV.

Law on Special Sales Tax, passed by the National Assembly on June 30, 1990, amended and added to on July 5, 1993, *reprinted in* FIL, FLRV.

Ordinance on Income Tax on High Income Earners passed on May 19, 1994, *reprinted in* FIL, FLRV.

State Council Ordinance on Residential Housing Land Tax (June 29, 1991), *reprinted in* FIL.

Law on Governing Taxes on Land-Use Right Assignment, promulgated July 5, 1994 [available on website in English].

Law on Value Added Tax, N° 02/1997/QH9, proclaimed by Presidential Order N° 57/L/CTN, May 22, 1997 (goes into effect Jan. 1, 1999), *reprinted in* Ministry of Finance, Law on Value Added Tax, Law on Business Income Tax (National Political Publishing House, Hanoi 1997) [in Vietnamese, English].

Law on Business Income Tax, N° 03/1997/QH9, proclaimed by Presidential Order N° 57/L/CTN, May 22, 1997 (goes into effect Jan. 1, 1999), *reprinted in id.*

Law on Foreign Investment, Nov. 12, 1996, proclaimed by Presidential Order N° 52/L/CTN (effective Nov. 23, 1996).

Yemen, Republic of (YEM)

Law N° 70 of 1991, The Production, Consumption, and Services Tax Law, amended by Presidential Decree N° 4 of 1995, Feb. 19, 1995.

Law N° 31 of 1991, Income Tax Law.

Zambia (ZMB)

The laws of Zambia are listed, and some are available in full text on the website of the Zambia Legal Information Institute (ZamLII) (http://lii.zamnet.zm:8000).

ITA—Income Tax Act 1966, *reprinted in* Unofficial Consolidation of the Income Tax Act, Republic of Zambia, Department of Taxes, Ministry of Finance (as amended to Mar. 31, 1988) *and in* 46 TLW (as amended to Apr. 1, 1996), amended by the following:

> Act Nº 17 of 1988 to amend the Income Tax Act.
> Act Nº 28 of 1988 to amend the Income Tax Act, Income Tax (Amendment) Act of 1989.
> Act Nº 15 of 1990 to amend the Income Tax Act.
> Act Nº 29 of 1990 to amend the Income Tax Act.
> Act Nº 12 of 1991 to amend the Income Tax Act.
> Act Nº 11 of 1992 to amend the Income Tax Act.
> Act Nº 4 of 1993 to amend the Income Tax Act.
> Act Nº 14 of 1994.
> Act Nº 2 of 1995.
> Act Nº 18 of 1995.
> Act Nº 27 of 1995.
> Act Nº 7 of 1996, Income Tax (Amendment) Act, 1996.

Act Nº 4 of 1995, Apr. 28, 1995, Value Added Tax Act, 1995 [available on website].

Value Added Tax (Commencement) Order, 1995, Supplement to the Republic of Zambia Government Gazette of Apr. 28, 1995, Government Printer.

Value Added Tax (Applications for Registration) (Nº 2) Order, 1995, Supplement to the Republic of Zambia Government Gazette of May 19, 1995, Government Printer.

Value Added Tax (Zero Ratings) Order, 1995, June 30, 1995, Government Printer.

Value Added Tax (Exemptions and Zero Ratings) Order, 1995, June 2, 1995, Government Printer.

Value Added Tax (Exemptions) Order, 1995, June 9, 1995, Government Printer.

Value Added Tax (Exemptions) (Nº 3) Order, 1995, July 14, 1995, Government Printer.

Value Added Tax (Exemptions) (Nº 4) Order, 1995, Supplement to the Republic of Zambia Government Gazette of Aug. 18, 1995, Government Printer.

Act Nº 12 of 1984, Property Transfer Tax Act, 1984, amended by Act Nº 4 of 1994.

Personal Levy Act (Cap. 432), amended by Act Nº 15 of 1993, Act Nº 8 of 1994.

Act Nº 17 of 1994, Stamp Duty (Repeal) Act.

Customs and Excise Act (Cap. 662).

Act Nº 28 of 1993, Apr. 30, 1993, Zambia Revenue Authority Act, 1993 [available on website].

Act Nº 39 of 1993, Sept. 8, 1993, The Investment Act, 1993 [available on website].

Act Nº 34 of 1994, Mineral Royalty Tax Act, 1994.

Zimbabwe (ZWE)

In addition to income and sales tax, estate duty, payroll taxes, property tax, real estate transfer tax, stamp duty, and company fees (registration and increase in authorized share capital) are imposed.

Income Tax Act (ch. 181), *reprinted in* The Income Tax Act, as amended on Dec. 31, 1994 (Government Printer, Harare), *reprinted in* TLW (as amended to Feb. 1989).

Sales Tax Act, Cap. 184 (as amended to Nov. 1984), *reprinted in* Sales Tax Act, Government Printer, *and in* Sales Tax Act [ch. 184] (publisher unknown) (as amended through 1994).

Act Nº 4 of 1996, Finance Act, 1996, 74 Government Gazette Nº 27 (May 1996).

Index